WITHDRAWAL

THE LITERATURE OF THE REBELLION

A

CATALOGUE

OF

BOOKS AND PAMPHLETS

RELATING TO THE

Civil War in the United States,

AND ON SUBJECTS GROWING OUT OF THAT EVENT,

TOGETHER WITH WORKS ON

AMERICAN SLAVERY,

AND ESSAYS FROM REVIEWS AND MAGAZINES ON THE SAME SUBJECTS.

COMPILED BY

JOHN RUSSELL BARTLETT,

NEGRO UNIVERSITIES PRESS
WESTPORT, CONNECTICUT

Originally published in 1866
by Draper and Halliday, Boston
and Sidney S. Rider & Bros., Providence

Reprinted in 1970 by
Negro Universities Press
A Division of Greenwood Press, Inc.
Westport, Connecticut

SBN 8371-3568-0

Printed in United States of America

PREFACE.

IN preparing this Bibliography of the Rebellion, the compiler has been at a loss where to begin his labors, inasmuch as events of great importance, which occurred long before the outbreak, had a direct bearing upon it, and require notice. The Raid at Harper's Ferry by John Brown; the contest for Freedom in Kansas; the working of the Fugitive Slave Law; the Missouri Compromise, and the long struggle between the Slave and Free States from the very adoption of the Federal Constitution, which finally culminated in the rebellion,—all seem to be a preparation for this event. With this view of the subject, the compiler has deemed it best that his catalogue should cover the whole ground of these several events, and should, consequently, include works relating to American Slavery. The historians of the rebellion, generally, have taken the same view, and have covered the field, beginning with the adoption of the Constitution in their preliminary remarks.

But, although it was determined to embrace works on this subject in the catalogue, it is, in this respect, far from complete, as the compiler did not commence till recently to collect works on American Slavery. But, notwithstanding the deficiencies in this department, he believes that his catalogue contains more titles on the subject than can be found elsewhere.

The catalogue will be found to include titles of the following :—

1. Books and Pamphlets relating to the Rebellion, and to topics connected therewith, published in the United States and Europe.

2. Congressional Reports; Reports and Documents from the Departments of the War and the Navy; Proceedings of Courts Martial; Communications from the Executive of the United States; Speeches in Congress, and all other publications of the general government, 1861-65, relating to the war.

3. Official publications of the several States covering the period of the war,—1861 to 1865,—embracing Messages of Governors; Reports of Adjutant and Quartermaster Generals; Rosters of Volunteers; Documents and Reports relative to Volunteers, Bounties, the Draft, etc.

4. Official publications of the British government relating to the war.

5. The publications of the United States Sanitary and United States Christian Commissions; the Loyal League of New York; the Union League of Philadelphia, etc.

6. Publications relating to the Harper's Ferry Invasion; the Fugitive Slave Law; the Missouri Compromise; Belligerent Rights at Sea; Foreign Relations; International Law; the Cotton Question, etc.

7. Works on American Slavery.

8. Essays relating to the rebellion from American and European Reviews and Magazines.

9. Proceedings of cities, towns and public bodies, together with Eulogies on the occasion of the Death of Abraham Lincoln.

Under these several heads are embraced Essays and Speeches on the State of the Country, Secession, Revenue, Taxation, National Banks, Currency, the National Debt, Habeas Corpus, Martial Law, Conscription, Prisoners of War, Confiscation, Slavery, Emancipation and Reconstruction; Orations, Addresses, Lectures and Sermons having reference to the War or to the topics above-mentioned; Eulogies and Memorials of the fallen; Biographies of Officers of the Army and Navy; Reports and Documents relating to National Armories, Navy Yards, the Enlargement of Canals for war purposes, Patent Fire-Arms, Armored Vessels; Reports of Societies for the aid of Soldiers and all objects connected with the war; Reports of Public Meetings for sustaining the Government during the progress of the war; Reports and Documents relative to Freedmen; Poems, etc.

Speeches in Congress are mentioned only when separately published. Among these are some of the best and most elaborate publications on the war, but more particularly on subjects to which the war has given rise, as the State of the Country, Taxation, Revenue, Currency, National Banks, Reconstruction, etc.

Another and much more numerous class of publications includes Discourses, Sermons, Lectures, Orations, Addresses and Speeches. Among these will be found productions of our most distinguished writers and speakers, embracing the best essays on the war, in which we find that event treated from every point of view. In a few instances, where articles of importance have been published only in the newspapers, it has been thought desirable to mention them.

Catalogue.

A BBOTT, Austin. Popular Government successful in a Great
Emergency. An Address delivered at Farmington, Maine, July
4, 1862. 8vo. pp. 8.

2. ABBOTT, A. O. (Lieutenant First New York Dragoons.) Prison
Life in the South, showing how we lived and were treated at
Libby, Macon, Savannah, Charleston, Columbus, Charlotte, Raleigh, Goldsboro' and Andersonville, during 1864 and 1865.
12 mo. pp. x. 374. New York: *Harper & Brothers*, 1865.

3. ABBOT, Edwin H. Love of Country. A Lecture, August 26,
1861. 8vo. pp. 122 to 139.

4. ABBOTT, J. S. C. South and North; or, impressions received
during a trip to Cuba and the South.
12 mo. pp. 352. New York: *Abbey & Abbott*, 1860.

5. —— An Address upon our National Affairs, delivered in Cheshire,
Conn., on the National Fast, January 4th, 1861.
8vo. pp. 16. New York: *Abbey & Abbott*, 1861.

6. —— Words of Patriotism and Wisdom now presented to the Freemen
of Connecticut for their consideration. 8vo. pp. 8.

7. —— The Military Hospitals at Fortress Monroe. *Harpers' Magazine, August*, 1864.

8. —— Heroic Deeds of Heroic Men. A Military Adventure. *Harpers' Magazine, December*, 1864.

9. —— The Siege of Vicksburg. *Harpers' Magazine*, 1865.

10. —— Grierson's Raid. *Harpers' Magazine, February*, 1865.

2

11. ABBOTT, J. S. C.   Siege and Capture of Fort Hudson.   *Harpers Magazine, March,* 1865.

12. ——Military Adventures beyond the Mississippi.   *Harpers' Magazine, April,* 1865.

13. —— The Change of Base.   *Harpers' Magazine, May,* 1865.

14. —— The Pursuit and Capture of Morgan.   *Harpers' Magazine, August,* 1865.

15. —— The History of the Civil War in America ; comprising a full and impartial account of the origin and progress of the Rebellion, of the various naval and military engagements, of the heroic deeds performed by armies and individuals, and of touching scenes in the field, the camp, the hospital and the cabin.   Illustrated with portraits, maps, diagrams and numerous steel engravings of battle scenes.

   2 vols. 8vo. pp. 493, 630.   NEW YORK : *Henry Bill,* 1865.

16. ABOLITION.   Minutes of the Proceedings of the Second Convention of Delegates from the Abolition Societies established in different parts of the United States, assembled in Philadelphia, on the seventh day of January, 1795, and continued by adjournments to the fourteenth of same month, inclusive.

   8vo. pp. 19.   PHIL.: 1795.   Reprinted, *Wilmington,* 1862.

17. ABOLITION PHILANTHROPY !   The Fugitive Slave Law too bad for Southern Negroes, but good enough for Free citizens of Foreign Birth !   Handcuffs for White Men !   Shoulder Straps for Negroes !   Voters read !

   8vo. pp. 4.   PHILADELPHIA : *Age Office.*

18. ABOLITION AND SECESSION; or Cause and Effect, together with the remedy for our sectional troubles.   By a Unionist.

   8vo. pp. 24.   N. YORK : *Van Evrie, Horton & Co.,* 1862.

19. ABOUT THE WAR.   Plain Words to Plain People by a Plain Man.

   8vo. pp. 16.   PHILADELPHIA, 1863.

20. ADAMS, CHARLES FRANCIS.   What makes Slavery a Question of National Concern ?   A Lecture delivered at New York, January 30, 1855.

   8vo. pp. 46.   BOSTON : *Little, Brown & Co.,* 1855.

21. —— Speech of, on the Union.   Delivered in the House of Representatives, January 31st, 1861.   8vo. pp. 8.

22. ADAMS, C. F. and Everett, Edward. The Union and the Southern Rebellion. Farewell Address of Mr. Adams to his constituents upon his acceptance of the Mission to England, and speech of Mr. Everett, at Roxbury, in behalf of the families of the volunteers.
8vo. pp. 18. LONDON : *Henry Stevens,* 1861.

23. ADAMS, Rev. E. E. The Temple and the Throne ; or, The True Foundations. A sermon preached in the North Broad St. Presbyterian Church, Philadelphia, Sept. 26. 1861.
8vo. pp. 28. PHILADELPHIA : *H. C. Peck,* 1861.

24. —— Government and Rebellion. A sermon preached Ap. 28, 1861.
8vo. pp. 23. PHILADELPHIA : *T. B. Pugh,* 1861.

25. ADAMS, F. COLBURN. The Story of a Trooper, with much of interest concerning the Campaign on the Peninsula, not before written. In four books. Book First.
12mo. pp. 127. N. YORK : *Dick & Fitzgerald,* 1864.

26. ADAMS, Rev. JOHN G. Our Country, and its Claims upon us, An Oration delivered before the municipal authorities and citizens of Providence, July 4, 1863.
8vo. pp. 30. PROVIDENCE : *Knowles, Anthony & Co.,* 1863.

27. ADAMS, JULIUS W. Letter to the Honorable Secretary of War. on the examination of officers for colored troops.
8vo. pp. 16. BROOKLYN : Sept 1st, 1863.

28. ADAMS, Rev. NEHEMIAH. A South-Side View of Slavery ; or Three Months in the South in 1854.
12mo. pp. 214. BOSTON : *T. R. Marvin,* 1854.

29. —— The Sable Cloud ; a Southern Tale with Northern Comments.
8vo. pp. 275. BOSTON : *Ticknor & Fields,* 1861.

30. ADAMS. Rev. R. S., Nineveh Threatened—A sermon preached in St. Andrews's Church, Brooklyn, Dec. 30, 1860.
8vo. pp. 16. N. YORK : *Mann & Stearns,* 1861.

31. ADAMS, Rev. WILLIAM, D. D. Prayer for Rulers, a duty of Christian Patriots. A discourse preached in the Madison Square Presbyterian Church, Jan. 4. 1861.
12mo. pp. 41. N. YORK : *Rudd & Carlton,* 1861.

32. ——Christian Patriotism.
8vo. pp. 21. N. YORK : *A. D. F. Randolph,* 1863.

33. **ADAMS, W. E.** The Slaveholder's War. An Argument for the North and the Negro.

8vo. pp. 24. MANCHESTER : *Un. and Emanc. Soc.,* 1863.

34. **ADDEY, MARKINFIELD,** " Little Mac," and how he became a Great General ; a Life of George Brinton McClellan, for young Americans. With Illustrations.

12mo. pp. 352. NEW YORK : *James G. Gregory,* 1864.

35. ADDRESS of the Democratic Members of Congress to the Democracy of the United States. 8vo pp. 8.

36. ADDRESS of the Democratic State Central Committee, August 11, 1863. Signed C. J. Biddle, Chairman.

8vo. pp. 8. PHILADELPHIA : *Age Office,* 1863.

37. ADDRESS of the Committee from the State of Missouri to President Lincoln. Dated September 30, 1863. pp. 12.

38. ADDRESS to the People, by the Democracy of Wisconsin, adopted in State Convention, at Milwaukee, Sept. 3, 1862. 8vo. pp. 8.

39. ADDRESS of the Union members of the Legislature to the People of Indiana, March, 1863. 8vo. pp. 15.

40. ADDRESS to the Democrats of Massachusetts, by a Jacksonian Democrat, George Sennott..

8vo. pp. 11. BOSTON : *James O. Bugle & Co.*

41. ADDRESS to the Democracy and People of the United States, by the National Democratic Executive Committee.

8vo. pp. 16. WASHINGTON : *McGill & Witherow,* 1860.

42. ADDRESS. The War, and how to End it, Address to the People of California, by One of Them.

8vo. pp. 38, SAN FRANCISCO : Nov. 1861.

43. ADDRESS to the People of Pennsylvania, issued by authority of Loyal Pennsylvanians of Washington, D. C., Sept. 1864.

8vo. pp. 15. WASHINGTON : *McGill & Witherow,* 1864.

44. ADDRESS to the Democracy of the United States, on the Duty of the Democratic Party, at this Crisis. 8vo. pp. 26.

45. ADDRESSES of the Hon. W. D. Kelley, Miss Anna E. Dickinson, and Mr. Frederic Douglas, at a Mass Meeting held at National Hall, Philadelphia, July 6, 1863, for the promotion of colored enlistments. 8vo. pp. 8

46. ADDRESS of the Loyal National League of the State of New York,

to the People of the State of New York. Convention assembled at Utica, October 20, 1863.

8vo. pp. 4.	*Loyal Publication Society, No.* 31, 1863.

47. —— The same. Royal 8vo. pp. 8.

48. ADDRESS of the Ohio Soldiers in the Army of the Cumberland, to the People of Ohio. Response of the People of North West Ohio to the Soldiers of Ohio, enrolled in the Army of the U. S.

8vo. pp. 10.	TOLEDO : *Pelton & Waggoner,* 1863.

49. ADDRESS from the Colored Citizens of Norfolk, Va., to the People of the United States. Also an account of the agitation among the Colored People of Virginia for Equal Rights. With an Appendix concerning the Rights of Colored Witnesses, before the State Courts.

8vo. pp. 26.	NEW BEDFORD, Mass., *E. Anthony & Sons,* 1865.

50. ADDRESS of the General Assembly of the Presbyterian Church in the Confederate States of America, to all the Churches throughout the earth, as reported by the Rev. J. H. Thornwell, from a Council appointed to prepare it, by the Assembly at Augusta, Ga., Dec. 1, 1861.

51. ADDRESS of the Congress to the people of the Confederate States. (Issued from Richmond, 1864.)

52. ADDRESS to the Soldiers of New Hampshire, from the Granite State Lincoln Club of Washington, D. C.

8vo. pp. 8.	WASHINGTON : *L. Towers,* 1864.

53. ADELA. Extract from a Despatch to Mr. Stewart, her Majesty's Chargè des Affaires at Washington, respecting the seizure of Mail Bags on board the " Adela."

Folio pp. 3.	LONDON : *Br. Parl. Papers, N. Amer.,* 1864.

54. AFRICAN'S RIGHT to citizenship, The.

8vo. pp. 31.	PHILADELPHIA : *James S. Claxton,* 1865.

55. AFRICAN SERVITUDE : When, why and by whom instituted. By whom and how long shall it be maintained ? Read and consider.

8vo. pp. 54.	N. YORK : *Davies & Kent,* 1860.

55.*AGNEW, DANIEL. Our National Constitution : its adaptation to a state of war or insurrection.

8vo. pp. 39.	PHILADELPHIA : *C. Sherman, Son & Co.,* 1863.

56. AGNEW, J. HOLMES. Reply to Prof. Tayler Lewis' Review of

Rev. Henry J. Van Dyke's Sermon on Biblical Slavery; also to his other articles on the same subject, published in " The World."
8vo. pp. 63.   N. YORK: *D. Appleton & Co.*, 1861.

57. AGNEW, J. HOLMES. The Coming Presidential Election. *Knickerbocker Magazine, June,* 1864.

58. —— The Country and the Clergy. *Knickerbocker Mag., Aug.*, 1864.

59. —— Presidential Election of 1864. *Knickerbocker Mag. Dec.*, 1864.

60. AIKMAN, Rev. WILLIAM. Government and Administration. A Sermon preached July 19, 1863, succeeding the secession riots in New York.
12mo. pp. 12.   WILMINGTON: *Henry Eckel,* 1863.

61. —— The Future of the Colored Race in America; being an article in the Presbyterian Quarterly Review, of July, 1862.
8vo. pp. 35.   N. YORK: *A. D. F. Randolph,* 1862.

62. AKERS, Mrs. ELIZABETH C. A Potomac Picture. *Northern Monthly, March,* 1864.

63. ALARM BELL, The. No. 1. By a Constitutionalist.
8vo. pp. 16.   N. YORK: *Baker & Goodwin,* 1863.

64. ALABAMA, PRIVATEER. Correspondence respecting the "Alabama"; also respecting the Bark "Maury," at New York, during the Crimean War; and the temporary Act of Congress, passed by the United States, at the instance of Great Britain, in 1838, to meet the case of the Rebellion in Canada. 8vo. pp. 56.

65. "ALABAMA." Correspondence Respecting.
Folio pp. 48.   LONDON: *Parl. Papers, N. America,* 1863.

66. ALABAMA. Legal Views of the Alabama Case, and Ship-Building for the Confederates. By Samuel Parker.
8vo. pp. 8.   MANCHESTER: *Union and Emanc. Society,* 1863.

67. ALABAMA. Correspondence respecting the "Alabama." (In continuation of Correspondence presented to Parl. in March, 1863.)
Folio pp. 57.   LONDON: *Parl. Papers, N. America,* 1864.

68. ALABAMA. Correspondence respecting the "Alabama." (In continuation of Papers presented to Parliament in Feb., 1864.)
Folio pp. 18.   LONDON: *Parl. Papers, N. America,* 1864.

69. ALABAMA. Narrative of the Cruise of the Alabama, and a list of her officers and men, by one of her crew.
8vo. pp. 16.   LONDON: 1864.

70. ALABAMA AND SUMTER. The Cruise of. From the private Journals and other Papers of Commander Semmes, C. S. N., and other officers. First and Second Editions.
   2 v. 12mo. LONDON: *Saunders, Otley & Co.*, 1864.

71. ALABAMA AND SUMTER. Narrative of the Cruise of. From the private Journals of, and Papers of Com. Semmes, C. S. N., and others.
   12mo. pp. 328. NEW YORK: *Carleton*, 1864.

72. ALABAMA AND SUMTER. The Log of. From the private Journals and other Papers of Commander Semmes, C. S. N., and other officers. Abridged from Library Edition.
   12mo. pp. xi and 297. LONDON: *Saunders, Otley & Co.*, 1864.

73. ALBANY. Correspondence in relation to the Public Meeting at, with Letter from Pres. Lincoln, dated June 12, 1860. 8vo. pp. 9.

74. ALBEMARLE, REBEL RAM. Letter from the Secretary of the Navy in regard to the Rebel Ram "Albemarle," which recently participated in the rebel attack on Plymouth.
   8vo. pp. 12. *House, Ex. Doc., No.* 53, 38*th Cong.*, 1864.

75. ALCOTT, L. M. Hospital Sketches.
   8vo. pp. 102. BOSTON: *James Redpath*, 1863.

76. ALDEN, HENRY M. Pericles and President Lincoln. *Atlantic Monthly for March*, 1863.

77. ALEXANDRIA. Report from the Joint Committee on the conduct of the War, on the "Military administration in the City of Alexandria,—and whether punishments of "a cruel and unusual character" are not inflicted without authority of law, in a place known as "the Slave Pen," in that city. *Senate, Report of Committee, No.* 54, 38*th Congress*, 1864.

78. ALEXANDER, Lt. Col. B. L. The Peninsular Campaign. *Atlantic Monthly for March*, 1864.

79. ALGER, FRANCIS. A petition to the National Government, embodying facts and statements in furtherance of the Claim of the late Cyrus Alger, for remuneration for certain inventions relating to Fuzes and Shells.
   8vo. pp. 69. WASHINGTON: *Franck Taylor*, 1862.

80. ALGER, WILLIAM R. Our Civil War, as seen from the Pulpit. A Sermon preached in Bulfinch St. Church, Boston, Apr. 28, '61.
   8vo. pp. 20. BOSTON: *Walker, Wise & Co.*, 1861.

81. ALGER, WILLIAM R. Public Morals; or the true Glory of a State. A Discourse delivered before the Legislative Departments of Massachusetts, at the annual election, January 1, 1862. 8vo. pp. 55.   BOSTON: *William White,* 1862.

82. ALLEN, ETHAN. A Discourse for the National Fast Day, June 1, 1865, on account of the Murder of our late President, and preached at St. Thomas's Church, Homestead, Maryland. 12mo. pp. 12.   BALTIMORE: *Wm. K. Boyle,* 1865.

83. ALLEN, Rev. ETHAN, D. D. A Sermon preached in Baltimore, Thanksgiving Day, August 6, 1863. (On Civil Government.) 12mo. pp. 11.

84. ALLEN, J. H. Africans in America, and their new Guardians *Christian Examiner, July,* 1862.

85. —— Our War Policy, and how it deals with Slavery. *Christian Examiner, September,* 1862.

86. —— The New War Policy, and the Future of the South. *Christian Examiner, November,* 1862.

87. —— The Peace Policy, how it is urged and what it means. *Christian Examiner, January,* 1863.

88. —— Later Phases of English Feeling. *Ch. Ex. March,* 1863.

89. —— The Thirty-Seventh Congress. *Ch. Exam., May,* 1863.

90. —— A Month of Victory and its Results. *Ch. Ex. Sept.,* 1863.

91. —— English Expositions of Neutrality. *Ch. Ex., Nov.,* 1863.

92. —— The Two Messages. *Christian Examiner, March,* 1864.

93. —— Federalism, and its present Tasks. *Ch. Ex., May,* 1864.

94. —— A Word on the War. *Christian Examiner, Sept.,* 1864.

95. —— American Expositions of Neutrality. *Ch. Ex., Nov.,* 1864.

96. —— The Eighth of November. *Ch. Ex., Jan.,* 1865.

97. —— The Fourth of March. *Christian Examiner, March,* 1865.

98. —— The Nation's Triumph and its Sacrifice. *Ch. Ex., May,* 1865.

99. ALLEN, STEPHEN M. Fibrilia, or Flax-Cotton. Address before the Massachusetts Legislative Agricultural Society, Boston, February 6, 1860. 8vo. pp. 11   BOSTON: *Wright & Potter,* 1860.

100. —— Fibrilia. An Address before the Class on Agriculture at Yale College, New Haven, February 18, 1860. 8vo. pp. 15.   BOSTON: *Wright & Potter,* 1860.

101. ALLEN, Stephen M. [Fibrilia.] Address before the Rhode Island Society for the Encouragement of Domestic Industry, at the State House, in Providence, February 2, 1860.

8vo. pp. 12.   Boston: *Wright & Potter,* 1860.

These three Addresses are sometimes put up together, with the general title of Fibrilia, or Flax- Cotton, with an Appendix containing directions for the culture and preparation of the Flax plant.

102. ALLEN, W. F. Democracy on Trial. *Chr. Ex. March,* 1863.

103. —— The Freedmen and Free Labor in the South. *Christian Examiner, May,* 1864.

104. ALLEN, Hon. William, of Ohio. Speech on Confiscation and Emancipation, delivered in the House of Representatives of the United States, April 24, 1862.

8vo. pp. 16.   Washington: *McGill, Witherow & Co.,* 1862.

105. ALLEN, William J., of Illinois. Speech upon the President's Message, delivered in House of Representatives, Jan. 27, 1864.

8vo. pp. 14.   Washington : *Constitutional Union,* 1864.

106. ALLISON, William B., of Iowa. Homesteads for Soldiers and Sailors in the Rebellious States. Speech delivered in the House of Representatives, May 4, 1864.

8vo. pp. 8.   Washington: *Gibson Brothers.*

107. Allotment System. United States Allotment System. Report to the President of the United States of the Commissioners for the State of New York. By T. Roosevelt, W. E. Dodge, Jun., and Theodore B. Bronson, Commissioners.

8vo. pp. 22.   N. York: *George F. Nesbitt & Co.,* 1862.

108. Almanac. The People's Military, for 1862.

8vo. pp. 116.   N. York: *Dexter & Co.*

See also Franklin Almanac.

109. The Ambulance System. Reprinted from the North American Review, January, 1864, and published for gratuitous distribution.

8vo. pp. 16.   Boston: *Crosby & Nichols,* 1864.

110. Ambulance System. Have we the best possible Ambulance System? Reprinted from the Christian Examiner Jan., 1864.

8vo. pp. 18.   Boston : *Walker, Wise & Co.,* 1864.

111. Ambulance System. A Brief Plea for, as drawn from the extra sufferings of the late Lt. Bowditch. By Henry I. Bowditch, M. D.

8vo. pp. 28.   Boston: *Ticknor & Fields,* 1863.

3

112. THE AMBULANCE SYSTEM. Communications from Dr. Bowditch to the Boston Post and the Boston Journal. Reprinted in three Broadsides, 1863.

113. AMERICAN ANTI SLAVERY SOCIETY, and its Auxiliaries. Platform of. 8vo. pp.   N. YORK: *American Anti Slavery Society*, 1860.

114. AMERICAN CHURCHES, The. The Bulwarks of African Slavery. By an American. Third Am. Edition enlarged by an Appendix. 8vo. pp. 48.   NEWBURYPORT: *Charles Whipple*, 1842.

115. AMERICAN DESTINY. What shall it be, Republican or Cossack? An Argument addressed to the people of the late Union, North and South.
8vo. pp. 14.   N. YORK: *Columbian Association*, 1854.

116. AMERICAN DESTINY, The Problem of, Solved by Science and History.
8vo. pp. 78.   N. YORK: *C. T. Evans*, 1860.

117. AMERICAN MONTHLY, formerly the *Knickerbocker Magazine.*

> Peace and its Consquences. *M. H. Troop, September,* 1864.
> Personal Liberty. *C. H. Whittlesey, September,* 1864.
> Personal Liberty. *C. H. Whittlesey, October,* 1864.
> History of Democratic Conventions. *October,* 1864.
> McClellan Redemptor. *October,* 1864.
> Our War Debt, and How to Pay it. *Prof. Lambert, November,* 1864.
> Repudiation. *November,* 1864.
> Presidential Election of 1864. *J. Holmes Agnew, December,* 1864.
> An Appeal for peace.
> Review of Goldwin Smith on Slavery. *W. D. Northend, Jan.,* 1865.
> Five Months in Dixie. *February,* 1865.
> Wendell Phillips. *April,* 1865.
> The President's Speech. *May,* 1865.
> The Cause of our Strife and the Remedy. *W. D. Northend,* 1865.

118. THE AMERICAN QUESTION: Secession, Tariff, Slavery.
12mo, pp. 73.   BRIGHTON: *H. Taylor*, 1862.

119. THE AMERICAN QUESTION, and How to Settle it.
Post 8vo. pp, 313.   LONDON: *S. Low & Co.*, 1863.

120. THE AMERICAN REVOLUTION. From the Edinburgh Review for October, 1862.

121. THE AMERICAN REBELLION. Some facts and Reflections for the consideration of the English People. By an American Citizen.
8vo. pp. 48.   LONDON ; *Beadle & Co.*, 1861.

122. AMERICAN THANKSGIVING DINNER, at St. James's Hall, London, November 26, 1863.

  8vo. pp. 94.   LONDON : *W. Ridgeway,* 2863.

  Includes the remarks made by the American Minister, Mr. Adams, Mr. Robert J. Walker, Mr. George Thompson, Mayor Pangborn, Captain Mayne Reid and others.

123. AMERICAN WAR. Essay on the American War. By " Americas."

  8vo. pp. 23.   LIVERPOOL : *Edward Howell,* 1865.

124. THE AMERICAN UNION shown to be the New Heaven and the New Earth, and its predicted Restoration to Life within four years from its Death.

  8vo. pp. 41.   NEW YORK : *J. Thompson,* 1865.

125. AMERICAN UNION COMMISSION. Speeches of Hon. W. Dennison, Rev. J. P. Thompson, D. D., Col. N. G. Taylor, of East Tennessee, Hon J. R. Doolittle, Gen. J. A. Garland, in the Hall of the Representatives, Washington, Feb. 12, 1865.

  8vo. pp. 43.   NEW YORK : *Sanford, Harrour & Co.,* 1865.

126. AMERICAN UNION COMMISSION : its Origin, Operations and Purposes. Organized to aid in the Restoration of the Union upon the basis of Freedom, Industry, Education and Christian Morality, Oct. 1865.

  8vo. pp. 24.   NEW YORK : *Sanford, Harrour & Co.,* 1866.

127. AMISTAD CAPTIVES. Africans taken in the Amistad. Congressional Document, containing the correspondence, &c., in relation to the captured Africans.

  8vo. pp. 48.   NEW YORK : *Anti Slavery Depository,* 1840.

128. AMISTAD CAPTIVES, A History of ; being an account of the capture of the Spanish schooner Amistad, by the Africans on board. Their voyage and capture near Long Island, New York ; with an account of the trials had in their cases. By John W. Barber.

  8vo. pp. 32.   NEW HAVEN : *E. L. & J. W. Barber,* 1840.

129. AMES, CHARLES G. Stand by the President. An Address delivered before the National Union Association of Cincinnati, March 6, 1863.

  8vo. pp. 14.   CINCINNATI : *Johnson, Stephens & Co.,* 1863.

130. —— The same work.   PHILADELPHIA : *King & Baird,* 1863.

131. ANDERSON, Col. CHARLES. The Cause of the War : Who brought it on, and for what purpose ?

  8vo. pp. 16.   *Loyal Publication Society, No.* 17, 1863.

132. ANDERSON, Col. CHARLES. Letter addressed to the Opera House Meeting, Cincinnati.
8vo. pp. 15. *Loyal Publication Society, No.* 21, 1863.

133. ANDERSON, Hon. LUCIEN, of Kentucky. Speech on the Democracy of Kentucky and their Allies in the North. *House of Representatives, March* 5, 1864. 8vo. pp. 15.

134. ANDERSON, Gen. ROBERT, Concurrent Resolutions of the Legislature of New York, in relation to.
House Mis. Doc., No. 65, 28*th Cong.,* 1864.

135. ANDERSON, Rev. W. C. The National Crisis. An Address delivered before the Young Men's Christian Association of San Francisco, Cal., at their Eighth Anniversary, Aug. 12, 1861.
8vo. pp. 10. SAN FRANCISCO : 1861.

136. ANDREW, JOHN A., Edward Everett, B. F. Thomas and Robert C. Winthrop. Addresses delivered at the Mass Meeting in aid of Recruiting, on Boston Common, August 27, 1862.
8vo. pp. 16. BOSTON: *J. E. Farwell & Co.,* 1862.

137. ANDREW, JOHN A. Address to the two Branches of the Legislature of the State of Massachusetts, January 5, 1861.
8vo. pp. 48. BOSTON: *William White,* 1861.

138. —— Address to the two Branches of the Legislature, May 14, 1861. Extra session.
8vo. pp. 24. BOSTON: *William White,* 1861.

139. —— Address to the two Branches of the Legislature of Massachusetts, January 3d, 1862.
8vo. pp. 75. BOSTON *: William White,* 1862.

140. —— Message, January 23, 1862. On the subject of an Act in Aid of the Families of Volunteers. 8vo. pp. 19. *Sen. Doc. No.* 10.

141. —— Message January 30, 1862. 8vo. pp. 3. *House Doc. No.* 50

142. —— Address to the Legislature of Massachusetts, Jan. 9, 1863.
8vo. pp. 80. BOSTON: *Wright & Potter,* 1863.

143. —— Letter to S. F. Wetmore, Indiana. 8vo. pp. 8. 1863.

144. —— Remarks to the Legislature of Massachusetts on the Death of President Lincoln, April 17, 1865. 8vo. pp. 8.

145. —— Address to the two Branches of the Legislature of Massachusetts, January 8, 1864.
8vo. pp. 88. BOSTON : *Wright & Potter,* 1864.

146. ANDREW, John A.   Address to the two Branches of the Legislature of Massachusetts, January 6, 1865.
8vo. pp. 140.   Boston : *Wright & Potter*, 1865

147. —— An Address on the occasion of Dedicating the Monument to Ladd and Whiting, members of the Sixth Regiment, M. V. M., killed at Baltimore, April 19, 1861.   Delivered at Lowell, Mass., June 17, 1865.
8vo. pp. 31.   Boston: *Wright & Potter*, 1865.

148. ANDREWS, Israel W.   Why is Allegiance due ?   and Where is it due ?   An Address before the National Union Association of Cincinnati, June 2, 1863.
8vo. pp. 30.   Cincinnati : *Moore, Wilstach & Co.*

149. ANDREWS, Prof. E. A.   Slavery and the Domestic Slave Trade in the U. S., in a series of letters addressed to the Executive Committee of the American Union, for the relief and improvement of the colored race.
12mo. pp. 201.   Boston: *Light & Stearns*, 1836.

150. ANDREWS, S. P.   The Great American Crisis. *Continental Monthly for December*, 1863, *January and March*, 1864.

151. Anglo-Californian.—The National Crisis.   A letter to the Hon. Milton S. Latham, Senator from California in Washington.
8vo. pp. 21.   San Francisco : *Towne & Bacon*, 1861.

152. Annual Report, Fifth Regiment, N. Y. S. M.   Jefferson Guard, Col. Louis Burger, for 1861.
8vo. pp. 8.   New York, *December* 21, 1861.

153. Annuaire des Deux Mondes.   Histoire des Etats-Unis, Presidence de M. Abraham Lincoln.   Vol. 11.   Paris, 1861.

154. —— Histoire des Etats-Unis, Presidence de M. Abraham Lincoln. Vol. 12.   Paris : 1862–1863.

155. ANTHONY, Elliott.   The Outlawry of a Race.   A Speech delivered in the Constitutional Convention of Illinois, Feb. 12, 1862, on the proposition to forever prohibit negroes or mulattoes from migrating into or settling in the State.   pp. 8.

156. —— Is a Constitution Convention a Legislature ?   A Speech delivered in the Constitution Convention of Illinois, February 17, 1862.   [Relative to the Abolition of Slavery by Congress.]
8vo. pp. 13.

157. ANTHONY, ELLIOTT. Shall the Privilege of the Writ of Habeas
     Corpus ever be Suspended in this State ? A Speech delivered
     in the Constitutional Convention of Illinois, 1862. 8vo. pp. 9.

158. AN APPEAL to the Conservative Men of all Parties. The Presi-
     dential Question. An important question : Shall the subject of
     Slavery forever prevent all useful Legislation, or shall it be set-
     tled by the doctrine of Non-Intervention? The Question fairly
     stated. pp. 16.

159. THE APPEAL of the Religious Society of Friends in Pennsylvania,
     New Jersey, Delaware, etc., to their Fellow-Citizens of the Uni-
     ted States, on behalf of the Colored Races.
     8vo. pp. 48.   PHILADELPHIA : *Friends' Bookstore*, 1859.

160. AN APPEAL to the People of the North. (Signed, A Voice from
     Kentucky.)
     8vo. pp. 16.   LOUISVILLE: *Hanna & Co.*, 1861.
                    This work went through five editions.

161. APPLETON, NATHAN. Letters to the Hon. Wm. C. Rives, of
     Virginia, on Slavery and the Union.
     8vo. pp. 17.   BOSTON : *J. H. Eastburn*, 1860.

162. ARGUELLES. Cuestion, Dulce—Zulueta— Arguelles.
     4to. pp. 39.   (HAVANA : 1865.)

     The subject is usually called, in the United States, the "Arguelles Case."
     In Cuba and Spain it is called the "Dulce-Zulueta-Arguelles Cues-
     tion," these three persons being prominent in the case.
        Mr. Arguelles was Secretary to Capt. General Dulce of Cuba. He was
     charged with being engaged in the Slave Trade; and escaping to New
     York, was, on demand of the Cuban authorities, surrendered by order of
     Mr. Seward, Secretary of State, and taken back to Cuba. This document
     contains letters, memorials to the Queen of Spain and to the President of
     the United States, and articles from the newspapers of Cuba, Spain and
     New York, on the subject, and is accompanied by an English translation.

163. ARIZONA. [Correspondence between Senor A. Ainsa of Arizona,
     W. H. Seward, Secretary of State, etc., relative to the schemes
     of the rebels in that territory and in Soñora.] Private. pp. 6.

164. ARKANSAS. Memorial of the Free State of Arkansas to Congress,
     and a Letter from W. D. Snow, Senator elect, to Hon. S. C.
     Pomeroy, showing the origin and history of the reörganized gov-
     ernment of Arkansas, etc.
     8vo. pp. 11.   WASHINGTON: *Chronicle Office*, 1865.

165. ARKANSAS. Report of the Committee on Elections, and the Credentials of T. M. Jacks and J. M. Johnson, claiming seats in the House of Representatives from Arkansas, 1865. pp. 9. *38th Congress, 2 Session, House Report, No. 18.*

166. ARMITAGE, Rev. THOMAS D. D. The past, present and future of the United States. A Discourse delivered in the Fifth Avenue Baptist Church, N. Y., Nov. 27, and repeated Dec. 18, 1862. 8vo. pp. 31. NEW YORK: *T. Holman*, 1862.

167. ARMITAGE, Rev. WILLIAM E. Unselfish Patriotism. A Sermon preached in St. John's Church, Detroit, Feb. 23, 1862. 8vo. pp. 16. DETROIT: *Richmond & Backus*, 1862.

168. ARMSTRONG, GEORGE D., DD. Pastor of the Presbyterian Church, Norfolk, Va. The Christian Doctrine of Slavery. 12mo. pp. 148. NEW YORK: *Charles Scribner*, 1857.

169. ARMSTRONG, Rev. JOHN J. An Oration delivered at Flushing, L. I., 4th of July, 1862. 8vo. pp. 24. NEW YORK: *Edwin O. Jenkins*, 1862.

170. —— An Oration delivered at Queens, L. I., July 4, 1861. 8vo. pp. 28. JAMAICA: (L. I.) *J. J. Brenton*, 1861.

171. ARMSTRONG, Rev. J. W. Oration delivered at Lowville, N. Y., July 4, 1861. 8vo. pp. 28.

172. ARMY OFFICERS stationed in and around Washington, drawing commutation for quarters and fuel. Letter of the Secretary of War in answer to a Resolution of the Senate, furnishing a statement. *Senate Ex. Doc., No. 15, 38th Cong., 1st Sept., (1864.)*

173. ARMY. Opinions of Hon. John M. Read, of the Supreme Court of Pennsylvania, in favor of the Constitutionality of the Act of Congress of March 3, 1863, "For Enrolling and Calling out the National Forces, and for other purposes." 8vo. pp. 31. PHILADELPHIA: *C. Sherman, Son & Co.*, 1864.

174. ARMY OF THE CUMBERLAND, Annals of, comprising Biographies, Descriptions of Departments, Accounts of Expeditions, Skirmishes, and Battles; also, its Police Record of Spies, Smugglers and prominent Rebel Emissaries; together with Anecdotes, Incidents, Poetry, Reminiscences, etc., and Official Reports of the Battle of Stone River. By an Officer. 8vo. pp. 671. PHILADELPHIA: *J. B. Lippincott & Co.*, 1863.

175. ARMY OF THE POTOMAC. The Defence of Richmond against the Federal Army under General McClellan. By a Prussian Officer in the Confederate Service. Translated from the *Koelnische Zeitung.*

 8vo. pp. 16 NEW YORK: *George F. Nesbitt & Co.*, 1863.

176. ARMY OF THE POTOMAC. History of its Campaigns. The Peninsular, Maryland, Fredericksburg. Testimony of its three Commanders, Maj. Gen. McClellan, Maj. Gen. Burnside, and Maj. Gen. Hooker, before the Congressional Committee on the Conduct of the War.

 8vo. pp. 32. NEW YORK: *Tribune Office*, 1863.

177. ARMY OF THE POTOMAC, Report of the Congressional Committee on the Operations of. Causes of its inaction and ill success. Its several Campaigns. Why McClellan was removed. The Battle of Fredericksburg. Removal of Burnside.

 8vo. pp. 30. NEW YORK: *Tribune Association*, 1863.

178. ARMY. Official Army List of the Western States for August, 1862, including Volunteers of Illinois, Indiana, Wisconsin, Minnesota, Michigan, Iowa, Missouri, Kansas, Nebraska and Colorado. Compiled and published with official sanction, by George B. Smith.

 12mo. pp. 176. CHICAGO: *John R. Walsh*, 1862.

179. ARMY PENSIONS. Instructions and Forms to be observed in applying for Army Pensions, under the Act of July 14, 1862.

 8vo. pp. 13. WASHINGTON: *Govt. Printing Office*, 1862.

180. ARMY AND NAVY, A Temperance Tract for.

 18mo. pp. 32. NEW YORK: *Evan. Knowledge Society*, 1865.

181. ARMY AND NAVY GAZETTE. Journal of the Regular and Volunteer Forces.

 Folio. NEW YORK; *commenced February*, 1862.

182. ARMY AND NAVY JOURNAL. Journal of the Regular and Volunteer Forces.

 Folio. NEW YORK: *commenced August*, 1863.

183. ARMY AND NAVY OFFICIAL GAZETTE.

  WASHINGTON: *commenced in July*, 1863,

184. ARMY REGISTER (Official,) for September, 1861. Published by Order of the Secretary of War, in compliance with a Resolution of the Senate, August 3, 1861.

 8vo. pp. 87. WASHINGTON: *Adjutant General's Office*, 1861.

185. ARMY REGISTER. The same for August, 1862. pp. 118.
186. —— The same for 1863. 8vo. pp. 151.
187. —— The same for 1864. 8vo. pp.
188. —— The same for 1865. 8vo. pp.
189. ARMY SERIES. [A Series of Small Tracts printed by the American Unitarian Association, for gratuitous distribution among the Soldiers of the United States Army.]

The following comprise the titles of the series.

No. 1. The Man and the Soldier. By George Putnam, D. D.
No. 2. The Soldier of the Good Cause. By Charles Eliot Norton.
No. 3. The Home to the Camp; an Address to the Soldiers of the Union. By John F. W. Ware.
No. 4. Liberty and Law. A Poem for the Hour. By Elbridge Jefferson Cutler.
No. 5. The Camp and the Field. By One of Our Chaplains.
No. 6. The Home to the Hospital. Addressed to the Sick and Wounded of the Army of the Union. By John F. W. Ware.
No. 7. A Letter to a Sick Soldier. By Robert Collyer.
No. 8. An Enemy within the Line. By S. H. Winkley.
No. 9. Wounded and in the Hands of the Enemy. By J. F. W. Ware.
No. 10. Traitors in Camp. By John F. W. Ware.
No. 11. A Change of Base. By John F. W. Ware.
No. 12. On Picket. By John F. W. Ware.
No. 13. The Rebel. By John F. W. Ware.
No. 14. To the Color. By John F. W. Ware.
No. 15. The Recruit. By John F. W. Ware.
No. 16. A Few Words with the Convalescent. By John F. W. Ware.
No. 17. The Reconnoissance. By John F. W. Ware.
No. 18. The Reveille. By John F. W. Ware.
No. 19. Rally upon the Rescue. By John F. W. Ware.

190. ARNOLD, E. G. Persecution of Volunteer Naval Officers. 8vo. pp. 30. PROVIDENCE: *A. Crawford Greene,* 1863.
191. ARNOLD, Hon. ISAAC N., of Illinois. Ship Canal from the Mississippi to Lake Michigan. Speech delivered in the House of Representatives, June 30, 1863. 8vo. pp. 8.
192. —— Reconstruction; Liberty the Corner Stone, and Lincoln the Architect. Speech delivered in the House of Representatives, March 19, 1864. 8vo. pp. 14. WASHINGTON: *L. Towers & Co.,* 1864.
193. —— Congressional Legislation. Speech at Metropolitan Hall, July 14, 1864. 8vo. pp. 16.
194. —— The Power, the Duty, and Necessity of destroying Slavery

4

in the Rebel States. A Speech delivered in the House of Representatives, January 6, 1864. 8vo. pp. 15.

195. ARNOLD, Hon. Isaac N., of Illinois. The same.
8vo. pp. 8.   Washington.

196. ARNOLD, R. Arthur. History of the Cotton Famine, from the Fall of Sumter to the passing of the Public Works Act.
8vo. pp. xiv and 570.   London: *Saunders & Otley*, 1864.

197. ARNY, W. F. M., Acting Governor of New Mexico. Message to the Legislative Assembly of the Territory, Dec. 2, 1862.
8vo. pp. 26.   Santa Fe: *Gazette Office*, 1862.

198. ARTHUR, T. S. Growler's Income Tax.
8vo. pp. 4.   *Loyal Publication Society, No.* 57, 1864.

199. ARTHUR, Rev. W. English Opinion on the American Rebellion.
8vo. pp. 4.   *Manchester Union and Emancipation Society.*

200. ASHLEY, J. M., of Ohio. Speech on the Rebellion, its Causes and Consequences; College Hall, Toledo, November 26, 1861.
8vo. pp. 16.

201. —— The Liberation and Restoration of the South. Speech in the House of Representatives, March 30, 1864. 8vo. pp. 15.

202. —— Amend the Constitution. It is the Way to Unity and Peace. Speech delivered in the House of Representatives, on Friday, January 6, 1865, on the Constitutional Amendment for the Abolition of Slavery.
8vo. pp. 22.   New York: *W. C. Bryant & Co.*, 1865.

203. —— The same. 8vo. pp. 8.

204. ASHMUN, Mr., of Massachusetts. Speech upon the Slavery Question, in the House of Representatives of the United States, March 27, 1850. pp. 16.

205. At Anchor. A Story of our Civil War. By an American.
12mo. pp. 311.   New York: *D. Appleton & Co.*, 1865.

206. ATKINSON, Rt. Rev. Thomas, Bishop of North Carolina, Extract from the Address of, before the Council of the Protestant Episcopal Church, held at Raleigh, Sept. 13, 1865. 8vo. pp. 13.

207. ATKINSON, Rev. T. A Sermon preached in the Congregational Church, in Westport, Connecticut, Sept. 22, 1861.
8vo. pp. 23.   New York: *Hall, Clayton & Medole*, 1861.

208. ATKINSON, Edward. The Future Supply of Cotton. *North American Review for April*, 1864.

209. ATKINSON, EDWARD. Report to the Boston Board of Trade on the Cotton Manufacture of 1862, March 1, 1863, 8vo. pp. 21.

210. ATLANTA. History of the Rebel Steam Ram " Atlanta," now on Exhibition, Philadelphia, for the Benefit of the Union Volunteer Refreshment Sâloon. November, 1863.

    12mo. pp. 10.   PHILADELPHIA : *George H. Ives.*

211. —— Another edition, pp. 4, PHILADELPHIA.

212. ATLANTIC MONTHLY for 1860–1861.

    The Election in November, 1860. October, 1800.
    The Question of the Hour. January, 1861.
    E Pluribus Unum. February, 1861.
    Charleston under Arms. April, 1861.
    The Reign of King Cotton. April, 1861.
    Brother Jonathan's Lament for Sister Caroline. May, 1861.
    The Ordeal by Battle. July, 1861.
    The United States and Europe. July, 1861.
    Washington as a Camp. July, 1861.
    Nat Turner's Insurrection. August, 1861.
    Advantages of Defeat. September, 1861.
    Health in the Camp. November and December, 1861.
    The Contrabands at Fortress Monroe. November, 1861.
    Denmark Vesey. An Account of the Slave Insurrection of 1822. June, '61.
    The New York Seventh Regiment. Our March to Washington. June, '61.
    The Pickens-and-Stealins Rebellion. June, 1861.

213. ATLANTIC MONTHLY for 1862.

    Fremont's Hundred Days in Missouri. Jan., February and March, 1862.
    Jefferson and Slavery. January, 1862.
    Taxation. March, 1862.
    Slavery, in its Principles, Development and Expediency. May, 1862.
    Chiefly about War Matters. Nathaniel Hawthorne. July, 1862.
    Gabriel's Defeat. T. W. Higginson. September, 1862.
    The Sanitary Condition of the Army. Edward Jarvis, M. D. Oct. 1862.
    Resources of the South. E. H. Derby. October, 1862.
    The Hour and the Man. C. C. Hazwell. November, 1862.
    Conventional Opinions of the Leaders of Secession November, 1862.
    The President's Proclamation. November, 1862.
    My Hunt after " The Captain !" O. W. Holmes. December, 1862.

214. ATLANTIC MONTHLY for 1863.

    A Reply to "The Affectionate and Christian Address of many thousands of Women in Great Britain and Ireland, to their Sisters, the Women of the United States of America. By Mrs. H. B. Stowe. Jan., '63.
    Iron-Clad Ships and Heavy Ordnance. Alexander L. Holley. Jan., '63.
    The Siege of Cincinnati. T. B. Read. February, 1863.
    The Last Cruise of the Monitor. Grenville M. Weeks. March, 1863.
    A Call to my Countrywomen. Abigail Dodge. March, 1863.

Pericles and President Lincoln. Henry M. Alden. March, 1863.
No Failure for the North. F. Wayland, Jr. April, 1863.
Shall we Compromise? D. A. Wasson. May, 1863.
The Claims to Service and Labor. R. Dale Owen. July, 1863.
Our General [Butler.] July, 1863.
The Freedmen of Port Royal. Edward L. Pierce. August, 1863.
The United States Armory. George B. Prescott. September, 1863.
Our Domestic Relations. Charles Sumner. September, 1863.
Letter to a Peace Democrat. F. Wayland. Jr. December, 1863.

215. ATLANTIC MONTHLY for the year 1864.

Beginning of the End. C. C. Hazwell. January, 1864.
Northern Invasions. E. E. Hale. February, 1864.
The Peninsular Campaign. Lt. Colonel B. L. Alexander, March, 1864.
Our Soldiers. Mrs. Furnace. March, 1864.
Fighting Facts and Fogies. C. C. Hazwell. April, 1864.
Our Progressive Independence. O. W. Holmes. April, 1864.
On Picket Duty. Poetry. Mrs. W. T. Johnson. April, 1864.
The Presidential Election. C. C. Hazwell. May, 1864.
Re-enlisted. Poetry. Lucy Larcom. May, 1864.
How to Use Victory. E. E. Hale. June, 1864.
Currency. George S. Lang. July, 1864.
The May Campaign in Virginia. C. C. Coffin. July, 1864.
The Heart of the War. J. G. Holland. August, 1864.
Our Recent Foreign Relations. G. M. Towle. August, 1864.
Regular and Volunteer Officers. Col. T. W. Higginson. Sept., 1864.
Before Vicksburg. George H. Boker. September, 1864.
Our Visit to Richmond. J. R. Gilmore. September, 1864.
The Ride to Camp. George H. Boker. October, 1864.
Democracy and the Secession War. October, 1864.
Leaves from an Officer's Journal. T. W. Higginson. November, 1854.
Our Last Day in Dixie. J. R. Gilmore. December, 1864.
Leaves from an Officer's Journal. Col. T. W. Higginson. Dec., 1864.
England and America. Goldwin Smith. December, 1864.
We are a Nation. J. T. Trowbridge. December, 1864.

216. ATLANTIC MONTHLY for the year 1865.

A Fortnight with the Sanitary. G. Reynolds. February, 1865.
The Cause of Foreign Enmity to the United States. E. P. Whipple, March, 1865.
Up the St. Mary's. Col. Higginson. April, 1865.
If Massa put Guns into our hands. Fitz Hugh Ludlow. April, 1865.
John Brown's Raid: How I got into it, and how I got out of it. June, '65.
Late Scenes in Richmond. June, 1875.
The Place of Abraham Lincoln in History. June, 1865.
Assassination. C. C. Hazwell, July, 1865.
The Chicago Conspiracy. July, 1865.
My Second Capture. August, 1865.
Reconstruction and Negro Suffrage. August, 1866.
Up the St. John's River. Colonel Higginson. September, 1865.

"Running at the Heads." Being an authentic account of the Capture of
Jefferson Davis. September, 1865.
Our Future Military System. September, 1865.
John Jordan. From the Head of Barne. October, 1865.
Abraham Lincoln. (A Poem.) October, 1865.
Clemency and Common Sense. A curiosity of literature, with a moral.
Charles Sumner. December, 1865.

217. THE ATTEMPT OF THE NORTH to Subdue the Southerners, and
the Attempt of Spain to Subdue the Netherlanders. Is there any
Analogy between them? An off-hand Enquiry. By the author
of "Uncle John's Cabin, next door to Uncle Tom's Cabin."
12mo. pp. 16.   LONDON: *Simpkin, Marshall & Co.*, 1865.

218. ATTERBURY, Rev. JOHN G. God in Civil Government. A
Discourse preached in the First Presbyterian Church, New Albany, November 27, 1862.
8vo. pp. 16.   NEW ALBANY: *George R. Beach*, 1862.

219. ATWATER, Rev. LYMAN H., Professor, College of New Jersey.
The War and National Wealth. Note to the same. *Princeton
Review for July*, 1864.

220. ATWOOD, Rev. E. S. In Memoriam. Discourses in commemoration of Abraham Lincoln, President of the United States,
delivered in Salem, April 16, and June 1, 1865.
8vo. pp. 31.   SALEM: *Gazette*, 1865.

221. AUGHEY, Rev. JOHN H. The Iron Furnace; or Slavery and
Secession.
12mo. pp. 296. Portrait. PHILA.: *W. S. & Alfred Martien*, '63.

222. AUGHEY, Rev. SAMUEL. The Renovation of Politics. A Discourse delivered in St. Paul's Evangelical Lutheran Church,
Lionville, Pa., January 4, 1861,
8vo. pp. 15.   WEST CHESTER: *E. F. James*, 1861.

223. AUTOBIOGRAPHY of a Female Slave.
12mo. pp. 401.   NEW YORK: *Redfield*, 1851.

224. AYCRIGG, B. (Chairman.) Duties of American Citizens.
Position of New Jersey. Dated Passaic, N. J., May, 3, 1865.
8vo. pp. 16.   NEW YORK: *E. O. Jenkins*, 1856.

225. AYER, I. WINSLOW. The Great Northwestern Conspiracy, in
all its startling details.
8vo. pp. 112.   CHICAGO: *J. R. Walsh*, 1865.

226. AYDELOTT, Rev. B. P.   Prejudice against Colored People.
     8vo. pp. 21.   CINCINNATI : *American Reform Society*, 1863.
227. —— The same work.   8vo. pp. 12.   CINCINNATI.

B ACON, G. W.   The Life and Administration of Abraham Lincoln ;
     with a general View of his Policy, as President of the United
     States.   Embracing the Leading Events of the War.   Also, the
     European Press on his Death.
     8vo. pp. 183.   LONDON : *Bacon & Co.*, 1865.
229. —— The Life and Speeches of President Andrew Johnson, with
     a Sketch of the Secession Movement, and his course in relation
     thereto ; also, his Policy as President of the United States.
     8vo. pp. 106.   LONDON : *Bacon & Co.*, 1865.
240. —— Bacon's Guide to American Politics ; containing the Federal
     and Confederate Constitutions.   Comparative Resources of the
     North and South.   Political Reports, etc.
     8vo. pp. 100.   LONDON ; *Bacon & Co.*, 1864.
231. B——, W. D., Correspondent of the Cincinnati Commercial.
     Rosecrans' Campaign with the Fourteenth Army Corps, or the
     Army of the Cumberland.   A Narrative of personal observations,
     with an Appendix, consisting of Official Reports of the Battle of
     Stone River.
     12mo. pp. 476.   CINCINNATI ; *Moore, Wilstach & Co.*, 1863.
232. BABCOCK, CHARLES.   British Honduras.   Central America.
     A plain Statement to the Colored People of the United States,
     who contemplate Emigration.
     8vo. pp. 16.   BOSTON : *For the author*, 1863.
233. BABCOCK, Rev. SAMUEL, Rector of St. Paul's Church, Dedham.
     A Discourse on the Death of President Lincoln, preached in the
     Orthodox Cong. Church, in Dedham, Mass., April 19, 1865.
     8vo. pp. 16.   DEDHAM : (Mass.) *John Cox, Jr.*, 1865.
234. BACON, Rev. LEONARD, DD.   Reply to Professor Parker's Let-
     ter in the Boston Post, to Rev. Leonard Bacon.   *From the New
     Englander, for April,* 1863.
235. —— The Jugglers Detected.   A Discourse delivered in the
     Chapel St. Church, New Haven, Dec. 30, 1860. With Appendix.
     8vo. pp. 39.   NEW HAVEN : *Thomas H. Pease*, 1861.

236. BACON, Rev. LEONARD, D. D. The Morality of the Nebraska Bill. *From the New Englander for May*, 1861. 8vo. pp. 32.

237. —— Conciliation. A Discourse at a Sunday Evening Service, July 20, 1862.
8vo. pp. 20. NEW HAVEN : *Peck, White & Peck*, 1862.

238. BACON, WILLIAM KIRKLAND, late Adjutant of the Twenty-Sixth Regiment of New York State Volunteers, Memorial of. By his Father.
18mo. pp. 139. BOSTON : *American Tract Society*, 1865.

239. BADGER, Rev. HENRY C. Brief Statement of the Sanitary Commission's Work. (For Circulation on the Pacific Coast.)
8vo. pp. 16. *California Branch Sanitary Commission*, 1864.

240. —— The Humble Conquerer. A Discourse commemorative of the Life and Services of Abraham Lincoln, preached to the Cambridgeport Parish, April 26, 1865.
8vo. pp. 18. BOSTON : *For the author*, 1865.

241. BAILEY, Hon. ALEXANDER H., of Oneida. Review of Gov. Seymour's Message. In Senate of New York, Jan. 29, 1863.
8vo. pp. 12. ALBANY ; *Weed, Parsons & Co.*, 1863.

242. BAILEY, Hon. JOSEPH. Speech on the Bill for the Issuing of additional Treasury Notes, delivered in the House of Representatives, January 18, 1862. 8vo. pp. 8.

243. BAILEY, Rev. RUFUS WILLIAM, of South Carolina. The Issue, presented in a Series of Letters on Slavery.
12mo. pp. 110. NEW YORK : *John S. Taylor*, 1837.

244. BAILEY, Rev. SILAS, DD. The Moral Significance of War. A Discourse delivered in the Baptist Meeting House, Franklin, Indiana, September 26, 1861.
8vo. pp. 20. INDIANAPOLIS : *Dodd & Co.*, 1861.

245. BAIRD, SAMUEL J., DD. Southern Rights and Northern Duties in the Present Crisis. A Letter to the Hon. William Penington.
8vo. pp. 32. PHILADELPHIA : *Lindsay & Blackston*, 1861.

246. —— Slavery and the Slave Trade. *Princeton Review, July*, '62.

247. —— The Union and the Constitution. *Danville Review for September and December*, 1863.

248. BAIRD, THOMAS H. Memorial praying for the enactment of

measures to preserve the Constitution and Union of the States, presented to the House of Representatives, February 7, 1863.

8vo. pp. 23.   PITTSBURG : *A. A. Anderson & Sons,* 1864.

249. A BAKE-PAN for the Dough-Faces. By one of them.

8vo. pp. 64.   BURLINGTON : (Vermont) *C. Goodrich,* 1854.

250. BAKER, J. L. Slavery.

8vo. pp. 19.   PHILADELPHIA : *J. A. Norton,* 1860.

251. BAKER, Hon. EDWARD D., Addresses on the Death of, delivered in the House of Representatives, on Wednesday, Dec. 11, 1861.

8vo. pp, 87.   WASHINGTON : *Government Printing Office,* 1862.

252. ——— Address on the Life and Character of, by Thomas Fitch. Delivered at Placerville, California, February 6, 1862.

8vo. pp. 7.   PLACERVILLE : *"Republican Office,"* 1862.

253. BAKER, JAMES L. Exports and Imports, as showing the relative Advancement of every Nation in Wealth, Strength and Independence.

8vo. pp. 30.   PHILADELPHIA : 1859.

254. BAKER, JOHN. Thè Rebellion. A Speech delivered in the Hall of Representatives, at Springfield, Illinois, February 4 ; Bloomington, March 20, and at Belleville, March 20, 1863.

8vo. pp. 32.   BELLEVILLE : (Illinois) *F. Hawes & Co.,* 1863.

255. BAKER, Mrs. O. S. Ladies' Loyal League. *Continental Monthly, July,* 1863.

256. BAKER, STEPHEN, of New York. Prompt Pay the Essential Principle of Credit. Speech in the House of Representatives, January 13, 1862. 8vo. pp. 8.

257. BALCH, F. B. Our Ambulance System. *Christian Examiner, January,* 1864.

258. BALDWIN, AUGUSTUS C. Address delivered before the Democracy of Orion, Michigan, July 4, 1863. 8vo. pp. 15.

259. BALDWIN, JOHN D. State Sovereignty and Treason. Speech in House of Representatives, March 5, 1864. 8vo. pp. 8.

260. BALL, CHARLES. Slavery in the United States; a Narrative of the Life and Adventures of a Black Man, who lived 40 years in Maryland, South Carolina and Georgia, as a Slave.

12mo. pp. 517.   NEW YORK : *John S. Taylor,* 1857.

261. BALL, L. CHANDLER. Our Federal Relations. Speech in the Assembly of New York. June 29, 1861. 8vo. pp. 8.

262. BALL, L. Chandler. War Meeting. Speech delivered at Hoosick Falls, April 24, 1861. 8vo. pp. 7.

263. —— Extract from a Speech delivered at South Hoosick, on the Raising of the American Flag, May 25, 1861. 8vo. pp. 8.

264. The Ballot Box the Palladium of our Liberties. By Jacob Barker.
8vo. pp. 65. New Orleans: *For the compiler, July,* 1863.

265. BALLOU, Adin. The Voice of Duty. An Address delivered at the Anti-Slavery Picnic at Westminster, Mass., July 4, 1843.
8vo. pp. 12. Milford: (Mass.) *Community Press,* 1843.

266. —— Violations of the Federal Constitution in the "Irrepressible Conflict" between the pro-Slavery and anti-Slavery Sentiments of the American People.
12mo. pp. 48. Milford: (Mass.) 1861.

267. BALME, Rev. J. R. American States, Churches and Slavery. Post 8vo. pp. lxviii and 546. Lond.: *Hamilton, Adams & Co.,* '63.

268. —— Letters on the American Republic; or Common Fallacies. and Monstrous Errors Refuted and Exposed.
12mo. pp. vii and 290. London: *Hamilton, Adams & Co.*

269. —— Synopsis of the American War.
12mo. pp. 547–776. London: *Hamilton, Adams & Co.,* 1865.

270. Baltimore, A. D. 1862; or How they act in Baltimore. By A Volunteer Zouave. (A Poem.) Fourth Edition.
12mo. pp. 12. Baltimore: *James S. Watters,* 1862.

271. Baltimore, A. D. 1862; or the Volunteer Zouave in Baltimore. By an Officer of the "Guard."
12mo. pp. 5. Baltimore: *J. Davis & Co.,* 1862.

272. Baltimore. Memorial of Charles Howard, W. H. Getchell, John W. Davis, Police Commissioners of Baltimore, to the Senate and House of Representatives of the United States. 8vo. pp. 16.

The above named memorialists were prisoners confined in Fort McHenry.

273. Baltimore. Communication from the Mayor of Baltimore, with the Mayor and Board of Police of Baltimore City. [Relative to the passing of United States Troops through that city.]
8vo. pp. 8. Frederick: *Elihu S. Riley,* 1861.

274. Baltimore. Memorial of the Mayor and City Council of Balti-

5

more to Congress, with accompanying Documents. [Relative to the suspending of the functions of the Board of Police.]
  8vo. pp. 20.   BALTIMORE : *Wm. M. Innes*, 1861.

275. BALTIMORE. Second Annual Report of the Executive Committee of the Union Relief Association of Baltimore, June 25, 1863.
  8vo. pp.   BALTIMORE : *J. W Woods*, 1863.
  For other works relating to Baltimore, see *Maryland.*

276. BANCROFT, GEORGE. Letter to the Honorable Luther Bradish, President of the New York Historical Society, on the Exchange of Prisoners during the American War of Independence.
  8vo. pp. 7.   NEW YORK : 1862.

277. Mr. BANCROFT and his Boston Critics. [Relative to the Exchange of Prisoners.] From a Boston Newspaper, February, 1862.
  8vo. pp. 4.

278. BANCROFT, GEORGE. Oration on the 22d of February, 1862. (The Pulpit and Rostrum, No. 29.)
                                 NEW YORK : *E. D. Barker*, 1862.

279. —— The League for the Union. Speeches of Hon. George Bancroft and James Miliken, Esq.
  8vo. pp. 20.   PHILADELPHIA : *W. S. & A. Martien*, 1863·

280. —— Oration pronounced in New York, at the Obsequies of Abraham Lincoln, April 25, 1865. The Funeral Ode by William Cullen Bryant. President Lincoln's Emancipation Proclamation. His last Inaugural Address, March 4, 1865. *Pulpit and Rostrum, No.* 34 *and* 35. 12mo. pp. 23.

281. BANK LAW. The United States. Bank Law. An act to provide a National Currency, secured by a pledge of United States Stocks, and to provide for the circulation and redemption thereof. Approved February 25, 1863.
  8vo. pp. 28.   NEW YORK : *D. Appleton & Co.*, 1863.

282. —— The same.
  8vo. pp. 28.   WASHINGTON : *Government Printing Office*, 1863.

283. BANK TAX and Bank Currency. An Appeal to the Congress of the U. S., by a Committee of New Jersey State Bank Officers.
  8vo. pp. 18.   TRENTON : (N. J.) *American Office*, 1864.

284. BANKS. Report of the Loan Committee of the associated Banks of the City of New York, June 12, 1862.
  8vo. pp. 45.   NEW YORK : *Hall & Clayton*, 1862.

285. BANKING ASSOCIATION and Uniform Currency Bill, with extracts from Reports of Secretary of the Treasury, submitted to Congress in December, 1861, and December, 1862. 8vo. pp. 36.

286. BANKS, Maj. General N. P.   Letter to the Hon. James H. Lane, Senator of Kansas.   (Relative to the Reconstruction of the of the Union.)   8vo. pp. 12.

287. —— The Reconstruction of States.   A Letter to Senator Lane. 8vo. pp. 23.   NEW YORK: *Harper & Brothers,* 1865.

288. —— Suggestions presented to the Judiciary Committee of the Senate of the U. S., relating to the State of Louisiana.   8vo. pp. 8.   38*th Congress, Senate Miscellaneous Document, No.* 9, 1865.

289. —— An Address delivered at the Custom House, New Orleans, on the 4th of July, 1865.   8vo. pp. 15.

290. BANKRUPTCY.   A Bill to establish a Uniform System of Bankruptcy throughout the United States.   Reported by the Hon. Thomas A. Jenckes, from the Select Committee on the Uniform System of Bankruptcy.   February 15, 1864.
8vo. pp. 29.   NEW YORK: *Dodge & Grattan,* 1864.

291. BANKRUPT LAW.   A Memorial to the Congress of the United States for a General Bankrupt Law.   New York, Oct. 1, 1861. 8vo. pp. 14.   NEW YORK: *Baker & Godwin,* 1861.

292. BANKRUPT LAW.   Proposed General Bankrupt Act for the United States, as prepared under the direction of a Committee of Merchants and Bankers in the City of New York, Nov. 30, 1861.
8vo, pp. 40.   NEW YORK: *John F. Trow,* 1861.

293. BANKRUPT LAW.   Speech on, delivered by the Hon. Thomas A. Jenckes, in the House of Representatives, June 1, 1864.
8vo. pp. 16.   WASHINGTON: *McGill & Witherow,* 1864.

294. BAPTISTS.   The Baptists of the North on the State of the Country.
8vo. pp. 11.   BROOKLYN: (N. Y.) May 27, 1861.

295. BARCLAY, Rev. CUTHBERT C.   Sermon on the Times.   A Sermon preached in St. Thomas' Church, Bethel, January 4, 1860. 8vo. pp. 19.   NEW HAVEN: *Tuttle, Morehouse & Co.,* 1861.

296. BARKER, Capt. AYERS C.   A Funeral Discourse preached in memory of, by Rev. C. M. Eggleston, Greenville, July 26, 1863. 8vo. pp. 19.   COXSACKIE: (N. Y.) *F. C. Dedrick*

297. **BARKER, Thomas H.**   Union and Emancipation.   A Reply to the Christian News Articles on Emancipation and War.
8vo. pp. 23.   Manchester : *Un. and Emancipation So'y*, 1863.

298. **BARNARD, Major J. G.**   Letter to the Editors of the National Intelligencer, in answer to the Charges against the United States Military Academy, in the Report of the Secretary of War, of July, 1861.
8vo. pp. 18.   New York : *D. Van Nostrand*, 1862.

299. **BARNARD, General J. G.**   The C. S. A. and the Battle of Bull Run.   (A Letter to an English Friend.)   With Maps.
8vo. pp. 136.   New York : *D. Van Nostrand*, 1862.

300. —— The Peninsular Campaign and its Antecedents, as developed by the Report of Maj. General George B. McClellan, and other published documents.
8vo. pp. 15.   Washington : *Union Cong. Committee*, 1864.

301. —— The same.   New York : *Van Nostrand*, 1863.

302. **BARNARD, F. A. P.**, of Missouri.   Letter to the President of the United States.   By a Refugee.
8vo. pp. 32.   New York : *C. S. Westcott & Co..* 1863.

303. **BARNES, Rev. Albert.**   An Inquiry into the Scriptural Views of Slavery.
12mo. pp. 384.   Philadelphia : *Perkins & Purves*, 1846.

304. —— The Church and Slavery.
12mo. pp. 196.   Philadelphia : *Parry & McMillan*, 1857.

305. —— The Conditions of Peace.   A Thanksgiving Discourse delivered in the First Presbyterian Church, Philadelphia, November 27, 1862.
8vo. pp. 63.   Philadelphia : *H. B. Ashmead*, 1863.

306. —— The State of the Country.   A Discourse delivered in the First Presbyterian Church of Philadelphia, June 1, 1865, the day appointed as a day of Humiliation and Mourning, in view of the Death of the President of the United States.
8vo. pp. 74.   Philadelphia : *H. B. Ashmead*, 1865.

307. **BARNES, David M.**   The Draft Riots in New York, July, 1863.   The Metropolitan Police.   Their Services during Riot Week.   Their Honorable Record.
8vo. pp. 117.   New York : *Baker & Godwin*, 1863.

308. BARNES, W. H.   The Drama of Secession; or Scenes from American History.

18mo. pp. 60.   INDIANAPOLIS: *Merrill & Co.*, 1862.

309. BARRETT, EDWARD, Lieut.   Commanding United Sates Navy. Temporary Fortifications prepared for the Naval Service.

8vo. pp. 14.   NEW YORK: *For the author*, 1863.

310. BARRETT, JOSEPH H.   Life of Abraham Lincoln; presenting his Early History, Political Career, and Speeches, in and out of Congress; also, a General View of his Policy as President of the United States, with his Messages, Proclamations, Letters, etc., and a Concise History of the War.

12mo. pp. 518.   CINCINNATI: *Moore, Wilstach & Co.*, 1864.

311. —— The same in German.   Ibid. 1864.

312. —— The same.   With an Account of the Scenes attendant upon his tragic and lamented Demise.

8vo. pp. 842.   CINNINNATI: *Moore, Wilstach & B.*, 1865.

313. BARROWS, WILLIAM.   Our War and our Religion, and their Harmony.   A Discourse delivered in the Old South Church, Reading, Massachusetts, March 2, 1862.

8vo. pp. 19.   BOSTON: *J. M. Whittemore & Co.*, 1862.

314. —— Honor to the Brave.   A Discourse delivered Aug. 23, 1863.

8vo. pp. 19.   BOSTON: *John M. Whittemore & Co.*, 1863.

315. —— The Standard of the Northern Army. *Boston Review, Vol.* 1.

316. —— The Present State of Our Country Historically developed. *Boston Review, Vol.* 2.

317. —— The Southern Insurrection. *Boston Review, Vol.* 2.

318. —— English Parties on American Affairs. *Boston Review, Vol.* 3.

319. —— The Sword and Christianity. *Boston Review, Vol.* 3.

320. —— The War and Slavery, and their Relations to each other.   A Discourse delivered in the Old South Church, Reading, Mass. December 28, 1862.

8vo. pp. 18.   BOSTON: *J. M. Whittemore & Co.*, 1863.

321. BARTLETT, JOHN RUSSELL.   History of the Great Conspiracy and Rebellion in the United States, gleaned from the Newspapers of the day.   Embracing a Daily Record of Events, Narratives, Letters, Military and Naval Orders, Official Reports and Documents, Speeches, Lectures, Statistics, Editorial Comments, etc.

Commencing in September, 1860, and continuing to end of the year 1865.

Folio 70 volumes.   PROVIDENCE, R. I.

This collection of newspaper cuttings includes the wood cuts, maps and plans from the various pictorial newspapers, and from other sources.

322. BARTLETT, JOHN RUSSELL. The Fugitive Poetry of the Rebellion, collected from the Newspapers of the day,—1860 to 1865. 2 vols. folio.

323. —— The Caricatures of the Rebellion, comprising the wood cuts from illustrated papers of New York and London.   3 vols. folio.

324. —— Pictorial Envelopes, relating to the Rebellion.   1 vol. folio.

325. —— Ballads of the Rebellion. (Each on a separate sheet.) 2 v. 4to.

326. —— Battle Scenes, Views and Portraits, illustrative of the Rebellion.   3 vols. atlas folio.

The above mentioned articles are uniformly bound in half morocco.

327. —— Memoirs of Rhode Island Officers who have rendered distinguished service to their country, in the contest of the Great Rebellion of the South.   With a History of each Rhode Island Regiment.   Illustrated with 30 Portraits engraved on steel.   4to. now in the press.

328 —— Literature of the Rebellion.   A Catalogue of Books and Pamphlets relating to the Great Rebellion of the United States, and to American Slavery.   (In press.)

8vo. pp.   PROVIDENCE : *Knowles, Anthony & Co.*, 1866.

329. —— Report to the General Assembly of the State of Rhode Island, on the Soldier's National Cemetery at Gettysburg, January, 1865.   8vo. pp. 6.

330. BARTLETT, WILLIAM A.   A portion of the Evidence submitted to the Senate, in the case of Wm. A. Bartlett, formerly a Lieutenant in the Navy of the United States.   (July, 1856.) 8vo. pp. 32.

331. BARTOL, Rev. C. A.   The Recompense.   A Sermon for Country and Kindred, delivered in the West Church, Aug. 24, 1862.

8vo. pp. 23.   BOSTON : *Ticknor & Fields*, 1862.

332. —— The Remission of Blood ; a Tribute to our Soldiers and the Sword.   Delivered in the West Church.

8vo. pp. 19.   BOSTON : *Walker, Wise & Co.*, 1862.

333. —— Conditions of Peace.   A Discourse delivered in the West Church in memory of David K. Hobart, June 14, 1863.

8vo. pp. 28.   BOSTON : *Walker, Wise & Co.*, 1863.

334. BARTOL, Rev. C. A. The Nation's Hour. A Tribute to Major Sidney Willard, delivered in the West Church, Dec. 21, 1862. 8vo. pp. 58. BOSTON: *Walker, Wise & Co.*, 1862.

335. —— The Purchase of Blood. A Tribute to Brig. Gen. Charles Russell Lowell, Jr. Spoken in the West Church, Oct. 30, 1864. 8vo. pp. 21. BOSTON: *John Wilson & Son*, 1864.

336. BASSETT, GEORGE W., of Ottowa Illinois. A Northern Plea for the right of Secession. 8vo. pp. 24. OTTAWA: (Ill.) *Free Trade Office*, 1861.

337. —— A Discourse on the wickedness and folly of the present War, delivered in the Court House, Ottawa, Ill., August 11, 1861. p. 24.

338. BASSETT, WILLIAM. Letter to a Member of the Society of Friends, in reply to objections against joining Anti-Slavery Societies. 12mo. pp. 41. BOSTON: *Isaac Knapp*, 1837.

339. THE BASTILE IN AMERICA; or Democratic Absolutism. By an Eye Witness. 8vo. pp. 19. LONDON: *Robert Hardwicke*, 1861.

340. THE BASTILES OF THE NORTH. By a Member of the Maryland Legislature. (Lawrence Sangston.) 8vo. pp. 136. BALTIMORE: *Kelly, Hedian & Co.*, 1863.

341. BATES, EDWARD, Attorney General. Opinion on Citizenship. 8vo. pp. 27. WASHINGTON *Government Printing Office*, 1862.

342. —— Opinion on the Validity of the Acceptances given by John B. Floyd, Secretary of War, to Russell, Majors and Waddell, now held by Peirce and Bacon. (1862.) 8vo. pp. 17.

343. BATTLE FIELDS OF THE SOUTH, from Bull Run to Fredericksburg, with Sketches of Confederate Commanders, and Gossip of the Camps. By an English Combatant. (T. E. C.) 8vo. pp. 517. NEW YORK: *John Bladburn*, 1864.

344. —— The same work. 2 vols. 8vo. pp. 339 and 399. LONDON: *Smith, Elder & Co.*, '63.

345. BAUGHER, H. L., DD., President of Pennsylvania College, The Christian Patriot. A Discourse to the Graduating Class of Pennsylvania College, September 15, 1861. 8vo. pp. 25. GETTYSBURG: *A. D. Buehler*, 1861.

346. THE BAY FIGHT., Mobile Bay, August 5, 1864. Reprinted from *Harper's Monthly*. 12mo. pp. 18.

347. BAXTER, WILLIAM. Pea Ridge and Prairie Grove; or Scenes and Incidents of the War of Arkansas.
16mo. pp. 262. CINCINNATI : *Poe & Hitchcock,* 1864.

348. BAXTER, W. E. (M. P.) The Social Condition of the Southern States of America. A Lecture delivered in the Commercial Exchange Hall, Dundee, November 5, 1862.
12mo. pp. 28. LONDON : *J. Nesbitt & Co.,* 1862.

349. BAYARD, Hon. JAMES A. Condition of the Country. Speech in the Senate of the United States, March 20, 21 and 22, 1861.
8vo. pp. 43. WASHINGTON : *H. Polkinhorn,*

350. —— Executive Usurpation. Speech in the Senate of the United States, July 19, 1861. pp. 24.

351. —— Executive Usurpation. In the Senate of the United States, July 19, 1861. 8vo. pp. 24.

352. —— Speech on the Expulsion of Mr. Bright. Delivered in the Senate of the United States, February 5, 1862. 8vo. pp. 16.

353. —— Abolition, and the Relation of Races. A Speech delivered in the Senate of the United States, April 3, 1862. pp. 18.

354. —— Abolition and the Relation of Races. Speech delivered in the Senate of the United States, April 2, 1862. pp. 15.

355. —— Two Speeches delivered in the United States Senate, February 28 and March 3, 1863, in opposition to the Conscription Bill, and the Bill to appoint a Dictator, entitled "An Act relating to Habeas Corpus, and regulating Judicial Proceedings in certain cases."
8vo. pp. 32. BALTIMORE : *W. M. Innes,* 1863.

356. —— Speech delivered in the Senate of the United States, Jan. 19, 1864, against the Validity of the Test Oath of July 2, 1862, with the subsequent Proceedings in the Senate, and his final Remarks before the resignation of his Seat. Also, a Letter addressed by Mr. Bayard to a Constituent, December 22, 1860.
8vo pp. 38. PHILADELPHIA : 1864.

357. BEACH, LEWIS. A Word or two about the War.
8vo. pp. 28. NEW YORK : *John F. Trow.*

358. BEADLE'S DIME KNAPSACK SONGSTER ; containing the choicest Patriotic Songs, together with many new and original ones, set to Old Melodies.
18mo. pp. 72. NEW YORK : *Beadle & Co.,* 1862.

359. BEADLE's MONTHLY. Ball's Bluff. A Ballad of the War. *Jan.,* '66.
360. —— The Prisoner of War in Texas. *January,* 1866.
361. BEALL. Trial of John Y. Beall, as a Spy and Guerrillero. By Military Commission.
8vo. pp. 94. NEW YORK : *D. Appleton & Co.,* 1865.
362. BEALL, JOHN Y., The Pirate Spy.
12mo. pp. 106. NEW YORK : *T. R. Dawley,* 1865.
363. BEAMAN, F. C., of Michigan. Provisional Governments over the Districts of Country now in Rebellion against the Lawful Authority of the United States. Speech in the House of Representatives, April 4, 1862. 8vo. pp. 7.
364. —— Reconstruction. A Speech in the House of Representatives, March 22, 1864, on the Bill to Guarantee to certain States, whose Governments have been usurped, or overthrown, a Republican Form of Government. 8vo. pp. 15.
365. BEASLEY, ROBERT E. A Plan to stop the present, and prevent future Wars ; containing a proposed Constitution for the General Government of the Southern States of North and South America.
12mo. pp. 24. RIO VISTA : (Cal.) *For the author,* 1864.
366. BEAUMONT, GUSTAVE DE, Marie, ou L'esclavage aux Etats-Unis. Tableau de Moeurs Americaines.
12mo. pp. 392. PARIS : *Charles Gosselin,* 1840.
367. BECKER, ALEXANDER R., M. D. Gun-Shot Wounds ; particularly those caused by newly-invented missiles. An Essay which received the Fiske Fund Premium of the Rhode Island Medical Society. Reprinted from the Boston Medical and Surgical Journal, February, 1865. 8vo. pp. 33.
368. BEECHER, EDWARD. A Narrative of the Riots at Alton ; in connection with the Death of Rev. Elijah P. Lovejoy.
12mo. pp. 169. ALTON : *George Holton,* 1838.
369. BEECHER, Rev. HENRY WARD. War and Emancipation. A Thanksgiving Sermon, preached in the Plymouth Church, Brooklyn, N. Y., Thursday, November 21, 1861. 8vo. pp. 31.
370. —— Freedom and War. Discourses on Topics suggested by the Times.
12mo. pp. 445. BOSTON : *Ticknor & Fields,* 1863.
371. —— The American Cause in England. An Address on the
6

American War. Delivered at Free Trade Hall, Manchester, England, October 9, 1863.

8vo. pp. 15.   NEW YORK: *Coutant & Baker*, 1863.

372. England and America. Speech at the Free Trade Hall, Manchester, October 9, 1863.

12mo. pp. 39.   BOSTON: *James Redpath*, 1863.

373. BEECHER, Rev. HENRY WARD. American Rebellion. Report of the Speeches of the Rev. Henry Ward Beecher, delivered at Public Meetings in Manchester, Glasgow, Edinburgh, Liverpool and London.

8vo. pp. 174.   MANCHESTER: *Union and Emanc. Soc'y*, 1864.

374. —— Oration at Raising the Old Flag over Fort Sumter, April 14, 1865. (Pulpit and Rostrum, No. 33.) pp. 24.

375. —— Presentation Memorial to Working Men. Oration at the Raising of "the Old Flag," at Sumter; and Sermon on the Death of Abraham Lincoln, President of the United States. Also, a Sketch of Mr. Lincoln by J. H. Estcourt.

8vo. pp. 55.   MANCHESTER: (Eng.) *A. Ireland & Co.*, 1865.

376. THE BEGINNING and the End. Dedicated to the Army of the Potomac. By your Humble Wagoner.

8vo. pp. 41.   NEW YORK: *John A. Gray & Green*, 1863.

377. BELL, JOHN. Speech on Slavery in the United States, and the Causes of the present Dissensions between the North and South. Delivered in the Senate, July 5 and 6, 1850. 8vo. pp. 30.

378. BELLEYME, ADOLPHE. La France et le Mexique.

8vo. pp. 23.   PARIS: 1863.

379. BELLOWS, HENRY W., DD. Duty and Interest identical in the present Crisis. A Sermon preached in All Soul's Church, April 14, 1861.

8vo. pp. 16.   NEW YORK: *Wynkoop, Hallenbeck & Co.*, 1861.

380. —— The State and the Nation, Sacred to Christian Citizens. A Sermon preached April 21, 1861.

8vo. pp. 16.   NEW YORK: *James Miller*, 1861.

381. —— The Advantage of Testing our Principles, compensatory of the Evils of Serious Times. A Discourse, February 17, 1861, before the Second Unitarian Society of Philadelphia.

8vo. pp. 26.   PHILADELPHIA: *C. Sherman & Son*, 1861.

382. BELLOWS, Henry W., D. D. The Valley of Decision. A Plea for unbroken Fealty on the part of the Loyal States to the Constitution and the Union, despite the Offences of the Rebel States. A Discourse preached September 26, 1861.

8vo. pp. 25. NEW YORK : *H. B. Price,* 1861.

383. —- President of the United States Sanitary Commission. Speech at the Academy of Music, Philadelphia, Tuesday evening, February 24, 1863.

8vo. pp. 32. PHILADELPHIA : *C. Sherman, Son & Co.,* 1863.

384. —— Unconditional Loyalty.

12mo. pp. 12. NEW YORK : *A. D. F. Randolph,* 1863.

385. —— The same. pp. 16. Ibid, 1863.

386. —— The War to end only when the Rebellion ceases.

8vo. pp. 16. NEW YORK : *Anson D. F. Randolph.*

387. —— The New Man for the New Times. A Sermon preached in All Souls' Church, June 1, 1864.

8vo. pp. 16. NEW YORK ; *James Miller,* 1865.

388. BEMAN, Nathan S. S., DD. Characteristics of the Age. A Discourse delivered in the First Presbyterian Church, Troy, N. Y., Thanksgiving Day, December 12, 1850.

8vo. pp. 32. TROY: (N. Y.) *Young & Heart,* 1851.

Among other topics discussed are American Slavery, Compromise, the Fugitive Slave Law, etc.

389. —— Antagonisms in the Moral and Political World. A Discourse delivered in the First Presbyterian Church, Troy, New York, on Thanksgiving Day, November, 18, 1858.

8vo. pp. 36. TROY : (N. Y.) *A. W. Scribner & Co.,* 1858.

390. —— Thanksgiving in the Times of Civil War ; being a Discourse delivered in the First Presbyterian Church, Troy, N. Y., November 28, 1861.

8vo. pp. 46. TROY : *A. W. Scribner & Co.,* 1861.

391. —— Our Civil War. The Principles involved. Its Cause and Cure ; being a Discourse delivered November 27, 1862.

8vo. pp. 52. TROY : (N. Y.) *A. W. Scribner & Co.,* 1863.

392. BEMENT, Ernest M. An Appeal to the Citizens of New York for the Organization of the Andrew Johnson Cavalry, for special service in East Tennessee.

8vo. pp. 12. NEW YORK ; *Wyncoop & Hallenbreck,* 1863.

393. BEMIS, George. Hasty Recognition of Rebel Belligerancy, and our Right to Complain of it.
8vo. pp. viii and 57. Boston : *A. Williams & Co.*, 1865.

394. —— Precedents of American Neutrality ; in Reply to the Speech of Sir Roundell Palmer, Attorney General of England, in the British House of Commons, May 13, 1864.
8vo. pp. viii and 83. Boston : *Little, Brown & Co.*, 1864.

395. BENEDICT, Hon. E. C. The War. Speech in the Assembly of the State of New York, April 6, 1864.
8vo. pp. 16. Albany : *Weed, Parsons & Co.*, 1864.

396. BENJAMIN, Judah P. Relations of States. Speech deliverd in the Senate of the United States, May 8, 1860, on the Resolutions submitted by the Hon. Jefferson Davis, March 1, 1860.
8vo. pp. 8. Baltimore : *Murphy & Co.*, 1860.

397. —— Speech on the Right of Secession. Delivered in the Senate of the United States, December 31, 1860. 8vo. pp. 16.

398. —— Intercepted Instructions to L. Q. C. Lamar, Styled Commissioner, etc. The African Slave Trade. The Secret Purpose of the Insurgents to Revive it.
8vo. pp. 34. Philadelphia : *C. Sherman & Son*, 1863.

399· BENJAMIN, S. G. W. Ode on the Death of Abraham Lincoln.
12mo. pp. 15. Boston : *William V. Spencer*, 1865.

400. BENTON, Thomas H. Historical and Legal Examination of that part of the Decision of the Supreme Court of the United States in the Dred Scott Case, which declares the unconstitutionality of the Missouri Compromise Act and the Self-Extension of the Constitution to Territories, carrying Slavery along with it.
8vo. pp. 193. New York : *D. Appleton & Co.*, 1857.

401. BERNARD, Mountague, M. A. On the Principle of Intervention. A Lecture delivered in the Hall of All Souls' College, (Oxford, England.)
8vo. pp. 36. Oxford and London : *J. H. & Jas. Parker*, 1860.

402. —— Two Lectures on the present American War.
8vo. pp. London : 1862.

403. BERRY, Rev. J. Romeyn. Christian Patriotism. A Sermon delivered in the Reformed Dutch Church of Kinderhook, June 23, 1861.
8vo. pp. 34. Albany : *Weed, Parsons & Co.*, 1861.

404. BETTLE, Edward. Notices of Negro Slavery, as connected with Pennsylvania. Memoirs of the Historical Society of Pennsylvania. Vol. 1. pp. 365.

405. The Bible on the Present Crisis. The Republic of the United States, and its Counterfeit Presentment; the Slave Power and the Southern Confederacy; the Copperhead Organization and the Knights of the Golden Circle; the Civil War in which they are involved; its duration and final results, described in Daniel and the Revelations, etc.
8vo. pp. 104. New York: *Sinclair Toucey.*

406. The Bible in the Army; a Statement of the Distribution of the Scriptures among the Military and Naval Forces of the Union, by the New York Bible Society, 1861.
8vo. pp. 31. New York: *Bible Society*, 1862.

407. BIDDLE, Hon. Charles J. The Alliance with the Negro. Speech in the House of Representatives of the United States, March 6, 1862. 8vo. pp. 8.

408 —— Speech in House of Representatives, June 2, 1862, on the Bill to appoint Diplomatic Representatives to the Republics of Hayti and Liberia. 8vo. pp. 8.

409. —— Soldiers Read!! Citizens Read!!! Address of the Democratic State Central Committee, September 19, 1863. Letter of Maj. Geo. A. Woodward. Letter of Judge Woodward.
8vo. pp. 8. Philadelphia: *Age Office*, 1863.

410. —— Address of the Democratic State Central Committee, Aug. 11, 1863. 8vo. pp. 8.

411. —— Eulogy upon the Hon. George Mifflin Dallas, delivered before the Bar of Philadelphia, February 11, 1865.
8vo. pp. 51. Philadelphia: *McLaughlin Brothers.*

412. BIGELOW, E. B. Internal Tax Simplified. Letter to the Hon. Thaddeus Stevens, Chairman of the Committee of Ways and Means. Dated, Washington: *March* 9, 1862. 8vo. pp. 8.

413. BIGELOW, John. Les Etats Unis d'Amerique en 1863; Leurs Histoire Politique; Leurs Resources Agricoles Industrielles et Commerciales.
8vo. pp. 557. Paris: *L. Hatchette & Co.*, 1863.

414. BIGLER, Hon. William. Speech on the State of the Union,

delivered in the Senate of the United States, January 21, 1861. 8vo. pp. 16.

415. BIGLER, Hon. WILLIAM, Address delivered at New Hope, Bucks Co., Pennsylvania, September 17, 1863.

8vo. pp. 13.   HARRISBURG: *Patriot Office*, 1863.

416. BILBO, Col. W. N. The Past, Present and Future of the Southern Confederacy. An Oration delivered in the City of Nashville, October 12, 1861.

8vo. pp. 47.   NASHVILLE: *J. D. W. Green & Co.*. 1861.

417. BINET, M. G. Neuf Mois aux Etats Unis d'Amerique.

12mo. pp. 184.   GENEVE: 1862.

8vo. pp. 122. WASHINGTON: *Government Printing Office*, 1865.

418. BINGHAM, JOEL F. The Hour of Patriotism. A Discourse delivered at the United States Service of the First Lafayette St., North, and Westminster Churches, Buffalo, November 27, 1862.

8vo. pp. 39.   BUFFALO: *Franklin Press*, 1862.

419. —— Great Providences toward the Loyal Part of this Nation. A Discourse delivered at the United Service of the Seven Presbyterian Congregations of Buffalo, Nov. 24, 1864, on the occasion of the Annual Thanksgiving of the State and the Nation.

8vo. pp. 59,   BUFFALO: *Breed, Butler & Co.*, 1864.

420. —— National Disappointment. A Discourse occasioned by the Assassination of President Lincoln, delivered in Westminster Church, Buffalo, May 7, 1865.

8vo. pp. 36.   BUFFALO: *Breed, Butler & Co.*, 1865.

421. BINGHAM, Hon. JOHN A., of Ohio. The Treasury Note Bill. Speech in the House of Representatives, Feb. 4, 1862. 8vo. p. 8.

422. —— Self-Preservation the Right and Duty of the General Government. The Rebel States but Organized Conspiracies; not Constitutional States, nor entitled to State Rights. Speech in the House of Representatives, March 12, 1862. 8vo. pp. 8.

423. —— Shall the Government surrender to the Rebellion? Speech in Reply to Hon. C. L. Vallandigham, delivered in the House of Representatives, January 14. 1863. 8vo. pp. 16.

424. BINGHAM, JOHN A., Special Judge Advocate. Argument in the Case of the Conspirators for the Assassination of President Lincoln. Delivered June 27, 28, 1865, before the Military Commission, Washington. D. C.

425. BINNEY, HORACE. The Privilege of the Writ of Habeas Corpus under the Constitution.
12mo. pp. 52.   PHILADELPHIA : *T. B. Pugh*, 1862.

426. —— The Privilege of the Writ of Habeas Corpus, under the Constitution. Second edition.
8vo. pp. 58.   PHILADELPHIA : *C. Sherman & Son*, 1862.

427. —— The Privilege of the Writ of Habeas Corpus, under the Constitution. Second Part.
8vo. pp. 50.   PHILADELPHIA : *C. Sherman & Son*, 1862.

428. —— A Reply to Horace Binney's Pamphlet on the Habeas Corpus. (Anonymous.)
8vo. pp. 40.   PHILADELPHIA : 1862.

429. —— Presidential Power over Personal Liberty. A Review of Horace Binney's Essay on the Writ of Habeas Corpus.
8vo. pp. 94.   *Imprinted for the author*, 1862.

430. —— A Review of Mr. Binney's Pamphlet on "the Privilege of the Writ of Habeas Corpus under the Constitution." By J. C. Bullett.
8vo. pp. 56.   PHILADELPHIA : *John Campbell*, 1862.

431. —— The Privilege of the Writ of Habeas Corpus under the Constitution. Third Part.
8vo. pp. 74.   PHILADELPHIA : *C. Sherman & Co.*, 1865.

For other Replies to Mr. Binney's Pamphlet, see *S. S. Nicholas, T. Jackson, David B. Brown, J. T. Montgomery* and *G. M. Wharton.*

432. —— Letter to the General Committee, of Invitation and Correspondence of the Union League of Philadelphia, June 25, 1863.
8vo. pp. 4.

433. BINNEY, WILLIAM. Oration on the Death of Abraham Lincoln. Delivered before the Municipal Authorities of the City of Providence, June 1, 1865. With the Proceedings on the Occasion.
8vo. pp. 56.   PROVIDENCE ; *Knowles, Anthony & Co.*, 1865.

434. BIRCH, JAMES H. Speech delivered in the House of Representatives, June 1, 1864, in his Contested Election Case with Austin A. King. 8vo. pp. 12.

435. BIRDSEYE, GEORGE W. Woman and the War. A Poem.
8vo. pp. 24.   NEW YORK : *J. Dickson*, 1865.

436. BIRNEY, James G.   Letter on Colonization, addressed to the Rev. Thornton J. Mills.

   18mo. pp. 46.   New York : *Anti Slavery Society*, 1838.

437. —— Examination of the Decision of the Supreme Court of the United States, in the Case of Strader, Gorham and Armstrong vs. Christopher Graham, December, 1850.   Concluding with an Address to the Free Colored People, advising them to remove to Liberia.

   8vo. pp. 46.   Cincinnati : *Truman & Spofford*, 1852.

438. —— Letter to Hon. John F. Driggs, August, 1863.   pp. 23.

439. The Birth and Death of Nations.   A Thought for the Crisis.

   12mo. pp. 33.   New York : *G. P. Putnam*, 1862.

440. BISHOP, Brig. Gen. Albert W.   An Oration delivered at Fayetteville, Kansas, July 4, 1865.

   8vo. pp. 27.   New York : *Baker & Goodwin*, 1865.

441. BISHOP, John Prentiss.   Thoughts for the Times.

   8vo. pp. 36.   Boston : *Little, Brown & Co.*, 1863,

442. BISHOP, Joel P.   Commentaries on the Criminal Law.

   2 vols 8vo.   Boston ; *Little, Brown & Co.*, 1865.

   This Third and greatly enlarged edition of Mr. Bishop's learned work embraces much that is applicable to the late Rebellion and matters that have grown out of it; including chapters, or legal discussions on Treason, Civil War, the Forum for the Trial of the Leaders of the Rebellion, Military Arrests, Suspension of the Writ of Habeas Corpus, the Jurisdiction of Congress over Seceded States, Extension of Franchise to Negroes, etc.

443. BITTINGER, Rev. J. B.   A Sermon preached before the Presbyterian Churches of Cleveland, on the National Fast Day, September 26, 1861.

   8vo. pp. 21.   Cleveland : *E. Cowles & Co.*, 1861.

444. BITTINGER, J. Q.   Caires on the Slave Power.   *North American Review for April*, 1863.

445. BLACK, Jeremiah S.   Speech at the Democratic Mass Convention, in Lancaster City, September, 17, 1863.

   8vo. pp. 7.   Harrisburg : *Patriot Office*, 1863.

446. Blacks and Mulattoes.   Report of the Senate Committee relative to the Immigration of the Blacks and Mulattoes into the State of Pennsylvania.   March 6, 1863.   8vo. pp. 4.

447. BLACKBURN, Rev. W. M.   Thanksgiving for Victory.   A Ser-

mon delivered in the Park Presbyterian Church, Erie, Pa., August 6, 1863. 8vo. pp. 24.

448. BLACKBURN, Rev. W. M. The Crime against the Presidency. A Sermon delivered Sunday, April 10, 1865, in the Fourth Presbyterian Church, Trenton, N. J.
8vo. pp. 24. TRENTON: (N. J.) *Murphy & Bechtet*, 1865.

449. BLACKWOOD MAGAZINE. The Disruption of the Union. *July*, '61.

450. —— Spence's American Union, *April*, 1862.

451. —— President Jefferson Davis. *September*, 1862.

452. —— Trollope's North America. *September*, 1862.

453. —— The Crisis of the American War. *November*, 1862.

454. —— A Month's Visit to the Confederate Head Quarters. *Jan.* '63.

455. —— Belligerent Rights at Sea, and the Changes proposed in them. *January*, 1863.

456. —— American State Papers. *May*, 1863.

457. —— The Battle of Gettysburg, and the Campaign in Pennsylvania. From the Diary of an English Officer present with the Confederate Army. *September*, 1863.

458. —— Our Rancorous Cousins. *November*, 1863.

459. —— Books on the American War. *December*, 1863.

460. —— Our Neutrality. *April*, 1864.

461. —— A Visit to the Cities and Camps of the Confederate States. *April*, 1864.

462. —— A Visit to the Cities and Camps of the Confederate States. Part II. *January and February*, 1865.

463. BLAINE, of Augusta. Speech in Reply to Mr. Gould of Thomaston, on the Confiscation Resolves, March 7, 1862.
8vo. pp. 12. AUGUSTA: *Journal Office*, 1862.

464. —— Speech in favor of Amending the Federal Constitution, by striking out the Clause which prohibits the Taxing of Exports. Delivered in the House of Representatives, March 2, '65. 8vo. p.4.

465. BLAIR, FRANCIS P., Jr. The Destiny of the Races on this Continent. An Address delivered before the Mercantile Library Association of Boston, Massachusetts, January 26, 1859.
8vo. pp. 38. WASHINGTON: *Buell & Blanchard*, 1859.

466. —— Fremont's Hundred Days in Missouri. Speech in the House of Representatives, March 7, 1862. 8vo. pp. 16.

7

467. BLAIR, FRANCIS P., Jr. Speech on the Policy of the President for the Restoration of the Union and Establishment of Peace. Delivered in the House of Representatives, April 11, 1862. 8vo. pp. 8.

469. —— Military appointment of. *Report No.* 110, 38*th Congress*, 1*st Session*, 1864.

470. —— Confiscation of Rebel Property. Speech in House of Representatives, February 5, 1864. 8vo. pp. 16.

471. —— The Jacobins of Missouri and Maryland. Speech delivered in the House of Representatives, Feb. 27, 1864. 8vo. pp. 14.

472. —— Secretary Chase scheming for the Presidency; his intrigues and official abuses. Speech in House of Representatives, April, 23, 1864. 8vo. pp. 15.

473. —— Message of the President of the United States, in relation to a military appointment of the Hon. Francis P. Blair, Jr., representing the First Congressional District of Missouri. pp. 2. *House of Representatives Ex. Doc., No.* 77, 38*th Cong.*, 1*st Sess.*

474. BLAIR INVESTIGATION CASE. Report of the Special Committee to investigate the charge made by the Hon. J. W. McClung, of Missouri, against F. P. Blair, Jr., of violating the laws in the matter of an alleged liquor speculation. *House of Representatives Report No.* 61, 38*th Congress*, 1*st Session*, 1864. pp. 75.

475. BLAIR, MONTGOMERY. Letter to the Meeting at Cooper Institute, March 6, 1862.

476. —— Comments on the Policy inaugurated by the President in a Letter and two Speeches, by Montgomery Blair, Postmaster General. 8vo. pp. 20.   NEW YORK: *Hall, Clayton & Co.*, 1863.

477. —— The Principles involved in the Rebellion. Speech at the Mass Meeting of the Loyal National League, Union Square, N. Y., on the Anniversary of the Assault on Sumter, April 11, 1863. 8vo. pp. 8.

478. —— Speech on the Revolutionary Schemes of the Ultra Abolitionists, and in defence of the Policy of the President, delivered at the Unconditional Union Meeting, Rockville, Md., Oct 3, 1863. 8vo. pp. 20.   NEW YORK: *D. W. Lee*, 1863.

479. —— Speech on the Causes of the Rebellion, and in support of the President's Plan of Pacification, delivered before the Legislature of Maryland, January 22, 1864.
8vo. pp. 22.   BALTIMORE : *Sherwood & Co.*, 1864.

480. BLAIR, Montgomery. Speech at the Cooper Institute, N. Y., to ratify the Union Nominations.
8vo. pp. 16. New York ; *D. W. Lee*, 1864.

481. —— The Monroe Doctrine. Speech at Hagarstown, Md., July 12, 1865 ; exposing the Alliance of the American Secretary of State with Louis Napoleon to overthrow the Monroe Doctrine, and establish a Despotism on this Continent. 8vo. pp. 23.

482. BLAKE, Hon. Harrison G., of Ohio. Freedom takes no step backwards. Speech delivered in the House of Representatives, February 19, 1861. 8vo. pp. 7.

483. —— Slavery in the District. Speech delivered in the House of Representatives, April 11, 1862. 8vo. pp. 4.

484. BLAKE, Henry N., Late Captain in the Eleventh Regiment Massachusetts Volunteers. Three years in the Army of the Potomac.
12mo. pp. 319. Boston: *Lee & Sheperd*, 1865.

485. BLAKE, Rev. Mortimer. The Issues of the Rebellion. A Sermon preached before the Taunton and Raynham Volunteers, Col. D. N. Couch commanding, June 2, 1861.
8vo. pp. 13. Taunton: *Republican Office*, 1861.

486. BLANCHARD, Charles, of Ottawa, Illinois. Remarks on Chief Justice Caton's Seymour Letter.
8vo. pp. 12. *Ottowa Republican*, 1863.

487. Les Blancs et les Noires en Amerique, et le Coton dans les deux Mondes.
8vo. pp. 43. Paris ; *Dentu*, 1862.
This work takes up the Rebellion in the United States in a humanitarian, political and economical point of view. It advises the South to free the Slaves and return to the Union.

488. BLEBY. Speech of Rev. Henry Bleby, Missionary from Barbadoes, on the Results of Emancipation in the British West Indian Colonies, delivered at the Celebration of the Massachusetts Anti-Slavery Society. July 31, 1858.
18mo. pp. 36. Boston. *R. F. Walcott*, 1858.

489. BLISS, Rev. T. E. "*Clarum et Venerabile Nomen.*" A Discourse commemorative of the Life and Character of Abraham Lincoln, late President of the United States. Delivered April 23, 1865.
8vo. pp. 16. Memphis: (Tenn.) *W. A. Whitmore*, 1865.

490. BLISS, Rev. Z.   The Extinction of Slavery a National Necessity, before the present conflict can be ended.   8vo. pp. 8.

491. BLODGETT, LORIN.   The Commercial and Financial Strength of the United States, as shown in the Balances of Foreign Trade and the increased production of staple articles.
8vo. pp. 39.   PHILADELPHIA : *King & Baird,* 1864.

492. —— The same, with Supplement.   King & Baird.   8vo. pp. 56.

493. —— The National Resources.   *North American Review, Jan.,* '65.

494. BLOW, Hon. HENRY T.   Missouri Question.   A Freedom Policy and Reconstruction.   Speech delivered in the City of Washington, December 16. 1863, on the Invitation of the National Union League.   8vo. pp. 13.

495. —— Speech in Reply to the Charges of Hon. F. P. Blair and the Postmaster General, in House of Rep., Feb. 23, 1864.   8vo. p. 16.

496. BLYDEN, Rev. E. W.   Address at the Annual Meeting of the Maine Colonization Society, June, 1862.   pp. 4.

497. BOARDMAN, Rev. GEORGE N.   Repentance of Sin and Restoration from Calamity.   A Sermon preached in the Presbyterian Church, Binghamton, September 26, 1861.
8vo. pp. 18.   BINGHAMTON : (N. Y.) *G. W. Reynolds,* 1861.

498. —— The Death of President Lincoln.   A Sermon preached in the Presbyterian Church, Binghamton, April 16, 1865.
8vo. pp. 16.   BINGHAMTON : (N. Y.) *F. N. Chace,* 1865.

499. BOARDMAN, HENRY A., DD.   The American Union.   A Discourse delivered December 12, 1850, the Day of the Annual Thanksgiving in Pennsylvania, and repeated December 19, in the Tenth Presbyterian Church, Philadelphia.
8vo. pp. 56.   PHILADELPHIA : *Lippincott, Gramb & Co.,* 1851.

500. —— The American Union.   A Discourse delivered December 12, 1850, and repeated December 19, 1860, in the Tenth Presbyterian Church, Philadelphia.   Seventh edition.
8vo. pp. 58.   PHILADELPHIA: *J. B. Lippincott & Co.,* 1860.

501. —— What Christianity demands of us at the Present Crisis.   A Sermon preached November 29, 1860.
8vo. pp. 28.   PHILADELPHIA , *J. B. Lippincott & Co.,* 1850.

502. —— The Federal Judiciary,   A Thanksgiving Discourse.
8vo. pp. 54.   PHILADELPHIA : *Wm. L. & A. Martien,* 1862.

503. BOARDMAN, Henry A., D. D. Thanksgiving in War. A Sermon preached in the Tenth Presbyterian Church, on the 28th of November, 1861.

    8vo. pp. 28.   PHILADELPHIA : *C. Sherman,* 1861.

504. —— The Sovereignty of God, the sure and only Stay of the Christian Patriot, in our National Troubles. A Sermon preached in the Tenth Presbyterian Church, Phila., September 4, 1862.

    8vo. pp. 31.   PHILADELPHIA : *W. S. & A. Martien,* 1862.

505. —— The Peace we Need, and How to Secure it. A Sermon preached June 1, 1865.

    8vo. pp. 32.   PHILADELPHIA : *James S. Claxton,* 1865.

506. BOARDMAN, H. A. Healing and Salvation for our Country from God alone. A Sermon preached on Thanksgiving Day, November 24, 1864.

    8vo. pp. 24.   PHILADELPHIA : *W. S. & A. Martien,* 1864.

507. Bob's Letter. From Cowan, Tennessee, Aug. 23, 1862.   pp. 6.

508. —— BOGEN, F. W. L'Empire François et les Etats Unis. Réponse à la Lettre à la Majesté Napoleon III.

    8vo. pp. 15.   NEW YORK.

509. BOKER, George H. Before Vicksburg. *Atlantic Monthly for September,* 1864.

510. —— The Ride to Camp. Ibid. for *October,* 1864.

511. —— Poems of the War.

    18mo. pp. 292.   BOSTON : *Ticknor & Fields,* 1864.

512. —— Our Heroic Themes. A Poem read before the Phi Beta Kappa Society of Harvard University, July 20, 1865.

    8vo. pp. 20.   BOSTON : *Ticknor & Fields,* 1865.

513. Bobolink Minstrel ; or Republican Songster. Edited by Geo. W. Bungay. " Lincoln and Liberty."

    12mo. pp. 72.   NEW YORK : *Hutchinson & Brother,* 1860.

514. BOKUM, Herman., Chaplain, U. S. A. The Testimony of a Refugee from East Tennessee. For gratuitous circulation.

    8vo. pp. 24.   PHILADELPHIA : 1863.

515. —— Das Zeugniss eines Flüchtlings von Ost Tennesse.

    8vo. pp. 23.   PHILADELPHIA : 1863.

516. BOLLES, Major J. A. With a Flag of Truce. *Harpers' Magazine, March,* 1864.

517. BOLLES, Major J. A. Escape from Fort Warren. Ib. *April,* '64.

518. BONNEFOUX, L.   Extracts from a Treatise on the Constitution of the United States.

> 8vo. pp. 31.   NEW YORK : *W. C. Bryant & Co.*, 1863.

519. BOOK OF COMMON PRAYER, and administration of the Sacraments and other Rites and Ceremonies of the Church in the Confederate States of America ; together with the Psalter.

> 24mo.   RICHMOND : (Va.) *J. W. Randolph*, 1863.
> Although this bears the imprint of Richmond, it also bears, inside, the name of a London Printing House.   It is like the ordinary Prayer Books, except that those passages in the prayers for the President of the United States are altered to "The President of the *Confederate States.*"   In one instance, however, the Confederate Churchmen deemed it more proper not to make a change.   This is in the prayer to be used at sea, in which the Almighty is asked to preserve them from the dangers of the sea, etc., that they "may be a safeguard unto the *United States.*"

520. BOOK OF COMMON PRAYER, Selections from, in use in the Protestant Episcopal Church, in the Confederate States of America.

> 8vo. pp.   CHARLOTTESVILLE : (Va.) *J. Alexander*, 1861.

521· THE BOOK FOR THE NATION and Times. By a Citizen U. S. N. A.

> 12mo. pp. 64.   PHILADELPHIA : *W. S. & A. Martien*, 1864.

522. BOOK OF THE PROPHET STEPHEN, son of Douglas.   Wherein marvellous things are foretold of the Reign of Abraham.

> 12mo. pp. 48.   NEW YORK : *Feeks & Baneker*, 1863.

523. BOOK OF THE PROPHET STEPHEN, son of Douglas.   Book 2d.

> 12mo. pp. 48.   NEW YORK : *J. F. Feeks*, 1864.

524. BOOLE, Rev. WM. H.   Antidote to Rev. H. J. Van Dyke's Pro-Slavery Discourse.   Delivered in the M. E. Church, Mount Vernon, New York, January 13, 1861.

> 8vo. pp. 34.   NEW YORK : *Edmund Jones & Co.*, 1861.

525. BOOMER, GEORGE BOARDMAN, Memoir of.

> (Private printed.)

> 12mo. pp. 284. Portrait. BOSTON : *Press of Rand & Avery,* '64.
> Brigadier General Boardman was born in Sutton, Massachusetts.   At an early age he took up his residence at St. Louis, Missouri.   Here he raised a regiment for the War and served in the Campaigns with General Grant. He fell before Vicksburg, on the 22d of May, 1863. The Memoir is by his Sister, Mrs. M. Amelia Stone, and is a volume of much interest.

526. BOOTH, JOHN WILKES. The Life, Capture and Crime of, and the Pursuit, Trial and Execution of his Associates.

> 8vo. pp. 64.   NEW YORK : *Dick & Fitzgerald*, 1865.

527. BOOTH, J. W. Private Confession of the Murderer of Lincoln. His connection with the Rebellion. The killing of a bosom friend of Booth's by Federal Soldiers after the Battle of Bull's Run. Their brutal conduct towards the victim's wife. Her brother and Booth then vow a terrible oath of Vengeance and Retribution. Booth is implicated in the slaying, in cold blood, of no less than twenty-six Federal Officers. His plans for assassinating the President, General Grant, and all the Members of the Cabinet, and to burn the Capitol at Washington; also the public buildings of New York, Boston and Philadelphia. This confession was given by the Assassin to a Confederate friend, who assisted in his concealment, and who escaped to New York after the capture of Booth by the officers of justice, arriving at Liverpool on Saturday last, on his way to Russia.

> The above is an advertisement of a catch-penny publication from a London paper.

528. BOOTH, ROBERT RUSSELL, DD. The Nation's Crisis and the Christian's Duty. A Sermon preached in the Mercer St. Presbyterian Church, New York, May 12, 1861.
8vo. pp. 24.   NEW YORK : *A. D. F. Randolph,* 1861.

529. —— Personal Forgiveness and Public Justice. A Sermon preached in the Mercer St. Presbyterian Church, New York, 23, 1865.
8vo. pp. 23.   NEW YORK: *A. D. F. Randolph,* 1865.

530. BORDER AND BASTILLE. By the Author of Guy Livingston.
12mo. pp. 291.   NEW YORK : *W. I. Fooley & Co.*

531. BORDER STATES. *McMillan's Magazine, June,* 1862.

535. BOSTON REVIEW, 1861. The Standard of the Northern Army. Rev. William Barrows. Vol. 1, pp. 398.

536. —— Gibeah. A Lesson for the Times. Vol. 1, p. 505.

537. BOSTON REVIEW, 1862. The Present State of the Country, Historically developed. Rev. William Barrows. Vol. 2, p. 69.

538. —— The Southern Insurrection ; its Elements and aspects. Rev. W. Barrows. p. 615.

539. BOSTON REVIEW, 1863. English Stories on American Affairs. Rev. W. Barrows. Vol. 3, p. 138.

540. —— The Sword and Christianity. do. Vol. 3, p. 252.

541. BOSTON REVIEW, 1864. Teachings of the Rebellion. Vol. 4, p. 376.
542. —— Our National Banner. Vol. 4, p. 581.
543. BOTTS, Hon. JOHN MINOR. The Past, the Present and the Future of our Country. Interesting and Important Correspondence between the Opposition Members of the Legislature of Virginia and John Minor Botts, January 17, 1860. 8vo. pp. 16.
544. —— Union or Disunion. Speech at Holcombe Hall, in Lynchburg, Va., October 18. 8vo. pp. 23.
545. BOURNE, GEORGE. Picture of Slavery in the United States of America.
   18mo. pp. 227.   MIDDLETOWN: *E. Hunt,* 1833.
546. BOURNE, WILLIAM OLAND. The Republic. A Poem.
   8vo. pp. 8.   NEW YORK: *Richard Brinkerhoff,* 1861.
547. —— Poems of the Republic. A Contribution to the Metropolitan Fair.
   8vo. pp. 48.   NEW YORK: *E. O. Jenkins,* 1864.
548. BOUTWELL, Hon. GEORGE S. Decisions on the Tax Law.
   8vo. pp. 24.   NEW YORK: *D. Appleton & Co.,* 1863.
549. —— An Address upon Secession, delivered at Charlestown, Mass., January 8, 1861.
   8vo. pp. 30.   BOSTON: *Ticknor & Fields,* 1861.
550. —— Speech upon the " Bill to Guarantee to certain States, whose Governments have been usurped or overthrown, a Republican form of Government." House of Representatives, May, 4, 1864. 8vo. pp. 16.
551. —— Confiscation of Rebel Property. Speech in House of Representatives, January 19, 1864. 8vo. pp. 8.
552. —— Emancipation; its Justice, Expediency and Necessity, as a means of securing a Speedy and Permanent Peace. An Address delivered in Tremont Temple, Boston, December 16, 1861.
   8vo. pp. 12.   BOSTON: *Wright & Potter,* 1861.
553. —— Speech delivered before the National Union League, Washington, June 16, 1863. 8vo. pp. 8.
554. BOWDITCH, HENRY I., M. D. A Brief Plea for the Ambulance System for the Army of the United States, as drawn from the extra sufferings of the late Lieut. Bowditch and a wounded Comrade.
   8vo. pp. 28.   BOSTON: *Ticknor & Fields,* 1863.

555. BOWDITCH, H. I., M. D.   An Apology for the Medical Profes
sion, as a means of developing the whole Nature of Man.   A
Valedictory Address to the Graduating Medical Class of Harvard
University, March 11, 1863.   With Additional Remarks on a Topic
of importance at the present hour.
8vo. pp. 52.   BOSTON : 1863.

556. BOWDITCH, WM. I.   The United States Constitution, a Pro-
Slavery Instrument according to the necessary meaning of its terms.
16mo. pp. 12.   *American Anti-Slavery Society.*

557. BOWEN, D.   The Conflict of the Brutal with the Human.   The
South against the Universe.   *Monthly Religious Mag., June,* '63.

558. BOWEN, FRANCIS.   Remarks on Specie Reserve and Bank
Deposits.   Communicated to the American Academy, November
31, 1861.   *Transactions American Academy, Vol.* viii.

559. BOWEN, JAMES L.   The Yankee Scout; or Haps and Mishaps
of the Border.
8vo. pp. 41.   NEW YORK : *American News Co.,* 1865.

560. BOWMAN, Col. S. M, and Lt. Col. R. B. IRWIN.   Sherman and
his Campaigns.   A Military Biography.   With eight Portraits,
Maps and Plans.
8vo. pp. 512.   NEW YORK : *C. B. Richardson,* 1865.

561. BOYD, A. H. H., DD.   Thanksgiving Sermon delivered in Winchester, Va., November 29, 1860.
8vo. pp, 20.   WINCHESTER : *J. H. Crum & Co.,* 1860.

562. BOYNTON, C. B., DD.   The Navies of England, France, America and Russia.   Being an Extract from a work on English and
French Neutrality, and the Anglo-French Alliance.
8vo. pp. 72.   NEW YORK : *John F. Trow,* 1865.

563. —— God's hand in the War.   A Sermon preached April 13 and
April 27, 1862.
8vo. pp 16.   CINCINNATI : *"Free Nation" Office,* 1862.

564. —— English and French Neutrality, and the Anglo-French Alliance, in their Relation to the United States and Russia.
8vo. pp.   CINCINNATI : *C. F. Vent & Co.,* 1864.

565. BOYNTON, THOMAS J.   Oration delivered at Key West, Florida, July 4, 1861.
8vo. pp. 23.   *Key West,* 1861.

8

566. BOYNTON, T. J.   A Letter to Colonel Commanding Joseph S. Morgan, Key West, Florida.   [Relative to the " removal of persons who have husbands, brothers, and sons in rebel employment."]
8vo. p. 8.

567. BRADLEY, Rev. G. S., Chaplain 22d Wisconsin.   The Star Corps ; or Notes of an Army Chaplain during Sherman's famous " March to the Sea."
12mo. pp. 204·   MILWAUKIE : *Jermain & Brightman*, 1865.

568. BRADNACK, Rev. I. R.   A Sermon for the Times, preached on the National Fast Day, September 26, 1861, Sandy Creek, N. Y.
8vo. pp. 30.   PULASKI : *Democrat Office*, 1861.

569. BRADSHAW, WESLEY.   The Angel of the Battle-Field.   A Tale of the Rebellion.
8vo. pp. 96.   NEW YORK : *American News Co.*, 1865.

570. —— The Volunteer's Roll of Honor.   A Collection of the Noble and Praiseworthy Deeds performed in the Cause of the Union, by the Heroes of the Army and Navy of the United States.
8vo. pp. 100.   PHILADELPHIA : *Barclay & Co.*, 1864.

571. BRAINERD, Rev. THOMAS, DD.   Patriotism aiding Piety.   A Sermon preached in the Third Presbyterian Church, Philadelphia, April 30, 1863.
8vo. pp. 32.   PHILADELPHIA : *W. F. Geddes*, 1863.

572. BRAKEMAN, Rev. N. L.   A Great Man Fallen   A Sermon preached in the Methodist Church, Baton Rouge, La., April 23, 1865, on the Death of Abraham Lincoln.   By the Post Chaplain.
8vo. pp. 32.   NEW ORLEANS : *Times Office*, 1865.

573. —— The same.   Third edition, with Notes and Appendix.

574. BRAMHALL, FRANK J.   The Military Souvenir.   A Portrait Gallery of Military and Naval Heroes.
2 vols. 4to.   NEW YORK : *J. C. Buttre*, 1863–66.
This is one of the most beautiful books published in the United States, connected with the War.   Each volume contains 75 Portraits, engraved on steel, of distinguished officers, accompanied by their biographies.

575. BRAMWILL, Rev.   The War in America.   A Sermon preached August 18, 1861, at St. Peter's Church, Congleton, England.
8vo. pp. 15.   COGLETON : *W. Burghope*, 1861.

576. BRAND, Rev. W. F.   Christ's Kingdom not of this World.   The Church viewed in its Relations to the State.   A Sermon.
8vo. pp. 16.   BALTIMORE : *James S. Waters*, 1862.

577. BRANDEGEE, Hon. Augustus. Speech on the Bill locating the Naval Station for Iron Clads at New London, Connecticut. Delivered in the House of Representatives, December 12, 1864.
8vo. pp. 26. Washington: *McGill & Witherow*, 1864.

578. BLAUNS, Rev. F. W. Joy in Tribulation. A Sermon preached in Baltimore, November 28, 1861.
8vo. pp. 15. Baltimore: *John D. Fay*, 1861.

579. BRAY, John. My Escape from Richmond. *Harpers' Magazine*, *April*, 1864.

580. BRECK, Robert L. The Habeas Corpus and Marshal Law. Prepared for the Danville Quarterly Review for December, '64.
8vo. pp. 39. Cincinnati: *R. H. Collins*, 1862.

581. BRECKENRIDGE, Rev. Robert J., DD. Discourse delivered at Lexington, Ky., January 4, 1861. The Day of National Humiliation.
8vo. pp. 23. Cincinnati: *Farrar & McLear*, 1861.

582. —— Four Articles on the State of the Country and the Civil War. Reprinted from the Danville Quarterly Review for 1861.
1. Our Country, its Perils—its Deliverance.
2. State of the Country.
3. Discourse delivered on the Day of National Humiliation, January 4, 1861.
4. The Civil War, its Nature and End.
8vo. pp. 218. Cincinnati ; *Office Danville Review* 1861.

583. —— Our Country and its Deliverance. From the Danville Review for March, 1861.
8vo. pp. 43. Cincinnati: *Office Danville Review*, 1861.

584. —— The Civil War; Its Nature and End. Danville Review, December, 1861.
8vo. pp. 33. Cincinnati: *Office Danville Review*, 1861.

585. —— Two Speeches on the State of the Country, at Cincinnati, May 20, 1862, and during a Debate in the Presbyterian General Assembly, Columbus, May 22, 1862.
8vo. pp. 44. Cincinnati: *Joseph P. Boyd*, 1862.

586. —— The Secession Conspiracy in Kentucky, and its Overthrow ; with the Relations of both to the General Revolt.

587 —— A Memoir of Civil and Political Events, Public and Private,

in Kentucky. To serve as a History of the Secession Conspiracy which had its centre in Kentucky. Commencing in 1859, and extending to the Overthrow of the Conspiracy and the breaking out of the Civil War in that State in 1861. *Danville Review. March, June and September,* 1862.

588. BRECKENRIDGE, Rev. R. J., D. D. Negro Slavery and the Civil War. *Danville Rev., Dec.,* 1862.

589. —— An Enquiry into the True Doctine of Human Society, Civil Government, the Magistracy and the Citizen, as Revealed by God, with special reference to the State of Public Affairs in America. *Danville Review, March,* 1863.

590. —— The Peril and Duty of the American People with respect to the Foreign Relations of the Country, Impending War with England and France, and the threatened Humiliation and Partition of the United States. *Danville Review, June,* 1863.

591. —— The Nation and the Insurgents; with special Reference to the Political, Military and Financial Interests of the Country, the Insurgent War, and the Foreign Relations of the United States, at the end of the year 1863. *Danville Review, December,* 1863.

592. —— The Nation's Success and Gratitude. The Substance of a Discourse delivered in Danville, Kentucky, November 26, 1863. *Danville Review, March,* 1864.

593. —— The same essay.
8vo. pp. 22.   PHILADELPHIA : *H. B. Ashmead,* 1864.

594. —— Treason—Slavery—Loyalty. Struggles in Kentucky during three years, succeeding the First Overthrow of the Secession Conspiracy in 1861. *Danville Review, September,* 1864,

595. —— The Peace Panic; Its Authors and Objects. Ibid.

596. —— The Great Deliverance and the New Career. An Oration delivered before the Phi Beta Kappa Society of Union College, Schenectady, New York, July 25, 1865.
8vo. pp. 32.   PHILADELPHIA : *J. S. Claxton,* 1865.

597. BRECKENRIDGE, S. M. Oration delivered at the Union Celebration, at Hannibal, Mo., July 4, 1862. 8vo. pp. 15.

598. BRECKENRIDGE, JOHN C. Address to the People of Kentucky. Dated Bowling Green, Kentucky, October 8, 1861.
8vo. pp. 4.   BALTIMORE : *"The South Office,"* 1862.

599. BREED, Rev. Wm. P. The National Nest-Stirring. A Discourse on the Times. Delivered in the West Spruce St. Presbyterian Church, May 5, 1861.

    8vo. pp. 15.   PHILADELPHIA : *H. B. Ashmead,* 1861,

600. —— The Lights which God hath showed us. A Thanksgiving Discourse, November 28, 1861.

    8vo. pp. 26.   PHILADELPHIA : *John Alexander,* 1861.

601. BRENTS, Major J. A. The Patriots and Guerrillas of East Tennessee and Kentucky. The Sufferings of the Patriots. Also the Experience of the Author as an Officer in the Union Army.

    8vo. pp. 171.   NEW YORK : *J. A. Brents,* 1863.

602. BREWER, John M. Prison Life. By John M. Brewer, late Reading Clerk of the Maryland Senate of 1860, 1861, and still later of Forts Delaware and Warren.

    8vo. pp. 31.   BALTIMORE : *S. S. Mills.*

603. BREWER, Urban C. The Bible and American Slavery. A Discourse delivered at the Christian Chapel, West Seventeenth St., New York, on January 4, 1863.

    8vo. pp. 30.   NEW YORK : *W. Reid Gould,* 1863.

604. BREWSTER, Benjamin H. Inauguration of the National Union Club. Speech at the Musical Fund Hall, Phila., March 11, '63.

    8vo. pp. 8.   PHILADELPHIA : *King & Baird,* 1863.

605. BRIGGS, George W., DD. Address at the Funeral of Brigadier General Frederic W. Lander, delivered at Salem, Massachusetts, March 5, 1862. *Salem Register, March* 10, 1862.

606. —— Eulogy on Abraham Lincoln, June 1, 1865. With the Proceedings of the City Council [of Salem] on the Death of the President.

    8vo. pp. 48.   SALEM, Mass., 1865.

607. BRIGHT, John. (M. P.) A Liberal Voice from England. Speech at Rochdale, December 4, 1861, on the American Crisis.

    8vo. pp. 13.   NEW YORK : *Rebellion Record,* 1862.

608. —— Speeches on the American Question. With a Biographical Introduction. By Frank Moore.

    12mo. pp. xv and 278.   BOSTON : *Little, Brown & Co.,* 1865.

609. BRACKETT, Colonel Albert G. History of the United States Cavalry, from the Formation of the Federal Government to the

1st of June, 1863. To which is added a list of all the Cavalry Regiments, with the names of their Commanders, which have been in the service since the breaking out of the Rebellion. 12mo. pp. 337. NEW YORK: *Harper & Brothers*, 1865.

610. BRIGHT, J. D., of Indiana. Speech on the Resolution proposed for his Expulsion. Senate, February 5, 1862. 8vo. pp. 8.

611. BRILLIANT. Proceedings of the Chamber of Commerce of the State of New York, on the Burning of the Ship Brilliant, by the Rebel Pirate Alabama, Tuesday, October 21, 1862. 8vo. pp. 22. NEW YORK: *J. W. Amerman*, 1862.

612. BRISTED, CHARLES ASTOR. Now is the Time to settle it. Suggestions on the present Crisis. 12mo. pp. 24. NEW YORK: *Martin B. Brown*, 1862.

613. BRITISH CONSULS. Correspondence Respecting the Removal of British Consuls from the so-styled Confederate States of America. *Parl. Papers, North Am., No. 13, London*, 1864. *Folio, pp.* 39.

614. [British.] Foreign Enlistment Act. Memorial from certain shipowners at Liverpool, suggesting an alleviation in. *British Parl. Papers, North America, No. 10, London*, 1862. *Folio, pp.* 2.

615. BRITISH PARLIAMENTARY PAPERS, also known as the "Blue Books," containing Papers and Reports presented to the Houses of Parliament by command of her Majesty, in 1862, relating to the Rebellion in the United States, or to Questions growing out of it. These papers are entered elsewhere, under the subjects to which they severally refer.

No. 1. Correspondence relating to the civil war in the United States of North America. Folio, pp.

No. 2. Extract of a Despatch from Her Majesty's Minister at Washington, dated December 6, 1861, enclosing papers relating to Foreign Affairs, laid before the Congress of the United States, at the opening of the session in 1861. 8vo, pp. 367.

No. 3. Correspondence respecting International Maritime Law. Addressed to the contending parties in the United States. Folio, pp. 37.

No. 4. Correspondence respecting the withdrawal by the Government of the United States, of Mr. Bunch's exequatur as Her Majesty's Consul at Charleston. Folio, pp. 27.

No. 5. Correspondence respecting the seizure of Messrs. Mason, Slidell, McFarland and Eustis, from on board the Royal Mail Packet, "Trent," by the commander of the United States Ship of War, "San Jacinto." Folio. pp. 37.

No. 6. Correspondence relating to the Steamers "Nashville" and "Tuscarora," at Southampton. Folio, pp. 30.

No. 7. Papers relating to the Imprisonment of Mr. Shaver at Fort Warren in Boston Harbor. Folio, pp. 9.

No. 8. Papers relating to the Blockade of the Ports of the Confederate States. Folio, pp. 126.

No. 9. Despatch from Lord Lyons respecting the obstruction of the Southern Harbors. Folio, pp. 1.

No. 10. Despatch from Lord Lyons respecting the Reciprocity Treaty. Folio, pp. 25.

No. 11. Papers respecting the "Emily St. Pierre,"of Liverpool. Folio, p.17.

No. 12. Further Correspondence relating to the Civil War in the United States of North America. Folio. pp. 5.

616. BRITISH PARLIAMENTARY PAPERS. *North America.* Presented, 1863.

No. 1. Correspondence relating to the Civil War in the United States of North America. Folio. pp. 53.

No. 2. Correspondence with Mr. Mason respecting Blockade and Recognition of the Confederate States. Folio, pp. 17.

No. 3. Correspondence respecting the "Alabama." Folio, pp. 48.

No. 5. Correspondence respecting instructions given to Naval Officers of the United States, in regard to Neutral Vessels and Mails. Folio, pp. 7.

No. 6. Correspondence with Mr. Adams respecting Neutral Rights and Duties. Folio, pp. 6.

No. 7. Correspondence respecting despatch of Letters by private ships to Matamoras. Folio, pp. 2.

No. 8. Correspondence with Mr. Adams respecting Confederate Agents in England. Folio, pp. 18.

No. 9. Correspondence with Mr. Adams respecting the Enlistment of British Subjects in the Federal Army. Folio, pp. 3.

No. 10. Extract from a Despatch to Mr. Stuart, Her Majesty's Chargé d'Affaires, at Washington, respecting the seizure of mail-bags on board the "Adela." Folio, pp. 3.

No. 11. Correspondence respecting trade with Matamoras. Folio, pp. 5.

No. 12. Correspondence respecting the seizure of the Schooner "Will o' the Wisp," by the United-States Ship of War "Montgomery," at Matamoras, June 3, 1862. Folio, pp. 46.

No. 13. Memorial from certain ship-owners of Liverpool, suggesting an alteration in the Foreign Enlistment Act. Folio, pp. 2.

No. 14. Correspondence respecting interference with trade between New York and the Bahamas. Folio, pp. 65.

617. BRITISH PARLIAMENTARY PAPERS. *North America.* Presented 1864.

No. 1. Correspondence respecting the "Alabama" (In continuation of Correspondence presented to Parliament in March, 1863.) Folio, pp. 57.

No. 2. Correspondence respecting the capture of the "Saxon" by the United States Ship "Vanderbilt." pp. 43.

No. 3. Correspondence respecting the "Alabama." (In continuation of Correspondence presented to Parliament in Feb., 1864.) Folio, pp. 18.

No. 4. Communications between the Collector of Customs, at Liverpool, and Messrs. Klingender & Co., respecting the shipment of Guns on board the "Gibraltar." (In continuation of Papers presented to Parliament in July, 1863.) Folio, pp. 3.

No. 5. Correspondence respecting iron-clad vessels building at Birkenhead. Folio, pp. 33.

No. 6. Correspondence respecting the "Tuscaloosa." Folio, pp. 32.

No. 7. Correspondence respecting the Enlistment of British Seamen at Queenstown on board the Ship of War "Kearsarge." Folio, pp. 10.

No. 8. Correspondence respecting Recruitment in Ireland for the Military Service of the United States. Folio, pp. 14.

No. 9. Papers relating to the Seizure of the United States Steamer "Chesapeake." Folio, pp. 96.

No. 10. Despatch from Lord Lyons referring to the alleged Report of the Secretary of the Navy of the so-called Confederate States. Folio. pp. 3.

No. 11. Return of the Claim of British Subjects against the United States' Government, from the commencement of the civil war to the 31st of March, 1864. Folio, pp. 18, Index 2.

No. 12. Further Correspondence respecting the Enlistment of British Seamen at Queenstown, on board of the United States Ship of War "Kearsarge." Folio, pp. 7.

No. 13. Correspondence respecting the removal of British Consuls from the so-styled Confederate States of America. Folio. pp. 39.

No. 14. Correspondence with Mr. Mason, Commissioner of the so-styled Confederate States of America. (In continuation of Papers presented to Parliament, March, 1863.) Folio, pp. 37.

No. 15. Papers respecting the Arrest and Imprisonment of Mr. James McHugh, in the United States. Folio, pp. 17.

No. 16. Further Papers respecting the Arrest and Imprisonment of Mr. James McHugh, in the United States. Folio. pp. 5.

No. 17. Correspondence respecting the Enlistment of British Subjects in the United States Army. Folio, pp. 59.

No. 18. Further Papers respecting the Arrest and Imprisonment of Mr. James McHugh, in the United States. Folio, pp. 6.

No. 19. Further Correspondence respecting the Enlistment of British Subjects in the United States Army. Folio, pp. 5.

618. BRITISH SYMPATHIES in the American Crisis. By an Irishman. 12mo. pp. 15.   DUBLIN: *Porteous & Gibbs*, 1863.

619. BRITISH VESSELS. Correspondence between the State Department and the Representative of Her Britannic Majesty's Government, in relation to the capture of British vessels sailing from one port to another, having on board articles contraband of war, intended for the use of the so called Confederate States.

8vo. pp. 29.   *37th Congress, 3d Session, Ex. Doc., No.* 27, 1863.

620. A BROADSIDE for the Times. By E. Pluribus Unum. 12mo. pp. 24.   NEW YORK: *James O. Noyes*, 1861.

621. BROCKETT, L. P., M. D. The Life and Times of Abraham Lincoln, President of the United States. Including his Speeches, Messages, Inaugurals, Proclamations, etc., etc. 8vo. pp. PHILADELPHIA : *Bradley & Co.*, 1865.

622. BROOKE, J. T. Short Notes on the Dred Scott Case. 8vo. pp. 29. CINCINNATI : *Moore, Wilstach & Co.*, 1861.

623. BROOKS, CHARLES. Some Reasons for the immediate establishment of a National System of Education for the United States. 8vo. pp. 22. *Loyal Publication Society, No.* 86, 1865.

624. BROOKS, Hon. JAMES. Speech before the Union Democratic Association, at 932 Broadway, December 30, 1862. 8vo. pp. 16.

625. —— "The Two Proclamations." Speech before the Democratic Union Association, September 29, 1862. 8vo. pp. 8.

626. —— Speech on the President's Message. House of Representatives, December, 1864. pp. 24.

627. —— The Currency ; its expansion. The Public Debt. The New York National Banks. Speech delivered in the House of Representatives, March 24, 1864. 8vo. pp. 8.

628. BROOKS, Rev. JAMES H. Subjection to Civil Rulers. The Christian's Duty. A Fast Day Sermon, preached April 30, 1863, at St. Louis. 8vo. pp. 16. ST. LOUIS : *Sherman Spencer*, 1863.

629. BROOKS, Rev. PHILLIPS. Our Mercies of Re-occupation. A Thanksgiving Sermon preached at Philadelphia, Nov. 26, 1863. 8vo. pp. 32. PHILADELPHIA : *W. S. & A. Martien*, 1863.

630. —— The Life and Death of Abraham Lincoln. A Sermon preached in Philadelphia, April 23, 1865. 8vo. pp. 24. PHILADELPHIA : *H. B. Ashland*, 1865.

631. BROOK, JEHIEL. Fugitive Slave Laws. A compilation of the Laws of the United States and of States, in relation to Fugitives from Labor. 8vo. pp. 32. WASHINGTON : *Taylor & Maury*, 1860.

632. BROOKLYN AND LONG ISLAND FAIR, History of. Feb. 22, 1864. 8vo. pp. 189. BROOKLYN : *Union Press*, 1864.

633. —— The same, with folding plates printed in colors. 4to. pp. 189. BROOKLYN : *Union Press*, 1864.

9

634. BROOM, W. W., of Manchester. An Englishman's Thoughts on the Crimes of the South, and the Recompense of the North.
8vo. pp. 24. NEW YORK: *Loyal Publication Soc'y, No.* 84, 1865.

635. BROOMALL, JOHN M., of Pennsylvania. On the Reconstruction of the Rebel States. Speech in House of Representatives, April 20, 1864. 8vo. pp. 16.

636. —— National Currency. Speech in the House of Representatives, February 7, 1865. pp. 16.

637. BROMWELL, R. H. The War in America. A Sermon.
12mo. pp. 15. CONGLETON: (England) 1861.

638. BROTHERHEAD, W. General Fremont, and the Injustice done him by Politicians and envious military Men.
8vo. pp. 10. PHILADELPHIA: *W. Brotherhead*, 1862.

639. BROUGH, JOHN. Speech at the Union Mass Meeting, Marietta, Ohio, June 10, 1863. pp. 8.

640. BROUGH, Hon. JOHN. Speech at Dayton, Ohio, July 4, 1863. President Lincoln on the Arrest of C. L. Vallandigham. President Lincoln's Reply to the Committee of Ohio Democrats, June 29, 1863.
8vo. pp. 31. CINCINNATI: *Moore, Wilstach & Co.*, 1863.

641. —— Die Dayton Rede des Achtbaren John Brough. President Lincoln's Erwiederung in Bezug auf die Verhaftung Vallandigham. 8vo. pp. 31.

642. BROWN, A. W., of East Rockport, Ohio. Sam's Fast, January 1, 1863. Awbron's Nationair. Song set for the day. Abe's Policy. Sambo's Call. New York, Dec. 1, 1862. 8vo. pp. 15.

643. BROWN, B. GRATZ. Freedom for Missouri. Letter to the "Weekly New Era," St. Joseph, Missouri. St. Louis, April 12, 1862. pp. 8.

644. —— Emancipation as a State Policy. Letter to the "Palmyra Courier." St. Louis, May 30, 1862. pp. 6.

645. —— Immediate Abolition of Slavery. Speech in Senate, March 8, 1864. pp. 16.

646. —— Let us have Genuine Freedom in Missouri. St. Louis, November 15, 1864. pp. 4.

647. —— Freedom and Franchise inseparable. A Letter to the Missouri Democrat. December 22, 1864. 8vo. pp. 8.

648. BROWN, B. G. Universal Suffrage. Address at St. Louis, September 22, 1865. 8vo. pp. 19.

649. BROWN's Three Years in the Kentucky Prisons. 1854 to 1857.
8vo. pp. 15.　　　　　CHICAGO: *Press & Tribune*, 1859.

650. BROWN, DAVID BOYER. Reply to Horace Binney on the Privilege of the Writ of Habeas Corpus under the Constitution. Second edition.
8vo. pp. 31.　　　PHILADELPHIA: *James Challen & Son*, 1862.

651. BROWN, FREDERICK T. A Sermon giving Thanks for Union Victories, preached in Georgetown, D. C., August 6, 1863.
8vo. pp. 15.　　　　WASHINGTON: *H. Polkinhorn*, 1863.

652. BROWN, Hon. GEORGE. The American War and Slavery. Speech.
8vo. pp. 16.　　　　　MANCHESTER: (Eng.) 1863.

653. BROWN, Mrs. H. E. Words of Cheer for the Christian Soldier.
18mo. pp. 64.　　　　　*American Tract Society.*

654. BROWN, Rev. HUGH. A Review of Rev. Dr. Raphael's Discourse on American Slavery as being consistent with the Hebrew Servitude of the Old Testament. A Sermon preached in the Baptist Church, Shushan, March 27, 1861.
8vo. pp. 39. NORTH WHITE CREEK: (N. Y.) *R. K. Crocker,* '61.

655. BROWN, ISAAC V. Biography of the Rev. Robert Finley, DD., of New Jersey, with an account of his agency as the author of the American Colonization Society; also a Sketch of the Slave Trade, etc.
12mo. pp. 336.　　　PHILADELPHIA: *John W. Moore*, 1857.

656. BROWN. THE JOHN BROWN INVASION. An authentic History of the Harper's Ferry Tragedy, with full details of the Capture, Trial and Execution of the Invaders, and all the incidents connected therewith.
8vo. pp. 112. Portrait.　　BOSTON: *James Campbell*, 1860.

657. —— The Life, Trial and Execution of Captain John Brown, known as "Old Brown of Ossawatamie," with a full account of the Attempted Insurrection at Harper's Ferry. Including Cooke's Confession, and the incidents of the Execution.
8vo. pp. 108.　　　　NEW YORK: *R. M. De Witt*, 1860.

658. —— Report of the Select Committee of the Senate appointed to

enquire into the late Invasion and seizure of public property at Harper's Ferry. With the Testimony taken before the Committee.

8vo. pp. 255.   *Senate Doc. 36th Cong., 1st Session, No.* 278.

659. BROWN, J. Speeches of Hon. A. C. Barstow, Rev. George T. Day, Rev. Augustus Woodbury, Hon. Thomas Davis, and Resolutions adopted at a Meeting of Citizens held in Providence, R. I., Dec. 2, 1859, on the occasion of the Execution of John Brown.

8vo. pp, 32.   PROVIDENCE : *Amsbury & Co.,* 1860.

660. —— John Brown, with a Photograph representing his execution. By Victor Hugo.

8vo. pp. 8.   PARIS : *Dentu,* 1861.

661. BROWN, JOHN THOMPSON. Speech in the House of Delegates of Virginia, on the Abolition of Slavery, January 18, 1832.

8vo. pp. 32.   RICHMOND : *C. H. Wynne,* 1860.

662. BROWN, R. T. The Mission of Nations. A Sermon preached at Greenwood, Indiana, November 27, 1862. 8vo. pp. 15.

663. —— The Christian Civilization. A Discourse delivered April 30, 1863, at Brownsburg, Indiana.

8vo. pp. 15.   INDIANAPOLIS : *"Daily Journal,"* 1863.

664. BROWN, Hon. WILLIAM A. A Historical Sketch of the early Movement in Illinois for the Legalization of Slavery. Read before the Chicago Historical Society, December 5, 1864.

8vo. pp. 43.   CHICAGO : *Goodman & Donnelly,* 1865.

665. BROWNE, JUNIUS HENRI. Four Years in Secessia. Adventures within and beyond the Union Lines; embracing a variety of Facts, Incidents and Romances of the War. Including the author's Capture at Vicksburg, May 3, 1863; his Imprisonment at Vicksburg; his Escape and perilous journey to the Union Lines.

8vo. pp. 450.   HARTFORD : *O. D. Case & Co.,* 1865.

The author was the Special War Correspondent of the New York Tribune.

666. BROWNELL, HENRY HOWARD. Lyrics of a Day; or Newspaper Poetry. By a Volunteer in the United States Service. Second edition.

12mo. pp. 194.   NEW YORK : *Carleton,* 1864.

One third of this volume is occupied with what the author calls " Votes and Bayonets; or Lays of the Civil War:" all of which have appeared in the

Leading Periodicals and Newspapers of the day, and been highly commended.

667. BROWNELL, H. H.   The Bay Fight at Mobile, August 5, 1864· *Harpers' Magazine, December,* 1864.

668. BROWNING, O. H., of Illinois.   Speech on the Confiscation of Property.   Senate, March 10, 1862.   8vo. pp. 16.

669. —— An Oration delivered on the occasion of the Celebration of our National Independence, at Quincy, Illinois, July 4, 1863. 8vo. pp. 19.   QUINCY : (Illinois) *Whig Press,* 1863.

670. BROWNLOW, W. G.   Sketches of the Rise, Progress and Decline of Secession ; with a Narrative of Personal Adventures among the Rebels. 12mo. pp. 458.   Portrait.   PHILADA.: *Geo. W. Childs,* 1862.

671. —— Sketch of Parson Brownlow, and his Speeches at the Academy of Music and Cooper Institute, New York, May, 1862. (Pulpit and Rostrum, September 1.) 12mo.   NEW YORK : *E. D. Barker,* 1862.

672. —— Governor of Tennessee.   Message and Inaugural Address to the Senate and House of Representatives.   Session of 1865. 8vo. pp. 23.   NASHVILLE : (Tenn.) *S. C. Mercer,* 1865.

673. BROWNLOW, MARTHA ; or the Heroine of Tennessee. 8vo. pp. 49.   PHILADELPHIA : *Barclay & Co.*

674. BROWNSON, ORESTES A.   The American Republic ; its Constitution, Tendencies and Destiny. 8vo. pp.   NEW YORK : *P. O'Shea,* 1866. The following articles, by him, from *Brownson's Review.*

676. —— The Great Rebellion.   July, 1861.

677. —— Slavery and the War.   October, 1861.

678. —— Archbishop Hughes on Slavery.   January, 1862.

679. —— The Struggle of the Nation for Life.   January, 1862.

680. —— State Rebellion ; State Suicide.   April, 1862.

681. —— Emancipation and Colonization.   April, 1862.

682. —— What the Rebellion Teaches.   July, 1862.

683. —— Confiscation and Emancipation.   July, 1862.

684. —— Slavery and the Church.   October, 1862.

685. —— The Seward Policy.   October, 1862.

686. —— Conscripts and Volunteers.   January, 1863.

687. —— The President's Message.   January, 1863.

688. BROWNSON, O. A. Mr. Conway and the Union. April, 1863.
689. —— Stand by the Government. July, 1863.
690. —— Are Catholics Pro-Slavery and Disloyal? July, 1863.
691. —— Catholics and the Anti-Draft Riots. October, 1863.
692. —— Return of the Rebellious States. October, 1863.
693. —— The Federal Constitution. January, 1864.
694. —— The President's Message and Proclamation. January, 1864.
695. —— General Halleck's Report. January, 1864.
696. —— Stevens on Reconstruction. April, 1864.
697. —— Abolition and Negro Equality. April, 1864.
698. —— The next President. April, 1864.
699. —— Military Matters and Men. April, 1864.
700. —— Lincoln, or Fremont? July, 1864.
701. —— General Fitz John Porter. July, 1864.
702. —— Liberalism and Progress. October, 1864.
703. —— Mr. Seward's Speech at Cleveland. October, 1864.
704. —— Are the United States a Nation? October, 1864.
705. —— Mr. Lincoln and Congress. October, 1854.
706. —— Chicago, Baltimore and Cleveland. October, 1864.
707. —— Seward's Speech at Auburn. October, 1864.
708. BRUCE, Rev. V. The Cloud of Human Experience a token of
     God's Protection. A Sermon delivered in St. Paul's Church,
     Hoboken, November 2, 1862.

     12mo. pp. 10.   HOBOKEN: *A. O. Evans*, 1863.

     Mr. Bruce has delivered several patriotic discourses which have been
       printed in the newspapers. His latest was to show " That the hand of
       God is discoverable in all the astounding events which have taken place
       in our country since the breaking out of the rebellion."

709. BUCHANAN, JAMES. Administration on the Eve of the Rebel-
     lion.

     8vo. pp. 296.   NEW YORK: *D. Appleton & Co.*, 1866.
710. BUCK, EDWARD. The Drift of the War.

     8vo. pp. 20.   BOSTON: *A. Williams & Co.*, 1861.
     These Papers were first published in the Boston Transcript, during the last
       six months of the year 1861.

711. BUCHER, Rev. T. P. Union National Fast Day Sermon, de-
     livered at Gettysburg, Penn., Friday, January 4, 1861.

     8vo. pp. 26.   GETTYSBURG: *H. C. Neinstadt*, 1861.

712. A BUGLE BLAST from the Army. What the Soldiers think of Northern Traitois. They will remember them when they return. The Voice of Loyal Democrats in the Army to Traitor Democrats at Home. 8vo. pp. 8.

713. THE BUGLE CALL. Devoted to the cause of our Sick and Wounded Soldiers. 4to. Chicago, 1865.

714. BULKLEY, C. H. Removal of Ancient Landmarks; or the Causes and Consequences of Slavery Extension. A Discourse preached at West Winsted, Conn., March 5, 1854. 8vo. pp. 23. HARTFORD: *Case, Tiffany & Co.*, 1854.

715. BULKLEY, EDWIN A. Wars and rumors of Wars. A Sermon preached at Groton, Massachusetts, April 21, 1861. 8vo. pp. 16. CAMBRIDGE: *Milke & Dillingham*, 1861.

716. BULL RUN. How Bull Run Battle was lost. The Ball's Bluff Massacre. Department of the West. *Fremont Tribune War Tracts.* pp. 8.

717. BULLARD, EDWARD F. The Nation's Trial. The Proclamation. Dormant Powers of the Government. The Constitution a Charter of Freedom, and not "a Covenant with Hell." 8vo. pp. 62. NEW YORK: *C. B. Richardson*, 1863.

718. BULLITT, J. C. A Review of Mr. Binney's Pamphlet on "The Privilege of the Writ of Habeas Corpus under the Constitution." 8vo. pp. 56. PHILADELPHIA: *John Campbell*, 1862.

719. BULLOCK, Hon. ALEXANDER H. Abraham Lincoln, the Just Magistrate, the Representative Statesman, the Practical Philanthropist. Address before the City Council and Citizens of Worcester, June 1, 1865. 8vo. pp. 49. WORCESTER: *Charles Hamilton*, 1865.

720. —— Massachusetts and the War Tax. Speech in the Massachusetts House of Representatives, April 10, 1862. 8vo. pp. 30. BOSTON: *Wright & Potter*, 1862.

721. BUNCE, O. B. Reconstruction. New York, 1862. pp. 11.

722. BUNSEN, C. C. J. The Law of Slavery in the United States. 8vo. pp. 12. BOSTON: *Little, Brown & Co.*, 1863.

723. BURCHARD, Rev. S. D. Providence in War. A Thanksgiving Discourse delivered in New York, November 28, 1861. (Pulpit and Rostrum, No. 23.)

724. BURKE, Edward. Tobacco Manufacture in the United States. A Report adopted in Convention of the Trade, held in New York, December 7 and 8, 1864.

8vo. pp. 33.   New York : *American News Co.*

725. BURKE, John. The Burden of the South, in verse; or Poems on Slavery. Grave, Humorous, Didactic and Satirical. By Rubek Sennora.

8vo. pp. 96.   New York : *Everardus Warner*, 1864.

726. BURLEIGH, William H. The Republican Pocket Pistol, a Collection of Facts, Opinions and Arguments for Freedom.

12mo. pp. 36.   New York : *H. Dayton*, 1860.

727. —— No Slave-Hunting in the old Bay State.

12mo. pp. 23.   *N. Y. American Anti-Slavery Society*, 1860.

728. BURNETT. Reply of the Judge Advocate, H. L. Burnett, to the Pleas of the Counsel for the accused to the Jurisdiction of the Military Commission, convened by Maj. General Hooker, in the case of the United States against Charles Walsh and others.

8vo. pp. 44.   Cincinnati : *Moore, Wilstach & Baldwin*, 1865.

729. BURNETT, Peter H. The American Theory of Government. considered with reference to the present Crisis.

8vo. pp. 93.   New York : *D. Appleton & Co.*, 1861.

730. BURNS, Anthony. A History. By Charles Emery Stevens.

12mo. pp. 295.   Boston : *J. P. Jewett & Co.*, 1856.

731. —— The Boston Slave Riot, and Trial of Anthony Burns, containing the Report of the Fanueil Hall Meeting ; the murder of Bachelder ; Theodore Parker's Lesson for the Day ; Speeches of Counsel ; Judge Loring's Decision, etc.

8vo. pp. 86.   Boston : *Fetridge & Co.*, 1854.

732. BURNS, James R. The Battle of Williamsburg, with Reminiscences of the Campaign, Hospital Experiences, Debates, etc.

16mo. pp. 119.   New York : *For the author*, 1865.

733. BURNS, Rev. Robert F. Address at St. Catherines, Canada West, on the occasion of the Death of President Lincoln, April 23, 1865.

8vo. pp.   St. Catherines : *E. S. Leavenworth*, 1865.

734. BURR, C. Chauncey. Speech in the Peace Convention, New York, June 3, 1863. pp. 4.

735. BURR, C. C.   The History of the Union and of the Constitution. Three Lectures on the Colonial, Revolutionary and Constitutional Periods of American History.
     8vo. pp. 92 and 4.   N. YORK: *Van Evrie, Horton & Co.*, 1863.

736. BURRITT, ELIHU.   A Plan of Brotherly Copartnership of the North and South, for the Peaceful Extinction of Slavery.
     18mo. pp. 48.   NEW YORK : *Dayton & Burdick*, 1856.

737. BURROWS, J. LANSING, DD.   Palliative and Prejudiced Judgments condemned.   A Discourse delivered in Richmond, Va., June 1, 1865, on account of the Assassination of President Lincoln.   With an Extract from a Sermon preached April 23, 1865, upon the Assassination of the President.
     8vo. pp. 12.   RICHMOND : (Va.) *Bulletin Office*, 1865.

738. BURTON, AMOS.   A Journal of the Cruise of the United States Ship Susquehanna, during the years 1860, 1861, 1862 and 1863.
     8vo. pp. 177.   NEW YORK: *E. O. Jenkins*, 1863.

739. BUSHNELL, HORACE, DD.   Popular Government by Divine Right.   A Thanksgiving Sermon, delivered in Hartford, Conn.
     8vo. pp. 16.   HARTFORD : *L. E. Hunt.*

740. —— The Census and Slavery.   A Thanksgiving Discourse, delivered in the Chapel at Clifton Springs, N. Y., Nov. 29, 1860.
     8vo. pp. 24.   HARTFORD : *Lucius E. Hunt*, 1860.

741. —— Reverses needed.   A Discourse delivered at Hartford on the Sunday after the Disaster at Bull Run.
     8vo. pp. 27.   HARTFORD : *L. E. Hunt*, 1861.

742. BUSTEED, RICHARD.   Speech delivered at Faneuil Hall, Boston, October 31, 1862, on the Issues of the War, and the Duty of Sustaining the Government.
     8vo. pp. 24.   NEW YORK: *O. S. Westcott & Co.*, 1862.

743. —— An Oration delivered at Huntington, L. I., July 4, 1862.
     8vo. pp. 21.   NEW YORK ; *O. S. Westcott & Co.*, 1862.

744. BUTLER, Maj. General B. F.   Letter to Hon. Daniel S. Richardson, dated Lowell, February 3, 1862.   8vo. pp. 8.

745. —— Character and Results of the War.   How to Prosecute and How to End it.
     8vo. pp. 28.   NEW YORK: *April* 2, 1863.

746. —— The same.   *Loyal Publication Society, No. 7, pp. 16.*
     10

747. BUTLER, Maj. Gen. B. F. The Same. Cincinnati, pp. 16.
748. —— The same. With General Butler's Address to the People of New Orleans. 8vo. pp. 28.
749. —— The same.
  8vo. pp. 32.   PHILADELPHIA : *Union League.*
750. —— The Life and Services of, Commander of the Military Department of Virginia and North Carolina; also, Commissioner for the Exchange of Prisoners.
  12mo. pp. 108. PHILADELPHIA : *T. B. Peterson & Bro.,* 1864.
751. BUTLER, Rev. C. M., DD. Funeral Address on the Death of Abraham Lincoln, delivered in Philadelphia, April 19, 1865.
  8vo. pp. 32.   PHILADELPHIA : *Henry B. Ashmead,* 1865.
752. BUTLER, C. W. North and South. *Continental Monthly, February,* 1864.
753. BUTLER, Rev. F. E. Our Prospects and Duties. A Sermon on the War, preached at Patterson, N. J., April 28, 1861.
  8vo. pp. 12.   PATTERSON : *Van Deerhoven & Irish,* 1861.
754. BUTLER, GEORGE B. The Conscription Act. A Series of Articles communicated to the Journal of Commerce.
  8vo. pp. 22.   *Loyal Publication Society, No.* 40, 1863.
755. BUTLER, Rev. J. G. The Martyr President. Our Grief and our Duty.
  8vo. pp. 14.   WASHINGTON : *McGill & Witherow,* 1865.

C. J. Slavery in the South; or What is our Present Duty to the Slaves.
  8vo. pp. 15.   BOSTON : *Prentiss & Deland,* 1862.
757. CADETS appointed to the Military Academy at West Point, during the year 1863. Report of Brig. Gen. Totten in relation to.
  8vo. pp. 4. *Ex. Doc., No.* 6, *38th Congress,* 1*st Session,* 1864.
758. CAIRNES, JOHN ELLIOT. The Slave Power. Its Character, Career and Probable Designs ; being an attempt to explain the real Issues involved in the American contest.
  8vo. pp. 171.   NEW YORK : *Carleton,* 1862.
759. —— The Revolution in America. A Lecture delivered before the Dublin Young Men's Christian Association. 12mo. pp. 48.

760. CAIRNES, J. E. The same.

12mo. pp. 43. DUBLIN : *Hodges, Smith & Co.*, 1862.

761. —— The same work. New York : T. J. Crowen, 1862. pp. 15.

762. —— Who are the Canters ? *Lond. Ladies' Eman. Soc.*, '63. *p.* 8.

763. CALDWELL, Rev. JOHN H. Slavery and Southern Methodism. Two Sermons preached in Newman, Georgia.

12mo. pp. 80. *Printed for the author*, 1865.

764. CALDWELL, Rev. SAMUEL L., DD. A Sermon preached in Providence, June 9, 1861, before the Second Regiment of Rhode Island Volunteers.

8vo. pp. 12. PROVIDENCE : *Knowles, Anthony & Co.*, 1861.

765. —— Oration delivered before the Municipal Authorities and Citizens of Providence, July 4, 1861.

8vo. pp. 23. PROVIDENCE : *Knowles, Anthony & Co.*, 1861.

766. CALIFORNIA on State Rights and the Rebellion. Resolutions of the Legislature of California on. *House Reps. Misc. Document, No.* 66, 38*th Congress*, 1864.

767. CALTHROP, S. R. Cambridge and Kingsley on American Affairs. *Christian Examiner, November*, 1863.

768. THE CAMP AND THE FIELD. By one of our Chaplains.

18mo. pp. 18. BOSTON : *American Unitarian Association*, 1861.

769. CAMP AND HOSPITAL, Manual for, containing Directions and Receipts for preparing and cooking the Army Rations ; also, Recipes for extra diet for the Sick, with Hospital Organization.

18mo. pp. 89. ST. LOUIS : *Pub. by Western San. Com.*, 1862.

770. CAMPBELL, ALEXANDER. The True American System of Finance, adapted to the Genius of our Institutions, the present wants of the Government and business interests of the Country, and a guaranty for the future Integrity of the Union. 8vo. pp. 8.

771. CAMPBELL, JOHN., A Douglas Democrat. Unionists versus Traitors. The Political Parties of Philadelphia ; or the Nominees that ought to be elected in 1861. pp. 24.

772. CAPEN, NAHUM. The Indissoluble Nature of the American Union, considered in connection with the assumed Right of Secession. A Letter to Hon. Peter Cooper of New York.

8vo. pp. 36. BOSTON : *A. Williams & Co.*, 1862.

773. CAPTURED AND ABANDONED PROPERTY in the Insurrectionar.

States. Letter from the Secretary of the Treasury to E. B. Washburn, in relation to.

8vo. p. 2. *H. Reps. Mis. Doc., No.* 78, 38*th Cong.* 1*st Ses.* 1864.

774. CAREY, EDWARD. The Confederation of the Nation. *Continental Monthly, June,* 1863.

775. CAREY, HENRY C. Letters to the President on the Foreign and Domestic Policy of the Union, and its Effects as exhibited in the Condition of the People and the State.

8vo. pp. 171. PHILADELPHIA: *M. Polock,* 1858.

776. —— The Slave Trade, Domestic and Foreign; Why it exists and how it may be extinguished.

12mo. pp. 426. PHILADELPHIA: *John A. Martien,* 1859.

777. —— The French and American Tariffs compared, in a Series of Letters addressed to Mons. Michael Chevalier.

8vo. pp. 29. PHILADELPHIA: *Collins,* 1861.

778. —— American Civil War. Correspondence with Mr. H. C. Carey of Philadelphia.

8vo. pp. 23. LONDON: *August, September,* 1861.

779. —— The Paper Question. Letters to the Hon. Schuyler Colfax, Speaker of the House of Representatives.

8vo. pp. 41. PHILADELPHIA: *Collins,* 1865.

780. —— The Farmer's Question. Letters to Schuyler Colfax.

8vo. pp. 24. PHILADELPHIA: *Collins,* 1865.

781. —— The Currency Question. Four Letters to the Hon. Schuyler Colfax. Philadelphia, 1865. 8vo. pp. 40.

782. —— The Railroad Question. Letter to the same. pp. 16.

783. —— The Iron Question. Letter Fifth. 8vo. pp. 18.

784. —— The Paper Question. The Iron Question. The Farmer's Question. Letters to the Hon. Schuyler Colfax.

8vo. pp. 41, 46, 24. PHILADELPHIA: *Collins,* 1865.

785, —— The Way to Outdo England without Fighting her. Letters to the Hon. Schuyler Colfax, on the Paper, the Iron, the Farmer's, the Railroad and the Currency Questions.

8vo. pp. 165. PHILADELPHIA: *Henry Carey Baird,* 1865.

786. CAREY, Rev. ISAAC E. The War an Occasion for Thanksgiving. A Discourse for Thanksgiving, preached at Keokuk, Iowa, November 28, 1861.

8vo. pp. 22. KEOKUK: (Iowa.) *Daily Gate City Print,* 1861.

787. CAREY, Rev. I. E.   God's Wonderful Doings in behalf of the Nation.   A Discourse preached on the National Thanksgiving Day, November 26, 1863, at Freeport, Illinois.
8vo. pp. 16.   FREEPORT: (Ill.) *Judson & McCluer*, 1863.

788. —— The Conflict and the Victory.   Two Discourses for the Times.   Preached November 6 and 24, 1864, at Freeport, Ill.
8vo. pp. 15.   FREEPORT: (Ill.) *Judson & McCluer*, 1864.

789. ——' Discourse on the Death of Abraham Lincoln.   Preached April 19, 1865, at Freeport, Illinois.   8v. pp. 8.

790. —— Abraham Lincoln.   The Value to the Nation of his Exalted Character.   A Sermon preached June 1, 1865, at Freeport.   p. 8.

791. CAREY, JAMES P.   Record of the Great Rebellion.   A Chronological History, from the Dawn of the Rebellion to the Dawn of Peace.
8vo. pp. 16.   NEW YORK: *Dick & Fitzgerald*, 1865

792. CARICATURES,   A Series of Twelve Caricatures of prominent political and military characters, engraved in outline.   Baltimore.
8vo.
Of this interesting series of caricatures, which were got up by secessionists in Baltimore, only 12 copies were struck off for friends, when the plates were destroyed for fear of exposing the artist.

793. CARLIER, AUGUSTE.   De L'Esclavage dans ses Rapports avec L'Union Americaine.
8vo. pp. 495.   PARIS: 1862.

794. CARLILE, JOHN S.   Speech in the Virginia State Convention, delivered Thursday, March 7, 1861.
8vo. pp. 29.   RICHMOND : *Whig Office*, 1861.

795. —— Speech on the Bill to Confiscate the Property and Free the Slaves of Rebels.   Senate, March 11, 1862.   8vo. pp. 13.

796. CARLISLE, Mr.   Synopsis of the Argument of, in the Prize Cases, before the Supreme Court of the United States, at December Term, 1862.   8vo. pp. 13.

797. CARNAHAN, Rev. D. T.   Oration on the Death of Abraham Lincoln, before the Citizens of Gettysburg, Pa., June 1, 1865.
8vo. pp. 24.   GETTYSBURG : *Aughinbaugh & Wible*, 1865.

798. CARPENTER, Rev. HUGH SMITH.   The Relations of Religion to the War.   A Sermon delivered September 26, 1861.
8vo. pp. 23.   NEW YORK: *W. A. Townsend*, 1861.

799. CARPENTER, Rev. H. S. The Final Triumph of Equity. A Sermon preached in Brooklyn, November 26, 1863.
8vo. pp. 28.   NEW YORK : *W. A. Townsend,* 1864.

800. CARPENTER, MAT. H. War Power outside the Constitution Review of Mr. Ryan's Address.
8vo. pp. 16.   MILWAUKIE : *Starr & Son,* 1862.

801. CARRINGTON, H. B. The Hour; the Peril; the Duty. An Address delivered at Columbus, Ohio, April 11 and 17, 1861.
8vo. pp. 16.   COLUMBUS : (Ohio) *Harris & Hurd,* 1861.

802. CARROLL, ANNA ELLA. (of Maryland) Reply to the Speech of the Hon. J. C. Breckenridge in the United States Senate, July 16, 1861, and in defence of the President's War Measures, Blockade of the Southern Ports, Suspension of the Writ of Habeas Corpus, etc.
8vo. pp. 15.   WASHINGTON : *H. Polkinhorn,* 1861.

803. —— The Relation of the National Government to Revolted Citizens defined. No power in Congress to Emancipate their Slaves or confiscate their property, proved. The Constitution, as it is, the only hope of the country. 8vo. pp. 16.

804. —— The War Powers of the General Government. pp. 24. '61.

805. CARTER, LUTHER C. "Propositions with my Imperfect Answers." Dated, Hermitage, Flushing, L. I., June 2, 1862. p. 14.
This pamphlet has no title. It consists of letters by four Propositions on Government, with the author's Answers, and is submitted to the public, "hoping to receive more perfect ones from the ready writers in our midst."

806. —— State of the Union. Speech in House of Representatives, February 27, 1861. pp. 8.

807. THE CARTRIDGE BOX, Published at the United States Army General Hospital, York, Penn. No. 1, March 1, 1864. 4to.

808. CARY, JOHN L. Slavery in Maryland briefly considered, with a preliminary Letter by Dr. Richard S. Stewart.
8vo. pp.   BALTIMORE : 1845.

809. —— Slavery and the Wilmot Proviso.
8vo. pp. 64.   BALTIMORE : 1847.

810. CASSERLY, EUGENE. The Issue in California. Letter of, to T. T. Davenport, Esq. Nevada County, California.
8vo. pp. 15.   SAN FRANCISCO : *Charles F. Robins,* 1861.

811. CATALOGUE of Books in all departments of Literature, Arts and Sciences, to be sold under the direction of Hiram Barney, Collector of the Port of New York, November 17, 1862.
8vo. pp. 95.   NEW YORK: 1862.
The above books comprised the Public Library at Beaufort, S. C. At the request of many gentlemen in New York, President Lincoln directed the books to be withdrawn and the sale stopped. They were subsequently removed to Washington and stored in the Smithsonian Institution, where they were destroyed by fire.

812. CATALOGUE of Autograph Letters, Documents and Signatures, Relics and Curiosities, etc., Donated to the Mississippi Valley Sanitary Fair, October 7 and 8, 1864.
8vo. pp. 37.   ST. LOUIS: *R. P. Studley & Co.*, 1864.

813. CAVADA, Col. F. F. Libby Life. Experiences of a Prisoner of War, in Richmond, Va., 1863–4.
12mo. pp. 221.   PHILADELPHIA: *King & Baird*, 1864.

814. CHACE, LESLIE, Jun. National Perils. Oration delivered at Columbia College Commencement, February 20, 1861.
8vo. pp. 6.   NEW YORK: *George F. Nesbitt & Co.*, 1861.

815. CHACE, Prof. THOMAS. An Address on the Character and Example of President Lincoln, delivered before the Athenæum and Everett Societies of Haverford College, 7th month, 6th, 1865.
8vo. pp. 35.   PHILADELPHIA: *Sherman & Co.*, 1865.

816. CHACE, WARREN. The American Crisis; or the Trial and Triumph of Democracy.
8vo. pp. 82.   BOSTON: *Bela Marsh*, 1862.

817. CHAFFIN, Rev. WILLIAM L. The President's Death and its Lessons. A Discourse, April 23, 1865, before the Second Unitarian Society of Philadelphia.
8vo. pp. 18.   PHILADELPHIA: *King & Baird*, 1865.

818. CHAMBERS, WILLIAM. American Slavery and Colour.
8vo. pp. 216.   LONDON: *W. & R. Chambers*, 1857.

819. CHAMBERLAIN, N. H. The Assassination of President Lincoln. A Sermon preached in Binghamton Conn., April 19, '65.
12mo. pp. 22.   NEW YORK: *G. W. Carlton*, 1865.

820. CHANCELLORSVILLE, The Battle of, and the Eleventh Army Corps.
8vo. pp. 48.   NEW YORK: *G. B. Teubner*, 1863.

821. CHANDLER, WM. W. The Soldier's Right to Vote. Who opposes it? Who favors it! or, The Record of the McClellan Cop-

perheads against allowing the Soldier who fights, the Right to Vote while fighting. pp. 15.

822. CHANDLER, Z.   Conduct of the War.   Speech in Senate, July 16, 1862. 8vo. pp. 16.

823. CHANDLER, Hon. LUCIUS H., of Virginia.   Speech in the House of Representatives of the United States, in defence of his claim to a seat in that body.   1864.   8vo. pp. 23.

824. CHANNING, WILLIAM E.   Slavery.
12mo. pp. 167.   BOSTON : *James Monroe & Co.,* 1835.

825. —— Review of the Remarks on Dr. Channing's Slavery, by a Citizen of Massachusetts.
8vo. pp. 48.   BOSTON : *James Monroe & Co.,* 1836.

826. —— Letter to James G. Birney.
12mo. pp. 37.   BOSTON : *James Monroe & Co.,* 1826.

827. —— A Letter to the Abolitionists.   With comments.
12mo. pp. 32.   BOSTON : *Isaac Knapp,* 1837.

828. —— A Letter to the Hon. Henry Clay, on the Annexation of Texas to the United States.
12mo. pp. 72.   BOSTON : *James Munroe & Co..* 1837.

829. —— The Duty of the Free States ; or Remarks suggested by the case of the Creole.
12mo. pp. 54.   BOSTON : *William Crosby & Co.,* 1842.

830. —— An Address delivered at Lenox, on the 1st of August, 1842, the Anniversary of Emancipation in the British West Indies.
8vo. pp. 36.   LENOX : (Mass.) *J. G. Stanley,* 1842.

831. —— Tribute to the American Abolitionists, for their Vindication of Freedom of Speech.
12mo. pp. 24.   NEW YORK : *Anti-Slavery Society,* 1861.

832. —— The Works of.   Tenth edition.
6 vols. 12mo.   BOSTON : *George R. Channing,* 1849.
Th following articles upon Slavery, Abolition, the Union and cognate subjects are in these volumes.
Vol. I. The Union.   Correspondence between John Quincy Adams, President of the United States, and several citizens of Massachusetts, concerning the Charge of a Design to Dissolve the Union, alleged to have existed
in that State.   Boston, 1829.
Vol. II. Slavery.
The Abolitionists.   A Letter to James G. Birney.
The Annexation of Texas to the United States.

Vol. V. Remarks on the Slavery Question in a Letter to Jonathan Phillips.
Vol. VI. Emancipation.—1840.
The Duty of the Free States; or Remarks suggested by the case of the Creole. Part 1. 1842.
The Duty of the Free States. Part 2. 1842.
An Address delivered at Lenox, August 1, 1842, the Anniversary of Emancipation in the British West Indies.

833. —— Memoir of, with Extracts from his Correspondence and Manuscripts.
3 vols. 12mo. BOSTON: *Crosby & Nichols*, 1848.

There is a great deal in these volumes showing how much Dr. Channing had exerted himself in the Cause of Freedom for the Slave, which does not appear in the books published during his life.

834. CHAPMAN, MARIA WESTON. Right and Wrong in Massachusetts.
18mo. pp. 175. BOSTON: *Henry L. Devereux*, 1840.

835. CHARLIE, the Drummer Boy. New York: *American Tract Society*. 8vo. pp. 16.

836. CHASE, S. P. The National Loan; embracing the Appeal in its behalf and the Laws authorizing it, with forms of Bonds, Insructions, etc., connected with the subscription.
8vo. pp. 23. WASHINGTON: *Government Printing Office*, 1861.

837. —— How the South rejected Compromise in the Peace Conference of 1861.
8vo. pp. 11. *Loyal Publication Society, No.* 37, 1863.

838. —— Liberty, or Slavery? Daniel O'Connell on American Slavery. Reply to O'Connell. 8vo. pp. 15.

839. CHASE, HENRY, and C. W. Sanborn, M. D. The North and the South. A Statistical View of the condition of the Free and Slave States, compiled from official documents.
12mo. pp. 134. BOSTON: *John P. Jewett*, 1855.

840. CHATTANOOGA. The Three Days' Battle of Chattanooga, 23d, 24th and 25th of November, 1863. An unofficial despatch from Gen. Meigs to the Hon. E. M. Stanton, Secretary of War. Accompanied by a Plan of the Battle.
8vo. pp. 10. NEW YORK: *Julius Bien & W. M. Franklin*, '64.

841. CHEEVER, Rev. GEORGE B. The Fire and Hammer of God's

11

Word against Slavery.   Speech at the Anniversary of the American Abolition Society, May, 1858.

    8vo. pp. 16.   NEW YORK: *American Abolition Society*, 1858.

842. CHEEVER, Rev. G. B.   The Sin of Slavery; the Guilt of the
Church, and the Duty of the Ministry.   An Address before the
Abolition Society at New York.

    12mo. pp. 23.   BOSTON : *J. P. Jewett & Co.*, 1858.

843. —— The True Christian Patriot.   A Discourse on the Virtues
and Public Services of the late Judge Jay, before the American
Peace Society.

    8vo. pp. 58.   BOSTON : *American Peace Society*, 1860.

844. —— The Guilt of Slavery and the Crime of Slaveholding demon-
strated from the Hebrew and Greek Scriptures.

    12mo. pp. 472.   BOSTON : *J. P. Jewett & Co.*, 1860.

845. —— The Salvation of our Country secured by Immediate Emancipation.   A Discourse delivered November 10, 1861.

    8vo. pp. 24.   NEW YORK : *John A. Gray*, 1861.

846. —— God's Way of Crushing the Rebellion.   A Sermon preached
at the Church of the Puritans, New York, September 29, 1861.

    18mo. pp. 20.   NEW YORK : 5 Beekman street, 1861.

847. —— Rights of the Colored Race to Citizenship and Representa-
tion, and the guilt and consequences of Legislation against them.
A Discourse delivered in the Hall of the Representatives of the
United States, in Washington, May 29, 1864.

    8vo. pp. 28.   NEW YORK: *Francis & Loutrel*, 1864.

848. CHEEVER, D. W.   Hygiene, with reference to the Military
Service. *North American Review, October*, 1863.

849. CHESAPEAKE,   Papers relating to the Seizure of.

    Folio, pp. 96.   *Parl. Papers, N. America, No. 9, London*, 1864.

850. CHESNEY, Capt, C. E. (R. E.)   Military View of recent Cam
paigns in Virginia and Maryland.

    Post 8vo. 2 vols.   LONDON : *Smith, Elder & Co.*, 1865.

851. CHESTER, Rev. JOHN.   The Lesson of the Hour.   Justice, as
well as Mercy.   A Discourse preached on the Sabbath following
the Assassination of the President, at Washington, D. C.

    8vo. pp. 16.   WASHINGTON : *Chronicle Print*, 1865.

852. CHESTNUT, JAMES W., of South Carolina.   Relations of States.

Speech delivered in the United States Senate, April 9, 1860, on the Resolutions submitted by the Hon. Jeff. Davis, Mar. 1, 1860. 8vo. pp. 24. BALTIMORE: *J. Murphy & Co.*, 1860.

853. CHEVALIER, M. M. France, Mexico and the Confederate States. Translated by William Henry Hurlbut. 8vo. pp. 16. NEW YORK: *C. B. Richardson*, 1863.

854. THE CHICAGO COPPERHEAD CONVENTION. The Treasonable and Revolutionary Utterances of the men who composed it. Extracts from all the notable Speeches delivered in and out of the National "Democratic" Convention. A Surrender to the Rebels advocated. A disgraceful and pusillanimous Peace demanded, etc. 8vo. pp. 16. WASHINGTON: *Cong. Union Committee*, 1864,

855. THE CHICAGO SANITARY COMMISSION. First and Second Reps. of. 8vo. pp. 30. CHICAGO: *Dunlop & Co.*, 1862.

856. CHICAGO CONVENTION, Spirit of. Extracts from all the notable Speeches delivered in and out of the National "Democratic" Convention. A Surrender to the Rebels advocated, etc. p. 58 to 71.

857. CHICAGO. Celebration of the 86th Anniversary of the Independence of the United States, at Chicago, July 4 1862. (Oration by B. F. Ayer; Poem by George W. Pettes.) 8vo. pp. 31. CHICAGO: 1862.

858. CHICAMAUGA, the Price of Chattanooga. A Description of the Strategic Plans, Marches and Battles of the Campaign of Chattanooga, with Map. 8vo. pp. 30. PHILADELPHIA: *J. B. Lippincott & Co.*, 1864.

859. CHIDLAW, Rev. W., Chaplain. A Thanksgiving Sermon, preached before the 39th Ohio Volunteers, at Camp Todd, Macon, Missouri, Nov. 28, 1861 ; and a Sketch of the Regiment. 12mo. pp. 24. CINCINNATI: *George Crosby*, 1861.

860. CHILD, DAVID LEE. The Despotism of Freedom. A Speech at the First Anniversary of the New England Anti-Slavery Society, January, 1834. 12mo. pp. 72. BOSTON: *Anti-Slavery Society*.

861. —— Rights and Duties of the United States relative to Slavery, under the Laws of War. No Military Power to return any Slave. "Contraband of War" inapplicable between the United States and their Insurgent Enemies. 12mo. pp. 48. BOSTON: *R. F. Walcutt*, 1861.

862. CHILD, Mrs. Anti-Slavery Catechism.
12mo. pp. 36. Newburyport: *Charles Whipple*, 1836.

863. —— An Appeal in favor of that class of Americans called Africans.
12mo. pp. 216. New York: *John S. Taylor*, 1836.

864. CHILD, L. Maria. The Duty of Disobedience to the Fugitive Slave Act. An Appeal to the Legislators of Massachusetts.
12mo. pp. 36. Boston: *American Anti-Slavery Society*, 1860.

865. —— Correspondence between Lydia Maria Child and Gov. Wise and Mrs. Mason, of Virginia.
12mo. pp. 28. Boston: *American Anti-Slavery Society*, 1860.

866. —— The Right Way and the Safe Way, proved by Emancipation in the British West Indies and elsewhere.
12mo. pp. 96. New York: 5 Beekman Street, 1860.

867. —— The Patriarchal Institution, as described by members of its own family.
12mo. pp. 55. New York: *American Anti-Slavery Society,* '60.

868. —— The Freedman's Book.
12mo. Boston: *Ticknor & Fields*, 1865.

869. CHIPMAN, John Logan. Address, on the State of the Union, before the Detroit Democratic Asso., Feb. 19, 1863. pp. 8.

870. CHITTENDEN, L. E. A Report of the Debates and Proceedings in the Secret Sessions of the Conference Convention for proposing amendments to the Constitution of the United States, at Washington, February, 1861.
8vo. pp. 626. New York: *D. Appleton & Co.*, 1864.

871. Christ in the Army. A Selection of the Sketches of the work of the United States Sanitary Commission, by various writers. Necessity, Organization, Principles, Sources of Supply. In the Camp, the Hospitals, Field Hospitals, at the Front, on the Battle Field, Prisoners. On the Moral Results of this War.
18mo. pp. 144. *For the Christian Commission*, 1865.

872. CHRISTIAN, Rev. L. H. Our Present Position. A Thanksgiving Discourse, delivered in Philadelphia, November 27, 1862.
8vo. pp. 46. Philadelphia: *Wm. S. & Alfred Martien*, 1862.

873. Christian Examiner. Present condition of the Free Colored People of the United States. By Jas. Freman Clarke. Mar., '59.

874. —— The War. By James F. Clarke. July, 1861.
England and America. By E. E. Hale. September, 1861.

875. CHRISTIAN EXAMINER. Africans in America, and their New Guardians. J. H. Allen. July, 1862.

Our War Policy, and how it deals with Slavery. J. H. Allen. September, 1862.

The New War Policy, and the Future of the South. J. H. Allen. November, 1862.

876. —— The Peace Policy, how it is urged and what it means. J. H. Allen. January, 1863.

Democracy on Trial. W. F. Allen. March, 1863.

Later Phases of English Feeling. J. H. Allen. March, 1863.

The Thirty-Seventh Congress. J. H. Allen. May, 1863.

A Month of Victory and its Results. J. H. Allen. Sept., 1863.

English Expositions of Neutrality. J. H. Allen. Nov., 1863.

Coleridge and Kingsley on American Affairs. S. R. Culthrop. November, 1863.

877. —— Our Ambulance System. By F. B. Balch. January, 1864.

The Two Messages. By J. H. Allen. January, 1864,

Federalism and its Present Tasks. By J. H. Allen. March, '64.

The Freedmen and Free Labor in the South. By W. F. Allen. May, 1864.

The American War as an English Question. By M. D. Conway. May, 1864.

A Word on the War. By J. H. Allen. July, 1864.

American Expositions of Neutrality. By J. H. Allen. Sep., '64

878. —— The Presidential Election. By E. E. Hale. Nov., 1864.

The Eighth of November. By J. H. Allen. January, 1865.

The Fourth of March. By J. H. Allen. March, 1865.

The Nation's Triumph and its Sacrifice. By J. H. Allen. May, 1865.

South Carolina one of the United States. September, 1865.

State Crimes and their Penalty. September, 1865.

The President's Reconstruction. November, 1865.

879. CHRISTIANITY, versus Treason and Slavery. Religion rebuking Sedition. 8vo. pp. 16. Philadelphia.

880. CHRISTY, DAVID. Lectures on African Colonization, and kindred subjects. COLUMBUS; *J. H. Riley & Co.,* 1853.

881. CHURCH, SANFORD E. Speech at Batavia, Oct. 13, 1863. p. 8.

882. CINCINNATI CONVENTION, October 18, 1864, for the organization of a Peace Party, upon State Rights, Jeffersonian, Democratic Principles, and for the promotion of Peace and Independent Nominations for President and Vice-President of the United States. 8vo. pp. 16.

883. CLAPP, Rev. A. H. God's Purpose in the War. A Sermon preached at Providence, R. I., May 12, 1861.
8vo. pp. 15. PROVIDENCE: *Knowles, Anthony & Co.*, 1861.

884. CLARIGUY, C. The Election of Mr. Lincoln. A Narrative of the contest in 1860, for the Presidency of the United States. Translated by Sir W. Jones.
8vo. pp. 90. LONDON: *J. Ridgeway*, 1861.

885. CLARIMONDE. A Tale of New Orleans Life, and of the Present War. By a Member of the New Orleans Washington Artillery.
8vo. pp. 79. RICHMOND: *L. A. Malsby*, 1863.

886. CLARK, ALEX. Memorial Sermon, preached on the National Funeral Day of Abraham Lincoln, April 19, 1865, at Cincinnati.
12mo. pp. 16. CINCINNATI: *Masonic Review Office*, 1865.

887. —— Christian Courage. A Sermon for the Times.
18mo. pp. 28. PHILADELPHIA: *W. S. Young*, 1862.

888. CLARK, B. C. Remarks upon United States Intervention in Hayti, with comments upon the correspondence connected with it.
8vo. pp. 36. BOSTON: *Eastburn's Press*, 1853.

889. CLARK, Hon. DANIEL. Eulogy on the Life and Character of Abraham Lincoln, before the City Government of Manchester, New Hampshire, June 1, 1865.
8vo. pp. 36. MANCHESTER: (N. H.) *Mirror Office*, 1865.

890. CLARK, Rev. FREDERICK G. Thankfulness, its Occasions and Responsibilities. A Sermon preached in New York, November 28, 1861.
8vo. pp. 27. NEW YORK: *Ivison, Phinney & Co.*, 1861.

891. —— Our National Restoration. A Sermon for the Times. June, 1862.
8vo. pp. 11. NEW YORK: *John A. Gray*, 1862.

892. —— Gold in Fire. Our National Position. A Sermon preached in New York on Thanksgiving Day, November 27, 1862,
8vo. pp. 20. NEW YORK: *J. H. Duyckinck*, 1862.

893. CLARK, Gaylord J. The Enemies of the Constitution and the Union. Peace or War! Speech delivered before the Democratic Club of Lockport, March 16, 1863. 8vo. pp. 15.

894. CLARK, Henry, of Poultney. A Biographical Sketch of Edward Crafts Hopson. Read before the Vermont Historical Society, January 25, 1865. 8vo. pp. 6.

895. CLARKE, Rev. James Freeman. The Rendition of Anthony Burns. Its causes and consequences. A Discourse on Christian Politics, delivered at Boston, June 4, 1854.
8vo. pp. 28. Boston: *Crosby, Nichols & Co.*, 1854.

896. —— A Discourse on the Aspects of the War, delivered in the Indiana-Place Chapel, Boston, on Fast Day, April 2, 1863.
8vo. pp. 36. Boston: *Walker, Wise & Co.*, 1863.

897. —— Order of Services at Indiana-Place Chapel, on Easter Sunday, April 16, 1865; being the Sunday after the Assassination of Abraham Lincoln.
12mo. pp. 24. Boston: *Walker, Fuller & Co.*, 1865.

898. CLARK, Rev. Joseph. The History and Theory of Revolutions. From the Princeton Review for April, 1862.
8vo. pp. 35. Philadelphia: *W. S. & Alfred Martien*, 1862.

899. CLARK, L. M. Letter to the Secretary of the Treasury, August 20, 1862. pp. 14.

900. CLARK, Peter H. The Black Brigade of Cincinnati. A Report of its Labors and a Muster-Roll of its Members; together with various Speeches, Orders, etc.
8vo. pp. 30. Cincinnati: *Joseph B. Boyd*, 1864.

901. CLARK, Rufus, DD. The Unity of American Nationality. A Discourse delivered in Albany, November 26, 1863.
8vo. pp. 42. Albany: *C. Van Benthuysen*, 1863.

902. —— A Discourse commemorative of the Heroes of Albany, who have fallen during the present war, in defence of our country, delivered at Albany, July 10, 1864.
8vo. pp. 50. Albany: *C. Van Benthuysen*, 1864.

903. CLARK, Rt. Rev. Thomas M., DD., Bishop of the Diocese of Rhode Island. The State of the Country. A Sermon delivered in Grace Church, Providence, November 25, 1860.
8vo. pp. 10. Providence: *Cooke, Danielson & Co.*, 1860

904. CLARK, Rt. Rev. T. M. The United States Sanitary Commission. A Discourse delivered in Providence, November 6, 1864. *Providence Journal, November* 12, 1864.

905. —— The Present War, and its Results. A Discourse delivered in Grace Church, Providence, November 24, 1864. *Providence Journal, November* 26, 1864.

906. —— A Plain Appeal to the People of the United States. 8vo. pp. 30. NEW YORK: *John F. Trow & Co.,* 1864.

907. CLARKE, WALTER, DD. The State of the Country. An Oration delivered at Buffalo, July 4, 1862. 12mo. pp. 20. BUFFALO; *Breed, Butler & Co.,* 1862.

908. CLAUDE, WILLIAM TELL. Address to the People of Anne Arundell County. (Maryland.) 8vo. pp. 7.

909. CLAY, CASSIUS M., Letter from. Slavery; the Evil— the Remedy. 8vo. pp. 4.

910. —— Speech before the Law Department of the University of Albany, New York, February 3, 1863. 8vo. pp. 24. NEW YORK; *Wyncoop & Co.,* 1863.

911. CLEAVELAND, ELISHA LORD. Love of Country. A Discourse preached in New Haven, Thanksgiving Day, November 29, and repeated December 9, 1860. 8vo. pp. 20. NEW HAVEN: *Thomas H. Pease,* 1860.

912. —— Our Duty in Regard to the Rebellion. April 3, 1863. 8vo. pp. 22. NEW YORK; *Hall, Clayton & Medole,* 1863.

913. CLEAVELAND, JOHN. Opinion as to the Liability, under the Act of April 29, 1863, to State Taxation on Loans to the United States, evidenced or secured by United States Government Stocks, held by New York Banking and Moneyed Corporations. 8vo. pp. 65. NEW YORK; *Hall, Clayton & Medrole,* 1863.

914. CLEMENS, JEREMIAH. Tobias Wilson; a Tale of the Gt. Rebellion. 8vo. pp. 179. PHILADELPHIA; *J. B. Lippincott & Co.,* 1865.

915. CLERGY, The, not Recruiting Agents, and the Churches not Recruiting Stations. A Letter to a Member of the Young Men's Christian Association. By Fromelden. New York. 8vo. p. 12.

916. CLEVELAND, Rev. W. NEAL. African Servitude. What is it? and what its moral Character? 8vo. pp. 27. NEW YORK: *D. Appleton & Co.,* 1861.

917. CLINE, A. J.   Secession unmasked; or an Appeal from the madness of Disunion to the Sobriety of the Constitution and common sense.

8vo. pp. 16.   WASHINGTON: *H. Polkinhorn*, 1861.

918. COATES, BENJAMIN.   Cotton Cultivation in Africa. Suggestions on the importance of the cultivation of Cotton in Africa, in reference to the Abolition of Slavery in the United States, through the organization of the African Colonization Society.

8vo. pp. 52.   PHILADELPHIA: *C. Sherman & Son*, 1868.

919. COBDEN, RICHARD.   Speech on the Foreign Enlistment Act, in the House of Commons.

8vo. pp. 25.   LONDON: *W. Ridgeway*, 1863.

920. COCHRAN, THOMAS F.   Address delivered at McSherrysville, Lower Chanceford Township, York Co., Penn., July 4, 1865.

8vo. pp. 24.   LANCASTER: (Pa.) *Pearson & Geist*, 1865.

921. COCHUT, A.   Les Finances et les Banques des Etats Unis depuis la Guerre. *Rev. des Deux Mondes, September*, 1862.

922. CODDINGTON, DAVID S.   The Military and Financial Policy of the National Goverpment.   Speech in the Assembly of New York, January 23, 1862.   8vo. pp. 5.

923. COFFIN, C. C.   The May Campaign in Virginia. *Atlantic Monthly, July*, 1864.

924. —— My Days and Nights on the Battle Field.   A Book for Boys. By Carlton.

18mo. pp. 312.   BOSTON: *Ticknor & Fields*, 1865.

925. —— Following the Flag.   From August, 1861, to November, 1862, with the Army of the Potomac.

18mo. pp. 336.   BOSTON: *Ticknor & Fields*, 1865.

Mr. Coffin is the writer of the spirited Letters from the Seat of War which appeared in the *Boston Journal.*

926. COFFIN, JOSHUA.   An Account of some of the principal Slave Insurrections, and others, which have occurred or been attempted, in the United States and elsewhere, during the last two centuries. Collected from various sources.

12mo. pp. 36.   *N. Y. American Anti-Slavery Society*, 1860.

927. COGGESHALL, S. W.   An Anti-Slavery Address.   Danielsonville, only 4, 1849.

12mo. pp. 57.   WEST KILLINGLY: *E. B. Carter*, 1849.

12

928. COGGESHALL, Wm. T.   The Journeys of Abraham Lincoln, from Springfield to Washington, 1861, as President Elect, and from Washington to Springfield, 1865, as President Martyred.
12mo. pp. 327.   Columbus : (Ohio) *Journal Office*, 1865.

929. COLFAX, Hon. Schuyler.   Fremont's Hundred Days in Missouri.   Speech in Reply to Mr. Blair of Missouri, in House of Representatives, March 7, 1862.   8vo. pp. 16.

930. —— Speeches in Reply to Messrs. Dwin and Blair's attacks on Gen. Fremont, in House of Representatives, April 21, 1862. 8vo. pp. 8.

931. —— Speech on his Resolution declaring Mr. Long, of Ohio, an unworthy member of the House.   House of Representatives, April 14, 1864.   8vo. pp. 8.

932. CALHOUN, Comr. John, U. S. Navy, Petition of, Protesting against the Action of the late Advising Board, and praying for Relief.
8vo. pp. 12.   Philadelphia ; *J. B. Chandler*, 1863.

933. COLLAMER, Jacob.   Speech on the Treasury Note Bill, in the Senate, February 12, 1862.   8vo. pp. 15.

934. —— On the Reconstruction of the Seceded States.   Speech made in the Senate of the United States, Feb. 6, 1865.   8vo. pp. 8.

935. COLLIER, Rev. Robert Laird.   Moral Heroism; its essentiality to the crisis.   A Sermon preached in Chicago, Aug. 3, 1862.
8vo. pp. 16.   Chicago : *Tribune Office*, 1862.

936. COLLINS, Elizabeth.   Memoirs of the Southern States.
12mo. pp.   Barnicott : *J. Russell Smith*, 1865.

937. COLLINS, John A.   Right and Wrong, amongst the Abolitionists of the United States ; with an introductory Letter by Harriet Martineau, with an Appendix.
8vo. pp. 76.   Glasgow : *George Gallie*, 1841.

938. —— The Anti-Slavery Picnick ; a collection of Speeches, Poems, Dialogues, and Songs for use in Schools and Anti-Slavery Meetings.
18mo. pp. 144.   Boston : *H. W. Williams*, 1842.

939. COLLINS, Thad. W.   Review of the Governor's Message. Speech in the House of Assembly of New York, March, 1863. 8vo. pp. 8.

940. COLLINS, William H., of Baltimore.   Address to the People of Maryland, December 20, 1860.

8vo. pp. 17.   Baltimore: *James Young*, 1861.

941. —— Second Address to the People of Maryland, Feb. 23, 1861. pp. 17.

942. —— Third Address to the People of Maryland, Sept. 2, '61. p. 24.

943. COLLYER, Robert.   The Battle Field of Fort Donelson.   A Narrative Sermon, preached in Chicago, March 2, 1862.   *Journal American Unitarian Association, April,* 1862.

944. —— A Letter to a Sick Soldier.   Boston.   pp. 14.

945. COLMAN, Rev. Geo. W.   Assassination of the President.   A Discourse on the Death of Abraham Lincoln, delivered at Acton, Mass., April 16, 1865.

8vo. pp. 15.   Boston: *S. Chesin*, 1865.

946. Colored Americans.   The Loyalty and Devotion of, in the Revolution and War of 1812.

12mo. pp. 24.   Boston: *R. F. Wallcut*, 1861.

947. Colored Freedmen.   First Annual Report of the Executive Board of the Association of Friends at Philadelphia and vicinity, for the Relief of Colored Freedmen.

8vo. pp. 39.   Birmingham: *White & Pike*, 1864.

948. Colored Enlistments.   Addresses of the Hon. W. D. Kelley, Miss Anna E. Dickinson, and Mr. Frederick Douglass, at a Mass Meeting held at Philadelphia, July 6, 1863, for the promotion of colored enlistments.   pp. 8.

949. Colored Men.   Proceedings of the National Convention of Colored Men, held in the city of Syracuse, N. Y., October 4, 5, 6 and 7, 1864.   With the Bill of Wrongs and Rights; and the Address to the American People.

8vo. pp. 62.   Boston: 1864.

950. Colored People's Educational Monument Association.   Celebration by, in memory of Abraham Lincoln, July 4, 1865, in Washington, D. C.

8vo. pp. 34.   Washington: *McGill & Witherow*, 1865.

951. Colored Refugees.   Report of a Committee of the Representatives of New York Yearly Meeting of Friends, upon the condition and wants of Colored Refugees.   pp. 30.

952. COLORED REFUGEES. Second Report of the Committee of the New York Yearly Meeting of Friends upon the condition of Colored Refugees, 5th month 27, 1863. pp. 15.

953. COLORED SCHOOLS. Report and Extracts relating to Colored Schools in the Department of the Tennessee and Arkansas, November 30, 1864.
12mo. pp. 20.   MEMPHIS: *Tenn. Freedmen Press*, 1862.

954. COLORED SUFFRAGE. Report to the Common Council [of Washington] by S. A. Peugh, from the Select Committee on the subject of Suffrage, November 6, 1865. pp. 6.

955. COLORED SCHOOLS. Reports relating to Colored Schools in Mississippi, Arkansas and Western Tennessee, April, 1865.
12mo. pp. 28.   MEMPHIS: (Tenn.) *Freedmen's Press*, 1865.

956. COLORED TROOPS and Military Colonies on Southern Soil. Notes by an Officer of the Ninth Army Corps.
8vo. pp. 16.   NEW YORK, 1863.

957. COLORS, Names of Battles to be placed on. General Orders, No. 20, of the Army of the Potomac, directing the names of the Battles, which the Regiments named may inscribe upon their colors or guidons for meritorious services performed by them. March 7, 1865. 12mo. pp. 26.

958. COLVER, Rev. NATHANIEL, DD. Slavery or Freedom must die. The Harper's Ferry Tragedy. A symptom of a Disease in the Heart of the Nation; or the power of Slavery to destroy the Liberties of the Nation, from which there is no escape but in the destruction of Slavery itself.
8vo. pp. 16.   CINCINNATI: *Office of Christian Luminary*, 1860.

960. [COLWELL, STEPHEN.] The South. A Letter from a friend in the North. With special reference to the effects of Disunion upon Slavery.
8vo. pp. 66.   PHILADELPHIA: *For the author*, 1850.

961. COLWELL, STEPHEN. The Claims of Labor, and their Precedence to the claims of Free Trade.
8vo. pp. 52.   PHILADELPHIA: *C. Sherman & Son*, 1861.

962. COLYER, VINCENT. Brief Report of the Services rendered by the Freed People to the United States Army in North Carolina in the Spring of 1862, after the Battle of Newbern.
8vo. pp. 64.   NEW YORK: *V. Colyer*, 1864.

963. COLYER, V.   Report to the Union League Club of New York, on the Reception and Care of the Soldiers returning from the War.   September 14, 1865.
8vo. pp. 56.   NEW YORK: *Club House,* 1865.

964. COMMERCE.   Report on the Commerce of the United States, and its most urgent necessities.
8vo. pp. 11.   NEW YORK: *John W. Amerman,* 1861.

965. COMMERCE. Additional Regulations concerning Commercial Intercourse with and in States declared in Insurrection.   January 26, 1864.   8vo. pp. 6.

966. COMMERCE.   War upon American Commerce, by subjects of Great Britain.
8vo. pp. 20.   B STON: *J. H. Eastburn,* 1864.

967. COMMERCIAL INTERCOURSE with and in States declared in Insurrection, and the collection of abandoned and captured property. Embracing the Treasury Department Circulars and Regulations; the Executive Proclamations and License; and the War and Navy Department Orders.
8vo. pp. 56.   WASHINGTON: *Government Printing Office,* 1863.

968. COMMERCIAL REPORTS received at the Foreign Office from her Majesty's Consuls.   Presented to both Houses of Parliament in May and June, 1865.
Royal 8vo. pp. 306.   LONDON: *Harrison & Sons,* 1865.
The Reports from the United States presenting the Commercial Statistics for 1863–64, and are of much interest.

969. COMSTOCK, Hon. GEORGE, of Syracuse.   Let us Reason Together.   8vo. pp. 16.

970. COMSTOCK, Judge GEO. F.   Speech delivered in the Brooklyn Academy of Music.   Campaign Document.   8vo. pp. 8.

971. CONCENTR TED FEED for Horses, Mules and Cattle.   Official Report of the Trial of, made by order of the Q. M. General, under the supervision of Capt. Edward L. Hartz, U. S. A.
8vo. pp 16.   WASHINGTON, 1863.

972. CONCESSIONS and Compromises.   Philadelphia, December 8, 1860.   8vo. pp. 14.

973. CONDUCT OF THE WAR.   Report of the Joint Committee on the Conduct of the present War.   *Senate, Report Com., No.* 41, 37*th Congress,* 2*d Session,* 1862.   *pp.* 8.

974. CONDUCT OF THE WAR, Report of the Joint Committee on. In Three Parts. Part I, The Army of the Potomac. Part II, Bull Run; Ball's Bluff. Part III, Western Department, or Missouri; Miscellaneous. 3 vols. 8vo. *Congressional Document, 37th Congress, 3d Session, Senate Report Com., No.* 108, 1863.

975. CONFEDERATE STATES. Statutes at Large. Public Laws of the Confederate States of America, passed at the First Session of the First Congress, 1862 ; carefully collated with the Originals at Richmond. Edited by James M. Matthews·
Royal 8vo. p. v. 1 to 56. Ind. ix. RICHMOND : *R. M. Smith,* '62.

976. —— Public Laws passed at the Second Session of the First Congress.
Royal 8vo. p. v. 57 to 92. Ind. ix. RICHMOND : *R. S. Smith,* '62.

977. —— Public Laws passed at the Third Session of the First Congress.
Ro. 8vo. p. viii. 93 to 170. Ind. xx. RICHMOND : *R. M. Smith,* '63.

978. —— Public Laws passed at the Fourth Session of the First Congress.
Royal 8vo. p. 171 to 252. Ind. xxiii. RICH.: *R. M. Smith,* 1864.

979. —— Public Laws passed at the First Session of the Second Congress.
Ro. 8vo. p. viii. 253 to 288. Ind. xii. RICHMOND: *R. M. Smith,* '64.

980. —— The Statutes at Large of the Provisional Government of the Confederate States of America, from the institution of the government, February 8, 1861, to its termination, February 18, 1862, inclusive. Arranged in chronological order, together with the Constitution for the Provisional Government, and the Permanent Constitution of the Confederate States, and the Treaties concluded by the Confederate States with Indian Tribes.
Ro. 8vo. p. xv. 1 to 411. Ind. xlvi. RICHMOND : *R. M. Smith,* '64.

981. —— Private Laws of the Confederate States of America, passed at the First, Second, Third and Fourth Sessions, of the First Congress, and First Session of the Second Congress.
Royal 8vo. pp. 18. RICHMOND : *R. M. Smith,* 1862–64.

982. CONFEDERATE STATES. Instructions for Collectors of Taxes, from C. G. Memminger, Secretary of the Treasury, Dated Richmond, May, 1863. 8vo. pp. 15.

983. CONFEDERATE CONFISCATION BILL. A Bill to be entitled An Act for the sequestration of the estate, property and effects of alien Enemies, and for the indemnity of citizens of the Confederate States, and persons aiding the same in the Existing War with the United States. September 3, 1861. 8vo. pp. 8.

984. CONFEDERATE STATES. An Act to impose Regulations upon the Foreign Commerce of the Confederate States, to provide for the Public Defence. 8vo. pp. 10.

985. —— Reports of the operations of the Army of Northern Virginia, from June, 1862, to and including the battle at Fredericksburg, December 13, 1862.

2 vols. 8vo. pp. 627 and 602. RICHMOND: *R. M. Smith,* 1864.

986. —— Report of Evidence taken before a Joint Special Committee of both Houses of the Confederate Congress, to investigate the affairs of the Navy Department.

8vo. pp. 472. RICHMOND: *George P. Evans & Co.,* 1862.

987. —— Official Reports of Battles. Published by an order of Congress.

8vo. pp. 562. RICHMOND: *R. M. Smith,* 1864.

988. —— The same work. New York: *C. B. Richardson,* 1864.

989. —— Papers relating to the Blockade of the Ports of. Fol. p. 126. (*Parliamentary Papers, North America, No.* 8,) *London,* 1862.

990. —— Correspondence with Mr. Mason respecting the Blockade and Recognition of the Confederate States.

Folio pp. 17. (*Parl. Papers, N. Am., No.* 2, *London,*) 1863.

991. CONFEDERATE AGENTS in England. Correspondence with Mr. Adams respecting.

Folio pp. 18. *Parl. Papers, N. America, No.* 8, *Lond.*: 1863.

992. CONFERENCE CONVENTION of the Commissioners from the several States, held, at the request of Virginia, at Washington, February, 1861. Report made to the General Assembly of Rhode Island, by the Commissioners on the part of the State.

8vo. pp. 9. PROVIDENCE: *Cooke & Danielson,* 1861.

993. CONGDON, CHARLES T. The Warning of War. A Poem delivered before the United Societies of Dartmouth College, New Hampshire, July 30, 1862.

8vo. pp. 29. NEW YORK: *Francis Hart & Co.,* 1862.

994. The Congressional Globe; containing the Debates and Proceedings of the 36th to the 39th Congress of the United States, inclusive. With Appendices containing Speeches, Important State Papers, Laws, etc. By W. C. Rives.
10 vols. 4to. Washington: *Globe Office,* 1860–1865.

These volumes cover the whole period of the war.

995. CONKLIN, Rev. C. Slavery Abolished. Its Relation to the Government.
8vo. pp. 20. Oberlin: (Ohio) *V. A. Shankland & Co.,* 1862.

997. CONKLIN, Rev. Luther. The Fast and the Feast. Discourses preached in East Bloomfield, New York, on the occasion of the National Fast, and Annual Thanksgiving.
8vo. pp. 23. Rochester: *A. Strong & Co.,* 1861.

998. CONKLING, Henry, M. D. An Inside View of the Rebellion; and American Citizens Text-Book.
8vo. pp. 23. Cincinnati: *Caleb Clark,* 1864.

999. CONKLING, Hon. Roscoe. The Supreme Court of the United States. Speech delivered in the House of Representatives, April 16, 1860. pp. 8.

1000. —— The State of the Union. Speech in House of Representatives, January 30, 1861.

1001. —— Privileges of the House of Representatives. Battle of Ball's Bluff. Speech delivered in the House of Representatives, January 6, 1862. 8vo. pp. 7.

1002. —— The Special Committee on Government Contracts. What has it done? Speech in the House of Representatives, April 29, 1862. 8vo. pp. 8.

1003. —— The Public Credit. Speech in the House of Representatives, February 4, 1862. pp. 8.

1004. [Connecticut Election, 1863.] Has this Administration done anything to put down the Rebellion? Does our History, since the breaking out of this Southern Conspiracy, encourage a Peace Policy or a War Policy? pp. 4.

1005. The Connecticut War Record. Edited by John M. Morris.
4to. New Haven: *Peck, White & Peck,* 1863.

Commenced in August, 1863, terminated in August, 1865.

1006. CONNECTICUT. Message of Governor Buckingham, to the Legislature of the State, May, 1861.
8vo. pp. 18. HARTFORD : *J. R. Hawley & Co.*, 1861.

1007. —— Annual Report for the Adjutant General for the year 1861.
8vo. pp. 115. HARTFORD : *J. R. Hawley & Co.*, 1861.

1008. —— Catalogue of the 1st, 2d, 3d, 4th and 5th Regiments Connecticut Volunteers, 1861.
8vo. pp. 117. HARTFORD : *Case, Lockwood & Co.*, 1861.

1009. —— Catalogue of the 6th, 7th, 8th, 9th, 10th and 11th Regiments of Infantry, and First Battalion of Cavalry, Connecticut Vols.
8vo. pp. 143. HARTFORD : *Case, Lockwood & Co.*, 1861.

1010. —— Message of Governor Buckingham, October Session, 1861.
8vo. pp. 7.

1011. —— Message of Gov. Buckingham, May, 1862.
pp. 24. NEW HAVEN : *Babcock & Sizer*, 1862.

1012. —— Annual Report of the Adjutant General for the year 1861.
8vo. pp. 115. HARTFORD : *J. R. Hawley & Co.*, 1862.

1013. —— Reports of the Quartermaster General (Col. John M. Hathaway, Col. J. B. Bunce and Col. W. A. Aiken) to the General Assembly, May Session, 1862.
8vo. pp. 59. HARTFORD : *J. R. Hawley & Co.*, 1862.

1014. —— Message of Governor Buckingham, accompanying the Report of Col. H. H. Osgood, giving the number of drafted men in the State, December 10, 1862.
8vo. pp. 45. NEW HAVEN : *Babcock & Sizer*, 1862.

1015. —— Catalogue of the twelfth and thirteenth Regiments Connecticut Volunteers, 1862.
8vo. pp. 45. HARTFORD : *Case, Lockwood & Co.*, 1862.

1016. —— Catalogue of Connecticut Volunteer Regiments, from the 14th to the 28th, inclusive, and Second Light Battery. Connecticut Volunteers for nine months. By Joseph D. Williams, Adjutant General.
8vo. pp. 327. HARTFORD : *Case, Lockwood & Co.*, 1862.

1017. —— Message of Governor Buckingham, May Sess., 1863. p. 20.

1018. —— Annual Report of the Adjutant General of Connecticut, for the year ending March 31, 1863.
8vo. pp. 333. HARTFORD : *J. M. Scofield & Co.*, 1863.

13

1019. CONNECTICUT. Report of the Quartermaster General, May, 1863. pp. 56.

1020. —— Report of Drs. Cogswell and White, special Agents to visit Connecticut sick and wounded Soldiers in the United States General Hospitals. pp. 10.

1021. —— Message of Governor Buckingham, Special Session, November, 1863. pp. 11.

1022. —— Annual Report of the Adjutant General of the State of Connecticut, for the year ending March 31, 1864.
8vo. pp. 356. HARTFORD : *J. M. Scofield & Co.*, 1864.

1023. —— Report of the Quartermaster General, May, 1864.
8vo. pp. 90. HARTFORD : *J. M. Scofield & Co.*, 1864.

1024. —— Report of the Paymaster General, to Governor, for the year ending March 31, 1864. pp. 20.

1025. —— Report of Drs. W. H. Coggeswell and W. M. White, State Agents for care of Soldiers. 8vo. pp. 4.

1026. —— Catalogue of Connecticut Volunteer Organizations, with additional enlistments and casualties, to July 1, 1864. Compiled from Records in the Adjutant General's Office and published by order of the Legislature. Horace J. Morse, Adjt. General.
8vo. pp. 847. HARTFORD : *Case, Lockwood & Co.*, 1864.

1027. —— Message of Governor Buckingham, May, 1865. 8vo. p. 19.

1028. —— Report of the Adjutant General for the year ending March 31, 1865.
8vo. pp. 494. NEW HAVEN : *Harrison, Hotchkiss & Co.*, 1865.

1029. —— Report of the Quartermaster General, May Session, 1865.
8vo. pp. 65. NEW HAVEN : *Harrison, Hotchkiss & Co.*, 1865.

1030. THE CONSCRIPTION. Also Speeches of the Hon. W. D. Kelley, of Pennsylvania, in House of Representatives, on the Conscription ; the way to obtain Peace ; and on arming the Negroes. With a Letter from Secretary Chase.
8vo. pp. 39. PHILADELPHIA : *For gratuitous distribution*, 1863.

1031. " THE CONSCRIPTION ACT." Will Laboring Men Vote for Seymour, and invite Civil War, Anarchy and Ruin ? pp. 4.

1032. CONSPIRACY TRIAL, for the Murder of the President and the attempt to overthrow the Government by the Assassination of its

Principal Officers. Edited, with an Introduction, by Ben. Perley Poore.

2 vols. 12mo.   BOSTON : *J. E. Tilden & Co.*, 1864.

1033. CONSPIRATORS. Trial and Execution of the Assassins and Conspirators at Washington, D. C., May and June, 1865, for the Murder of President Lincoln.

8vo. pp.   PHILADELPHIA : *T. B. Peterson & Bros.*, 1865.
See also *John A. Bingham* for argument in the case.

1034. —— Les Procès des Conspirateurs de Washington.

4to.   NEW YORK : *H. de Mareil*, 1865.

1035. THE CONSTITUTION and the Union. Speeches delivered at the American Union Breakfast, given in Paris, May 29, 1861, at the Grand Hotel du Louvre.

8vo. pp. 24.   PARIS : *E. Brière*, 1861.

1036. CONSTITUTION. Amendments of the Constitution submitted to the consideration of the American People. 8vo. pp. 89. *Loyal Publication Society, No.* 83.

1037. CONSTITUTION des Etats Unis, suivie de Conseils de Washington au Peuple Americaines.

8vo. pp. 32.   PARIS : *Dentu*, 1862.

1038. THE CONSTITUTION of the United States ; also a Document entitled "The Constitution of the Confederate States." Arranged in parallel columns, with the differences indicated, for convenient reference and comparison.

8vo. pp. 24.   CINCINNATI : *E. Watkin*, 1862.

1039. THE CONTINENTAL MONTHLY. The Situation. January, 1862.
Among the Pines. J. R. Gilmore. January, 1862.
The Lesson of War. January, 1862.
Song of Freedom. January, 1862.
What to do with the Darkies. A new and original plan to save the Union on Southern Principles. January, 1862.
The Slave Trade in New York. January, 1862.

1040. —— Our War and our Want. February, 1862.
Among the Pines. J. R. Gilmore. February, 1862.
Mr. Seward's Published Diplomacy. February, 1862.
Our Danger and its Cause. February, 1862.

1041. —— Southern Aids to the North. March, 1862.

CONTINENTAL MONTHLY. Is Cotton our King? March, 1862.
Gen. Patterson's Campaign in Virginia. March, 1862.
The Lesson of the Hour. (Poetry.) March, 1862.
Among the Pines. J. R. Gilmore. March, 1862.
Active Service; or Campaigning in Western Virginia. Mar., '62.
A Cabinet Session. March, 1862.

1042. CONTINENTAL MONTHLY. The War between Freedom and
Slavery in Missouri. April, 1862.
Beaufort; Past, Present and Future. April, 1862.
General Lyon. April, 1862.
Among the Pines. J. R. Gilmore. April, 1862.
Southern Aids to the North. April, 1862.

1043. —— What shall we do with it? May, 1862.
State Rights. May, 1862.
The Knights of the Golden Circle. May, 1862.
Columbia's Safety. May, 1862.

1044. —— The Constitution and Slavery. Rev. C. E. Lord. June, '62.
Desperation and Colonization. Charles G. Leland. June, 1862.
Monroe to Farragut. Charles G. Leland. June, 1862.
Among the Pines. J. R. Gilmore. June, 1862.

1045. —— What shall be the end? July, 1862.
Bone Ornaments. (Poetry.) July, 1862.
For the Hour of Triumph. (Poetry.) July, 1862.
Among the Pines. J. R. Gilmore. July, 1862.
Newbern as it was and is. July, 1862.
Our Brave Times. July, 1862.
The Crisis and the Parties. July, 1862.
Slavery and Nobility vs. Democracy. July, 1862.

1046. —— Among the Pines. J. R. Gilmore. August, 1862.
Southern Rights. August, 1862.
The Last Ditch. August, 1862.
Rewarding the Army. August, 1862.
Corn is King. August, 1862.

1047. —— The Soldier and the Civilian. September, 1862.
Anthony Trollope on America. September, 1862.
Up and Act. September, 1862.
The Negro in the Revolution. September, 1862.
National Unity. September, 1862.

1048. CONTINENTAL MONTHLY. The Constitution as it is—The Union
   as it was! C. S. Henry. October, 1862.
  A Military Nation. Charles G. Leland. October, 1862.
  Southern Hate of the North. Horace Greeley. October, 1862.
  The Union. Robert J. Walker. October, 1862.
  Our Wounded. C. K. Tuckerman. October, 1862.
  A Southern Review. Charles G. Leland. October, 1862.
1049. —— The Causes of the Rebellion. F. P. Stanton. Nov., 1862.
  The Union. Robert J. Walker. November, 1862.
  The Proclamation. Charles G. Leland. November, 1862.
  Aurora. Horace Greeley. November, 1862.
1050. —— The Union. Robert J. Walker. December, 1862.
  Something we have to think of and to do. C. S. Henry.
   December, 1862.
  An Englishman in South Carolina, December, 1860–July, 1862.
   December, 1862.
  The Causes of the Rebellion. F. P. Stanton. December, 1862.
  On Guard. John G. Nicolay. December, 1862.
  The Obstacles to Peace. Horace Greeley. December, 1862.
  Thank God for all. (Poetry.) Charles G. Leland. Dec., 1862.
  The Freed Men of the South. F. P. Stanton. December, '62.
1051. —— Consequences of the Rebellion. F. P. Stanton. Jan., '63.
  The Union, No. 4. New York and Virginia compared. R. J.
   Walker. January, 1863.
  American Destiny. John Stahl Patterson. January, 1863.
  An Englishman in South Carolina. January, 1863.
1052. —— Our National Finances. Robert J. Walker. Feb, 1863.
  A Trip to Antietam. Charles W. Loring. February, 1863.
  American Destiny. John Stahl Patterson. February, 1863.
  Nullification and Secession. Robert J. Walker. February, '63.
1053. —— Dead. (Poetry.) February, 1863.
  The Consequences of the Rebellion. February, 1863.
  The Captain of 1863, to his Men. Mary E. Nealey. Feb., '63.
  The Lady and her Slave. February, 1863.
1054. —— European Opinion. F. P. Stanton. March, 1863.
  Montgomery in Secession Time. March, 1863.
  The Union. Robert J. Walker. March, 1863.
  The Soldier's Burial. March, 1863.

1055. CONTINENTAL MONTHLY. How the War affects Americans. F.
　　　　P. Stanton. Apr.,'63.
　　　The Return. (Poetry.) Edward S. Rand, Jr. April, 1863.
　　　The Union. Robert J. Walker. April, 1863.
　　　Down in Tennessee.
　　　Flag of our Sires. (Poetry.) Robert J. Walker. April, 1863.
　　　Our Present Position ; its Dangers and its Duties. April, 1863.
1056. —— In Memoriam. Richard Wolcott. May, 1863.
　　　A Winter in Camp. E. G. Hammond. May, 1863.
　　　National Ode, suggested by the President's Proclamation of Jan-
　　　　　uary 1, 1863. May, 1863.
　　　The Surrender of Forts Jackson and St. Phillip, on the Missis-
　　　　　sippi. F. H. Gerdes. May, 1863.
　　　The Value of the Union. W. H. Muller. May, 1863.
　　　The Destiny of the African Race in the United States. Rev. J.
　　　　　M. Sturtevant. May, 1863.
　　　The Union. Robert J. Walker. May, 1863.
　　　The Causes and Results of the War. Lieut. Egbert Phelps.
1057. —— The Value of the Union. W. H. Muller. June, 1863.
　　　The Navy of the United State. June, 1863.
　　　Virginia. (Poetry.) June, 1863.
　　　The Confederation and the Nation. Edward Carey. June, '63.
　　　How Mr. Lincoln became an Abolitionist. S. B. Gookins.
　　　　　June, 1863.
1058. —— Emancipation in Jamaica. Rev. C. C. Starbuck. July, '62.
　　　Ladies' Loyal League. Mrs. O. S. Baker. July, 1863.
　　　The Third Year of the War. F. P. Stanton. July, 1863.
1059. —— Our Future. Lieut. Egbert Phelps. August, 1863.
　　　Jefferson Davis and Repudiation. Robt. J. Walker. Aug., '63.
　　　Dying in the Hospital. Mary E. Nealey. August, 1863.
1060. —— Southern Hate of New England. Miss Virginia Sher-
　　　　　wood. September, 1863.
　　　Reconnoisance near Fort Morgan, and Expedition in Lake Pon-
　　　　　chartrain and Pearl River, by the Mortar Flotilla of
　　　　　Capt. D. D. Porter, U. S. N. F. H. Gerdes. Sept., '63.
　　　The Great Riot. Edward R. Freeland. September, 1863.
　　　Jefferson Davis and Repudiation. Robert J. Walker. Sept., '63.

1061. CONTINENTAL MONTHLY. Jefferson Davis ;—Repudiation, Recognition, and Slavery. Hon. Robt. J. Walker. Oct., 1863.
Thirty Days with the New York 71st Regiment. October, '63.
Currency and the National Finances. J. Smith Homans. October, 1863.
The Restoration of the Union. Hon. F. P. Stanton. Oct., '63.
American Finances and Resources. Hon. Robert J. Walker. October, 1863.

1062. —— The Defence and Evacuation of Winchester. F. P. Stanton. November, 1863.
The Two Southern Mothers. (Poetry.) Isabella McFarland. November, 1863.
Letters to Prof. S. F. B. Morse. Rev. D. Henry. Nov., 1863.
Patriotism and Provincialism. H. Clay Preuss. November, '63.

1063. —— The Nation. H. Miller Thompson. December, 1863.
The Sleeping Soldier. E. N. Pomeroy. December, 1863.
The Great American Crisis. S. P. Andrews. December, '63.
Reconstruction. Henry E. Russell. December, 1863.
Virginia. H. T. Tuckerman. December, 1863.

1064. —— Retrospective. Rev. D. Henry. January, 1864.
The Great Struggle. January, 1864.
American Finances and Resources. Robert J. Walker. Jan.,'64.
Union not to be maintained by Force. F. P. Stanton. Jan.,'64.
The Great American Crisis. S. P. Andrews. January, 1864.
The Conscription Act of March 3. L. M. Haverstick. Jan., '64.

1065. —— The Treasury Report of Mr. Secretary Chase. F. P. Stanton. February, 1864.
Thomas Jefferson, as seen by the Light of 1863. J. Sheldon. February, 1863.
North and South. Charles W. Butler. February, 1864.

1066. —— American Finances and Resources, No. 3. Robert J. Walker. March, 1864.
The issues of the War. John Stahl Patterson. March, 1864.
The Great American Crisis, No. 3. Stephen P. Andrews. March, 1864.
American Finances and Resources, No. 4. Robert J. Walker. March, 1864.

1067. CONTINENTAL MONTHLY. English and American Taxation. Egbert Hurd. April, 1864.

Our Government and the Blacks. W. H. Kimball. April, '64.

Jefferson Davis and Repudiation of Arkansas Bonds. Hon. R. G. Walker. April, 1864.

1068. —— American Finances and Resources. Hon. Robert J. Walker. May, 1864.

Our Domestic Relations; or How to treat the Rebel States. Charles Russell. May, 1864.

The War a Contest for Ideas. Henry Everett Russell. May, '64.

1069. —— An Army; its Organization and Movements. Lieut. Col. C. W. Tolles. June, 1864.

1070. —— An Army, its Organization and Movements, 2d Paper. Lieut. Col. C. W. Tolles. July, 1864.

American Slavery and Finances. Robert J. Walker. July, '63.

Life on a Blockader. July, 1864.

Lookout Mountain. (Poetry.) Alfred B. Street. July, 1864.

James Fenimore Cooper on Secession and State Rights. July, 1864.

Recognition. Virginia Vaughan. July, 1864.

American Civilization. Lieut. Egbert Phelps. July, 1864.

1071. —— American Civilization; Second Paper. Lieut. Egbert Phelps. August, 1864.

Our Martyrs. (Poetry.) Kate Putnam. August, 1864.

Negro Troops. H. Everett Russell. August, 1864.

Battle of the Wilderness. E. A. Warriner. August, 1864.

An Army; its Organization and Movements. Third Paper. Lieutenant Col. C. W. Tolles. August, 1864.

1072. —— Our Domestic Affairs. George Wurts. September, 1864.

The Constitutional Amendment. Henry E. Russell. Sept., '64.

Averill's Raid. (Poetry.) Alfred B. Street. September, 1864.

An Army; its Organization and Movements, 4th Paper. Lieut. Colonel C. W. Tolles. September, 1864.

1073. —— Some Uses of a Civil war. Hugh Miller Thompson. October, 1864.

The North Carolina Conscript. Isabella McFarland. Oct., '64.

Coming up at Shiloh. October, 1864.

Our Great America. January Leader.

1074. CONTINENTAL MONTHLY. The Progress of Liberty in the United States. Rev. A. D. Mayo. November, 1864.
Fly-Leaves from the Life of a Soldier. November, 1864.
The Two Platforms. Henry E. Russell. November, 1864.

1075. —— An Army; its Organization and Movements, 5th Paper. Lieut. Colonel Tolles. December, 1864.

1076. —— Letter of the Hon. R. J. Walker, in favor of the Re-election of Abraham Lincoln. December, 1864.

1077. CONTRABAND'S RELIEF COMMISSION, of Cincinnati, Ohio, Report by the Committee of, proposing a Plan for the occupation and government of vacated territory in the Seceded States.
8vo. pp. 16.   CINCINNATI: *Gazette Office*, 1863.

1078. CONVENTION. Massachusetts National Democratic Convention. Speeches of Gen. Cushing, Gen. Whitney, B. F. Hallett, J. H. Wright, Dr. George B. Loring and others. Sept. 12, 1860.
8vo. pp. 72.   BOSTON: *Beals, Greene & Co.*, 1860.

1079. —— Presidential Election, 1864. Proceedings of the National Union Convention, held in Baltimore, June 7 and 8, 1864.
8vo. pp. 94.   NEW YORK: *Baker, Godwin & Co.*, 1864.

1080. —— (Conference,) held at Washington, February, 1861. Official Journal of. By Crafts J. Wright, Secretary.
8vo. pp. 93.   WASHINGTON: *McGill & Witherow*, 1861.

1081. CONWAY, MONCURE D., of Virginia. The Golden hour.
12mo. pp. 160.   BOSTON: *Ticknor & Fields*, 1862.

1081.* CONWAY, M. D. The American War as an English Question. *Christian Examiner, May*, 1864.

1082. —— The Rejected Stone; or Insurrection and Resurrection in America. By a Native of Virginia.
12mo. pp. 132.   BOSTON: *Walker, Wise & Co.*, 1861.

1083. —— Personal Recollections of President Lincoln. (London.) *Fortnightly Review for May* 15, 1865.

1084. —— North and South, and Slavery. A Lecture in the Free Trade Hall, Manchester, (England,) June 21, 1863. 12mo. p. 11.

1085. CONWAY, MARTIN F. The War. A Slave Union or a Free? Speech delivered in the House of Representatives, Dec. 12, '61.
12mo.   NEW YORK: *E. D. Barker*, 1862.

1086. —— Shall the War be for Union and Freedom, or Union and Slavery? Speech in House of Rep., Dec., 12, 1861. 8vo. p. 15.

14

1087. CONWAY, M. F. The War a Reactionary Agent. A Speech delivered in the House of Representatives, January 27, 1863 8vo. pp. 15.

1088. CONWAY, Thomas W. The Freedmen of Louisiana. Final Report of the Bureau of Free Labor, Department of the Gulf, to Major General Canby.

8vo. pp. 37.   New Orleans : *Times Office*, 1865.

1089. CONYNGHAM, Capt. D. P. Sherman's March through the South ; with Sketches and Incidents of the Campaign.

12mo. pp. 431.   New York : *Sheldon & Co.*, 1865.

1090. COOK, Rev. J. T. Sermon on the Origin of the War, delivered at Genesee, Illinois, July 13, 1862.

8vo. pp. 16.   Genesee : (Ill.) 1862.

1091. —— Fast Day Discourse, preached at the M. E. Church, Syca- more, June 1, 1865, on God's government over men and nations, and the Duty of Recognizing that government. *Syracuse Repub- lican, June* 14, 1865.

1092. COOK, Joel. The Siege of Richmond. A Narrative of the Military Operations of Major General George B. McClellan, dur- ing the months of May and June, 1862.

12mo. pp. 358.   Philadelphia : *George W. Childs*, 1862.

1093. COOKE, Rev. C., DD. A Sermon on the Life and Death of Abraham Lincoln, delivered at Smyrna, Delaware, June 1, 1865.

12mo. pp. 24.   Philadelphia : *John Richards*, 1865.

1094. COOKE, & Co., Jay. How to organize a National Bank, under Secretary Chase's Bill.

8vo. pp. 40.   Philadelphia : *Ringwalt & Brown*, 1863.

1095. COOMBS, J. J. Speech at the Union League Reading Room, Washington, D. C., September 1, 1863. 8vo. p. 16.

1096. COOMBE, Rev. P. A Sermon on the Divine Origin of Civil Government, and the Sinfulness of Rebellion. Delivered in Philadelphia, June 30, 1861.

8vo. pp. 24.   Philadelphia : *Barnard & Jones*, 1861.

1097. COOPER, Rev. David M. (Grand Haven, Mich.) Obituary Discourse on occasion of the Death of Noah Henry Ferry, Major of the Fifth Michigan Cavalry, killed at Gettysburg, July 3, '63.

8vo. pp. 46. Portrait.   New York : *John F. Trow*, 1863.

1098. COOPER, Rev. JACOB, Prof. of Greek, Centre College, Kentucky. The Loyalty demanded by the present Crisis. *Danville Review, March,* 1864.

1099. —— The same. Philadelphia. *Loyal League,* 1864.

1100. —— Perjury exemplified in Secession. *Danville Rev., June,*'64.

1101. —— Slavery in the Church Courts. *Danville Review, Dec.,* '64.

1102. COOPER, Rev. JAMES. The Death of President Lincoln. A Memorial Discourse delivered in West Philadelphia, Apr. 16,'65. 8vo. pp. 24.   PHILADELPHIA : *J. B. Rodgers,* 1865.

1103. COOPER, JAMES FENIMORE, on Secession and State Rights. *Continental Monthly for July,* 1864.

1104. COOPER, PETER. Letter to Abraham Lincoln, President of the United States, on Slave Emancipation, January, 1862. 8vo. pp. 8.   *Loyal Publication Society, No. 23,* 1863.

1105. —— The Death of Slavery. Letter from Peter Cooper to his Excellency, Horatio Seymour, Governor of the State of N. York. 8vo. pp. 12.   *Loyal Publication Society, No. 28,* 1863.

1106. COOPER'S SHOP Volunteer Refreshment Saloon, First Annual Report of.   Philadelphia, May 26, 1862. 8vo. pp. 8.   PHILADELPHIA : *Collins,* 1862.

1107. —— Second Annual Report of, Philadelphia, May 26, 1863. p. 8.

1108. —— Third Annual Report, May, 1864. pp. 8.

1109. —— Fourth Annual Report, Philadelphia, May 26, 1865. 8vo. pp. 16.   PHILADELPHIA : *Collins,* 1865.

1110. COPPEE, HENRY. Grant, and his Campaigns. A Military Biography. 8vo. pp. 500. Portraits. NEW YORK : *C. B. Richardson,* '66.

1111. —— Sherman and his Campaigns. A Military Biography. 8vo. pp. 512. Portraits. N. YORK : *C. B. Richardson,* 1866.

1112. COPPERHEAD. Ye Sneak ycleped Copperhead. A Satirical Poem. 18mo. pp.   PHILADELPHIA : *A. Winch,* 1863.

1113. COPPERHEADS, the Votes of, in the Congress of the U. S.   p. 8.

1114. COPPERHEAD MINSTREL. A choice collection of Democratic Poems and Songs, for the use of Political Clubs and the Social Circles. 12mo. pp. 60.   NEW YORK : *Feeck & Bancker,* 1863.

1115. COPPERHEAD CONSPIRACY in the North West. An Exposé of the Treasonable Order of the "Sons of Liberty," Vallandigham, Supreme Commander. For the Cong. Committee, 1864. pp. 8.

1116. —— The same. pp. 8. New York : *J. A. Gray & Son*, 1864.

1117. THE COPPERHEAD CATECHISM. For the instruction of such Politicians as are of tender years. Carefully compiled by divers learned and designing men. Authorized, and with admonitions, by Fernando, the Gothamite, High Priest of the Order of Copperheads.
12mo. pp. 30. NEW YORK : *Sinclair Toucey*, 1864.

1118. COPPERHEADS, Ye Book of.
Oblong 8vo. wood cuts. PHILADELPHIA : *Fred. Leopoldt*, 1863.

1119. CORCORAN, General. His Captivity.
8vo. pp. 100. PHILADELPHIA : *Barclay & Co.*, 1862.

1120. CORDOVA, R. J. de. A Lecture on War, Foreign and Civil, and the Blessings of Union and Peace. Delivered in New York, December 8, 1860.
8vo. pp. 7. NEW YORK : *M. Ellinger*, 1860.

1121. CORNELL, Rev. WILLIAM. "Our Thanksgivings." A Sermon preached at Freehold, N. J., August 6, 1863.
8vo. pp. 15. FREEHOLD : *James S. Yard*, 1863.

1122. CORNING, JAMES LEONARD, of Milwaukie. Religion and Politics. A Discourse delivered on Thanksgiving Day, November 29, 1860.
8vo. pp. 23. MILWAUKIE : *Strickland & Co.*, 1860.

1123. CORNING, Rev. W. H. Our Epoch ; its Significance and History. A Discourse preached at Whitehall, New York, November 29, 1860.
8vo. pp. 17. WHITEHALL : *Chronicle Office*, 1860.

1124. CORNISH, S. E., and T. S. Wright. The Colonization Scheme considered, in its Rejection by the Colored People, in its Tendency to uphold caste, in its unfitness for Christianizing and civilizing the Aborigines of Africa, etc.
8vo. pp. 26. NEWARK : *Aaron Guest*, 1840.

1125. CORRESPONDENCE relating to the purchase and fitting out of the Steamship "United States," and the building and fitting out of the Steamship of the Line " General Admiral."
8vo. pp. 8. NEW YORK : *Hall & Clayton*, 1863.

1126. CORRESPONDENCE on the subjects of Mediation, Arbitration, or other Measures looking to the Termination of the existing Civil War; communicated by the President of the United States, February 12, 1863. *37th Congress, 3d Session, Ex. Doc., No.* 38.

1127. COSSHAM, HANDEL. America; Past, Present and Future. A Lecture.
12mo. pp. 65–90. LONDON; *Fred. Fitman,* 1863.

1128. —— The American War. Facts and Fallacies. A Lecture delivered in Bristol, (England,) February 12, 1864.
12mo. pp. 98–127. LONDON: *Fred. Pitman,* 1864.

1129. COSTI, AN. MICHELO, Publicist of Venice, Italy. Memoir on the Trent Affair.
8vo. pp. 23. WASHINGTON: (D. C.) *McGill & Witherow,* 1865.

1130. COTTON. Cheap Cotton and Free Labor. By a Cotton Manufacturer.
8vo. pp. 52. BOSTON: *A. Williams & Co.,* 1861.

1131. —— The Same. Second edition, Boston: *A. Williams & Co.,* 1861. *pp.* 54.

1132. COTTON. The Great Cotton Question: Where are the Spoils of the Slave? Addressed to the Upper and Middle Classes of Great Britain. By A.
8vo. pp. 21. CAMBRIDGE: (Eng.) *Macmillan & Co.,* 1861.

1133. COTTON. Report of the Special Committee of the Chamber of Commerce of the State of New York, on the Confiscation of Cotton in the Southern States by the Government.
8vo. pp. 12. NEW YORK: *J. W. Amerman,* 1865.

1134. COTTON IS KING; or the Culture of Cotton and its relation to Agriculture, Manufactures and Commerce; to the Free Colored People, and to those who hold that Slavery is sinful. By an American.
12mo. pp. 210. CINCINNATI: *Moore, Wilstach & Co.,* 1855.

1135. COTTON MANUFACTURE. Statistics from the Seventh Annual Report of the Boston Board of Trade. pp. 16. Boston; *T. R. Marvin & Son,* 1861.

1136. THE COWARDS' CONVENTION. (The Chicago Convention,—Two Governments and the Results. Chaos come again, etc.) Letters to the Editor of the New York Times.
8vo. pp. 16. *Loyal Publication Society, No.* 63, 1864.

1137. CO.VAN, EDGAR. The Forfeiture and Confiscation of Rebel Property in the Confederate States. Speech in Senate, March 4, 1862. 8vo. pp. 16.

1138. COWLES, Rev. SYLVESTER. Conflict of Races. A Sermon preached in Randolph, New York, Oct., 12, 1862. 8vo. pp. 16.

1139. COX, Hon. S. S. Conciliation and Nationality. Speech delivered in the House of Representatives, Jan. 14, 1861. pp. 16.

1140. —— Our English Relations. Speech in House of Representatives, December 17, 1861. pp. 8.

1141. —— Speech in vindication of Gen. McClellan from the attack of Congressional War Critics, in the House of Representatives of the United States, January 31, 1862. pp. 16.

1142. —— Puritanism in Politics. Speech before the Democratic Union Association, January 13, 1863.
8vo. pp. 14.   NEW YORK: *Van Evrie, Horton & Co.*, 1863.

1143. —— Shall the Constitution be repealed? Confiscation or Conciliation. Speech on the Joint Resolution Explanatory of the Confiscation Act. House of Reps., January 14, 1864. pp. 16.

1144. —— The Nation's Hope in the Democracy. Historic Lessons for Civil War. Speech on the Bill to Guarantee to certain States, whose Government is usurped or overthrown, a Republican form of Government. House of Rep., May, 1864. 8vo. p. 16.

1145. —— Speeches on the Tariff and other Economical Questions, delivered in Congress. Extracted from his forthcoming volume of " Eight Years in Congress." 8vo. pp. 31–61.

1146. —— Eight Years in Congress, from 1857 to 1865. Memoir and Speeches.
8vo. pp. 442.   NEW YORK: *D. Appleton & Co.*, 1869.
This volume is intended to present an exposition of the motives and principles which actuated a constitutional opposition to the Government during the progress of the Rebellion. It comprises Speeches connected with finance, those which accuse the North of sedition and sectionalism, which discuss the question of fugitives from foreign lands and the right of asylum, speeches on foreign affairs, on Secession and the war, on the amendment of the Constitution abolishing Slavery, and on the proposition to admit the Cabinet into Congress.

1147. COXE, Rev. A. CLEVELAND, DD. Truth and our Times. The Baccalaureate Sermon preached in Calvary Church, June 30, '63.
8vo. pp. 17.   NEW YORK; *C. Alvord*, 1863.

1148. COXE, Rev. A. C., DD.   Unjust Reproaches in Public Calamity, viewed as part of the Divine Discipline.   A Sermon preached in Calvary Church, November 26, 1863.
8vo. pp. 21.   NEW YORK: *C. A. Alvord*, 1863.

1149. COZZENS, F. S.   Pope's Proclamation.   Dated, Washington, July 15, 1862.   pp. 4.

1150. —— Col. Peter A. Porter.   A Memorial delivered before The Century Club in December, 1864.
8vo. pp. 54.   NEW YORK: *D. Van Nostrand*, 1865.

1151. CRAFTS, W. A.   The Southern Rebellion ; being a History of the United States, from the commencement of President Buchanan's Administration.
4to. vol. 1, pp. viii and 648.   BOSTON: *S. Walker*, 1864.

1152. CRAIG, IRA.   The Essence of Slavery.
12mo. pp. 8.   LONDON: *Ladies' Emancipation Society*, 1863.

1153. CRAIG, Rev. W. B.   Our Sins, Individual and National.   A Sermon preached in New Bloomfield, Penn., September 7, 1862.
8vo. pp. 29.   PHILADELPHIA: *C. Sherman & Son*, 1862.

1154. CRAIG, WHEELOCK.   Our Duties at this Crisis.   A Sermon preached in the Trinitarian Church, New Bedford, Apr. 21, 1861
8vo. pp. 8.   NEW BEDFORD ; *Mercury Press*, 1861.

1155. CRAIK, Rev. JAMES.   The Union.   National and State Sovereignty allied essential to American Liberty.   A discourse delivered in Frankfort, Kentucky, December 19, 1859.
8vo. pp. 36.   LOUISVILLE: *Morton & Griswold*, 1860.

1156. CRANE, Rev. C. B.   Sermon on the Occasion of the Death of President Lincoln.   Preached in Hartford, Conn., April 16, '65.
8vo. pp. 29.   HARTFORD: *Case, Lockwood & Co.*, 1865.

1157. CRAVENS, J. A., of Indiana.   Speech on the President's Message.   Delivered in the House of Reps., Dec. 8, 1862. 8vo. pp. 8.

1158. CRESWELL, JOHN A.   Speech on the proposed amendment to the Constitution of the United States, in the House of Representatives of the United States, January 5, 1865.   pp. 16.

1159. CRESWELL UNMASKED.   8vo. p. 7.   [Maryland, 1864.]

1160. THE CRISIS.   8vo. pp. 95.   New York: *D. Appleton & Co.*, '63.

1161. THE CRISIS.   8vo. pp. 48.   New York: *W. B. Smith & Co.*, '60.

1162 THE CRISIS.   (By T. Packer Scott.) Dec., 1860.   8v. pp. 7.

1163. CRITTENDEN, J. J.　Speech on his Resolutions.　Delivered in the Senate of the United States, January 7, 1861.　8vo. pp. 8.

1164. —— Speech on the Confiscation of Rebel Property.　House of Representatives, April 23, 1862.　8vo. pp. 8.

1165. —— Speech on the Abolition of Slavery in the District of Columbia, April 11, 1862.　8vo. pp. 16.

1166. THE CRITTENDEN and other Resolutions.　A Review of.　Addressed to the South and to every adherent of the Constitution.　8vo. pp. 20.　　　　　　NEW YORK: *Dodge & Grattan*, 1861.

1167. CROCKER, SAMUEL L.　Eulogy upon the Character and Services of Abraham Lincoln, late President of the U. S., June 1, '65.　8vo. pp. 28.　　　　　　BOSTON : *John Wilson & Son*, 1865.

1168. CROMELIEN. R.　On the Great American Rebellion.　Tri-Party War of 1861 and 1862.　8vo. pp. 8.

1168.* CROMWELL, HENRY S., M. D.　Lincoln ; Died April 15, A. D. 1865.　(A Poem.)　Broadside.　New London, Conn.

1169. CROMWELL, SIDNEY.　Political Opinion in 1776 and 1863.　A Letter to a Victim of Arbitrary Arrests and "American Bastiles."　8vo. pp. 19.　　　　　NEW YORK: *Anson D. F. Randolph*, 1863.

1170. CROSBY, ALPHEUS.　The Present Position of the Seceded States, and the Rights and Duties of the General Government in respect to them.　An Address to the Phi Beta Kappa Society, Dartmouth College, July 19, 1865.　8vo. pp. 16.　　　　　　BOSTON: *G. C. Rand & Avery*, 1865.

1171. CROSBY, EDWARD N.　The Letter of a Republican to Prof. S. F. B. Morse, February 25, 1863, and Prof. Morse's Reply, March 2, 1863.　8vo. pp. 12.

1172. CROSBY.　A Memorial of Lieut. Franklin Butler Crosby, of the Fourth Regiment United States Artillery, who was killed at Chancellorsville, Va.　May 3, 1863.　32mo. pp. 69.　　　　　　NEW YORK: *A. D. F. Randolph*, 1864.

1173. CROSBY, JOHN E.　Life of Abraham Lincoln.　12mo. pp. 276.　　　　　PHILADELPHIA : *John E. Potter*, 1865.

1174. CROSBY, EDWARD N.　Our Country versus Party Spirit ; being a Rejoinder to the Reply of Professor Morse.　8vo. pp. 14.　　　　　POUGHKEEPSIE : *Platt & Schram*, 1863.

1175. CROSS, ANDREW B.　The War and the Christian Commission.　pp. 56.

1176. CROSS, A. B. Battle of Gettysburg and the Christian Commission 8vo. pp. 32. BALTIMORE: *Sherwood & Co.*

1177. CROUNSE, J. L. Our Army Correspondent. *Harpers' Magazine, October,* 1863.

1178. CROWELL, JOSEPH T. Speech against the Anti-War Resolutions, in the Senate of New Jersey, January 22, 1863. pp. 9.

1179. CROZIER, Rev. H. P. Sermon upon the Death of Solomon W. Price, Continental Guard at Port Royal, S. C., preached at Huntington, New York, Dec. 22, 1861. *The Long-Islander for January* 3, 1862.

1180. —— Sermon at the Funeral of Sergeant Arnold Wood, who was killed at Charles City, Va., December 13, 1863. Preached at Huntington. *Long-Islander, January* 15, 1864.

1181. —— The Nation's Loss. A Discourse on the Life, Services and Death of Abraham Lincoln. Delivered at Huntington, L. I., April 9, 1865.
8vo. pp. 16. NEW YORK: *John A. Gray & Green,* 1865.

1182. CRUISE of the United States Ship Hartford, 1862–63; being a Narrative of all the Operations since going into commission, in 1862, until her return to New York in 1863. From the private Journal of William C. Holton, by B. S. Osbon.
12mo. pp. 81. NEW YORK: *L. W. Paine,* 1863.

1183. CRUMMELL, Rev. ALEX. The Relations and Duties of Free Colored Men in America to Africa. A Letter to Charles B. Dunbar, M. D., of New York.
8vo. pp. 54. HARTFORD: *Case, Lockwood & Co.,* 1861.

1184. CUDWORTH, Rev. WARREN H. Eulogy on the Life, Character and Public Services of the late President Abraham Lincoln, delivered at East Boston, May 8, 1865; with a Record of the other Proceedings.
8vo. pp. 27. BOSTON: *Wright & Potter,* 1865.

1185. —— History of the First Massachusetts Regiment. 8vo. Boston : *George Fuller & Co.,* 1866.

1186. CUMBERLAND. Annals of the Army of the Cumberland; comprising Biographies, Descriptions of Departments, Accounts of Expeditions, Skirmishes and Battles; also its Police Record of Spies, Smugglers, etc. By an Officer.
8vo. pp. 671. PHILADELPHIA: *J. B. Lippincott & Co.,* 1863.

15

1187. CUMBERLAND, Army of., History of the Old Second Division, Commanders McCook, Till and Johnson.

8vo.   CHICAGO : *Church & Goodman,* 1864.

1188. CUMMINGS, ALEXANDER. Letter in Reply to the Report of the Van Wyck Committee. Presented to Congress March 6, 1862. 8vo. pp. 8.

1189. CURTIN, Gov. A Black Record. Gov. Curtin's Portrait drawn by a Black Republican Editor. Who clothed our Soldiers in shoddy? Who plundered our Brave Volunteers? Voters, read! pp. 4. Philadelphia: *Age Office.*

1190. CURTIS, B. R. Executive Power.

8vo. pp. 31.   BOSTON: *Little, Brown & Co.,* 1862.

1191. The same. pp. 29, Boston: *Little, Brown & Co.,* 1862.

1192. The same. pp. 15. New York: [*Office of the World.*]

1193. CURTIS, GEORGE TICKNOR. An Argument against the Constitutional validity of the Legal Tender Clause, contained in the Act of Congress of February 25, 1862, authorizing the issue of Treasury Notes. Delivered in the Supreme Court of New York, November 18, 1862.

8vo. pp. 24.   NEW YORK: *W. C. Bryant & Co.,* 1862.

1194. —— An Oration delivered on the 4th of July, 1862, before the Municipal Authorities of Boston.

8vo. pp. 46.   BOSTON: *J. E. Farwell & Co.,* 1862.

1195. —— The true condition of American Loyalty. A Speech delivered before the Democratic Union Association, March 28, 1863. 8vo. pp. 11.

1196. CURTIS, GEORGE WILLIAM. The Duty of the American Scholar to Politics and the Times. An Oration delivered August 5, 1856, before the Literary Societies of Wesleyan University, Middletown, Connecticut.

8vo. pp. 46.   NEW YORK: *Dix, Edwards & Co.,* 1856.

1197. CURTIS, L. Civil Government an Ordinance of God. A Sermon delivered in Colchester, April 21, 1861.

8vo. pp. 15.   HARTFORD: *O. F. Jackson,* 1861.

1198. CUSHMAN, Miss Major PAULINE. The Romance of the Great Rebellion ; the Mysteries of the Scout Service. A genuine and faithful Narrative of the Thrilling Adventures, Hairbreadth Escapes, and Final Capture and Happy Rescue by the Union Forces.

12mo. pp. 32.   New York : *Wyncoop & Hallenbeck*, 1864.

1199. CUSHMAN, Rev. R. S.   Resolutions and Discourse occasioned by the Death of Abraham Lincoln, at Manchester, Vermont, April 19, 1865.

8vo. pp. 20.   Manchester : *For the Committee*, 1865.

1200. CUTLER, Ebenezer.   The Right of the Sword.   A Thanksgiving Discourse, at Worcester, Mass., November 21, 1861.

8vo. pp. 24.   Worcester : *Henry J. Howland*, 1861.

1201. CUTLER, Elbridge Jefferson.   Liberty and Law.   A Poem for the Hour.

18mo. pp. 11.   Boston : *American Unitarian Association*, 1862.

1202. CUTLER, Hon. R. King.   The Two Speeches of, on the matter of Mr. Thomas P. May, arraigned at the Bar of the Louisiana State Constitutional Convention for contempt, July 22 and 23,'64.

8vo. pp. 21.   New Orleans : *Rea's Press*, 1864.

1203. ——— Address to the Citizens of Louisiana.   Proceedings in Congress.   The Louisiana Delegation.   The President, Cabinet and Congress.   The Louisiana Constitution.   Compensation and Negro Suffrage.

8vo. pp. 22.   New Orleans : *Rea's Press*, 1865.

1204. CUTLER, W. P., of Ohio.   Slavery, a Public Enemy, and ought therefore to be destroyed ; a Nuisance that must be abated. Speech in the House of Representatives, April 23, 1862. pp. 12.

1205. Cyclopædia,   The Annual Cyclopædia and Register of Important Events, for the year 1861 to 1865.

4 vols Royal 8vo.   New York : *D. Appleton & Co.*, 1861–65.

The portions of each volume devoted to the United States embrace the operations of the armies, their organization, numbers and condition. The debates of Congress on all important questions; the messages of the President, and public documents of the government; finances; commercial and diplomatic intercourse; emancipation, peace, &c.

1206. CUTTER, Rev. Edward F.   Eulogy on Abraham Lincoln, delivered in Rockland, Maine, April 19, 1865.

8vo. pp. 16.   Boston : *D. C. Colesworthy*, 1865.

D ADMUN, Rev. J. W.   Union League Melodies; a collection of Patriotic Hymns and Tunes.   Original and Selected.

12mo. pp. 32.   Boston: *Benjamin D. Russell,* 1864.

1208. DAGGETT, O. E.   A Sermon on the Death of Abraham Lincoln, April 15, 1865, preached in Canandagua, New York, April 16, 1865.

8vo. pp. 16.   Canandagua: (N. Y.) *N. J. Milliken,* 1865.

1209. The Daily Campaign Record.   Published at Memphis, Tennessee, October, 1864.

1210. DALE, Rev. James W.   Northern Hearts embrace Southern Homes.   Two Sermons: 1, Abolitionism in its Fruits. 2, Abolitionism in its Morals ; or is the relation of Master and Servant a Sin, per se?

8vo. pp. 46.   Philadelphia: *C. Sherman & Son,* 1861.

1211. DAILEY, Mrs. Charlotte F.   Report upon the Disabled Rhode Island Soldiers; the names, condition and in what Hospital they are.   Made to Gov. Sprague, January 7, 1863.

8vo. pp. 24.   Providence: *Alfred Anthony,* 1863.

1212. DALLAS, George M.   Eulogy on, see C. J. Biddle.

1213. DALY, Hon. Charles P.   Are the Southern Privateersmen Pirates?   Letter to the Hon. Ira Harris.

8vo. pp. 13.   New York: *James B. Kirker,* 1862.

1214. DANA, R. H., Jr.   Enemy's Territory and Alien Enemies. What the Supreme Court decided in the Prize cases.

8vo. pp. 11.   Boston: *Little, Brown & Co.,* 1864.

1215. —— Speech at a Meeting of Citizens held in Faneuil Hall, June 21, 1865, to consider the subject of Re-organization of the Rebel States.   8vo. pp. 4.

1216. -—— An Address upon the Life and Services of Edward Everett, delivered before the Municipal Authorities and Citizens of Cambridge, February 22, 1865.

8vo. pp. 70.   Cambridge: (Massachusetts,) 1865.

1217. —— The same work on large paper.   (Fifty copies printed.)

4to. pp. 70.   Cambridge: (Massachusetts,) 1865.

1218. DANA, Rev M. M. G.   National Life, its Characteristics and Perils.   A Discourse preached Nov. 27, 1862, at Winsted, Ct.

8vo. pp. 15.   New York: *Sackett & Cobb,* 1862.

1219. DANDY, Rev. W. G. American Nationality. A Sermon delivered in Lexington, Kentucky, August 5, 1863. 8vo. pp. 8.

1220. DANIELS, J. M. Life of Stonewall Jackson. From Official Papers, Contemporary Narratives, and Personal Acquaintance. Crown 8vo. pp. 305. LONDON : *Low*, 1863.

1221. DANVILLE REVIEW. The Peril and Duty of the American People with respect to the Foreign Relations of the Country. By R. J. Breckenridge, DD., June, 1863.

Chaplaincy in the Army. F. W. Landis. June, 1863.

The Union and the Constitution. Rev. S. J. Baird. Sept., 1863.

The Nation and the Insurgents. Rev. R. J. Breckenridge. December, 1863.

1222. —— The Nation's Success and Gratitude. Rev. R. J. Breckenridge. March, 1864.

The Loyalty demanded by the Present Crisis. Rev. Jacob Cooper. March, 1864.

Disloyalty in the Church. Rev. George Morrison. March, 1864.

Perjury exemplified in Secession. Jacob Cooper. June, 1864.

The Peace Panic ; its Authors and Objects. September, 1864.

Slavery in the Church Courts. Jacob Cooper. December, 1864.

Enmities and Barbarities of the Rebels. December, 1864.

1223. DARLING, Rev. HENRY, DD. Slavery and the War. A Historical Essay.
8vo. pp. 48. PHILADELPHIA : *J. B. Lippincott & Co.*, 1863.

1224. —— Grief and Duty. A Discourse delivered in Albany, April 19, 1865, the day of the Funeral Obsequies of President Lincoln.
8vo. pp. 24. ALBANY : *S. R. Gray*, 1865.

1225. DASCOMB, Rev. A. B. A Discourse preached at Waitsfield, Vermont, in honor of our late Chief Magistrate, April 23, 1865.
8vo. pp. 23. MONTPELIER : *Walton's Press*, 1865.

1226. DAVIDSON, Rev. ROBERT, DD. A Nation's Discipline ; or Trials, not Judgments. A Discourse delivered September 26, 1861, in New York.
8vo. pp. 24. NEW YORK : *W. S. Dorr*, 1861.

1227. —— Piety Compatible with the Military Life.
8vo. pp. 296–306. *National Preacher, Sermon* 21, *Vol.* 1, 1862.

1228. DAVIDSON, Rev. R., DD. The Lessons of the Hour. A Discourse upon the Death of Abraham Lincoln, delivered in Huntington, L. I., Apr. 19, 1865.
8vo. pp. 12.   HUNTINGTON: (Long Island,) 1865.

1229. DAVIS, ANDREW JACKSON. Defeats and Victories; their Benefits and Penalties. A Lecture delivered in N. Y., Jan. 11, 1863.
12mo. pp. 24.   NEW YORK: *A. J. Davis & Co.*, 1863.

1230. DAVIS, Admiral C. H. The Navy of the United States. *North American Review, April*, 1864.

1231. DAVIS, Hon. GARRETT. The War not for Emancipation or Confiscation. A Speech delivered in the U. S. Senate, January 23, 1862.
12mo. pp. 55–65.   NEW YORK: *E. D. Barker*, 1862.

1232. —— Speech in which he gives a Sketch of the Political History of Massachusetts. Senate, February 16 and 17, 1864. 8vo. p. 39.

1233. DAVIS, Hon. HENRY WINTER. Address delivered at Baltimore, October 16, 1861, at the request of a large number of Merchants, Mechanics and Business Men generally.   pp. 16.

1234. —— The Southern Rebellion and the Constitutional Powers of the Republic for its Suppression. An Address delivered before the Mercantile Library Association, Brooklyn, Dec. 26, 1861.
12mo.   NEW YORK: *E. D. Barker*, 1862.

1235. —— Speech at Concert Hall Philadelphia, Sept. 24, 1863. p. 29.

1236. —— Speech on the President's Colonization and Compensation Scheme, delivered in House of Reps., Feb. 25, 1864. 8vo. pp. 8.

1237. —— Speech of, at Concert Hall, Philadelphia, September 24, 1863. 8vo. pp. 29.

1238. —— Speech; and the Debate on his Amendment to the Miscellaneous Bill, prohibiting the Trial of Citizens by Military Commission; in the House of Reps., March 2 and 3, 1865.
8vo. pp. 32.   WASHINGTON: *Lemuel Towers*, 1865.

1239. DAVIS, HENRY WINTER, Portrait of, by his own hand. His political Inconsistencies daguerreotyped in colors warranted not to fade, as his principles have always done, under the corroding touch of time. 8vo. pp. 16.

1240. —— Read and Judge for yourself. A Review of the pamphlet of Henry Winter Davis, entitled the Origin, Purposes and Principles of the American Party. (Signed Madison.) 8vo. pp. 14.

1241. DAVIS, Jefferson.   Message to the Confederate Sates, November 18, 1861.   pp. 2.

1242. —— An Address to the People of the Free States by the President of the Southern Confederacy, Dated Richmond, January 5, 1863. *Broadside.*

1243. —— Life of, by a South Carolinian.
8vo. pp. 96.   London : *G. W. Bacon*, 1865.

1244. —— State Papers, Messages, Proclamations, Letters, Speeches, etc., during the progress of the War. 8vo. Richmond.

1245. DAVIS, Nath'l W.   The Writ of Habeas Corpus.   Speech in the House of Assembly of New York, March 5, 1863.   pp. 10.

1246. DAVIS, T. T., of New York.   Speech on Military and Post Roads, in the House of Reps., March 23, 1864.   pp. 8.

1247. DAVIS, William M., of Pennsylvania.   The War; its Cause and Cure.   Speech in House of Reps., March 6, 1862. 8vo. p. 8.

1248. DAWES, Hon. Henry L., of Massachusetts.   Government Contracts.   Speech delivered in the House of Representatives, January 13, 1862.   pp. 8.

1249. —— Defence of the Committee on Government Contracts. Speech in House of Representatives, April 25, 1862. 8vo. p. 15.

1250. DAWSON, John L., of Pennsylvania.   Speech in the House of Representatives, February 24, 1864, on the State of the Union. pp. 29.

1251. DAY, Rev. P. B.   A Tribute to the Memory of Lieut. John Howard Worcester, in a Discourse delivered at Hollis, N. H., January 24, 1864.
8vo. pp. 16.   Nashua : *Telegraph Office*, 1864.

1252. —— A Discourse on Victory and its Dangers, delivered in Hollis, N. H., Fast Day, April 13, 1865.
8vo. pp. 20.   Concord : *McFarland & Jencks*, 1865.

1253. —— A Memorial Discourse on the Character of Abraham Lincoln, delivered at Hollis, N. H., on the day of the National Fast, June 1, 1865.
8vo. pp. 20.   Concord : *McFarland & Jencks*, 1865.

1254. DAY, Samuel Phillips.   Down South; or an Englishman's Experience at the Seat of the American War.
2 vols. 8vo.   London : *Hurst & Blackett*, 1862.

1255. The Days of Sixty-Three.
  12mo. pp. 54. Philadelphia : *For the Sanitary Comm.* 1864.

1256. DeAHNA, Col. Charles H. Report of the Committee on Military Affairs, on the petition of. *House of Representatives, Report No.* 124, *38th Congress, 1st Session,* 1864. *pp.* 17.

1257. DEAN, Gilbert. The Emancipation Proclamation and Abitrary Arrests. Speech in the House of Assembly of New York, February 12, 1863. 8vo. pp. 15.

1258. DEAN, Rev. Sidney. The War, and the Duty of a Loyal People. A Sermon preached in Providence, R. I., July 27, 1862.
  8vo. pp. 16. Providence : *Pierce & Budlong,* 1862.

1259. —— Eulogy on the occasion of the Burial of Abraham Lincoln, delivered in the City of Providence, April 19, 1865.
  8vo. pp. 23. Providence : *H. H. Thomas & Co.,* 1863.

1260. The Defence of the Great Lakes ; its necessity, and the quickest, cheapest, and best way to accomplish it.
  8vo. pp. 16. Ithaca : (N. Y.) *Andrews, McChain & Co.,* 1863.

1261. DeFOREST, Capt. J. W. The First Time under Fire. *Harpers' Magazine, September,* 1864.

1262. —— Sheridan's Battle of Winchester. *Harpers' Mag., Dec.,* '64.

1263. —— Sheridan's Victory at Middletown. Ibid. *February,* 1865.

1264. DEFREES, John, D. Remarks of, before the Indiana Club of Washington, D. C., August 1, 1864. 8vo. pp. 14.

1265. DeHAERNE, Le Chanoine. La Question Americaine dans ses rapports avec les Mœurs, L'Esclavage, L'Industrie et la Politique.
  8vo. pp. 72. Brussels : *La Revue Belge,* 1862.

1266. —— The American Question. Translated by Thomas Ray.
  8vo. pp. 114. London : *W. Ridgeway,* 1863.

1267. DELAWARE. Inaugural Address of William Cannon, upon taking the Oath of Office as Governor of Delaware, January 20, 1863.
  8vo. pp. 30. Wilmington : *Henry Eckle,* 1863.

1268. —— Illegal Arrests. Special Message of Governor Cannon, March 3, 1863. Also, the Governor's Proclamation, March 11, 1863. 8vo. pp. 8.

1269. —— Special Message of Governor Cannon, January 12, 1864.
  8vo. pp. 8.

1270. DELAWARE. Special Message of Governor Cannon, July 28, 1864. p. 11.

1271. —— Message of Governor Cannon, January 3, 1865. pp. 16.

1272. —— Argument of Samuel Harrington, Jr., and Col. Bowman, U. S. A., in defence of Edwin Wilmer, Provost Marshal of Delaware, before a Court Marshal in Washington, June 2, 1865. 8vo. pp. 39.   PHILADELPHIA: *King & Baird,* 1865.

1273. —— A History of the Delaware Department of the Great Central Fair for the United States Sanitary Commission, at Philadelphia, June, 1864. 8vo. pp. 34.   WILMINGTON: *James B. Riggs,* 1864.

1274. DELAWARE Farmer's Union Almanac for the year 1865. 4to. pp. 36.   PHILADELPHIA: *King & Baird,* 1865.
     Full of patriotic sentiment, and very severe on the Copperheads.

1275. DELEON. La Vérité sur les Etats Confédérés d'Amérique. Par Edwin De Leon ; ex Agent Diplomatique et Consul Général des Etats Unis. 8vo. pp. 32.   PARIS: *E. Dentu,* 1862.

1276. DELMAR, ALEXANDER. Gold Money and Paper Money. 8vo. pp. 42.   NEW YORK: *A. D. F. Randolph,* 1863.

1277. —— The Life of George B. McClellan. 12mo. pp. 109.   NEW YORK: *T. R. Dawley,* 1864.

1278. DELORME, EMILE NOUETTE. Les Etats Unis et l'Europe. Rupture de l'Union. Reconnoisance du Sud. Abolition de l'Esclavage. 8vo. pp. 30.   PARIS: *Dentu,* 1863.

1279. DELPHINE. Solon; or the Rebellion of '61. A Domestic and Political Tragedy. 8vo. pp. 74.   CHICAGO: *S. P. Rounds,* 1862.

1280. DEMAREST, JAMES, Jr. Thanksgiving Sermon. A Sermon preached in Hackensack, N. Y., November 28, 1861. 8vo. pp. 16.   HACKENSACK: *Bergen Co. Patriot,* 1861.

1281. —— The Present Duty of American Christians. A Sermon preached July 7, 1861. 8vo. pp. 15.   NEW YORK: *J. A. Gray,* 1861.

1282. DEMING, Hon. HENRY C., of Connecticut. Speech on the President's Plan for State Renovation, Feb. 27, 1864. 8vo. p. 16.

16

1283. DEMING, Hon. H. C.   Our Decisive Battle.   Speech delivered in the Town Hall, at Suffield, Conn., Fast Day, April 14, 1865. *Broadside.*

1284. —— Eulogy on Abraham Lincoln, before the General Assembly of Connecticut, at Allyn Hall, June 8, 1865.
8vo. pp. 58.   HARTFORD: *A. N. Clark & Co.,* 1864.

1285. DEMOCRACY.   The Disloyal and the War.   Its Record as made by its Leaders, its Presses, its Legislators, and Party Conventions.   8vo. pp. 32.

1286. DEMOCRACY WITH TREASON,   The Complicity of.   Its Record for Ohio.   (August, 1865.)   8vo. pp. 16.

1287. THE DEMOCRATIC Anti-Abolition State Rights Association, of the City of New York.   New York, 1863.   8vo. pp. 32.

1288. DEMOCRATIC CONVENTION, held at the Cooper Institute, New York, November 1, 1862.   4to. pp. 24.   *Iron Platform, Extra.*

1289. DEMOCRACY OF INDIANA, Appeal to.   Together with the Resolutions of the 66th, 93d and 34th Indiana Regiments; and a Speech of A. H. Stephens, of Georgia.   pp. 8.

1290. DEMOCRATIC LEAGUE.   Circular, N. York, June, 1862.   4to. p. 4.
This Circular was the first announcement of the formation and objects of the "Democratic League," which is claimed to be the first of all the "Leagues" formed for sustaining the government against the "Confederate" Treason. It is signed by C. P. Kirkland, Thomas Ewbank, Henry O'Reilly, Lorenzo Sherwood, and others.

1291. DEMOCRATS.   Northern Democrats.   What Traitors say.   8vo.

1292. DEMOCRATIC PARTY.   The Record of 1860–1865.   I, Secession and Reconstruction.   II, Opposition.   Philadelphia.   pp. 39.

1293. DEMOCRATIC PLATFORM.   People's Resolutions.   A Republican Form of Government: definition, Manhood Suffrage.
8vo. pp. 15.   NEW YORK: *C. S. Westcott & Co.,* 1865.

1294. THE DEMOCRATIC PLATFORM.   General McClellan's Letter of Acceptance.   pp. 8.

1295. THE DEMOCRATIC TIMES.   Chapter 1, A Dishonorable Peace with Rebellion!   The Dissolution of the Union.   Perpetual War ending in Anarchy or Military Despotism, etc.   8vo. pp. 4.

1296. A DEMOCRATIC PEACE offered for the Acceptance of Pennsylvania Voters.   Philadelphia, 1864.   8vo. pp. 13.

1297. DEMOCRATIC STATESMEN and Generals to the Loyal Sons of the

Union. Views of Generals Grant, Sherman, Dix, Wood, Butler, Edward Everett, J. A. Griswold, etc.

8vo. pp. 14. ALBANY : *Weed, Parsons & Co.*, 1864.

1298. DENNIS, Wm. L. An Oration delivered before the Authorities and Citizens of Newport, Rhode Island, July 4, 1865.

8vo. pp. 32. PHILADELPHIA : *E. C. Mackley & Son*, 1865.

This oration relates wholly to the rebellion.

1298.* DENISON, C. W. Illustrated Life, Campaigns and Public Services of Philip H. Sheridan.

12mo. pp 197. PHILADELPHIA : *T. B. Peterson*, 1866.

1299. DeNORMANDIE, Rev. James. Christian Peace. A Discourse delivered on the occasion of the National and State Thanksgiving, November 24, 1864, at Portsmouth, New Hampshire.

8vo. pp. 14. PORTSMOUTH : *C. W. Brewster*, 1864.

1300. —— The Lord Reigneth. A Few Words, April 16, 1865, at Portsmouth, N. H., after the Assassination of Abraham Lincoln.

12mo. pp. 8.

1301. DENSLOW, Van Buren. Fremont and McClellan ; their Political and Military Careers reviewed ; their Birth, Education and early Associations, Political Affinities, etc.

8vo. pp. 32. YONKERS : (N. Y.) *Office of the Clarion*, 1862.

1302. DePEYSTER, J. Watts. Winter Campaign ; the Test of Generalship.

12mo. pp. 24. NEW YORK : *C. G. Stone*, 1862.

1303. —— Secession in Switzerland and in the United States, compared ; being the Annual Address, October 20, 1863, before the Vermont Historical Society.

8vo. pp. 72. CATSKILL : *Joseph Joesbury*, 1864.

1304. —— Practical Strategy, as illustrated by the achievement of the Austrian Field Marshal Traun.

8vo. pp. 64. CATSKILL : *Joseph Joesbury*, 1863.

1305. DERBY, E. Hascett. Cotton and the Cotton Trade. *North American Review, January*, 1861.

1306. —— Resources of the South. *Atlantic Monthly, October*, 1862.

1307. DESPOTISM ; or the Last Days of the American Republic. By Invisible Sam.

12mo. pp. 463. NEW YORK : *Hall & Wilson*, 1856.

1308. DESSAULLES, L'hon L. A. La Guerre Américaine, son Origine et ses vrais Causes. Lecture Publique faite à l'Institute Canadien le 14 Décembre, 1864.
18mo. pp. 75.   Montreal : *Typ. du Journal "Le Pays,"* 1865.

1309. DEW, Prof. Thomas R. Review of the Debate in the Virginia Legislature, 1831–32. 1, Debate on the Abolition of Slavery. 2, Letter of Appomattox to the People of Virginia, on the Abolition of Slavery. (See Pro-Slavery Argument, pp. 288 to 490.) Philadelphia, 1852.

1310. DEWEY, Orville. A Talk with the Camp.
18mo. pp. 16.   New York : *A. D. F. Randolph*, 1863.

1311. —— A Sermon preached on the National Fast Day, Boston.
12mo. pp. 22.   Boston : *Ticknor & Fields*, 1861.

1312. DEXTER, Rev. Henry Martin. What ought to be done with the Freedmen and with the Rebels? A Sermon preached in Boston, April 23, 1865.
8vo. pp. 36.   Boston : *Nichols & Noyes*, 1865.

1313. Diary. (A) Four months of Prison Life of 1st Maryland Regiment, at Lynchburg and Richmond, by a Sergeant of the 1st Maryland, a Prisoner.
8vo. pp. 24.   Baltimore : *Sherwood & Co.*, 1863.

1314. Diary of the Great Rebellion. A Summary of each day's events, from the inauguration of the Rebellion at Charleston, S. C., December 20, 1860, to the first of January, 1862.
16mo. pp. 64.   Washington : *Bixler & Winchester*, 1862.

1315. Dialogue between an Old-fashioned Jackson Democrat and a Copperhead. 8vo. pp. 4.

1316. DICEY, Edward. Six months in the Federal States.
2 vols. post 8vo.   London : *Macmillan & Co.*, 1863.

1817. DICKINSON, Hon. Daniel S. The Union. An Address before the Literary Societies of Amherst College, July 10, 1861.
8vo. pp. 22.   New York : *James G. Gregory*, 1861.

1318. —— Great Speech to the Democracy in Mass Meeting Assembled at Wyoming County, Pennsylvania, August 19, 1861, on the Existing Rebellion. 8vo. pp. 8.

1319. —— Address delivered at Hartford on the 17th September, 1861, the Anniversary of the adoption of the Constitution of the United States, September 17, 1787.

8vo. pp. 15. HARTFORD : 1861.

1320. DICKINSON, Hon. D. S. The Duty of Loyal Men. Speech at the Union Meeting in New York, October 9, 1862. Seymour Democracy dissected. 8vo. pp, 15.

1321. —— No Compromise with Treason nor "Pause," in the Contest. Speech at Albany, New York, May 29, 1863. *Albany Journal, May* 30, 1863.

1322. DICKERSON, EDWARD N. The Navy of the United States. An Exposure of its Condition and the Causes of its Failure.

8vo. pp. 80. NEW YORK : *J. A. Gray* & *Greene,* 1864.

1323. —— The Steam Navy, of the United States ; its past, present and future. A Letter to the Hon. Gideon Welles, Sec. of the Navy.

8vo. pp. 20. NEW YORK : *J. A. Gray* & *Greene,* 1863.

1324. DICKSON, WILLIAM M. That we may have Peace we must now make War. Address at Cincinnati, September 23, 1863.

8vo. pp. 31. CINCINNATI : *Robert Clarke* & *Co.,* 1863.

1325. DICKSON, Rev. Dr., of Lewisburg, Pa. State of the Country. *Evangelical Quarterly Review, Vol.* xiii.

1326. DILL, Rev. Dr. The American Conflict. A Lecture.

12mo. pp. 24. BELFAST : (Ire.) *Whig Office,* 1863.

1327. DILLON, JOHN B., of Indiana. An Inquiry into the Nature and Uses of Political Sovereignty.

8vo. pp. 30. INDIANAPOLIS : *" Journal"* Co., 1860.

1328. A DIPLOMAT on Diplomacy. (Signed California.) 8vo. pp. 8.

1329. THE DIPLOMATIC YEAR ; being a Review of Mr. Seward's Foreign Correspondence of 1862. By a Northern Man. Second edition, with a Postscript.

8vo. pp. 71. PHILADELPHIA : *John Campbell,* 1863.

1330. DISTURBED CONDITION of the Country. Reports of the Select Committee of Thirty-three on.

8vo. pp. 71. WASHINGTON : *Thomas H. Ford,* 1861.

1331. DISUNION and its Results to the South. A Letter from a Resident in Washington to a Friend in South Carolina, February 18, 1861. pp. 23.

1332. DITTERLINE, T. Sketch of the Battle of Gettysburg, July

1, 2, and 3, 1863; with an account of the movements of the respective Armies for some days previous thereto.

8v. pp. 24. NEW YORK: *C. A. Alvord*, 1863.

1333. DIVEN, Hon. A. S., of New York. Speech on the Appropriation Bill and the Confiscation of Rebel Property. House of Representatives, January 22, and May 12, 1862. 8vo. pp. 16.

1334. —— The Surrender of Mason and Slidell. Speech delivered in House of Representatives, January 7, 1862. pp. 6.

1335. DIX, Rev. MORGAN, Asst., Rector of Trinity Church, New York. The Way of God in the Storm. A Sermon preached in St. Paul's Chapel, New York, April 21, 1861.

8vo. pp. 15. NEW YORK: *F. J. Huntington*, 1861.

1336. —— God's Mercies towards the Nation. A Sermon delivered Thanksgiving Day, 1861.

8vo. pp. 16. NEW YORK: *F. J. Huntington*, 1861.

1337. —— The Death of President Lincoln. A Sermon preached in New York, April 19, 1865.

8vo. pp. 16. CAMBRIDGE: *Riverside Press*, 1865.

1338. DIXON. Despotic Doctrines declared by the United States Senate Exposed, and Senator Dixon unmasked.

8vo. pp. 24. HARTFORD: *Case, Lockwood & Co.*, 1863.

1339. DIXON, JAMES, of Connecticut. Speech on the Legal Effects of Acts or Ordinances of Secession. Senate, June 25, 1862. pp. 8.

1340. DOANE, Rev. W. CROSWELL. The Statesman and the State. In uno, plura; E Pluribus Unum. The Oration at Burlington, February 22, 1862.

8vo. pp. 21. PHILADELPHIA: *J. B. Chandler*, 1862.

1341. —— The Sorrow of Lent, for Sin and not for Suffering. A Sermon preached February 22, 1863, at Burlington, N. Jersey.

8vo. pp. 14. PHILADELPHIA: *J. B. Chandler*, 1863.

1343. DODGE, ABIGAIL E. (Gail Hamilton.) A Call to my Countrywomen. Reprinted from the Atlantic Monthly, March, 1863.

12mo. pp. 12. NEW YORK: *G. W. Wood*, 1863.

1344. —— The same. 8vo. pp. 25. N. York: *A. D. F. Randolph*,'63.

1345. —— Tracts for the Times. Courage.

8vo. pp. 4. NEW YORK: *C. B. Richardson*, 1863.

1346. DODGE, WILLIAM E. Influence of the War on our National Prosperity. A Lecture delivered in Baltimore, March 13, 1865. 8vo. pp. 29. NEW YORK: *Wm. C. Martin*, 1865.

1347. DODGE, WILLIAM S. The History of the Old Second Division, Army of the Cumberland, Commanders McCook, Sill and Johnson. Portraits and maps.
8vo. p. 450. CHICAGO: *Church & Goodman*, 1864.

1348. DODGE, W. C. Memorial to the Secretary of War; or How to strengthen our Army and crush the Rebellion, with a saving of Life and Treasure.
8vo. pp. 12. WASHINGTON: *McGill & Witherow*, 1864.

1349. DOGGETT, Rev. THOMAS. Community of Guilt. A Sermon preached on Fast Day, at Groveland, N. H., Sept. 26, 1861.
8vo. pp. 16. HAVERHILL: *E. G. Frothingham*, 1861.

1350. —— Sermon delivered at Niagara Falls, April 19, 1865, on the Death of Abraham Lincoln. *Niagara Falls Gazette, Apr. 26, '65.*

1351. DOOLITTLE, Hon. J. R. Speech on Emancipation and Colonization. Delivered in the U. S. Senate, March 19, 1862. 8vo. pp. 8.

1352. —— The Rebels, and not the Republican Party, destroyed Slavery. Speech delivered in the U. S. Senate, Februay 9, 1864. 8vo. pp. 7.

1353. DORR, BENJAMIN, DD. The American Vine. A Sermon on occasion of the National Fast, January 4, 1861.
8vo. pp. 32. PHILADELPHIA *Collins*, 1861.

1354. DORR, JAMES A. Justice to the South. An Address by a Member of the New York Bar, October 8, 1856. 8vo. pp. 12.

1355. DOSTIE, Dr. A. P. Freedom versus Slavery. Address delivered before the Free State Union Association, of New Orleans, January 2, 1864. 8vo. pp. 8.

1356. —— The Political Position of Thomas J. Durant, of Louisiana. A Letter from, to Hon. Henry L. Dawes, Chairman of the Committee on Elections, of the House of Representatives.
8vo. pp. 8. NEW ORLEANS: *True Delta Office*, 1864.

1357. DOUGHERTY, DANIEL. The Peril of the Republic the Fault of the People. An Address before the Senate of Union College, Schenectady, July 20, 1863.
8vo. pp. 28. PHILADELPHIA: *J. B. Lippincott & Co.* 1863.

1358. DOUGLASS, FREDERICK. Eulogy on the late Hon. William Jay, delivered on the Invitation of the Colored Citizens of New York, May 12, 1859.

8vo. pp. 32.   ROCHESTER : *A. Strong & Co.*, 1859.

1359. ―― My Bondage and Freedom. With an Introduction by Dr. James McCune Smith.

12mo. pp. 464.   AUBURN: *Miller & Orton*, 1855.

1361. DOUGLAS. Observations on Senator Douglas's Views of Popular Sovereignty, as expressed in Harper's Magazine for September, 1859.

8vo. pp. 24.   Second edition.   WASHINGTON: *T. L. Magill*, '59.

1362. ―― Life of Stephen A. Douglas, U. S. Senator from Illinois.

12mo. pp. 12.   BALTIMORE : *John P. Des Forges*, 1860.

1363. ―― "See, the Conquering Hero comes." Principles of Stephen A. Douglas illustrated in his Speeches. 8vo. pp. 16.

1364. ―― Political Record of Stephen A. Douglas, on the Slavery Question. A Tract issued by the Illinois State Central Committee. pp. 16.

1365. ―― Eulogy upon, delivered at the Smithsonian Institute, Washington, July 3, 1861. By John W. Forney.

8vo. pp. 28.   PHILADELPHIA : *Ringwalt & Brown*, 1861.

1366. DOUGLASS, WM. The Heresy of Secession. Speech delivered at Booneville, Missouri, May 7, 1862.

8vo. pp. 16.   ST. LOUIS : *George Knapp & Co.*, 1862.

1367. DOY, JOHN, of Laurence, Kansas. The Narrative of. "A plain, unvarnished Tale."

12mo. pp. 132.   NEW YORK : *Thomas Holman*, 1860.

1368. DRAFT. All about the Draft. How it will be made. Every Man's exact chance. The Quota for New York State. Exemptions. Physical Disabilities, etc.

18mo. pp. 16.   NEW YORK : *Sinclair Toucey*, 1862.

1369. THE DRAFT ; or Conscription Reviewed by the People.

8vo. pp. 8.   PROVIDENCE : *For the author*, 1863.

1370. DRAINESVILLE. Letter from the Secretary of War, in answer to a Resolution of the House of Representatives, transmitting report of the engagement at Drainesville. *House of Representatives, Ex. Document, No.* 59, *37th Cong., 2d Ses.*, 1862.   8vo. pp. 22.

1371. DRAKE, CHARLES D., of St. Louis. The Union; its nature and its Assailants. Speech delivered at a Union Meeting, at the City of Louisiana, Missouri, July 4, 1861. The Nature of the Union. State Sovereignty. Jeff. Davis's Message. National and State Allegiance. Allegiance to King Cotton, etc.
8vo. pp. 16. ST. LOUIS: *Republican Office*, 1861.

1372. —— Address of, delivered at the Union Commemoration of the Birth Day of Washington, in St. Louis, Feb. 22, 1862. 8vo. p. 8.

1373. —— The Rebellion; its origin and life in Slavery. Position and Policy of Missouri. Speech delivered in Mercantile Library Hall, April 14, 1862. 8vo. pp. 8.

1374. —— The Rebellion; its character, motive, and aim. Oration of Charles D. Drake, delivered at Washington, July 4, 1862. 8vo. pp. 12.

1375. —— The War of Slavery upon the Constitution. Address on the Anniversary of the Constitution, delivered in St. Louis, September 17, 1862. pp. 7.

1376. —— The Proclamation of Emancipation. Speech delivered in Turner's Hall, St. Louis, January 28, 1863. 8vo. pp. 7.

1377. —— Camp Jackson; its History and Significance. Oration at St. Louis, May 14, 1863, on the Anniversary of the Capture of Camp Jackson. To which is subjoined his Reply to the Missouri Republican's Attack upon him, on account of that Oration.
8vo. pp. 16. ST. LOUIS: *Democrat Office*, 1863.

1378. —— Immediate Emancipation in Missouri. Speech of, delivered in the Missouri State Convention, June 16, 1863. 8vo. pp. 12.

1379. —— The Missouri State Convention, and its Ordinance of Emancipation. Speech of, delivered in St. Louis, July 9, 1862. 8vo. pp. 8.

1380. —— The Wrongs to Missouri and Loyal People. Speech before the Mass Convention at Jefferson City, Sept. 1, 1863. 8vo. p. 13.

1381. —— Address of the Committee from the State of Missouri to President Lincoln. Dated, September 30, 1863. pp. 12.

1382. —— Letter from the Executive Committee of the Missouri Delegation to President Lincoln. Washington, Oct. 3, 1863. pp. 7.

1383. —— Slavery's Destruction, the Union's Safety. A Speech before the Freedom Convention in Louisville, Ky., Feb. 22, 1864. p. 9.

17

1384. DRAKE, C. D.　The Decisive Struggle ; its Nature and its Issues.　Speech before the National Union Association, at Cincinnati, October 1, 1864.　pp. 16.

1385. —— Union •and Anti-Slavery Speeches delivered during the Rebellion.
12mo. pp. 431.　　　　　CINCINNATI : *Applegate & Co.,* 1864.

1386. DRAKE, RICHARD.　Revelations of a Slave Smuggler ; being the Autobiography of Capt. Richard Drake, an African trader for fifty years—from 1807 to 1857 ; with a Preface by his Executor, Rev. H. Byrd West.
8vo. pp. 98.　3 folding plates.　N. YORK : *R. M. De Witt,* 1860.

1387. DRAPER, Prof. J. W.　A History of the American Civil War.
3 vols. 8vo.　(In press.)　NEW YORK : *Harper & Brothers,* 1865.

1388. DRED SCOTT.　Report of the Decision of the Supreme Court of the United States, and the Opinions of the Judges thereof, in the case of Dred Scott versus John F. A. Sandford, December term, 1856.
8vo. pp. 239.　　　　WASHINGTON : *Cornelius Wendell,* 1857.

1389. —— The same.　New York : *D. Appleton & Co.,* 1857.

1390. —— Historical and Legal Examination of the Decision of the Supreme Court of the United States in the Dred Scott Case.
8vo. pp. 193.　　　　NEW YORK : *D. Appleton & Co.,* 1857.

1391. —— An Examination of the Case of Dred Scott vs. Sandford, and a full and fair Exposition of the Decision of the Court, and of the Opinions of the majority of the Judges.　By the Hon. Samuel A. Foot, late Judge of the Court of Appeals.
8vo. pp. 19.　　　　NEW YORK : *W. C. Bryant & Co.,* 1859.

1392. DRESSER, HORACE E.　The Battle Record of the American Rebellion.
8vo. pp. 72.　　　　　　　NEW YORK : *S. Toucey,* 1863.

1393. DREW, BENJAMIN.　A North-Side View of Slavery.　The Refugee ; or the Narratives of Fugitive Slaves in Canada, related by themselves ; with an Account of the History and Condition of the Colored Population of Upper Canada.
12mo. pp. 387.　　　　　BOSTON : *J. P. Jewett & Co.,* 1856.

1394. DRISLER, HENRY.　Bible View of Slavery, by John H. Hopkins, Bishop of Vermont.　Examined by H. Drisler.　Part 1.

Bible View of Slavery Reconsidered. Letter to the Rt. Rev. Bishop Hopkins, by Louis C. Newman.

8vo. pp. 20 and 14.   *Loyal Publication Society, No.* 39, 1863.

1395. DRUMM, Rev. JOHN H., DD. Assassination of Abraham Lincoln, President of the United States. A Sermon preached April 19, 1865, at Bristol, Pennsylvania.

8vo. pp. 21.   BRISTOL: *W. Bache,* 1865.

1396. DRUMMER BOY. A Story of Burnside's Expedition.

8vo. pp. 334.   BOSTON: *J. E. Tilton & Co.,* 1863.

1397. THE DRUMMER BOY. A Story of the War. In verse. By Cousin John.

12mo. pp. 48.   BOSTON: *Crosby & Nichols,* 1862.

1398. DOANE, Rev. RICHARD B. A Sermon preached in St. John's Church, Providence, April 10, 1865, the day for the Funeral Obsequies of President Lincoln.

8vo. pp. 15.   PROVIDENCE: *H. H. Thomas & Co.,* 1865.

1399. DUDLEY, JOHN S. Discourse preached in Middletown, Conn., and on Sabbath morning after the Assassination of President Lincoln.

8vo. pp. 28.   MIDDLETOWN: *D. Barnes,* 1865.

1400. DUELL, Hon. R. H., of New York. Position of Parties. Speech delivered in the House of Representatives, April 12, 1860. 8vo. pp. 8.

1401. DUFFIELD, GEO. Our National Sins to be repented of, and the Grounds of Hope for the Preservation of our Federal Constitution and Union. A Discourse delivered January 4, 1861.

8vo. pp. 40.   DETROIT: *Free Press Office,* 1861.

1402. —— Secession, its Causes and Cure. A Thanksgiving Discourse. The Rule of Providence applicable to the present Circumstances of our Country. Delivered in Detroit, November 28, 1860.

8vo. pp. 31.   DETROIT: *Free Press Office,* 1860.

1403. —— Pastoral Letter of the Synod of Michigan. Signed by George Duffield, Chairman; Alanson Scofield, and Elder Wood, Committee. 8vo. pp. 11.

1405. —— Courage in a good Cause; or the Lawful and Courageous Use of the Sword. A Sermon delivered April 21, 1861. 8vo. pp. 38. *T. B. Pugh.*

1406. DUFFIELD, G. Humiliation and Hope; or the Christian Patriot's Duty in the present Crisis of our National Affairs. A Discourse delivered November 14, 1862.
8vo. pp. 24.   DETROIT: *O. S. Gulley*, 1862.

1407. —— The Nation's Wail. A Discourse delivered in Detroit, the 16th of April, 1865, the day after receiving the intelligence of the brutal Murder of President Lincoln.
8vo. pp.   DETROIT: *Advertiser Office*, 1865.

1408. DUGANNE, Col. A. J. H. March to the Capitol. 4to. *N. Y. J. Robins*, 1862.

1409. —— Camps and Prisons. Twenty months in the Department of the Gulf.
12mo. pp. 424.   NEW YORK: *Subscribers' Edition*, 1865.

1410. DuHAILLY. Une Station sur les Côtes d'Amérique. 3 Parts. *Revue des deux Mondes, October, November and December*, 1862.

1411. DUNBAR, EDWARD E. The Mexican Papers containing the History of the Rise and Decline of Commercial Slavery in America.
8vo. pp. 278.   NEW YORK: *Rudd & Carlton*, 1861.

1412. DUNNING, Rev. HOMER N. Our National Trial. A Sermon preached at the Union Meeting of the Churches of Gloversville, November 28, 1861.
8vo. pp. 19.   GLOVERSVILLE: *George W. Heaton*, 1861.

1413. —— Providential Design of the Slavery Agitation. A Sermon preached January 4, 1861.
12mo. pp. 18.   GLOVERSVILLE: *A. Peirson*, 1861.

1414. —— The Strangeness of God's Ways. A Sermon preached before the Churches of Gloversville, November 24, 1864.
8vo. pp. 15.   GLOVERSVILLE: *George W. Heaton*, 1865.

1415. DUNNING, Rev. H. Address delivered on the occasion of the Funeral Solemnities of the late President of the United States, in Baltimore, April 18, 1865.
8vo. pp. 12.   BALTIMORE: *J. W. Woods*, 1865.

1416. —— The Nameless Crime. A Discourse delivered in Baltimore, April 23, 1865.
8vo. pp. 12.   BALTIMORE: *J. W. Woods*, 1865.

1417. DUNNING, Rev. H. The Assassination; its Lessons to Young

Men.   A Discourse delivered in the First Constitutional Presbyterian Church, May 7, 1865.

8vo. pp. 12.   BALTIMORE : *John W. Woods,* 1865.

1418. DURAND, CALVIN.   Letter from the Secretary of State, addressed to, February 1, 1864.   8vo. pp. 11.

1419. DURHAM, A. A.   The Devil's Confession in his Dying Hour. A Miraculous Revelation of the Nature and Cause of the Present Rebellion and War.   A Speedy Termination of the War.   The Union to be Restored.

8vo. pp. 12.   DE QUOIN : (Ill.) *R. R. Fleming,* 1863.

1420. DURYEA, Rev. JOSEPH T.   Loyalty to our Government.   A Divine Command and a Christian Duty.   A Sermon preached in Troy, New York, April 28, 1861.

8vo. pp. 28.   TROY : *A. W. Scribner & Co.,* 1861.

1421. —— Civil Liberty.   A Sermon preached August 6, 1863.

8vo. pp. 29.   NEW YORK : *J. A. Gray,* 1863.

1422. DUTIES.   Our Remaining Duties.   8vo. pp. 8.   (No date.)

1423. DUTTON, Rev. S. W. S.   Ought Treason against the Government of the United States to be punished?   *New Englander.*

1424. DUVAL, ALFRED.   [Memorial] to the Honorable Cotton Supply Association, Manchester, England.   Baltimore, February, 1861.   8vo. pp. 14.

1425. DUVERGIERE DE HAURANNE E.   Huit mois en Amérique à la fin de la Guerre—lettres et notes de Voyage.   *Rev. des Deux Mondes, August and September,* 1865.

1426 DUYCKINCK, E. A.   History of the War for the Union, Civil Military and Naval.   Illustrated by Alonzo Chappel.

3 vols. 4to.   NEW YORK : *Johnson, Fry Co.,* 1865.

1427. DWIGHT, EDMUND.   A Plan for Military Education of Massachusetts.

8vo. pp. 16.   BOSTON : *Little, Brown & Co.,* 1862.

1428. DWIGHT, HENRY O.   How we Fought at Atlanta.   *Harpers' Magazine, October,* 1864.

1429. DWINELL, Rev. ISRAEL E.   Hope for our Country.   A Sermon preached in the South Church, Salem, October 19, 1862.

8vo. pp. 19.   SALEM : *C. U. Swasey,* 1862.

1430. DYE, JOHN SMITH.   The Adder's Den : or Secrets of the Great

Conspiracy to overthrow Liberty in America. Depravity of Slavery. Two Presidents secretly assassinated by poison. Together with the dying Struggles of the Great Rebellion.
8vo. pp. 128.   NEW YORK; *The Author*, 1864.

1431. DYER, DAVID. Discourse occasioned by the Assassination of Abraham Lincon; delivered in the Albany Penitentiary, a military prison of the United States, April 19, 1865.
8vo. pp. 20.   ALBANY : *Edward Leslie*, 1865.

EARLE, PLINY, M. D. Lessons from the Past. A Poem delivered at the Annual Meeting of the Alumni Association of Friends' Yearly Meeting School, at Newport, R. I., 1861.
8vo. pp. 16.   PROVIDENCE : *Knowles, Anthony & Co.*, 1881.

1433. EASTON, Rev. H. A Treatise on the Intellectual Character and Civil and Political Condition of the Colored People of the United States, and the Prejudice exercised towards them.
8vo. pp. 54.   BOSTON : *Isaac Knapp*, 1837.

1434. EAST TENNESSEE. Report of the Committee for Relief to, for the State of New York.
8vo. pp. 30.   NEW YORK : *J. W. Amerman*, 1865.

1435. EATON, EDWARD BYRON. California and the Union. (A Poem.)
12mo. pp. 10.   LONDON : *Headley & Co.*, 1863.

1436. —— "The Crisis." Its Solution—the Causes—their Removal. A Lecture delivered at Oxford, England, by permission of the Reverend, the Vice-Chancellor, March 14, 1863.
8vo. pp. 32.   LONDON : *Headley & Co.*, 1863.

1437. EBONY IDOL. A Novel.
8vo. pp. 283.   NEW YORK : *D. Appleton & Co.*, 1860.

1438. ECCLESTINE, J. B. A Compendium of the Laws and Decisions relating to Mobs, Riots, Invasion, Civil Commotion, Insurrection, etc., as affecting Fire Insurance Companies in the United States.
8vo. pp. 112.   NEW YORK : *Grierson & Ecclestine*, 1863.

1439. THE ECHO FROM THE ARMY. What our Soldiers say about the Copperheads.
8vo. pp. 7.   *Loyal Publication Society, No.* 2, 1864.

1440. EDDY, Daniel C., DD. Liberty and Union, Our Country; its Pride and its Peril. A Discourse delivered in Boston, August 11, 1861.

8vo. pp. 32. BOSTON : *James M. Hewes*, 1861.

1441. —— Secession, a Natural Crime and Curse. A Discourse delivered in Philadelphia, on the National Fast Day, April 30, 1863. Philadelphia : 1863.

1442. —— The Martyr President. A Sermon preached before the Baldwin Place Church, April 16, 1865.

18mo. pp. 23. BOSTON : *Graves & Young*, 1865.

1443. EDDY, Rev. Richard. History of the Sixteenth Regiment New York State Volunteers, from its organization in July, 1861, to its Reception at Ogdensburg, as a Veteran Command, January 7, 1864.

12mo. pp. xii and 360. PHILADELPHIA : *For the author*, 1865.

1444. —— Three Sermons preached in the First Universalist Church, Philadelphia, April 16, April 19 and June 1, (Relating to the War.)

8vo. pp. 27. PHILADELPHIA : *H. W. Smith*, 1865.

1445. EDDY, T. M. The Patriotism of Illinois Illustrated.

Vol. 1, 8vo. pp. 608. CHICAGO : *Clarke & Co.*, 1865.

1446. EDDY, Zachariah. Secession; Shall it be Peace or War? A Fast Day Sermon, delivered in Northampton, April 4, 1861.

8vo. pp. 21. NORTHAMPTON : *Trumbull & Gere*, 1861.

1447. EDGAR, Rev. C. H. Earthquakes : Instrumentalities in the Divine Government. A Sermon preached in Easton, Pennsylvania, November 29, 1860.

8vo. pp. 19. EASTON : (Penn.) *Lewis Gordon*, 1860.

1448. —— Germs of Growth ; or Elements and Evidences of National Permanence. A Sermon preached in Easton, Pennsylvania, November 28, 1861.

8vo. pp. 30. NEW YORK : *Baker & Godwin*, 1861.

1449. —— The Curse of Canaan Rightly Interpreted ; and kindred Topics. Three Lectures delivered in the Reformed Dutch Church, Easton, Penn., January and February, 1862.

8vo. pp. 48. NEW YORK : *Baker & Godwin*, 1862.

The subjects of these Lectures are,—1, The Curse of Canaan; by whom and on whom pronounced. 2, The Negro; concerning his Color. 3, The Future of the Cushite.

1450. EDGAR, Rev C. H Three Sermons occasioned by the Assassination of President Lincoln, preached in Easton, Pennsylvania,
April 16, 19 and 23, 1865.

8vo. pp. 20.   EASTON : (Pa.) *Free Press Office*, 1865.
The titles of these Sermons are, 1, The Assassination of President Lincoln;
its Significance. 2, Loss and Gain. 3, The Majesty of Law.

1451. —— God's Help the Ground of Hope for our Country. A Sermon preached on the Day of National Thanksgiving, November
24, 1864, at Easton, Pennsylvania.

8vo. pp. 25.   NEW YORK : *Baker & Godwin*, 1864.

1452. —— Josiah and Lincoln, the Great Reformers. A Tribute to
the Worth and Work of our Martyr President, delivered on Fast
Day, June 1, 1865.

8vo. pp. 12.   EASTON : *Lewis Gordon*, 1865.

1453. EDGE, FREDERICK MILNES. Major General McClellan and
the Campaign on the Yorktown Peninsular. With Maps.

8vo. pp. 203.   LONDON : *Trubner & Co.*, 1865.

1454. —— The same work.

8vo. pp. 201.   NEW YORK : *Loyal Pub. Soc., No.* 81, 1865.

1456. —— An Englishman's View of the Battle between the Alabama
and the Kearsarge.

12mo. pp. 48.   NEW YORK : *A. D. F. Randolph*, 1864.

1457. EDGERTON, Hon. SIDNEY, of Ohio. Speech on the State of
the Union, delivered in the House of Representatives, January
31, 1861. 8vo. pp. 8.

1458. EDINBURGH REVIEW. The United States under the President-
ship of Mr. Buchanan. October, 1660.

1459. —— The Election of President Lincoln and its Consequences.
April, 1861.

The Disunion of America. October, 1861.

1460. —— Belligerents and Neutrals. January, 1862.

The American Revolution. October, 1862.

1461. —— The Negro Race in America. January, 1864.

1462. —— The Last Campaign in America. January, 1865.

1463. EDMONDS, S. EMMA E. Nurse and Spy in the Union Army ;
comprising the Adventures and Experience of a Woman in the
Hospitals, Camps and Battle Fields.

8vo. pp. 384. Illustrated. HARTFORD : *S. Williams & Co.*,'65.

1464. EDWARDS, Rev. Henry L. Discourse commemorative of our Illustrious Martyr, delivered in South Abington, Massachusetts, June 1, 1865.

8vo. pp. 16.   Boston: *Wright & Potter*, 1865.

1465. EDWARDS, Thomas M. Treasury Note Bill. Speech delivered in House of Representatives, Feb. 6, 1862. 8vo. pp. 8.

1466. EELLS, Rev. W. W. How and Why we give Thanks. A Thanksgiving Sermon preached in Pittsburgh, Nov. 26, 1865.

8vo. pp. 20.   Pittsburgh: *W. S. Haven*, 1864.

1467. EGAR, Rev. John H., DD. The Christian Patriot. A Sermon delivered in Grace Church, Galena, in May, 1861. By the Rector.

8vo. pp. 12.   Quincy: (Ill.) *Whig Press*, 1863.

1468. —— The Martyr President. A Sermon preached in the Church of St. Paul, Leavenworth, Kansas, June 1, 1865.

8vo. pp. 16.   Leavenworth: *Bulletin Office*, 1865.

1469. EGERTON, Hon. Jos. K., of Indiana. The Relations of the Federal Government to Slavery. Speech delivered at Fort Wayne, Indiana, October 30, 1860.

8vo. pp. 64.   Fort Wayne: *Dawson*, 1861.

1470. —— Letter of a Citizen of Indiana to the Hon. John J. Crittenden, on the Anti-Slavery Policy of President Lincoln, and the Duty of the National Democracy, March 21, 1862. 8vo. pp. 8.

1471. —— Confiscation. Speech delivered in the House of Representatives, January 28, 1864. pp. 8.

1472. —— Speech delivered in the House of Reps., June 15, 1864. 8vo. pp. 8.

1473. —— Speech at Ligonier, July 20, 1864, before the Democratic Cong. Convention of the Tenth District of Indiana. *Broadside*

1474, —— Reconstruction. Speech in the House of Representatives, February 20, 1865. pp. 16.

1475. EGGLESTON, Rev. Nathaniel H. Have we a Government? A Sermon preached at Stockbridge, Mass., January 20, 1860. *Berkshire County Eagle, January* 31, 1860.

1476. —— The Riot and the Conscription Act. A Sermon preached at Stockbridge, Aug. 2, 1863. *Berkshire Co. Eagle, Aug.* 13, '63.

1477. —— Reasons for Thanksgiving. A Discourse to the Congregational Church and Society, in Stockbridge, Mass., Nov. 21, 1861.

8vo. pp. 21.   Pittsfield: (Mass.) *H. Chickering*, 1861.

18

1478. EGGLESTON, Rev. C. M.   A Funeral Discourse in memory of Capt. Ayers C. Barker, 120th Regiment N. Y. S. V., killed at the Battle of Gettysburg, July 2, 1863.

12mo. pp. 19.   COXSAKIE: (N. Y.) *F. C. Dedrick,* 1863.

1479. —— The Riot and Conscription Act.   A Sermon preached at Stockbridge, August 2, 1863.   *Berkshire Co. Eagle, Aug.* 13,'63.

1480. EHREHART, Rev. CHARLES J.   A Discourse delivered in St. Peter's Evangelican Lutheran Church, Middletown, Pennsylvania, November 27, 1862.

8vo. pp. 23.   LANCASTER: (Pa.) *E. H. Thomas & Son,* 1862.

1481. ELDER, Dr. WILLIAM.   Debt and Resources of the United States, and the Effect of Secession upon the Trade and Industry of the Loyal States.

8vo. pp. 32.   PHILADELPHIA: *Ringwalt & Brown,* 1863.

1482. —— How the Western States can become the Imperial Power in the Union.

8vo. pp. 23.   PHILADELPHIA: *Ringwalt & Brown,* 1865.

1483. —— How our National Debt can be paid.   The Wealth, Resources and Power of the People of the United States.

8vo. pp. 15.   PHILADELPHIA: *Sherman & Co.,* 1865.

1484. ELDRIDGE, JOSEPH, DD.   Does the Bible sanction Slavery? A Discourse delivered at Norfolk, Connecticut, February 24, 1861.   Litchfield, 1861.

1485. ELEMENTS OF DISCORD in Secessia.   The Vulgarity of Treason. Extracts from Rebel Organs.

8vo. pp. 16.   *Loyal Publication Society, No.* 15, 1863.

1486. ELIOT.   A Letter to the Hon. Samuel A. Eliot, Representative in Congress from Boston, in Reply to his Apology for voting for the Fugitive Slave Bill.   By Hancock.

8vo. pp. 57.   BOSTON: *Crosby & Nichols,* 1851.

1487. ELIOT, J. H.   News from the War.   *Knickerbocker Magazine, September,* 1863.

1488. ELIOT, THOMAS D., of Mass.   Objects of the War.   Speech in House of Representatives, December 12, 1861.   8vo. pp. 8.

1489. —— Address to his Constituents.   First Congressional District of Massachusetts.   pp. 8.

1490. —— Speech delivered in House of Representatives, February

10, 1864, on the Bill for the establishment of a Bureau of Freedmen's Affairs: 8vo. pp. 16.

1491. ELIOT, Rev. W. G., DD. Loyalty and Religion. A Discourse
for the Times, delivered at St. Louis, August 18, 1861.
8vo. pp. 12. St. Louis: *George Knapp & Co.*, 1861.

1492. —— Washington's Birth Day. Patriotism. 8vo. pp. 4.

1493. —— A Sermon preached at the Installation of the Rev. A. D.
Mayo as Pastor of the Church of the Redeemer, Cincinnati, June
3, 1863. *Christian Register, June* 20, 1863.

Both these Discourses relate to the Rebellion.

1494. —— Loyal work in Missouri. *North American Rev., April,* '64.

1495. ELLET, Charles, Jun. The Army of the Potomac, and its
Mismanagement. Respectfully addressed to Congress.
8vo. pp. 19. Washington: *L. Towers & Co.*, 1861.

1496. —— Military Incapacity and what it costs the Country. Military Incapacity has caused the loss of one Campaign; shall we
allow it to cause the loss of another?
8vo. pp. 15. New York: *Ross & Toucey*, 1862.

1497. ELLIOTT, E. B. On the Military Statistics of the United
States of America; especially those which relate to the Mortality,
the Sickness and other Casualties, and to certain Physiological
Characteristics of the Soldiers in the existing Volunteer Service.
4to. p. 44. and 3 eng. tables. Berlin: (Prus.) *R. V. Decker,*'63.

1498. ELLIOTT, Samuel M. The Highland Brigade, November,
1861. 8vo. pp. 29.

1499. ELLIS, Charles Mayo. The Power of the Commander-in-
Chief to declare Marshal Law, and decree the Emancipation, as
shown from B. R. Curtis, Esq.
8vo. pp. 24. Boston: *A. Williams & Co.*, 1862.

1500. ELLIS, George E., DD. "The Preservation of the United
States." A Discourse delivered in Charlestown, on November
29, 1860.
8vo. pp. 29. Charlestown: *Abram E. Cutter*, 1860.

1501. —— The Nation's Ballot and its Decision. A Discourse delivered in Cambridgeport and in Charlestown, November 13, 1864;
being the Sunday following the Presidential Election.
8vo. pp. 18. Boston: *W. V. Spencer*, 1864.

1502. ELLIS, G. E DD Is Emancipation to be the Object, or the Result of our War? A Discourse delivered in Charlestown, on the National Fast Day, September 26, 1861. *Ch. Register, Oct.* 12, 1861.

1503. ELLIS, Rev. RUFUS. The Holy War. *Monthly Religious Magazine, April,* 1861.

1504. —— The Opportunities of the Present War. Ibid. *Feb.,* 1862.

1505. —— Peace not always possible. Ibid. *October,* 1862.

1506. —— The Cause of National Disaster. Ibid. *April,* 1863.

1507. —— Christian Patriotism. Ibid. *September,* 1864.

1508. —— Our National Ideal. Ibid. *January,* 1864.

1509. —— Ought the War to go on. Ibid. *October,* 1864.

1510. —— Address on the occasion of the Burial of President Lincoln, delivered in Boston, April 19, 1865. Ibid. *May,* 1865.

1511. ELLIS, THOMAS T., M. D. Leaves from the Diary of an Army Surgeon; or Incidents of Field, Camp, and Hospital Life. 12mo. pp. 312. NEW YORK: *John Bradburn,* 1863.

1512. ELLISON, THOMAS. Slavery and Secession in America, Historical and Economical; together with a practical Scheme of Emancipation. Second Edition, enlarged. With a Reply to the Fundamental Arguments of Mr. James Spence, contained in his work on "the American Union." 12mo. pp. xxxv. and 371. LONDON: *Sampson, Low & Son,* '62.

1513. ELLSWORTH, LYON and BAKER. The Patriot's Offering; or the Life, Services and Military Career of the Noble Trio. 12mo. pp. 108. NEW YORK: *Baker & Godwin,* 1862.

1514. ELMENDORF, Rev. J. J. Loyalty. A Voice from the Sanctuary concerning the Civil War. 8vo. pp. 16. NEW YORK: *H. B. Durand,* 1863.

1515. ELMORE, F. H. The Anti-Slavery Examiner, No. 8. Correspondence between the Hon. F. H. Elmore and Jas. G. Birney. 8vo. pp. 68. NEW YORK: *American Anti-Slavery Soc.,* 1838.

1516. ELY, ALFRED. Enlargement of Canal Locks of New York, for National Defence. Speech delivered in the House of Representatives, June 30, 1862. 8vo. pp. 13.

1517. —— Journal of. A Prisoner in Richmond. Edited by Charles Lanman. 12mo. pp. 359. Portrait. NEW YORK: *D. Appleton & Co.,* '62.

1518. ELY, S. W. Union— Secession. The Case plainly stated. Order or Anarchy ; "That's the Question." Cincinnati, July 29, 1861. pp. 8.

1519. EMANCIPATION, The War and Slavery ; or Victory only through. 8vo. pp. 8. BOSTON: *R. F. Wallcut*, 1861.

1520. —— Proceedings of the Emancipation Convention held at Jefferson City, June, 1862. 8vo. pp. 8.

1521. —— Constitution and By-Laws of the General Emancipation Society of Missouri. Adopted, St. Louis, April 8, 1862. 8vo. pp. 16. ST. LOUIS: *Democrat Job Office*, 1862.

1522. —— Immediate Emancipation in Maryland. Proceedings of the Union State Central Committee, Baltimore, December 16, 1863. 8vo. pp. 20. BALTIMORE: *Bull & Tuttle*, 1863.

1523. —— The Power of the Commander-in-Chief to declare Martial Law and decree Emancipation ; as shown from B. R. Curtis. By Libertas. 8vo. pp. 24. BOSTON: *A. Williams & Co.*, 1862.

1524. EMANCIPATION AND COLONIZATION, Report of the Select Committee on, with an Appendix. 8vo. pp. 83. WASHINTON: *Government Printing Office*, 1862.

1525. EMERSON, R. W. An Address delivered in Concord, Mass., August 1, 1844, on the Anniversary of the Emancipation of the Negroes in the British West Indies. 8vo. pp. 34. BOSTON : *James Munroe & Co.*, 1844.

1526. EMERSON, G., M. D. Cotton in the Middle States; with Directions for its easy Culture. 8vo. pp. 12. PHILADELPHIA : *H. L. Butler*, 1862.

1527. EMIGRATION. Report of the Special Committee of the Union League Club, on Emigration, May 12, 1864. 8vo. pp. 19. NEW YORK : *Club House*, 1864.

1528. —— Report on Emigration by a Special Committee of the Chamber of Commerce of the State of New York, January 5, 1865. With Appendix of Documents. 8vo. pp. 32. NEW YORK: *J. W. Amerman*, 1865.

1529. ENGINEERS. Memorial of the United States Naval Engineers, to the 38th Congress of the United States. First Session. 8vo. pp. 14. NEW YORK : *C. A. Alvord*, 1864.

1530. ENGLAND AND AMERICA. From the Princeton Review for January, 1862.
8vo. pp. 31.   PHILADELPHIA : *W. S. & Alfred Martien,* 1862.

1531. ENGLISH NEUTRALITY. Is the Alabama a British Pirate?
8vo. pp. 36.   NEW YORK : *A. D. F. Randolph,* 1863.

1532. ENROLLMENT LAWS of the United States, for calling out the National Forces. Approved March 3, 1864, and amended February 24, 1864. Official and complete.
18mo. pp. 48.   NEW YORK : *J. W. Fortune,* 1864.

1533. THE EQUALITY of all Men before the Law, claimed and defended, in Speeches by W. D. Kelley, Wendell Phillips and Frederick Douglass, etc. 8vo. pp. 42.

1534. ESTCOURT, J. H. Rebellion and Recognition, Slavery, Sovereignty, Secession and Recognition considered.
8vo. pp. 28. MANCHESTER ; (Eng.) *Un. and Eman. So.,* 1863.

1535. —— Prefatory Sketch of Abraham Lincoln ; with Mr. Beecher's " Sumter Oration " and Eulogy. Manchester, England, 1865.

1536. ESTVAN, B., (Colonel of Cavalry in the Confederate Army.) War Pictures from the South.
2 vols. post 8vo.   LONDON : 1863.

1537. —— The same work.
8vo. pp. 352.   NEW YORK : *D. Appleton & Co.,* 1863.

1538. ETHERIDGE, Hon. EMERSON. State of the Union. A Speech delivered in the House of Representatives, Jan. 23, 1861. p. 15.

1539. EVANGELICAL QUARTERLY REVIEW, published at Gettysburg, Pennsylvania. Prof. M. L. Stœver, Editor. Vol. xiii.
Our National Crisis. Rev. Dr. Reynolds, of Chicago.
State of the Country. Rev. Dr. Dickson, of Lewisburg, Penn.
Slavery among the Ancient Hebrews ; translated from the German by Rev. Dr. Schmidt, New York.
Ministry of the Gospel in Time of War ; translated from the German by the Rev. G. A. Wenzel. Philadelphia.

1540. —— Vol. XIV. Christianity and Politics ; from the German, by Rev. G. A. Wenzel.
The Universal Fatherhood of God, and the Universal Brotherhood of Man, God's Argument against Oppression. Prof. Tyler. Amherst, Massachusetts.

1541. EVANGELICAL QUARTERLY REVIEW. XV. Battle of Gettysburg. Prof. Jacobs.

Responsibilities of the American Citizen. Hon. G. C. Maund.

1542. —— XVI. The Hand of God in the War. Rev. Dr. Conrad, of Chambersburg, Pennsylvania.

Politics and the Pulpit. Prof. Zeigler, of Pennsylvania.

The United States Christian Commission. Prof. L. M. Stœver.

1543. EVANS, ESTWICK, for the Presidency. To the People of the United States. Washington, April, 1864.

1544. —— Letter to the President of the United States. Dated, Washington, October, 1862. 8vo. pp. 8.

1545. EVANS, Dr. THOMAS W. La Commission Sanitaire des Etats Unis, son origine, son organisation et des résultats avec une notice sur les Hopitaux Militaires aux Etats Unis, et sur la réforme sanitaire dans les avinces Européennes.

Royal 8vo. pp. 178, with 5 plates. PARIS: *E. Dentu*, 1865.

1546. EVERETT, Rev. CHARLES CARROLL. A Sermon preached on the Assassination of Abraham Lincoln.

8vo. pp. BANGOR: *Berry & Burr*, 1865.

1547. —— Eulogy on Abraham Lincoln, late President of the United States, delivered before the Citizens of Bangor, June 1, 1865.

8vo. pp. 30. BANGOR: *Samuel S. Smith*, 1865.

1548. EVERETT, EDWARD. Success of our Republic. An Oration delivered in Boston, July 4, 1860. (Pulpit and Rostrum, No. 14.)

1549. —— The Great Issues before the Country. An Oration delivered in the New York Academy of Music, on the 4th of July,'61.

8vo. pp. 52. NEW YORK: *G. Q. Colton*, 1861.

1550. —— The Questions of the Day. [Same Oration as the above.] Pulpit and Rostrum, Nos. 21 and 22.

1551. —— An Address delivered before the Union Agricultural Society of Adams, Rodman and Loraine, Jefferson County, New York, September 12, 1861.

8vo. pp. 23. CAMBRIDGE: *H. O. Houghton*, 1861.

1552. —— The Monroe Doctrine. From the New York Ledger.

8vo. pp. 11. *Loyal Publication Society, No.* 34, 1863.

1553. —— The Monroe Doctrine. Letter of John Quincy Adams Balance of Power in Europe.

8vo. pp. 17. NEW YORK: *W. C. Bryant & Co.*, 1863.

1554. EVERETT, E. An Address delivered at the Inauguration of the Union Club, April 9, 1863.

8vo. pp. 61. BOSTON: *Little, Brown & Co.*, 1863.

1555. —- The same. 12mo. pp. 64. *Little Brown & Co.*, 1863.

1556. —— An Oration delivered on the Battle-Field of Gettysburg, (November 19, 1863,) at the consecration of the Cemetery, etc.

8vo. pp. 48. NEW YORK: *Baker & Godwin*, 1863.

1557. —— Address at the consecration of the National Cemetery at Gettysburg, 19th November, 1863; with the Speech of President Lincoln, and the other Exercises of the occasion; accompanied by an account of the Origin of the Undertaking, and of the Arrangement of the Cemetery Grounds, and by a Map of the Battle-Field, etc.

8vo. pp. 87. BOSTON: *Little, Brown & Co.*, 1864.

1558. EWART, DAVID, of Columbia, S. C. A Scriptural View of the moral relations of American Slavery. 1849. Revised and amended in 1859.

8vo. pp. 12. CHARLESTON: (S. C.) *Walker, Evans & Co.*, 1859.

1559. EWBANK, THOMAS. Inorganic Forces ordained to supercede Human Slavery. Originally read before the American Ethnological Society.

8vo. pp. 32. NEW YORK: *Wm. Everdell & Sons*, 1860.

1560. EWER, Rev. F. C. Discourse on the National Crisis, delivered at St. Ann's Church, New York, May 5, 1861.

8vo. pp. 19. NEW YORK: *George F. Nesbitt & Co.*, 1861.

1561. —— A Rector's Reply to sundry requests and demands for a Political Sermon. Preached in New York the 16th Sunday after Trinity, 1864.

8vo. pp. 23. NEW YORK: *Francis Hart & Co.*, 1864.

1562. EWING, THOMAS. Letter to Benjamin Stanton, Lieutenant Governor of Ohio, relative to charges brought against our Generals who fought the Battle of Shiloh, April 6, 1862.

8vo. pp. 12. COLUMBUS: (Ohio,) *R. Nevins*, 1862.

1563. —— The same work.

8vo. pp. 24. COLUMBUS: *R. Nevins*, 1862.

1564. EXCISE TAX LAWS. Suggestions of Amendments recommended by a Convention of United States Assessors, holden at Cleveland, Ohio, December 16, 17 and 18, 1863.

8vo. pp. 20.   BOSTON: *George O. Rand & Avery,* 1864.

1565. EXEMPTION CLAUSE of the Enrolment Act, Message from the President in relation to.   June 8, 1864.   pp. 2.

1566. EYMA, XAVIER.   La République Américaine, ses Institutions, ses Hommes.

2 vols, 8vo. pp. 770.   PARIS: *Michel Levy Frères,* 1861.

FABENS, JOSEPH WARREN.   Facts about Santo Domingo, applicable to the Present Crisis.   An Address before the American Geographical and Statistical Society, New York, April 3, 1862.

8vo. pp. 32.   NEW YORK: *G. P. Putnam,* 1862.

1568. FAIRBANKS, CHARLES.   The American Conflict as seen from a European Point of View.   A Lecture delivered at St. Johnsbury, Vermont, June 4, 1863.

8vo. pp. 44.   BOSTON: *George O. Rand & Avery,* 1863.

1569. FAIRS.   Spirit of the Fair.   Folio.   N. York: *John F. Trow,*'64.

1570. —— Our Daily Fare.   Folio.   Philadelphia, 1864.

1571. —— The Boatswain's Whistle.   Published at the National Sailors' Fair, Boston.   (November 9 to the 19, 1864.)   Folio, 1864.

1572. FAIR.   History of the Great Western Sanitary Fair.

8vo. pp. 578.   CINCINNATI: *O. F. Vent & Co.,* 1865.

See also Philadelphia Central Fair.

1573. FALLACIES OF FREEMEN, and Foes of Liberty.   A Reply to "The American War, the Whole Question Explained."

8vo. pp. 36.   MANCHESTER: *Union and Emanc. Society,* 1863.

1574. FANNING, Col. DAVID.   (A Tory in the Revolutionary War with Great Britain); giving an account of his Adventures in North Carolina, from 1775 to 1783.   Printed for private distribution only.   1861.   In the first year of the Independence of the Confederate States of America.   4to.

A copy of this book in the Library of Yale College is a presentation copy to Jefferson Davis, from the Editor, and bears the following note: "Hon. Jefferson Davis, this *first* printed book, in the *first* year of the Independence of the Confederacy, to its *first* President, is respectfully presented by John H. Wheeler."

19

1575. FARQUHAR, Rev. JOHN. The Claims of God to Recognition, in the Assassination of President Lincoln. A Sermon preached in the Chanceford Presbyterian Church, York County, Pennsylvania, and at Fawn, York County.

8vo. pp. 23.　　　　　　　LANCASTER: *Pearsall & Geist,* 1865.

1576. FARRAR, Judge. The Trial of the Constitution. *North American Review, October,* 1863.

1577. FARRAR, C. C. S., of Bolivar County, Mississippi. The War, its Causes and Consequences.

12mo. pp. 260.　　　　　CAIRO : (Ill.) *Blelock & Co.,* 1861.

1578. FAUCHET, M. Message of President Lincoln transmitting Correspondence relative to the attempted seizure of M. Fauchet, Envoy Extraordinary and Minister Plenipotentiary of France, by the Commander of the British Sloop-of-War Africa, within the waters of the United States.

8vo. pp. 53.　　　37th *Cong., 3d Session, Ex. Doc., No.* 4, 1862.

This Correspondence was called for, from its bearing on the case of the seizure of Mason and Slidell.

1579. FAULKNER, Hon. C. J., of Virginia. Speech on the Compromise, the Presidency, Political Parties. Delivered in the House of Representatives, August 2, 1852.

8vo. pp. 15.　　　　　　WASHINGTON: *Globe Office,* 1852.

1580. FAULKNER'S History of the Revolution in the Southern States ; including the Special Messages of President Buchanan. The Ordinances of Secession of the six Withdrawing States, etc.

8vo. pp. 94.　　　　NEW YORK : *For the booksellers,* 1861.

1581. FAY, THEODORE S. " Die Sklavenmacht. Blicke in die Geschichte der Vereinigten Staaten von Amerika zur Erklärung der Rebellion 1860–65."

8vo. pp.　　　　　　　　　　　BERLIN: 1865.

" The Slave Power: A Glance at the History of the United States in its con nection with the Rebellion of 1860 and '65."

1582. FEDERALS and Confederates ; for what they Fight. The true Issue of the American Civil War, stated by B. D.

8vo. pp. 16.　　　　　　　　LONDON : *Job Candwell.*

1583. FELT, Lieut. GEORGE H., 55th New York S. M. Proceedings. of a Court of Inquiry, convened by Special Order, No. 85. Headquarters, Department of Washington.

8vo. pp. 64.　　　　NEW YORK : *Willard Felt & Co.,* 1863.

1584. FERRAND, JACQUES. John Brown mort l'affranchissement des Noirs.

16mo. pp. 106. PARIS : 1861.

1585. FERRER DE COUTE, JOSE. The Question of Slavery conclusively and satisfactorily solved, as regards Humanity at large, and the Permanent interests of Present Owners.

8vo. pp. 312. NEW YORK : *S. Hallett,* 1865.

1586. FERRIS, ISAAC, DD. The Duties of the Times. Preached on the National Thanksgiving, August 6, 1863, in the University Place Presbyterian Church.

8vo. pp. 24. NEW YORK : *John A. Gray & Green,* 1863.

1587. FERRY. Obituary Discourse on the occasion of the Death of Noah Henry Ferry, Major of the Fifth Michigan Cavalry, killed at Gettysburg, July 3, 1863. By Rev. David M. Cooper.

8vo. pp. 46. Portrait. NEW YORK : *J. F. Trow,* 1863.

1588. FESSENDEN, S. C., of Maine. Issues of the Rebellion. Speech in House of Representatives, January 20, 1862. pp. 8.

1589. —— Speech on the Abolition of Slavery in the District of Columbia. Senate, April 1, 1862. pp. 8.

1590. —— The Issues of United States Notes. Feb. 12, 1862. pp. 15.

1591. A FEW WORDS for Honest Pennsylvania Democrats. pp. 16.

1592. A FEW WORDS to Loyal Democrats, by one who knows and who honors them. 8vo. pp. 24. Philadelphia.

1593. A FEW WORDS in behalf of the Loyal Women of the United States, by One of Themselves. New York, May, 1863.

8vo. pp. 23. *Loyal Publication Society, No.* 10, 1863.

1594. A FEW PLAIN WORDS with the rank and file of the Union Armies. *Union Congressional Committee,* 1864. 8vo. pp. 8.

1595. FIELD, Hon. R. S., of New Jersey. Speech on the discharge of State Prisoners, in the Senate of the United States, January 7, 1862. pp. 16.

1596. —— A Charge to the Grand Jury in the District Court of the United States for the District of New Jersey, April 21, 1863.

8vo. pp. 24. TRENTON : (N. J.) *State Gazette,* 1862.

1597. FINANCE. A Letter addressed to the House Committee of Ways and Means, June 1, 1862. 8vo. pp. 7.

1598. —— The Financial Credit of the United States. How it can be sustained. A Report made to the American Geographical and Statistical Society, January 16, 1862. pp. 22.

1599. FINANCE. Our National Finances. What shall be done? Boston, November 15, 1862. 8vo. pp. 12.

1600. —— The National Finances. The Second Letter to the Secretary of the Treasury, and to the Senate and House of Representatives of the United States, on the subjects of Cheap Money, the Proposed War Tax, Demand Treasury Notes, etc. By a Patriot.
8vo. pp. 8.   NEW YORK: *Baker & Godwin,* 1862.

1601. —— National. By W. 8vo. pp. 24.

1602. —— Appeal to Congress and to the People of the United States. Some facts and texts for their consideration on the Financial Condition of the Country. 8vo. pp. 12.

1603. —— Our National Finances. A serious Comedy. This Comedy never was played, and probably never will be played. It always has been played and always will be played, and is at present being played, and may become a Tragedy.
12mo. pp. 36.   NEW YORK: *For the author, Feb.* 15, 1864.

1604. FINANCIAL AFFAIRS in the United States during the first Two Years of the Southern Insurrection. By a Member of the Chamber of Commerce.
8vo. pp. 10.   NEW YORK: *J. W. Amerman,* 1862.

1605. THE FINANCIAL CREDIT of the United States; how can it be sustained. Report of a Committee of the American Geographical and Statistical Society, January 16, 1862. 8vo. pp. 29.

1606. FINANCIAL POLICY of the Government. Some considerations upon. By John P. McGregor. Milwaukie, November, 1862. 8vo. pp. 16.   MILWAUKIE: *Starr & Son,* 1862.

1607. THE FINANCIAL SITUATION. To Abraham Lincoln, the United States Senators, Congressmen, the People, and especially the Farmers of the United States. Signed, "A Patriot." New York, January 9, 1865. 8vo. pp. 15.

1608. FINANCIAL SCHEMES for the Government. *Bankers' Magazine, March,* 1862. *pp.* 8.

1609. FINANCIAL SUGGESTIONS. By H. M. S. New York, December 10, 1864. pp. 3.

1610. FIREY, Lewis P. Speech in the Senate of Maryland, February 5, 1862, on the Compromise Resolutions proposed by him. 8vo. pp. 11.

1611. The First Duty of a Citizen. [Showing the importance of a deeper interest by the people in the elections.] pp. 8.

1612. Fiscal Convention, (The.) Hints for the People in pro-forma Debates of a Convention of Delegates from different Classes and Interests; with a Platform of Principles unanimously recommended to the National Government.
8vo. pp. 90. New York: *J. M. Sherwood*, 1865.

1613. FISCH, Georges. Les Etats Unis en 1861.
12mo. pp. 238. Paris: *Dentu*, 1862.

1614. FISH, Rev. George. Nine months in the United States during the Crisis; with an Introduction by the Hon. Arthur Kinnaird, M. P., and a Preface by the Rev. W. Arthur.
8vo. pp. xiii. 166. London: *James Nisbet & Co.*, 1863.

1615. FISHBACK, William M. Letter to the Hon. James H. Lane giving a detailed account of his conduct during the present Rebellion, and in defence of himself against the Charge of Disloyalty. *Senate Doc., No.* 129, *38th Cong., 1st Ses.,* 1864. *pp.* 4.

1616. FISHER, Geo. Adams. The Yankee Conscript; or Eighteen months in Dixie. With an Introduction by the Rev. William Dickson.
12mo. pp. Philadelphia : *J W. Daughaday*, 1864.
Narrative of the author's experience as a compulsory soldier in the rebel army.

1617. FISHER, Prof. George P. National Faults. A Sermon delivered in Yale College on Fast Day, April 6, 1860.
8vo. pp. 14. New Haven: *Tuttle & Morehouse*, 1860.

1618. FISHER, Herbert W. Considerations on the Origin of the American War.
12mo. pp. vi and 97. London: *Macmillan & Co.*, 1865.

1619. FISHER, James H., of Buffalo, N. Y. The Federal Constitution; its Claims upon the Educated Men of the Country. An Address before the Alumni of Hobart College. Delivered in Geneva, July 16, 1862. 8vo. pp. 6.

1620. FISHER, J. Francis. The Degradation of our Representative System and Reform.
8vo. pp. 57. Philadelphia: *C. Sherman & Co.*, 1863.

1621. FISHER, Richard S. A Chronological History of the Civil War in America.
8vo. pp. 160. New York : *Johnson & Ward,* 1863.

1622. FISHER, Sidney Geo. The Trial of the Constitution.
8vo. pp. 391. Philadelphia : *J. B. Lippincott & Co.,* 1862.

1623. —— The Bible and Slavery. *North American Rev., Jan.,* 1864.

1624. —— Duties on Exports. Ibid. *July,* 1865.

1625. —— Reply to a pamphlet recently published by Sidney George Fisher, Esq., entitled " A National Currency."
8vo. pp. 18. Philadelphia : *John Campbell,* 1865.

1626. FISHER, Rev. S. W., DD. Light in Darkness. A Discourse delivered in Clinton, N. Y., before the Methodist, Baptist and Congregational Churches, November 27, 1862.
8vo. pp. 23. Clinton : *M. D. Raymond,* 1862.

1627. FISKE, John O. A Sermon on the Present National Troubles, delivered in the Winter Street Church, January 4, 1861.
8vo. pp. 19. Bath : *Daily Times Office,* 1861.

1628. FITCH, Charles E. The National Problem. An Oration delivered at Delphi, New York, July 4, 1861.
12mo. pp. 19. Syracuse : *Summers & Co.,* 1861.

1629. FITCH, Thomas. Address on the Life and Character of Colonel Edward D. Baker, at Placerville, Cal., February 6, 1862.
8vo. pp. 7. Placerville : *Republican Office,* 1862.

1630. FITZGERALD, Ross. (Captain in the Imperial Austrian Service.) A Visit to the Cities and Camps. of the Confederate States.
12mo. pp. vi and 300. Map. Lond. : *W. Blackwood & Sons,* '65.

1631. The Five Cotton States and New York; or Remarks upon the Social and Economical Aspects of the Southern Political Crisis, January, 1861. 8vo. pp. 64.

1632. The Flag of Truce. By the Chaplain.
12mo. pp. 12. Baltimore : *James Young,* 1862.

1633. The Flag of Truce. Dedicated to the Emperor of the French, by a White Republican.
Post 8vo. pp. 52. London : *J. Ridgeway,* 1862.

1634. FLANDERS, Henry. Must the War go on? An Inquiry whether the Union can be restored by any other means than

War, and whether Peace upon any other basis, would be safe or durable?

8vo. pp. 23. PHILADELPHIA : *W. S. & Alfred Martien*, 1863.

1635. FLETCHER, Lieut. Colonel. (Scot's Fusileer Guard's.) History of the American War.

2 vols. 8vo. Plans of Battles. LONDON : *Richard Bentley*, 1865.

1636. FLETCHER, JOHN. Studies on Slavery. In Easy Lessons. Compiled into eight studies, and subdivided into short lessons for the convenience of readers.

8vo. pp. 637. NATCHEZ : *Jackson Warner*, 1852.

"The author has analyzed the fountain of Moral Philosophy, and detected the bitter waters of error so industriously infused by the eloquent pens of Dr. Samuel Johnson, Dr. Paley, Dr. Channing, Dr. Wayland, Mr. Barnes and others." *Extract from the Publisher's Preface.*

1637. FLETCHER, Rev. JOSEPH. The American War. A Lecture.

8vo. pp. 16. MANCHESTER : (Eng.) *W. Irwin & Co.*, 1863.

1638. FLETCHER, Governor THOMAS C. Inaugural Message to the 23d General Assembly of the State of Missouri, Jan. 2, 1865.

8vo. pp. 13. JEFFERSON CITY : *W. A. Curry*, 1865.

1639. —— Missouri's Jubilee. Speech delivered in the State Capital, on the reception, by the Legislature, of the news of the passage of the Convention Ordinance abolishing Slavery in Missouri.

8vo. pp. 8. JEFFERSON CITY : *W. A. Curry*, 1865.

1640. FLORIDA EXPEDITION. Report of the Joint Committee on the Conduct of the War, on the Origin, Progress and Results of the late Expedition to Florida. *Senate Report, Committee, No. 47, 38th Congress, 1st Session*, 1864. 8vo. pp. 25.

1641. FLORIDA. Historical Sketch of the Third Annual Conquest of Florida. Captain Le Diable. "And behold, the whole herd ran violently * * * * and perished."—*Matthew.*

12mo. pp. 19. (Privately printed.) PORT ROYAL : S. C., 1864.

A Satire upon the operations of the Union army in the occupancy of Florida.

1642. FLOYD'S ACCEPTANCES. Opinion of Charles B. Goodrich upon the Acceptances of J. B. Floyd, Secretary of War, 1861.

8vo. pp. 21. WASHINGTON : *Scammell & Co.*, 1862.

1643. —— Case of Pierce and Bacon. Memorial to Congress. [Relative to the Acceptances of J. B. Floyd, Sec. of War.] 8vo. p. 20.

1644. —— Opinion of Edward Bates, Attorney General, on the validity of the Acceptances given by J. B. Floyd, Secretary of War, to Russell, Majors and Waddell.

8vo. pp. 17. WASHINGTON: *Government Printing Office*, 1862.

1645. FLOYD'S ACCEPTANCES. Memorial of Duncan, Sherman & Co. to Congress, January, 1863. (Relative to the Acceptances of John B. Floyd.) 8vo. p. 8.

1646, FOCHT, Rev. D. H. Our Country. A Sermon delivered by special appointment, in New Bloomfield, Penn., July 22, 1860.

8vo. pp. 71.   GETTYSBURG: (Pa.) *H. C. Neinstedt,* 1862.

1647. —— A Reply to the Charge of the Hon. James H. Graham, 1862. (Appended to the foregoing.) 8vo. pp. 8.

1648. FOCHT, D. H. Our National Day. An Address delivered at Ikesburg, Penn., on the 4th day of July, 1862.

8vo. pp. 28.   SELINSGROVE: *Kirchenbote Office,* 1862.

1649. FŒDERAL MONTHLY. A Party of the Future. A. J. H. Duganne. August, 1865.

Friends of America in England. August, 1865.

1650. —— Re-instatement and Suffrage. September, 1865.

Friends of America in England. September, 1865.

1651. —— Atlantic Monthly and Negro Suffrage. J. N. A. Oct.,'65.

State Taxation and United States Securities. October, 1865.

Review of Grant's Army. Jacques Bonhomme. October, 1865.

Manassas. A. J. H. Duganne. October, 1865.

The Future of our Country. H. C. Whittlesey. October, 1865.

1652. FOOT, Hon. S. Remarks to the Second Vermont Regiment, on the occasion of their departure from the city of New York, for the Seat of War, June 25, 1861. *National Republican, Washington, July* 6, 1861.

1653. FORD, SALLY ROCHESTER. Raids and Romances of Morgan and his Men.

12mo. pp. 417.   NEW YORK: *Charles B. Richardson,* 1864.

1654. FORD, Rev. WILLIAM. American Republicanism; its Success, its Perils, and the Duty of its present Supporters. Sermon delivered before the Citizens of Brandon, September 26, 1861.

8vo. pp. 24.   RUTLAND: *George A. Tuttle & Co.,* 1861.

1655. FOREIGN CONSPIRACY against the U. S. 8vo. pp. 43. (No date.)

1656. FORSTER, W. E. Speech on the Slaveholder's Rebellion, and

Prof. Goldwin Smith's Letter on the Morality of the Emancipation Proclamation.

8vo. pp. 15. MANCHESTER : *Union and Emancipation So.*, '63.

1657. FORTIFICATIONS. Report of the Committee on Military Affairs, upon Permanent Fortifications and Sea-Coast Defences.

8vo. pp. 528. *House of Representatives, Report No.* 86, 37th *Congress, 2d Session*, 1862.

1658. FORT LAFAYETTE LIFE, 1863-4. In Extracts from the " Right Flanker," a manuscript sheet circulating among the Southern Prisoners in Fort LaFayette, in 1863-4.

8vo. pp. 102. LONDON : *Simpkins, Marshall & Co.*, 1864.

1659. FORT ADAMS. Papers accompanying Joint Resolution in relation to the arming ot Fort Adams, Narragansett Bay. 37th *Congress, 2d Session Miscellaneous Document, No.* 79.

1660. FORTNIGHTLY REVIEW, 1865. Personal Recollections of President Lincoln, by M. D. Conway.

The Last six Days of Secession. Hon. Frank Lawley.

1661. FOSTER. Exposition of the Conduct of Charles Henry Foster, in regard to the Election of Congressmen from the Second District of North Carolina, on January 1, 1863. pp. 15.

1662. FOSTER, Hon. L. F. S., of Connecticut. Speech in the Senate of the United States on the Bill to repeal the Fugitive Slave Law, April 20, 1864. 8vo. pp. 16.

1663. FOSTER, JOHN W. War and Christianity irreconcilable. An Address to Christians.

8vo. pp. 46. PROVIDENCE : *For the author*, 1861.

1664. FOSTER, JOHN T. Four Days at Gettysburg. *Harpers' Magazine, February,* 1864.

1665. FOWLER. Rev. HENRY. Character and Death of Abraham Lincoln. A Discourse preached at Auburn, N. Y., Apr. 23, '65.

8vo. pp. 16. AUBURN : (N. Y.) *W. J. Moses*, 1865.

1666. FOWLER, JOHN, Jun. An Address on the Death of President Lincoln, delivered at New Rochelle, Westchester County, New York, April 20, 1865.

8vo. pp. 28. NEW YORK : *John A. Gray & Green,* 1865.

1667. FOWLER, P. H., DD. National Destruction threatens us ; and

20

Repentance of Sin and Reformation our only Hope of Escape.
A Discourse delivered in Utica, New York, July 28, 1861.
8vo. pp. 16.   UTICA : (N. Y.) *Roberts*, 1861.

1668. FOWLER, WM. C. The Sectional Controversy ; or Passages in
the Political History of the United States ; including the Causes
of the War between the Sections.
8vo. pp. 269.   NEW YORK : *C. Scribner*, 1863.

1669. FRANCIS, VALENTINE MOTT, M. D. The Fight for the Union.
A Poem.
8vo. pp. 14.   NEW YORK : *J. F. Trow*, 1863.

1670. LA FRANCE, le Mexique et les Etats Confédérés.
8vo. pp. 42.   PARIS : 1863.

1671. FRANKLIN ALMANAC, (The Old,) for the years 1862, 1863, 1864,
1865 and 1866.   Philadelphia : *A. Wince.*

This Almanac contains an excellent Diary of the Rebellion from its beginning.

1672. FRANKLIN, S. F.   Life and Character of Abraham Lincoln.
A Memorial Oration, delivered at Franklin, N. Y., June 1, 1865.
8vo. pp. 16.   DELHI : *Sturtevant & Co.*, 1865.

1673. FRANKLIN, Rev. THOMAS L.   Fast Day Sermon on the
Death of President Lincoln, preached at Mount Morris, New
York, April 20, 1865. *Union and Constitution, Mount Morris,
New York, May* 11, 1865.

1674. FRANKLIN, Maj. General WILLIAM B.   Reply to the Report
of the Joint Committee of Congress on the Conduct on the War,
submitted to the public on the 6th of April, 1863.   With a map.
8vo. pp. 31.   NEW YORK : *D. Van Nostrand*, 1863.

1675. FRANSIOLI, Rev. JOSEPH, (of St. Peter's Catholic Church,
Brooklyn, N. Y.) Patriotism, a Christian Virtue. A Sermon
preached July 26. 1863. *Loyal Pub. So., No.* 24, 1863.   *pp.* 8.

1676 FRAZER'S MAGAZINE.   The Contest in American.   By John
Stuart Mill.   February, 1862.
Universal Suffrage in the United States, and its Consequences.
July, 1862.
North and South.   The Controversy in a Colloquy.   Sept., 1862.
North and South.   The Two Constitutions.   October, 1862.
North and South ; or Who is the Traitor.   November, 1862.

1677. —— Negroes and Slavery in the United States,   February, '63.

An American Refugee in London. June, 1863.

England and America. October, 1863.

1678. FRAZER'S MAGAZINE Three Years of War in America. June, 1864.

1679. —— Virginia, First and Last. March, 1865.

Regulars and Volunteers. April, 1865.

A Visit to Gen. Butler and the Army of the James. Apr., 1865.

The Assassination of President Lincoln. June, 1865.

1680. FREE NEGROISM ; or the Results of Emancipation in the North and the West India Islands. Idleness of the Negro, his Return to Savageism, and the effect of Emancipation upon the Laboring Classes.

8vo. pp. 32. NEW YORK : *Van Evrie, Horton & Co.*, 1862.

1681. FREEDMAN, JOHN J. Is the Act entitled " An Act for enrolling and calling out the National Forces, and for other purposes," passed March 3, 1863, Constitutional or not ?

8vo. pp. 62. NEW YORK : *George S. Diossy*, 1863.

1682. FREEDMEN. First Annual Report of the Educational Commission for Freedmen. May, 1863.

8vo. pp. 22. BOSTON : *Prentiss & Deland*, 1863.

1683. —— The same, with Extracts from Letters of Teachers.

8vo. pp. 28. BOSTON : *David Clapp*, 1863.

1684. —— Extracts of Letters received by the Educational Commission, Boston, from Teachers at Port Royal and its vicinity.

4to. pp. 4.

1685. —— Second Series of Extracts from the same. 4to. pp. 4.

1686. —— Third Series of Extracts from the same. June 17, 1863.

4to. pp. 4.

1687. —— Fourth Series of Extracts from the same. Jan. 1, 1864.

1688. —— New England Freedmen's Aid Society. Second Annual Report of. (Educational Commission.) Presented Apr. 21, '64.

8vo. pp. 86. BOSTON : *Office of the Society*, 1865.

1689. —— First Annual Report of the National Freedmen's Relief Association of the District of Columbia. 8vo. pp. 8.

1690. —— Semi-Annual Report of the Volunteer Teachers of Washington and vicinity, 1864.

1691. FREEDMEN'S INQUIRY COMMISSION, (American.) Preliminary

Report touching the Management and Condition of Emancipated
Refugees, made to the Secretary of War, June 30, 1863.
8vo. pp. 40.   New York : *John F. Trow*, 1863.

1692. Freedmen's Inquiry Commission. Report of the Secretary of
War, communicating the Preliminary, and also the Final Report
of the American Freedmen's Inquiry Commission. By R. Dale
Owen, J. McKayes, and Samuel G. Howe, Commissioners.
8vo. pp. 110.   *Sen. Ex. Doc., No.* 53, 38*th Cong.,* 1*st Sess.,* '64.

1693. Freedmen. Statistics of the operations of the Executive Board
of Friends' Association of Philadelphia and its vicinity, for the
Relief of Colored Freedmen ; with the Report of Samuel R.
Shepley, President of the Board, of his Visit to the Camps of the
Freedmen on the Mississippi River.
12mo pp. 33.   Philadelphia: *Inquirer Office*, 1864.

1694. —— Northwestern Freedmen's Aid Commission, Second Annual Report of, presented at Chicago, April 13, 1865.
8vo. pp. 24.   Chicago : *James Barnet*, 1865.

1695. —— First Annual Report of the National Freedmen's Relief
Association. New York, February 19, 1863. 4to. pp. 3.

1696. —— Monthly Report of same, No. 2. 4to. pp. 4.

1697. —— Annual Report of the Port Royal Relief Committee. Philadelphia, March 26, 1863.

1698. —— Annual Report of the Superintendent of Negro Affairs in
North Carolina, 1864. With an Appendix, containing the History and Management of the Freedmen up to June 1, 1865. By
Horace James, Superintendent.
8vo. pp. 64.   Boston : *W. F. Brown & Co.*, 1865.

1699. —— Report of a Committee of the Representatives of New
York Yearly Meeting of Friends, upon the Wants of Colored
Refugees. [New York, 1863.] 8vo pp. 30.

1700. —— Second Report, 5th month 27, 1863. [New York.] pp. 15.

1701. —— Report of the General Superintendent of Freedmen. Department of the Tennessee and State of Arkansas, for 1864.
8vo. pp. 98.   Memphis : (Tenn.) 1865.

1702. —— Report and Extracts relating to the Colored Schools in the
Department of the Tennessee and State of Arkansas, Nov. 30,'64.
12mo. pp. 20.   Memphis : *Freedmen's Press*, 1864.

1703. FREEDMEN. Final Report of Freedmen Schools in the Department of Tennessee and Arkansas, lately under the supervision of Colonel John Eaton, Jr. 1864–5.

8vo. pp. 19. VICKSBURG : (Miss.) *Freedmen Press*, 1865.

1704. FREEDMEN OF LOUISIANA. Annual Report of Thomas W. Conway, Superintendent of Bureau of Free Labor, Department of the Gulf, to Major General Hurlbut. New Orleans, 1864.

1705. —— Final Report of the Bureau of Free Labor, Department of the Gulf, to Maj. General E. R. S. Canby, Commanding. By Thomas W. Conway, General Superintendent.

8vo. pp. 37. NEW ORLEANS: *Times Office*, 1865.

1706. FREEDMEN. Report of the Board of Education for Freedmen, Department of the Gulf, for the year 1864.

8vo. pp. 27. NEW ORLEANS : *Office of the True Delta*, 1865.

1707. —— Conference between Secretary Stanton, General Sherman and Freedmen in Savannah. February 12, 1865.

8vo. pp. NEW YORK: 1865.

1708. FREEDMEN'S RELIEF. Report of the Com. of the Contraband's Relief Commission of Cincinnati, Ohio, proposing a Plan for the occupation and government of vacated territory in the Seceded States.

8vo. pp. 16. CINCINNATI: *Gazette Office*, 1863.

1709. FREEDMEN. Rights of the Colored Race to Citizenship and Representation ; and the Guilt and Consequences of legislation against them. By the Rev. George B. Cheever.

8vo. pp. 28. NEW YORK : *Francis & Loutrel*, 1864.

1710. —— Proceedings of the National Convention of Colored Men, held in Syracuse, N. Y., October, 1864 ; with the Bill of Wrongs and Rights, and the Address to the American People.

8vo. pp. 62. BOSTON : 1864.

1711. —— First Annual Report of the Executive Committee of Barnard Freemen's Aid Society, Dorchester, Mass., 1865.

1712. —— Annual Meeting of the North Western Freedmen's Aid Commission, Chicago, 1864.

1713. —— Minutes of Conventions of Freedmen's Commissions, Indianapolis, July, 1864.

1714. —— Annual Report of the Pennsylvania Freedmen's Relief Association, Philadelphia, March, 1864.

1715. FREEDMEN. Report of the National Freedmen's Relief Association, New York, 1864.

1716. —— Condition of the Freedmen of Mississippi. By James E. Yeatman. December 17, 1863.

1717. —— Report of Meeting to consider the condition of the Freed People of South Carolina; with Speeches of Bishop Potter and others. Philadelphia, November 3, 1863.

1718. —— Extracts from Reports of Superintendents of Freedmen. Compiled by the Rev. Joseph Warren. Vicksburg, June, 1864.

1719. —— The Negroes and Africans as Freedmen and Soldiers. 8vo. pp. 30. LONDON : *Ladies' Emancipation Society,* 1864.

1720. —— Facts concerning the Freedmen. Their Capacity and Destiny. Collected and published by the Emancipation League. 8vo. pp. 12. BOSTON: *Commercial Printing House,* 1863.

1721. —— Report of the Committee on Territories upon a bill " to set apart a Portion of the State of Texas for the use of persons of African descent. *Senate Report Committee, No.* 8, 38*th Congress,* 1*st Session,* 1864. *pp.* 4.

1722. —— Report of the minority of the Select Committee on Emancipation relative to the Bill to establish a Bureau of Freedmen's Affairs, January 20, 1864. *House of Representatives, Report No.* 2, 38*th Congress,* 1*st Session,* 1864. *pp.* 4.

1723. —— First Annual Report of the Executive Committee of Barnard Freedmen's Aid Society, of Dorchester, Mass., 1865.

1724. —— The First Annual Report of the Education Board of the Association of Friends at Philadelphia and its vicinity, for the Relief of Colored Freedmen. 8vo. pp. 39. BIRMINGHAM: (Eng.) *White & Pike,* 1864.

1725. —— of Port Royal, South Carolina, Official Reports of, by Edward L. Pierce. *Rebellion Record.*

1726. FREEDMEN AT FORTRESS MONROE. Report of the General Superintendent of Negro Affairs, Lieut. Colonel J. Burnham Kinsman, June 1, 1864.

1727. —— Mission of the Freed Contrabands at Fortress Monroe. Supplement to the American Missionary, October, 1861.

1728. —— Military Districts. Letter from the Secretary of War *Executive Document,* 37*th Congress, March* 25, 1862.

1729. —— Contrabands at Fortress Monroe. *Atlantic Monthly, Nov.*, '61.

1730. FREEDMEN'S AFFAIRS. Speech of the Hon. W. D. Kelley on, delivered in the House of Reps., February 23, 1864. 8vo. pp. 8

1731. FREEDMAN'S AID SOCIETY, Letter of, to President Lincoln. 8vo. pp. 15. WASHINGTON: *McGill & Witherow*, 1863.

1732. FREEDMEN'S (Western) BULLETIN. Chicago, 1864–5. 8vo. A Monthly Journal, the first number issued in July, 1864.

1733. THE FREEDMEN'S RECORD. Boston, 1865. 8vo.

A monthly periodical, published in Boston, the organ of the New England Freedmen's Aid Society. The work commenced in January, 1865.

1734. THE NATIONAL FREEDMAN, New York.

1735. THE FREEDMAN'S HARP; being a Selection of Patriotic Hymns, designed to excite a greater love for Freedom and a deeper hatred to Slavery; with President Lincoln's Proclamation of Liberty. 12mo. pp. 36. PROVIDENCE: *A. Crawford Greene.*

1736. FREEDMAN'S SAVING and Trust Company. An Act to Incorporate, Approved March 3, 1865. 8vo. pp. 8. NEW YORK: *W. C. Bryant & Co.*, 1865.

1737. FREED PEOPLE. Brief Report of the Services rendered by the Freed People to the United States Army in North Carolina, in the Spring of 1862, after the Battle of Newbern. 8vo. pp. 63. NEW YORK: *Vincent Colyer*, 1865.

For other works relating to Freedmen, see *Atlantic Monthly, Colored Americans, Colored Enlistments.*

1738. FREELAND, EDWARD B. The Great Riot. *Continental Monthly for September*, 1863.

1739. FRELIGH, J. H., of Tennessee. Union or Secession; Which is best? 8vo. pp. 35. MEMPHIS: *January*, 1861.

1740. FRELINGHUYSEN, FREDERICK T. Oration by. Obsequies of Abraham Lincoln, in Newark, N. J., April 19, 1865. 8vo. pp. 23. NEWARK: (N. J.) *Advertiser Office*, 1865.

1741. FREMANTLE, Lieut. Colonel, (Coldstream Guards.) Three months in the Southern States, April to June, 1863. 8vo. pp. vii and 316. LONDON: *Blackwood & Sons*, 1863.

1742. —— The same work. 8vo. pp. 309. NEW YORK: *John Bradburn*, 1864.

1743. FREMOND, Sarah Parker. The Negroes and Anglo-Africans, as Freedmen and Soldiers.
12mo. pp. 30. London: *Ladies' Emancipation Society*, 1864.

1744. FREMONT, Jessie Benton. The Story of the Guard; A Chronicle of the War.
12mo. pp. 227. Boston: *Ticknor & Fields*, 1863.

1745. FRENCH, Rev. Edward W. Our Present Duty. A Sermon preached in South Bergen, N. Jersey, July 20, 1862.
8vo. pp. 16. New York: *W. C. Bryant & Co.*, 1862.

1746. Friends in New England. Memorial to the General Assembly of Rhode Island in relation to bearing Arms, 1863. Record of a Special Meeting of Sufferings, held in Boston, 30th 7th month, 1863, relative to the Conscription Law. Proceedings of a Meeting for Sufferings, held in Providence, R. I., 24th of 3d month, 1863. 4to. 3 sheets.

1747. Friends. Epistle to the Members of the Yearly Meeting of Friends, held at Philadelphia, (18th of 12th month, 1863.)
12mo. pp. 12. Philadelphia: *W. K. Bellows*, 1863.

1748. FROST, Mrs. J. Blakeslee. The Rebellion in the United States; or the War of 1861; being a complete History of its Rise and Progress.
8vo. pp. 192. Hartford: 1862.

1749. FROTHINGHAM, Rev. O. B. The Let-Alone Policy. A Sermon, June 9, 1861.
12mo. pp. 16. New York: 5 Beekman street, 1861.

1750. —— The Morality of the Riot. A Sermon at Ebbitt Hall, July 19, 1863.
12mo. pp. 20. New York: *David G. Francis*, 1863.

1751. —— Seeds and Shells. A Sermon preached in New York, November 17, 1861.
8vo. pp. 22. New York: *Wyncoop & Co.*, 1862.

1752. —— New Year's Gifts of the Spirit. A Discourse.
8vo. pp. 25–44. New York: *David G. Francis*, 1865.
This Discourse has reference to the great successes that attended the Union Armies during a short period previous to January, 1865.

1753. —— The Murdered President. *The Friend of Progress for June*, 1865.

1754. FRY Rev. Jacob. Trembling for the Ark of God; or, the

Danger and Duty of the Church, in the present Crisis. A Sermon preached in the First Lutheran Church, Carlisle, Pennsylvania, December 30, 1860.

8vo. pp 21. *E. Cornman*, 1861.

1755. FUGITT, Rev. James P. The Union of Patriots for the sake of the Union. An Oration on the Union. Delivered at Catonsville, June 30, 1860.

8vo. pp. 16. Baltimore : *Joseph Robinson*, 1860.

1756. —— Our Country and Slavery. A friendly Word to the Rev. Francis Hawks, DD., and other Northern Clergymen.

8vo. pp. 36. Baltimore: *Joseph Robinson*, 1861.

1757. —— Shall the Federal Government instigate a Servile War? Is Slaveholding Constitutional and Scriptural?

8vo. pp. 35. Baltimore : *John D. Toy*, 1862.

1758. —— A Plea for Peace. A Sermon preached in Baltimore, September 26, 1861.

8vo. pp. 17. Baltimore : *John D. Toy*, 1861.

1759. —— Is Slaveholding Constitutional and Scriptural?

8vo. pp. Baltimore : *John D. Toy*, 1862.

1760. Fugitive Slave Laws. A Compilation of the Laws of the United States and of States, in relation to Fugitives from Labor.

8vo. pp. 32. Washington : *Taylor & Maury*, 1860.

1761. FULLER, Rev. Dr. Mercy Remembered in Wrath. A Sermon preached on Fast Day, September 26, 1861.

8vo. pp. 24. Baltimore : *Henry Taylor*, 1861.

1762. FULLER, Richard. Our Duty to the African Race. An Address delivered at Washington, D. C., January 21, 1851.

8vo. pp. 17. Baltimore : *W. M. Innes*, 1851.

1763. FULLERTON, Alexander, Jun. Coercion a Failure, Necessarily and Actually. Philadelphia, 1863. 8vo. pp. 16.

1764. FULTON, Rev. J. D. "Who is my Neighbor?" A Sermon preached in the Baptist Church, Albany, N. Y., September 14, 1862. 8vo. pp. 8.

1765. FUNK, Mr. Copperheads under the Heel of an Illinois Farmer. 1863. pp. 3.

1766. FURNESS, Rev. Wm. H. The Blessing of Abolition. A Dis-

21

course delivered in the First Congregational Unitarian Church, July 1, 1860.

8vo. pp. 26.   PHILADELPHIA : *C. Sherman & Sons,* 1860.

1767. FURNESS, Rev. W. H. Our Duty as Conservatives. A Discourse delivered in Philadelphia, November 25, 1860, occasioned by the threatened Secession of some of the Southern States.

8vo. pp. 20.   PHILADELPHIA : *C. Sherman & Sons,* 1860.

1768. —— A Discourse on the occasion of the National Fast, September 26, 1861.

8vo. pp. 20.   PHILADELPHIA : *T. B. Pugh,* 1861.

1769. —— The Declaration of Independence. A Discourse delivered June 29, 1862.

8vo. pp. 18.   PHILADELPHIA : *C. Sherman & Sons,* 1862.

1770. —— A Thanksgiving Discourse, delivered in Philadelphia, April 13, 1862, in accordance with the recommendation of the President of the United States.

8vo. pp. 17.   PHILADELPHIA : *T. B. Pugh,* 1862.

1771. —— England and America. A Discourse delivered December 22, 1861.

8vo. pp. 15.   PHILADELPHIA : *Privately printed,* 1861.

1772. FURNESS, Rev. W. H. A Word of Consolation for the Kindred of those who have fallen in Battle ; together with the Funeral Services at the Burial of Lieut. A. W. Peabody, Sept. 26,'62.

8vo. pp. 23.   PHILADELPHIA : *Crissey & Markley,* 1862.

1773. —— Our American Institutions. A Thanksgiving Discourse, August 6, 1863.

8vo. pp. 21.   PHILADELPHIA : *T. B. Pugh,* 1863.

1774. —— A Voice of the Hour. A Discourse, January 10, 1864.

8vo. pp. 15.   PHILADELPHIA : *Crissey & Markley,* 1864.

1775. FURNESS, Mrs. Our Soldiers. *Atlantic Monthly, March,* '64.

1776. THE FUTURE of the Country. By a Patriot. 8vo. pp. 28.

GADDIS, Rev. M. P. Sermon upon the Assassination of Abraham Lincoln, delivered at Cincinnati, April 16, 1865.

8vo. pp. 15.   CINCINNATI : *Times Office,* 1865.

1778. GAGE, WILLIAM L. The War ; its Necessity, and its relation to Christian Duty. A Discourse before the New Hampshire Volunteers, May 5, 1861. 8vo. pp. 4.

1779. GAIL, G. W., of Baltimore. Suggestions for Taxing Tobacco for the use of the Tobacconists' National Association.
8vo. pp. 16. BALTIMORE: *John Murphy & Co.*, 1865.

1780. GALLATIN, JAMES. Two Letters to the Hon. S. P. Chase, Secretary of the Treasury.
8vo. pp. 21. NEW YORK; *Privately printed*, 1861.

1781. —— Letter to Wm. P. Fessenden on Financial Affairs. New York, June 14, 1862. 4to. pp. 3.

1782. —— Government Finances and the Currency. Letters to Hon. David Wilmot, United States Senator from Pennsylvania.
8vo. pp. 31. NEW YORK: *Hall, Clayton & Co.*, 1862.

1783. —— Letter to the Hon. Wm. P. Fessenden. The proposed United States Banking System, and further Issues of Legal Tender.
8vo. pp. 11. NEW YORK: *J. W. Amerman*, 1863.

1784. —— Letter to Hon. Samuel Hooper of Massachusetts, on the National Finances and Currency.
8vo. pp. 8. NEW YORK: *Hall, Clayton & Medole*, 1863.

1785. —— The National Debt, Taxation, Currency, and Banking System of the United States; with Remarks on the Report of the Secretary of the Treasury.
8vo. pp. 61. NEW YORK: *Hosford & Ketcham*, 1864.

1786. —— The National Finances, Currency, Banking, etc.; being a Reply to a Speech in Congress, by Hon. Samuel Hooper.
8vo. pp. 34. NEW YORK: *Clayton & Medole*, 1864.

1787. —— Letter on Financial Affairs, to A. Stockley, Esq., President of the Bank of Smyrna. New York, June 24, 1865. 4to. pp. 2.

1788. GALLAUDET, Rev. THOMAS. A Discourse delivered on the National Fast Day, September 26, 1861.
8vo. pp. 8. NEW YORK: *Henry Spear*, 1861.

1789. GANNETT, Rev. EZRA S. Relation of the North to Slavery. A Discourse preached in Boston, June 11, 1854.
8vo. pp. 23. BOSTON: *Crosby, Nichols & Co.*, 1854.

1790. —— Repentance amidst Deliverance and Mobs. Two Discourses preached July 12 and July 19, 1863.
8vo. pp. 31. BOSTON: *Crosby & Nichols*, 1863.

1791. GANNETT, W. C. The Freedmen of Port Royal. *North American Review, July*, 1865.

1792. GANS, Hon. G. W. The War for the Union; or the Rights of the Republic. November 19, 1861. 8vo. pp. 7.

1793. GANTT, Brig. General E. W., C. S. A. Address at Little Rock, Arkansas, October 7, 1863. pp. 29.

1794. GARDNER, DANIEL. A Treatise on the Law of the American Rebellion, and our True Policy, Domestic and Foreign. 8vo. pp. 20. NEW YORK: *J. W. Amerman*, 1862.

1795. —— A Treatise on the Martial Power of the President of the United States. 8vo. pp. 8.

1796. GARDNER, D. T. The Fall of Fort Morgan. A Poem. Delivered at the Celebration of the Birthday of Washington, by the Cooper Union, February 20, 1865. 18mo. pp. 8.

1797. GARDNER, H. W., Agent of the Providence Steam Engine Company. Correspondence with the Secretary of the Navy, relative to certain Work for the Navy. pp. 15.

1798. GARFIELD, JAMES A., of Ohio. Treason in Congress. Speech in Reply to Alexander Long, in favor of Abandoning the War and Recognizing the Southern Confederacy. House of Representatives, April 8, 1864. 8vo. pp. 8.

1799. GARRARD, T. T. (General.) Letter from the Secretary of War, transmitting papers relative to Claim for the Destruction of Salt Works, by Order of Gen. Buell, in 1862. *House of Representatives, Ex. Document, 38th Cong., 1st Ses.*, 1864. pp. 30.

1800. GARRETT, AUGUSTA B. A Raid on the Evening's Camp. *Knickerbocker Magazine, April*, 1863.

1801. GARREY, EMILE. Grandeur et Avenir des Etats Unis. 8vo. pp. 48. PARIS: *Dentu*, 1863.

1802. GARRISON, Rev. J. F. The Teachings of the Crisis. Address delivered in Camden, N. J., on the occasion of the Funeral of Abraham Lincoln, April 19, 1865. 8vo. pp. 20. CAMDEN: (N. J.) *S. Chew*, 1865.

1803. GARRISON, WILLIAM LLOYD, Selections from the Writings and Speeches of, with an Appendix. 12mo. pp. 416. BOSTON: *R. F. Wallcut*, 1852.

1804. —— The "Infidelity" of Abolitionism. 12mo. pp. 12. NEW YORK: *American Anti-Slavery Soc.*, 1860.

1805. GARRISON, W. L.   The Abolitionists and their relations to the War.   A Lecture delivered in the Cooper Institute, New York, January 14, 1862.   (Pulpit and Rostrum, No. 26.)

1806. GARVER, Rev. D.   Our Country in the Light of History.   An Address before the Alumni Association of Pennsylvania College, Gettysburg, Penn., September 18, 1861.
8vo. pp. 32.   GETTYSBURG : *A. D. Beuhler*, 1861.

1807. GASPARIN, AGENOR DE.   Les Etats Unis en 1861.   Un Grand Peuple qui se Relève.
12mo. pp. 415.   PARIS : *Michel Levy Frères*, 1862.

1808. —— The Uprising of a Great People.   The United States in 1861.   Translated from the French by Mary L. Booth.
12mo. pp. 263.   NEW YORK : *C. Scribner*, 1861.

1809. —— The same work, abridged from the French, and translated by the Rev. J. McClintock, DD., with Appendices.
12mo. pp. 82.   LONDON : *Sampson, Low & Co.*, 1861.

1810. —— Une Parole de Paix, sur le différence entre l'Angleterre et les Etats Unis.
8vo. pp. 31.   PARIS : *Michel Levy Frères*, 1862.

1811. —— A Word of Peace on the American Question.   Translated from the French by the Rev. J. McClintock, DD.
12mo. pp. 24.   LONDON : *Sampson, Low & Co.*, 1861.

1812. —— L'Amérique devant L'Europe, Principes et Intérêts.
8vo. pp. 553.   PARIS : *Michel Levy Frères*, 1862.

1813. —— America before Europe.   Principles and Interests.   Translated by Mary L. Booth.
12mo. pp. 419.   NEW YORK : *C. Scribner*, 1862.

1814. —— Réponse de M. M. DeGasparin, Laboulaye, Martin et Cochin, à la Ligue Loyale de New York.
8vo. pp. 20.   *Loyal Publication Society, No.* 41, 1864.

1815. —— Reply to Messrs. Agenor de Gasparin. Ed. Laboulaye, Henri Martin, Augustin Cochin, to the Loyal National League of New York ; together with the Address of the League.
8vo. pp. 30.   *Loyal Publication Society, No.* 42, 1864.

1816. —— The same.   12mo. pp. 17.   Liverpool : *D. Marples*, 1864.

1817. —— Antwort der Herren A. de Gasparin, Ed. Laboulaye und anderer Freunde Amerikas in Frankreich an die Loyal National League.

8vo. pp. 11. *Loyal Publication Society, No.* 43, 1864.

1818. GAY, GEORGE H., M. D. A few Remarks on the Primary Treatment of Wounds received in battle. A Report to the Surgeon General of Massachusetts.

8vo. pp. 8. BOSTON: *David Clapp,* 1862.

1819. GAYLORD, Rev. WM. L. The Soldier, God's Minister. A Discourse delivered in Fitzwilliam, N. H., October 5, 1862.

8vo. pp. 21. FITCHBURG: *"Rollstone Office,"* 1862.

1820. GEER, Capt. J. J. Beyond the Lines; or a Yankee Prisoner loose in Dixie. With an Introduction by Rev. Alexander Clark.

12mo. pp. PHILADELPHIA : *J. W. Daughaday,* 1863.

1821. GENERALS, MAJOR AND BRIGADIER, who are without Commands equal to a Brigade ; also the number of Major and Brigadier Generals who are in Command of Departments and Posts in the Loyal States. Report of the Secretary of War. *Senate Executive Document, No.* 5, 38*th Congress,* 1*st Sess.,* 1863. 8vo. pp. 6.

1822. GENERAL AID SOCIETY for the Army, Buffalo, N. Y., First Annual Report of. January 1, 1862, to January 1, 1863.

8vo. pp. 15. BUFFALO : *Franklin Press,* 1863.

1823. GENERAL OFFICERS, A List of, nominated to the United States Senate during the Session of July, 1861, and January, 1862. *Confidential, April* 7, 1862. pp. 10.

1824. GENERAL ORDERS of the War Department, from January 18, 1861, to December 26, 1861. Numbers 1 to 110.

1825. GENERAL ORDERS of the War Department, from January 6, 1862, to December 30, 1862. Numbers 1 to 217.

1826. GENERAL ORDERS of the War Department, from January 2, 1863, to December 28, 1863. Numbers 1 to 400.

1827. GENERAL ORDERS of the War Department, from January 1, 1864, to December 29, 1864. Numbers 1 to 300.

The Orders are all issued from the Adjutant General's Office, now Department, at Washington.

1828. GENERAL ORDERS, Department of the East. Headquarters, New York City. Jan. 12, 1862, to Dec. 30, 1864. Nos. 1 to 102.

1829. GENERAL ORDERS of the War Department; embracing the years 1861, 1862 and 1863, adapted for the use of the Army and Navy of the United States. Chronologically Arranged, with an Alphabetical Index. By T. O'Brien and O. Diefendorf.

2 v. 8vo. p. xxiv, 472 & xxxi, 710. N. YORK: *Daly & Miller,* '64.

1830. GERDES, F. H. The Surrender of Forts Jackson and St. Phillip, on the Mississippi. *Continental Monthly, April,* 1863.

1831. —— Reconnoisance near Fort Morgan, and Expedition to Lake Ponchartrain and Pearl River, by the Mortar Flotilla of Capt. D. D. Porter, U. S. N. September, 1863.

1832. A GERM of severe Ethical Analysis, Pure Philosophy and Inflexible Truth. The Corner Stone of Patriotism. Government and Nationality, and the only Practical Basis for restored Peace. Danbury, Connecticut, 1862. pp. 7.

1833. GETTYSBURG. Mr. Everett's Address at the Consecration of the National Cemetery, November 19, 1863; with the Address of President Lincoln, and the other Exercises on the occasion.

8vo. pp. 87. BOSTON: *Little, Brown & Co.,* 1864.

1834. —— An Oration delivered on the Battle Field of Gettysburg, (November 19, 1863,) at the Consecration of the Cemetery prepared for the Interment of the Remains of those who fell in the Battles of July 1, 2 and 3, 1863, by Edward Everett; to which is added Details of the Ceremonies, Description of the Battle Field, Details of the Battles, etc.

8vo. pp. 48. NEW YORK: *Baker & Godwin,* 1863.

1735. —— Report of the Operations of the Sanitary Commission, during and after the Battles at Gettysburg, July 1, 2 and 3, 1854.

8vo. pp. 29. NEW YORK: *W. C. Bryant & Co.,* 1863.

1836. —— Sketch of the Battles of. By J. C. Ditterline. 8vo. p. 24.

1837. —— Three Weeks at Gettysburg.

12mo. pp. 24. NEW YORK: *A. D. F. Randolph,* 1863.

1838. —— Leaves from the Battle Field of Gettysburg. A Series of Letters from a Field Hospital. By Mrs. Edmund A. Souder.

12mo. pp. 142. PHILADELPHIA: *Clayton Press,* 1864.

1839. —— Names of the Officers and Privates who fell in the Battle of Gettysburg, and in the Skirmishes incident thereto, or who died of wounds received in that Battle.

Folio pp. 153. *Printed for the National Cemetery Association.*

Thirty copies of this volume were printed by order of the Commissioners of the Soldiers' National Cemetery Association. It includes the names of all the Officers and Privates who are buried in the Soldiers' Cemetery, as far as known. Copies were sent to the Adjutant General of each State, whose Regiments were in the Battle of Gettysburg, in order that they might complete the List of the men killed, from the official returns.

1840. GETTYSBURG. Report of the Select Committee relative to the Soldiers' National Cemetery : together with the accompanying Documents, as reported by the House of Representatives of Pennsylvania, March 31, 1864.

8vo. pp. 108.   HARRISBURG : *Singuly & Myers*, 1864.
With Map of the Battle Field and Plan of the Cemetery.

1841. —— Proceedings of the Commissioners of the Soldier's National Cemetery Association, held at Philadelphia, on the 7th of December, 1864.

8vo. pp. 8.   PROVIDENCE : *Knowles, Anthony & Co,*, 1864.

1842. —— Charter and Proceedings of the Board of Commissioners of the Soldiers' National Cemetery Association.

8vo. pp. 20.   PROVIDENCE : *Knowles, Anthony & Co.*, 1864.

1843. —— Notes on the Rebel Invasion of Maryland and Pennsylvania, and the Battle of Gettysburg, July 1, 2 and 3, 1863. By M. Jacobs.

12mo. pp. 47.   PHILADELPHIA : *J. B. Lippincott & Co.*, 1864.

1844. —— Report of the Committee recommending that a Pension be granted to John L. Burns, of Gettysburg.

8vo. pp. 2.   *Sen. Rep. Com., No.* 13, 38*th Cong.*, 1*st Sess.*,'64.
Mr. Burns, an aged citizen of Gettysburg, was the only person of that place who took up arms, and joined the Federal Army in its defence.

1845. —— Our Campaign around Gettysburg; being a Memorial of what was endured, suffered and accomplished by the 23d Regiment, (N. Y. S. N. G.) and other Regiments, during the Second Rebel Invasion of the Loyal States, in June and July, 1863.

12mo. pp. 168.   BROOKLYN : *A. H. Rome & Brothers*, 1864.

1846. —— Sketch of the Battles of. Compiled from the personal Observation of eye-witnesses. See *Ditterline.*

1847. —— Report to the Governor of the State of Michigan, on the Soldiers' National Monument at Gettysburg, 1864. 8vo. pp. 6.

1848. —— Report of W. G. Veazey, Agent of the State of Vermont, in relation to the National Cemetery, 1864. pp. 3.

1849. GETTYSBURG. Report of the Hon. Paul Dillingham, Commissioner of Vermont, on the National Cemetery, September 28, 1864. pp. 6.

1850. —— First Annual Report of the Commissioners composing the Board of Managers of the Soldiers' National Cemetery, at Gettysburg, Pennsylvania, made December 7, 1864.
8vo. pp. 32. PHILADELPHIA : *King & Baird,* 1864.

1851. —— Ceremonies of the Laying of the Corner Stone of the Soldiers' National Monument at, July 4, 1865. *Soldiers' Casket, August,* 1865.

1852. —— Report of the Committee, [of the State of Maine,] on the Soldiers' National Cemetery, 1865. pp. 8.

1853. —— Revised Report of the Select Committee relative to the Soldiers' National Cemetery, at Gettysburg ; with the accompanying Documents, as reported to the House of Representatives of Pennsylvania.
8vo. pp. 212. HARRISBURG : *Singerly & Myers,* 1865.

1854. —— Oration of Major General O. O. Howard and Speech of Governor Curtin, at the Laying of the Corner Stone of the Monument in the Soldiers' National Cemetery, at Gettysburg, July 4, 1865 ; with the other Exercises of the occasion.
8vo. pp. GETTYSBURG : *Auginbaugh & Wible,* 1865.

1855. —— Report of John R. Bartlett, Commissioner of Rhode Island, to the General Assembly of Rhode Island, on the Soldiers' National Monument, January, 1866. pp. 6.

1856. —— Proceedings and Second Annual Report of the Commissioners of the Soldiers' National Cemetery, for the year ending November 30, 1865.
8vo. pp. 28. GETTYSBURG : *J. E. Wible,* 1865.

1857. GHOLSON, Hon. THOMAS S., of Virginia. Speech on the Policy of Employing Negro Troops, and the Duty of all Classes to aid in the Prosecution of the War. Delivered in the House of Representatives of the Confederate States, February 1, 1865.
8vo. pp. 20. RICHMOND : *G. P. Evans & Co.,* 1865.

1858. GIBBONS, CHARLES. Oration before the Union League of Philadelphia, on July 4, 1865.
8vo. pp. 32. PHILADELPHIA : *King & Baird,* 1865.
22

1859. GIDDINGS, Joshua R. The Exiles of Florida; or the Crimes committed by our Government against the Maroons, who fled from South Carolina and other Slave States, seeking protection under Spanish Laws.

12mo. pp. 338. Columbus: (Ohio) *Follett, Foster & Co.*, 1858.

1860. —— History of the Rebellion; its Authors and Causes.

8vo. pp. 498. New York: *Follett, Foster & Co.*, 1864.

1861. GILES, Rev. Chauncey. The Problem of American Nationality, and the Evils which hinder its Solution. A Discourse delivered April 30, 1863.

8vo. pp. 24. Cincinnati: *Wrightson & Co.*, 1863.

1862. —— The True Source of National Prosperity. A Discourse delivered on Thanksgiving Day.

8vo. pp. 22. New York: *C. S. Westcott & Co.*, 1864.

1863. GILLETT, Rev. Ezra H. Thanksgiving Sermon preached at Harlem, November 27, 1862.

8vo. pp. 16. New York: *A. J. Brady*, 1863.

1864. GILLETT, A. D, DD. God seen above all National Calamities. A Sermon on the Death of President Lincoln, April 13, 1865. Preached at Washington, D. C.

8vo. pp. 15. Washington: *McGill & Witherow*, 1865.

1865. GILLMORE, Maj. General Q. A. Official Report to the United States Engineer Department of the Siege and Reduction of Fort Pulaski, Georgia, February, March and April, 1862. Illustrated by Maps and Engraved Views.

8vo. pp. 96. New York: *D. Van Nostrand*, 1862.

1866. —— Engineer and Artillery Operations against the Defences of Charleston Harbor in 1863; comprising the Descent upon Morris Island, the Demolition of Fort Sumter, the Reduction of Forts Wagner and Gregg, with Observations on Heavy Ordnance, Fortifications, etc. Illustrated by 76 Plates.

8vo. pp. 353. New York: *D. Van Nostrand*, 1865.

1867. GILMER, John A., of North Carolina. Speech on the State of the Union, delivered in the House of Representatives, January 26, 1861. 8vo. pp. 8.

1868. GILMORE, J. R. (Edmund Kirk.) My Southern Friends.

12mo. pp. 308. New York: *Carleton*, 1863.

1869. GILMORE, J. R. Among the Pines ; or South in Secession Time. 12mo. pp. 310. NEW YORK: *J. R. Gilmore,* 1862.

1870. —— Down in Tennessee and back by way of Richmond. 12mo. pp. 282. NEW YORK: *Carleton,* 1864.

1871. —— The Poor Whites of the South. *Harpers' Mag., June,* '64.

1872. —— Our Visit to Richmond. *Atlantic Monthly, Sept.,* 1864.

1873. —— Our Last Day in Dixie. Ibid. *December,* 1864.

1874. —— John Jordan. From the Head of Bame. Ibid. *Oct.,* 1865.

1875. —— Rebel Terms of Peace. Visit to the Rebel Capital with Col. Jacques. What Jeff. Davis said. The North must yield— the South Nothing. 8vo. pp. 7.

1876. —— Patriotic Boys, and Prison Pictures. 12mo. pp. 306. BOSTON: *Ticknor & Fields,* 1865.

1877. GLADSTONE, T. H. The Englishman in Kansas ; or Squatter Life and Border Warfare. With an Introduction by Fred Law Olmsted. 12mo. pp. 328. NEW YORK: *Miller,* 1857.

1878. GLAZIER, Lieut. MILLARD W. The Capture, the Prison Pen, and the Escape ; giving an account of Prison Life in the South, at Richmond, Danville, Salisbury, Andersonville, etc. 12mo. pp. 343. ALBANY: *S. R. Gray,* 1865.

1879. GLOVER, Rev. L. M., DD. Our Country Vindicated. A Thanksgiving Discourse, delivered November 29, 1860. Jacksonville, Illinois. 8vo. pp. 23. JACKSONVILLE: *Catlin & Co.,* 1860.

1880. —— National Sin and Retribution. A Discourse, Jan. 4, 1861. 8vo. pp. 19. JACKSONVILLE: *Catlin & Co.,* 1861.

1881. —— The Character of Abraham Lincoln. A Discourse delivered April 23, 1865, at Strawn's Hall, Jacksonville, Illinois. 8vo. pp. 21. JACKSONVILLE: *Journal Office,* 1865.

1882. GLOVER, SAMUEL T. Slavery in the United States ; Emancipation in Missouri. Speech at the Ratification Meeting, St. Louis, July 22, 1863. 8vo. pp. 18. ST. LOUIS: *Daily Union Office,* 1863.

GLYNDON, HOWARD, see *Laura C. Redden.*

1883. GODDARD, S. A. Reply to Mr. Lindsay's Speech at Sunderland, August, 1864, on the American Questions. 8vo. pp. 16. BIRMINGHAM: (Eng.) *E. C. Osborne.*

1884. GODKIN.   The Democratic View of Democracy. *North American Review, July,* 1865.

1885. GODWIN, Benjamin, DD.   Lecture on Slavery.
12mo. pp. 258.   Boston : *James B. Dow,* 1836.

1886. GOEPP, Charles.   The National Club on the Reconstruction of the Union, February 4, 1864.
8vo. pp. 16.   New York : *G. B. Teubner,* 1864.

1887. Gold.   The Price of Gold and the Presidency.   Considerations for the People.
8vo. pp. 19.   New York : *Dodge & Grattan,* 1864.

1888. GOLDSMITH, M.   A Report on Hospital Gangrene, Erysipelas, and Pyrmia, as observed in the Departments of the Ohio and the Cumberland.
8vo. pp. 94.   Louisville : *Bradley & Gilbert,* 1863.

1889. GOLOVIN, Ivan.   Stars and Stripes ; or American Impressions.
12mo. pp. 312.   London : *W. Freeman,* 1856.

> "The object of this book," the author says, " is to show that the United States are pursuing a wrong way in their politics and morals, falsely interpreting their destination, and losing sight of the principles which presided at their formation."

1890. GOODELL, Rev. William.   The Nationalities.   Their Origin, Elements, Mission, Responsibilities, Duties and Destinies.   A Discourse delivered in Williamsburg, New York, (and in other places,) April 28 to September 1, 1861.   12mo. pp. 15.

1891. —— Our National Charters ; for the Million.   With Notes, showing their bearing on Slavery, and the relative Power of the State and National Governments.
8vo. pp. 144.   New York : *J. W. Alden,* 1862.

1892. GOODFELLOW, Rev. William.   Discourse on the Death of Abraham Lincoln, delivered at Buenos Aires, (South America,) June 11, 1865.
8vo. pp. 25.   Buenos Aires : *German Printing Office,* 1865.

1893. GOODLOE, Daniel R.   The Southern Platform ; or Manual of Southern Sentiment on the subject of Slavery.
Royal 8vo. pp. 95.   Boston : *John P. Jewett & Co.,* 1858.

1894. GOODRICH, Frank B.   The Tribute Book.   A Record of the Munificence, Self-Sacrifice, and Patriotism of the American People, in defence of their Integrity as a Nation, during the War for the Union. Illustrated by 147 engravings.

Royal 8vo. pp. 512. NEW YORK : 1865.

1895. GOODRICH, Rev. WM. H. A Sermon on the Christian Necessity of War, preached in Cleveland, April 21, 1861.

8vo. pp. 15. CLEVELAND : *Fairbanks, Benedict & Co.*, 1861.

1896. —— The Education of Divine Providence. A Sermon. 8vo. p. 7.

1897. GOODWIN, Dr. Speech in Reply to Dr. Hawks, Dr. Mahan and others, delivered in Convention, October 14, 1862.

18mo. pp. 35. NEW YORK : *John A. Gray*, 1862.

1898. GOODWIN, DANIEL R. Southern Slavery, in its Present Aspects ; containing a Reply to a late work of the Bishop of Vermont, on Slavery.

12mo. pp. 343. PHILADELPHIA : *J. B. Lippincott & Co.*, 1864.

1899. GOODWIN, THOMAS S. The Natural History of Secession ; or Despotism and Democracy at Necessary, Eternal, Exterminating War.

12mo. pp. 328. NEW YORK : *John Bradburn*, 1864.

1900. GOOKINS, S. B. How Mr. Lincoln became an Abolitionist. *Continental Monthly for June*, 1863.

1901. GORDON, GEORGE. In the Matter of George Gordon's Petition for Pardon. [Indicted and Convicted for the violation of the Fugitive Slave Law, in Ohio, in 1861.]

8vo. pp. 56. CINCINNATI : *Gazette Company*, 1862.

1902. GORDON, Rev. W. R., DD. The Peril of our Ship of State. A Sermon preached on Fast Day, January 4, 1861. The Folly of our Speculations. A New Year's Sermon, January 6, 1861. Strictures on a Sermon by Rev. H. J. Van Dyke, on the Character and Influence of Abolitionism.

8vo. pp. 38. NEW YORK : *John A, Gray*, 1861.

1903. —— Reliance on God our Hope of Victory. A Sermon, September 26, 1861.

8vo. pp, 30. NEW YORK : *John A. Gray*, 1861.

1904. —— (Pastor of the Reformed Protestant Dutch Church of Schraalenburg, N. J.) The Sin of Reviling, and its work. A Funeral Sermon, occasioned by the Assassination of President Lincoln, April 14, 1865.

8vo. pp. 24. NEW YORK : *John A. Gray & Green*, 1865.

1905. GOULD, CHARLES. Financial Scheme for the Government.
Read before the American Geographical Society. *Bankers'
Magazine, March*, 1862.

1906. THE GOVERNING RACE. A Book for the Time, and for all
Times. By H. O. R.
8vo. pp. 102.   WASHINGTON : *Thomas McGill*, 1860.

1907. GOVERNMENT. The Trial of our Democratic Form of Government. The Great Question now to be solved. Is a Democratic
Government a Possible Thing, or must we have a Despotism?
8vo. pp. 12.   PHILADELPHIA : *C. Sherman & Son*, 1863.

1908. —— Modern Government, and its True Mission. A Few Words
for the American Crisis. 1862. 8vo. pp. 16.

1909. "GOVERNMENT, or no Government;" or, The Question of State
Allegiance. A Tract for Churchmen.
8vo. pp. 8.   MOBILE : *Farrow & Dennett*, 1861.

1910. GOVERNMENT CONTRACTS. Report of the Special Committee of
the House, appointed to enquire into all the Facts and Circumstances connected with Contracts and Agreements by, or with,
the Government, growing out of its Operations in suppressing the
Rebellion, December 7, 1861. 8vo. pp. 1109. *House of Representatives, 37th Congress, 2d Session, Report No.* 2, 1861.

1911. —— Report of the Special Committee of the House of Representatives. (Report, continuation of the Journal and Testimony.)
8vo. pp. Report, lxxxiv; Journal, xiv. Testimony, Part 2. Purchase of Army Supplies, pp. 1615. *House of Representatives,
37th Congress, Report No.* 2, 1861–62.

1912. GOVERNOR. Wreck of the Steamer Governor, and Search for
the United States Ship Vermont by the Frigate Sabine. Letter
from the Secretary of the Navy in relation thereto. *House of
Representatives, Ex. Doc., No.* 139, 37th Congress, 2d Ses., 1862.
p. 23.

1913. GRAHAM, Rev. D. M. The Rebellion and Prospects of the
Union. *Free Will Baptist Quarterly, October*, 1863.

1914. THE GRAND MISTAKES. No place or date. 8vo. pp. 4.

1915. GRAND-GUILLOT, A. La Reconnaissance du Sud.
8vo. pp. 30.   PARIS : *E. Dentu*, 1862.
A defence of the right of the South to secede,

1916. GRANGER, Rev. A. H.   The Voice of Christ in the Storm. A Sermon delivered in Providence, April 21, 1861.

8vo. pp. 16.   PROVIDENCE: *Knowles, Anthony & Co.,* 1861.

1917. GRANT, Capt. J. W.   The Flying Regiment.   Journal of the Campaign of the 12th Regiment Rhode Island Volunteers.

12mo. pp. 152.   PROVIDENCE: *S. S. Rider & Brother,* 1865.

1918. GRANT, Major General.   Hero of Fort Donaldson, Vicksburg, and Chattanooga, etc.   Life and Services as a Soldier.

12mo. pp. 66.   PHILADELPHIA: *T. B. Peterson & Brothers,* '64.

1919. GRANT, Lieut. General, U. S.   Sketch of the Life of.   By Prof. Coppée.   From the U. S. Service Magazine.

8vo. pp. 10.   NEW YORK: *C. B. Richardson,* 1864.

1920. —— Life and Campaigns of, by Julian K. Larke, with Portrait and Illustrations.

8vo. pp. 469 and 40.   NEW YORK: *Derby & Miller,* 1864.

1921. —— Report of, 1864–65.

8vo. pp. 77.   NEW YORK: *D. Appleton & Co.,* 1865

1922. —— The same.   Washington: *Govt. Printing Office,* 1866.

1923. GRANT and his Campaigns.   A Military Biography.   By Prof. Coppée.

8vo. pp.   NEW YORK: *C. B. Richardson,* 1866.

1924. GRATTAN, T. C.   England and the Disrupted States of America.

8vo. pp. 49.   LONDON: *Ridgeway,* 1861.

1925. GRAY, Rev. E. H.   A Discourse on the Imperative Duties of the Hour, delivered in Washington, D. C., July 5, 1863.

8vo. pp. 15.   WASHINGTON: *H. Polkinhorn,* 1863.

1926. THE GREAT ISSUE, To be decided in November next.   Shall the Constitution and the Union stand, or fall?   Shall Sectionalism triumph?   Lincoln and his Supporters.   Washington.   pp. 24.

1927. THE GREAT MASS MEETING of Loyal Citizens, at Cooper Institute, March 6, 1863.   Speeches of Judge Daley and others.

8vo. pp. 16.   *Loyal Publication Society,* 1863.

1928. THE GREAT SURRENDER to the Rebels in Arms.   The Armistice, Washington, 1864.   pp. 8.

1929. GREBLE, JOHN T., Lieut. U. S. A.   Remarks of Rev. Dr. Brainerd at the Funeral of.

8vo. pp. 7.   PHILADELPHIA: *G. T. Stockdale,* 1861.

1930. GREELEY, HORACE. A History of the Struggle for Slavery Extension, or Restriction of the United States, from the Declaration of Independence to the present day.
Royal 8vo. pp. 164. NEW YORK : *Dix, Edwards & Co.,* 1856.

1931. —— Southern Hate of the North. *Continental Monthly, October,* 1862.

1932. —— Aurora. Ibid. *November,* 1862.

1933. —— The Obstacles to Peace. Ibid. *December,* 1862.

1934. —— The American Conflict. A History of the Great Rebellion in the United States of America, 1860–64. Its Causes, Incidents and Results. Intended to exhibit especially its Moral and Political Phases ; with the Drift and Progress of American Opinion, respecting Human Slavery, from 1776 to the close of the War for the Union.
2 vols. 8vo. Illustrations. HARTFORD : *O. D. Case & Co.,* '64.

1935. GREELEY, BEECHER, GARRISON, etc., the Great Perversionists of the Constitution. Jeff. Davis and the Rebels justified by the Friends of Freedom. The Constitution interpreted in favor of Criminals and the worst form of Oppression, etc., 1864. p. 8.

1936. GREEN-BACK to his Country Friends. To the Constituents of the 37th Congress, now assembled in Washington. New York, June 20, 1862. pp. 17.

1937. GREEN, JOHN A., Jr. Letter to the Publisher of the Daily Courier and Union. An Appeal for Peace. Syracuse, N. Y., May, 1861. pp. 14.

1938. GREENE, Mrs. FRANCES. Shahmah in Pursuit of Freedom ; or the Branded Hand.
12mo. pp. 599. NEW YORK : *Thatcher & Hutchinson,* 1858.

1939. GREENHOW, Mrs. ROSE. My Imprisonment and the First Year of Abolition Rule at Washington. With Portrait.
Post 8vo. pp. x, 352. LONDON : *Richard Bentley,* 1863.

1940. GRENARD, LEO. Shots from the Monitor ; or Facts for the Times.
12mo. pp. 22. NEW YORK : *Sinclair Toucey,* 1864.

1941. —— A Book for the Times ; or Shots from the Monitor.
8vo. pp. 22. NEW YORK : *Sinclair Toucey,* 1863.

1942. GRIFFITHS, JULIA. Autographs for Freedom.
12mo. pp. 309. AUBURN : *Alden, Beardsley & Co.,* 1854.

1943. GRIMES, Rev. J. S. The National Crisis. A Sermon preached at Columbia, Penn., January 4, 1861.
8vo. pp. 16. WRIGHTSVILLE : *Robert W. Smith*, 1861.

1944. —— The Nation's Last Hope. A Sermon preached in the First Presbyterian Church, on the day of National Humiliation, August 4, 1864.
8vo. pp. 20. NEW CASTLE : (Pa.) *E. S. Durban*, 1864.

1945. GRIMES, JAMES W., of Iowa. Achievements of the Western Naval Flotilla. Remarks in Senate, March 13, 1862. 8vo. p. 8.

1946. —— The Surrender of Slaves by the Army. Speech delivered in the Senate of the United States, April 14, 1862. 8vo. pp. 7.

1947. GRIMKE, A. E. Appeal to the Christian Women of the South. *Anti-Slavery Examiner, Vol.* 1, 1836.

1948. —— Letters to Catherine E. Beecher, in Reply to an Essay on Slavery and Abolitionism.
18mo. pp. 129. BOSTON : *Isaac Knapp*, 1838.

1949. GRIMKE, THOMAS S. Oration on the Absolute Necessity of Union, and the Folly and Madnesss of Disunion, delivered 4th of July, 1809, by Thomas S. Grimké ; and Speech of T. S. Grimké, December, 1828, on the Constitutionality of the Tariff and on the True Nature of State Sovereignty, both dedicated to the People of South Carolina.
12mo. pp. 129. CHARLESTON : (S. C.) *W. Riley*, 1829.

1950. GRINNELL, JOSIAH B., of Iowa. Early and Modern Democracy Reviewed. Speech in the House of Representatives, March 5, 1864. 8vo. pp. 14.

1951. GRISWOLD, Hon. S. O. Speech on the Resolutions relative to the Suspension of the Writ of Habeas Corpus and Arrest of Disloyal Persons. Delivered in the Ohio House of Representatives, January 29, 1863. 8vo. pp. 7.

1952. GROSS, CHARLES T. A Reply to Horace Binney's Pamphlet on Habeas Corpus.
8vo. pp. 40. PHILADELPHIA : 1862.

1953. GUERNSEY, A. H. Iron Clad Vessels. *Harpers' Magazine, September*, 1862.

1954. GUERRE D'AMERIQUE. Campagne du Potomac. Mars–Juillet, '62.
8vo. pp. 211. Map. PARIS : *Michel Levy Frères*, 1863.

23

1955. LA GUERRE CIVILE en Amérique et l'Esclavage. Par F. C.
8vo. pp. 31. PARIS : *E. Dentu*, 1861.

1956. LA GUERRE CIVILE aux Etats Unis. Impuissance du Nord, l'Indépendance du Sud inévitable. Par A. D. revenu tout récemment des Etats Unis.
8vo. pp. 32. PARIS : *E. Dentu*, 1862.

1957. GUION, Rev. ELIJAH. Sermon on the Scriptural, Ecclesiastical and Political Obligations, in regard to the use of certain Prayers in the Liturgy of the Protestant Episcopal Church, preached in New Orleans, April 9, 1864.
8vo. pp. 25. NEW ORLEANS : 1864.

1958. GUNCKEL, LEWIS B. Speech in the Senate of Ohio, March 2, 1863, on the Resolutions in favor of the Union. 8vo. pp. 11.

1959. GURLEY, J. A., of Ohio. The War must be prosecuted with more vigor. Speech in House of Representatives, January 29, 1862. pp. 8.

1960. —— Confiscation and Emancipation, May 26, 1862. pp. 8.

1961. —— Money and Paper. Bank Bill. Soldiers must be paid. Why not Paid. Speech in House of Reps., Jan. 15, 1863. p. 8.

1962. GURLEY, Rev. L. B. Sermon on the Victory at Fort Donelson, and Moral Aspects of the Rebellion. Delivered in Galion, Ohio, February 23, 1862.
8vo. pp. 28. CINCINNATI : *Methodist Book Concern*, 1862.

1963. GURLEY, Rev. P. D., DD. Man's Projects and God's Results. A Sermon preached, August 6, 1863, the Day of National Thanksgiving.
8vo. pp. 20. WASHINGTON : (D. C.) *Wm. Ballantyne*, 1863.

1964. —— Sermon preached at Washington, D. C., on the occasion of the Death of President Lincoln. June 1, 1865. pp. 16.

1965. GUROWSKI, ADAM. Diary, from March 4, 1861, to November 12, 1862.
12mo. pp. 315. BOSTON : *Lee & Shepard*, 1862.

1966. —— Diary, from November 18, 1862, to October 18, 1863.
12mo. pp. 348. NEW YORK : *Carleton*, 1864.

1967. GUTHRIE, Dr. W. E. Oration on the Death of Abraham Lincoln. Addressed to the American People.
12mo. pp. 9. PHILADELPHIA : *John Penington & Son*, 1865.

HABEAS Corpus. Facts and Authorities on the Suspension of the Privilege of the Writ of Habeas Corpus. 8vo. pp. 20.

1969. —— The Benefit of the Writ of Habeas Corpus is naturally Suspended until granted, and the Suspension is lawful until made unlawful. 8vo. pp. 6.

1970. —— The Suspending Power and Writ of.
8vo. pp. 48. PHILADELPHIA : *James Campbell*, 1862.

1971. —— [The Act, the Writ and the Privilege.] Its Death, and how it came by it. (Poetical.)
4to. pp. vii. PHILADELPHIA : *John Doe*, 1862.

1972. —— The Privilege of the Writ of Habeas Corpus, under the Constitution of the United States. In what it consists. How it is allowed. How it is suspended. It is the Regulation of the Law, etc.
8vo. pp. 16. PHILADELPHIA : *John Campbell*, 1862.
For other works relating to Habeas Corpus, see *H. Binney, S. S. Nicholas, N. K. Hall.*

1973. HACKETT, HORATIO B. Christian Memorials of the War ; or Scenes and Incidents illustrative of Religious Faith and Principle, Patriotism and Bravery in our Army ; with Historical Notes.
12mo. pp. 252. BOSTON : *Gould & Lincoln*, 1864.

1974. HACO, DION. Sue Munday, the Guerrilla Spy.
18mo. pp. 66. NEW YORK : *T. R. Dawley*, 1865.

1975. —— Osgood, the Demon Refugee.
18mo. pp. 92. NEW YORK : *T. R. Dawley*, 1865.

1976. —— Larry, the Army Dog Robber.
18mo. pp. 106. NEW YORK : *T. R. Dawley*, 1865.

1977. —— Cheatham, or the Swamp Dragons.
12mo. pp. 94. NEW YORK : *T. R. Dawley*, 1865.

1978. —— Perdita, the Demon Refugee's Daughter.
12mo. pp. 93. NEW YORK : *T. R. Dawley*, 1865.

1979. —— Hawks, the Conscript.
12mo. pp. 106. NEW YORK : *T. R. Dawley*, 1865.

1980. —— Rob. Cobb Kennedy, the Incendiary Spy.
12mo. pp. 71. NEW YORK : *T. R. Dawley*, 1865.

1981. —— J. Wilkes Booth, the Assassinator of President Lincoln.
12mo. pp. 102. NEW YORK : *T. R. Dawley*, 1865.

1982. HAGUE, WILLIAM. Christianity and Slavery. A Review of Correspondence by Dr. Fuller and Dr. Wayland.
12mo. pp.   BOSTON: 1847.

1983. HAGUE, WM., and KIRK, E. N. Addresses at the Annual Meeting of the Educational Commission for Freedmen, May 28, 1863.
8vo. pp. 16.   BOSTON: *David Clapp*, 1863.

1984. HAHN, Hon. MICHAEL. Manhood the Basis of Suffrage. Speech before the National Equal Suffrage Association of Washington, November 17, 1855.

1985. HALDEMAN, R. J. African Slavery regarded from an unusual Stand-Point. Territorial Abstractions ignored as now immaterial, and a more Radical Issue raised. Address to the Democracy of Pennsylvania. pp. 8.

1986. HALE, E. E. The Desert and the Promised Land. A Sermon.
12mo. pp. 22.   BOSTON: *C. C. P. Moody*, 1863.

1987. —— The Future Civilization of the South. A Sermon preached April 13, 1862, at the South Congregational Church, Boston.
12mo. pp. 17.

1988. —— The Desert and the Promised Land. A Sermon.
12mo. pp. 22.   HARTFORD: *L. E. Hunt*, 1863.

1989. —— England and America. *Christian Examiner, Sept.,* 1861.

1990. —— The Presidential Election. Ibid. *November,* 1864.

1991. —— Northern Invasions. *Atlantic Monthly, February,* 1864.

1992. —— How to use Victory. Ibid. *June,* 1864.

1993. HALE, Hon. JOHN P. Speech on the State of the Union, January 31, 1861. pp. 16.

1994. —— Speech on the Purchase of Vessels by George D. Morgan. Senate, February 7, 1862. pp. 8.

1995. —— Speech on the Abolition of Slavery in the District of Columbia. Delivered in the U. S. Senate, March 18. 1862. pp. 8.

1996. —— Frauds and Corruption of the Navy Department. A Speech delivered in the Senate of the United States, January 21 and 31, and February 1 and 17, 1865. 8vo. pp. 32.

1997. HALL, A. OAKEY. Horace Greeley decently Dissected, in a Letter on Horace Greeley, addressed to Joseph Hoxsie, Esq., republished by popular request.
8vo. pp. 38.   NEW YORK: *Ross & Toucey*, 1862.

1998. HALL, Rev. CHARLES H., DD. A Mournful Easter. A Discourse delivered in Washington, D. C., April 19, 1865.
8vo. pp. 15.   WASHINGTON : *Gideon & Pearson*, 1865.

1999. HALL, CHARLES W. Court Martial.
8vo. pp. 28.   CINCINNATI : *Robert Clarke & Co., Oct.*, 1863.

2000. HALL, GORDON, DD. President Lincoln's Death ; its Voice to the People. A Discourse preached in Northampton, Apr. 19, '65.
8vo. pp. 16.   NORTHAMPTON : (Mass.) *Trumbull & Gere*, 1865.

2001. —— Divine Mercy a Cause for Humiliation. A Discourse preached on the occasion of the State Fast, April 13, 1865.
8vo. pp. 15.   NORTHAMPTON : (Mass.) *Trumbull & Gere*, 1865.

2002. HALL, MARSHALL, DD. The Two-Fold Slavery of the United States ; with a Project of Self-Emancipation. With two Maps.
18mo. pp. 158.   LONDON : *Adam Scott*, 1854.

2003. HALL, Rev. NEWMAN. No War with America. A Lecture on the Affair of the Trent. Delivered at Surrey Chapel, London, December 9, 1861.
12mo. pp. 8.   LONDON : *Eliot Stock*, 1861.

2004. —— The American War. A Lecture to working Men.
12mo. pp. 31.   LONDON : *James Nisbet & Co.*, 1862.

2005. —— The American War. A Lecture delivered in London, October 20, 1862.
12mo. pp. 48.   NEW YORK : *Anson D. F. Randolph*, 1862.

2006. —— The same. pp. 32. Boston : *American Tract Society*.

2007. —— A Reply to the Pro-Slavery Wail.
8vo. pp. 15.   LONDON : *John Sents*, 1863.

2008. —— The Pro-Slavery Religion of the South. To the Editors of " Good Words," " The Evangelical Magazine," and other Religious Periodicals which have admitted the Appeal from the Clergy of the Confederate States.
8vo. pp. 2.   MANCHESTER : (Eng.) *Un. and Emanc. Society*.

2009. —— A Lecture on the Assassination of Abraham Lincoln, preached at Surrey Chapel, London, May 14, 1865.
8vo. pp. 16.   BOSTON : *Bartlett & Halliday*, 1865.

2010. HALL, Judge N. K., of the United States District Court for the Northern District of New York, a Habeas Corpus, in the case of

Rev. Judson Benedict; and Documents and Statements of Facts relating thereto.

8vo. pp. 34.   BUFFALO : *Joseph Warren & Co.*, 1862.

2011. HALL, Judge N. K.   The same work.

pp. 15.   New York: *Argus Office*, 1862.

2012. HALL, NATHANIEL.   Slavery and its Hero Victim. Its Iniquity. A Sermon preached in Dorchester, December 11, 1859.

8vo. pp. 19.   BOSTON : *John Wilson & Son.*, 1859.

2013. —— The Man; the Deed; the Event.   A Sermon preached in the First Church, Dorchester, December 4, 1859.

8vo. pp. 18.   BOSTON: *John Wilson & Son*, 1859.

2014. —— The Proclamation of Freedom.   A Sermon preached in Dorchester, January 4, 1863.

8vo. pp. 15.   BOSTON : *Crosby & Nichols*, 1863.

2015. HALL, Rev. P.   Dangers and Duties of the Present Hour.   A Sermon preached at Indianapolis, Ind., April 28, 1861.

8vo. pp. 15.   INDIANAPOLIS: " *Journal Co.*," 1861.

2016. —— What shall we do?   A Sermon delivered Jan. 13, 1861.

8vo. pp. 16.   INDIANAPOLIS : *"Journal Co.,"* 1861.

2017. HALL, Rev. SAMUEL H.   The Tried Stability of our Government, a Cause for Thanksgiving.   A Sermon preached in Oswego, New York, November 28, 1861.

8vo. pp. 18.   NEW YORK : *A. D. F. Randolph*, 1861.

2018. HALL, W. A., of Missouri.   Remarks on the Slavery Question. House of Representatives, May 13, 1862.   8vo. pp. 8.

2019. HALL, W. W., M. D.   Take care of your Health.   Advice to Soldiers.

16mo. pp. 16.   BOSTON : *American Tract Society.*

2020. —— Soldiers' Health.   Third edition.   N. York : 1862. 8vo. p. 31.

2021. HALLAM, Rev. ROBERT A.   National Unity.   A Sermon preached in New London, on the Day of the National Fast, September 26, 1861.

8vo. pp. 15.   NEW LONDON : *D. S. Ruddock.*

2022. HALLECK, H. W., General-in-Chief.   Annual Report of.   Dated, Washington, D. C., November 15, 1863.   (Accompanying Report of the Secretary of War.)   8vo. pp. 15 to 46.

2023. HALLECK, Gen. H. W.   Report reviewed in the Light of Facts.

8vo. pp. 23.   NEW YORK : *Anson D. F. Randolph*, 1862.

2024. HALLECK, General, and Gen. Burnside. A Reprint, with additions of two Articles originally communicated to the Providence Journal, December 18, 1863, and July 16, 1864·
8vo. pp. 23.   BOSTON: *John Wilson & Co.*, 1864.

2025. HALPINE, Col. CHARLES G. Life and Adventures, Songs, Services and Speeches of Private Miles O'Reilley, 47th Regiment New York Volunteers.
12mo. pp. 237.   NEW YORK: *Carlton*, 1864.

2026. —— Poem, at the Laying of the Corner Stone of the Soldiers' National Monument at Gettysburg, July 4, 1865.   pp. 5.

2027. HALSTEAD, M. Caucuses of 1860. A History of the National Political Conventions of the Current Presidential Campaigns; being a complete Record of the Business of all the Conventions, etc.
8vo. pp. 232.   COLUMBUS: *Follett, Foster & Co.*, 1860.

2028. HALSTED, O. S., Jun.,   Finance. A Letter addressed to the House Committee of Ways and Means, Jan. 1, 1862.   8vo. p. 7.

2029. —— Finance, No. 3. Should the Interest on the National Debt be forced by Congressional Enactment to be paid in Coin? Would such a Measure, at this time, be wise or just, patriotic, politic or possible?   8vo. pp. 5.

2030. HAMILTON, Col. AND. JACKSON. Origin and Objects of the Slaveholders's Conspiracy against Democratic Principles, as well as against the National Union.
8vo. pp. 16.   NEW YORK: *Baker & Godwin,* 1862.

2031. —— On the Condition of the South, under Rebel Rule, and the Necessity of early Relief to the Union Men of Western Texas.
8vo. pp. 19.   NEW YORK: *National War Com.*, 1862.

2032. —— Letter to the President of the United States.   New York: *Loyal Publication Society.*   8vo. pp. 18.

2033. —— The same.   No imprint.   pp. 18.

2034. HAMILTON, A. J., Military Governor. An Address to the People of Texas.
8vo. pp. 19.   NEW ORLEANS: *"Era" Office*, 1864.

2035. HAMILTON, JAMES A. State Sovereignty. Rebellion against the United States by the People of a State is its Political Suicide.
8vo. pp. 32.   NEW YORK: *Baker & Godwin*, 1862.

2036. HAMILTON, J. A.   The Constitution Vindicated.   Nationality;
      Secesssion ; Slavery.
         8vo. pp. 12.   NEW YORK : *Loyal Publication Society*, 1864.
2037. HAMILTON, JOHN C.   The Slave Power; its Heresies and
      Injuries to the American People.   A Speech, November, 1864.
         8vo. pp. 23.   NEW YORK : *J. A. Gray & Green*, 1864.
2038. —— The same.   8vo. pp. 23.   *Loyal Publication Society.*
2039. —— Coercion completed ; or Treason Triumphant.
         8vo. pp. 25.   NEW YORK : *W. C. Bryant & Co.*, 1864.
2040. —— The same.   8vo. pp. 25.   *Loyal Publication Society.*
      HAMILTON, GAIL, see *Abigail Dodge.*
2041. HAMILTON, Rev. C.   The Problem of Freedom and Slavery
      in the United States.   A Lecture before the Literary and Scien-
      tific Institution of Smyrna.   (Turkey.)
         8vo. pp. 28.   SMYRNA : *Damian*, 1862.
2042. HAMMOND, CHARLES.   A Sermon on the Life and Character
      of Abraham Lincoln, preached at Monson, Massachusetts, on the
      occasion of the National Fast, June 1, 1865.
         8vo. pp. 21.   SPRINGFIELD : *S. Bowles & Co.*, 1865.
2043. HAMMOND, E. G.   A Winter in Camp.   *Continental Monthly,
      May*, 1863.
2044. HAMMOND, J. H., late Governor of South Carolina.   Two Let-
      ters on Slavery in the United States, addressed to Thomas Clark-
      son, Esq.   From the *South Carolinian*, 1845.   8vo. pp. 39.
         See also, under Slavery, the work entitled "The Pro-Slavery Argument."
2045. HAMMOND, WILLIAM A., Surgeon General.   A Statement of
      the Causes which led to the dismissal of Surgeon General Wil-
      liam A. Hammond, from the Army ; with a Review of the Evi-
      dence adduced before the court.
         8vo. pp. 73.   NEW YORK : *September*, 1864.
2046. —— Defence of Brig. General William A. Hammond, Surgeon
      General United States Army.   8vo. pp. 66.
2047. —— Reply of the Judge Advocate, John A. Bingham, to the
      Defence of the Accused, before a General Court Martial for the
      Trial of Surgeon General Hammond.
         8vo. pp. 64.   WASHINGTON : *Government Printing Office*, 1864.
2048. HAMMOND, WM. G.   Abraham Lincoln.   A Eulogy delivered

at Anamosa, Iowa, on the day of the State Fast, April 27, 1865.
8vo. pp. 16.   DAVENPORT: *Luse & Griggs*, 1865.

2049. HANAFORD, Mrs. P. A.   The Young Captain.   A Memorial of Captain Richard C. Derby, 15th Regiment Massachusetts Volunteers, who fell at Antietam.
16mo. pp. 226.   BOSTON: *Degen, Estes & Co.*, 1865.

2050. —— Our Martyred President, Abraham Lincoln: Born February 12, 1809; Died April 15, 1865.
8vo. pp. 24.   Portrait.   BOSTON: *B. B. Russell & Co.*, 1865.

2051. HANDY, Rev. ISAAC W. K.   Our National Sins.   A Sermon delivered in the First Presbyterian Church, Portsmouth, Va., January 4, 1861.
8vo. pp. 20.   PORTSMOUTH: *Transcript Office*, 1861.

2052. HANNAFORD, EBEN.   In Hospital after Stone River.   *Harpers' Magazine, November*, 1863.

2053. [HARCOURT, Mr.]   Belligerent Rights of Maritime Capture. By Historicus.
8vo. pp. 4 and 22.   LIVERPOOL: *Webb & Hunt*, 1863.

2054. —— "Letters by, on some Questions of International Law. Reprinted from the [London] Times," with considerable additions.
8vo. pp. xiii and 98.   LONDON: *Macmillan & Co.*, 1863.

2055. —— American Neutrality.   From the London Times of December 22, 1864.
8vo. pp. 11.   NEW YORK: 1865.

2056. HARDING, A., of Kentucky.   Speech on Emancipation of Slaves in Rebel States.   House of Reps., Dec. 17, 1861.   p. 16.

2057. —— Speech on the President's Two Proclamations, and the Two Rebellions, in the House of Reps., January 21, 1863.   pp. 15.

2058. HARDINGE, EMMA.   America and her Destiny.   Inspirational Discourse, given extemporaneously, at Dodworth's Hall, New York, August 25, 1861, through Emma Hardinge, by the Spirits.
8vo. pp. 15.   NEW YORK: *Robert M. De Witt*, 1861.

2059. —— The Great Funeral Oration on Abraham Lincoln.   Delivered April 16, 1865, at Cooper Institute, New York, before upwards of three thousand persons.
8vo. pp. 28.   NEW YORK: *American News Company*, 1865.

2060. HARDINGE, Mrs. (Belle Boyd.)   In Camp and Prison.

24

Written by Herself; with an Introduction by a Friend to the South.

2 v. post 8vo. pp. xxvi, 571.   LONDON : *Saunders & Otley*, 1865.

2061. HARDINGE, Mrs.   The same.

12mo. pp. 464.   NEW YORK : *Brelock & Co.*, 1865.

The *New York Evening Post* of August 3, 1865, in an account of this book, gives the following notice of its author: " Belle Boyd was a young woman of Martinsburg, Virginia; good-looking, as we have been told by officers upon whom she has exercised her charms, ready-witted, impetuous, and a determined enemy of the Union, as she does not omit to tell us in this book. She was notorious as a skillful spy for Stonewall Jackson and other Rebel Generals, and she closed her career by seducing one Hardinge, a lieutenant of our Navy, who fell in love with her; for her sake, suffered the escape of a prisoner in his hands, and afterward deserted to the enemy and married Miss Boyd."

2062. HARLAN, Hon. JAMES, of Iowa.   State of the Union.   Speech in the Senate, January 11, 1861.   8vo. pp. 15.

2063. —— Service of the Militia.   Speech in Senate, July 11, 1862. 8vo. pp. 16.

2064. —— The Constitution upheld and maintained.   Speech in the United States Senate.   8vo. pp. 8.

2065. —— Legal Title to Property in Slaves.   Speech on the Amendment to the Constitution, delivered in the United States Senate, April 6, 1864.   8vo. pp. 7.

2066. —— Retaliation on Rebel Prisoners.   Speech in the Senate of the United States, January 28, 1865.   *Washington Globe, January* 30, 1865.

2067. HARPER'S FERRY.   Rise and Progress of the Bloody Outbreak at Harper's Ferry.

8vo. pp. 20.   NEW YORK : *Democratic Vigilant Association.*

HARPER'S FERRY INVASION.   For other works on, see *John Brown, Victor Hugo, Henningsen.*

2068. HARPERS' MAGAZINE, for 1862.

A Soldier's Letter.   Fitz James O'Brien.   March, 1862.
Early Secessionists.   B. J. Lossing.   March, 1862.
Camp Life at the Relay [House.]   G. Haven.   April, 1862.
The Contest in America.   From Frazer's Magazine.   J. Stuart Mill.   April,'62.
Early Disunionists.   B. J. Lossing.   May, 1862.
South Carolina Nullification.   Ibid.   August, 1862.
Iron-Clad Vessels.   A. A. Guernsey.   September, 1862.
The People and the Government.   Rev. Samuel Osgood.   November, 1862.

2069. HARPERS' MAGAZINE for 1863.

The Home and the Flag. Rev. Samuel Osgood. April, 1863.
Some Secession Leaders. George M. Towle. April, 1863.
Two Weeks at Port Royal. June, 1863.
The Battle of Antietam. George L. Noyes. August, 1863.
The Religious Life of a Negro Slave. Charles A. Raymond. August, 1863.
Harbor Defence.
The First Cruise of the Monitor "Passaic." Edgar Holden, M. D. Oct., '63.
The Army Correspondent. L. L. Crounse. October, 1863.
The Religious Life of the Negro Slave. C. A. Raymond. Oct. and Nov., '63.

2070. HARPERS' MAGAZINE for 1864.

In Hospital after Stone River. E. Hannaford. January, 1864.
Four Days at Gettysburg. John T. Foster. February, 1864.
With a Flag of Truce. Major John A. Bolles. March, 1864.
Escape from Fort Warren. Ibid. April, 1864.
My Escape from Richmond. John Brag. April, 1864.
The Second Division at Shiloh. Daniel McCook. April, 1864.
The Second Division at Shiloh. Ibid. May, 1864.
Three Trophies from the War. Helen Pierson. June, 1864.
The Poor Whites of the South. J. R. Gilmore. June, 1864.
The Drummer Boy's Burial. Miss Julia R. Dorr. July, 1864.
The Fortunes of War. Dr. Robert Tomes. July, 1864.
In "Dixie." A Southern Refugee. July, 1864.
Three Years in Montgomery. W. Hedges. July, 1864.
The Military Hospitals at Fortress Monroe. J. S. C. Abbott. August, 1864.
The First Time under Fire. J. W. DeForrest. September, 1864.
How we Fight at Atlanta. Henry C. Dwight. October, 1864.
A Cruise on the Sassachas. Edgar Holden. November, 1864.
Heroic Deeds of Heroic Men. A Military Adventure. J. S. C. Abbott. Dec.,'64.
Sheridan's Battle of Winchester. J. W. DeForest. December, 1864.
The Bay Fight, Mobile Bay, August 5, 1864. Henry A. Brownell. Dec., '64.

2071. HARPERS' MAGAZINE for 1865.

Grierson's Raid. J. S. C. Abbott. February, 1865.
The Siege of Vicksburg. Ibid. January, 1865.
Sheridan's Victory of Middletown. J. W. DeForest. February, 1865.
Siege and Capture of Fort Hudson. J. S. C. Abbott. March, 1865.
Military Adventures beyond the Mississippi. Ibid. April, 1865.
Recollections of General Sherman. W. F. G. Shanks. April, 1865.
The Change of Base. J. S. C. Abbott. May, 1865.
The Pursuit and Capture of Morgan. Ibid. August, 1865.
Under Fire at Charleston. J. R. G. Peck. August, 1865.
Recollections of Sheridan. J. S. Sparks. August, 1865.
Sherman's Great March. October, 1865.
Jefferson Davis. Gen. Jordan, of Gen. Beauregard's Staff. October, 1865.
The Raising of the Frigates. October, 1865.
Fighting Joe Hooker. October, 1865.

2072. HARPERS' Pictorial History of the Great Rebellion. New York, 1864–66.

2073. HARPER, CHANCELLOR, on Slavery. (The Pro-Slavery Argument.) Philadelphia. pp. 98.

2074. HARRIS, ELISHA, M. D. The Sanitary Commission. *North American Review, April,* 1864.

2075. HARRIS, Hon. IRA. The Expulsion of Senator Bright. Speeches in the Senate of the United States, January 24 and February 25, 1862. 8vo. pp. 7.

2076. —— Confiscation of Rebel Property. Speech in the Senate of the United States. April 14, 1862. pp. 8.

2077. HARRIS, Hon. J. MORRISON, of Maryland. State of the Union. Speech delivered in the House of Reps., Jan. 29, 1861. 8vo. p. 8.

2078. HARRIS, Lieut. WM. C. Prison Life in the Tobacco Warehouse at Richmónd. By a Ball's Bluff Prisoner.
12mo. pp. 175. PHILADELPHIA : *G. W. Childs,* 1862.

2079. HARRISON, Hon. RICHARD A. The Principles of Representation in Congress. Substance of Remarks made in the House of Representatives, February 27, 1862.

2080. —— The Suppression of the Rebellion. Speech in House of Representatives, June 23, 1862. 8vo. pp. 8.

2081. —— Oration delivered at Pleasant Valley, Ohio, July 14, 1863.
12mo. pp. 22. LONDON : (Ohio) *"Union Print,"* 1863.

2082. " HARVEY BIRCH." Facts and Law in the case of the Ship Harvey Birch. Burned [by the Rebel Cruiser Nashville,] November 19, 1861, off Ireland.
8vo. pp. 25. NEW YORK : *John W. Amerman,* 1862.

2083. HARWOOD, EDWIN, DD. Canaan, Shem and Japheth. A Sermon preached in Trinity Church, New Haven, Oct. 25, 1863.
8vo. pp. 28. NEW HAVEN : *T. H. Pease,* 1863.

2084. [HASSAN, Dr., U. S. A.] Our Military Experience, and what it suggests.
8vo. pp. 24. BALTIMORE : *Cushing & Bailey,* 1863.

2085. HASTED, FREDERICK. A copy of a Letter written to the President of the United States [Franklin Pierce] on Slave Emancipation. Dated Indianapolis, Ind., Dec. 2, 1854. pp. 8.

2086. HASTINGS, Major DAVID K. Record of the Trial of, by Court Martial.
8vo. pp. 293. *House of Representatives, 38th Congress, 2d Session, Executive Document, No.* 54, 1865.

2087. HASTINGS, Samuel D.   Address before the Hastings Invincibles, 30th Regiment Wis. Vols., Nov. 9, 1862.   Madison, Wis. 8vo. pp. 22.   Madison: *Willard G. Roberts*, 1862.

2088. HATCH, Cora L. V. S.   In Memoriam. [President Lincoln.] *The Friend of Progress, June*, 1865.

2089. HATHAWAY, Warren. A Discourse occasioned by the Death of Abraham Lincoln.   Preached at Coxsackie, April 19, 1865. 8vo. pp. 24.   Albany: *J. Munsell*, 1865.

2090. HAUT, Marc de.   La Crise Américaine, ses causes, ses résultats probables, ses rapports avec l'Europe et la France. 8vo. pp. 168.   Paris: *Dentu*, 1862.

2091. HAUTEFEUILLE, L. B.   Propriétés Privées des sujets Belligérants sur mer. 8vo. pp. 39.   Paris: *A. Franck*, 1860.

2092, —— Quelques Questions de Droit Internation Maritime appropos à la Guerre d'Amérique. 8vo. pp. 74.   Leipzig: *A. Franck*, 1861.
 An Essay on Maritime Rights, particularly with reference to privateers, and the blockade.

2093. —— De la Legalité des Blocus Americaines.   From the *Revue Contemporaine, February* 28, 1863.

2094. —— Nécessité d'une Loi Maritime pour régler les rapports des Neutres et des belligérants. 8vo. pp. 32.   Paris: *Revue Contemporaine*, 1862.

2095. HAVEN, Rev. E. O. The American Crisis. *Qr. Rev., Oct.*, '62.

2096. HAVEN, Rev. Gilbert.   The Cause and Consequence of the Election of Abraham Lincoln.   A Thanksgiving Sermon, delivered November 1, 1860. 8vo. pp. 44.   Boston: *J. M. Hewes*, 1860.

2097. —— Camp Life at the Relay.   *Harpers' Magazine, May*, 1862.

2098. HAVENS, J. S.   The Usurpations of the Federal Government. Speech on the subject of Arbitrary Arrests, and the Suspension of the Writ of Habeas Corpus.   Delivered in the Assembly at Albany, February 17, 1863.   8vo. pp. 8.

2099. HAVENS, Hon. Palmer E.   Review of Governor Seymour's Message, in the Assembly, (of N. Y.) Feb. 6, 1863.   8vo. p. 12.

2100. —— Arbitrary Arrests.   Speech in the House of Assembly, of New York, March 5, 1863.   8vo. pp. 7.

2101. HAVERSTICK, L. M. The Conscription Act of March 3, 1863. *Continental Monthly, January,* 1864.

2102. HAWES, J., DD. North and South; or Four Questions Considered: What have we done? What have we to do? What have we to hope? What have we to fear? A Sermon preached at Hartford, September 26, 1861.

8vo. pp. 31. HARTFORD : *Case, Lockwood & Co.,* 1861.

2103. HAWKES, Rev. T. H. Our National Trials a Cause for Thankfulness. A Sermon preached in Cleveland, Nov. 28, '61.

8vo. pp. 24. CLEVELAND : *Fairbanks, Benedict & Co.,* 1861.

2104. HAWKINS, Col. RUSH C. Ninth Regiment New York Volunteers. "Hawkins' Zouaves." Testimonial to.

8vo. pp. 9. NEW YORK : *Latimer Brothers & Seymour,* 1863.

2105. HAWKINS, Rev. WM. G. Lunsford Lane ; or another Helper from North Carolina.

12mo. pp. 305. BOSTON : *Crosby & Nichols,* 1863.

2106. HAWLEY, B., DD. Truth and Righteousness Triumphant. A Discourse Commemorative of the Death of President Lincoln, preached in Albany, April 20, 1865.

8vo. pp. 20. ALBANY : *J. Munsell,* 1865.

2107. HAWTHORNE, NATH'L. Chiefly about War Matters. *Atlantic Monthly, July,* 1862.

2108. HAYDEN, WILLIAM B. The Institution of Slavery, viewed in the Light of Divine Truth. A Lecture delivered in Portland, March 17, 1861.

8vo. pp. 28. PORTLAND : *David Tucker,* 1861.

2109. HAZARD, ERSKINE. Thoughts on Currency and Finance, September, 1863. 8vo. pp. 8.

2110. HAZARD, ROWLAND G. Our Resources. A Series of articles on the Financial and Political Condition of the United States.

8vo. pp. 32. LONDON : *Trübner & Co.,* 1864.

The papers contained in this pamphlet are as follows: Taxation for war purposes. Taxation and paper Issue. Compensation to slaveholders. Our Financial Policy. Our Resources in men and money. Our Financial Prospects. The Woman's Covenant. Contraction and Expansion.

2111. —— Financiën en Hulpbronnen der Vereenigde Staten. *Amsterdam Courant, December* 8, 1864.

2112. —— The same, in Jj-en Amstelbode. December 17, 1864.

2113. HAZARD, R. G. The same. Amsterdam, 1864. 8vo. pp. 4.

The above are Dutch translations of extracts from Mr. Hazard's Essays, entitled "Our Resources."

2114. HAZARD, Thomas R. National American Party. A Constitutional Manual for; in which is examined the Question of Negro Slavery, in connection with the Constitution of the United States. By a Northern Man with American Principles. 8vo. pp. 30. PROVIDENCE: *A. C. Greene*, 1856.

2115. HAZELTINE, Lieut. Colonel. The Prisoner of the Mill; or Captain Hayward's Body Guard. 8vo. pp. 46. NEW YORK: *American News Company*, 1864.

2116. —— The Border Spy; or the Beautiful Captive of the Rebel Camp. A Story of the War. 8vo. pp. 40. NEW YORK: *Sinclair Toucey*, 1864.

2117. HAZEWELL, C. C. The Hour and the Man. *Atlantic Monthly November*, 1862.

2118. —— Beginning of the End. Ibid. *January*, 1864.

2119. —— Fighting Facts and Fogies. Ibid. *April*, 1864.

2120. —— The Presidential Election. Ibid. *May*, 1864.

2121. —— Assassination. Ibid. *July*, 1865.

2122. HEACOCK, J. W. Speech in favor of a Vigorous prosecution of the War; Sustaining the Administration in its Emancipation Policy, and advocating an extensive and general use of the Negro in the Army and Navy. 8vo. pp. 15. ALBANY: *Weed, Parsons & Co.*, 1863.

2123. HEADLEY, J. T. The Great Rebellion. A History of the Civil War in the United States. 2 vols. 8vo. HARTFORD: *Hurlbut, Williams & Co.*, 1863.

2124. —— Grant and Sherman; their Campaigns and Generals. Comprising an account of Battles and Sieges, Adventures and Incidents; including Biographies of the Prominent Generals. 8vo. p. 608. Portraits and maps. N. Y.: *E. B. Trent & Co.*'65.

2125. HEADLEY, Rev. P. C. The Patriot Boy; or the Life and Career of Major General Ormsby M. Mitchell. 12mo. pp. 278. NEW YORK: *W. H. Appleton*, 1864.

2126. —— The Hero Boy; or the Life and Deeds of Gen. Grant. 12mo. pp. 340. NEW YORK: *W. H. Appleton*, 1864.

2127. HEADLEY, Rev. P. C.   Life and Military Career of Maj. Gen. W. T. Sherman.
12mo. pp. 368.   NEW YORK: *W. H. Appleton*, 1865.

2128. —— Boy's Life of Vice-Admiral Farragut.
16mo. pp. 350.   NEW YORK: *W. H. Appleton*, 1865.

2129. —— Boy's Life of General P. H. Sheridan.
16mo. pp. 350.   NEW YORK: *W. H. Appleton*, 1865.

2130. HEBBARD, W. WALLACE.   The Night of Freedom.   An Appeal, in verse, against the Great Crime of our Country : Human Bondage.
8vo. pp. 42.   BOSTON : *Samuel Chesin*, 1857.

2131. HEDGE, Rev. F. H., DD.   To your Tents, O Israel.   A Sermon for the Times.   *Boston Evening Transcript, May* 3, 1861.

2132. —— Nationality.   *Religious Magazine, December*, 1861.

2133. —— " God in the Destiny of Nations."   A Sermon preached at Brookline, Mass., Sept. 7, 1862.   *Christian Register, Sept.*, 1862.

2134. —— The National Wickedness.   A Discourse delivered in Brookline, September 26, 1861.
12mo. pp. 19.   BOSTON : *Walker, Wise & Co.*, 1861.

2135. —— The Sick Woman.   A Sermon for the Time.
8vo. pp. 16.   BOSTON : *Prentiss & Deland*, 1863.

2136. —— A Thanksgiving Discourse, preached at the First Church in Brookline, November 26, 1863.   *Boston Daily Advertiser, November* 28, 1853.

2137. —— The National Entail.   A Sermon preached to the First Congregational Church in Brookline, 3d of July, 1864.
8vo. pp. 19.   BOSTON : *Wright & Potter*, 1864.

2138. HELMER, C. D.   Two Sermons.   1, Signs of our National Atheism.   2, The War begun.   Preached in Plymouth Church, April 21 and 28, 1861.
8vo. pp. 25.   MILWAUKIE : *Terry & Cleaver*, 1861.

2139. —— The Stars and Stripes.   A Poem pronounced before the Phi Beta Kappa Society, Yale College, July 30, 1862.
8vo. pp. 23 to 47.   NEW HAVEN : *E. Haynes*, 1862.

2140. HELPER, HINTON ROWAN.   The Impending Crisis of the South ; how to meet it.
12mo. pp. 413.   NEW YORK : *Burdick Brothers*, 1857.

2141. HELPER, H. R. Compendium of the Impending Crisis of the South.
12mo. pp. 214. NEW YORK: *A. B. Burdick*, 1860.

2142. HENDERSEN, J. B., of Missouri. Speech on the Abolition of Slavery. Senate, March 27, 1862. 8vo. pp. 15.

2143. —— Speech on the National Currency, May 6, 1864. pp. 16.

2144. —— Funeral Oration delivered at Louisiana, Missouri, April 23, 1865. *Missouri Democrat, May* 3, 1865.

2145. HENDERSON, Rev. A. W. Glad Tidings for the Hospital. Light and Comfort from the Old Testament. (Embraced in eleven small Tracts.) New York: *American Tract Society.*

2146. —— Remember ; a Word for Soldiers.
18mo. pp. 48. NEW YORK : *American Tract Society.*

2147. HENDERSON, Rev. GEO. D., Chaplain U. S. N. Naval Academy, Annapolis. Address on the Death of General Nathaniel Lyon. Delivered at Manhattan, Kansas, September 26, 1861.
8vo. pp. 8. LEAVENWORTH: (Kansas,) 1861.

2148. HENDERSON, Hon. J. B., of Missouri. Speech on the Confiscation of Property. Delivered in the House of Representatives, April 8, 1862. 8vo. pp. 16.

2149. —— Speech delivered before a Mass Meeting of the Citizens of Marion and Ralls Counties, at Hannibal, Missouri, August 20, 1862. 8vo. pp. 8.

2150. HENDERSON, J. STANLEY. Missing Jo ; or The Mystery of Camp White. A Tale of the Tents.
8vo. pp. 36. NEW YORK: *Beadle & Co.*, 1865.

2151. HENNINGSEN, Gen. C. F. Letter in Reply to the Letter of Victor Hugo, on the Harper's Ferry Invasion ; with an Extract from the Letter of the Rev. Nathan Lord, and an Article from the London "Times" on Slavery.
8vo. pp. 32. NEW YORK : *Davies & Kent*, 1860.

2152. HENRY, C. S. Patriotism and the Slaveholders' Rebellion.
8vo. pp. 34. NEW YORK: *D. Appleton & Co.*, 1861.

2153. —— Among the Pines. *North American Review, Oct.*, 1862.

2154. —— The Constitution as it is. The Union as it was. *Continental Monthly, October*, 1862.

2155. —— Something we have to think of and to do. Ibid. *Dec.*, '62.

25

2156. HENRY, C. S. Letters to Professor S. F. B. Morse. Ibid. *Nov.,* 1863.

2157. —— Retrospective. Ibid. *January,* 1864.

2158. HENRY, GUSTAVUS A., of Tennessee. Speech in the Senate of the Confederate States, Nov. 29, 1864. Richmond. 8vo. pp. 13.

2159. HEPWORTH, GEORGE H. The Whip, Hoe and Sword; or the Gulf Department in '63.
8vo. pp. 298.   BOSTON : *Walker, Wise & Co..* 1864.

2160. HERBERT, SIDNEY. McClellan Melodist. A Collection of Patriotic Campaign Songs, in favor of the Constitution and the Union, the election of Gen. McClellan, the Restoration of the Federal Authority, etc.
12mo. pp. 32.   NEW YORK : *B. W. Hitchcock,* 1864.

2161. HERRICK, ANSON. The Disunion Policy of the Administration. Speech made in House of Representatives, March 26, 1864. 8vo. pp. 14.

2162. HEWES, GEORGE WHITFIELD. Ballads of the War.
12mo. pp. 147.   NEW YORK : *Carlton,* 1862.

2163. HEYWOOD, Rev. J. H. The Spirit and Duty of Christian Citizenship. A Sermon preached in Louisville, Kentucky, September 15, 1861.
8vo. pp. 12.   LOUISVILLE : *Maxwell & Co.,* 1862.

2164. HIBBARD, Rev. J. R. War in Heaven. A Sermon preached April 21, 1861.
12mo. pp. 15.   CHICAGO : *Tribune Office,* 1861.

2165. —— A Spiritual Ground of Hope for the Salvation of the Country. A Discourse delivered in the New Jerusalem Temple, August 6, 1863.
8vo. pp. 24.   CHICAGO : *Tribune Office,* 1862.

2166. —— A Sermon on the Causes and Uses of the Present Civil War, delivered in Chicago, April 11, 1862. 8vo. pp. 8.

2167. HICKMAN, Hon. JOHN, of Penn. Southern Sectionalism. Speech delivered in the House of Representatives, May 1, 1860. 8vo. pp. 8.

2168. HICKOK, Rev. M. J. The Mission of Calamity. A Thanksgiving Sermon preached in Scranton, Pa., November 27, 1862.
8vo. pp. 28.   NEW YORK : *John F. Trow,* 1862.

2169. HICKS, Hon. THOMAS H. Addresses on the Death of, delivered in the Senate and House of Representatives of the United States, on Wednesday, February 14, 1865.

8vo. pp. 48. WASHINGTON: *Government Printing Office*, 1865.

2170. HIGGINSON, Col. T. W. Gabriel's Defeat. *Atlantic Monthly, September*, 1862.

2171. —— Regular and Volunteer Officers. Ibid. *September*, 1864.

2172. —— Leaves from an Officer's Journal. Ibid. *November*, 1864.

2173. —— Leaves from an Officer's Journal. Ibid. *December*, 1864.

2174. —— Up the St. Mary's River. Ibid. *June*, 1865.

2175. —— Up the St. John's River. Ibid. *September*, 1864.

2176. HILDRETH, R. The "Ruin" of Jamaica. *Anti-Slavery Society*. 12mo. pp. 12.

2177. —— Despotism in America; or an Inquiry into the Nature and Results of the Slave-holding in the United States.

12mo. pp. 186. BOSTON: *Whipple & Damrell*, 1840.

2178. HILL, ALFRED C. Macpherson, the Great Confederate Philosopher and Southern Blower. A Record of his Philosophy, his Career as a Warrior, etc., and subsequent election as Governor of Louisiana.

12mo. pp. 209. NEW YORK: *James Miller*, 1864.

2179. HILL, A. F. Our Boys. The Personal Experience of a Soldier in the Army of the Potomac.

12mo. pp. 402. PHILADELPHIA: *John E. Potter*, 1864.

2180. —— Our Boys; or the Rich and Racy Scenes of Army and Camp Life, as seen and participated in by One of the Rank and File.

12mo. pp. PHILADELPHIA: *Potter*, 1865.

2181. HILL, ALONZO. Revelation by Fire. A Sermon preached in Worcester, August 17, 1862, after the Burial of William Hudson, a Private in the 25th Reg. of Massachusetts Volunteers.

8vo. pp. 23. BOSTON: *John Wilson & Son*, 1862.

2182. —— In Memoriam. A Discourse preached in Worcester, October 5, 1862, on Lieut. Thomas Jefferson Spurr, 15th Massachusetts Volunteers, who, mortally wounded at Antietam, died at Hagerstown, September 27.

8vo. pp. 32. BOSTON: *John Wilson & Son*, 1862.

2183. HILL, Rev. Thomas. (President of Harvard College.) The Sin of Silence. A Sermon preached in the Unitarian Church at Waltham, April 13, 1865. Waltham: *Free Press, May* 2, 1865.

2184. HILLARD, G. S. Life and Campaigns of George B. McClellan, Major General United States Army.
18mo. pp. 396.   Philadelphia : *J. B. Lippincott & Co.*, 1864.

2185. —— Life of General McClellan. *Am. Monthly Mag., July,* '64.

2186. HILLHOUSE, Thomas. The Conscription Act Vindicated.
8vo. pp. 27.   Albany : *Weed, Parsons & Co.*, 1863.

2187. HINGELEY, Rev. E. The Character and Greatness of Abraham Lincoln. A Discourse delivered April 23, 1865, at Monongahela City, Pennsylvania. pp. 15.

3188. History, A, of every attempt at Resistance to the Federal Government.
8vo. pp. 32.   New York : *William E. Chapin,* 1861.

2189. HITCHCOCK, Rev. R. D. Our National Sin. A Sermon preached on the Day of the National Fast, September 26, 1861, in New York.
8vo. pp. 24.   New York : *Baker & Godwin,* 1861.

2190. —— Thanksgiving for Victories. A Discourse delivered in Plymouth Church, Brooklyn, September 11, 1864.
8vo. pp. 7.   New York : *J. A. Gray & Greene,* 1864.

2191. HITCHCOCK, Rev. Henry L. God acknowledged in the Nation's Bereavement. A Sermon delivered in Hudson, Ohio, on the day of the Obsequies of Abraham Lincoln, April 19, 1865.
8vo. pp.   Cleveland : *Fairbanks, Benedict & Co.,* 1865.

2192. HODGE, Rev. Charles, DD. The State of the Country. From the *Princeton Review, January,* 1861. 8vo. pp. 32.

2193. —— The Church and the Country. *Princeton Review, Apr.,*'61.

2194. —— The General Assembly. The State of the Country. Ibid. *July,* 1861.

2195. —— England and America. Ibid. *January,* 1862.

2196. —— The War. Ibid. *January,* 1863.

2197. —— President Lincoln. Ibid. *July,* 1865.

2198. HODGES, Rev. Charles E. Disunion our Wisdom and our Duty. *Anti-Slavery Tracts, No.* 11. 16mo. pp. 12.

2199. HODSDON, Adjutant General. Major General Berry. *The Northern Monthly, March,* 1864.

2200. HODSDON, Adjutant General. Major General O. O. Howard. Ibid. *April,* 1864.

2201. HOGE, Mrs. Address delivered at a Meeting of Ladies, at Brooklyn, L. I., March, 1865, in aid of the Northwestern Fair. 8vo. pp. NEW YORK: *Sanford, Harroun & Co.,* 1865.

2202. HOGE, Rev. WM. J., DD. A Discourse delivered in New York, on the Resignation of his Charge, July 21, 1861. 8vo. pp. 26. NEW YORK: *Baker & Godwin,* 1861.

2203. HOIT, T. W. The Right of American Slavery. Southern and Western Edition. 8vo. pp. 51. ST. LOUIS: *L. Bushnell,* 1860.

2204. HOLCOMB, JUDSON, and W. S. IRWIN. The Chaplet of Freedom. A Biography of President Lincoln, Vice-President Hamlin, and every Representative and Senator who voted for the Amendment of the Constitution of the United States, passed by the 38th Congress, abolishing Slavery. In Press.

2205. HOLDEN, EDGAR, M. D. The First Cruise of the Monitor "Passaic." *Harpers' Magazine, October,* 1863.

2206. —— The Cruise of the Sassachus. *Harpers' Mag., Nov.,* 1864.

2207. HOLDEN, WM. S., of Indiana. Confiscation; Emancipation. Speech in House of Representatives, May 23, 1862. 8vo. pp. 8.

2208. HOLLAND, J. G. The Heart of the War. *Atlantic Monthly, August,* 1864.

2209. —— Eulogy on Abraham Lincoln, late President of the United States, pronounced at Springfield, Mass., April 19, 1865. 8vo. pp. 18. SPRINGFIELD: *L. J. Powers,* 1865.

2210. —— Life of Abraham Lincoln. 8vo. pp. 544. SPRINGFIELD: *Gurdon Bill,* 1866.

2211. HOLLAND, Col. JOHN C. Speech at the Union Mass Meeting, Rockville, Montgomery Co., Maryland, Oct. 3, 1863. 8vo. pp. 8.

2212. HOLLEY, ALEXANDER L. Iron Clads and Heavy Ordnance. *Atlantic Monthly, January,* 1863.

2213. HOLMAN, WILLIAM S., of Indiana. Frauds on the Treasury. Speech in the House of Representatives, April 29, 1862. 8vo. pp. 16. WASHINGTON: *McGill & Witherow,* 1862.

2214. HOLMES, Rev. JOHN McC. The Crisis and its Claims. A Sermon preached October 19, 1862, at Brooklyn, L. I. 8vo. pp. 16. NEW YORK: *Samuel Booth,* 1862.

2215. HOLMES, Oliver W. My Hunt after the Captain. *Atlantic Monthly, December,* 1862.

2216. —— Our Progressive Independence. Ibid. *April,* 1864.

2217. —— Oration delivered before the City Authorities at Boston, on the 87th Anniversary of the National Independence.
8vo. pp. 30.   Philadelphia: 1863.

2218. —— The same. 8vo. pp. 60 Boston: *J. E. Farwell & Co.,* '63.

2219. HOLMES, Stephen, Jr. The Guerillas of the Osage: or the Price of Loyalty on the Border.
8vo. pp. 45.   New York : *American News Co.,* 1864.

2220. HOLMES. A Soldier of the Cumberland; Memoir of Mead Holmes, Jr., Sergeant of Company K, 21st Regiment Wisconsin Volunteers. By his Father; with an Introduction by John S. Hart, LL. D.
18mo. pp. 240. Portrait.   *American Tract Society,* 1864.

2221. HOLT, Hon. Joseph. Speeches recently delivered in the cities of Boston and New York, on the Present Crisis in the Affairs of the Republic.
8vo. pp. 20.   Washington : *H. Polkinhorn,* 1861.

2222. —— Letter from, upon the Policy of the General Government ; Pending Revolution, its objects, its probable results if successful, and the Duty of Kentucky in the Crisis. Second edition.
8vo. pp. 28.   Washington: *H. Polkinhorn,* 1861.

2223. —— The same. Louisville, Ky. 8vo. pp. 15. *Bradley & Gilbert,* 1861.

2224. HOLT, Joseph, Edward Everett and Com. Charles Stuart. Letters on the Present Crisis.
8vo. pp. 45.   Philadelphia : *Wm. S. & Alfred Martien,* 1861.

2225. —— A Magnificent Argument. The Union Forever. A Kentuckian Speech. pp. 16.

2226. —— Address at Irving Hall, New York, September 5, 1861.
8vo. pp. 4.   Baltimore : *J. W. Woods,* 1861.

2227. —— Speech at Irving Hall, N. York, September 5, 1861. pp. 8.
New York : *Putnam.*

2228. —— The Fallacy of Neutrality. An Address to the People of Kentucky, delivered at Louisville, July 13, 1861 ; also his Letter to J. F. Speed, Esq.
8vo. pp. 31.   New York : *James G. Gregory,* 1861.

2229. HOLT, J.   Speech to the Troops of Indiana, and the Chamber of Commerce, New York.

8vo. pp. 8.   DETROIT: (Mich.) *H. Barns & Co.*

2230. —— Review, by the Judge Advocate General, of the Proceedings, Findings and Sentence of a General Court Marshal, held in Washington, for the Trial of Maj. Gen. Fitz John Porter.

8vo. pp. 31.   WASHINGTON: *Chronicle Office*, 1863.

2231. —— Report of the Judge Advocate General on the "Order of American Knights," or "Sons of Liberty." A Western Conspiracy in aid of the Southern Rebellion.

8vo. pp. 16.   WASHINGTON: *Government Printing Office*, 1864.

2232. —— Reply to Hon. Montgomery Blair, late Postmaster General, September 13, 1865.   pp. 12.

2233. —— Treason and its Treatment.   Remarks at a Dinner in Charleston, S. C., on the Evening of the 14th of April, 1865, after the Flag-Raising at Fort Sumter.

8vo. pp. 8.   NEW YORK: *Young Men's Repub. Union*, 1865.

2234. HOMANS, J. SMITH.   A Few Plain Words to England and her Manufacturers, read before the American Geographical and Statistical Society, February 27, 1862.   8vo. pp. 8.

2235. —— Currency, and the National Finances. *Continental Monthly, October*, 1863.

2236. HOOKER, JOHN.   Letter to my Friends of the Legal Profession throughout the State [of Connecticut] who adhere to the Democratic Party.   Dated Hartford, March 7, 1863.

8vo. pp. 8.   *New England Loyal Publication Society.*

2237. HOOPER, SAMUEL, of Mass.   Speech on the Treasury Note Bill, House of Representatives, Feb. 3, 1862.   8vo. pp. 8.

2238. —— Speech of, on Finances.   Delivered in the House of Representatives, Washington, January 19, 1863.   8vo. pp. 8.

2239. —— The Necessity of regulating the Currency of the Country. A Speech in the House of Reps., April 6, 1864.   8vo. pp. 15.

2240. HOPE, A. J. B. BERESFORD.   England; the North and the South.

8vo: pp. 40.   LONDON: *James Ridgeway*, 1862.

2241. —— The Social and Political Bearings of the American Disruption.

8vo. pp. 42.   LONDON: *W. Ridgway*, 1863.

2242. HOPE, A. J. B. B. A Popular View of the American Civil War. 8vo. pp. 27. LONDON: *W. Ridgway*, 1861.

2243. HOPKINS, JOHN BAKER. Introduction to the Hon. James William's "The South Vindicated," etc. Lond. 8vo. p. xii, 40.

2244. HOPKINS, JOHN HENRY, DD. The American Citizen; his Rights and Duties, according to the Spirit of the Constitution of the United States.
12mo. pp. 459. NEW YORK: *Prudney & Russell*, 1857.

2245. —— Bible View of Slavery. (A Letter to G. M. Wharton and others, in reply to a Note from them, requesting the Bishop's Views on the Christian Aspect of Slavery.) Burlington, Vermont, May 2, 1863. 8vo. pp. 16.

2246. —— Review of a "Letter from the Rt. Rev. John H. Hopkins, DD., LL. D., Bishop of Vermont, on the Bible View of Slavery." By a Vermonter.
8vo. pp. 28. BURLINGTON: *Free Press Office*, 1861.

2247. —— Review of Bishop Hopkins' Bible View of Slavery, by a Presbyter of the Church, in Philadelphia. Phila. 8vo. pp. 15.

2248. —— Remarks on Bishop Hopkins' "Letter on the Bible View of Slavery." (No place.) 8vo. pp. 20.

2249. —— Bible View of Slavery, by John H. Hopkins, DD., Bishop of Vermont," Examined. By Henry Drisler.
8vo. pp. 20. NEW YORK: *C. S. Westcott & Co.*, 1862.

2250. —— Bible View of Slavery reconsidered. A Letter to the Rt. Rev. Bishop Hopkins. 2d edition, enlarged. (Signed, Biblicus.)
8vo. pp. 15. PHILADELPHIA: *H. B. Ashmead*, 1863.

2251. —— Bishop Hopkins' Letter on Slavery Ripped up, and his Misuse of the Sacred Scriptures Exposed. By a Clergyman of the Protestant Episcopal Church.
12mo. pp. 44. NEW YORK: *John F. Trow*, 1863.

2252. —— The Bishop of Vermont's Protest, and Draft of a Pastoral Letter. 8vo. pp. 16.

2253. —— Protest of the Bishop and Clergy of the Diocese of Pennsylvania, against Bishop Hopkins' Letter on African Slavery. September, 1863. 4to. pp. 3.

2254. —— The Views of Judge Woodward and Bishop Hopkins on Negro Slavery at the South. Illustrated from the Journal of a Residence on a Georgia Plantation, by Mrs. Kemble. Phila.,'63.

2255. HOPKINS, J. H., DD. Bible View of Polygamy. To the Rt. Rev. J. H. Hopkins, Bishop of Vermont. Signed, Mizpah. [Henry C. Lea.] 8vo. p. 4.

2256. —— A Scriptural, Ecclesiastical and Historical View of Slavery, from the days of Abraham to the Nineteenth Century. Addressed to the Rt. Rev. Alonzo Potter, DD. 12mo. pp. 376. NEW YORK : *W. I. Pooley*, 1864.

2257. HOPKINS, MARK, DD. The Living House, on God's Method of Social Unity. A Baccalaureate Sermon, delivered at Williamstown, Mass., August 3, 1862. 8vo. pp. 26. BOSTON : *T. R. Marvin & Son*, 1862.

2258. HOPKINS, WILLIAM. Speech on the Joint Resolutions on the State of the Country, in the Pennsylvania House of Representatives, April 9, 1863. pp. 4.

2259. HOPKINS, Rev. T. M. A Discourse on the Death of Abraham Lincoln, delivered in Bloomington, Ind., Apr. 19, 1865. 8vo. p 7.

2260. HOPPER, Rev. EDWARD. Republican Homes. An Address delivered before the Association of the Alumni of the University of the City of New York, June 19, 1861. 8vo. pp. 27. *University Press*, 1861.

HOPSON, EDWARDS C., see *Henry Clark*.

2261. HORNBLOWER, W. H. The Duty of the General Assembly to all the Churches under its care. A Vindication of the minority in opposition to the Resolutions on the State of the Country. 8vo. pp. 10. PATERSON : *A. Mead*, 1861.

2262. HORSFORD, E. N. The Army Ration ; how to diminish its weight and Bulk, etc. 8vo. pp. 42. NEW YORK : *D. Van Nostrand*, 1864.

2263. HORTON, V. B., of Ohio. Speech on the Treasury Note Bill. House of Representatives, February 5, 1862. 8vo. pp. 8.

2264. HOSMER, FRANK K. The Color-Guard ; being a Corporal's Notes of Military Service in the Nineteenth Army Corps. 8vo. pp. 244. BOSTON : *Walker, Wise & Co.*, 1864.

2265. —— The Thinking Bayonet. 12mo. pp. vi and 326. BOSTON : *Walker, Fuller & Co.*, 1865.

2266. HOSMER, GEORGE W., DD. Report of Delegates from the General Aid Society for the Army, at Buffalo, N. Y., to visit the

26

Government Hospitals, and the Agencies of the Sanitary Commission.

8vo. pp. 16.   BUFFALO : *Franklin Press*, 1862.

2267. HOSPITAL LIFE, Notes of, from November, 1861, to August, '63.
12mo. pp. 210.   PHILADELPHIA : *J. B. Lippincott & Co.*, 1864.

2268. HOSPITAL TRANSPORTS. A Memoir of the Embarkation of the Sick and Wounded from the Peninsula of Virginia, in the Summer of 1862.

12mo. pp. 167.   BOSTON : *Ticknor & Fields*, 1863.

2269. HOTALING, SAMUEL. The Questions in the Canvass considered by a Merchant of New York. Speech before the Young Men's Republican Union, October 29, 1860.

8vo. pp. 12.   NEW YORK : *Baker & Godwin*, 1860.

2270. HOTCHKISS' Rifle Projectiles, and the manner of using them.
18mo. pp. 13.   *Ordnance Department*, 1862.

2271. HOUGH, FRANKLIN B. History of Duryee's Brigade, during the Campaign in Virginia, under General Pope, and in Maryland, under General McClellan, in the Summer and Autumn of 1862.

8vo. pp. 200.   ALBANY : *J. Munsell*, 1864.

2272. HOUGHTON, EDWIN B. History of the Campaigns of the Seventeenth Maine Regiment. (In press.) Portland, Maine.

2273. HOVEY, Rev. HORACE C. The National Fast. A Sermon preached at Coldwater, Michigan, January 4, 1861.

8vo. pp. 12.   COLDWATER : *Republican Print*, 1861.

2273.* —— Freedom's Banner. A Sermon preached to the Coldwater Light Artillery and Zouave Cadets, April 28, 1861.

8vo. pp. 11.   COLDWATER : *Republican Print*, 1861.

2274. —— Loyalty. A Sermon preached in Northampton, February 22, 1863.

8vo. pp. 16.   NORTHAMPTON : *Metcalf & Co.*, 1863.

2275. HOWARD, F. R. Fourteen months in American Bastiles.
8vo. pp. 89.   BALTIMORE : *Kelly, Hedian & Piet*, 1863.

2276. HOWARD, Hon. J. M., of Michigan. Speech on the Confiscation of Property, in the Senate of the United States, April 18, 1862. 8vo. pp. 16.

2277. —— Speech, January, 1864, on the Motion to expel Mr. Davis of Kentucky, for offering a Series of Resolutions in the Senate, tending to incite insurrection. pp. 15.

2278. HOWARD, Hon. J. M. Speech on the Joint Resolution for the recognition and readmission to the Union of Louisiana. Delivered in the Senate of the United States, Feb. 25, '65. 8vo. pp. 15.

2279. HOWARD, Rev. MARTIN S. Christian Patriotism. A Sermon delivered in South Dartmouth, January 20, 1861. New Bedford: *Standard, February* 2.

2280. —— The Divine Sanction. The Basis of Human Success. A Sermon preached in South Dartmouth, Nov. 27, 1862.
8vo. pp. 23. NEW BEDFORD : (Mass.) *Edmund Anthony,* 1862.

2281. —— Protection in the Family, in Society, and in the State. A Sermon preached in South Dartmouth, April 7, '64. 8vo. pp. 8.

2282. HOWARD, MARK. Despotic Doctrines, declared by the United States Senate, exposed; and Senator Dixon unmasked.
8vo. pp. 24. HARTFORD : *Case, Lockwood & Co.,* 1863.

2283. HOWARD, Major General O. O. Oration at the Laying of the Corner Stone of the Monument in the Soldiers' National Cemetery, at Gettysburg, July 4, 1865 ; with the Speech of Governor Curtin, and other Exercises of the occasion.
8vo. pp. 60. GETTYSBURG : *Auginbaugh & Wible,* 1865.

2284. HOWARD, Col. PERCY. The Barbarities of the Rebels, as shown in their Cruelty to the Federal Wounded and Prisoners ; in their Outrages upon Union Men ; in the Murder of Negroes, and in their unmanly Conduct throughout the Rebellion.
8vo. pp. 40. PROVIDENCE : (R. I.) *For the author,* 1863.

2285. HOWE, M. A. DEWOLFE. Loyalty in the American Republic. What is it ? and What its Object ? A Discourse delivered in Philadelphia, November 26, 1863.
8vo. pp. 19. PHILADELPHIA : *J. S. McCalla,* 1863.

2286. —— A Reply to the Letter of Bishop Hopkins, addressed to Dr. Howe, in the Print called "The Age," of December, 1863.
8vo. pp. 18. PHILADELPHIA : *King & Baird,* 1864.

2287. HOWE, S. G., M. D. A Letter on the Sanitary Condition of the Troops in the neighborhood of Boston, to the Governor of Massachusetts.
8vo. pp. 16. WASHINGTON: *Government Printing Office,* 1861.

2288. HOWE, S. G., M. D.   A Letter to Mrs., and other Loyal Women, touching the matter of Contributions for the Army, and other matters connected with the War.
8vo. pp. 28.   BOSTON : *Ticknor & Fields*, 1862.

2289. HOWE, Hon. T. O., of Wisconsin.   The State and the National, Governments.   Speech in the Assembly Chamber, March 29, 1860.   pp. 16.

2290. —— The Authority of the Nation, Supreme and Absolute; that of the State, Subordinate and Conditional.   Speech in the Senate of the United States, January 10, 1866.   pp. 20.

2291. —— Speech on the Issue of United States Notes, February 12, 1862.   pp. 14.

2292. —— Speech on his Bill to aid in restoring Order and preserving the Public Peace, within the Insurrectionary Districts.   United States Senate, May 26, 1862.

2293. —— An Address before the American Iron Association, delivered in Chicago, May 24, 1865.
8vo. pp. 18.   CHICAGO : *John A. Norton*, 1865.

2294. —— The same.   8vo. pp. 19.   Green Bay : *Robinson Bro.*, '65.

2295. HOW THE WAR WAS COMMENCED.   An Appeal to Documents. Southern Democrats, especially, quoted.   (From the Cincinnati Daily Commercial.)
8vo. pp. 16.   *Loyal Publication Society, No. 46*, 1864.

2296. —— Wie der Krieg angefangen wurde.   (The same as the foregoing, in German.)
8vo. pp. 15.   *Loyal Publication Society, No. 53*, 1864.

2297. HOWLETT, Rev. T. R.   The Dealings of God with the Nation. A Discourse delivered in Washington, D. C., on the Day of Humiliation and Prayer, June 1, 1865.
8vo. pp. 7.   WASHINGTON : *Gibson Brothers*, 1865.

1298. HOWSON, HENRY.   American Jute.   Paper read at the monthly Meeting of the Franklin Institute, Philadelphia, October 16, 1862.
8vo. pp. 8.   PHILADELPHIA : *Howson's Office*, 1862.

2299. HOYT, JAMES.   God with the Nation.   A Thanksgiving Sermon delivered November 27, 1862, in Orange, New Jersey.
12mo. pp. 26.   ORANGE : *N. J. Edward Gardner*, 1862.

2300. HUBBARD, Rev. A. C. A Thanksgiving Sermon preached at the First Baptist Church, on November 27, 1862.
8vo. pp. 16. SPRINGFIELD : *Bailhache & Baker*, 1862.

2300.* HUBBELL, WILLIAM W. Letter to the Chairman of the Naval Commitee. House of Reps., Dec. 12, 1860. 12mo. p. 23.

2301. —— Testimony and Brief of Facts, etc., on behalf of William Wheeler Hubbell, Esq., in support of his claim on the Government, for payment for the use of his improvements in Explosive Shells and Fuses.
8vo. pp. 79 and Index. PHILADELPHIA : *King & Baird*, 1861.

2302. —— Claim for remuneration for use of Explosive Shell. Statement relative to, from Bureau of Ordnance. 12mo. pp. 23.

2303. —— Reply to the pamphlet headed, " Bureau of Ordnance and Hydrography, Washington, 1862," in relation to his Claim for Patent Explosive Shell and Fuse, used for the great Guns of the Ships and Gun Boats. pp. 8.

2304. —— The Path of Washington. The Way to secure Peace and establish Unity as One Nation. 8vo. pp. 28.

2305. HUDSON, E. M. The Second War of Independence in America. Translated by the Author from the Second enlarged and revised German edition. With an Introduction by Bolling A. Pope.
8vo. pp. LONDON : 1863.

2306. HUDSON, WILLIAM. Revelation by Fire. A Sermon preached at the Burial of, by Rev. Alonzo Hill, in Worcester, Aug. 17,'62.
8vo. pp. 23. BOSTON : *John Wilson & Son*, 1861.

2307. HUDSON, Rev. H. N. Christian Patriotism. A Sermon preached in St. Clement's Church, New York, Jan. 4, 1861.
12mo. pp. 27. NEW YORK : *F. D. Harriman*, 1861.

2308. HUGHES, Archbishop. A Sermon on the Civil War in America, delivered August 17, 1862, on his return to America from Europe.
8vo. pp. 4. PHILADELPHIA : *T. B. Peterson*, 1862.

2209. HUGHES, HENRY. A Report on the African Apprentice System, read at the Southern Commercial Convention.
8vo. pp. 15. VICKSBURG : 1859.

2210. HUGHES, THOMAS. The Cause of Freedom ; Which is its Champion in America, the North or the South ?
8vo. pp. 16. LONDON : *William Wisley*, 1863.

2311. HUGO, Victor. John Brown ; with a Photograph Representation of his Execution.
8vo. pp. 8. Paris : *E. Dentu,* 1861,

2312. HUMPHREYS, E. R. Education of Officers, Preparatory and Professional.
8vo. pp. 40. Boston : *Lee & Shepard,* 1862.

2313. HUMPHREY, Rev. Heman, DD. Charges against Slavery. Extracts from a Discourse delivered at Pittsfield, Jan. 4, 1861.
18mo. pp. 32. Boston : *American Tract Society.*

2314. HUNT, Capt. E. B. Union Foundations ; a Study of American Nationality as a Fact of Science.
8vo. pp. 61. New York: *D. Van Nostrand,* 1863.

2315. HUNT, Ezra M. The War and its Lessons.
8vo. pp. 35. New York : *F. Somers,* 1862.

2316. —— Words about the War ; or Plain Facts for Plain People.
8vo. pp. 39. New York : *F. Somers,* 1861.

2317. HUNT, Major Henry J. Report of Light Battery, Me. Second Artillery, U. S. A. Battle of Bull Run, July 21, 1861. pp. 4.

2318. HUNT, Dr. James. The Negro's Place in Nature. A Paper read before the London Anthropological Society.
8vo. pp. 27. New York : *Van Evrie, Horton & Co.,* 1864.

2319. HUNT, Noah H. The End of Strife. A Thanksgiving Discourse preached in Baltimore, Md., December 7, 1865.
8vo. pp. 16. Baltimore : *Wm. K. Boyle,* 1865.

2320. HUNTER, General D. Letter to Edwin M. Stanton, Secretary of War. (Called forth by the Resolution of Mr. Wickliffe, of Kentucky.)
8vo. pp. 4. Boston : *Emancipation League,* 1862.

2321. HUNTER, R. M. T., of Virginia. Speech on the Resolution proposing to retrocede the Forts, Dock-Yards, etc., to the State applying for the same. Senate, Jan. 11, 1861. 8vo. pp. 16.

2322. —— The Ruling Passion strong in Death. Speech of Senator Hunter on the Bill for Arming the Slaves. *Broadside, Manchester, England.*

2323. HUNTINGTON, F. D., DD. A Nation's Look towards God. A Sermon. *New York Christian Times, September* 27, 1862.

2324. —— God's Way in the War. A Sermon preached in Emmanuel Church, Boston, April 30, 1863. *Boston Ch. Witness, May,* '63.

2325. HUNTINGTON, F. D., D. D.   Personal Humiliation demanded by the National Danger.   A Sermon delivered at Emmanuel Church, April 24, 1864.

12mo. pp. 16.   BOSTON: *E. P. Dutton & Co.*, 1864.

2325.* HURD.   The Law of Freedom and Bondage in the U. S.

2 vols. 8vo. pp. 617, 800.   BOSTON: *Little, Brown & Co.*, 1863.

2326. HURD, EGBERT.   English and American Taxation.   *Continental Monthly, April,* 1864.

2327. HURLBERT, WM. HENRY.   Gen. McClellan and the Conduct of the War.

12mo. pp. 312.   Map.   NEW YORK: *Sheldon & Co.*, 1864.

2328. HUSBAND, J. L.   Our National Finances.   8vo. pp. 8.   Philadelphia, 1864.

2329. HUTCHINS, Hon. JOHN, of Ohio.   Speech on the Bill for the Release of certain persons held to service or labor, in the District of Columbia.   Delivered in the House of Representatives, April 11, 1862.   8vo. pp. 7.

2330. HUTCHINS, ROBERT C.   The Usurpation of the Federal Government.   The Dangers of Centralization.   Speech in the House of Assembly of New York, February 26, 1863.

8vo. pp. 16.   ALBANY: *Atlas and Argus Print*, 1863.

2331. HUXSON, A. B., U. S. A.   Contributions to the Rhymes of the War.   May, 1865.

12mo. pp. 25.   BALTIMORE: *J. D. Toy*, 1865.

I AM A SOLDIER.   [Advice to a Soldier.]   8vo. pp. 8.

2333. ILLINOIS STATE SANITARY BUREAU, Report of, May, 1863.   8vo. pp. 10.

2334. ILLINOIS.   Inaugural Address of Richard Yates, Governor, January 14, 1861.   pp. 24.

2335. —— Annual Report of the Adjutant General of, for 1861–62.

8vo. pp. 383.   SPRINGFIELD: *Baker & Philips*, 1863.

2335.* —— Message of Gov. Yates to the General Assembly, January 5, 1863.

8vo. pp. 64.   SPRINGFIELD: *Baker & Phillips*, 1863.

2336. ILLINOIS. The Impending Contest. The Issues of the Campaign. The Question for True Union Men. Shellabarger and Cox contrasted. 8vo. pp. 16. *Springfield Republican.*

2337. INCIDENTS of American Camp Life; being events which have actually transpired during the present Rebellion.
12mo. pp. 72. NEW YORK: *T. R. Dawley,* 1862.

2338. —— The same, enlarged. 12mo. pp. 104. New York: *Dawley.* ·

2338.* INCIDENTS of the Civil War in America.
8vo. pp. 100. NEW YORK : *Frank Leslie,* 1862.

2339. INCOME TAX, Regulations for the Assessment of, May, '63. pp. 4.

2340. INDIAN TRUST BONDS. (Abstracted.) Report of the Select Committee in relation to the Fraudulent Abstraction of certain Bonds, held by the Government in trust for the Indian Tribes, and to whom was referred the Communication of Hon. John B. Floyd, late Secretary of War. 8vo. pp. 352. *36th Congress, 2d Session, House of Representatives, Report No.* 68.

2341. INDIANA. Prospectus of the Proposed Loan of the State of Indiana, for War Purposes. New York, 1861. 8vo. pp. 10.

2342. —— The Soldier of, in the War for the Union.
8vo. pp. 142. INDIANAPOLIS : *Merrill & Co.,* 1864.

2343. —— Report of the Adjutant General of, 1861–62.
8vo. pp. 339. INDIANAPOLIS : *J. J. Bingham,* 1863.

2344. —— Report of Special Agents, Pay Agents, et al., Visiting Troops, etc.
8vo. pp. 220. INDIANAPOLIS : *Joseph J. Bingham,* 1863,

2345. —— Report of the State Paymaster of the Indiana Volunteer Militia, December 31, 1862. 8vo. pp. 7.

2346. —— Report of J. P. Liddall, Draft Commissioner. pp. 39.

2347. —— Report of John C. New, Quartermaster Gen., Nov., 1862.
8vo. pp. 14. INDIANAPOLIS : *J. J. Bingham,* 1863.

2348. —— Message of Governor Morton, January 9, 1863.
8vo. pp. 32. INDIANAPOLIS : *Joseph J. Bingham,* 1863.

2349. —— Report of the Quartermaster General, May 1, 1862.
8vo. pp. 27. INDIANAPOLIS : *Joseph J. Bingham,* 1863.

2350. —— Report of Pay Agents, December 31, 1862. 8vo. pp. 4.

2351. —— Report of W. H. H. Terrell, Financial Secretary, to the Governor, May, 1864.
8vo. pp. 25. INDIANAPOLIS : *Joseph J. Bingham,* 1864.

2352. INDIANA. Report of Indiana Military Agencies, to the Governor. 8vo. pp. 76. INDIANAPOLIS : *W. R. Holloway*, 1865.

2353. —— Report of the Indiana Sanitary Commission, Jan. 2, 1865. 8vo. pp. 132. INDIANAPOLIS : *W. R. Holloway*, 1865.

2354. —— Proceedings of the Indiana Sanitary Convention, held in Indianapolis, Indiana, March 2, 1864.
8vo. pp. 76. INDIANAPOLIS : *Journal*, 1864.

2355. —— Message of the Governor of Indiana, Jan. 6, '65. 8vo. p. 33.

2356. —— Message of the Governor of Indiana, Special Session, November 15, 1865. pp. 26.

2357. —— Report of Ashel Stone, Quartermaster Gen., Jan. 1, 1865. 8vo. pp. 86. INDIANAPOLIS : *W. W. Holloway*, 1865.

2358. —— Report of Laz. Noble, Adjutant General, from Jan. 1, 1863, to November 12, 1864. pp. 33.

2359. —— Report of the Allotment Commissioner, on the transmission of money to Soldiers. 8vo. pp. 23.

2360. INGERSOLL, CHARLES. A Letter to a Friend in a Slave State. By a Citizen of Pennsylvania.
8vo. pp. 60. PHILADELPHIA, 1862.

2361. —— An Undelivered Speech on Executive Arrests, Dec., 1862. 8vo. pp. 98. PHILADELPHIA, 1862.

2362. —— A Letter to a Friend in a Slave State. By a Citizen of Philadelphia.
8vo. pp. 60. PHILADELPHIA : *James Campbell*, 1862.

2363. INGERSOLL, J. R. Secession Resisted.
8vo. pp. 38. PHILADELPHIA : *King & Baird*, 1861.

2364. —— Secession, a Folly and a Crime. pp. 29. Phila., 1861.

2365. —— Separazione una Follia, ed un Diletto. Discorso del Lodevole J. R. Ingersoll di Filadelfia. Traduzione dall' Inglese di C. G. Moroni.
8vo. pp. 29. PHILADELPHIA : *King & Baird.*

2366. AN INQUIRY into the Causes and Cost of Corrupt State Legislation. By a Citizen of Philadelphia.
8vo. pp. 32. PHILADELPHIA, 1863.

2367. INTERIOR CAUSES of the War. The Nation Demonized, and its President a Spirit Rapper. By a Citizen of Ohio.
8vo. pp. 115. NEW YORK : *M. Doolady*, 1863.

27

2268. INTERNAL REVENUE. Report of the Commissioner of Internal Revenue, on the Operations of the Internal Revenue System, for the year ending June 30, 1863.

8vo. pp. 241. WASHINGTON: *Government Printing Office,* 1864.

2369. INTERNAL REVENUE LAWS, An Act amendatory of, and for other purposes. Approved March 3, 1863.

8vo. pp. 23. WASHINGTON: *Government Printing Office,* 1863.

2370. INTERNATIONAL MARITIME LAW, Correspondence respecting.

Folio, pp. 27. (*Parl. Papers, N. Am., No. 3.*) *London,* 1862.

2371. INTERNATIONAL LAW. War and Peace.

8vo. pp. 10. NEW YORK: *Sinclair Toucey,* 1863.

2372. IOWA. Message of Governor Abram A. Hammond, January 11, 1861. 8vo. pp. 13.

2373. —— Special Message of Gov. Kirkwood, May 21, '61. 8vo. p. 7.

2374. ——- Report of the Adjutant General of the State of Iowa, for the year ending December 31, 1861.

8vo. pp. 494. DES MOINES: *F. W. Palmer,* 1862.

2375. —— Biennial Message, delivered to the Iowa General Assembly, by Governor S. J. Kirkwood, January 14, 1862.

8vo. pp. 19. DES MOINES: *F. W. Palmer,* 1862.

2376. —— Inaugural Address to the General Assembly of the State of Iowa, by Gov. S. J. Kirkwood, January 15, 1862.

8vo. pp. 12. DES MOINES: *F. W. Palmer,* 1862.

2377. —— Special Message delivered to the House of Representatives of the State of Iowa, by Gov. Kirkwood, February 6, 1862.

8vo. pp. 20. DES MOINES: *F. W. Palmer,* 1862.

2378. —— Report of the Adjutant General and Acting Quartermaster General, January 1, 1863.

2 vols. 8vo. DES MOINES: *F. W. Palmer,* 1863.

2379· —— Report of the Adjutant General and Acting Quartermaster General of the State of Iowa, Jan. 1, 1863, to Jan. 11, 1864.

8vo. pp. xliv. 799. DES MOINES: *F. W. Palmer,* 1864.

2380. —— Inaugural Address delivered to the Tenth General Assembly of the State of Iowa, by Governor William M. Stone.

8vo. pp. 20. DES MOINES ; *F. W. Palmer,* 1864.

2381. —— Report of the Adjutant General and Acting Quartermaster General, January 11, 1864, to January 1, 1865.

8vo. pp. xx and 1502. DES MOINES: *F. W. Palmer,* 1865.

2382· IOWA. History of the Southern Iowa Soldiers' Fair, at Burlington, Iowa, from September 26 to October 1, 1864.
8vo. pp. 14. BURLINGTON: (Iowa) *Hawke Eye Press*, 1865.

2383. —— First Annual Festival of the Scott County Old Soldiers' Association, October 4, 1865. Oration of the Rev. H. N. Powers. Addresses of Governor Saunders and Gov. G. H. Baker. *Davenport Gazette, October 4, 1865.*

2384. IRELAND AND AMERICA. A Letter to the O'Donoghue, M. P., by an American Citizen. "England's Difficulty is Ireland's Opportunity."
8vo. pp. 18. NEW YORK: *P. O'Shea*, 1862.

2385. IRISH, DAVID. Observations on a living and effectual Testimony against Slavery; introduced with some remarks upon excess and superfluity, recommended to the consideration of the Society of Friends.
12mo. pp. 30. NEW YORK: *For the author*, 1836.

2386. —— Self-Justification; Self-Condemnation. A Dialogue.
12mo. pp. 17. NEW YORK: *For the author*, 1836.

2387. IRON-CLAD SHIPS. Letter from the Secretary of the Navy to the Committee on Naval Affairs, in relation to Iron-Clad Ships, Ordnance, etc. 8vo. pp. 6. *House of Representatives, Miscellaneous Document, No. 82, 37th Congress, 2d Session, 1862.*

2388. IRWIN, Rev. WILLIAM. A Sermon preached April 16, 1865, the day after the Death of President Lincoln, at Rondout, N. Y.
8vo. pp. 20. NEW YORK: *John A Gray & Green*, 1865

JACKSON, President ANDREW. Proclamation against the Nullification Ordinance of South Carolina, Dec. 11, 1832. 8vo. pp. 20.

2390. JACKSON. Testimonials to the Life and Character of the late Francis Jackson, President of the Mass. Anti-Slavery Society.
12mo. pp. 36. BOSTON: *R. F. Wallcut*, 1861.

2391. JACKSON, JAMES W., the Alexandria Hero—the Slayer of Ellsworth, the First Martyr in the Cause of Southern Independence; containing a full account of the circumstances of his heroic Death, and the many remarkable incidents in his eventful Life, constituting a true History—more like romance than reality.
8vo. pp. RICHMOND: *West & Johnston*, 1863.

2393. JACKSON, Stonewall, Life of. From Official Papers, Contemporary Narratives, and Personal Acquaintance. By the Hon. J. M. Daniels.
12mo. pp.   Richmond : 1863.

2394. —— The same, with Portrait.
12mo. pp. 305.   New York : *C. B. Richardson,* 1863.

2395. —— The same. With Portrait.
Crown 8vo. pp. 305.   London : *S. Low,* 1863.

2396. JACKSON, Rev. John Walter. The Sentiments and Conduct proper to the present Crisis in our National Affairs. A Sermon preached at Philadelphia, April 21, 1861.
8vo. pp. 13.   Philadelphia : *Collins,* 1861.

2397. —— The Union ; Constitution ; Peace. A Thanksgiving Sermon, delivered in Harrisburg, Pa., August 6, 1863.
8vo. pp. 33.   Harrisburg : *Telegraph Office,* 1863.

2398. JACKSON, Tatlow. Martial Law ; What is it ? and Who can declare it ?
8vo. pp. 19.   Philadelphia : *John Campbell,* 1862.

2400. —— Authorities cited, antagonistic to Horace Binney's Conclusions on the Writ of Habeas Corpus.
8vo. pp. 8.   Philadelphia : *John Campbell,* 1862.

2401. JACKSON, William A., Colonel of the 18th Regiment New York Volunteers, who died at Washington, November 11, 1861. Memoir of.
8vo. pp. 40.   Albany : *Joel Munsell,* 1862.

2402. JACOBS, M. Notes on the Rebel Invasion of Maryland and Pennsylvania, and the Battle of Gettysburg, July 1, 2 and 3, '63.
12mo. pp. 47.   Philadelphia : *J. B. Lippincott & Co.,* 1864.

2403. —— The Battle of Gettysburg. *Emanc. Qr. Review, Vol.* xv.

2405. JACOBS, Col. Richard T., Lieut. Governor of Kentucky, and Col. Frank Wolford, one of the Presidential Electors of that State. Information in relation to the arrest of, communicated to Congress by the President, *Senate Executive Document,* 16, *38th Congress, 1st Session,* 1865. 8vo. pp. 25.

2406. JAGGER, William. Information, acquired from the best authority, with respect to the Institution of Slavery.
8vo. pp. 28.   New York : *R. Craighead,* 1856.

2407. JAMES, EDWIN. Suggestions for an Act to establish a uniform System of Bankruptcy Laws throughout the United States. 8vo. pp. 32. NEW YORK: *Baker & Godwin,* 1864.

2408. —— Oration delivered before the Young Men's Association of Brooklyn, New York, on July 4, 1863. 8vo. pp. 23. NEW YORK: *Baker & Godwin,* 1863.

2410. —— A Letter to the Artisans and Operatives of the City of New York. NEW YORK: *Baker & Godwin,* 1863.

2411. JAMES, HORACE, The Two Great Wars of America. An Oration delivered in Newbern, N. C., before the 25th Regiment Massachusetts Volunteers, July 4, 1862. 8vo. p. 30. BOSTON: *W. F. Brown & Co.*

2412. —— The Christian Patriot, A Sermon. Worcester, 1861. 8vo. pp. 7.

2413. JAMES, HENRY. The Social Significance of our Institutions. An Oration delivered at Newport, R. I., July 4, 1861. 8vo. pp. 47. BOSTON: *Ticknor & Fields,* 1861.

2414. JANVIER, FRANCIS DE HAES. The Sleeping Sentinel. 12mo. pp. 19. PHILADELPHIA : *T. B. Peterson & Bros.,* 1863.

2416. JAQUES, JOHN W. Three Years' Campaign in the 9th New York State Militia. Southern Rebellion. 12mo. pp. 198. NEW YORK: *Hilton & Co.,* 1865.

2417. JARVIS, EDWARD, M. D. The Sanitary Condition of the Army of the United States. *Atlantic Monthly, October,* 1862.

2418. JAY, JOHN. Thoughts on the Duty of the Episcopal Church, in relation to Slavery. A Speech delivered in the New York Anti-Slavery Convention, February 12, 1839. 16mo. pp. 11. NEW YORK: *Piercy & Reed,* 1839

2419. —— The Progress and Results of Emancipation in the English West Indies. A Lecture before the Philomathean Society of New York. 8vo. pp. 39. NEW YORK: *Wiley & Putnam,* 1842.

2420. —— Caste and Slavery in the American Church. 8vo. pp. 51 NEW YORK : *Wiley & Putnam,* 1843.

2421. —— America Free, or America Slave. An Address on the State of the Country, at Bedford, Westchester County, New York, October 8, 1856. 8vo. pp. 20.

2422. JAY, J. The American Church and the African Slave Trade. Speech in the New York Diocesan Convention of the Protestant Episcopal Church, September 27, 1860 ; with a Note of the Proceedings had in that Council on the subject.

8vo. pp. 30.   NEW YORK : *Roe Lockwood & Sons,* 1860.

2423. —— The Great Conspiracy. An Address delivered at Mount Kisco, Westchester County, New York, July 4, 1861.

8vo. pp. 50.   NEW YORK : *James G. Gregory,* 1861.

2424. —— The same. Second edition. New York : *Randolph,* 1863. 8vo. pp. 50.

2425. —— The Rise and Fall of the Pro-Slavery Democracy, and the Rise and Duties of the Republican Party. Address to the Citizens of Westchester County, N. York. Delivered at Bedford, November 5, 1860.

8vo. pp. 45.   NEW YORK : *Roe Lockwood & Co.,* 1861.

2426. —— Address to the Citizens of Westchester County, on the Approaching State Election. " The New York Election and the State of the Country." Morissania, N. Y., Oct. 30, 1862.

8vo. pp. 24.   NEW YORK : *John F. Trow,* 1862.

2427. —— The Church and the Rebellion. Letter to the Rector and Vestry of St. Matthew's Church, Bedford ; with a Preface in Reply to the Rectors. Speech from the Chancel, June 21, 1863, touching the recent visit of a Clergyman of doubtful loyalty.

8vo. pp. 37.   BEDFORD : (Westchester Co., N. Y.,) 1863.

2428. —— Judge Jay's Portrait at White Plains. Correspondence in reference to its original Acceptance by the County of Westchester, and the recent attempt to remove it from the Court House.

8vo. pp. 24.   NEW YORK : *James G. Gregory,* 1863.

2429. —— Letter on the recent relinquishment of the Monroe Doctrine, New York, March 30, 1863. 8vo. pp. 8.

2430. —— Our Triumph and our Duties. Remarks at the Celebration Dinner of the East Brooklyn Union Campaign Club. December 22, 1864. pp. 6.

2431. —— The Narrowness of the Call for the Baltimore Convention. A Letter to the Hon. Edwin D. Morgan, Chairman of the Republican Committee, appointed at Chicago in 1860, on the Call for Presidential Convention at Baltimore, on the 7th June, 1864.

8vo. pp. 13.   NEW YORK : *Baker & Godwin,* 1864.

2432. JAY, J. The Great Issue. An Address. *Loyal Publication Society, No.* 75. New York, 1864. pp. 32.

2433. —— Dawson's Federalist. Letter from John Jay. 8vo. pp. 8.

2434. —— New Plottings in aid of the Rebel Doctrine of State Sovereignty. Mr. Jay's Second Letter on Dawson's Introduction to the Federalist. Exposing his Falsification of the History of the Constitution ; its Libels on Duane, Livingston, Jay and Hamilton, and its relation to recent efforts of Traitors at home, and Foes abroad, to maintain the Rebel Doctrine of State Sovereignty, etc. 8vo. pp. 54 and viii. NEW YORK : *A. D. F. Randolph,* 1864.

2435. —— The Great Issue. An Address delivered before the Union Campaign Club, of East Brooklyn, N. Y., October 27, 1864. 8vo. pp. 32.   NEW YORK : *Baker & Godwin,* 1864.

2436. —— The Constitutional Principles of the Abolitionists, and their endorsement by the American People. A Letter to the American Anti-Slavery Society, December 30, 1833. 8vo. pp. 12.   NEW YORK : 1864.

2437. —— Our Duty to the Freedmen. Remarks at the Inaugural Meeting of the American Freedmen's Aid Union, at the Cooper Institute, May 9, 1865. pp. 7.

2438. JAY, WILLIAM. An Inquiry into the Character and Tendency of the American Colonization, and American Anti-Slavery, Societies. 12mo. pp. 202.   NEW YORK : *Leavitt, Lord & Co.,* 1835.
For a reply to this work, see *Reese.*

2439. —— A View of the Action of the Federal Government in behalf of Slavery. 12mo. pp. 217.   NEW YORK : *J. S. Taylor,* 1839.

2440. —— A Letter to the Right Rev. L. Silliman Ives, Bishop of the Protestant Episcopal Church in North Carolina, occasioned by his late Address to the Convention of the Diocese. 8vo. pp. 32.   NEW YORK : *William Harned,* 1848.

2441. —— Letter to Hon. William Nelson, M. C., on Mr. Clay's Compromise. 12mo. pp. 22.   NEW YORK : *W. Harned,* 1850.

2442. —— Reply to the Remarks of Rev. Moses Stuart, on Hon. John Jay, and an examination of his Scriptural Exegesis, contained in his recent Pamphlet entitled, " Conscience and the Constitution." 8vo. pp. 22.   NW YORK : *J. A. Gray,* 1850.

2443. —— A Letter to the Committee chosen by the American Tract Society to inquire into the Proceedings of its Executive Committee, in relation to Slavery. 1857. 8vo. pp. 38.

2444. —— An Examination of the Mosaic Laws of Servitude.
8vo. pp. 56.   New York: *M. W. Dodd*, 1854.

2445. —— Letter respecting the American Board of Commission for Foreign Missions, and the American Tract Society. (Relating to Slavery.)
8vo. pp. 16.   New York: *Lewis J. Bates*, 1853.
—— for Eulogies on, see *G. B. Cheever, F. Douglass and A. H. Partridge.*

2447. JENCKES, Hon. Thomas A., of Rhode Island. The Bankrupt Law. Speech delivered in the House of Reps., June 1, 1864.
8vo. pp. 16.   Washington: *McGill & Witherow*, 1864.

2448. —— A Bill to establish a Uniform System of Bankruptcy throughout the United States. Reported through Mr. Jenckes, from the Select Committee, February 15, 1864.
8vo. pp. 24.   New York: *Dodge & Grattan*, 1864.

2449, JENKINS, Rev. John, DD. Thoughts for the Crisis.
8vo. pp. 24   Philadelphia: *J. B. Lippincott & Co.*, 1861.

2450. JENKINS, J. Foster, M. D. Relations of War to Medical Science. The Annual Address before the Westchester County (N. Y.) Medical Society, June 19, 1863.
8vo. pp. 16.   New York: *Bailliere Brothers*, 1863.

2451. JENKINS, Robert, DD. "Show my People their Transgressions." A Fast Day Discourse, preached in Philadelphia, September 26, 1861.
8vo. pp. 32.   Philadelphia: *C. Sherman & Son*, 1861.

2452. JERMON, J. Wagner. Abraham Lincoln and South Carolina.
8vo. pp. 15.   Philadelphia: *D. E. Thompson*, 1861.

2453. JOHNS, Right Rev. J. Sermon delivered at Richmond on the occasion of the Funeral of the Rt. Rev. Wm. Meade, DD., March 17, 1862.
8vo. pp.   Baltimore: *Entz & Bash*, 1862.

2454. JOHNSON, Hon. Andrew. Speech on the proposed Expulsion of Mr. Bright. Senate, January 31, 1862.
8vo. pp. 15.   Washington: *Globe Office*, 1862.

2455. JOHNSON, Gov. ANDREW, and Gov. Wright of Indiana. Interesting Debate at the Reception of, at the State Capital of Pa. 8vo. pp. 32.   HARRISBURG : (Pa.) *George Bergner*, 1863.

2456. JOHNSON, ANDREW, Life, Speeches and Services of. 12mo. pp. 15–214. PHILADELPHIA : *T. B. Peterson & Bros.*,'65.

2457. —— President of the United States, Life and Speeches of. Edited by Frank Moore.

12mo. pp. xlviii & 493. Portrait. BOST.: *Little, Brown & Co.*,'65.

The following are among the Speeches in this volume : On the Constitutionality and Righteousness of Secession; delivered in the Senate, December 19 and 20, 1860. On the State of the Union; delivered in the Senate, February 5 and 6, 1861. Reply to Senator Lane of Oregon; delivered in the Senate, March 2, 1861. Speech at Cincinnati, Ohio, June 20, 1861. On the War for the Union; delivered in the Senate, July 27, 1861. On the proposed Expulsion of Mr. Jesse D. Bright, January 31, 1862. Appeal to the People of Tennessee, March 18, 1862. Speech to the Colored People of Nashville, Tenn., 1864.

2457.* —— The Life and Public Services of. Including his State Papers, Speeches and Addresses. By John Savage.

8vo. pp. 408, 130, 19.   NEW YORK : *Derby & Miller*, 1866.

2458. JOHNSON, A. B. The advanced Value of Gold, Suspended Specie Payments, Legal Tender Notes, Taxation, and National Debt, investigated impartially.

8vo. pp. 32.   ITHACA : (N. Y.) *Curtiss & White*, 1862.

2459. JOHNSON, Rev. E. S. Sermon delivered June 1, 1865, in consequence of the Assassination of Abraham Lincoln, at Harrisburg, Pennsylvania. 8vo. pp. 11.

2460. JOHNSON, Rev. HERRICK. The Nation's Duty. A Thanksgiving Sermon preached in the Third Presbyterian Church, Pittsburgh, November 27, 1862.

8vo. pp. 26.   PITTSBURGH : *W. S. Haven*, 1862.

2461. —— The Shaking of the Nations. A Sermon preached at Pittsburgh, September 11, 1864.

8vo. pp. 27.   PITTSBURGH : *W. S. Haven*, 1864.

2462. —— The Banners of a Free People set up in the name of their God. A Thanksgiving Sermon preached at Pittsburg, Nov. 24,'64.

8vo. pp. 34.   PITTSBURGH : *W. S. Haven*, 1864.

2463. —— God's Ways Unsearchable. A Discourse on the Death of President Lincoln, preached in Pittsburgh, Pa., April 23, 1865.

8vo. pp. 11,   PITTSBURGH : *W. G. Johnson & Co.*, 1865.

2464. JOHNSON, Rev. HERRICK. Sergeant Slasher; or the Border Feud. A Romance of the Tennessee Mountains.
8vo. pp. 41. NEW YORK: *American News Company*, 1865.

2465. JOHNSTON, JAMES DALE. The Contemplated Secession from the Federal Republic of North America, by the Southern States. Detroit, December 9, 1860. 8vo. pp. 7.

2466. JOHNSON, JAMES F. The Suspending Power, and Writ of Habeas Corpus.
8vo. pp. 48. PHILADELPHIA: *John Campbell*, 1862.

2467. JOHNSON, OLIVER. and George F. White. Correspondence between. With an Appendix.
12mo. pp. 48. NEW YORK: *Oliver Johnson*, 1841.

2468. JOHNSON, REVERDY. Remarks on Popular Sovereignty, as maintained and denied respectively by Judge Douglass, and Attorney General Black. By a Southern Citizen.
8vo. pp. 48. BALTIMORE: *Murphy & Co.*, 1859.

2469. —— The same. Baltimore: *Murphy* & *Co.*, 1859. 8vo. pp. 40.

2470. —— Review of the Proceedings of the Court of Enquiry on Colonel S. D. Miles's (U. S. A.) Case. By R. Johnson and R. H. Gillette. 8vo. pp. 62.

2471. —— A Brave Soldier, a True Patriot, a Noble Man, defended against partisan malice. Reply of Reverdy Johnson to the Paper which Judge Advocate Holt furnished to the President, urging General Porter's condemnation. 8vo. pp. 56.

2472. —— A Reply to the Review of Judge Advocate General Holt, of the Proceedings, Findings and Sentence of the General Court Martial, in the Case of Major General Fitz John Porter; and a Vindication of that Officer.
8vo. pp. 88. BALTIMORE: *John Murphy* & *Co.*, 1863.

2473. —— Report of, as Commissioner of the United States, in New Orleans; transmitted by the President of the United States to the Senate, under a Resolution of December 15, 1862. 8vo. pp. 64. *37th Congress, 3d Session, Executive Document, No.* 16.

2474. —— Speech in support of the Resolution to amend the Constitution so as to abolish Slavery. Delivered in the Senate of the United States, April 5, 1864. 8vo. pp. 22.

2475. JOHNSON, REVEDY. An Argument to establish the Illegality of Military Commissions in the United States, and especially "of the one organized for the Trial of the Parties charged with conspiring to Assassinate the late President and others; presented to that Commission, June 19, 1865.

8vo. pp. 31. BALTIMORE : *John Murphy & Co.,* 1865.

2476. JOHNSON, S. M. The Dual Revolutions : Anti-Slavery and Pro-Slavery.

8vo. pp. 48. BALTIMORE : *W. M. Innes,* 1863.

2477. JOHNSON, WILLIAM. An Address on the Aspect of National Affairs and the Right of Secession, March 16, 1861.

8vo. pp. 42. CINCINNATI : *Rickey & Carroll,* 1861.

2478. JOHNSON, Hon. WM., of Ohio. Speech on the Bill to Provide Homesteads on the Forfeited and Confiscated Lands of Rebels. House of Representatives, May 4, 1864. 8vo. pp. 8.

2479. JOHNSON, Mrs. W. T. On Picket Duty. *Atlantic Monthly, April,* 1864.

2480. [JOINVILLE, LE PRINCE DE.] Guerre d'Amérique. Campagne du Potomac. Mars—Juillet, 1862.

12mo. pp. 211. Map. PARIS : *Michel Levy Frères,* 1863.

2481. —— The same work. New York : 1863.

2482. —— The Army of the Potomac ; its Organization, its Commander, and its Campaign. Translated from the French ; with Notes by William Henry Herbert.

8vo. pp. 118. Map. NEW YORK : *A. D. F. Randolph,* 1862.

2483. JONES, BEN., of East Tennessee. Speech, November 20, 1863. 12mo. pp. 16.

2484. JONES, Rev. CHARLES J. The Providence and Purpose of God in our National History. A Thanksgiving Sermon preached at Staten Island, November 26, 1863.

8vo. pp. 23. NEW YORK : *J. A. Gray & Green,* 1863.

2485. —— A Hopeful View of National Affairs. A Thanksgiving Sermon, preached at Staten Island, September 11, 1864.

18mo. pp. 23. NEW YORK : *Edward O. Jenkins,* 1864.

2486. JONES, ERNEST. The Slaveholders' War. A Lecture delivered at Ashton-under-Lyne, (England) November 6, 1863.

12mo. pp. 44. MANCHESTER : *Union and Emanc. Soc'y,* 1863.

2487. JONES, ERNEST. Oration on the American Rebellion, delivered at Rochdale, England, March 7, 1864.

8vo. pp. 16.   ROCHDALE: (Eng.) *G. Howarth,* 1863.

2488. JONES, J. B. Wild Southern Scenes. A Tale of Disunion and Border War.

12mo. pp. 502.   PHILADELPHIA : *T. B. Peterson & Brother.*

2489. —— (Clerk in the Confederate States War Office.) A Secret Diary of the Transactions of the War Department of the Confederate States Government, during the whole period of its existence, until the Evacuation of Richmond and Surrender of Gen. Lee ; embracing copies of all important Documents and Despatches pertaining to the War Office.

2 vols. 8vo.   PHILADELPHIA : *J. B. Lippincott & Co.,* 1866.

2490. JONES, JOHN RICHTER. Slavery sanctioned by the Bible. The First Part of a general Treatise on the Slavery Question.

8vo. pp. 34.   PHILADELPHIA : *J. B. Lippincott & Co.,* 1861.

2491. JONES. The Experience of Thomas Jones, who was a Slave for forty-three years. Written by a Friend as given to him by Brother Jones.

8vo. pp. 47.   BOSTON : *Daniel Laing, Jr.*

2392. JONES, WILLIAM D. Mirror of Modern Democracy. A History of the Democratic Party, from its organization in 1825, to its last great achievement, the Rebellion of 1861.

8vo. pp. 270.   NEW YORK : *N. C. Miller,* 1864.

2493. A JOURNAL of Incidents connected with the Travels of the Twenty-Second Regiment Connecticut Volunteers, for nine months. In verse. By an Orderly Sergeant.

8vo. pp. 28.   HARTFORD : *Williams, Wiley & Waterman,* 1863.

2494. JOY, JAMES F. Messrs. Trade and Chandler. The Senatorship. Detroit, January 5, 1863. pp. 4.

2495. —— The Testimony of Gen. Hitchcock and the Peninsular Campaign. Detroit, February 4, 1865. 8vo. pp. 14.

2496. JUDD, A. B. "Union for the sake of the Union." Speech on the State of the Country, in the Legislature of Conn., July 9, '62.

8vo. pp. 24.   HARTFORD : *O. F. Jackson,* 1862.

2497. JUDSON, E. Z. C. (Ned Buntline.) Life in the Saddle ; or The Cavalry Scout.

8vo. pp. 81.   NEW YORK : *F. A. Brady,* 1864.

2498. JULIAN, Hon. GEO. W., of Indiana. The Cause and Cure of our National Troubles. Speech in the House of Representatives January 14, 1862.

8vo. pp. 15. WASHINGTON: *Scammell & Co.*, 1862.

2499. JULIAN, Hon. G. W. Confiscation and Liberation. Speech in House of Representatives, May 23, 1862. 8vo. pp. 8.

2500. —— The Rebellion; the Mistake of the Past, the Duty of the Present. February 18, 1863. 8vo. pp. 8.

2501. —— Homesteads for Soldiers on the Lands of Rebels. Speech in the House of Representatives, March 18, 1864. 8vo. pp. 8.

2502. —— Radicalism and Conservatism; the Truth of History vindicated. Speech in the House of Reps., Feb. 7, 1865. pp. 7.

2503. —— Dangers and Duties. Reconstruction and Suffrage. Speech in the House of Reps., Indianapolis, Ind., November 17, 1865.

8vo. pp. 16. CINCINNATI: *Gazette Office*, 1865.

2504. —— Suffrage in the District of Columbia. Speech in the House of Representatives, January 16, 1865. pp. 8.

2504.* JUDKIN, GEORGE, DD. Civil Government an Ordinance of God. A Lecture for the Times, delivered in Philadelphia, October 27, 1861.

8vo. pp. 23. PHILADELPHIA: *J. B. Chandler*, 1861.

2505. —— Political Fallacies. An Examination of the False Assumptions, and refutation of the Sophistical Reasonings which have brought on this Civil War.

12mo. pp. 332. Portrait, NEW YORK: *Charles Scribner*, 1863.

K. G. C. An Authentic Exposition of the Origin, Objects and secret Work of the organization known as the Knights of the Golden Circle. Published by the U. S. National U. C., Feb., 1862. 8vo. p. 16.

2507. KANSAS and the Constitution. By "Cecil."

8vo. pp. 16. BOSTON: *Damrell & Moore*, 1856.

2508. KANSAS. Message of President Buchanan, communicating Correspondence between the Executive Department and the present Governor of Kansas, and between the Executive and any other Governor of Kansas, or other Officer of the Government there.

8vo. pp. 134. *35th Cong., 1st Sess., Sen. Ex. Doc., No.* 8, 1857.

2509. KANSAS. Subduing Freedom in. Report of the Congressional Committee, presented in the House of Rep.. July 1, 1865. 8vo. pp. 31.

2510. KANSAS. Information for Immigrants to. By Thomas H. Webb. 12mo. pp. 118.   BOSTON: *Alfred Mudge & Son,* 1857.

2511. —— Annual Message of Gov. G. M. Bebee, Jan. 10, '61. pp. 8.

2512. —— Report of the Adjutant General of, Dec. 31, '63. p. 95, 148.

2513. —— Report of the Adjutant General, for the year 1864. 8vo. pp. 111 and 714.   LEAVENWORTH: *Hubbell & Co.,* 1865.

2514. KASSON, JOHN A., of Iowa. Speech on the Amendment to the Constitution, delivered in the House of Representatives, January 10, 1865. pp. 16.

2515. KEARSARGE. Correspondence respecting the Enlistment of British Seamen on board the U. S. Ship-of-War "Kearsarge." Folio, pp. 10.   *Parl. Papers, N. Am., No.* 7, *London,* 1864.

2516. —— Further Correspondence respecting the Enlistment of British Seamen at Queenstown, on board the United States Ship-of-War "Kearsarge." Folio, pp. 7.   *Parl. Papers, North America, No.* 12, 1864.

2517. KEDAR, OBED. A Vision. The Cause and Progress of the present War, and its Final Termination foretold, July 4, 1861. 8vo. pp. 13.   COLUMBUS, 1862.

2518. KEELING, Rev. R. J. The Death of Moses. A Sermon preached in Trinity Church, April 23, 1865, as a Tribute of Respect to the Memory of Abraham Lincoln. 8vo. pp. 16.   WASHINGTON: *W. H. & O. H. Morrison,* 1865.

2519. KEILER VOUCHERS. Petition of the Adams Express Company to the Secretary of War, praying the reversal of the Decision of the United States Commission, at St. Louis, on the "Keiler" Vouchers, held by the Company for certain parties in Cincinnati. 8vo. pp. 11.   NEW YORK: *G. F. Nesbitt & Co.,* 1862.
    Relating to clothing furnished for the Soldiers by Mr. Keiler, a contractor in St. Louis.

2519.* KEITH, Rev. O. B. An Address delivered at the Funeral Solemnities of President Lincoln, Jenkinton, April 19, 1865. 8vo. pp. 8.   PHILADELPHIA: *King & Baird,* 1865.

2520. KELLY, GEORGE FOX. Eight months in Washington; or Scenes behind the Curtain. Corruption in high places, and Villainy unparalleled on earth. Cause and Cure of the present Rebellion; or the People versus their Servants. A Despotism in active operation. Darkness of blackness before us. 8vo. p. 38.

2521. KELLEY, Hon. WM. D., of Pennsylvania. The Recognition of Hayti and Liberia. In House of Reps., June 3, '62. 8vo. pp. 8.

2522. —— Remarks in opposition to the employment of Slaves in Navy Yards, Arsenals, Dock Yards, etc., and in favor of the Pacific Railroad. 8vo. pp. 8.

2523. —— The Trent Case, and the means of averting Foreign War. Speech in the House of Reps., January 7, 1862. pp. 7.

2524. —— The Way to attain and secure Peace. Speech in the House of Representatives, December 19, 1862. 8vo. pp. 8.

2525. —— The Policy of the Administration. Speech, January 31, 1862. 8vo. pp. 7.

2527. —— Remarks in Reply to the Opponents of the Conscription Bill, in the House of Representatives, Feb. 24, 1863. pp. 7.

2526. —— Replies of, to George Northrop, Esq., in the Joint Debate, in the Fourth Congressional District.
8vo. pp. 89. PHILADELPHIA: *Collins,* 1864.

2528. —— United States versus William Smith. Piracy Case. Speech of Hon. William D. Kelley.
8vo. pp. 13. PHILADELPHIA: *King & Baird.*

2529. —— Speech of, on Freedmen's Affairs. Delivered in the House of Representatives, February 23, 1864. 8vo. pp. 8.

2530. —— Have Faith in God and the People. Speech delivered in the House of Representatives, June 15, 1864. pp. 8.

2531. —— The Practice of Justice our only Security for the Future. Remarks in support of his proposed Amendment to the Bill " To Guaranty to certain States, whose Governments have been usurped or overthrown, a Republican Form of Government. In the House of Representatives, January 16, 1865.
8vo. pp. 23. WASHINGTON: 1865.

2532. —— The same work. 8vo. pp. 61. New York: *Loyal Publication Society, No.* 82.

2533. —— Report from the Select Committee to investigate the Assault upon the Hon. W. D. Kelley, by A. P. Field, a citizen of Louisiana. pp. 33. 38*th Cong.,* 2*d Sess., House Report, No.* 10, '65.

2534. —— The Safeguards of Personal Liberty. An Address delivered at Concert Hall, Thursday Evening, June 22, 1865.
8vo. pp. 16.   PHILADELPHIA : *Merrihew & Son,* 1865.
See also, *Northrup-Kelley Debate.*

2535. KELLOGG, Rev. CHARLES D. The Duties of the Hour. A Discourse preached at Wilmington, Delaware, on the occasion of the National Thanksgiving, August 6, 1863.
8vo. pp. 16.   WILMINGTON : *Henry Eckel,* 1863.

2536. KELLOGG, F. W., of Michigan. Reciprocity Treaty. Speech in House of Representatives, May 25, 1864. pp. 8.

2537. KELLOGG. ROBERT H. Sixteenth Connecticut Volunteers. Life and Death in Rebel Prisons, principally at Andersonville and Florence, S. C.
12mo. pp. 399. Illustrated.   HARTFORD : *L. Stebbins,* 1865.

2538. KELLOGG, WILLIAM. Confiscation of Rebel Property. Speech in House of Reps., May 24, 1862,   8vo. pp. 16.

2539. —— Speech on the Treasury Note Bill, delivered in the House of Representatives, February 6, 1862. 8vo. pp. 8.

2540. KELSO, ISAAC. The Stars and Bars ; or the Reign of Terror in Missouri.
12mo. pp. 324.   BOSTON : *A. Williams & Co.,* 1862.

2541. KEMBLE, FRANCES ANNE. Journal of a Residence on a Georgia Plantation, in 1838–39.
8vo. pp. 337.   NEW YORK : *Harper & Brothers,* 1863.

2542. KEMBLE. What became of the Slaves on a Georgia Plantation ? Great Auction Sale of Slaves at Savannah, Georgia, March 2 and 3, 1859. A Sequel to Mrs. Kemble's Journal,
8vo. pp. 20.

2543. KENDALL, R. C., of Maryland. Cotton and Common Sense. A Treatise on Perennial Cotton.
8vo. pp. 32.   NEW YORK : *Mapes & Lockwood,* 1862.

2544. KENNEDY, JOHN P. The Great Drama ; an Appeal to Maryland. Baltimore. 8vo. pp. 16.

2545. —— The Border States, their Power and Duty in the present disordered condition of the Country.
8vo. pp. 46.   BALTIMORE : 1861.

2546. —— The same. 8vo. pp. 47. Phil.: *J. B. Lippincott & Co.,*'65.

2547. KENNEDY, J. P.   Mr. Ambrose's Letters on the Rebellion.
18mo. pp.   NEW YORK: *Hurd & Houghton*, 1865.

2548. KENNEDY, Rev. JOHN.   Hebrew Servitude and American Slavery.   An Attempt to prove that the Mosaic Law furnishes neither a basis nor an apology for American Slavery.
8vo. pp.   LONDON: *Jackson, Walford & Hoddern*, 1863.

2549. KENNEDY, Col. WM.   Proceedings of the Democratic Republican General Committee of the City of New York, relative to the Death of.   8vo. pp. 6.

2250. KENRICK, JOHN.   Horrors of Slavery.   In Two Parts.
18mo. pp. 59.   CAMBRIDGE: *Hilliard & Metcalf*, 1817.

2551. KENTUCKY.   Annual Report of the Adjutant General of the State of Kentucky, for the year 1863.
8vo. pp. 232.   FRANKFORT: *W. E. Hughes*, 1864.

2552. —— Annual Report of the Quartermaster General for 1863–64.
8vo. pp. 42.   FRANKFORT: *State Printing Office*. 1865.

2553. —— Minority Report of the Committee on the proposed Amendment of the United States Constitution, Feb. 14, 1865.   pp. 8.

2554. —— Response of the Adjutant General of Kentucky in regard to the Federal Enrollments in the State, March 1, 1865.
8vo. pp. 20.   FRANKFORT: *G. D. Prentice*, 1865.

2555. KEOGH, JAMES, DD.   Catholic Principles of Civil Government.
8vo. pp. 20.   CINCINNATI: *Catholic Telegraph*, 1862.

2556. KERR, HENRY T.   Remarks before the Committee of Ways and Means, on the subject of the Tariff on Silk Manufactures, March 3, 1864.   8vo. pp. 20.

2557. KETCHUM, HIRAM.   Oration delivered at New Haven, July 4, 1861,
8vo. pp. 30.   NEW HAVEN: *T. J. Stafford*, 1851.

2558. KETTELL, THOMAS PRENTICE.   Southern Wealth and Northern Profits, as exhibited in Statistical Facts and Official Figures; showing the necessity of union to the future prosperity and welfare of the Republic.
8vo. pp. 173.   NEW YORK: *Geo. W. & J. A. Wood*, 1860.

2559. —— Notes on "Southern Wealth and Northern Profits."
8vo. pp. 31.   PHILADELPHIA: *C. Sherman & Son*, 1831.
An anonymous Tract in reply to the previous one.

29

2560. KELLETT, T. P. The History of the War Debt of England; the History of the War Debt of the United States, and the two compared. New York. 8vo. pp. 16.

2561. KILLDARE, The Black Scout.
18mo. pp. 106.   NEW YORK: *T. R. Dawley,* 1865.

2562. KIMBALL, Rev. HENRY. The Ship of State bound for Tarshish. A Sermon preached in Sandwich, November 21, 1861.
8vo. pp. 15.   BOSTON: *George C. Rand & Avery,* 1861.

2563. —— A Discourse commemorative of Major Charles Jarvis, of the 9th Vermont Vols., delivered at his Funeral at Weathersfield Bar, Vermont, December 13, 1863.
8vo. pp. 24.   NEW YORK: *E. O. Jenkins,* 1864.

2564. KIMBALL, WM. H. Our Government and the Blacks. *Continental Monthly, April,* 1864.

2565. KING, A. British Sympathies in the American Crisis. A Letter on the Address of the Protestant Pastors of France to the Christian Ministers of all denominations in Great Britain and Ireland.
12mo. pp. 15.   DUBLIN: *Porteous & Gibbs,* 1863.

2566. KING, T. BUTLER. Lettre à son Exc. M. le Ministre du Commerce.
8vo. pp. 48   PARIS: *Dubuisson & Co.,* 1861.

2567. KINGSBURY, HARMON. The Slavery Question settled. Man-Stealing, Legitimate Servitude, etc.
12mo. pp. 36.   NEW YORK: *John A. Gray,* 1862.

2568. KINGSLEY, VINE WRIGHT. French Intervention in America; or a Revue de La France, Le Mexique, et les Etats Confédérés.
8vo. pp. 22.   NEW YORK: *C. B. Richardson,* 1863.

2569. KINSMAN, Lieut. Colonel J. BURNHAM, General Superintendent of Negro Affairs, Department of Virginia and North Carolina. Circular Order No. 1. Fort Monroe, Virginia, January 1, 1864. 4to. pp. 3.

KIRKE, EDMUND, see *J. R. Gilmore.*

2570. KIRKLAND, CHARLES P. The Coming Contraband; a Reason against the Emancipation Proclamation, not given by Mr. Justice Curtis, to whom it is addressed, by an Officer in the Field.
12mo. pp. 21.   NEW YORK: *G. P. Putnam,* 1862.

2571. KIRKLAND, C. P. A Letter to the Hon. B. R. Curtis, late Judge of the Supreme Court of the United States, in Review of his recently published pamphlet on the " Emancipation Proclamation " of the President.

8vo. pp, 21.   NEW YORK : *Latimer Bros. & Seymour*, 1862.

2572. —— The same.   Second edition.

8vo. pp. 20.   NEW YORK : *A. D. F. Randolph*, 1863.

2573. —— The Destiny of our Country.

8vo. pp. 71.   NEW YORK : *Anson D. Randolph*, 1864.

2574. —— Liability of the Government of Great Britain for the Depredations of Rebel Privateers on the Commerce of the United States, considered.

8vo. pp. 37.   NEW YORK : *A. D. F. Randolph*, 1863.

2575. —— A Letter to Peter Cooper on " The Treatment to be extended to the Rebels, individually," and " The Mode of Restoring the Rebel States to the Union."   With an Appendix containing a reprint of a Review of Judge Curtis's Paper on the Emancipation Proclamation.   With a Letter from President Lincoln.

8vo. pp. 46 and 20.   NEW YORK : *A. D. F. Randolph*, 1865.

2576. KNAPP, W. H.   Resistance to Evil.   A Discourse delivered to the Barton Square Society at Salem, September 6, 1862.

12mo. pp. 13.   BOSTON : *John Wilson & Son*, 1863.

2577. KNICKERBOCKER MAGAZINE for 1861.   New York.

A Few Words about the War.   January.
What are we Fighting for?   July.
Before and after the Battle.   A Day and Night in Dixie.   G. P. Putnam.   Sept.
Emancipation ; its Influence on the Rebellion, and Effect on the Whites.   Sinclair Toucey.   October.
Servile Insurrection.   C. G. Leland.   November.
Words to the West.   Ibid.   October.
Tour through the Cotton States.   October, November and December.
Strike boldly.   C. G. Leland.

2578. KNICKERBOCKER MAGAZINE, for 1862.

The Opening Scenes of the Rebellion.   April.
The President's Emancipation Proclamation.   November.
Slavery, Colonization and the Constitution.   November.
Resources of the North and South compared.   November.
The Union Soldier.   December.
The Effects of a Separation on the South ; and the National Duty.   Dec.

2579. KNICKERBOCKER MAGAZINE, for 1863.

The President's Message and the War.   January.

A Raid on the Enemy's Camp. Augusta B. Garrett. April.

Way Down in Dixie. August.

Fredericksburg. Wilford Wylley. September.

News from the War. J. H. Elliott. September.

2580. KNICKERBOCKER MAGAZINE, for 1864.

Our Lookout Mountain. Lieut. W. L. English. January.

The Rebel Surgeon. January.

The Issue between North and South. N. Lord, DD. March and April.

The Negro; his Nature and Destiny. April.

Theories of Reconstruction. May.

Causes and Dangers of Social Excitements. June.

The Coming Presidential Election. J. Holmes Agnew. June.

For a continuation of the Knickerbocker, see *American Monthly.*

2581. KNOX, Rev. JOHN. L. M. A Sermon for the Times. Preached in Aid of Jacobins in Maryland.

8vo. pp. 8. BALTIMORE : *For the author,* 1864.

A hit at Mr. Blair and the Maryland Conservatives. The name of the author is an assumed one.

2582. KNOX, THOMAS W. Camp Fire and Cotton Field. Southern Adventure in Time of War. Life with the Union Armies, and Residence on a Louisiana Plantation.

8vo. pp. NEW YORK: *Blelock & Co.,* 1865.

2583. KRAMER, Dr. J. THEOPHILUS, of New Orleans. The Slave Auction.

18mo. pp. 48. BOSTON : *Robert F. Walcutt,* 1859.

2584. KRAUTH, CHARLES P., DD. The Two Pageants. A Discourse delivered in Pittsburgh, Pa., June 1, 1865.

8vo. pp. 23. PITTSBURGH: *W. S. Haven,* 1865.

2585. KREBS, Rev. Dr. H A Sermon in memory of Abraham Lincoln, President of the United States. Assassinated on Good Friday, April 14, 1865. Delivered in St. Louis, Missouri. From the German. 8vo. pp. 8.

2586. —— Rede zum Andenken an Abraham Lincoln. Ermordet am Charfreitage, April 14, 1865, A. D. Gebalten am 19 April, 1865, dem Tage des Leichenzuges, 12 Uhr Mittags in der Kirche zum Heiligen Geiste in St. Louis. 8vo. pp. 7.

LABOULAYE, Edward. Les Etats Unis et La France.
    8vo. pp. 72.   Paris: *E. Dentu*, 1862.

2588. —— The United States and France.
    8vo. pp. 14.   Boston: *Advertiser Office*, 1862.

2589. —— Pourquoi le Nord ne peut accepter la séparation.
    8vo. pp. 9.   New York: *Messenger Fr. et America*. 1863.

2590. —— Why the North cannot accept Separation.
    8vo. pp. 16.   New York: *C. B. Richardson*, 1863.

2591. —— Upon whom rests the Guilt of the War? Separation. War
    without end.
    8vo. pp. 19.   New York: *W. C. Bryant & Co.*. 1863.

2592. —— The same. 12mo. pp. 14. Edinburgh: *Murray & Gibb*, '63.

2593. LACOMBE, H. Mercier de. Le Mexique et les Etats Unis.
    8vo. pp. 162.   Paris: *E. Dentu*, 1863.

2594. LACONTURE, Edward. Mémoire à sa Majesté l'Empereur
    Napoléon III. La Vérité sur la guerre d'Amérique.
    8vo. pp. 16.   Paris: *Dentu*, 1862.

2595. LADOR, J. A. In Memoriam. An Address 8vo. Cahawba,
    Alabama, 1861.

2596. The Lady Lieutenant. A Wonderful, Startling and Thrilling
    Narrative of the Adventures of Miss Madeline Moore, who, in
    order to be near her lover, joined the army, was elected Lieuten-
    ant and fought in Western Virginia.
    8vo. pp. 40.   Philadelphia: *Barclay & Co.*, 1862.

2597. Ladies' National League, of St. Louis. Report of the Organ-
    ization of, with their Constitution and Pledge.
    8vo. pp. 18.   St. Louis: (Mo.) *Democrat Office*, 1863.

2598. Ladies' Aid Society of Philadelphia, Annual Report of.

2599. Ladies' Union Relief Association of Baltimore, First An-
    nual Report of.
    8vo. pp. 18.   Baltimore: *W. M. Innes*, 1862.

2600. LAMBERT, Prof. Our War Debt, and How to pay it. *Amer-
    ican Monthly, November*, 1864.

2601. LAMON, Ward H. Marshal of the District of Columbia.
    [Washington, 1862.] pp. 18.

2602. LAMSON, Rev. Wm. God Hiding Himself in Times of Trouble. A Sermon preached in Brookline, Mass., April 2, 1863. 8vo. pp. 26. Boston: *Gould & Lincoln,* 1863.

2603. LANDER, Gen. F. W. Ceremonies at the Funeral of, in Salem, Mass. With the Address on the occasion, by G. W. Briggs, DD., March 5, 1862. *Salem Register, March* 10, 1862.

2604. LANDIS, R. W. Chaplaincy in the Army. *Danville Review, June,* 1863.

2605. LANE, Hon. Joseph, of Oregon. Speech in Reply to Senator Johnson, in the Senate of the U. S., December 19. 1860. pp. 8.

2606. LANE, Hon. J. H. Vindication of the Policy of the Administration. Speech in the Senate, February 16, 1864, on the Bill to set apart a portion of Texas for the use of Persons of African descent. 8vo. pp. 16.

2607. —— Speech at Waterbury, Conn., December 28, 1863. pp. 8.

2608. LANE, H. L., of Indiana. Speech on the Resolution to expel Hon. Jesse D. Bright from his seat in that Body. Senate, January 21, 1862. 8vo. pp. 8.

2609. —— Speech on the Discharge of State Prisoners. Senate, December 18, 1862. 8vo. pp. 16.

2610. LANG, George S. Currency. *Atlantic Monthly, July,* 1864.

2611. LANGEL, A. Les Causes et les Caractères de la guerre civile aux Etats Unis. *Rev. des Deux Mondes, March,* 1861.

2612. —— La Guerre Civile aux Etats Unis le Gouvernment Fédéral. Ibid. *October,* 1863.

2613. —— Les Etats Unis pendant la Guerre. Ibid. *December,* 1864, *May and July,* 1865.

2614. —— Le Président des Etats Unis—Abraham Lincoln. Ibid. *May,* 1865.

2615. LANSING, Hon. W. E., of New York. Confiscation and Emancipation. Speech in the House of Reps., May 21, '62. 8vo. p. 8.

2616. LARIMORE, J. W. An Evening with the Chaplain. Dedicated to the Ninth Regiment Iowa Cavalry. 18mo. pp. 46. Boston: *American Tract Society.*

2617. LARKE, Julian K. Life and Campaigns of General Grant; with Portrait and Illustrations. 8vo. pp. 469 and 40. New York: *Derby & Miller,* 1864.

2618. LARNED, Edwin C. The New Fugitive Slave Law. Speech in Reply to Hon. S. A. Douglas, delivered in the city of Chicago, October 25, 1850.

8vo. pp. 16. Chicago: *Democrat Office*, 1850.

2619. —— The Great Conflict. What has been gained, and What remains to be done. Oration delivered at Aurora, Illinois, on the 4th July, 1865.

8vo. pp. 23. Chicago: *H. A. Newcombe & Co.*, 1865.

2620. LATHAM, Hon. George, of West Virginia. Reconstruction. A Speech delivered in the House of Reps., Jan. 8, 1866. pp. 8.

2621. LATHAM, Hon. Milton S. Speech on the President's Message. "The Mission of Peace from Virginia." Delivered in the United States Senate, February 1, 1861. 8vo. pp. 15.

2622. LATROBE, John H. B. African Colonization. An Address at the Anniversary of the American Colonization Society, Washington, January 21, 1862.

8vo. pp. 16. Washington: *H. S. Bowen*, 1862.

2623. [LATROBE, John H. B.] Three Great Battle.

8vo. pp. 35. Baltimore: *Printed (not pub) by John B. Toy.*
This pamphlet contains accounts of the Battles of Buena Vista; the Seven Days' Battle on the Peninsula, June 26 to July 2, 1862; and the Battle of Gettysburg.

2624. LAURENS, Henry. South Carolina Protest against Slavery; being a Letter from Henry Laurens, second President of the Continental Congress, to his Son, Colonel John Laurens, dated, Charleston, S. C., August 14, 1776. Now first published from the original.

8vo. pp. 34. New York: *G. P. Putnam*, 1861.

2625. LAURIE, Rev. Thomas. Government is of God. A Sermon preached in Dedham and West Roxbury, May 12, 1861.

12mo. pp. 27. Boston: *S. O. Thayer*, 1861.

2626. —— Three Discourses preached in West Roxbury, Mass., April 13, 19, and 23, 1865. 1, Fast Day. (Relating to the rebellion.) 2, On the Death of Abraham Lincoln. 3, On the same subject.

8vo. pp. 40. Dedham: (Mass.) *John Cox, Jr.*, 1865.

2627. LAW, John, of Indiana. Speech on the Bill "Emancipating Slaves of Rebels," and the Bill "Confiscating the Property of Rebels." In the House of Representatives, May 23, 1862. pp 8.

2628. LAWLEY, Hon. FRANK. The Last Six Days of Secessia. *London Fortnightly Review, September,* 1865.

2629. LAWRENCE. Border and Bastile.

8vo. pp. xii, 277.   LONDON : *Tinsley, Brothers & Co.,* 1863.

2629.* —— The same. 12mo. pp.   New York, 1863.

2630. LAWRENCE, Lt. Col A. GALLATIN. Fort Fisher. [A Poem.]

8vo. pp. 11.   PROVIDENCE : *For the author,* 1865.

2631. LAWRENCE, Hon. WILLIAM BEACH. L'Industrie Française, et l'esclavage des nègres aux Etats Unis. Lettre au rédacteur en chef du Journal des Débats.

8vo. pp. 16.   PARIS : *E. Dentu,* 1860.

This essay awakened much interest in Europe, and was translated for, and published in, the *London Morning Chronicle,* under the following title:

2632. —— French Commerce and Manufactures, and Negro Slavery in the United States. Letter to the Editor of the " Journal des Debats." 8vo. pp. 16.

2633. —— Belligerent Rights at Sea. Letter Dated July 20, 1861, to John Westlake, Esq., Secretary of the International Law Department of the Social Science Association. *London Law Magazine, November,* 1861. pp. 81–99. Published also in the Transactions of the National Association for the Promotion of Social Science, 1861. pp. 794–802.

2634. —— On Contraband of War. Letter to John Westlake, dated May 23, 1862. Transactions of the Mutual Association for the Promotion of Social Science. pp. 900.

2635. —— Elements of International Law. By Henry Wheaton. 2d edition, by Wm. Beach Lawrence.

2 vols. 8vo.   BOSTON and LONDON : 1863.

The notes to this edition, by Mr. Lawrence, have reference to many topics, which have a bearing upon, or are connected with, questions growing out of the rebellion. See also in the Index, " Civil War in America."

2636. —— International Law. Letter from the Hon. Wm. Beach Lawrence to John Westlake, Esq., September 22, 1863. *London Law Magazine, November,* 1863. pp. 138–150. *Mémorial Diplomatique,* 1863. pp. 454. Parif. *Monthly Law Reporter, November,* 1863. pp. 12–22.

2637. LAWS OF WAR, and Martial Law ; comprising a few Extracts from General Halleck's Work on International Law, and their application to passing events.

12mo. pp. 15. BOSTON: *A. Williams & Co.*, 1863.

2638. LAWYER, Rev. JOHN O. Our Country; its Peace, Prosperity and Perpetuity. A Sermon preached in Coeymans, New York, November 27, 1862.

8vo. pp. 24. ALBANY: (N. Y.) *S. R. Gray*, 1863.

2639. LEACH, J. M., of North Carolina. State of the Union. Speech of J. M. Leach, in the House of Reps., Feb. 7, 1861. pp. 8.

2640. A LEAF FOR THE PEOPLE. Absolute Submission to a Rebel Conspiracy, or War. 8vo. pp. 4.

2641. LEAVITT, JOSHUA. The Monroe Doctrine.

8vo. pp. 50. NEW YORK: *Sinclair Toucey*, 1863.

2642. LEAVITT, Rev. W. S. God, the Protector and Hope of the Nation. A Sermon preached on Thanksgiving Day, Nov. 27, '62.

8vo. pp. 18. HUDSON: *Bryan & Webb*, 1862.

2643. —— A Sermon preached April 9, 1865, the Sunday after the Capture of Richmond.

8vo. pp. 18. HUDSON: *Bryan & Webb*, 1865.

2644. LEAVY, Hon. C. S. L., and F. Thomas, of Maryland, on the Indemnification Bill. Speeches in the House of Representatives, February 18, 1863. pp. 16.

2645. LECOMPTON CRISIS. Private and Confidential on Government Matters. Grand Mass Meeting at Tammany Hall, March 4, 1858, to strengthen the President; called by Stuart Brown, Henry Grinnell and 3100 others. Secret Circular. 8vo. pp. 14.

2646. LECOMTE, FERDINAND. Guerre des Etats Unis d'Amérique. Rapport au departement militaire Suisse précédé d'un discours à la société militaire fédérale réunie à Berne le 18 août, 1862.

8vo. pp. 216. 2 Maps. PARIS: *Ch. Tancra*, 1863.

2647. —— The War in the United States. Report to the Swiss Military Department; preceded by a Discourse to the Federal Military Society.

18mo. pp. 148. NEW YORK: *D. Van Nostrand*, 1863.

2648. LEE, ALFRED, (Bishop of Delaware.) The Christian Citizen's Duty in the Present Crisis. A Discourse delivered in Wilmington, Delaware, April 21, 1861.

18mo. pp. 16. WILMINGTON: *Henry Eckle*, 1861.

30

2649. LEE, A.   God to be Glorified in the Fires.   Thanksgiving Discourse, delivered in St. Andrew's Church, Wilmington, Nov. 27, 1862.
12mo. pp. 16.   WILMINGTON : *Henry Eckle,* 1862.

2650. LEEDS, S. P.   " Thy Kingdom Come ; Thy Will be done."   A Discourse, September 26, 1861, at Dartmouth College.
8vo. pp. 31.   WINDSOR : (Vermont) *Bishop & Tracy,* 1861.

2651. —— Remarks made by the Pastor, March 9, 1862, after the President's Emancipation Message.   8vo. pp. 3.

2652. —— Address at the Funeral of Capt. Lorenzo D. Gove, slain by the Rebels in Virginia.   Hanover, N. H.   pp. 12.

2653. LEGRAND, JOHN C.   Letter to Reverdy Johnson, on the Proceedings at the Meeting held at Maryland Institute, January 10, 1861.   8vo. pp. 8.

2654. LELAND, CHARLES G.   Desperation and Colonization.   *Continental Monthly, June,* 1862.

2655. —— Monroe to Farragut.   (Poetry.)   Ibid.   *June,* 1862.

2656. —— A Military Nation.   Ibid.   *October,* 1862.

2657. —— A Southern Review.   Ibid.   *October,* 1862.

2658. —— The Proclamation.   Ibid.   *November,* 1862.

2659. —— Thank God for all.   Ibid.   *December,* 1862.

2660. —— Centralization, or " State Rights."
8vo. pp. 14.   NEW YORK : *C. T. Evans,* 1863.

2661. LEMMON SLAVE CASE.   New York Court of Appeals.   Report of the Case.   The People of the State of New York, on the relation of Louis Napoleon, Respondents, against Jonathan Lemmon, of Virginia, Appellant.
8vo. pp. 146.   NEW YORK : *W. H. Tinson,* 1860.

2662. LEON, EDWIN DE.   La Vérité sur les Etats Confédérés d' Amérique.
8vo. pp. 32.   PARIS : *E. Dentu,* 1862.

2663. LENG, WILLIAM C.   The American War.   The Aims, Antecedents and Principles of the Belligerents.   A Lecture delivered December 10, 1862, in Dundee.
8vo. pp. 38.   DUNDEE : " *Advertiser Office,*" 1863.

2664. LESLIE, STEPHEN.   An American Protectionist.   *McMillan's Magazine, December,* 1862.

2665. THE LESSON OF ST. DOMINGO. How to make the War short and the Peace righteous. From the "New York Tribune," of May 27, 1861.

12mo. pp. 24.   BOSTON : *A. Williams & Co.*, 1861.

2666. LETCHER, Governor. Message to the Virginia Legislature, January 6, 1862.

2667. LETTER to an English Friend, on the Rebellion in the United States, and on British Policy.

8vo. pp. 28.   BOSTON : *Ticknor & Fields*, 1862.

2668. A LETTER from an Elder in an Old School Presbyterian Church, to his son at College, on Secession.

8vo. pp. 24.   NEW YORK : 1863.

2669. LETTER addressed to a Congressman. Union and Liberty. Power of Congress in relation to the Slaves ; with a Form of Enactment in conformity thereto. 8vo. pp. 8.

2670. A LETTER to the Hon. Rufus Choate, by a Conservative Whig. The Duty of Conservative Whigs in the Present Crisis.

8vo. pp. 21   BOSTON : 1856.

2671. LETTERS on the Presidency.

8vo. pp. 56.   LOUISVILLE : (Kentucky) 18–.

2672. LETTER to Gov. Bradford, by a Marylander. Balt., 1863. p. 21.

2673. LETTER from a Gentleman in Baltimore, Md., to a friend in New York, on the subject of Slavery. [By J. J. Speed.] 1841. p. 91.

2674. LETTER, A, To an English Friend, on the American War.

8vo. pp. 24.   NEW YORK : *A. D. F. Randolph*, 1863.

2675. LETTER to an English Friend, on the Rebellion in the United States, and on British Policy.

8vo. pp. 28.   BOSTON : *Ticknor & Fields*, 1862.

2676. LETTERS. Three Letters from a South Carolinian, relating to Secession, Slavery and the Trent Case.

8vo. pp. 22.   LONDON : *Smith, Elder & Co.*, 1862.

2677. LETTERS OF LOYAL SOLDIERS. Part 1, What General Grant says of the Administration ; What Gen. Dix says of the Rebellion ; What Gen. Sickles says of Peace ; What Gen. Hooker says of the Election. Part 2, How Gen. Sherman proclaimed Peace at Atlanta ; How Gen. McCall pronounced for Peace in Pennsylvania, etc.

8vo. pp. 16. NEW YORK : *Loyal Publication Society, No.* 64, '64.

2678. LETTERS FROM EUROPE, touching the American Contest, and acknowledging the receipt, from Citizens of New York, of presentation Sets of the " Rebellion Record."
8vo. pp. 27. NEW YORK: *Loyal Publication Society, No.* 70, '64.

2679. LETTRE à Napoleon III sur l'Esclavage aux Etat du Sud.　Par un Créole de la Louisiane.　(E. M.)
8vo. pp. viii, 160.　　　　　　　　　PARIS: *Dentu,* 1862.

2680. LEWIS, JOSEPH J., Commissioner of Internal Revenue.　Letter to a Member of Congress, on the National Currency.
8vo. pp. 15.　　　　　PHILADELPHIA: *King & Baird,* 1865.

2681. LEWIS, Rev. ROBERT W.　Christian Thanksgiving Perpetual. A Sermon preached at Sheldon, Vermont, Nov. 28, 1861.
8vo. pp. 14.　　　　　BURLINGTON: *W. H. & C. A. Hoyt,* 1861.

2682. LEWIS, TAYLER, LL. D.　State Rights.　A Photograph from the Ruins of Ancient Greece.
12mo. pp. 96.　　　　　　　ALBANY: *J. Munsell,* 1864.

2683. —— The same.　With appended Dissertations on the Ideas of Nationality, of Sovereignty, and the Right of Revolution.
8vo. pp. 97.　　　　ALBANY: *Weed, Parsons & Co.,* 1865.

2684. LIBERIA.　The Land of Promise to Free Colored Men.
8vo. pp. 31.　　　　　WASHINGTON: *H. S. Bowen,* 1861.

2685. LIBERTY.　The Liberty Papers.　No. 1.　No. 2, Liberty, a Divine Inalienable Right.　No. 3, Liberty; all hail.　No. 4, Liberty, a Power among the Nations.　New York, 1861.　4 sheets.

2686. LIBERTY.　The Image and Superscription on every Coin issued by the United States of America, Proclaim Liberty throughout all the Land, unto all the Inhabitants thereof.　12mo. pp. 120. *Slave Laws,* 21.　1839.

2687. THE LIBERTY BELL, by Friends of Freedom.
12mo. pp. 256.　　　BOSTON: *Mass. Anti-Slavery Fair,* 1845.

2688. LIDELL, JOHN A., M. D.　On Gun-shot Wounds of Arteries, Traumalic Hemorrhage and Traumalic Aneurism.
8vo. pp. 24.　　　WASHINGTON: *McGill & Witherow,* 1863.

2689. LIEBER, FRANCIS, LL. D.　What is our Constitution,—League, Pact or Government?　Two Lectures on the Constitution of the United States, concluding a Course on the Modern State.　Delivered in the Law School of Columbia College, during the Winter of 1860 and 1861. To which is appended an Address on Secession, written in the year 1851.

8vo. pp. 48. NEW YORK: *For the Trustees,* 1861.

2690. LIEBER, F., LL. D. Guerilla Parties, considered with reference to the Laws and Usages of War. Written at the request of Major General Halleck, and printed for the use of the Army.

12mo. pp. 22. NEW YORK: *D. Van Nostrand,* 1862.

2691. —— A Song on our Country and her Flag. Written after the Raising of the Flag on Columbia College, New York, on the Great " Flag Day." Printed by the Students. 8vo. pp. 2.

2692. —— No Party now—but all for our Country. Address read at the Meeting of the Loyal National League, New York, April 11, 1863.

8vo. pp. 12. PHILADELPHIA: *Crissy & Markley,* 1863.

2693. —— The same. *Loyal Pub. Society, No.* 16, 1864. pp. 8.

2694. —— Instructions for the Government of Armies of the United States, in the Field. Revised by a Board of Officers. " General Order No. 100. Adjutant General's Office."

12mo. pp. 36. NEW YORK: *D. Van Nostrand,* 1863.

2695. —— Plantations for Slave Labor the Death of the Yeomanry. 8vo. pp. 8.

2696. —— The same. *Loyal Publication Society, No.* 29. pp. 8.

2697. —— A Code for the Government of Armies in the Field, as authorized by the Laws and Usages of War on Land. 8vo. p. 25.

2698. —— The Argument of the Secessionists. A Letter to the Union Meeting, held in New York, September 30, 1863.

8vo. pp. 7. *Loyal Publication Society, No.* 35, 1863.

2699. —— Lincoln oder McClellan? An die Deutschen in Amerika. *Loyal Publication Society, No.* 59, 1864.

2700. —— Lincoln, or McClellan. Appeal to the Germans in America. Translated from the German by T. C.

8vo. pp. 8. *Loyal Publication Society, No.* 67, 1864.

This appeal was written several weeks before the letter of Alexander H. Stephens, to some friends in Georgia, and the Report of Judge Advocate Holt on the Conspiracy of this country.

2701. —— An Address on Secession, delivered in South Carolina in the year 1851.

8vo. pp. 12. *Loyal Publication Society, No.* 77, 1864.

234   *CATALOGUE.*

2702. LIEBER, F., LL. D. A Letter to Hon. E. D. Morgan, Senator of
the United States, on the Amendment to the Constitution of the
United States abolishing Slavery. Resolutions passed by the
New York Union League Club, concerning Conditions of Peace
with the Insurgents. *Loyal Publication Society, No. 79.* pp. 4.

2703. —— Amendments of the Constitution, submitted to the Consideration of the American People.
8vo. pp. 39.   *Loyal Publication Society, No. 83, 1865.*

2704. LIFE IN THE SOUTH, from the Commencement of the War. By
a Blockaded British Subject. Being a Social History of those
who took part in the Battles, from a personal Acquaintance with
them in their own Homes. From the Spring of 1860 to August,
1862. By S. L. J.
2 vols, post 8vo. pp. 427 and 404. LOND.: *Chapman & Hall,* '63.

2705. LIFE IN THE UNION ARMY; or Notings and Reminiscences of a
Two Years' Volunteer. A Rhythmical History of the Fifteenth
New York Volunteer Engineers. By Don Pedro Quaerendo
Reminisco, a Private in the Ranks.
8vo. pp. 147.   NEW YORK: *Dexter, Hamilton & Co.,* 1863.

2706. THE LIGHT AND DARK of the Rebellion.
12mo. pp. 303.   PHILADELPHIA: *George W. Childs,* 1863.

2707. LINCOLN, ABRAHAM. Debates between the Hon. Abraham
Lincoln and Hon. Stephen A. Douglas, in the celebrated Campaign in 1858, in Illinois. 8vo. Columbus, 1860.

2708. —— Abraham Lincoln and South Carolina. By Rev. J. W.
Jermon.
8vo. pp. 15.   PHILADELPHIA: *D. E. Thompson,* 1865.

2709. LINCOLN'S (President) VIEWS. The Truth from an Honest
Man. The Letter of the President. An important Letter on
the Principles involved in the Vallandigham Case. Correspon-
pence in relation to the Democratic Meeting at Albany, N. Y.
8vo. pp. 16.   PHILADELPHIA: *King & Baird,* 1863.

2710. —— On the Arrest of C. L. Vallandigham, June 12, 1863.
8vo. pp. 8.   CINCINNATI, 1863.

2711. —— Reply to the Committee of Ohio Democrats, June 29, 1863.

2712. —— Erwiederung in Bezug auf die Verhaftung Vallandigham's.
8vo. pp. 12,   CINCINNATI, 1863.
A German translation of the two previous tracts.

2713. LINCOLN, Abraham, President of the United States. Inaugural Message, March 4, 1861.

2714. —— Message to the two Houses of Congress, Dec. 3, '61. p. 20.

2715. —— Message to the two Houses of Congress, Dec. 1, 1862.

2716. —— Message to the two Houses of Congress, December, 1862. 8vo. pp. 20. WASHINGTON: *Government Printing Office*, 1863.

2717. —— Message, Dec. 8, '63, accompanied by a Proclamation. p. 15.

2718. —— Message to the two Houses of Congress, Dec, 6, '64. p. 14.

2719. —— Message in answer to a Resolution of the Senate, communicating Correspondence with the Working Men of England. *37th Congress, Executive Document No. 49,* 1863. pp. 6.

2723. —— Correspondence with Committee at Albany, New York, (Erastus Corning and others.) With Resolutions passed at the Meeting. 8vo. pp. 9.

2724. —— The Opinions of, upon Slavery and its Issues; indicated by his Speeches, Letters, Messages and Proclamations. pp. 16. (Washington, 1864.)

2725. —— President Lincoln and General Grant; or Peace and War. Mr. Lincoln's View of Democratic Strategy. Letter of General Grant, dated at City Point, Va., August 16, 1864. *Broadside.*

2726. —— Trial of Abraham Lincoln by the Great Statesmen of the Republic. A Council of the Past on the Tyranny of the Present. The Spirit of the Constitution on the Bench. Abraham, Prisoner at the Bar, his own Council. 8vo. pp. 28. NEW YORK: *Metropolitan Record*, 1863.

2727. —— Character of, and the Constitutionality of his Emancipation Policy. 8vo. pp. 16. (Boston, 1863.)

2728. —— God Bless Abraham Lincoln! A Solemn Discourse by a Local Preacher. Dedicated to the Faithful. For General Distribution at Five cents a copy. 8vo. p. 16.

The sentiments of this pamphlet are directly the reverse from what would be inferred from its title.

2729. —— Letters on President Lincoln. Questions of National Policy to Gen. McClellan, Horace Greeley, Fernando Wood. To the Albany Committee, to Governor Seymour, and to the Springfield Meeting. 12mo. pp. 22. NEW YORK: *H. H. Lloyd & Co.*, 1863.

2730. [LINCOLN, A.] Africanus I; his Secret Life revealed under the Mesmeric Influence. Mysteries of the White House. 12mo. pp. 57. NEW YORK: *J. F. Feeks.*

2731. LINCOLN AND JOHNSON Campaign Song Book; containing forty pages of Soul-stirring Pieces, written expressly for the Campaign. 12mo. pp. 38. NEW YORK: *American News Company,* 1864.

2732. LINCOLN AND JOHNSON CLUB'S Union Campaign Songster. 24th Ward, Philadelphia. pp. 12.

2733. LINCOLNIANA; or Humors of Uncle Abe. Second Joe Miller. By Andrew Adderup. Springfield, Illinois. 16mo. pp. 91. NEW YORK: *J. F. Feeks,* 1864.

2734. LINCOLN CATECHISM, (The.) Wherein the Eccentricities and Beauties of Despotism are fully set forth. 12mo. pp. 46. New York: *J. F. Feeks.*

2734.* LINCOLN. Psychometrical Examination of Abraham Lincoln, by A. J. Davis. *Friend of Progress, June,* 1865.

2735. LINCOLN, ABRAHAM, The Private and Public Life of. 18mo. pp. 96. NEW YORK: *Beadle & Co.,* (No date.)

2736. —— 8vo. pp. 12. No date. (Philadelphia.)

2737. —— The only authentic Life of Abraham Lincoln, alias " Old Abe." Sold everywhere, 1864. pp. 16.

2738. —— Life of, by Frank Crosby. 12mo. pp. 276. PHILADELPHIA: *John E. Potter,* 1865.

2739. —— The Life, Speeches and Public Services of. " Wigwam edition." 12mo. pp. 117. NEW YORK: *Rudd & Carleton,* 1860.

2740. —— The Life of, by Abott A. Abott. 12mo. pp. 100. NEW YORK: *T. R. Dawley,* 1864.

2741. —— The Private and Public Life of; comprising a full Account of his early Years. By O. J. Victor. 18mo. pp. 98. NEW YORK: *Beadle & Co.,* 1864.

2742. —— The Life and Martyrdom of. 12mo. pp. 203. PHILADELPHIA: *T. B. Peterson & Brother.*

2743. —— The Life and Times of. By L. P. Brockett. 8vo. pp. 700. PHILADELPHIA: *Bradley & Co.,* 1865.

2744. —— Abraham Lincoln. A Study. 16mo. pp. 32. LIVERPOOL: (England) 1865.

2745. LINCOLN, A. The Martyr President. A Poem, by R. H. Newell.
8vo. pp. 43. NEW YORK: *Carleton*, 1865.

2746. —— Life of, by Joseph H. Barrett.
8vo. pp. 518. CINCINNATI: *Moore, Wilstach & Co.*

2747. —— Life of, by the Rev. J. G. Holland.
8vo. pp. 344. SPRINGFIELD: *Gurdon Bill*, 1866.

2748. —— Life of, by the Hon. J. H. Raymond.
12mo. pp. 83. NEW YORK: *Derby & Miller*, 1864.

2749. —— History of the Administration of. By Hon. J. H. Raymond.
12mo. pp. 496. NEW YORK: *Derby & Miller*, 1864.

2750. —— Vida de Abran Lincoln Decimo—sesto Presidente de los Estados Unidos. Precidida de una introduccion por D. F. Sarmiento.
12mo. Int. xlviii. Text pp. 306. N. Y.: *D. Appleton & Co.*, 66.

2751. —— The President's Words. A Selection of Passages from the Speeches, Addresses and Letters of Abraham Lincoln.
12mo. pp. 186. BOSTON: *Walker, Fuller & Co.*, 1865.

2752. —— Sermons preached in Boston on the Death of Abraham Lincoln. Together with the Funeral Service in the East Room of the Executive Mansion at Washington.
12mo. pp. 381. BOSTON: *J. E. Tilton & Co.*, 1865.

2753, ——· Our Martyr President. Voices from the Pulpit of New York and Brooklyn. Oration by Hon. George Bancroft, etc.
12mo. pp. 420. NEW YORK: *Tibbals & Whiting*, 1865.

2754. —— A Memorial of Abraham Lincoln, late President of the United States.
4to. pp. 153. BOSTON: *Ticknor & Fields*, 1865.

2755. —— Memorial Record of the Nation's Tribute to Abraham Lincoln. Compiled by B. F. Morris.
8vo. pp. 272. WASHINGTON: *W. H. & O. H. Morrison*, 1865.

2756. —— Poetical Tributes to the Memory of Abraham Lincoln.
8vo. pp. xi, 306. Portrait. PHIL.: *J. B. Lippincott & Co.*, 1865.

2757. THE LINCOLN MEMORIAL. A Record of the Life, Assassination and Obsequies of the Martyred President.
8vo. pp. 288. NEW YORK: *Bunce & Huntington*, 1865.

2758. LINCOLN. President Abraham Lincoln. A Memoir, with his Opinion on Secession; Extracts from the United States Constitu-

31

tion, etc., to which is appended an Historical Sketch of Slavery. Reprinted, by permission, from the [London] *Times.* Lond. 8vo.

2759. LINCOLN. Notes on the Lincoln Families of Massachusetts, with some account of the Family of Abraham Lincoln. By the Hon. Solomon Lincoln, of Hingham.

8vo. pp. 60. BOSTON: *D. Clapp & Son,* 1865.

2760. —— The Journeys of Abraham Lincoln, from Springfield to Washington, 1861, as President Elect; and from Washington to Springfield, 1865, as President Martyred. By William T. Coggeshall.

12mo. pp. 327. COLUMBUS: (Ohio) *Journal Office,* 1865.

2761. —— In Memoriam. 8vo. New York: *Trent, Filmer & Co.,*'65.
Contains Mr. Lincoln's Farewell Speech on leaving Springfield for Washington, Proclamation of Emancipation, Addresses at Gettysburg, November 19, 1863, Inaugural Address, 1865.

2762. LINCOLNIANA. In Memoriam.

4to. pp. 346. BOSTON: *Wm. V. Spencer,* 1865.
Contains Sermons, Eulogies, Speeches and Letters, with a List of Publications relating to the Assassination, Death and Obsequies of President Lincoln.

2763. —— Le Président des Etats Unis. Abraham Lincoln. *Revue des Deux Mondes, May,* 1865.

2764. —— Abraham Lincoln, sa naissance, sa vie, sa mort.

Folio pp. 96. PARIS: *Charlien Fréres,* 1865.

2764.* —— Von der Holzart zum Präsidentenstuhl oder Lebensgeschichte des Volksmannes Abraham Lincoln.

8vo. pp. 32. BERLIN; *C. F. Conrad,* 1865.

2764.** —— der Wiederhersteller der Nordameri-Kanischen Union und der grosze Kampf der Nord und Südstaaten wahrend der Jahne, 1861–65. Von Dr. Mar Lange.

8vo. pp. 260. LEIPZIG: *Otto Spamer,* 1866.

PROCEEDINGS OF CITIES, TOWNS AND PUBLIC BODIES ON THE OCCASION OF THE DEATH OF ABRAHAM LINCOLN.

2765. ATHENÆUM CLUB, New York. Commemorative Proceedings of, April 1865.

Royal 8vo. pp. 36. Port. *For the Athenæum Club,* 1865.

2766. BALTIMORE. Proceedings of the City Council of.

8vo. pp. 24. BALTIMORE: 1865.

2767. BERLIN, Prussia. Funeral Observances, etc., by German. English and American Ministers. With Speeches on the occasion. 8vo. pp. 39.

2768. BOSTON. A Memorial of Abraham Lincoln, late President of the United States. Proceedings of City Council. Meeting at Faneuil Hall, and Eulogy by Chas. Sumner. Ro. 8vo. p. 163. BOST.: *By Order of City Council,* 1865.

2769. BOSTON. Proceedings of the City Council of, April 17, 1865.
8vo. pp. 35.   BOSTON: 1865.

2770. BUENOS AYRES. Tribute to the Memory of Abraham Lincoln, by the American Citizens resident in Buenos Ayres, South America.
8vo. pp. 25. BUENOS AYRES: *German. Pr. Office,* 1865.
Contains the proceedings of the Meeting, the Resolutions adoped; Remarks by the Hon. R. C. Kirk, and the Address by the Rev. William Goodfellow.

2771. BUFFALO, New York. In Memoriam. 8vo. pp. 36.

2772. BUNKER HILL MONUMENT ASSOCIATION. Proceedings of, June 17, 1865.

2773. HISTORICAL SOCIETY OF PENNSYLVANIA. Proceedings of, April 24, 1865. 8vo. pp. 4.

2774. NEW LONDON, Connecticut. Funeral Observances at, April 19, 1865. With the Addresses of the Rev. G. B. Wilcox and Rev. Dr. Field.
8vo. pp. 34.   NEW LONDON: 1865.

2775. NEW YORK. Obsequies at Union Square, April 25, 1865. pp. 16.

2776. PHILADELPHIA. Proceedings and Resolutions of City Councils, Saturday, April 15, 1865, and Thursday, April 20, 1865. 8vo. pp. 8.

2777. PORTSMOUTH, New Hampshire. Account of the Obsequies at, April 19, 1865. With the Eulogy of the Rev. A. J. Paterson.
8vo. pp. 30.   PORTSMOUTH: 1865.

2778. PROVIDENCE, R. I. Proceedings of the City Council of, June 1, 1865. With the Oration of Wm. Binney, Esq.
8vo. pp. 56. PROVIDENCE: *Knowles, Anthony & Co.,*'65.

2779. RIO JANEIRO. Proceedings and Resolutions of a Meeting at.

2780. SACO, Maine. Proceedings of the Town of, April 19, 1865 ; with the Eulogy of R. P. Tapley, Esq.
8vo. pp. 27. BIDDEFORD, 1865.

2780.* ST. JOHN, New Brunswick. Proceedings at, June 2, 1865. With Memorial Address by C. M. Ellis, Esq. p. 65

2781. SPRINGFIELD, Massachusetts. Observances of the City Authorities of; with the Eulogy of the Rev. Dr. Holland, April 19, 1865.
8vo. pp. 32. SPRINGFIELD : *Samuel Bowles & Co.*, 1865.

2782. ST. CATHERINES, Canada West. Proceedings of Public Meetings at, April 23, 1865; with Discourse of the Rev. R. Norton, and Address by the Rev. R. F. Burns.
8vo. pp. 40. ST. CATHERINES : *E. J. Leavenworth*, 1865.

2783. TROY, New York. A Tribute of Respect by the Citizens of Troy, New York, to the Memory of Abraham Lincoln ; with Proceedings and Eulogy.
8vo. pp. xl and 342. ALBANY : *J. Munsell & Co.*, 1865.

2784. —— The same. Imp. 4to. (50 copies.) Albany : *J Munsell & Co.*, 1865.

2785. UNION LEAGUE OF PHILADELPHIA. Proceedings of, April 15, 1865.
8vo. pp. 22. PHILADELPHIA : 1865.

2786. WASHINGTON. Proceedings of a Meeting of Ministers of all Denominations in the District of Columbia, April 17, 1865. With the Remarks of the Rev. Dr. Gurley, and Reply of President Johnson.
8vo. pp. 14. WASHINGTON : *McGill & Witherow*, 1865.

2787. WASHINGTON. Celebration by the Colored People's Education Monument Association, July 4, 1865. pp. 33. Washington, 1865.

2788. LINCOLN, ABRAHAM. Eulogies, Sermons, Orations and Poems upon.

1. Allen, Rev. Ethan. Homestead, Baltimore Co., Maryland, June 1, 1865.
2. Andrew, Hon. John A. Message to Legislature of Mass., July 17, 1865.
3. Atwood, Rev. E. S. Salem, Massachusetts, April 16, 1865.
4. Atwood, Rev. E. S. Salem, Massachusetts, June 1, 1865.

5. Babcock, Rev. Samuel D. Dedham, Massachusetts, April 19, 1865.
6. Badger, Rev. Henry C. Cambridgeport, Massachusetts, April 23, 1865.
7. Bain, Rev. J. W. Canonsburg, Pennsylvania, June 1, 1865.
8. Baldridge, Rev. S. C. Friendsville, Illinois, April 23, 1865.
9. Bancroft, Hon. George. New York, N. Y., April 25, 1865.
10. Bancroft, Hon. George. Article in Atlantic Monthly, June, 1865.
11. Bancroft, Hon. George. Oration, delivered before the Houses of Congress, Feb. 12, 1866.
12. Barnes, Rev. Albert. Philadelphia, Pennsylvania, June 1, 1865.
13. Barnes, Rev. Samuel. Baltimore, Maryland, April 19, 1865.
14. Barr, Rev. T. H. Canaan Centre, Ohio, April 19, 1835.
15. Bartol, Rev. C. A., DD. Boston, Massachusetts, June 1, 1865.
16. Beecher, Rev. Henry Ward. Brooklyn, New York.
17. Benjamin, S. G. W. Ode on the Death of Abraham Lincoln.
18. Bingham, Rev. J. C. Neshanock and Hopewell, Penn., June 1, 1865.
19. Bingham, Joel F. Buffalo, New York, May 7, 1865.
20. Binney, William. Providence, Rhode Island, June 1, 1865.
21. Binns, Rev. William, Birkenhead, England, April 30, 1865.
22. Blackburn, Rev. W. M. Trenton, New Jersey, April 16, 1665.
23. Bliss, Rev. T. E. Memphis, Tennessee, April 23. 1865.
24. Boardman, Rev. George N. Philadelphia, Pennsylvania, April 16, 1865.
25. Boardman, Rev. George N. Philadelphia, Pennsylvania, April 19, 1865.
26. Boardman, Rev. H. A., DD. Philadelphia, Pennsylvania, June 1, 1865.
27. Booth, Rev. Robert Russell, DD. New York, New York, April 23, 1865.
28. Boutwell, Hon. George S. Lowell, Massachusetts, April 19, 1865.
29. Brakeman, Rev. N. L. Baton Rouge, Louisiana, April 23, 1865.
30. Briggs, Rev. George W., DD. Salem, Massachusetts, June 1, 1865.
31. Brooks, Rev. Phillips. Philadelphia, Pennsylvania, April 23, 1865.
32. Broome, W. W. Abraham Lincoln's Character, sketched by English Travellers.
33. Bulkley, Rev. E. A. Plattsburg, New York, April 19, 1865.
34. Bullock, Hon. Alexander H. Worcester, Massachusetts, June 1, 1865.
35. Burns, Rev. Robert F. St. Catherines, Canada West, April 23, 1855.
36. Burgess, Rev. Chalon. Panama, New York, April 30, 1866.
37. Burrows, Rev. J. Lansing, DD. Richmond, Virginia, April 23, 1865.
38. Butler, Rev. C. M., DD. Philadelphia, Pennsylvania, April 19, 1865.
39. Butler, Rev. H. E. Keeseville, New York, April 23, 1865.
40. Butler, Rev. J. G. Washington, D. C., April 16, 1865.
41. Carey, Rev. Isaac E. Freeport, Illinois, April 19, 1865.
42. Carey, Rev. Isaac E. Freeport, Illinois, June 1, 1865.
43. Carnahan, Rev. D. T. Gettysburg, Pennsylvania, June 1, 1865.
44. Chaffin, Rev. Wm. L. Philadelphia, Pennsylvania, April 23, 1865.
45. Chamberlain, Rev. N. H. Birmingham, Connecticut, April 19, 1865.
46. Chase, Professor Thomas. Haverford College, Penn., July 6, 1865.
47. Chester, Rev. John. Washington, D. C., April 16, 1865.
48. Clark, Rev. Alexander. Cincinnati, Ohio, April 19, 1865.
49. Clark, Hon. Daniel. Manchester, New Hampshire, June 1, 1865.
50. Clark, Henry. Poultney, Vermont, April 19, 1865.

51. Clark, Rev. James Freeman, DD. Boston, Massachusetts, April 16, 1865.
52. Co'fax, Hon. Schuyler. South Bend, Indiana, April 24, 1865.
53. Coddington, David S. Charleston, South Carolina, May 6, 1865.
54. Colman, Rev. George W. Acton, Massachusetts, Apr'l 16, 1865.
55. Cooke, Rev. C., DD. Smyrna, Delaware, June 1, 1865.
56. Cooper, Rev. James. Philadelphia, Pennsylvania, April 16, 1865.
57. Craig, Rev. W. New Bedford, Massachusetts, April 23, 1865.
58. Crane, Rev. C. B. Hartford, Connecticut, April 16, 1865.
59. Crocker, Samuel L., Jun., Esq. Taunton, Massachusetts, June 1, 1865.
60. Cromwell, Henry S. Poem. 1865. Broadside.
61. Crozier, Rev. Henry P. Huntington, New York, April 19, 1865.
62. Cudworth, Rev. Warren H. East Boston, Massachusetts, May 8, 1865.
63. Cushman, Rev. R. S. Manchester, Vermont, April 19, 1865.
64. Cutter, Rev. E. F. Rockland, Maine, April 19, 1865.
65. Daggett, Rev. O. E. Canandaigua, New York, April 16, 1865.
66. Darling, Rev. Henry, DD. Albany, New York, April 19, 1865.
67. Dascomb, Rev. A. B. Waitesfield, Vermont, April 23, 1865.
68. Dailey, J. P. Flemington, New Jersey, April 19, 1865.
69. Davidson, Rev. R., DD. Huntington, New York, April 19, 1865.
70. Davis, Hon. Noah. Albion, New York, April 19, 1865.
71. Day, Rev. P. B. Hollis, New Hampshire, June 1, 1865.
72. Dean, Rev. Sidney. Providence, Rhode Island, April 19, 1865.
73. Deming, Hon. Henry Champion. Hartford, Connecticut, June 8, 1865.
74. DeNormandie, Rev. James. Portsmouth, New Hampshire, April 16, 1865.
75. Dexter, Rev. Henry Martyn. Boston, Massachusetts, April 23, 1865.
76. Dix, Rev. Morgan, S. T. D. New York, New York, April 19, 1865.
76.* Douglass, Frederick. Washington, D. C., February 12, 1866.
77. Drumm, Rev. J. H., M D. Bristol, Pennsylvania, April 16, 1865.
78. Duane, Rev. Richard B. Providence, Rhode Island, April 19, 1865.
79. Dudley, Rev. John S. Middletown, Connecticut, April 16, 1865.
80. Duffield, Rev. George. Detroit, Michigan, April 16, 1865.
81. Dunning, Rev. H. Baltimore, Maryland, April 19, 1865.
82. Dunning, Rev. H. Baltimore, Maryland, April 23, 1855.
83. Dunning, Rev. H. Baltimore, Maryland, May 7, 1865.
84. Dyer, Rev. D. Albany, New York, April 19, 1865.
85. Eddy, Rev. Daniel C., DD. Boston, Massachusetts, April 16, 1865.
86. Eddy, Rev. Richard. Philadelphia, Pennsylvania, April 16, 1865.
87. Eddy, Rev. Richard. Philadelphia, Pennsylvania, April 19, 1865.
88. Eddy, Rev. Richard. Philadelphia, Pennsylvania, June 1, 1865.
89. Eddy, T. M., DD. Waukegan, Illinois, April 16, 1865.
90. Edgar, Rev. Cornelius H., DD. Easton, Pennsylvania, April 16, 1865.
91. Edgar, Rev. Cornelius, DD. Easton, Pennsylvania, April 19, 1865.
92. Edgar, Rev. Cornelius, DD. Easton, Pennsylvania, April 23, 1865.
93. Edgar, Rev. Cornelius, DD. Easton, Pennsylvania, June 1, 1865.
94. Edwards, Rev. Henry L. South Abington, Massachusetts, June 1, 1865.
95. Egar, Rev. John H., BD. Leavenworth, Kansas, June 1, 1865.
96. Einhorn, Rev. D., DD. (In German.) Philadelphia, Penn., April 19, 1865.
97. Ellis, C. M. St. John, New Brunswick, June 1, 1865.

98. Ellis, Rev. Rufus. Boston, Massachusetts, June 16. 1865.
99. Everett, Rev. Charles Carroll. Bangor, Maine, April 16, 1865.
100. Everett, Rev. Charles Carroll. Bangor, Maine, April 19, 1865.
101. Everett, Rev. Charles Carroll. Bangor, Maine, June 1, 1865.
102. Farquhar, Rev. John. Lower Chanceford, Pennsylvania, June 1, 1865.
103. Field, Rev. Thomas P., DD. New London, Connecticut, April 19, 1865.
104. Field, Hon. R. S. Trenton, New Jersey, February 12, 1866.
105. Fowler, Rev. Henry Auburn, New York, April 23, 1865
106. Fowler, John, Jun. New Rochelle, New York, April 23, 1865.
107. Frelinghuysen, F. T., Esq. Newark, New Jersey, April 19 1865.
108. Franklin Thomas L. Mount Morris, New York, April 20, 1865.
109. Frothingham, Rev. O. B. "The Murdered President," in Friend of Progress, June, 1865.
110. Fuller, Rev. Richard, DD. Baltimore, Maryland, June 1, 1865.
111. Gaddis, Rev. M. P. Cincinnati, Ohio, April 16, 1865.
112. Garrison, Rev. J. F., M. D. Camden, New Jersey, April 19, 1865.
113. Gear, Rev. D. L. Philadelphia, Pennsylvania, April 23, 1865.
114. Gillette, Rev. A. G., DD. Washington, D. C., April 23, 1865.
115. Glover, Rev. L. M., DD. Jacksonville, Illinois, April 23, 1865.
116. Goodfellow, Rev. William. Buenos Aires, South America, June 11, 1865
117. Gordon, Rev. W. R., DD. Schraalenberg, New Jersey, April 14. 1865.
119. Gurley, Rev. P. D., DD. Washington, D. C., April 19, 1865.
120. Gurley, Rev. P. D., DD. Washington, D. C., June 1, 1865.
121. Guthrie, Dr. W. E. Philadelphia, Penn., April 25, 1865
122. Hall, Rev. Charles H. Washington, D. C., April 19, 1865.
123. Hall, Rev. Gordon, DD. Northampton, Massachusetts, April 19, 1865.
124. Hall, Rev. Newman. Surrey Chapel, London, England, May 14, 1865.
125. Hamill, Samuel M., DD. Lawrenceville, New Jersey, June 1, 1865.
126. Hammond, Rev. Charles. Monson, Massachusetts, June 1, 1865.
127. Hammond, William G. Davenport, Iowa, April 27, 1865.
128. Hanaford, Mrs. P. A. "The Martyred President." Boston.
129. Hardinge, Miss Emma. New York, N. York, April 16, 1865.
130. Hatch, Mrs. Cora L. V. Poem, "Friend of Progress."
131. Hathaway, Rev. Warren. Coxsackie, New York, April 19, 1865.
132. Haven, E. C. Ann Arbor, Michigan, April 19, 1865.
133. Haven, Rev. Gilbert. Boston, Massachusetts, April 23, 1865.
134. Hawley, Rev B., DD. Albany, New York, April 23, 1865.
135. Hayden, Mrs. C. A. A Tribute to Abraham Lincoln. A Poem.
136. Hayden, Rev. W. B. Cincinnati, Ohio.
137. Hepworth, Rev. G. H. Boston, Massachusetts, April 23, 1865.
138. Hepworth, Rev. G. H. Boston, Massachusetts.
139. Hibbard, A. G. Detroit, Michigan, April 16.
140. Hingeley, Rev. E. Monongahela City, Pennsylvania, April 23 1865.
141. Hitchcock, Rev. Henry L. Hudson, Ohio, April 19, 1865.
142. Hodge, Rev. C., DD. From the Princeton Review.
143. Hoffman, Rev. E. A. Brooklyn, New York, April 26, 1865.
144. Holland, Rev. E. A., DD. Springfield, Massachusetts, April 19, 1865.
145. Hockheimer, Rev. H. Baltimore, Maryland, April 19, 1865. (In German.)

146. Hockheimer, Rev. H.   Baltimore, Maryland, June 1, 1865.   (In German.)
147. Hopkins, Rev. T. M.   Bloomington, Indiana, April 19, 1865.
148. Howlett, Rev. T. R.   Washington, D. C., June 1, 1865.
149. "In Memoriam."   Abraham Lincoln.   New York.
150. Irwin, Rev. William.   Rondout, New York, April 16, 1865.
151. Ives, Rev. Alfred.   Castine, Maine, April 16.
152. Janeway, Rev. J. L.   Flemington, New Jersey, April 19.
153. Jeffrey, Rev. R., DD.   Philadelphia, Pennsylvania, June 1, 1865.
154. Johnson, Rev. Herrick.   Pittsburgh, Pennsylvania, April 23, 1865.
155. Johnson, Rev. E. S.   Harrisburg, Pennsylvania, June 1, 1865.
156. Johnson, Rev. Samuel.   Lynn, Massachusetts, April 19, 1865.
157. Johnson, Rev. William M.   Stillwater, New York, April 16, 1865.
158. Jordan, Rev. E. S.   Cumberland Center, Maine, June 1, 1865.
159. Keeling, Rev. R. J.   Washington, D. C., April 23, 1865.
160. Keith, Rev. O. B.   Jenkentown, Pennsylvania, April 19, 1865.
161. Kip, William Ingraham, DD.   Hombourg-les-Bains, Germany.   June 1, '65.
162. Krauth, Rev. Charles P., DD.   Pittsburgh, Pennsylvania, June 1, 1865.
163. Krebs, Rev. Hugo, DD.   St. Louis, Missouri, April 14, 1865.
164. Krebs, Rev. Hugo.   (German.)   St. Louis, Missouri.   April 19, 1865.
165. Krummacher, Dr.   Berlin, May 4.   (In German.)
166. Lamb, Rev. E. E.   Rootstown, Ohio, April 23.
167. Laurie, Rev. Thomas.   West Roxbury, Massachusetts, April 19, 1865.
168. Laurie, Rev. Thomas.   West Roxbury, Massachusetts, April 23, 1865.
169. Laurie, Rev. Thomas.   West Roxbury, Massachusetts, June 1, 1865.
170. Lowe, Rev. Charles.   Charlestown, South Carolina, April 23, 1865.
171. Lowrie, Rev. John M.   Fort Wayne, Indiana, April 16, 1865.
172. Ludlow, Rev. J. M.   Albany, New York, April 23, 1865.
173. Mac El'Rey, Rev. J. H., M. D.   Wooster, Ohio, April 16, 1865.
174. McCauley, Rev. James.   Baltimore, Maryland, June 1, 1865.
175. McClintock, John, DD.   New York, New York, April 19, 1865.
176. Mac Donald, James M., DD.   Princeton, New Jersey, June 1, 1865.
177. Maple Leaves from Canada, see Rev. *Robert Norton* and Rev. *R. Burns.*
178. Marshall, Rev. Joseph, U. S. A.   Norfolk, Virginia, April 29, 1865
179. Mayo, Rev. A. D.   Cincinnati, Ohio, April 16, 1865.
180. Mayo, Rev. A. D.   Cincinnati, Ohio, April 19, 1865.
181. Miller, Hon. S. F.   Franklin, New York, June 1, 1865.
182. Mitchell, Rev. S. S.   Harrisburg, Pennsylvania, April 19, 1865.
183. Morais, Rev. S.   Philadelphia, Pennsylvania, June 1, 1865.
184. Morehouse, Rev. H. L.   East Saginaw, Michigan, April 19, 1865.
185. Morgan, Rev. William F., DD,   New York, New York, April 16, 1865.
186. Myers, Hon. Leonard.   Philadelphia, Pennsylvania, June 15, 1865.
187. Murdock, Rev. D.   New Milford, Connecticut, April, 23, 1865.
188. Nadal, Rev. B. H., DD.   Washington, D. C., June 1, 1865.
189. Nason, Rev. Elias.   Boston, Massachusetts, May 3, 1865.
190. Nelson, Rev. Henry A.   Springfield, Illinois, May 7, 1865.
191. Newell, Robert.   "The Martyr President."   A Poem.
192. Niccolls, Rev. Samuel J.   St. Louis, Missouri, April 23, 1865.
193. Niles, Rev. H. E.   York, Pennsylvania, April 19, 1865.

194. Noble, Rev. Mason. Newport, Rhode Island, April 19, 1865.
195. Norton, Rev. Robert. St. Catherines, Canada West, April 23, 1865.
196. Paddock, Rev. Wilbur F. Philadelphia, Pennsylvania, April 23, 1865.
197. Parke, Rev. N. G. Pittston, Pennsylvania, June 1, 1865.
198. Parker, Rev. Henry E. Concord, New Hampshire, April 16, 1865.
199. Patterson, Rev. A. J. Portsmouth, New Hampshire, April 19, 1865.
200. Patterson, Hon. James W. Concord, New Hampshire, June 1, 1865.
201. Patterson, Robert M. Philadelphia, Pennsylvania.
202. Pettee, Rev. J. Abington, Massachusetts, April 19, 1865.
203. Pierce, Rev. J. D. North Attleboro', Massachusetts, April 19. 1865.
204. Post, Rev. Jacob. Harrison Landing, Virginia, April 23, 1865.
205. Potter, Rev. William J. New Bedford, Massachusetts, April 16, 1865.
206. Potter, Rev. William J. New Bedford, Massachusetts, April 19, 1865.
207. Potter, Rev. William J. New Bedford, Massachusetts, June 1, 1865.
208. Potter, Rev. William J. New Bedford, Massachusetts, June 4, 1865.
209. Preston, Rev. William, DD. Pittsburgh, Pennsylvania, April 19, 1865.
210. Prime, Rev. G. Wendell. Detroit, Michigan, April 16, 1865.
211. Putnam, Rev. George, DD. Roxbury, Massachusetts, April 19, 1865.
212. Quint, Rev. Alonzo H. New Bedford, Massachusetts, April 16, 1865.
213. Rankin, Rev, J. E. Charlestown, Massachusetts, April 19, 1865.
214. Ray, Rev. Charles. Wyoming, New York, April 19, 1865.
215. Reed, Rev. S. Edgartown, Massachusetts, April 19, 1865.
216. Reed, Rev. V. D, DD. Camden, New Jersey, April 30, 1865.
217. Reynolds, Rev. J. V., DD. Meadville, Pennsylvania, June 1, 1865.
218. Rice, Rev. Daniel. Lafayette, Indiana, April 19, 1865.
219. Rice, Rev. N. L. New York, New York, April 19, 1865.
220. Robbins, Rev. Frank L. Philadelphia, Pennsylvania, April 23, 1865.
221. Robinson, Rev. Charles S. Brooklyn, New York, April 16, 1865.
222. Russell, Rev. Peter. Eckley, Pennsylvania, April 30, 1865.
223. Russell, Rev. Peter. Eckley, Pennsylvania, June 1, 1865.
224. Sabine, Rev. William T. Philadelphia, Pennsylvania, April 16, 1865.
225. Salisbury, Rev. S. West Alexandria, Ohio, April 30, 1865.
226. Sample, Rev. Robert F. Bedford, Pennsylvania, April 23, 1865.
227. Sanborn, Rev. R. S. Ripon, Wisconsin, April 23, 1865.
228. Saunders, R. S. Island No. 40. Tennessee. April 25, 1865.
229. Searing, Rev. E. Milton, Wisconsin. June 1, 1865.
230. Sedgwick, Hon. Charles B. Syracuse, New York, April 19, 1865.
231. Seiss, Rev. Joseph A., DD. Philadelphia, Pennsylvania, June 1, 1865.
232. Sherman, Surgeon S. N., U. S. V. Grafton, West Virginia, April 19, 1865.
233. Simon, Rev. Dr. Berlin, Prussia, April 30, 1865. (In German.)
234. Simpson, Rev. Matthew, DD. Springfield, Illinois, May 4, 1865.
235. Slater, Rev. Edward C., DD. Paducah, Kentucky, April 19, 1865.
236. Smith, Rev. H., DD. Buffalo, New York, April 23, 1865.
237. Snively, Rev. W. A. Pittsburg, Pennsylvania, April 16, 1865.
238. Spaeth, Rev. A. Philadelphia, Pennsylvania, April 19, 1865. (In German.)
239. Spear, Rev. Samuel T., DD. Brooklyn, New York, April 23, 1865.
242. Sprague, Rev. J. N. Caldwell, New Jersey, June 1, 1865.
243. Sprague, Rev. William B., DD. Albany, New York, April 16, 1865.

32

244. Starr, Rev. Frederick, Jun. Pennyan, New York, April 16, 1865.
245. Starr, Rev. Frederick, Jun. St. Louis, Missouri, May 14, 1865.
246. Steiner, Lewis H. Frederick, Maryland, April 23, 1865.
247. Stewart, Rev. Daniel, DD. Johnston, New York, April 16, 1865.
248. Stewart, Rev. Daniel, DD. Johnston, New York, April 19, 1865.
249. Stoddard, R. H. An Horatian Ode. New York.
250. Stoever, Professor M. L. Abraham Lincoln. Congregational Quarterly.
251. Stone, Rev. Andrew L., DD. Boston, Massachusetts, April 16, 1865.
252. Storrs, Rev. Richard S., Jun., DD. Brooklyn, New York, June 1, 1865.
253. Strong, Rev. J. D. San Francisco, California, April 16, 1865.
254. Sturz, J. F. Berlin, Prussia. May 4. (In German.)
255. Sumner, Hon. Charles. Boston, Massachusetts, June 1, 1865.
256. Sutphen, Rev. Morris C. Philadelphia, Pennsylvania, April 16, 1865.
257. Swaim, Rev. Thomas, DD. Flemington, New Jersey, April 19, 1865
258. Swain, Rev. Leonard. Providence, Rhode Island, April 16, 1865.
259. Sweetzer, Rev. Seth. Worcester, Massachusetts, April 23, 1865.
260. Swing, Rev. David. Hamilton, Ohio, April 16, 1865.
261. Symmes, Rev. J. G. Cranbury, New Jersey, June 1, 1865.
262. Szold, Benjamin. (German.) Baltimore, Maryland, June 1, 1865.
263. Tapley, Rufus P. Saco, Maine, April 19, 1865.
264. Tappan, Rev. Henry P., DD. Berlin, Prussia, May 4, 1865.
265. Tappan, Rev. H. P., DD. Same in German.
266. Taylor, Rev. A. A. E. Georgetown, D. C., June 1, 1865.
267. Thomas, Rev. A. G., U. S. A. Philadelphia, Pennsylvania, April 19, 1865.
268. Thompson, Rev. Joseph P., DD. New York, New York, April 30. 1865.
269. Thompson, Rev. John C. Pittstown, Pennsylvania, June 1, 1865.
270. Thompson, Rev. Henry P. Peapack, New Jersey, April 16, 1865.
271. Timlow, Rev. Heman R. Rhinebeck, New York, April 19, 1865.
272. Tucker, Rev. J. T. Holliston, Massachusetts, June 1, 1865.
273. Twomblay, Rev. A. S. Albany, New York, April 16, 1865.
274. Tyler, Rev. G. P. Brattleboro, Vermont, April 19, 1865.
275. Tyng, Stephen H., DD. New York, New York, April 20, 1865.
276. Vincent, Rev. Marvin R. Troy, New York, April 23, 1865.
277. Walden, Rev. Treadwell. Philadelphia, Pennsyivania, April 16, 1855.
278. Walden, Rev. T. Philadelphia, Pennsylvania, April 19, 1865.
279. Wallace, Rev. C. C. Placerville, California, April 19, 1865.
280. Wayman, Rev. James. Liverpool. England, May 7, 1865.
281. Webb, Rev. E. B. Boston, Massachusetts, April 16, 1865.
282. Weiss, Rev. J. Article in "Friend of Progress." June, 1865.
283. Wells, Rev. Theodore W. Bayonne, New Jersey, April 23, 1865.
284. Wentworth, Rev. J. B. Buffalo, New York, April 23, 1865.
285. Westall, John. "In Memoriam." A Poem.
286. White, Rev. Erskine N. New Rochelle, New York, June 1, 1865.
287. White, Rev. Pliny H. Coventry, Vermont, April 23, 1865.
288. Wilcox, Rev. G. B. New London, Connecticut, April 19, 1865.
289. Williams, Rev. Robert H. Frederick City, Maryland, April 29, 1865.
290. Williams, Rev. Robert H. Frederick City, Maryland, June 1, 1865.
291. Williams, Hon. Thomas. Pittsburgh, Pennsylvania, June 1, 1865.

292. Williams, Rev. William R., DD. New York, New York, April 16, 1865.
293. Wilson, Rev. William T. Albany, New York, April 19, 1865.
294. Windsor, Rev. W. Davenport, Iowa, Juna 1, 1865.
295. Winsor, Rev. John H. Saco, Maine, June 1, 1865.
296. Woodbury, Rev. Augustus. Providence, Rhode Island, April 16, 1865.
297. Woodbury, Rev. Augustus. Providence, Rhode Island, June 1, 1865.
298. Wortman, Rev. Denis. Schenectady, New York, April 16, 1865.
299. Yard, Rev. Robert B. Newark, New Jersey, June 1, 1865.
300. Yourtee, Rev. S. L. Springfield, Ohio, April 19, 1865.

2789. LINCOLN, Jarius. Anti-Slavery Melodies, for the Friends of Freedom. Prepared for the Hingham Anti-Slavery Society. 12mo. pp. 96. Hingham: *Elijah B. Gill,* 1843.

2790. LINCOLN, William S. Alton Trials, of Winthrop S. Gilman, who was indicted, with Enoch Long and others, for a Riot on the night of the 7th November, 1837, while engaged in defending a Printing Press from an attack by an armed Mob. 12mo. pp. 158. New York: *John F. Trow,* 1838.

2791. LITTLE, Mrs. Sophia L. Thrice through the Furnace. A Tale of the Times of the Iron Hoof. 12mo. pp. 190. Pawtucket; (R. I.) *A. W. Pearce,* 1852.

2792. LIVERMORE, George. An Historical Research respecting the Opinions of the Founders of the Republic, on Negroes as Slaves, as Citizens, and as Soldiers. 8vo. pp. xviii and 184. Boston: *A. Williams & Co.,* 1862.

2793. —— The same. Royal 8vo. Boston: *J. Wilson & Son,* 1862.

2794. —— The same. 4to. (50 copies printed.) Boston: *J. Wilson & Son,* 1862.

2795. Loan Committee of the Associated Banks of the City of New York. Report, June 12, 1862. 8vo. pp. 45. New York: *Hall, Clayton & Co.,* 1862.

2796. Loans and the Currency, Acts of Congress relating to, from 1842 to 1863. pp. 74 and 8. New York.

2797. LOGAN, Major General John A. Speech at Duquoin, Illinois, July 31, 1863, on his return to Illinois after the Capture of Vicksburg. 8vo. pp. 32

2798. —— The same, in German. 8vo. pp. 33. Cincinnati.

2799. —— Speech on his return to Illinois, after the Capture of Vicksburg. 8vo. pp. 32. Cincinnati: *Caleb Clark,* 1863.

2800. —— Great Union Speech in Chicago, August 10, 1863. pp. 16.

2801. London Quarterly Review. Democracy on its Trial. July,'61.

2802. —— The American Crisis. January, 1862.

2803. —— The American War. Fort Sumter to Fredericksburg. April, 1863.

2804. —— The Prospects of the Confederates. April, 1864.

2805. —— The United States as an Example. January, 1865.

2806. —— The Close of the American War. July, 1865.

2807. LONG, Alexander. The Policy of the Administration. Speech delivered in the House of Reps., Feb. 7, 1865. 8vo. pp. 16.

2808. LONGYEAR, J. W. Speech on the Reconstruction of the Union. House of Reps., April 30, 1864. pp. 8.

2809. LOPER, R. F., to Hon. E. M. Stanton, Secretary of War, in self-defence against the aspersions of the Senate Committee. 8vo. pp. 32. Philadelphia, 1863.

2810. LORD, Rev. C. E. Sermons on the Country's Crisis, delivered in Mount Vernon, New Hampshire, April 28, 1861.
8vo. pp. 29. Milford: *Boutwell's Office,* 1864.

2811. LORD, Charles E. Slavery, Secession and the Constitution. An Appeal to our Country's Loyalty. Boston, Oct., 1862. p. 58.

2812. A'LORD, Corporal G. (Company G, 125th Regt. New York Volunteers.) A short Narrative of the Military Experience of, etc. With a brief Sketch of the War.
12mo. pp. 64. *Sold by the author,* 1863.

2813. LORD, Eleazer. Six Letters on the Necessity and Practicability of a National Currency, and the Principles and Measures essential to it.
12mo. pp. 53. New York: *A. D. F. Randolph,* 1862.

2814. —— National Currency. A Review of the National Banking Law.
12mo. pp. 41. New York: *A. D. F. Randolph,* 1863.

2815. LORD, Henry W. The Highway of the Seas in Times of War.
8vo. pp. 56. London: *Macmillan & Co.,* 1862.

2816. LORD, John C., DD. "The Higher Law," in its application to the Fugitive Slave Bill. A Sermon on the Duties men owe to God and to Governments. Delivered in Buffalo.
8vo. pp. 16. New York: 1851.

2817. —— The Justice of our National Cause, and the Momentous

Issues of our Nation, the Church and the World, which are involved in the Result of the present Civil War. 1861. pp. 8.

2818. LORD, J. C., DD. The Dead of the Present War. A Funeral Discourse, delivered at Buffalo, June 28, 1862.
8vo. pp. 28. BUFFALO : *Martin Taylor*, 1861.

2819. —— Causes and Remedies of the Present Convulsions. A Discourse delivered January 4, 1861.
8vo. pp. 25. BUFFALO : *Joseph Warren & Co.*, 1861.

2820. —— A Sermon on the Character and Influence of Washington, before the Union Continentals, of Buffalo, February 22, 1863.
8vo. pp. 22. BUFFALO : *A. M. Clapp & Son*, 1863.

2821. LORD, NATHAN, DD. A Northern Presbyter's Second Letter to Ministers of the Gospel of all denominations, on Slavery.
8vo. pp. 99. BOSTON : *Little, Brown & Co.*, 1855.

2822. —— The Issue between North and South. *Knickerbocker Magazine, March and April*, 1864.

2823. LORD, Rev. WM. H. A Sermon on the Causes and Remedy of the National Troubles, preached at Montpelier, Vt., April 4, 1861.
8vo. pp. 22. MONTPELIER : *E. P. Walton*, 1861.

2824. LORING, CHARLES G., and Edwin W. Field. Correspondence on the present Relations between Great Britain and the United States of America.
8vo. pp. 153. BOSTON : *Little, Brown & Co.*, 1862.

2825. —— Neutral Relations of England and the United States.
8vo. pp. 116. BOSTON: *Wm. V. Spencer*, 1863.

2826. —— England's Liability for Indemnity. Remarks on the Letter of " Historicus," dated November, 1863. Printed in the London " Times," November 7.
8vo. pp. 46. BOSTON: *William V. Spencer*, 1864.

2827. LORING, CHARLES W. A Trip to Antietam. *Continental Monthly, February*, 1863.

2828. LORING, Dr. GEO. B. Oration at the Celebration at Salem, July 4, 1862.
8vo. pp. 30. BOSTON: *J. E. Farwell*, 1862.

2829. LOSSING, BENSON J. The League of States.
8vo. pp. 28. NEW YORK: *C. B. Richardson*, 1863.

2830. —— Early Secessionists. *Harpers' Magazine, March*, 1862.

2831. LOSSING, B. J.   Early Disunionists.   Ibid.   *May,* 1862.

2832. —— South Carolina Nullification.   Ibid.   *August,* 1862.

2833. LOTHIAN, The Marquis of.   The Confederate Secession.

Post 8vo. pp. 226.   EDINB. and LOND.: *Blackwood & Sons,* 1864.

Contents: The Right of Secession. The North and the South. Presidential Election. The Battle of the Tariffs. The Question of Siavery. The Battle of the Territories. Secession. The Rights of War. The Question of Recognition.

2834. LOTHROP, S. K., DD.   The Causes, Principles and Results of the present Conflict.   A Discourse delivered before the Ancient and Honorable Artillery Company, in its CCXXIII Anniversary, June 3, 1864.

8vo. pp. 70.   BOSTON: *Alfred Mudge,* 1861.

2834.* LOUISIANA.   Proceedings of the Louisiana State Convention (English and French); together with the Ordinances passed by said Convention, and the Constitution of the State as amended.

8vo. pp. 330.   NEW ORLEANS: *J. O. Nixon,* 1861.

2835. —— Letter of the Governor of the State of, communicating the Credentials of Charles Smith and R. King Cutler to the Congress of the United States ; with copies of the Proceedings of the General Assembly of Louisiana on their Election.   *Senate Document No.* 1, 38*th Congress,* 2*d Session,* 1864.

2836. —— Address of Gov. Allen to the Citizens of, July 5, 1864.

2837. —— Inaugural Address of Michael Hahn, Governor, at New Orleans, March 4, 1864.   8vo. pp. 4.

2838. —— Message of the Governor, October 7, 1864.   pp. 13.

2839. —— Rules and Regulations of the Convention for the Amendment and Revision of the Constitution, 1864.   pp. 8.

2840. —— Report of the Board of Education for Freedmen, for the year 1864.   8vo. pp. 27.

2841. —— Auditor's Report on the State Constitutional Convention of 1864.   8vo. pp. 8.

2842. —— Grand Celebration in honor of the Passage of the Ordinance of Emancipation, by the Free State Convention, May 11, 1864. Held in New Orleans, June 11 ; with the Programme, Proceedings and Speeches.

8vo. pp. 32.   NEW ORLEANS: *H. R. Lathrop,* 1864.

2843. —— Letter from Major Gen. Banks to J. H. Lane, Senator of Kansas, (relating to the New Constitution of Louisiana.) p. 12.

2844. LOUISIANA. Debates in the Convention for the Revision and Amendment of the Constitution. Assembled at Liberty Hall, New Orleans, April 6, 1864.

8vo. pp. 643. NEW ORLEANS: *W. R. Fish*, 1864.

2845. —— Official Journal of the Proceedings (English and French) of the Convention for the Amendment and Revision of the Constitution.

8vo. pp. 184 and x., NEW ORLEANS: *W. R. Fish*, 1864.

2846. —— Journal Official des Travaux de la Convention réunie pour réviser et amender la Constitution.

8vo. pp. 187 and x. NOUVELLE ORLEANS: *W. R. Fish*, 1864.

2847. —— Platform of the Free State Party, Jan. 30, 1865. pp. 4.

2848. —— Proceedings of the Convention of the Republican Party, at New Orleans, September 25, 1865, and of the Executive Committee of the Friends of Universal Suffrage. 8vo. pp. 50.

2848.*. —— Annual Message of Governor Allen, January, 1865.

2849. LOUISIANA ELECTIONS. Memorials of the citizens of Louisiana remonstrating against the admission of Senators and Representatives, from the State of Louisiana, and the Reception of any Electoral Vote from that State for President and Vice-President of the United States, etc., *Sen. Mis. Doc.*, *38th Cong.*, *2d Ses.*, *No. 2 & 6*, 1864. *pp* 4.

2850. LOUNSBERY, Rev. EDWARD. The Refuge in the Day of Calamity. A Sermon preached in Philadelphia, Sept. 7, 1862.

8vo. pp. 12. PHILADELPHIA: *Ringwalt & Brown*, 1862.

2851. LOVE, Maj. General of the Indiana Legion, Report of.

8vo. pp. 72. INDIANAPOLIS: *Joseph J. Bingham*, 1863.

2852. LOVE, ALFRED H. An Appeal in vindication of Peace Principles, and against Resistance by Force of Arms. A Review in opposition to an Address by Wm. J. Mullen.

8vo. pp. 17. PHILADELPHIA: *Maas & Vodges*, 1862.

2853. LOVEJOY, OWEN. There is no Property in Man. A Speech in the House of Reps., February 17, 1858. pp. 8.

2854. —— State of the Union. Speech in the House of Representatives, January 23, 1861. pp. 8.

2855. —— Conduct of the War. Speech, House of Representatives, January 6, 1862. pp. 7.

2856. LOVEJOY, O. Confiscation of Rebel Property. Remarks in Reply to Messrs. Crittenden and Wickliffe, in House of Representatives, April 24, 1862. pp. 8.

2857. —— and W. M. Dunn. Remarks on the Bill to authorize the President to enlist Soldiers of African Descent. House of Representatives, January 29 1863. pp. 8.

2858. LOVEJOY. Addresses on the Death of, in the Senate and House of Representatives of the United States, March 28, 1864.
8vo. pp. 60. WASHINGTON: *Government Printing Office*, 1864.

2859. LOW, HENRY R. The Governor's Message Reviewed. Senate, January 28, 1863.
8vo. pp. 24. ALBANY: *Weed, Parsons & Co.*, 1863.

2860. LOWE, Rev. CHARLES. Death of President Lincoln. A Sermon delivered in Charleston, S. C., April 23, 1865.
12mo. pp. 24. BOSTON: *Am. Unitarian Association*, 1865.

2861. —— The Condition and Prospects of the South. A Discourse delivered in Somerville, Mass., June 4, 1865.
8vo. pp. 8. BOSTON: *Walker, Fuller & Co.*, 1865.

2862. LOWE, Gov. E. LOUIS. Letter to the Virginia Legislature. Dated, Ashland, Virginia, December 16, 1861. pp. 4.

2863. LOWELL, Brig. General CHARLES RUSSELL. The Purchase of Blood. A Tribute to, by C. A. Bartol.
8vo. pp. 21. BOSTON: *John Wilson & Son*, 1864.

2864. LOWELL, JAMES RUSSELL. The President's Policy. From the North American Review, January, 1864. 8vo. pp. 22.

2865. —— The same. 8vo. pp. 22. Philadelphia, 1864.

2866. —— Gen. McClellan's Report. *N. American Review, Apr.*, 1864.

2867. —— The Next General Election. Ibid. *October*, 1864.

2868. —— Reconstruction. Ibid. *April*, 1865.

2869. LOWELL, R. T. S. The Better Am. Opinion. Ibid. *July*, '62.

2870. LOWREY, GROSVENOR P. The Commander-in-Chief. A Defence, upon Legal Grounds, of the Proclamation of Emancipation, and an Answer to Ex-Judge Curtis's pamphlet, entitled " Executive Power."
12mo. pp. 31. NEWYORK: *G. P. Putnam*, 1862.

2871. LOWRIE, Rev. JOHN M. The Lessons of our National Sorrow. A Discourse delivered at Fort Wayne, Ind., April 19, 1865.
8vo. pp. 16. FORT WAYNE : *Jenkinson & Hartman*, 1865.

2872. Loyal Citizens at Cooper Institute. The Great Mass Meeting of, March 6, 1863.

8vo. pp. 16. *Loyal Publication Society, No.* 3, 1863.

2873. To Loyal Democrats. Who are the Sympathizers with the Rebellion? What the Rebels say. pp. 7.

2874. Loyal International Bulletin. Good News! Good News from Home.

12mo. pp. 16. Providence : *By the author*, 1862.

2875. Loyal Leagues. Proceedings of the Convention of Loyal Leagues, held at Mechanics Hall, Utica, May 26, 1863.

8vo. pp. 68. New York : *W. C. Bryant & Co.*, 1863.

2876. The Loyal National Union Journal, Brownsville, Texas, April, 1864.

2877. Loyal National League. Letter to Count Gasparin, Edward Laboulaye, Henri Martin, Augustin Cochin, and other Friends of America, in France. pp. 10.

2878. —— Proceedings at the Organization of, New York, March 20, 1863. Speeches by Gen. Cochrane, Gen. Hamilton, and Senator Foster.

8vo. pp. 47. New York : *C. S. Westcott & Co.*, 1863.

2879. —— Opinions of Prominent Men concerning the Great Questions of the Times, expressed in their Letters to the Loyal National League.

8vo. pp. 72. New York : *C. S. Westcutt*, 1863.

2880. —— The Great Questions of the Times, discussed in a brief Report of Proceedings at the Great Inaugural Mass Meeting, New York, on the Anniversary of Sumter, April 11, 1863.

8vo. pp. 32. New York : *Loyal National League*, 1863.

2881. Loyal Publication Society. Proceedings of the First Anniversary Meeting of, February 13, 1864.

8vo. pp. 24. New York : *Loyal Publication Society, No.* 44.

2882. —— Proceedings of the Second Anniversary, Feb. 11, 1865.

8vo. pp. 30. New York : *Loyal Publication Society, No.* 78.

2883. —— List of Pamphlets issued. (These are not numbered in the order in which they appear here, but will be found elsewhere under the names of their respective authors, with fuller titles.)

1. Future of the Northwest. By Robert Dale Owen.
2. Echo from the Army. Extracts from Letters of Soldiers.

33

3. Union Mass Meeting, Cooper Institute, March 6, 1863. Speeches of Brady, Van Buren, etc.
4. Three Voices: the Soldier, Farmer and Poet.
5. Voices from the Army. Letters and Resolutions of Soldiers.
6. Northern True Men. Addresses of Connecticut Soldiers—Extracts from Richmond Journals.
7. Speech of Major-General Butler. Academy of Music, N. York, April 2, '63.
8. Separation; War without End. Ed. Laboulaye.
9. The Venom and the Antidote. Copperhead Declarations. Soldiers' Letters.
10. A few words in behalf of Loyal Women of the United States. By One of Themselves.
11. No Failure for the North. Atlantic Monthly.
12. Address to King Cotton. Eugene Pelletan.
13. How a Free People Conduct a long War. Stillé.
14. The Preservation of the Union, a National Economic Necessity.
15. Elements of Discords in Secessia. By William Alexander, Esq., of Texas.
16. No Party, now, but all for our Country. Francis Lieber.
17. The Cause of the War. Col. Charles Anderson.
18. Opinions of the Early Presidents and of the Fathers of the Republic upon Slavery, and upon Negroes as Men and Soldiers.
19. Einheit und Freiheit, von Hermann Raster.
20. Military Despotism! Suspension of the Habeas Corpus! &c.
21. Letter addressed to the Opera-House Meeting, Cincinnati. By Col. Charles Anderson.
22. Emancipation is Peace. By Robert Dale Owen.
23. Letter of Peter Cooper on Slave Emancipation.
24. Patriotism. Sermon by the Rev. Joseph Fransioli, of St. Peter's (Catholic) Church, Brooklyn.
25. The Conditions of Reconstruction. By Robert Dale Owen.
26. Letter to the President. By Gen. A. J. Hamilton, of Texas.
27. Nullification and Compromise; a Retrospective View. By John Mason Williams.
28. The Death of Slavery. Letter from Peter Cooper to Gov. Seymour.
29. Slavery Plantations and the Yeomanry. Francis Lieber.
30. Rebel Conditions of Peace. Extracts from Richmond Journals.
31. Address of the Loyal Leagues, Utica, October 20, 1863.
32. War Power of the President—Summary Imprisonment. By J. Heermans.
33. The Two Ways of Treason.
34. The Monroe Doctrine. By Edward Everett, &c.
35. The Arguments of Secessionists. Francis Lieber.
36. Prophecy and Fulfillment. Letter of A. H. Stephens—Address of E. W. Gantt.
37. How the South Rejected Compromise, &c. Speech of Mr. Chase in Peace Conference of 1861.
38. Letters on our National Struggle. By Brig. Gen. Thomas Meagher.
39. Bible View of Slavery, by John H. Hopkins, DD., Bishop of the Diocese of Vermont. Examined by Henry Drisler.
40. The Conscription Act; a Series of Articles. By George B. Butler.

41. Réponse de M. M. De Gasparin, Laboulaye, &c.
42. Reply of Messrs. Gasparin, Laboulaye, and others.
43. Antwort der Herren De Gasparin, Laboulaye, Martin, Cochin, an die Loyal National League.
44. Proceedings of First Ann. Meet. of the Loyal Pub. So., Feb. 13, 1864.
45. Finances and Resources of the United States. By H. G. Stebbins.
46. How the War Commenced. From Cincinnati Daily Commercial.
47. Result of Serf Emancipation in Russia.
48. Resources of the United States. By S. B. Ruggles.
49. Patriotic Songs. A Collection by G. P. Putnam.
50. The Constitution Vindicated. By James A. Hamilton.
51. No Property in Man. By Charles Sumner.
52. Rebellion, Slavery and Peace. By N. G. Upham.
53. How the War Commenced. (Germ. Trans.) Dr. F. Schutz, for the Society.
54. Our Burden and our Strength. By David A. Wells.
55. Eman. Slave and his Master. (Germ. Trans.) By Dr. F. Schutz, for the Soc'y.
56. The Assertions of a Secessionist. By Alexander H. Stephens.
57. Growler's Income Tax. By T. S. Arthur, Philadelphia.
58. Emancipated Slave and his Master. By James McKaye.
59. Lincoln or McClellan. (German.) By Francis Lieber.
60. Peace through Victory. (Sermon). By Rev. J. P. Thompson.
61. Sherman vs. Hood. Broadside. By the Secretary.
62. The War for the Union. By William Swinton.
63. Letter on McClellan's Nomination. By Hon. Gerrit Smith.
64. Letters of Loyal Soldiers. Parts 1, 2, 3, 4. By the Secretary.
65. Submissionists and their Record. Parts 1 and 2. By the Secretary.
66. Coercion Completed; or Treason Triumphant. By John C. Hamilton.
67. Lincoln or McClellan. (English.) By Francis Lieber.
68. The Cowards' Convention. By Charles Astor Bristed.
69. Whom do the English Wish Elected? By Frederick Milne Edge.
70. Collection of Letters from Europe. By G. P. Putnam.
71. Lincoln or McClellan. (Dutch Translation.)
72. Address of Dr. Schutz, at Philadelphia, October 5, 1865.
73. Loyalty and Sufferings of East Tennessee. By N. G. Taylor.
74. The Slave Power. By J. C. Hamilton.
75. The Great Issue. Address by John Jay.
76. Sufferings of U. S. Prisoners of War. By U. S. Sanitary Commission.
77. On Secession. Delivered by Dr. Lieber, in South Carolina, in 1851.
78. Proceedings of Second Annual Meet. of the Loyal Pub. So., Feb. 11, 1865.
79. To Hon. E. D. Morgan, on Amendment of Const. By Francis Lieber.
80. America for Free Working Men. By C. Nordhoff.
81. General McClellan's Campaign. By F. M. Edge.
82. Speech on Reconstruction. By Hon. Wm. D. Kelley.
83. Amendments of the Constitution. By Francis Lieber.
84. Crimes of the South. By W. W. Broom.
85. Lincoln's Life and its Lessons. By Rev. J. T. Thompson.
86. National System of Education. By C. Brooks.
87. Gasparin's Letter to President Johnson.

2884. LOYAL WOMEN OF THE REPUBLIC. Proceedings of the Meeting of, held in New York, May 14, 1863.
8vo. pp. 86.   NEW YORK: *Blair & Co.*, 1863.

2885. LOYALTY and Disloyalty.
8vo. pp. 8.   [PHILADELPHIA:] *Ringwalt & Brown.*

2886. LOYALTY; What is it? To whom or what due? [Baltimore,'63.]

2887. LOYALISTS, (The.) Ammunition. pp. 16. Philadelphia.

2888. LOYD, THOMAS E., President of the Board of Aldermen. Speech on the Question of Negro Suffrage in the District of Columbia, December 14, 1865. pp. 8.

2889. LOWREY, GROSVENOR P. The Commander-in-Chief. A Defence, upon legal grounds, of the Proclamation of Emancipation; and an Answer to Ex-Judge Curtis's Pamphlet, entitled " Executive Power."
12mo. pp. 34.   NEW YORK: *G. P. Putnam*, 1863.

2890. —— English Neutrality. Is the Alabama a British Pirate?
8vo. pp. 36.   NEW YORK: *Anson D. F. Randolph*, 1863.

2891. LUCKENBACK, Rev. W. H.   On Magnifying God's Work. A Discourse preached in Rhinebeck, November 28, 1861.
8vo. pp. 24.   ALBANY: *J. Munsell*, 1861.

2892. LUDLOW, J. M. A Sketch of the History of the United States, from Independence to Secession ; to which is added, The Struggle for Kansas, by Thomas Hughes.
8vo. pp. xx, 404.   CAMBRIDGE: *Macmillan & Co.*, 1862.

2893. —— The Southern Minister, and his Slave Convert.
8vo. pp. 4.   MANCHESTER: *A. Ireland & Co.*

2894. —— American Slavery. *London Ladies' Emancipation So.,*'64.

2895. LUDLOW, Rev. JAMES M. Sermon commemorative of National Events, delivered in Albany, April 23, 1865.
8vo. pp. 27.   ALBANY: *Weed, Parsons & Co.*, 1865.

2896. LUDLOW, FITZ HUGH. If Massa put Guns into our hands. *Atlantic Monthly, April,* 1864.

2897. LUNDY, Rev. J. P.   Loyalty to Government.   Preached in Emanuel Church, Holmesburg, April 21, 1861.
12mo. pp. 14.   PHILADELPHIA: *Lindsay & Blackstone*, 1861.

2898. —— Review of Bishop Hopkins' Bible View of Slavery. By a Presbyter of the Church in Philadelphia. pp. 15.

2899. LUNT, George. Washington and our own Times. A Lecture in aid of the Public Library, Newburyport, Feb. 22, 1861.

12mo. pp. 29.   Boston: *Crocker & Brewster*, 1861.

2900. LUTHER, Jr. Right and Wrong of the Boston Reformers; showing them to be a bad Remedy.

18mo. pp. 42.   New England: *Published by the author*, 1841.

2901. LYLE, Rev. W. W. (11th Regiment Ohio Vols.) Light and Shadows of Army Life. A Picture from the Battlefield, the Camp and the Hospital.

12mo. pp. 403.   Cincinnati: *R. W. Carroll & Co.*, 1865.

2902. LYON, Brig. General N. Obituary Addresses of Messrs. Pomeroy, Dixon and Foster, on the Death of. United States Senate, December 20, 1861.

8vo. pp.   Washington: *Globe Office*, 1861.

LYON, Brig. General F. For Eulogy on, see *Henderson*.

2904. Lyrics for Freedom, and other Poems. Under the auspices of the Continental Club.

12mo. pp. xvi and 243.   New York: *Carlton*, 1862.

MACDILL, David, DD. Three Questions: Why was the Continent of America not discovered till so late a period? Have we, the People of the United State, an Infidel or a Heathen System of Government? Does the Constitution of the United States sanction Slavery?

8vo. pp. 25.   Oquaka: (Illinois) *Plaindealer Office*, 1863.

2906. MACDONALD, Rev. J. M., DD. Prayer for the Country. A Discourse preached November 29, 1860, in Princeton, N. J.

8vo. pp.   New York: *John F. Trow*, 1860.

2907. —— Charles Hodge Dod. A Memorial containing, in substance, the Address delivered in Princeton, New Jersey, Aug. 31, 1864.

12mo. pp. 36.   New York: *Robert Carter & Brothers*, 1864.

The subject of this memorial was Assistant Adjutant General in the Army of the Potomac, on the Staff of Major General Hancock. He died at City Point, Virginia.

2908. —— President Lincoln; his Figure in History. A Discourse delivered in Princeton, N. J., June 1, 1865.

8vo. pp. 23.   New York: *Charles Scribner*, 1865.

2909. MAC EL'REY, Rev. J. H., M. D.   The Substance of Two Discourses occasioned by the Assassination of the President.   The Position, the Lesson, and the Duty of of the Nation.   Delivered in Wooster, Ohio.

8vo. pp. 24.   WOOSTER : (Ohio) *Republican Press,* 1865.

2910. MACK, Hon. A. W.   Speech on the Slavery Question, in the State Senate (of Illinois,) January 20, 1865.

8vo. pp. 20.   SPRINGFIELD : *Baker & Phillips,* 1865.

2911. MACKENZIE, ROBERT.   America and her Army.

8vo. pp. 60.   LONDON : *T. Nelson & Sons,* 1865.

2912. MACON, NATH'L.   The Destruction of the Union is Emancipation.   Letters to Charles O'Connor.

8vo. pp. 38.   PHILADELPHIA : *John Campbell,* 1862.

2913. —— Letters to Charles O'Connor.   Dated at Montgomery, Alabama, August 24 to October 5, 1860,

8vo. pp. 38.   PHILADELPHIA : *John Campbell,* 1862.

2914. MADDEN, R. R.   A Letter to Wm. E. Channing, on the subject of the abuse of the Flag of the United States in Cuba, and the advantage taken of its Protection, in promoting the Slave Trade.

8vo. pp. 32.   BOSTON : *Wm. D. Ticknor,* 1839.

2915. MAGIE, Rev. DAVID, DD.   Public Thanksgiving.   A Sermon preached in Elizabeth, New York, November 28, 1861.

8vo. pp. 23.   NEW YORK : *Francis Hart & Co.,* 1861.

2916. —— A Sermon delivered in Elizabeth, New York, August 6, 1863. on occasion of the Public Thanksgiving to commemorate the Victories to the Federal Arms.

8vo. pp. 28.   NEW YORK : *Francis Hart & Co.,* 1863.

2917. MAHAN, Dr.   Speech.   [Before the Protestant Episcopal Convention.]   8vo. pp. 16.

2918. —— Second Speech.   8vo. pp. 16.

2919. MAHONY, D. A.   The Prisoner of State.

12mo. pp. 414.   NEW YORK : *Carlton,* 1863.

2920. —— The Four Acts of Despotism, comprising : 1, The Tax Bill, with all the Amendments. 2, The Finance Bill. 3, The Conscription Act. 4, The Indemnity Bill. With Introductions and Comments.

8vo. pp. 160.   NEW YORK : *Van Evrie, Horton & Co.,* 1863.

2921. MAINE, Defences of.   [A Letter from John A. Poor, Commis-

sioner of Maine, to the Secretary of War, January 31, 1862.]
Privately printed. pp. 26.

2922. MAINE. Address of Governor Washburn to the Legislature of the
State of Maine, January 3, 1861.
8vo. pp. 25. AUGUSTA: *Stevens & Seward,* 1851.

2923. —— Address of Governor Washburn, April 22, 1861. pp. 7.

2924. —— Annual Report of the Adjutant General, Dec. 1, '60. p. 32.

2925. —— Address of Governor Washburn, January 2, 1862.
8vo. pp. 30. AUGUSTA: *Stevens & Sayward,* 1862.

2926. —— Annual Report of the Adjutant Gen., for the year 1861.
8vo. pp. 633 and Appx. AUGUSTA: *Stevens & Sayward,* 1862.

2927. —— Annual Report of the Adjutant Gen., for the year 1862.
8vo. pp. 164 and Appx. AUGUSTA: *Stevens & Sayward,* 1863.

2928. —— Report of John A. Poor, Commissioner, in relation to the
Defence of Maine, December 12, 1862. pp. 50.

2929. —— Annual Report of the Adjutant Gen , for the year 1863.
8vo. pp. 947 and Appx. AUGUSTA: *Stevens & Sayward,* 1863.

2930. —— Report on the Gettysburg Soldiers' Cemetery. pp. 8.

2931. —— Address of Gov. Coney to the Legislature, Jan. 5, 1865.

2932. MALCOM, Rev. HOWARD. Signs of the Times favorable to
Peace. An Address before the American Peace So., May 26,'62.
8vo. pp. 14. BOSTON: *American Peace Society,* 1862.

2933. MANDEVILLE, G. HENRY. My Country. A Discourse delivered at Newburgh, N. Y., Nov. 28 and December 8, 1861.
8vo. pp. 22. NEWBURGH: *E. M. Ruttenber,* 1861.

2934. MANN, HORACE. Speech on the Right of Congress to Legis-
late for the Territories of the United States, and its Duty to
exclude Slavery therefrom. House of Reps., June 30, 1848.
8vo. pp. 31. BOSTON: *Wm. B. Fowle,* 1848.

2935. —— Speech on Slavery in the Territories, and the Consequence
of a Dissolution of the Union, in the House of Reps., Feb. 15,'50.
8vo. pp. 35. BOSTON: *Redding & Co.,* 1850.

2936. —— Speech on the Fugitive Slave Law, delivered at Lancaster,
Mass., May 19, 1851. 8vo. pp. 16.

2937. —— Slavery; Letters and Speeches.
12mo. pp. 564. BOSTON: *B. B. Mussey & Co.,* 1851.

2938. MANN, W. W. What are we coming to; or The Veil removed.
Peace,—Reconciliation,—Reconfederation. Feb., 1863. pp. 8.

2939. MANNING, Rev. J. M. Peace under Liberty. Oration before the City Authorities of Boston, on the 4th of July, 1865.
8vo. pp. 54. BOSTON: *J. E. Farwell & Co.*, 1865.

2940. MANSFIELD, E. D. The Issues and Duties of the Day. 1, The Republic on Trial. 2, Why it is on Trial. 3, The actual Condition of Affairs. 4, The Issues of the Day. 5, Our Duties to the Country.
8vo. pp. 15. CINCINNATI: *Caleb Clark,* 1864.

2941. —— The United States Military Academy at West Point.
8vo. pp. 48. *American Journal of Education, March,* 1863.

2942. MANSFIELD, Gen. JOSEPH K. F. Discourse on the Death of. By Rev. John L. Dudley, Middletown, Ct., Sept. 28, 1862.
8vo. pp. 31. MIDDLETOWN: *D. Barnes,* 1862.

2943. MARCH, DANIEL. Steadfastness and Preparation in the Day of Adversity. A Sermon preached in Philadelphia, Sep. 14, '62.
8vo. pp. 20. PHILADELPHIA: *C. Sherman & Son,* 1862.

2944. —— The Presidential Election. Sermon in Phil., Nov. 6, 1864.

2945. MARGINALIA; or Gleanings from an Army Note-Book. By Personne. Columbia, South Carolina, 1864. 8vo.

2946. MARINE CORPS. Letters from Naval Officers in relation to.
8vo. pp. 39. WASHINGTON: *D. C. Franck Taylor,* 1864.

2947. —— List of Officers of the Navy and Marine Corps, who, between December 1, 1860, and Dec. 1, 1863, left the service.
8vo. pp. 12. *Senate Ex. Doc., No,* 3, *38th Cong., 1st Ses.,* 1863.

2948. MARINE ENGINES. Report of Mr. A. H. Rice, from the Committee on Naval Affairs, in relation to the Plans and Structure of the Marine Engines for the Navy.
8vo. pp. 48. *38th Cong., 2d Sess., House Report No.* 8, 1865.

2949. MARSH, LEONARD. Review of a Letter from Bishop Hopkins, Vermont, on the Bible View of Slavery.
8vo. pp. 28. BURLINGTON: *Free Press,* 1861.

2950. —— On the Relations of Slavery to the War; and on the Treatment of it necessary to permanent Peace. A few Suggestions for thoughtful and Patriotic Men. 8vo. pp. 8.

2951. MARSHALL, JAMES. The Nation's Inquiry. A Discourse delivered in the Chesapeake General Hospital, Fort Monroe, Virginia, April 30, 1863.
8vo. pp. 34. PHILADELPHIA: *King & Baird,* 1863.

2952. MARSHALL, J. The Nation's Changes. A Discourse delivered in the Chesapeake General Hospital, November 26, 1863.
8vo. pp. 30. BALTIMORE : *John F. Wiley,* 1863.

2953. —— The Nation's Prospects of Peace. A Discourse at the Officers' General Hospital, September 11, 1864.
8vo. pp. 32. PHILADELPHIA : *King & Baird,* 1864.

2954. —— The Nation's Gratitude. A Discourse delivered at the United States General Hospital, November 24, 1864.
8vo. pp. 32. PHILADELPHIA : *King & Baird,* 1865.

2955. —— The Nation's Grief. Death of Abraham Lincoln. A Discourse delivered in Norfolk, Virginia, April 29, 1865.
8vo. pp. 40. SYRACUSE : (N. Y.) *Journal Office,* 1865.

2956. MARSHALL, E. C. Are the West Point Graduates Loyal?
18mo. pp. 8. NEW YORK : *D. Van Nostrand,* 1862.

2957. MARTIN, H. MARCE. La Revolution Américaine. From La *Revue Contemporaine, December* 15, 1862. Paris.

2958. MARTIN, Hon. JONAS, of Kentucky. Speech on the subject of Federal Relations, in House of Representatives of Kentucky, February 12, 1863. pp. 8.

2959. MARTIN, Rev. THOMAS M. The National Crisis. A Sermon preached in Philadelphia, on the 4th July, 1861. pp. 16.

2960. MARTINEAU, HARRIET. Views of Slavery and Emancipation, from "Society in America."
8vo. pp. 79. NEW YORK : *Piercy & Read,* 1837

2961. —— Manifest Destiny of the American Union. Reprinted from *Westminster Review,* 1857.

2962. —— The Brewing of the American Storm. From *Mac William's Magazine, June,* 1862.

2963. MARTYRS. To the Memory of the Martyrs; Abraham, Franklin, Peter Hueston, Wm. Jones, James Costello, and others, Slain in the Riots of July, in New York. Funeral Services, New York, September 20, 1863. pp. 8.

2964. MARYLAND. Message of Governor Hicks, in Extra Session, 1861. (With Correspondence with the Authorities at Wash'n.)
8vo. pp. 24. FREDERICK : *E. S. Riley,* 1861.

2965. —— Correspondence between the Governor of Maryland and the Sheriff of Frederick County. pp. 4.

34

2966. MARYLAND. Report of the Board of Police of Baltimore, in Extra Session, 1861. pp. 8 and 48.

2967. —— Copy of Proposed Amendment to the Constitution of the United States. April 30, 1861. pp. 4.

2968. —— Report of the Adjutant General, May 8, 1861, pp. 16.

2969. —— Report of the Committee on Federal Relations, in regard to the calling of a Sovereign Convention. May 9, 1861. pp. 22.

2970. —— Communication from the Mayor and Board of Police of Baltimore. (May 10, 1861.) pp. 8.

2971. —— Report of the Committee upon the Messages of the Governor, in regard to the Arbitrary Proceedings of the United States Authorities. 8vo. pp. 8.

2972. —— Report in regard to the $70,000 Appropriation. pp. 5.

2973. —— Petition of Richard B. Carmichael and others against the Adjournment of the Legislature, sine die. pp. 5.

2974. —— Report of the Police Commissioners of Baltimore; with accompanying Documents, August, 1861. pp. 37.

2975. —— Report and Resolutions to the General Assembly, upon the Reports of the Police Commissioners and the Mayor and Council of Baltimore. pp. 26. 1861.

2976. —— Address to the People of Maryland. by the General Assembly, in Extra Session. pp. 4.

2977 —— Report of the Commissioners appointed to wait on the President of the United States. pp. 4.

2978. —— Message of the Governor in relation to Disarming the State Militia, in Extra Session, 1862. pp. 4.

2979. —— Report of the Peace Commissioners appointed to wait on Presidents Lincoln and Davis, by the General Assembly, 1861.

2980. —— Report of the Committee on the Message of the Governor, giving his reasons for disarming the State Militia. pp. 7.

2981. —— Protest of the General Assembly against the Illegal Arrest and Imprisonment, by the Federal Government, of Citizens of Maryland. pp. 4.

2982. —— Message of Gov. Hicks, December, 1861. pp. 15.

2983. —— Journal of the Proceedings of the Senate of Maryland at a Special Session, December, 1861.
8vo, pp. 569.   ANNAPOLIS: *Schley & Cole*, 1861.

2984. MARYLAND. Inaugural Address of Gov. Bradford, Jan. 8, 1862. 8vo. p. 15.

2985. —— Journal of the Procedings of the House of Delegates, at a Special Session, December, 1861.

    8vo. pp. 117.   ANNAPOLIS: *Thomas J. Wilson*, 1861.

2986. —— Journal of the Proceedings of the House of Delegates of the January Session, 1862.

    8vo. pp. 992.   ANNAPOLIS: *Thomas J. Wilson*, 1862.

2987. —— Preamble and Resolutions in regard to the Objects of the Present War, passed by the General Assembly, Dec. 23, '61. p. 4.

2988. —— Correspondence between S. Teackle Wallis, Esq., and the Hon. John Sherman of the United States Senate, concerning the Arrest of the Members of the Maryland Legislature, and the Mayor and Police Commissioners of Baltimore, in '61. 8vo. p. 31.

2989. —— Message of Governor Bradford to the General Assembly of Maryland, with Documents, January Session, 1864.

    8vo. pp. 87.   ANNAPOLIS: *Bull & Tuttle*, 1864.

Documents accompanying the Governors's Message:

Report of Sebastian F. Streeter, Military Relief Agent.

Col. John S. Berry's Report of Gettysburg Cemetery Proceedings.

Resolutions of State of Kansas in Response to the Resolutions of Maryland Legislature. February 14, 1863.

Governor of Massachusetts enclosing Report of Distribution of $7,000, appropriated by the Maryland Legislature, for the Relief of Sufferers in the Riot of the 19th of April, 1861, in Baltimore. March 16, 1863.

Resolutions from the State of Delaware on Federal Relations.

Resolutions of Kentucky Legislature transmitted for the purpose of being laid before the General Assembly of Maryland. March 11, 1863.

Letter to the President, [from Gov. Bradford,] on the subject of Slave Enlistments. Dated, Annapolis, September 28, 1863.

Governor's Proclamation on the subject of the late election, embodying a copy of Gen. Schenck's Order, No. 53. (November 2, 1863.)

Letter from Major General Dix, to the Judges of Election in Carroll County. Dated, Baltimore, November 1, 1861.

Opinion of the Hon. Reverdy Johnson, about proclaiming the Members of Congress. Washington, 23d November, 1863.

Various Statements, Memorials and Reports from Citizens and Officers, relative to the Election in Maryland in November, 1864.

Report of the Commissioners appointed to disburse the $50,000 appropriated for the Relief of Families of Maryland Volunteers.

Minority Report of the Senate Committee in regard to compensating Loyal Citizens of Maryland for property taken or destroyed by the armies of the United States, or the so-called Confederate States.

Report of the Committee on Elections of the State of Maryland, January Session, 1864.

2990. MARYLAND. Message of the Governor of, January Sess., 1864. pp. 38.

2991. —— Journal of the Proceedings of the Senate of Maryland, January Session, 1864.

8vo. pp. 564. ANNAPOLIS : *Mittag & Sneary,* 1864.

2992. —— Journal of the Proceedings of the House of Delegates, January Session, 1864.

8vo. pp, 1144. ANNAPOLIS : *Bull & Tuttle,* 1864.

2993. —— Documents accompanying the Governor's Message to the Legislature of Maryland, January, 1864.

Report on Contested Elections in Somerset County, together with the Testimony. pp. 104. Annapolis: *Bull & Tuttle,* 1864.

Minority Report on the Contested Elections in Somerset County, January Session, 1864.

2994. —— Message of Gov. Bradford, Jan. Session, 1865. pp. 32.

2995. —— Inaugural Address of the Hon. Thomas Swann, Governor Elect of Maryland, January 11, 1865. 8vo. pp. 15.

2996. —— Communication from Major General Lew. Wallace, in relation to the Freedmen's Bureau, to the General Assembly.

8vo. pp. 95. ANNAPOLIS : *Richard P. Bayly,* 1865.

2997. —— The Debates of the Constitutional Convention, assembled at Annapolis, April 27, 1864.

3 vols. 8vo. ANNAPOLIS : *Richard P. Bayly,* 1864.

2998. —— Proceedings of the State Convention of Maryland to frame a Constitution. Commenced at Annapolis, April 27, 1864.

8vo. pp. 856. ANNAPOLIS : *Richard P. Bayly,* 1864.

2999. —— Evidence in the Contested Election, in the case of Ridgely vs. Grason, to the General Assembly.

8vo. pp. 285. ANNAPOLIS : *Richard P. Bayly,* 1865.

3000. —— Report of the Committee on the Contested Election Case of Ridgely vs. Grason. 8vo. pp. 7.

3001. —— Minority Report in the same case. pp. 3.

Much interesting matter connected with the position and movements of parties at the outbreak of the Rebellion, as well as of the military movements in Maryland, are brought out in the testimony before this Committee. The documents referred to, accompany the Message of the Governor of Maryland, January Session, 1865.

3002. —— Report of the Committee on Elections, in the case of Hart B. Holton vs. Littleton Maclin, with accompanying Evidence. pp. 31.

3003. MARYLAND. Protest of Hart B. Holton against the taking of further Testimony in the case of Holton vs. Maclin. pp. 7.

3004. —— Minority Report of the Committee, in the case of the Contested Seat of Holton vs. Maclin. pp. 8.

> Like the previous case of Ridgely vs. Grason, the seat of the member elect, Mr. Maclin, was contested on the ground that he was ineligible according to the Constitution of Maryland, in having given aid and comfort to the enemy in the Rebellion.

3005. —— Memorial of Citizens of Somerset County, contesting the Seat of Levin L. Waters to the General Assembly of Maryland. 8vo. pp. 4. ANNAPOLIS : *R. P. Bayly*, 1865.

> The defendant is charged with "giving comfort, countenance and support to those engaged in armed hostility to the United States." That he permitted a rebel flag to be raised near the door of his printing office; that he publicly rejoiced at the defeat of the armies of the United States, at the Battles of Bull Run and Ball's Bluff, etc., etc.

3006. —— Colonization of the Free Colored Population of Maryland, and of such Slaves as may hereafter become free. Statement of Facts.
12mo. pp. 16. BALTIMORE: *J. Robinson*, 1832.

3007. —— The Free Negro Question in.
8vo. pp. 28. BALTIMORE : *J. W. Woods*, 1859.

3008. —— The Position of. Letter of William Price of Baltimore.
8vo. *J. Murphy & Co.*, (No date.)

3009. —— Addresses of William H. Collins to the People of Maryl'd.
8vo. pp. 17, 17 and 24. BALTIMORE : *James Young*, 1860–61.

3010. —— Proceedings and Speeches at a Public Meeting of the Friends of the Union, in the City of Baltimore, Jan. 10, 1861.
8vo. pp. 56. BALTIMORE: *John D. Toy*, 1861.

3011. —— Address of the Union State Central Committee of Maryland. (Written by Brantz Mayer.)
8vo. pp. 8. BALTIMORE : *J. W. Woods*, 1861.

3012. —— The Emancipation Problem in Maryl'd. By B. Mayer. p. 4.

3013. —— Secret Correspondence illustrating the condition of affairs in Maryland.
8vo. pp. 42. BALTIMORE : 1862.

> One of the rarest publications of the rebels. It was privately printed and circulated in Baltimore.

3014. —— Address of the Unconditional Union State General Committee, to the People of Maryland, September 16, 1863.
8vo. pp. 20. BALTIMORE : *Sherwood & Co.*, 1863.

3015. MARYLAND. Address of the Union State Central Committee ; with the Proceedings at Temperance Temple, Aug, 26, 1863. pp. 16.

3016. —— Immediate Emancipation in Maryland. Proceedings of the Union State Central Committee, at a Meeting held in Temperance Temple, Baltimore, December 16, 1863. pp. 20.

3017. —— Maffitt against Goldsborough. The Record compared by the Unconditional Union State Central Committee, Oct. 7, 1863. 8vo. pp. 13. BALTIMORE : *Sherwood & Co.*, 1863.

3018. —— Emancipation in Maryland. Commemoration of, in Philadelphia, November 1, 1864. Folio, pp. 4.

3019. —— No compensation for Slaves in, 1864. pp. 4.

3020. —— The Union State Executive Committee versus the Union City Convention. 8vo. pp. 4. 1864.

3021. —— The Great Drama. An Appeal to Maryland, by John P. Kennedy. pp. 16.

3022. MASON AND SLIDELL, Correspondence relative to the case of. (Between Mr. Seward, Mr. Adams, Lord Lyons and Mr. Thouvenel.) 8vo. pp. 15.

3022.* —— A Legal View of the seizure of. 1861. pp. 27.

3023. MASON, Rev. CHARLES, DD. A Discourse delivered on the National Fast Day, January 4, 1861, in Boston.
8vo. pp. 18. BOSTON : *David Clapp*, 1861.

3024. MASON, RICHARD R. Slavery in America. An Essay for the Times.
8vo. pp. 34. BOSTON : *Crocker & Brewster*, 1853.

3025. MASSACHUSETTS. Address of Gov. Andrew to the two branches of the Legislature, January 5, 1861.
8vo. pp. 46. BOSTON : *William White*, 1861.

3026. —— Address of Governor Andrew to the two branches of the Legislature. Extra Session, May 14, 1861.
8vo. pp. 24. BOSTON : *William White*, 1861.

3027. —— Report of the Quartermaster General Feb. 1, 1862. p. 10.

3028. —— Proceedings in the Legislature upon the Act of the State of Maryland appropriating $7,000 for the families of those belonging to the Sixth Regiment of Mass. Volunteers, who were killed or disabled by wounds, in the Riot at Baltimore, April 19, 1861.
8vo. pp. 15. BOSTON : *Wright & Potter*, 1862.

3029. MASSACHUSETTS. Correspondence of Gov. Andrew and others relative to the recruiting of Troops for the Department of New England, 1862. 8vo. pp. 86.

3030. —— Address of Gov. Andrew to the two branches of the Legislature, January 3, 1862.
8vo. pp. 75. BOSTON: *William White,* 1862.

3031. —— Correspondence relating to the Recruiting of Troops for the Department of New England. 1862. pp. 86.

3032. —— Annual Report of the Adjutant General, Quartermaster General, Surgeon General and Master of Ordnance, for 1862.
8vo. pp. 470, 10, 28 and 19. BOSTON: *Wright & Potter,* 1863.

3033. —— Letter from Gov. Andrew to S. F. Wetmore of Indiana, in answer to the Question raised by the popular branch of the Legislature of that State, "Why Massachusetts has not sent to the field during the Present War, as many Men as have been sent by Indiana." Dated, Boston, February 3, 1863. pp. 8.

3034. —— Address of Gov. Andrew to the Legislature, January 9, 1863. pp. 80.

3035. —— Address of Gov. Andrew to Legislature, November 11, 1863. p. 24.

3036. —— Annual Reports of the Adjutant General, with Reports from the Quartermaster General, Surgeon General and Master of Ordnance, for the year 1863.
8vo. pp. 1022, 8, 22 and 20. BOSTON: *Wright & Potter,* 1864.

3037. —— Address of Gov. Andrew to the two branches of the Legislature, January 8, 1864.
8vo. pp. 88. BOSTON: *Wright & Potter,* 1864.

3038. —— Address of His Excellency, John A. Andrew, to the two branches of the Legislature of Massachusetts, January 6, 1865.
8vo. pp. 140. BOSTON: *Wright & Potter,* 1865.

3039. —— Annual Report of Adjutant General, Quartermaster General, Surgeon General, and Master of Ordnance, for the year ending December 31, 1864.
8vo. pp. 1099, 80. BOSTON: *Wright & Potter,* 1865.

3040. MASSIE, Rev. JAMES W. The Case Stated. The Friends and Enemies of the American Slave.
8vo. pp. 8. MANCHESTER, 1863.

3041. MASSIE, J. W. International Sympathies. Report of the Farewell Meeting for Dr. Massie, of London. New York, Sept. 27, '63. 8vo. pp. 31. NEW YORK : *Anson D. F. Randolph,* 1863.

3042. —— America, the Origin of the Present Conflict ; her Prospect for the Slave and her Claim for Anti-Slavery Sympathy. Illustrated by Incidents of Travel through the United Sates in 1863. 8vo. pp. viii, 477. LONDON : *John Snow,* 1865.

3043. MATLOCK, Rev. ROBERT. The Loyalty of the Episcopal Church vindicated. An Address, November 5, 1865 ; with Resolutions adopted by the Vestry of the Church. 8vo. pp. 34. PHILADELPHIA : *L. G. Leisenring,* 1865.

3044. MATTHEWS, Rev. JAMES. Religious Instruction in the Army. *Princeton Review, July,* 1863.

3045. MAUND, G. C. Responsibilities of the American Citizen. An Address before the Alumni of Pennsylvania College, Aug. 10,'64. 8vo. pp. 23. GETTYSBURG : *H. C. Neinstadt,* 1864.

3046. —— The same. *Evangelical Quarterly Review, Vol.* XV.

3046.* MAURER, U. Betrachtungen über die amerikanische Frage und ihre wahrscheinliche Lösung. 8vo. pp. 16. DARMSTADT : *Gustav G. Lange,* 1862.

3047. MAURY, Capt. M. F. Letter on American Affairs, addressed to Rear-Admiral Fitz Roy, of England. Richmond, August, 1861. 8vo. pp. 10.

3048. —— Letter on American Affairs. J. C. Breckenridge's Address to the People of Kentucky. Ex-Governor Lowe's Letter to the Virginia Legislature. Address of George N. Saunders to the Democracy of the Northwest. Gov. Letcher's Message to the Virginia Legislature. Message of Jefferson Davis to the Confederate Congress, November 18, 1861. pp. 36.

3049. MAY, GEORGE T. Suggestions towards a Navy. 8vo. pp. 16. NEW YORK : *Beadle & Company,* 1862.

3050. MAY, CHARLES S. Sustain the Government. Speech in the Senate of the State of Michigan, February 9, 1863. 8vo. pp. 22. LANSING : *John A. Kerr & Co.,* 1863.

3051. —— Union, Victory and Freedom. Speech delivered in the Hall of Representatives, Lansing, January 25, 1864. pp. 22.

3052. MAYER, BRANTZ. Address of the Union Central Committee of Maryland. Baltimore, 1861. pp. 8.

3053. MAYER, B.   The Emancipation Problem in Maryland.   pp. 4. 1862.

3054. MAYHAM, S. L.   Speech on the Condition of the Country, in Assembly, New York, March 2, 1863.   pp. 12.

3055. MAYNADIER, Lieut. Colonel WM., U. S. Army.   Reply to the Charges in the Report of the Potter Committee, Washington.

3056. MAYNARD, Hon. HORACE.   An Oration before the Order of United Americans, at New York, February 22, 1861.
8vo. pp. 32.   NEW YORK: *C. E. Gildersleve*, 1861.

3057. —— How, by Whom and for What was the War begun? Speech in Nashville, March 20, 1862.   pp. 24.

3058. —— Speech on the Claim of Joseph Segar to a Seat in the House.   House of Representatives, Feb. 11, 1862.   8vo. pp. 8.

3059. —— Speech on the Negro Enlistment Bill, in the House of Representatives, January 31, 1862.   8vo. pp. 12.

3060. —— The Punishment of Treason.   Speech delivered in the House of Representatives, March 23, 1862.   8vo. pp. 12.

3061. —— An Address to the Slaveholders of Tennessee, delivered in Nashville, on the 4th of July, 1863.   8vo. pp. 23.

3062. MAYO, A. D.   The Personal Liberty Bill.   An Address to the Legislature and People of New York.
12mo. pp. 17.   ALBANY: *Weed, Parsons & Co.*, 1859.

3063. —— East and West.   8vo. pp. 33.

3064. —— American Dangers and Duties.   Tracts for the Times.
12mo. pp. 19.   ALBANY: *Weed, Parsons & Co.*, 1861.

3065. —— Herod, John and Jesus; or American Slavery, and its Christian Cure.   A Sermon delivered at Albany.
8vo. pp. 29.   ALBANY: *Weed, Parsons & Co.*, 1860.

3065.* —— The Scholar's Vocation in the New Republic.   Address before the Union Literary Soc., of Antioch College, June 30, '63.
8vo. pp. 28.   CINCINNATI: *Robert Clark & Co.*, 1863.

3066. —— The Progress of Liberty in the United States.   *Continental Monthly, November*, 1864.

3067. —— The Nation's Sacrifice.   Abraham Lincoln.   Two Discourses, delivered April 16 and April 19, 1865, in Cincinnati, O.
8vo. pp. 28.   CINCINNATI: *Robert Clarke & Co.*, 1865.

3068. —— The Republic of Peace.   A Discourse delivered on the

35

occasion of the National Fast, June 1, 1865, at Cincinnati. New York, *Christian Enquirer, June* 17, 1865.

3069. McARONE. The Life and Adventures of Jeff. Davis. 12mo. pp. 31.   NEW YORK : *J. C. Haney & Co.*, 1865.

3070. M'BRIDE, of Oregon. Navy Appropriation Bill. Speech in House of Representatives, Feb. 19, 1864. 8vo. pp. 16.

3071. McCABE, J. D. The Aid-de-Camp. A Romance of the War. Richmond, 1863.

3072. McCALL, General. The Seven Days' Contests. Pennsylvania Reserves on the Peninsula. Official Reports of the part taken by his Division in the Battles of Mechanicsville, Gaines's Mills and the New Market Cross-Roads ; with the Statements of Gens. Meade and Porter, and Col. Stone and others. pp. 10.

3073. —— The same, in *Rebellion Record.* New York, 1864.

3074. —— Sequel to Report of the Pennsylvania Reserves. pp. 4.

3075. McCALL, Rev S. Who is responsible for Public Calamities? A Sermon preached in Old Saybrook, Conn., April 28, 1861. 8vo. pp. 20.   NEW YORK : *Hall, Clayton & Co.*, 1861.

3076. McCARTY GUN. Report of the Committee appointed to investigate the capacities and advantages of. 8vo. pp. 10.   NEW YORK : *S. S. Motley*, 1862.

3077. M'CARTY, Rev. J. H. The American Union. A Discourse delivered in Concord, N. H., May 11, 1862. 8vo. pp. 29.   CONCORD : (N. H.) *Fogg, Hadley & Co.*, 1862.

3078. McCAULEY, Rev. JAMES A. Character and Services of Abraham Lincoln. A Sermon preached in Baltimore, June 1, 1865. 8vo. pp. 16.   BALTIMORE : *John D. Toy*, 1865.

3079. McCLELLAN, Maj. General GEORGE B., from August 1, 1861, to August 1, 1862. By a Military Man who never saw General McClellan. 8vo. pp. 26.   NEW YORK : *H. Dexter*, 1862.

3080. McCLELLAN'S CAMPAIGN. Reprinted from the World of August 7, 1862. " There is Justice in History." 8vo. pp. 12.   NEW YORK : *Anson D. F. Randolph*, 1862.

3081. McCLELLAN. Letter from the Secretary of War, on the subject of the occupation of the " White House " in Va., July 8, '62. 8vo. pp. 7.   *Ho. of Reps. Ex. Doc.*, 145, 37*th Cong, 2d Ses.*, '62.

3082. McCLELLAN AND FREMONT. A Reply to "Fremont and McClellan, their Political and Military Careers reviewed. By Antietam.

8vo. pp. 16. NEW YORK: *Sinclair Toucey*, 1862.

3083. McCLELLAN, GEORGE B. Report concerning the Organization and Operation of the Army of the Potomac, while under his command, and of all Army Operations while he was Commander-in-Chief.

8vo. pp. 242. *H. of Rep. Ex. Doc., No.* 15, *38th Con., 1st Ses.*,'63.

3084. —— Army of the Potomac. Report, August 4, 1863. With an account of the Campaign in Western Virginia. (250 copies printed.)

Royal 8vo. pp. 484. NEW YORK: *Sheldon & Co.*, 1864.

3085. —— West Point Battle Monument. History of the Project to the Dedication of the Site, June 15, 1864. Oration of General McClellan.

12mo. pp. 37. NEW YORK: *Sheldon & Co.*, 1864.

3086. —— How McClellan took Manassas. A Poem.

4to. pp. 6. Privately printed. NEW YORK: 1864.

3087. —— Mai-Jour (Translated May-Day) General George Barnum McClellan, Militant-Homeopath to the Army of the Confederates. Attacked after his own Mode through Parallels.

16mo. pp. 32. NEW YORK: *American News Co.*, 1864.

3088. —— A Brief Sketch of the Life and History of, with Incidents in his Career. New York, 1864. pp. 10.

3089. —— Letter of Acceptance, together with his West Point Oration.

8vo. pp. 8. NEW YORK: *E. P. Patten*, 1864.

3090. —— Oration at West Point.

8vo. pp. 30. NEW YORK: *C. S. Westcutt & Co.*, 1862.

3091. —— The Life of, by Alexander Delmar.

12mo. pp. 109. NEW YORK: *T. R. Dawley*, 1864.

3092. —— Only authentic Life of George Brinton McClellan, alias, Little Mac. With an account of his numerous Victories, from Phillipi to Antietam. *American News Co.* 12mo. pp. 16.

3093. McCLELLAN CAMPAIGN MELODIST. A Collection of Patriotic Songs. By Sidney Herbert.

16mo. pp. 32. NEW YORK: *American News Co.*, 1864.

3094. McCLELLAN Democratic Presidential Campaign Songster. No. 1, McClellan and Pendleton.
16mo. pp. 72.   NEW YORK: *J. F. Feeks*, 1864.

3095. —— Little Mac Campaign Songster.
16mo. pp. 72.   NEW YORK: *T. R. Dawley*, 1864.

3096. "McCLELLAN; Who is he, and What has he done;" and Little Mac, "From Ball's Bluff to Antietam." Both in one. Revised by the Author. By an Old-Line Democrat.
12mo. pp. 14.   NEW YORK: *American News Co.*, 1864.

3097. —— "Leave Pope to get out of his Scrape." McClellan's Despatches. 8vo. pp. 8.

3098. McCLELLAN's RECORD. His Sympathy with the South. Read for yourselves. Cincinnati, 1864. pp. 12.

3099. McCLELLAN. Ben Wade on McClellan; and Gens. Hooker and Heintzelman's Testimony. A Crushing Review of Little Napoleon's Military Career. From the Cincinnati Gazette. p. 8.

3100. McCLELLAND, Hon. ROBERT. Letter on the Crisis.
8vo. pp. 11.   DETROIT: *December* 31, 1860.

3101. McCLUNE, J. H. Camp Life. The Sayings and Doings of Volunteers.
8vo. pp. 36.   BALTIMORE: *J. D. Toy*, 1862.

3102. McCLURG, JOSEPH W. Missouri Home Guards. Speech in House of Representatives, December 22, 1863. 8vo. pp. 8.

3103. —— Speech in Reply to the Personalities of his Colleagues, Blair and King. House of Representatives, March 9, 1864. pp. 16.

3104. —— Speech in House of Representatives, March 23, 1864, to refute the Charges of Forgery alleged by Mr. Blair against B. R. Bonner, Treasury Agent at St. Louis. pp. 8.

3105. —— Speech on motion to print the Evidence and Report of the Investigating Committee, in the case of the alleged Charge against Hon. F. P. Blair, April 29, 1864. pp. 16.

3106. McCOOK, Col. DANIEL. The Second Division at Shiloh. *Harpers's Magazine, May,* 1864.

3107. McCORMICK, RICHARD C. The Patriotism of the Plough. An Address before the Queens County Agricultural Society, at Flushing, Long Island, October 3, 1861.
8vo. pp. 31.   HEMPSTEAD: *For the Society,* 1861.

3108. McCORMICK, R. C. The Duty of the Hour. An Oration delivered at Jamaica, Long Island, July 4, 1863.
8vo. pp. 36. NEW YORK: *George A. Whitehorme*, 1864.

3109. McCOSKRY, Rev. SAMUEL A. The Duties of the Church in Times of Trial; and the Ground of her Confidence. The Sermon preached before the General Convention of the Protestant Episcopal Church in New York, October 1, 1862.
8vo. pp. 19. NEW YORK: *Baker & Godwin*, 1862.

3110. —— Trust in God, the Strength of a Nation. A Sermon preached in Detroit, January 4, 1861.
8vo. pp. 16. DETROIT: *"Free Press,"* 1861.

3111. McCLINTOCK, JOHN, DD. Discourse delivered on the day of the Funeral of President Lincoln, April 19, 1865, in New York.
8vo. pp. 35. NEW YORK: *J. M. Bradstreet & Son*, 1865.

3112. McCULLOCH, Mr. HUGH, and the Secretaryship of the Treasury.
8vo. pp. 8. WASHINGTON: *March* 1, 1865.

3113. —— Our National and Financial Future. Address at Fort Wayne, Indiana, October 11, 1865. pp. 16.

3114. McDONOUGH, JOHN, of New Orleans. Self-Emancipation. A Successful Experiment on a large Estate in Louisiana. Completed in 1840. 8vo. pp. 24.

3115. McDOUGALL, J. A. Speech on the Arrest of Gen. Stone, and the Rights of the Soldier and Citizen. Senate, April 22, 1862. pp. 32.

3116. —— Speech on the Expulsion of Mr. Bright, in the Senate, January 31, 1862. pp. 7.

3117. —— Speech on the Confiscation of Property, delivered in the Senate of the United States, March 12, 1862. pp. 29.

3118. —— French Interference in Mexico. Speech in the Senate of the United States, February 3d, 1864. pp. 30.

3119. McDOWELL, IRWIN, Major General. Statement of, in Review of the Evidence before the Court of Inquiry, instituted at his request in Special Order 353.
8vo. pp. 64. WASHINGTON: *L. Towers & Co.*, 1863.

3120. THE McELROY PRIZE COMPOSITIONS. Our Country; by Mary H. Cutter and Mary T. Reed. Woodbridge, July 4, 1863.
8vo. pp. 16. NEW YORK: *W. C. Bryant & Co.*, 1863.

3121. McFALLS, Rev. T. B.   We still Live as a Nation.   A Thanksgiving Sermon, delivered November 28, 1862.   Wash'n.   pp. 8.

3122. McFARLANE, Isabella.   The North Carolina Conscript. *Continental Monthly, October,* 1864.

3123. M'FARREN, Rev. Samuel, DD.   Modern Slavery destitute of a Divine Warrant.   A Sermon preached at Unity, April 14, '63. 8vo. pp. 16.   Pittsburg: *W. S. Haven,* 1863.

3124. McGIFFERT, Rev. J. N.   Our Duty to our Country in the Present Crisis.   A Discourse delivered in Sanquoit, May 5, '61. 8vo. pp. 20.   Utica: (N. Y.) *DeWitt C. Grove,* 1862.

3125. —— A Sermon delivered in Manlius, N. York, Sept. 29, 1861. Syracuse : *D. J. Halsted,* 1861.

3126. —— A Discourse delivered at Clayville, June 4, 1863, at the Funeral of Corp. Robert Pettee, of the 5th Reg. N. Y. Vols. p. 8.

3127. McGILL, Rev. Alexander J.   Sinful, but not Forsaken.   A Sermon preached in New York, January 4, 1861. 8vo. pp. 22.   New York: *John F. Trow,* 1861.

3128. —— American Slavery, as Viewed and Acted on by the Presbyterian Church, in the United States. 8vo. pp. 72.   Philadelphia: *Presbyterian Board of Ed.,* 1865.

3129. —— The Hand of God with the Black Race.   A Discourse before the Pennsylvania Colonization Society. 8vo. pp. 19.   Philadelphia: *Wm. F. Geddes,* 1862.

3130. McGINLEY, Rev. Wm. A.   Rational Triumph; or the Danger of Victory.   A Discourse delivered in Shrewsbury, Mass., upon the occasion of the Federal Triumphs over the Victories of February, 1862. 8vo. pp. 25.   Worcester: *Edward R. Fiske,* 1862.

3131. McGREGOR, John P.   Some Considerations upon the Financial Policy of the Government. 8vo. pp. 16.   Milwaukie: *Starr & Son,* 1862.

3132. McHENRY, George.   Cotton Trade; its Bearing upon the Prosperity of Great Britain, and Commerce of the American Republics, considered in connection with the System of Negro Labor in the Confederate States. 8vo. pp. lxix, 292.   London: *Saunders & Otley,* 1863.

3133. —— Statement of Facts on the Cotton Crisis.   8vo.   Richmond. 1864.

3134. McILVAINE, Rev. J. H.   American Nationality.   *Princeton Review, October,* 1861.

3135. McILVAINE, Charles P., DD.   Pastoral Letter of the Bishops of the Protestant Episcopal Church of the United States, to the Clergy and Laity.   Delivered before the General Convention, New York, October 17, 1862.
8vo. pp. 14.   New York: *Baker & Godwin,* 1862.

3136. McJILTON, Rev. J. N.   God's Controversy with the People of the United States.   A Sermon delivered in Balt., Sept. 26, '61
12mo. pp. 32.   Baltimore: *Joseph Robinson,* 1861.

3137. —— A Nation making light of Religion in the Time of its Calamities.   A Sermon preached November 27, 1862.
12mo. pp. 24.   Baltimore: *J. W. Bond & Co.,* 1862.

3138. —— Our National Degeneracy the Cause of our National Troubles.   A Sermon preached in Baltimore, November 28, 1861.
12mo. pp. 27.   Baltimore: *J. W. Bond & Co.,* 1861.

3139. —— The Prayer of the Republic in the Visitation of Calamity upon its Sins.   A Sermon, April 30, 1863.
12mo. pp. 21.   Baltimore: *J. W. Bond & Co.,* 1863.

3140. McKAGE, James.   The Birth and Death of Nations.   A Thought for the Crisis.
8vo. pp. 10.   New York: *G. P. Putnam,* 1862.

3141. —— The Mastership and its Fruits; the Emancipated Slave Face to Face with his Old Master.   A Supplementary Report of the Hon. E. M. Stanton, Secretary of War.
8vo. pp. 38.   *Loyal Publication Society, No.* 57, 1864.

3142. —— The same in German
8vo. pp. 31.   *Loyal Publication Society, No.* 55, 1864.

3143. McKEON, Hon. John.   The Administration Reviewed. Speech before the Democratic Union Asso., N. York, Oct. 29, 1862.
8vo. pp. 15.   New York: *Van Evrie, Horton & Co.,* 1862.

3144. McKEON, Rev. Silas.   Heroic Patriotism.   A Sermon delivered at Bradford, Vt., April 28, 1861, in the presence of the Bradford Guards.
8vo. pp. 16.   Windsor: (Vermont) *Chronicle Office,* 1860.

3145. M'KIM, J. Miller.   The Freedmen of South Carolina.   An Address delivered July 9, 1862,
8vo. pp. 32.   Philadelphia: *Willis P. Hazard,* 1862.

3146. McKINSTRY, Brig. General J., Vindication of. 8vo. pp. 102.

3147. McLEON, ALEXANDER, Jr. The Clemency of the Divine Government, a Cause for Thanksgiving. A Sermon preached in Fairfield, Connecticut.
8vo. pp. 16.   NEW YORK: *George W. Wood,* 1861.

3148. McLEOD, Rev. ALEXANDER. Negro Slavery Unjustifiable. A Discourse, 1862. 11th edition, with an Appendix.
8vo. pp. 48.   NEW YORK : *Alexander McLeod,* 1863.

3149. McLEOD, Prof. DANIEL. The Rebellion in Tennessee. Observations on Bishop Otey's Letter to the Hon. William H. Seward.
8vo. pp. 11.   WASHINGTON : *McGill, Witherow & Co.,* 1862.

3150. McMAHON, T. W. Cause and Contrast; an Essay on the American Crisis.
8vo. pp.   RICHMOND : *West & Johnston,* 1862.

3151. McMILLAN's MAGAZINE. The Border States. June, 1862.
The Brewing of the American Storm. Harriet Martineau. June, 1862.
An American Protectionist. Stephen Leslie. December, 1862.

3152. McPHEETERS, Rev. S. B. The Complete Correspondence between Union Members of Pine St. Presbyterian Church, and their Pastor, on the subject of Slavery. St. Louis, June, 1862. pp. 18.

3153. McPHERSON, Hon. EDWARD. Disorganization and Disunion. Speech in the House of Reps., February 24, 1860. pp. 8.

3154. —— The Disunion Conspiracy. Two Speeches in the House of Representatives, January 23, and February 14, 1862.
8vo. pp. 16.   WASHINGTON ; *Scammell & Co.,* 1861.

3155. —— The Rebellion. Our Relations and Duties. Speech in House of Representatives, February 14, 1861. 8vo. pp. 7.

3156. —— The Administration and its Assailants. June 5, 1862.

3157. —— Remarks on a Bill to Reörganize the Staff attached to Divisions of the Army of the U. S., March 6, 1862. pp. 7.

3158. —— The Political History of the United States of America, during the Great Rebellion. November 6, 1860, to July 4, '64.
8vo. pp. viii and 440.   WASHINGTON : *Philip & Solomons,* '64.

3159. —— Political History of the United States of America during the Great Rebellion ; Including a classified Summary of the Legislation of the Second Session of the Thirty-Sixth Congress, the Three Sessions of the Thirty-Seventh Congress, the First Session of the Thirty-Eighth Congress ; with the Votes thereon, and the important Executive, Judicial and Politico-Military Facts of that eventful Period ; together with the Organization, Legislation and General Proceedings of the Rebel Administration ; and an Appendix containing the principal political Facts of the Campaign of 1864 ; a Chapter on the Church and the Rebellion, etc Second edition.

8vo. pp. 653. WASHINGTON : *Philip & Solomons*, 1865.

Mr. McPherson is Clerk of the House of Representatives, Washington.

3160. McSHEA, Hon. JOHN, Jr.   The War, its Causes and the Remedy.   Speech in the House of Assembly, New York, April 11, 1863.   pp. 16.

3161. MEAD.   The Soldier's Sacrifice.   (A Biographical Sketch of Henry H. Mead, 10th Connecticut Volunteers.)   pp. 4.

3162. MEAGHER, Brig. Gen. THOMAS F.   Letters on our National Struggle, addressed to the Dublin "Irishman" and "Citizen."
8vo. pp. 15. *Loyal Publication Society, No.* 38, 1863.

3163. —— The last Days of the 69th in Virginia.   A Narrative in Three Parts, with a Portrait.
8vo. pp. 15. NEW YORK : *Office of "Irish American."*

3164. MEANS, Rev. J. O.   Soldiers and their Mothers.
18mo. pp. 32. *American Tract Society.*

3165. MEDALS.   Names of petty Officers and Seamen in the United States Naval Service to whom Medals have been awarded, who have distinguised themselves by their gallantry in action, or by extraordinary heroism.   Navy Department, December 31, 1864.   General Order No. 45.   12mo. pp. 18.

3166. THE MEDIATOR between North and South ; or the Seven Pointers of the North Star.   Thoughts of an American in the Wilderness.
8vo. pp. 11. BALTIMORE : *C. H. Anderson*, 1863.

3167. MEDICAL STAFF of the Army, A Plea for.   8vo. pp. 16.

3168. MEIER, ADOLPHUS.   United States Treasury Notes to be the Circulation of the Country, in lieu of Bank Notes.
8vo. pp. 8. ST. LOUIS : *R. P. Studley & Co.*, 1861.

36

3169. MELLEN, W. P.   Report relative to leasing abandoned plantations and affairs of the Freed People in First Special Agency.
8vo. pp. 19.   WASHINGTON : *McGill & Witherow,* 1864.

3170. MEMORIAL reported to have been laid before the "General
Council" of the Bishops, Clergy and Laity of the Protestant
Episcopal Church in the Confederate States of America, held in
St. Paul's Church, Augusta, Georgia, November 22, 1862. pp. 8.
An amusing squib.

3171. MEN OF THE TIME ; Being Biographies of Generals Butler,
Banks, Burnside, Baker, Stevens, Wilcox, Weber.
12mo. pp. 100.   NEW YORK : *Beadle & Company,* 1862.

3172. —— Being Biographies of Generals Halleck, Pope, Siegel, Corcoran, Prentiss, Kearny, Hatch, Augur.
12mo. pp. 100.   NEW YORK : *Beadle & Co.,* 1862.

3173. MENZIES, JOHN W.   Speech on the Military Academy Bill.
House of Representatives, January 27, 1862. 8vo. pp. 8.

3174. MERCER, Rev. ALEXANDER G., DD.   American Citizenship.
Its Fault and their Remedies.   A Sermon preached Jan 4, 1861.
8vo. pp. 41.   BOSTON : *Little, Brown & Co.,* 1861.

3175. THE MERCHANTS' MAGAZINE for 1861.
Cotton and Cotton Manufacture.   July, 1861.
The Southern Harbors of the United States.   July, 1861.
The Cotton Question.   October, 1861.
The Manchester Cotton Supply Association.   November, 1861.
Cotton and its Culture.   December, 1861.

3176. THE MERCHANTS' MAGAZINE for 1862.
International Law vs. The Trent and San Jacinto.   January, 1862.
The Cotton Question.   January, April and June, 1862.
A National Currency and Banking System.   February, 1862.
Harbor Defences on Great Lakes and Rivers.   April, 1862.
Laws relating to the Excise Tax.   September, 1862.
Federal Finances examined and considered in reference to the present Issues
of Paper Money.   December, 1862.
The Advanced Value of Gold.   December, 1862.

3177. THE MERCHANTS' MAGAZINE for 1863.
The Past and Future of the West.   The Effect of this War on the Mississippi.
The West as the Center of Manufactures.   April, 1863.
Paper Money.   The Lessons of History.   July, 1863.
Legal Tender United States Notes.   Decisions of the First and Seventh Dis-
tricts of the Supreme Court of New York.   July, 1863.
Considerations concerning the Effect and probable Consequence to result from
the establishment of Banks under the Act to provide a National Cur-
rency.   October, 1863.

Liability of the British Government for the Depredations of Rebel Privateers on the Commerce of the United States, considered. By Charles P. Kirkland. November, 1863.

Are the United States Treasury Notes a Legal Tender?

3178. THE MERCHANTS' MAGAZINE for 1864.

Decision of the Court of Appeals of New York. January, 1864.

The National Revenue. By Hon. Amasa Walker. February, 1864.

Tobacco Duties and Taxation. February, 1864.

The Age of Greenbacks. Debt and Currency. March, 1864.

Our National Finances. Contraction vs. Inflation. May, 1864.

Legal Tender Notes. Has Congress the Power to make Notes a Legal Tender? Opinion of Judge Spotswood, of Philadelphia. May, 1864.

The Ex-Secretary of the Treasury and his Successor. July, 1864.

The National Debt and National Resources. October, 1864.

National Savings and National Taxation. December, 1864.

3179. MERRILL & Co. The Soldier of Indiana in the War for the Union. 8vo. pp. 142. INDIANAPOLIS: *Merrill & Co.*, 1864.

3180. MERRILL, Corporal W. H., 27th Regiment New York Volunteers. Five months in Rebeldom; or Notes from the Diary of a Bull Run Prisoner, at Richmond. 8vo. pp. 64. ROCHESTER: (N. Y.) *Adams & Dalney*, 1862.

3181. MERRIMAC. Die Panzerschiffe Merrimac und Monitor und das Seegefecht in den Hampton Roads am 8 und 9 Marz, 1862. Royal 8vo. pp. 12. DARMSTADT: *Gustav Georg Lange*, 1862.

3182. —— Der Seekampf zwichen den Panzerschiffen Merrimac und Monitor auf der Rhede von Hampton. 8vo. pp. 16. LEIPZIG: *G. Poenicke*, 1862.

3183. MERRIMAN CASE. Opinion of Chief Justice Roger Brooke Taney in. 8vo. pp. BALTIMORE: *J. Murphy & Co.*, 1861.

3184. —— Habeas Corpus. The Proceedings in the Case of John Merriman, of Maryland, before the Hon. R. B. Taney, Chief Justice of the Supreme Court of the United States. 8vo. pp. 24. BALTIMORE: *Lucas Brothers*, 1861.

3185. —— Decision of Chief Justice Taney in the Merriman Case, upon the Writ of Habeas Corpus. 8vo. pp. 16. PHILADELPHIA: *John Campbell*, 1862.

3186. MERSHON, Rev. STEPHEN L. Causes for Thanksgiving in the midst of Civil War. A Discourse delivered at East Hampton, Long Island, November 28, 1861. 8vo. pp. 24. NEW YORK: *Nesbitt & Co.*

3187. METHODIST QUARTERLY REVIEW. The Future of a Cotton State Confederacy. J. B. Woodruff. July, 1861.
3188. —— The American Crisis. Rev. E. O. Haven, DD. Oct. 1862.
3189. —— Methodism and the War. Rev. W. P. Strickland, U. S. A. July, 1863.
3190. —— The War for the Union. Capt. Jas. F. Rusling. April, '64.
3191. METROPOLITAN FAIR, New York, in aid of the United States Sanitary Commission. pp. 16.
3192. —— Catalogue of Paintings and other Works of Art, to be sold at auction in, for the benefit of the Sanitary Commission.
8vo. pp. 13. NEW YORK: *G. F. Nesbitt & Co.*, 1864.
3193. —— Catalogue of the Museum of Flags, Trophies and Relics relating to the Revolution, the War of 1812, the Mexican War and the present Rebellion.
8vo. pp. 109. NEW YORK: *Charles O. Jones*, 1864.
3194. —— Catalogue of the Art Exhibition at. 4to. pp. 18.
3195. —— Catalogue of Articles contained in the Museum and Curiosity Shop.
8vo. pp. 18. NEW YORK: *Baker & Godwin*, 1864.
3195.* METROPOLITAN RECORD, Articles from the.
8vo. pp. 130. NEW YORK: *Office of the Metro. Record*, 1863.
3196. THE MEXICAN EMPIRE and the American Union.
8vo. pp. 12. BOSTON: *Geo. C. Rand & Avery*, 1865.
3197. MEYER, ALBERTUS. The Introduction of Paper Money involves the Abolishment of Taxation. Dated, Oakland, California, March, 1865. 8vo. pp. 12.
3198. MEYNARDIE, E. J. The Siege of Charleston; a Discourse. 8vo. Columbia, S. C., 1864.
3199. MICHIGAN FIRST REGIMENT. Incidents, Marches, Battles and Camp Life; and the Adventures of the Author, known as the Indiana Banker, who was fifer in Company "F," and made such remarkable Time in leaving Bull's Run.
8vo. pp. DETROIT: *Printed for the Author*, 1861.
3200. MICHIGAN. Gov. Blair's Inaugural Message to the Legislature, for the year 1861.
8vo. pp. 24. LANSING: *Hosmer & Kerr*, 1861.
3201. —— Message of the Governor, Extra Session, Jan. 2,'62. p. 11.

3202. MICHIGAN. Annual Report of the Adjutant General, Dec, 24, 1861. pp. 47.

3203. —— Report of the Quartermaster General, November 30, 1861.

3204. —— Message of Gov. Blair, January 7, 1863. pp. 31.

3205. —— Report of the Quartermaster General for 1862. pp. 24.

3206. —— Report of the Adjutant General, 1862. pp. 95.

3207. —— The same, with a Supplementary Report containing the Casualties in Battle, Deaths by Disease, Discharged from Service, etc., of the Private Soldiers from this State, from the beginning of the War to the 31st of December, 1862.
8vo. pp. 309. LANSING: *John A. Kerr & Co.*, 1863.

3208. —— Annual Report of the Adjutant General (John Robertson) for the year 1863.
8vo. pp. 501. LANSING: *John A. Kerr & Co.*, 1864.

3209. —— Governor's Message, January 10, 1864. pp. 18.

3210. —— Report of the Quartermaster General for 1863. pp. 19.

3211. —— Gov. Blair's Message, January 4, 1865.
8vo. pp. 26. LANSING: *John A. Kerr & Co.*, 1865.

3212. —— Inaugural Message of Gov. Crapo, January 4, 1865.
8vo. pp. 34. LANSING: *John A. Kerr & Co.*, 1865.

3213. —— Report of the Quartermaster General for 1864.
8vo. pp. 38. LANSING: *John A. Kerr & Co.*, 1865.

3214. MILES, Col. D. H., U. S. A. Review of the Proceedings of the Court of Enquiry Case of, by Reverdy Johnson and R. H. Gillette. 8vo. pp. 62.

3215. —— Message of the President of the United States, with copies of the Charges, Testimony and Finding of the recent Court of Inquiry, in the Case of Col. Dixon H. Miles, U. S. A.
8vo. pp. 56. *Sen. Ex. Doc. No. 7. 37th Cong., 2d Session*, 1861.

3216. MILITARY, Medical and Surgical Essays ; prepared for the United States Sanitary Commission. Edited by William A. Hammond, M. D., Surgeon General U. S. A.
8vo. pp. viii, 552. PHILADELPHIA : *J. B. Lippincott & Co.*
These essays are prepared by eminent medical men, selected for their presumed acquaintance with the subjects upon which they were desired to write, and were originally published as separate monographs for distribution to the Medical Officers of the army.

3217. MILITARY. Report on a Bill to prevent Officers of the Army and Navy, and other persons in the military and naval service of the United States, from interfering in Elections in the States.

8vo. pp. 52. *Sen. Rep. Com. No.* 14, 38*th Cong.*, 1*st Sess.*, 1864.

3218. THE MILITARY and Naval Situation, and the glorious Achievements of our Soldiers and Sailors.

8vo. pp. 15. WASHINGTON: *Union Congressional Com.*, 1864.

3219. MILITARY DESPOTISM. Suspension of the Habeas Corpus. Curses coming home to roost.

8vo. pp. 16. *Loyal Publication Society, No.* 20, 1863.

3220. MILITARY LAWS of the Confederate States. 8vo. Richmond, 63.

3221. MILITARY SYSTEM of the Republic of Switzerland; or how to raise an efficient army, without offering bounty or resorting to draft.

8vo. pp. 15. WASHINGTON: *Franck Taylor*, 1864.

3222. MILITIA. Laws of the United States, for the Government of the Militia of the District of Columbia; and the United States Rules and Articles of War, as now modified; with explanatory Notes.

8vo. pp. 48. BALTIMORE: *John Murphy & Co.*, 1861.

3223. —— The Militia of the United States. What it has been and what it should be.

8vo. pp. 130. BOSTON: *T. R. Marvin & Son*, 1864.

3224. MILL, J. STUART. The Contest in America. *Frazer's Mag.*,'62.

3225. —— The Contest in America.

12mo. pp. 32. BOSTON: *Little, Brown & Co.*, 1862.

3226. —— The same. *Harpers' Magazine, April*, 1862.

3227. —— The Slave Power; its Character, Career, and probable Designs. Being an attempt to explain the Real Issues involved in the American Contest.

8vo. pp. 16. NEW YORK: *T. J. Crowen*, 1862.

3228. —— and Thomas Hare. True and False Democracy. Representation of all, and Representation of the majority only. A brief Synopsis of Recent Publications on the subject.

8vo. pp. 16. BOSTON: *Prentiss & Deland*, 1862.

3229. MILLER, LEO. The Great Conflict; or. Cause and Cure of Secession. Delivered in Providence, R. I., December 8, 1861.

8vo. pp. 24. BOSTON: *Bela Marsh*, 1862.

3230. MILLER, Rev. MARMADUKE. Slavery and the Union. A Lecture.

12mo. pp. 46. MANCHESTER: *Union and Emanc. Soc.*, 1863.

3231. MILLER, Rev. L. MERRILL. The Union a Blessing. It must be preserved. A Sermon delivered April 28, 1861. Ogdensburg, New York.

8vo. pp. 8.   OGDENSBURGH: "*Advance Office*," 1861.

3232. —— Perfect through suffering. A Thanksgiving Sermon delivered November 28, 1861. 8vo. pp. 8.

3233. —— The Spirit of our Fathers, The Nation's Hope. An Oration delivered at Ogdensburgh, July 4, 1861. pp. 12.

3234. MILLER, SAMUEL. Prayer for our Country. Three Sermons. 1, The Righteous War of a Christian People. 2, National Prayer. 3, The Union Prayer Meeting.

8vo. pp. 46.   PHILADELPHIA: *Henry B. Ashmead*, 1862.

3235. MILLIROUX, J. F. Confédération Américaine. Revue de son Passé, conjectures, suggestions.

8vo. pp. 48.   PARIS: *E. Dentu*, 1861.

3236. —— Aperçus sur les Institutions et les Moeurs des Américains.

8vo. pp. 173.   PARIS: *E. Dentu*, 1862.

3237. MILLS, Rev. ROBERT C. The Southern States Hardened until Ruined. A Sermon preached in Salem, April 13, 1865.

8vo. pp. 21.   BOSTON: *J. M. Hewes*, 1865.

3238. MINIERES, ERNEST BELLOT DES. La Question Américaine suivi d'un Appendice sur le Coton, le Tabac, et le Commerce générale des ancien Etats Unis.

8vo. pp. 74.   PARIS: *Dentu*, 1861.

3239. MINNESOTA. Message of Gov. Ramsay, 1861. pp. 31.

3240. —— Message of Governor Ramsay, January 9, 1862.

8vo. pp. 32.   ST. PAUL: *W. R. Marshall*, 1862.

3241. —— Report of the Adjutant General.

8vo. pp. 300.   ST. PAUL: *W. R. Marshall*, 1862.

3242. —— Message of Gov. Ramsay, September 9, 1862. pp. 15.

3243. —— Message of Gov. Ramsay, January 7, 1863. pp. 32.

3244. —— Appendix to Adjutant General's Report.

8vo. pp. 392.   ST. PAUL: *W. R. Marshall*, 1863.

3245. —— Report of the Adjutant General, Dec. 15, 1862. pp. 160.

3246. —— Message of Governor Swift, January 11, 1864. pp. 33.

3247. —— Inaugural Address of Gov. Miller, Jan. 13, 1864. pp. 11.

3248. —— Report of the Adjutant General, 1864. pp. 298.

3249. MINNESOTA. Report of the Adjutant General, 1864.

    8vo. pp. 61. Appx. 211.   ST. PAUL: *Frederick Driscoll,* 1864.

3250. —— Message of Gov. Miller, January 4, 1865.

    8vo. pp. 30.   ST. PAUL: *Frederick Driscoll,* 1865.

3251. —— Annual Report of the Adjutant General, December, 1864.

    8vo. pp. 411.   ST. PAUL: *Frederick Driscoll,* 1865.

3252. MINT. Annual Report of the Director of the Mint, (Hon. James Pollock,) for the fiscal year ending June 30, 1861.

    8vo. pp. 39.   PHILADELPHIA: *Bryson,* 1861.

3253. —— Annual Report for the year ending June 30, 1862.

    8vo. pp. 38.   PHILADELPHIA: *James H. Bryson,* 1862.

3254. —— Annual Report for the year ending June 30, 1863.

    8vo. pp. 40.   PHILADELPHIA: *Bryson & Son,* 1864.

3255. —— Annual Report for the year ending June 30, 1864.

    8vo. pp. 43.   PHILADELPHIA: *Bryson & Son,* 1865.

These reports are interesting, connected with the finances of the country, and the production of the precious metals during the war.

3256. MISCEGENATION. The Theory of the Blending of the Races applied to the American White Man and Negro.

    12mo. pp. 72.   NEW YORK: *Dexter, Hamilton & Co.,* 1863.

3257. MISSOURI. Adj't General's Report of the State Militia, for 1861.

    8vo. pp. 9 and Tables.   ST. LOUIS: 1862.

3258. —— Message of Governor Gamble, December 30, 1862. pp. 20.

3259. —— Annual Report of the Adjutant Gen., Dec., 1862. pp. 12.

3260. —— Official Report of Missouri Troops, for 1862. pp. 204.

3261. —— Report of the Quartermaster General for 1863.

    8vo. pp. 44. Tables clxxviii.   ST. LOUIS: 1864.

3262. —— Report of the Adjutant General for 1863.

    8vo. pp. 168, 124 and 493.   ST. LOUIS: (Missouri) 1864.

3263. —— Report of the Adjutant General, December 31, 1864.

    8vo. pp. 414.   JEFFERSON CITY: *W. A. Curry,* 1865.

3264. MITCHELL, D. W. Ten Years in the United States.

    Post 8vo. pp. 332.   LONDON: *Smith, Elder & Co.,* 1862.

3265. MITCHELL, JAMES. Letter to the President of the United States, on the relation of the White and African Races in the United States; showing the Necessity of the Colonization of the latter.

    8vo. pp. 28. WASHINGTON: *Government Printing Office,* 1862.

3266. MITCHELL, J. Report on Colonization and Emigration, made to the Secretary of the Interior.

8vo. pp. 29. WASHINGTON ; *Government Printing Office*, 1862.

3267. MITCHELL, Rev. JOHN. The Sower Blessed. A Discourse delivered on Thanksgiving Day, at West Galway, Nov. 29, 1860.

8vo. pp. 14. AMSTERDAM: (New York) *"Recorder Office,"* '61.

3268. MITCHELL, O. P. The Olive Branch. Near Plum Valley, Sierra County, California.

8vo. pp. 97. MARYSVILLE, 1862.

3269. MITCHELL, Rev. S. S. Eulogy on President Lincoln, delivered at Harrisburg, Pennsylvania, April 19, 1865.

3270. THE MONEY QUESTION, in 1813 and 1863. What some did then, others are seeking to do now. By a Loyal Citizen.

12mo. pp. 11. NEW YORK: *Anson D. F. Randolph*, 1863.

3271. MONEY BY STEAM. John Law; his Body moulders in the ground, but his Soul is marching on. MDCCCLXIV. New York, April 30, 1864. 8vo. pp. 40.

3272. THE "MONITOR" IRON CLADS. "The Truth is mighty and it will prevail."

8vo. pp. 17. BOSTON: *S. H. Eastburn*, 1864.

3273. MONTHLY RELIGIOUS MAGAZINE for 1861 and 1862.

The Holy War. Rev. Rufus Ellis. April, 1861.
The Opportunities of the present. Rev. Rufus Ellis. February, 1862.
Peace not always possible. Rev. Rufus Ellis. October, 1862.

3274. MONTHLY RELIGIOUS MAGAZINE for 1863.

The Cause of National Disaster. Rev. Rufus Ellis. April.
The Conflict of the Brutal with the Human. The South against the Universe. D. Bowen. June.
Home Duties in Time of War. Rev. T. B. Daggett. December.

3275. MONTHLY RELIGIOUS MAGAZINE for 1864.

Our National Ideal. Rev. Rufus Ellis. January.
A Day at Annapolis. J. F. W. Ware. February.
A Glimpse at the Army; the Hospitals and the Freedmen. April.
The War as affecting our Views of Death. July and August.
Christian Patriotism. Rev. Rufus Ellis. September.
Ought the War to go on. Rev. Rufus Ellis. October.
The Nation's Ballot and Decision. December.

3276. MONTAGU, Lord ROBERT. A Mirror in America.

8vo. pp. 108. LONDON: *Saunders, Otley & Co.*, 1861.

37

3277. MONTALAMBERT, Count de. Le Victoire du Nord. Printed in " Le Correspondant." Paris, June, 1865.

3278. —— The Victory of the North. Translated and published in the New York Evening Post. June 23, 1865.

3279. MONTGOMERY, Captain CHARLES S. In Memoriam. Sermon delivered by the Rev. Dr. R. B. Claxton, in St. Luke's Chapel, Rochester, New York. 8vo. unpaged.

Captain Montgomery, commanding the Fifth Regiment of New York Infantry, was killed in action in Hatcher's Run, before Petersburg, Virginia, on the 6th of February, 1865.

3280. MONTGOMERY, JOHN. The Writ of Habeas Corpus, and Mr. Binney.
8vo. pp. 29. PHILADELPHIA : *John Campbell*, 1862.

3281. MOODY, LORING. The Destruction of Republicanism, the Object of the Rebellion. The Testimony of Southern Witnesses.
8vo. pp. 20. BOSTON ; *Emancipation League*, 1863.

3282. MOORE, Rev. D., Jr. A Thanksgiving Sermon preached in Buffalo, New York, November 28, 1861.
12mo. pp. 25. BUFFALO : *Breed, Butler & Co.*, 1861.

3283. MOORE, FRANK. Heroes and Martyrs ; Notable Men of the Time. Biographical Sketches of the Military and Naval Heroes, Statesmen and Orators, distinguished in the American Crisis of 1861–62. With Portraits on Steel.
4to. pp. NEW YORK : *G. P. Putnam*, 1862.

3284. —— The Rebellion Record. A Diary of American Events, with Documents, Narratives, Incidents, Poetry, etc. Illustrated with Portraits on steel, and Maps and diagrams.
8 vols. Royal 8vo. NEW YORK : *G. P. Putnam*, 1861–62.

The most valuable collection of original materials which has appeared on the Rebellion. As a work of reference it is unsurpassed.

3285. —— Rebel Rhymes and Rhapsodies.
18mo. pp. 316. NEW YORK : *G. P. Putnam*, 1864.

3286. —— Lyrics of Loyalty.
18mo. pp. xvi, 336. NEW YORK : *G. P. Putnam*, 1864.

3287. —— Songs of the Soldiers.
18mo. pp. xv, 316. NEW YORK : *G. P. Putnam*, 1864.

3288. —— Personal and Political Ballads.
18mo. pp. xv, 368. NEW YORK : *G. P. Putnam*, 1864.

3289. MOORE, F.   The Portrait Gallery of the War ; Civil, Military and Naval.   A Biographical Record.   60 steel Portraits.
Royal 8vo. pp. iv, 353.   NEW YORK: *Derby & Miller*, 1864.

3290. —— Life and Speeches of Andrew Johnson, President of the United States.
12mo. pp. xlviii and 493.   BOSTON : *Little, Brown & Co.*, 1865.

3291. —— Spirit of the Pulpit, North and South.

3292. —— Anecdotes, Poetry and Incidents of the War, North and South.

3293. —— Speeches of John Bright, M. P., on the American Question. With a Memoir.

3294. —— Women of the War, their Heroism and life Sacrifices.

3295. MOORE, GEORGE H.   Historical Notes on the Employment of Negroes in the American Army of the Revolution.
8vo. pp. 24.   NEW YORK : *C. T. Evans*, 1862.

3296. MOORE, Rev. HENRY D.   Our Country ; Its Sin and its Duty. A Discourse delivered in Portland, Maine, Sept. 26, 1861.
8vo. pp. 21.   PORTLAND : *Hezekiah Packard*, 1861.

3297. MOORE, JAMES, M. D.   Kilpatrick and our Cavalry ; comprising a Sketch of the Life of General Kilpatrick, with an account of the Cavalry Raids, Engagements under his command, from the beginning of the Rebellion to the Surrender of Johnson.
12mo. pp. 245.   NEW YORK : *W. J. Widdleton*, 1865.

3298. MOORE, MADELINE.   The Lady Lieutenant.   A Wonderful, Startling and Thrilling Narrative of the Adventures of, who, in order to be near her lover, joined the army, and fought in Western Virginia.
8vo. pp. 40.   PHILADELPHIA : *Barclay & Co.*

3299. MOORE, Rev. W. W.   The Non-Essentialism and the War. The Non-Essentialism of the American Church, the Cause of our present National Calamity.
8vo. pp. 20.   CHICAGO : *J. W. Dean*, 1863.

3300. MOOREHEAD, Hon. J. K., of Penn.   The Perpetuity of the Union.   A Speech in the House of Reps., March 26, 1864.
8vo. pp. 8.   WASHINGTON : *McGill & Witherow*, 1864.

3301. MORAIS, Rev. S.   An Address on the Death of Abraham Lincoln, delivered before the Congregation, Mikvé Israel, of Philadelphia, at their Synagogue.
8vo. pp. 7.   PHILADELPHIA : *Collins*, 1865.

3302. MOREHOUSE, H. L.   Evil, its own Destroyer.   A Discourse delivered in the City of East Saginaw, April 19, 1865, on the Death of Abraham Lincoln.

8vo. pp. 16.   East Saginaw: *Enterprise Office,* 1865.

3303. MORFORD, Henry.   Shoulder Straps.   A Novel of New York and the Army, 1862.

8vo. pp. 482.   Philadelphia: *T. B. Peterson.*

3304. —— Democracy and the Nation.   A Poem delivered on the 4th of July, 1863, before the Tammany Society, New York.   With Oration of the Hon. H. C. Murphy, and Proceedings on the occasion.

8vo. pp. 67.   New York: *Baptist & Taylor,* 1863.

3305. MORGAN, Geo. D.   Report of the Committee on Naval Affairs, relative to the Employment of, to purchase vessels for the Government.   *Senate Rep. Com. No.* 9, *37th Cong., 2d Sess.,* 1862.

3306. MORGAN, General G. W.   Report of the Occupation of Cumberland Gap.   *House of Representatives, Executive Document, No.* 94, *38th Congress, 2d Session,* 1864.   pp. 19.

3307. MORGAN, Rev. Wm. F.   In Memoriam.   Joy Darkened.   Sermon preached in St. Thomas' Church, New York, April 16, 1865.   Order of Services, April 19.   The Prolonged Lament.   Sermon preached April 23, 1865.   8vo. pp. 47.

3308. —— Discourses upon Christian Duties in connection with National Dangers.

12mo. pp. 27.   New York: *Wm. M. Taylor,* 1861.

3309. —— MORRELL, Daniel J.   Letter showing the amount of direct and indirect Taxes on American Iron, as compared with the import Duties levied upon Foreign Iron.

8vo. pp. 12.   Philadelphia: *Sherman & Co.,* 1865.

3310. MORRILL, Justin S.   The Impolicy of making paper a Legal Tender.   Speech in House of Reps., February 4, 1862.   pp. 4.

3311. —— Tax Bill.   Speech delivered in House of Representatives, April 19, 1864.   8vo. pp. 7.

3312. —— Modern Democracy.   The Extension of Slavery in our own Territory or by the acquisition of Foreign Territory, wrong, Morally, Politically and Economically.   Speech in the House of Representatives, June 6, 1860.   pp. 8.

3313. MORRILL, of Vermont, and KELLEY of Penn.   Remarks in reply to Mr. Voorhees of Indiana, in H. of Rep. May 21,'62. p. 4.

3314. MORRILL, Hon. L. M.   Speech on the Confiscation of Property.   Delivered in the U. S. Senate, May 1, 1862.   pp. 8.

3315. MORRIS, EDWARD S.   Second Address to the Colored People of Pennsylvania ; with Remarks for my own Race.
8vo. pp. 24.   PHILADELPHIA : *James H. Bryson,* 1863.

3316. MORRIS, ROBERT.   The Organization of the Public Debt and a Plan for the Relief of the Treasury.
8vo. pp. 22.   NEW YORK : *James Miller,* 1863.

3317. MORRIS, ROBERT, LL. D.   The Wounded Soldier ; or Coming Home to Die. "The Cedar Spring."   An Incident of Stone River. "The Wounded Soldier." Poems.
Several other patriotic poems, have appeared, from the pen of the same author.

3318. MORRIS, WALKER.   An Address to the People of the United States, and particularly of the Slave States.
8vo. pp. 50.   LOUISVILLE : *Bradley & Gilbert,* 1862.

3319. MORRISON, Rev. GEO.   Disloyalty in the Church. *Danville Review, March,* 1864.

3320. MORRISON, MARION.   A History of the Ninth Regiment Illinois Volunteer Infantry.
8vo. pp. 95.   MONMOUTH : (Ill.) *John S. Clark,* 1864.

3321. MORRISON, Col. W. R.   Speech delivered at Edwardsville, Ill., Oct. 13, 1863. (Against the Administration of Mr. Lincoln.)
8vo. pp. 19.   ST. LOUIS : *George Knapp & Co.,* 1863.

3322. MORSE, SIDNEY E.   Premium Questions on Slavery ; each admitting of a Yes or No Answer ; addressed to the Editors of the New York Independent and New York Evangelist.
8vo. pp. 30.   NEW YORK : *Harper & Brothers,* 1860.

3323. —— A Geographical, Statistical and Ethical View of the American Slaveholders' Rebellion.
8vo. pp. 19.   NEW YORK : *A. D. F. Randolph,* 1863.

3324. MORTON, Rev. JAMES.   The School Boy's Oration on the State of the Country. New York, March 24, 1863. pp. 4.

3325. MORTON, Governor O. P.   Letter to James Winslow, Esq., of New York, touching the payment of Interest on the Funded Debt of Indiana.
8vo. pp. 14.   INDIANAPOLIS : 1863.

3326. MORTON, Gov. O. P.   Reconstruction and Negro Suffrage.
Speech at Richmond, Va., September 29, 1863.. 8vo. pp. 23.

3327. MOSEBY, JACK, the Guerilla Chief. By Lt. Col. ——.
12mo. pp. 106.   NEW YORK: *T. R. Dawley*, 1864.

3328. MOTLEY, JOHN LOTHROP.   The Causes of the American Civil
War. A Letter to the London Times.
8vo. pp. 36.   NEW YORK: *James G. Gregory*, 1861.

3329. —— The same. pp. 24. New York: *D. Appleton & Co.*, 1861.

3330. —— The same. (Pulpit and Rostrum, No. 20.)

3331. —— The same. pp. 30. London, 1861.

MOUNTAINEER, for works by, see *Charles Wright.*

3332. MULLER, NICLAS.   Zehn Gepanzerte Sonnete.   Mit einer
Widmung an Ferdinand Freiligrath, und einem nachklang.
" Die Union, wie sie sein soll." Im November, 1862.
8vo. pp. 15.   NEW YORK: *Nic. Muller*, 1862.

3333. MULLER, W. H.   The Value of the Union.   *Continental
Monthly, June*, 1863.

3334. MURDOCK, Rev. D.   Eulogy on President Lincoln, at New
Milford, Connecticut, April 23, 1865.

3335. MUNICIPALIST. Addenda to the Municipalist. Letter xxiv. 12mo.

3336. MURDOCK, Rev. DAVID.   Death of Abraham Lincoln. A Sermon preached in New Milford, Conn., April 23, 1865. pp. 16.

3337. MURDOCK, JAMES E.   Patriotism in Poetry and Prose ; being
Passages from Lectures and Patriotic Readings. Also, Poems
by T. Buchanan Read, George H. Boker, and other American
Authors, commemorative of the Gallant Deeds of our Noble Defenders on Land and Sea.
8vo. pp. 172.   PHILADELPHIA: *J. B. Lippincott & Co.*, 1864.

3338. MURDOCK, Rev. JOHN N.   Our Civil War. Its Causes and
and its Issues. A Discourse delivered in Brookline, Massachusetts, August 6, 1863.
12mo. pp. 23.   BOSTON: *Wright & Potter*, 1863.

3339. MURPHY, Hon. HENRY C.   Remarks upon that portion of
the Message of Gov. Seymour, relating to Military Arrests, delivered in the Senate [of the State of N. York] March 6, 1863.
8vo. pp. 25.   ALBANY: *Comstock & Casssidy*, 1863.

3340. —— Oration delivered at the Annual Celebration of the 87th

Anniversary of American Independence, at Tammany Hall, New York. With Poem by Henry Morford. July 4, 1863.

8vo. pp. 67. NEW YORK: *Baptist & Taylor*, 1863.

3341. MURRAY, Hon. HENRY A. Lands of the Slave and the Free; or Cuba, the United States and Canada.

2 vols. post 8vo. LONDON: *John W. Parker & Son*, 1855.

3342. MURRAY, Rev. JAMES O. Loyalty to Country and its Duties. A Sermon delivered in Cambridge, September 15, 1861.

8vo. pp. 28. CAMBRIDGE: *Allen & Farnham*, 1861.

3343. MYER, Col. ALBERT J. A Manual of Signals, for the use of Signal Officers in the Field.

8vo. pp. 148. WASHINGTON: (D. C.) 1864.

3344. MYERS, AMOS, of Penn. Speech on the Constitutionality and Necessity of a Draft. House of Reps., Feb. 3, 1864. pp. 8.

3345. MYERS, JOHN C. A Daily Journal of the 192d Regiment of Pennsylvania Volunteers, commanded by Col. Wm. B. Thomas, in the service of the United States for one hundred days.

12mo. pp. 203. Portrait. PHILADEL.: *Crissy & Markley*, 1865.

3346. MYERS, Hon. LEONARD. Abraham Lincoln. Memorial Address, delivered June 15, 1865, before the Union League of the 13th Ward.

8vo. pp. 15. PHILADELPHIA: *King & Baird*, 1865.

3347. MYSTERY REVEALED: or the Way to Peace. [Richmond.]

NADAL, B. H., DD. The War in the Light of Divine Providence. A Fast Day Sermon.

8vo. pp. 20. NEW HAVEN: *Tuttle, Morehouse & Co.*, 1863.

3349. —— Eulogy on President Lincoln. Washington, June 1, 1865.

3350. NAGLEE, Brig. General HENRY M. Report of the part taken by the First Brigade, Casey's Division, in the Battle of Seven Pines, May 31, 1862. With the official Report of Gen. Casey.

8vo. pp. PHILADELPHIA: *Collins*, 1862.

3351. —— Report of his Command of the District of Virginia: with the Correspondence between Gen. Naglee and the Mayor and Common Council of the City of Portsmouth, referred to in the Report.

8vo. pp. 39. PHILADELPHIA: *J. B. Lippincott & Co.*, 1863.

3352. NAGLEE, Brig. Gen. H. M.   Correspondence with the Mayor and Common Council of the City of Portsmouth.

8vo. pp. 20.   PHILADELPHIA : *J. B. Lippincott & Co.*, 1863.

3353. —— A Chapter from the Secret History of the War.   A Letter to W. D. Kelley, Philadelphia.   pp. 4.

3354. —— Second Chapter from the Secret History of the War.   A Letter to the Hon. Wm. D. Kelley.   pp. 4.

3355. —— Letter to Wm. A. Atkinson, Esq., Chairman of the State Executive Committee, Dover.   pp. 4.

3356. NASON, Rev. ELIAS.   Eulogy on Abraham Lincoln, delivered before the New England Historic Genealogical Society, Boston, May 3, 1865.

8vo. pp. 28.   BOSTON : *W. V. Spencer*, 1865.

3357. —— Our Obligation to defend the Government of the Country. A Discourse on the War, at Exeter, N. H., April 21, '62.   pp. 6.

3358. —— A Sermon on the War, preached to the Soldiers at Exeter, New Hampshire, May 19, 1861.   pp. 4.

3359. —— A brief Record of Events in Exeter, N. H., during the year 1861 : together with the Names of the Soldiers of this town in the War.

8vo. pp. 16.   EXETER : *Samuel Hale*, 1862.

3360. —— Record of Events in Exeter, 1862 ; with the Names of the Soldiers of the town.   pp. 20.

NATIONAL ARMORIES AND FOUNDERIES.   Soon after the War commenced, there was a general call for another great National Armory and Foundry in the West.   Memorials from various cities and towns were sent to Congress, setting forth the advantages they possessed for such an establishment, as follows :

3361. NATIONAL ARMORY.   The National Foundry for the West. Where shall it be located?   A Letter to Hon. John Sherman, U. S. Senator from Ohio, by the Rev. William J. Clark.

8vo. pp. 17.   CINCINNATI : *Bradley & Webb*, 1862.

3362. —— Does the Country require a National Armory and Foundry west of the Allegany Mountains?   If it does, where should they be located?

8vo. pp. 60.   PITTSBURGH : *W. S. Haven*, 1862.

3363. —— Memorial to Congress upon the subject of a National Armory; with the Preamble and Resolutions adopted by the Common Council of the City of Alton, December 2, 1861.

8vo. pp. 8.   ALTON: (Ill.) *L. A. Parks & Co.*, 1861.

3364. NATIONAL ARMORY. Memorial of Burlington Island Asso. pp. 4.

3365. —— Memorial to the Government of the United States, from Chicago, Illinois, setting forth the advantages of that city as a site for a National Armory and Foundry, November, 1864.

8vo. pp. 22. Map.   CHICAGO: *Beach & Barnard*, 1861.

3366. —— A Memorial from the Citizens of Columbus, on the subject of an Armory and Arsenal, to be established at Columbus, Ohio.

8vo. pp. 22.   COLUMBUS: *Richard Nevins*, 1862.

3367. —— Iron is King. Hollidaysburg a suitable site for the National Foundry and Armory, and for all kinds of Iron Manufacture.

8vo. pp. 8.   PITTSBURGH: *W. S. Haven*, 1862.

3368. —— A Memorial of the Board of Trade and Common Council of the City of Indianapolis, to Congress, in regard to the location of a Western National Armory. pp. 4.

3369. —— Memorial to Congress for the establishment of a National Foundry and Gun-Boat Yard at Ironton, Ohio.

8vo. pp. 14.   WASHINGTON: *H. Polkinhorn*, 1862.

3370. —— A Memorial from the city of Milwaukie, on the subject of a Naval Depot, an Armory and an Arsenal.

8vo. pp. 15.   MILWAUKIE: *Starr & Son*, 1861.

3371. —— Memorial to the Government of the United States from Pittsburgh, setting forth the advantages of that city, as a site for a National Armory and Foundry.

8vo. pp. 15. With a Map. PITTSBURGH: *W. S. Haven*, 1861.

3372. —— An Appeal to Congress by the Citizens of Rock Island and Moline, Illinois, and Davenport, Iowa, in favor of a National Armory on Rock Island, Illinois.

8vo. pp. 14. Map.   ROCK ISLAND: *Argus Office*, 1861.

3373. —— Memorial to Congress from Toledo, Ohio, setting forth the advantages of that city as a site for a National Armory and Foundry, December, 1861.

8vo. pp. 8. Map.   TOLEDO: *Pelton & Waggoner*.

3374. NATIONAL ADVOCATE, [New Orleans.] Suspension of, by order of Maj. Gen. Butler. (Special Order No. 513.) pp. 11.

38

3375. NATIONAL BANK. The First of a Series of a work in favor of the Constitutionality of a National Bank. By The Belarius of Cymbeline.

8vo. pp. 31.					WASHINGTON : *L. Towers & Co.,* 1862.

3376. NATIONAL BANK CURRENCY ACT. Report on its Defects and its Effects.

8vo. pp. 18.					NEW YORK : *C. S. Westcutt & Co.,* 1863.

3377. NATIONAL BANKS. An Examination into the Prospective Effects of the National Banks upon the Public Welfare. N. York, December 1, 1863.

8vo. pp. 23.					NEW YORK : *Hall, Clayton & Medole.*

3378. NATIONAL CURRENCY. An Act proposed by a New York State Banker. pp. 3.

3379. —— An Act to provide for, secured by a Pledge of U. S. Bonds, and to provide for the Circulation and Redemption thereof. Approved June 3, 1864.

8vo. pp. 28.					WASHINGTON : *Government Office,* 1864.

3380. —— What is Needed. Suggestions by a Practical Banker.

8vo. pp. 48.					PHILADELPHIA : *W. & A. Martien,* 1863.

3381. —— Some Strictures on an Act to provide, secured by a Pledge of United States Stocks.

8vo. pp. 18.					BOSTON : *John Wilson & Son,* 1863.

3382. OUR NATIONAL CONSTITUTION. Its adaption to a State of War or Insurrection.

8vo. pp. 39.					PHILADELPHIA : *C. Sherman, Son & Co.,* 1863.

3383. NATIONAL GUARD. Notes on the Colors of the National Guard; with some Incidental Passages of the History of the Regiment. Prepared at the request of " The Veterans of the National Guard."

Imperial 8vo. pp. 55. NEW YORK : *From an Amateur Press,*'64.

3384. NATIONAL UNION CLUB, Philadelphia. Articles of Association and Constitution of.

12mo. pp. 12.					PHILADELPHIA : *King & Baird,* 1863.

3385. THE NATIONAL FREEDMAN. A Monthly Journal of the National Freedmen's Relief Association. • New York, 1865.

3386. THE NATIONAL CLUB on the Reconstruction of the Union, February 4, 1864.

8vo. pp. 16. Map.					NEW YORK : *G. B. Teubner,* 1864.

3387. NATIONAL REPUBLICAN CONVENTION. Proceedings of, held at Chicago, May 16, 17 and 18, 1860. For President, Abraham Lincoln, of Illinois. 8vo. pp. 44.

3388. NATIONAL UNITY, American Society for promoting. Society Rooms, Bible House, Astor Place, New York.
8vo. pp. 60 and 6.   NEW YORK: *John F. Trow.*

3389. NATIONAL UNION ASSOCIATION, of Ohio.
This Association published many patriotic tracts, but the compiler of this work has been unable to procure from it, either its publications or the titles of them.

3390. NATION'S SIN AND PUNISHMENT, or the Hand of God visible in the overthrow of Slavery. By a Chaplain of the U. S. Army, who has been thirty years a resident of the Slave States.
12mo. pp. 274.   NEW YORK: *M. Doolady,* 1864.

3391. NATIONAL WAR COMMITTEE of the Citizens of N. Y., Reports of.
No. 1. Report of the Committee to visit the Governors of the Loyal States, to press forward the new Levies to the seat of War. 8vo. pp. 6.
No. 2. Report of the Committee on the Militia and Defences of the State of New York, September 11, 1862. 8vo. pp. 5.
No. 3. Report of the Proceedings of the National War Committee of the Citizens of New York, September 22, 1862. pp. 9.
No. 4. Report of the Committee appointed to examine a Plan to provide for greater efficiency in Ambulance and Hospital Corps. Sept. 22, '62. 8vo. p. 4.
No. 5. Report of the National War Committee of the Citizens of New York, on Army Organization and Depot Camps. September 23, 1862. 8vo. pp. 12.
No. 6. Report of the Committee appointed to take into consideration the condition of Western Texas. September 29, 1862. 8vo. pp. 17.
No. 7. Speech of the Hon. Andrew Jackson Hamilton of Texas, late Representative of Texas, in the 36th Congress, on the Condition of the South under Rebel Rule, and the Necessity of early Relief to the Union men of Western Texas, October 3, 1862. 8vo. pp. 19.
No. 8. Memorial to the Governor of the State of New York, on the Condition of the Artillery in this Harbor. 8vo. pp. 4.
No. 9. Report of the Committee who visited Washington on the Affairs of Western Texas. October 20, 1862. 8vo. pp. 15.
No. 10. Report of the Committee to ask the attention of the President to the complaints of General Sigel. New York, October 20, 1862. 8vo. pp. 2.
No. 11. Report of the Committee appointed to consider the Wiard Inventions, (viz: Iron-Clad Gunboats, Forts and Spherical Cannon.) Nov. 6, '62. 8vo. p. 3.
No. 12. Report of the Committee who presented the Report on Ambulance and Camp-Hospital Corps to the authorities in Washington. September 30, 1862. 8vo. pp. 3.
No. 13. Report of the Committee who submitted the Memorial on the condition of the Artillery in New York Harbor, to the Governor of the State of New York. November 1, 1862. 8vo. pp. 2.

No. 14. Report of Hiram Walbridge on the considerations which render a Proclamation to the South expedient on the landing of the National Forces in Texas. October 30, 1862. 8vo. pp. 6.

3392. NAVAL GENERAL COURT-MARTIAL, Navy Yard of Charlestown, Mass. The United States against Franklin W. Smith. Argument of the Judges Advocate.

8vo. pp. 139. BOSTON: *Farwell & McGlener*, 1865.

The accused in this case was charged with "Fraud upon the United States," and "Wilful neglect of duty as a Contractor."

3393. NAVAL CONSTRUCTION. Interrogatories on. pp. 3.

3394. NAVAL ACADEMY. Letter from the Secretary of the Navy in relation to the removal of the Naval Academy from Annapolis to Newport, R. I. *Sen. Ex. Doc., No.* 35, 37*th Con., 2d Sess.,* '62.

3395. —— Report of the Committee to "inquire if the Superintendent of the Naval Academy, or any of the Officers connected with the Government or instruction thereof, have allowed or countenanced in the young men under their charge, any manifestation of feelings or sentiments hostile to the Government of the United States, and whether any of the Officers of said Academy have manifested any sentiments of like character."

8vo. pp. 20. *Sen. Rep. Com. No.* 68, 37*th Cong., 2d Sess.,* 1862.

3396. NAVAL DEFENCES. Report of the Committee, on "the cheapest, most expeditious. and reliable mode of placing Vessels-of-War upon Lake Ontario and the other great lakes,—and for the purpose of establishing water communication adapted to vessels of war from other waters to the lakes," etc.

8vo. pp. 16. *H. of Reps., Rep. No.* 4, 37*th Con., 3d Sess.,* 1863.

See, also, *Ship Canals, Niagara Ship Canal, S. B. Ruggles.*

3397. NAVAL SUPPLIES. Report of the Committee, in relation to Naval Supplies. *Sen. Rep. Com. No.* 45, 38*th Cong., 1st Ses.,* 1864.

3398. —— Report from the Select Committee, (Mr. Hale, Chairman,) on Naval Supplies.

8vo. pp. 231. *Sen. Rep. Com. No.* 99, 38*th Cong., 1st Sess.,* '64.

3399. —— Letter from the Secretary of the Navy, in relation to the purchase of Supplies for the Navy by that Department, February 16, 1864. pp. 32. 38*th Cong., 1st Sess., Ho. Ex. Doc., No.* 40.

3400. NAVY YARD, etc. Report on the "Circumstances attending the Surrender of the Navy Yard at Pensacola, and the Destruction of the Property of the United States at the Navy Yard at Norfolk, and at the Armory at Harper's Ferry, etc.

8vo. pp. 21. Sen. Rep. Com. No. 37, 37th Cong., 2d Sess., 1862.

3401. THE NAVY IN CONGRESS. Speeches of the Hon. Messrs. Grimes, Doolittle and Nye, of the Senate. And the Hon. Messrs. Rice, Pike, Griswold and Blow, of the House of Representatives.

8vo. pp. 53. WASHINGTON **:** *Franck Taylor, 1865.*

3402. NAVY. Report of the Secretary of the Navy, (the Hon. Gideon Welles,) with an Appendix containing Reports from Officers and List of Vessels purchased, built, etc., December 2, 1861.

8vo. pp. 157. WASHINGTON ; *Government Printing Office,* '62.

3403. —— Report of the Secretary of the Navy, with an Appendix, containing Reports from Officers, December, 1862.

8vo. pp. 530. WASHINGTON: *Government Printing Office,* '63.

3404. —— Report of the Secretary of the Navy. Dec. 1, 1862. p. 44.

3405. —— Report of the Secretary of the Navy, with an Appendix, containing Reports from Officers. December, 1863.

8vo. pp. 586. WASHINGTON: *Government Printing Office,* '63.

3406. —— Report of the Secretary of the Navy, with an Appendix containing the Reports from Officers. December 5, 1864.

8vo. pp. 48. WASHINGTON: *Government Printing Office,* 1864.

3407. —— Report of the Sec. of the Navy, December 5, 1864.

8vo. pp. xlviii. Appx. 1259. WASH.: *Govt. Pr. Office,* 1864.

The Reports of the Secretary of the Navy which accompany the President's Messages, contain the Reports of the Chiefs of Bureaus, and accompanying Papers.

3408. —— Report of the Secretary of the Navy, (Hon. Gideon Welles) in relation to Armored Vessels.

8vo. pp. 607. WASHINGTON: *Government Printing Office,* '64.

This Report comprises the various reports of Boards, and of officers appointed to examine Iron-Clads and Monitor vessels. Also the reports from the North Atlantic, the South Atlantic, the Western Gulf, and the Mississippi Squadrons; of all the operations by them, including, not only the general engagements and battles, but the details of the particular voyages of every iron-clad vessel employed in the Navy, on the sea and rivers.

3409. —— Report of the New York Chamber of Commerce on the Memorial of Officers of the United States Navy to Congress, for increase of pay. January, 1866. 8vo. pp. 7.

3410. NAVY AND MARINE CORPS. Report of the Secretary of the

Navy; with a List of Officers of the Navy and Marine Corps, who, between the first day of December, 1860, and the first of December, 1863, left the service, with the grade and rank of each. *Senate Ex. Document, 38th Congress, 1st Session,* 1863. pp. 12.

3411. THE NAVY OF THE UNITED STATES. An exposure of its condition, and the Causes of its failure. By Edward N. Dickinson.
8vo. pp. 80.   NEW YORK : *J. A. Gray & Greene,* 1864.

3412. NAVY. A Tract for the Navy. "Say your Prayers in Fair Weather."
18mo. pp. 32.   NEW YORK : *Protestant Episcopal So.,* 1865.

3413. —— Assimilated Rank of the Officers of the United States Navy, proposed by the Board on Regulations. 1864. 8vo. pp. 18.

3414. —— Hand-Book of the United States Navy; being a compilation of all the principal Events in the History of every vessel in the United States Navy, from April, 1861, to May, 1864. Compiled by B. S. Osbon.
8vo. pp. 277.   NEW YORK : *D. Van Nostrand,* 1864.

3415. —— Facts concerning. Philadelphia, 1863. pp. 14.

3416. NAVY REGISTER. Register of the Commissioned, Warrant and Volunteer Officers of the Navy of the United States, including Officers of the Marine Corps and others. January 1, 1863.
8vo. pp.   WASHINGTON : *Government Printing Office,* 1863.

3417. —— The same, to January 1, 1864.
8vo. pp. 289. WASHINGTON : *Government Printing Office,* '64.

3418. —— The same, to January 1, 1865.
8vo. pp. 335. WASHINGTON : *Government Printing Office,* '65.

3419. —— [Rebel.] Register of the Commissioned and Warrant Officers of the Navy of the Confederate States, to January 1, 1863.

3420. NAVY YARD. Majority and minority Reports of the Board of Officers appointed under the Act approved July 15, 1862, entitled "An Act to authorize the Secretary of the Navy to accept League Island, in the Delaware River, for Naval purposes.
8vo. pp. 29. *Senate Ex. Doc. No.* 9, *37th Cong., 3d Sess.,* 1862.

3421. —— Statements relating to a Navy Yard in the Delaware, for the construction and equipment of Iron-Clad Steamships of War, proposed to be established at League Island.
8vo. pp. 27.   PHILADELPHIA : *Collins,* 1862.

3422. NAVY YARD. Report of the Board of Officers appointed to decide between League Island and New London, for a Naval Station. Shall the Secretary of the Navy locate it at League Island in defiance of the Report.   pp. 10.

3423. —— Statement of Facts, with accompanying Documents, presented before the Committee appointed by the Secretary of the Navy to examine New London Harbor.

8vo. pp. 16.   NEW LONDON: *Starr & Farnum,* 1862.

3424. —— A brief Review of the Navy Yard Question; showing that New London has the advantage of defensibility, fresh water, iron, coal, freedom from ice, &c.

8vo. pp. 32, Map.   NEW LONDON: *Starr & Farnum,* 1863.

3425. —— The Report of a Joint Select Committee of the Legislature of Connecticut, on the proposed Navy Yard at New London.

8vo. pp. 16.   NEW HAVEN: *Babcock & Sizer,* 1862.

3426. —— Report of the Committee " to enquire into and report upon the expediency of the establishment of a new Yard for the construction, docking and repair of Iron, Iron-Clad and other vessels, and the proper site for its location."

8vo. pp. 54. *Ho. of Reps. Rep. No.* 100, 38*th Con.,* 1*st Ses.,* '64.

3427. —— Report of the minority of the Naval Committee, in favor of occupying League Island for a station for the construction, cleansing and repair of Iron and Armed Vessels.

8vo. pp. 40.   PHILADELPHIA: *Commercial List Office,* 1864.

3428. —— A Review of the minority Report, on the Navy Yard Question; with an Appendix containing Letters from Major General John A. Dix and others.

8vo. pp. 36.   NEW LONDON: *Starr & Farnum,* 1864.

3429. —— A Reply to the minority Report of Messrs. Kelley and Moorehead, on Sites for Navy Yards; with a brief Comment on the Testimony before the Naval Committee.

8vo. pp. 86. Map.   NEW LONDON: *D. S. Ruddock,* 1864.

3430. —— Reports of the Secretary of the Navy, and the Commission by him appointed, on the proposed new Iron Navy-Yard at League Island.

8vo. pp. 56.   PHILADELPHIA: *Collins,* 1863.

3431. —— Memorial of the Citizens of Cairo and vicinity, relating to the permanent location of a Western Navy and Dock Yard and Naval Depot.

8vo. pp. 5.   Cairo : (Illinois) *News Company*, 1864.

3432. Navy Yard. Resolutions of the Chamber of Commerce of the State of New York, in favor of the establishment of a Navy Yard and Depot at New London, Connecticut.

8vo. pp. 2.   *Sen. Mis. Dec., No.* 122, 38*th Cong.*, 1*st Sess.*, 1864.

3433. NAYLOR, Charles.   Speech on the Bill imposing additional Duties, as depositaries, in certain cases, on Public Officers. House of Representatives of United States, October 13, 1837.

8vo. pp. 31.   Philadelphia : *King & Baird*, 1862.

3434. Nebraska.   Proceedings of a Public Meeting of the Citizens of Providence, March 7, 1854, to protest against Slavery in Nebraska; with the Addresses of the Speakers.

8vo. pp. 32.   Providence : *Knowles, Anthony & Co.*, 1854.

3435. Nebraska. A Poem.   Personal and Political.

12mo. pp. 42.   Boston: *J. P. Jewett & Co.*, 1854.

3436. Needle Pickets of the city of Quincy, Illinois.   Constitution and By-Laws of; together with a Report of their Proceedings from May 31, 1861, to May 31, 1862.

8vo. pp. 16.   Quincy : (Illinois) *Whig Press*, 1862.

3437. —— Second Annual Report of, for the year 1863.

8vo. pp. 16.   Quincy : (Illinois) *For the society*, 1863.

3438. —— Third Annual Report of, for 1864.   pp. 16.

3439. —— Fourth Annual Report of, for 1865.   pp. 16.

> The object of the "Needle Pickets" was similar to that of the Sanitary Commission; to furnish supplies of clothing, bedding and hospital stores; also, to aid the families of soldiers.

3440. Negro.   What shall we do with the Negro ?   A Tract for the Times.   By Caius Urbanus, of St. Louis, Missouri.

8vo. pp. 36.   St. Louis : *George J. Jones*, 1862.

3441. —— The Ancient Story of the Negro Race.   Mar. 28, '63.   p. 24.

3442. Negroes.   What shall be done with the Confiscated Negroes ? The Question discussed and a Policy proposed, in a Letter to Hon. Abraham Lincoln, Gen. Scott, W. H. Seward, Archbishop Hughes, Edward Everett and all other Patriots.   8vo. pp. 15.

3443. Negro.   The 'Negro Pew;' being an Inquiry concerning the propriety of Distinction in the House of God, on account of color.

12mo. pp. 108.   Boston: *Isaac Knapp*, 1837.

3444. NEGROES AND RELIGION. The Episcopal Church at the South. Memorial to the General Convention of the Protestant Episcopal Church in the United States of America. pp. 4.

3445. NEGRO SOLDIERS, Washington and Jackson on. General Banks on the Bravery of Negro Troops. Poem. The Second Louisiana. By George H. Boker. pp. 15. Philadelphia.

3446. —— General Washington and General Jackson on. 8vo. pp. 8. PHILADELPHIA: *H. Carey Baird,* 1863. NEGROES. See also *Colored Men, Freedmen, and Slavery.*

3447. NELSON, Hon. THOMAS A. R., of Tennessee. Speech on the Disturbed Condition of the Country. 8vo. pp. 16. WASHINGTON: *H. Polkinhorn.*

3448. NESMITH, Hon. J. W., of Oregon. Speech on Reconstruction, in the Senate of the United States, January 18, 1866. pp. 14.

3449. NEUTRAL VESSELS AND MAILS. Correspondence respecting Instructions given to Naval Officers of the U. S. in regard to. Folio pp. 7. (*Parl. Papers, N. Am., No. 5,*) *London,* 1863.

3450. NEUTRAL RIGHTS AND DUTIES. Correspondence with Mr. Adams respecting. Folio pp. 6. (*Parl. Papers, N. America, No. 6,*) *London,* 1863.

3451. NEVILLE, Rev. EDMUND, DD. Rebellion and Witchcraft. A Thanksgiving Sermon preached in Trinity Ch., Newark, N. J. 8vo. pp. 16. NEWARK: (N. J.) 1861.

3452. NEWCOMB, SIMON. A Critical Examination of our Financial Policy during the Southern Rebellion. pp. 222. NEW YORK: *D. Appleton & Co.,* 1865.

3453. NEWELL, R. H. The Martyr President. (A Poem.) 8vo. pp. 43. NEW YORK: *Carleton,* 1865.

3453.* NEW ENGLAND LOYAL PUBLICATION SOCIETY.

The issues of this Society are in the form of Broadsides, many of which occupying four or five closely printed columns of a folio sheet, would make a pamphlet of from 12 to 16 octavo pages each. Their regular edition has numbered fifteen hundred copies, though, in some instances, it has been much greater. According to the Report of the Executive Committee of the Society, eight hundred and seventy-four copies of the publications are sent regularly to newspapers, some of which copy largely from the documents. The remainder of the edition are sent to Associations, individuals, American Ministers, Consuls and distinguished men abroad.

3454. —— Report of the Executive Committee of, May 1, 1865. 8vo. pp. 27. BOSTON: 1865.

39

3455. NEW ENGLAND SOLDIERS' RELIEF ASSOCIATION. Minutes of the Organization and Proceedings of.
8vo. pp. 62.   NEW YORK: *Root, Anthony & Co.,* 1862.

3456. —— Report of the Superintendent of, December, 1862.
12mo. pp. 18.   NEW YORK : *Francis & Loutrel,* 1862.

3467. NEWHALL, Rev. FALES HENRY. National Exaltation. The Duties of Christian Patriotism. A Discourse at Roxbury, January 4, 1861.
8vo. pp. 16.   BOSTON : *John M. Hewes,* 1861.

3468. NEWHALL, WALTER S., Captain 3d Reg. Penn. Cavalry. A Memoir.
8vo. pp. 140.   PHILADELPHIA : *For the Sanitary Com.,* 1864.

3469. NEW JERSEY. Duties of American Citizens. Position of New Jersey. Signed, by order of the Committee, B. Aycrigg. Passaic, New Jersey, May 3, 1865.
8vo. pp. 16.   NEW YORK : *E. O. Jenkins,* 1865.

3470. —— Message of Governor Olden, January 10, 1861.

3471. —— Inaugural Address of Joel Parker, as Governor of the State of New Jersey. January 20, 1863.
8vo. pp. 22.   TRENTON: (New Jersey) 1863.

3472. —— Report of the Adjutant General for 1863. pp. 32.

3478. THE NEW GOSPEL of PEACE, according to St. Benjamin.
12mo. pp. 47.   NEW YORK: *S. Toucey,* 1864.

3479. —— according to Abraham. Revelations ; a Companion to.
12mo. pp. 36.   NEW YORK: *Feeks & Bancker,* 1863.

3481. NEWMAN, F. W. Character of the Southern States of America. Letter to a Friend who joined the Southern Independence Association.
8vo. pp. 14.   MANCHESTER: (Eng.) *Union and Eman. So.,* '63.

3482. NEWSPAPERS AND PERIODICALS.
Albany Army Letter. Albany, New York, 1863. Folio.
Army and Navy Gazette. New York. Folio.
Army and Navy Journal. New York. Folio.
Army and Navy Official Gazette. Washington. 4to.
The Bugle Call. Chicago, Illinois. 4to.
The Boatswain's Whistle. Boston. 4to.
The Campaign for the Union. Boston, 1864. 4to.
The Cartridge Box. U. S. Army General Hospital, York, Penn. Folio.
The Connecticut War Record. New Haven, Connecticut. 4to.

The Daily Campaign Record. Memphis, Tennessee. 4to.
The Freedmen's Bulletin. Chicago, Illinois. 8vo.
The Freedmen's Record. New York, monthly. 8vo.
The Iron Platform. New York. 4to.
The Loyal National Union Journal. Brownsville, Texas. Folio.
Minnesota, (The First.) Berryville, Virginia, 1862. 4to.
National Freedman. Boston. 8vo.
Our Camp Journal. 26th Michigan Infantry. 4to.
Our Daily Fare. Philadelphia. 4to.
Spirit of the Fair. New York. 4to.
The Roll Call. Washington, D. C. 4to.
The Third Rhode Island Cavalry. New Orleans. 4to.
The Soldier's Casket. Philadelphia. 8vo.
The Southern Spy. Baltimore.
The Union League Gazette. Philadelphia. Folio.
The Volunteer. New York. 8vo.
The War Eagle. Columbus, Kentucky. 8vo.
West Philadelphia Hospital Register. Philadelphia. 4to.

3483. NEW ORLEANS PICAYUNE. Extracts from the editorial columns
of. Read and circulate.
8vo. pp. 23. NEW YORK: *James Clarke*, 1861.

3484. THE NEW YANKEE DOODLE, by Dan (not Bev.) Tucker. Dedicated to the United States Volunteers.
12mo. pp. 23. WASHINGTON: *O. H. Morrison*, 1861.

3485. NEW ORLEANS. Reports of the Naval Engagements on the Mississippi River, resulting in the capture of Forts Jackson and
St. Philip and the city of New Orleans.
8vo. pp. 107. WASHINGTON: *Government Printing Office*, '62.

3486. —— Reports of the Minority and Majority of the Financial
Commission of New Orleans, under Special Orders No. 69, issued
by General Banks, March 18, 1864.
8vo. pp. 21. With Tables. NEW ORLEANS: *Era Office*, 1864.

3487. —— City Celebration of the Anniversary of the National Independence at, July 4, 1864.
8vo. pp. 24. NEW ORLEANS: *Era Office*, 1864.

3488. NEWTON, Rev. RICHARD, DD. God's Marvellous Doings for
the Nation. A Sermon preached on Thanksgiving Day. Philadelphia, August 6, 1863.
8vo. pp. 16. PHILADELPHIA: *W. F. Murphy & Sons*, 1863.

3489. —— The English and American Rebellion compared and contrasted. An Address delivered at the University of Pennsylvania, December 4, 1865.

8vo. pp. 37. PHILADELPHIA: *King & Baird,* 1866.

3490. NEW YORK. Official Report of the Great Union Meeting, held in the city of New York, December 19, 1859.

8vo. pp. 176. NEW YORK: *Davies & Kent,* 1859.

3491. —— Report of the Select Committee on the Petition to prevent Slave Hunting in the State of New York, Feb. 11, 1860. p. 11.

3492. —— Report of the Board of State Officers on " An Act to authorize the embodying and equipment of Volunteer Militia," etc. With the Minutes of their meetings, April 16 to December 16, 1861. pp. 214.

3493. —— Annual Report of the Judge Advocate General, December 13, 1861. 8vo. pp. 11.

3494. —— Message of Governor Morgan, January 7, 1862.

8vo. pp. 74. ALBANY: *C. Benthuysen,* 1862.

3495. —— Report of the Surgeon General, Dec. 31, 1861. pp. 56.

3496. —— Annual Report of the Adjutant General for the year 1861.

8vo. pp. 735. ALBANY: *C. Van Benthuysen,* 1862.

3497. —— The Militia Law. Passed April 23, 1862.

8vo. pp. 110. ALBANY: *Weed, Parsons & Co.,* 1862.

3498. —— Annual Report of the Adjutant General for the year 1862.

8vo. pp. 1181. ALBANY: *Comstock & Cassidy,* 1863.

3499. —— Annual Report of the Surgeon General for 1862.

8vo. pp. 72. ALBANY: *Comstock & Cassidy,* 1863.

3500. —— The Conscription Act vindicated, by Thomas Hillhouse, late Adjutant General.

8vo. pp. 27. ALBANY: *Weed, Parsons & Co.,* 1863.

3501. —— Annual Report of the Quartermaster Gen., Dec. 31, 1862.

8vo. pp. 188. ALBANY: *Comstock & Cassidy,* 1863.

3502. —— Annual Report of the Paymaster Gen, Dec. 31, '62. p. 28,

3503. —— Report of Samuel B. Ruggles, Commissioner in respect to the enlargement of the Canals for National Purposes.

8vo. pp. 105. ALBANY: *Comstock & Cassidy,* 1863.

3504. —— Annual Message of Gov. Seymour, January 7, 1863.

8vo. pp. 48. ALBANY: *Comstock & Cassidy,* 1863.

3505. —— Presentation of Regimental Colors to the Legislature.

8vo. pp. 52.

3506. NEW YORK. Report of the Adjutant General for the year 1863. 2 vols. 8vo. ALBANY: *Comstock & Cassidy*, 1864.

3507. —— Report of the Commissary General for 1863. 8vo. pp. 123. ALBANY: *Comstock & Cassidy*, 1864.

3508. —— Proceedings attending the Presentation of Regimental Colors to the Legislature, April 20, 1864. 8vo. pp. 82. ALBANY: *Van Benthuysen*, 1864.

3509. —— Report of the Judge Advocate General, upon the Errors and Frauds of the Enrollment. 8vo. pp. 27. ALBANY: *Comstock & Cassidy*, 1863.

3510. —— First Annual Report of (L. L. Doty) Chief of the Bureau of Military Statistics, January 26, 1864. 8vo. pp. 212. ALBANY: *Comstock & Cassidy*, 1864.

3511. —— Report of the Surgeon General. pp. 28.

3512. —— Annual Report of the Quartermaster General, December 31, 1863. 8vo. pp. 106.

3513. —— Communication from Major General Dix, relative to the Arrest of Hawley D. Clapp, (charged with frauds in bounties to recruits) April 11, 1864. pp. 22.

3514. —— An. Report of the Inspector Gen., Jan. 5, '64. 8vo. pp. 140.

3515. —— Roster of the National Guard of the State. 8vo. pp. 225. *Senate Document, No.* 50, 1864.

3516. —— Digest of Taxation. Report on the State Assessment Laws, by the Joint Select Committee, 1862. 8vo. pp. 272. ALBANY: *Weed, Parsons & Co.*, 1863.

3517. —— Report of the Adjutant General, January 12, 1865. 2 vols. Vol. 1, pp. 461. ALBANY: *C. Van Benthuysen*, 1865.

3518. —— Presentation of Flags of New York Volunteer Regiments, and other organizations, to Governor Fenton, July 4, 1865. Royal 8vo. pp. 249. ALBANY: *Weed, Parsons & Co.*, 1865.

3519. NEW YORK STATE VOLUNTEERS. A Record of the Commissioned Officers, Non-Commissioned Officers and Privates of the Regiments organized in the State of New York, and called into the service of the U. S., to assist in suppressing the Rebellion. 3 vols. 4to. ALBANY: *Comstock & Cassidy*, 1864.

3520. NEW YORK. Proceedings of an Union Meeting, held in New York, (December 15, 1860.) An Appeal to the South. 8vo. pp. 36. NEW YORK: *John H. Duyckinck*, 1860.

3521. NEW YORK. The Life of Slavery, or the Life of the Nation? Mass Meeting of the Citizens of New York, at the Cooper Institute, March 6, 1862. 4to. pp. 11.

3522. —— Proceeding at the Mass Meeting in Union Square, 15th of July, 1862.

3523. —— Great Union War Ratification Meeting, at the Cooper Institute, October 8, 1862. One Country! One Constitution! One Destiny. Speeches of W. Curtis Noyes, D. S. Dickinson and Lyman Tremaine. 8vo. pp. 19.

3523.* —— Loyal Meeting of the People to support the Government, prosecute the War, and maintain the Union ; at the Cooper Institute, March 6, 1863.
8vo. pp. 52.   NEW YORK : *G. F. Nesbitt & Co.*, 1863.

3524. —— The same. Another edition. pp. 80. *Nesbitt & Co.*

2525. NEW YORK RIOTS. Report of the Merchant's Committee for the relief of Colored People suffering from the Riots in the city. July, 1863.
8vo. pp. 48.   NEW YORK : *George A. Whitehorne*, 1863.

3526. NEW YORK. To the Legislature of the People. pp. 18. (no date.)

3527. NEW YORK MEDICAL ASSOCIATION for the supply of Lint, Bandages, etc., to the United States Army. July 25, 1861.
8vo. pp. 32.   NEW YORK : *By the Association*, 1861.

3528. NEW YORK Resolutions of the Chamber of Commerce, on National Affairs. 1862. pp. 4.

3529. NEW "REIGN OF TERROR," in the Slaveholding States, for 1859–60.
12mo. pp. 144.   NEW YORK : *Am. Anti-Slavery Society*, 1860.

3530. THE NIAGARA SHIP CANAL ; its Military and Commercial Necessity.
8vo. pp. 15.   With 2 Maps.   NEW YORK : 1863.

3531. —— Proposition. Speech of A. X. Parker of St. Lawrence. In Assembly, 1864. 8vo. pp. 7.

3532. —— Report of the Committee on Commerce and Navigation, (of the Senate of the State of New York) on the Bill to Incorporate. pp. 16.

3533. NIAGARA. Engineers' Opinion of the Marine Railway around the Falls of Niagara.
8vo. pp. 13–34.   NEW YORK : *W. C. Bryant & Co.*, 1865.

3534. NIAGARA. Argument in favor of a Marine Railway around the Falls of Niagara, by Charles C. Woodman. February, 1865. pp. 19.

3535. NIAGARA STEAMER, chartered for the Banks Expedition in 1862. Letter of the Secretary of War, with information relative thereto. *Senate Executive Doc. No.* 12, *38th Cong., 1st Sess.,* 1864. pp. 8.

3536. NIBLACK, Hon. W. E. State of the Union. Speech delivered in the House of Representatives, January 31, 1861. 8vo. pp. 7.

3537. NICCOLLS, Rev. S. J. Thanksgiving. A Sermon preached in Chambersburg, November 28, 1861.
8vo. pp. 8. CHAMBERSBURG: (Pa.) *Repository Office,* 1861.

3538. NICHOLAS, S. S. Martial Law. Part of a Pamphlet first published in 1842, over the Signature of a Kentuckian.
8vo. pp. 31. PHILADELPHIA: *John Campbell,* 1862.

3539. —— A Review of the Argument of President Lincoln and Attorney General Bates, in favor of Presidential Power to suspend the Privilege of the Writ of Habeas Corpus.
8vo. pp. 38. LOUISVILLE: (Ky.) *Bradbury & Gilbert,* 1861.

3540. —— Martial Law. Part of a Pamphlet published in 1842.
8vo. pp. 16. LOUISVILLE: (Ky.) *Bradbury & Gilbert,* 1861.

3541. —— Habeas Corpus. The Law of War and Confiscation.
8vo. pp. 29. LOUISVILLE: *Bradbury & Gilbert,* 1862.

3542. —— Habeas Corpus. A Response to Mr. Binney.
8vo. pp. 20. LOUISVILLE: *Bradbury & Gilbert,* 1862.

3543. —— Emancipation,—White and Black. 8vo. pp. 13.

3544. NICHOLS, G. W. The Story of the Great March; from the Diary of a Staff Officer.
12mo. pp. 394. NEW YORK: *Harper & Brothers,* 1865.

3545. NILES, Rev. H. E. Address on the occasion of President Lincoln's Obsequies, in York, Penn., April 19, 1865.
8vo. pp. 8. YORK: (Pa.) *Hiram Young,* 1865.

3546. NILES, Rev. WILLIAM A. Our Country's Peril and Hope. A Sermon delivered January 4, 1861, at Corning, N. Y.
8vo. pp. 30. CORNING: (N. Y.) *E. E. Robinson,* 1861.

3547. NINET, J. La Question du Cotton en Angleterre depuis la crise Américaine. *Revue de Deux Mondes, March,* 1861.

3548. NINTH ARMY CORPS. Report of the Committee to Recruit. February to August, 1864.
8vo. pp. 16. NEW YORK: *J. W. Amerman,* 1864.

3549. NIXON, John T.　The Rebellion; its origin, and the means of suppressing it.　Speech in House of Reps., April 11, 1862.　p. 8.

3550. NOBLE, Rev. Frederick A.　Blood, the Price of Redemption. A Discourse delivered in the House of Hope, Nov. 22, 1862. 8vo. pp. 21.　　　　　　　St. Paul: *Press Company*, 1862.

3551. NOBLE, Rev. Mason.　Sermon delivered in the United States Naval Academy, on the day of the Funeral of the late President. 8vo. pp. 16.　　　　　　　Newport: *Geo. T. Hammond*, 1865.

3552. NOBLE, Warren P.　Speech on the Causes of the Rebellion. In House of Representatives, June 6, 1862.　pp. 8.

3553. NOEL, Baptist Wriothesley.　Rebellion in America. Post 8vo. pp. xix, 494.　　　　London: *Nisbet & Co.*, 1863.

3554. No Failure for the North.　From the "Atlantic Monthly." 8vo. pp. 23.　　　　*Loyal Publication Society No.* 11, 1863.

3555. No Party Now, but all for our Country. 8vo. pp. 12.　　　　Philadelphia: *Crissy & Markley*, 1863.

3557. NORDHOFF, Charles.　Secession is Rebellion.　Rebellion cannot succeed.　The Union is indissoluble, except by consent of all the States.　An open Letter to the Rev. A. A. Lipscomb, of Alabama. 8vo. pp. 20.　　　　　New York: *Baker & Godwin*, 1860.

3558. —— The Freedmen of South Carolina; some account of their appearance, character, condition and customs. Royal 8vo. pp. 27.　　　　New York: *C. T. Evans*, 1863.

3559. —— America for Free Working Men.　How Slavery injures the Free Working Man.　The Slave-Labor System and Free Working Man's worst Enemy. 8vo. pp. 39.　　　　New York: *Harper & Brothers*, 1865.

3560. —— The same.　pp. 39.　(Loyal Publication Society No. 80.)

3561. NORFOLK.　Address of the Merchants of the City of Norfolk, Virginia, to General Naglee; and his Reply.　October, 1863. pp. 8.　Philadelphia.

3562. North American Review for 1861.
Cotton, and the Cotton Trade.　E. Haskett Derby.　January.
Slavery; its Origin and its Remedy.　By the Editor.　April.
The Right of Secession.　July.
Habeas Corpus and Martial Law.　Joel Parker.　October.

3563. North American Review for 1862.
Loyalty.　By the Editor.　January.

The Domestic and Foreign Relations of the United States. Joel Parker. Jan.
English and French Views of the American Rebellion. April.
Constitutional Law. April.
International Law. Joel Parker. July.
The Better American Opinion. D. Holland. R. T. S. Lowell. July.
Count de Gasparin. J. P. Thompson. October.
The Character of the Rebellion, and the Conduct of the War. Joel Parker.
October.
Among the Pines. C. S. Henry. October.

3564. NORTH AMERICAN REVIEW for 1863.
Cairnes on the Slave Power. J. Q. Bittinger. April.
The Trial of the Constitution. Judge Farrar. October.
Hygeine, with reference to the Military Service. D. W. Cheever. October.

3565. NORTH AMERICAN REVIEW for 1864.
The Bible and Slavery. Sidney G. Fisher. January.
The Ambulance System. Col. F. W. Palfrey. January.
Immorality in Politics. Charles Eliot Norton. January.
The Sanitary Commission. January.
The President's Policy. James Russell Lowell. January.
The Sanitary Commission. Elisha Harris, M. D. April.
The Navy of the United States. Admiral C. H. Davis. April.
The Future Supply of Cotton. Edward Atkinson. April.
Loyal Work in Missouri. William G. Eliot, DD. April.
Gen. McClellan's Report. James Russell Lowell. April.
The Next General Election. James Russell Lowell. October.
The Constitution and its Defects. July.
The Navy of the United States. July.
Our Soldiers. July.
A National Currency. July.
The Rebellion; its Causes and Consequences. July.

3566. NORTH AMERICAN REVIEW for 1865.
Abraham Lincoln. Charles Eliot Norton. January.
The National Resources. L. Blodgett. January.
America and England. Charles Eliot Norton. April.
Free Missouri. Rev. T. M. Post, DD. April.
Reconstruction. James Russell Lowell. April.
The Freedmen at Port Royal. W. C. Gannett. July.
The Democratic View of Democracy. E. L. Godkin. July.
Duties on Exports. Sidney G. Fisher. July.

3567. NORTH BRITISH REVIEW. The American Conflict. Nov., '62.

3568. —— The Disintegration of Empires. May, 1863.

3569. —— The Cotton Famine. August, 1864.

3570. THE NORTH AND THE SOUTH Misrepresented and misjudged ; or a Candid View of our present Difficulties and Danger, and their Causes and Remedy.
8vo. pp. 48. PHILADELPHIA : *For the author*, 1861.
40

3571. NORTHRUP-KELLEY DEBATE. The Joint Debates between George Northrup, Esq., Democratic, and Hon. Wm. D. Kelley, Republican, Nominees for Congress in the Fourth Congressional District of Pennsylvania. (First Debate.)
8vo. pp. 12. PHILADELPHIA: *J. Campbell*, 1864.

3572. —— Reply of Hon. William D. Kelley to George Northrop, Esq., Philadelphia, September 23, 1865. pp. 8.

3573. —— The Second Joint Debate between George Northrop, Esq., and Hon. William D. Kelley, September 26, 1864. pp. 12.

3574. —— Speech of W. D. Kelley, September 26, 1864.

3575. —— The Third Joint Debate between George Northrop, Esq., and Hon. William D. Kelley. September 28, 1864. pp. 12.

3576. —— Speech of W. D. Kelley, September 28, 1864. pp. 12.

3577. —— Fourth Joint Debate. Mr. Northrup's Reply. Sept. 29, '64.

3578. —— Speech of Hon. William D. Kelley, at Spring Garden Institute, September 29, 1864. 8vo. pp. 11.

3579. —— Fifth Joint Debate between, October 3, 1864. Opening of George Northrup. pp. 16.

3580. —— Speech of Hon. Wm. D. Kelley, October 3, 1864.

3581. —— Sixth Joint Debate, Oct. 4, 1864. Reply of George Northrup. pp. 13.

3582. —— Speech of Hon. Wm. D. Kelley, October 4, 1864. pp. 12.

3583. —— Seventh Joint Debate, Oct. 6, 1864. Opening of George Northrup, Esq. pp. 16.

3584. —— Reply of Hon. Wm. D. Kelley, Oct. 6, 1864. pp. 11.

3585. —— Eighth Joint Debate. Mr. Northrup's Reply, October 7, 1864. pp. 12.

3586. —— Closing Speech of Hon. Wm. D. Kelley, Oct. 7. '64. p. 11.

3587. —— NORTH AND SOUTH. By the White Republican of " Frazer's Magazine."
8vo. pp. 336. LONDON: *Chapman & Hall*, 1863.

3588. THE NORTH AND THE SOUTH. Slavery and the Union. Reprinted from the New York Tribune.
8vo. pp. 40. NEW YORK: *Tribune Office*, 1854.

3589. NORTHEND, W. D. Review of Goldwin Smith on Slavery. *American Monthly, January,* 1865.

3590. —— The Cause of our Strife, and the Remedy. Ibid. 1865.

3591. NORTHERN TRUE MEN, and Southern Traitors. Address and Resolutions of the Connecticut Soldiers. Extracts from Richmond Journals.
8vo. pp. 8. *Loyal Publication Society, No.* 30.

3592. NORTHWESTERN SANITARY COMMISSION, Report of, for the months of September, October, November and December, 1863.
8vo. pp. 33. CHICAGO: *Dunlop, Lowell & Spaulding,* 1865.

3593. NORTON, CHARLES ELIOT. The Soldier of the good Cause.
18mo. pp. 14. BOSTON: *American Unitarian Association,* '62.

3594. —— Immorality in Politics. *North American Review, Jan.* '64.

3595. —— Abraham Lincoln. Ibid. *January,* 1865.

3596. —— America and England. Ibid. *April,* 1865.

3597. NORTON, Rev. ROBERT. God's Discipline of Nations. A Sermon on the Death of President Lincoln, preached at St. Catherines, Canada West, April 23, 1865.
8vo. pp. 17. ST. CATHERINES: *Leavenworth,* 1865.

3598. NOTT, Col. CHARLES C. The Coming Contraband; a reason against the Emancipation Proclamation, not given by Mr. Justice Curtis.
8vo. pp. 21. NEW YORK: *G. P. Putnam,* 1862.

3599. —— Sketches of the War. A Series of Letters to the North Moore Street School, New York.
12mo. pp. 174. NEW YORK: *C. T. Evans,* 1863.

3600. NOTT, SAMUEL. Slavery, and the Remedy; or Principles and Suggestions for a Remedial Code.
8vo. pp. 118. BOSTON: *Crocker & Brewster,* 1856.

3601. —— The Present Crisis; with a Reply and Appeal to European Advisers.
8vo. pp. 43. BOSTON: *Crocker & Brewster,* 1860.

3602· NOYES, Capt. GEORGE F. Oration at the Celebration of the National Independence, by Doubleday's Brigade, at Camp opposite Fredericksburg, Virginia, July 4, 1862.
8vo. pp. 16. PHILADELPHIA: *Crissy & Markley,* 1862.

3603. —— The Bivouac and the Battle Field; or Campaign Sketches in Virginia and Maryland.
18mo. pp. 339. NEW YORK: *Harper & Brothers,* 1863.

3604. NOYES, GEORGE L. The Battle of Antietam. *Harpers' Magazine, August,* 1863.

OAKLEY, Rev. P. D.   The War; its Origin, Purpose, and our Duty respecting it.   A Sermon preached at Jamaica, L. I., July 1, '61.   8vo. pp. 23.   New York: *John A. Gray*, 1861.

3606. Objects of the Rebellion, and Effects of its success upon Free Laborers and Civilization.   By a Member of the Cincinnati Bar.
8vo. pp. 32.   Cincinnati: *Wrightson & Co.*, 1863.

3607. O'BRIEN, Fitz James.   A Soldiers Letter.   *Harpers' Magazine, March*, 1862.

3608. Observations on the Rev. Dr. Gannett's Sermon, entitled "Relation of the North to Slavery."
8vo. pp. 29.   Boston: *Redding & Company*, 1854.

3609. Occasional, Numbers 1 to 10.   A Series of Tracts under this title, published by the American Reform Tract and Book Society, Cincinnati, Ohio.
   No. 1. Our Country's greatest Danger, and true Deliverance. pp. 8.
      2. What are we fighting for? By James A. Thorne. pp. 8.
      3. Catechism for Free Working Men. By the Son of a Blacksmith. pp. 4.
      4. Not Careful, but Prayerful. pp. 4.
      5. Slavery in Rebellion. An Outlaw; How to deal with it. pp. 12.
      6. Christianity and War. By Rev. E. T. Robinson. pp. 16.
      7. Home Words for the Soldiers. pp. 4.
      8. Emancipation. By the Rev. A. L. Stone, Boston. pp. 12.
      9. The Captain of our Salvation. By Chaplain Horace James. pp. 8.
      10. The Church and the Country; being the Action of Ecclesiastical Bodies, on the State of the Country. pp. 20
      11. Mitchell, General O. M. Views for Freedom. pp. 4.

3610. O'CONNELL, Daniel, Upon American Slavery; with other Irish Testimonies.
12mo pp. 45.   New York: *Anti-Slavery Society*, 1860.

3611. O'CONNOR, J. D.   Speech in the Ohio Senate, February 28, 1863, on the Conduct of the Administration.   8vo. pp. 8.

3611.* O'FLANAGAN, John.   The Continuation of a Government Fraud.
8vo. pp. 20.   New York: 1862.

3612. Ohio.   Message of Governor Dennison, January 7, 1861. pp. 32.

3613. —— Report of the Quartermaster General for 1861. pp. 34.

3614. —— Message of Governor Dennison, January 6, 1862; with accompanying Documents. pp. 98.

3615. OHIO. Inaugural Message of Governor Tod, January 13, 1862.

3616. —— Report of the Commissary General for 1861. pp. 28.

3617. —— Report of the Adjutant General for 1861. pp. 98.

3618. —— Report of the Quartermaster General for 1861. pp. 34.

3619. —— Message of Governor Tod to the General Assembly, January 5, 1863; with accompanying Documents.
8vo. pp. 132.   COLUMBUS: *Richard Nevins,* 1863.

3620. —— Report of the Adjutant General for the year 1862.
8vo. pp. 140.   COLUMBUS: *Richard Nevins,* 1862.

3621. —— Report of the Quartermaster General for 1862.
8vo. pp. 68.   COLUMBUS: *Richard Nevins,* 1863.

3622. —— Inaugural Address of James D. Cox, Governor of Ohio, January 8, 1866. 8vo. pp. 10.

3623. —— Annual Message of John Brough, Governor, January 3, 1865; with accompanying Documents.
8vo. pp. 156.   COLUMBUS: *Richard Nevins,* 1865.

3624. —— Annual Report of the Adjutant General, for the year ending December 31, 1864.
8vo. pp. 287.   COLUMBUS: *Richard Nevins,* 1865.

3625. —— Report of Commissioners of Morgan Raid Claims.
8vo. pp. 453.   COLUMBUS: *Richard Nevins,* 1865.

3626. —— Report of the Quartermaster General, for 1864.
8vo. pp. 59.   COLUMBUS: *Richard Nevins,* 1865.

3627. —— Surgeon General's Report, November 5, 1864.

3628. OHIO ARMY REGISTER of Ohio Volunteers in the Service of the United States, from the Official Records.
8vo. pp. 74.   COLUMBUS: *Ohio State Journal,* 1862.

3629. —— The same for July, 1862. 8vo. pp. 85.

3630. OHIO BOYS IN DIXIE. The Adventures of twenty-two Scouts sent by Gen. Mitchell to destroy a Railroad; with a Narrative of their barbarous treatment by the Rebels, and Judge Holt's Report.
8vo. pp. 47.   NEW YORK: *Miller & Mathews,* 1863.

3631. THE OLD CONTINENTAL, and the New Greenback Dollar. p. 8.

3632. OLDHAM, Hon. W. S., of Texas. Speech on the Resolutions of the State of Texas, concerning Peace, Reconstruction and Independence. In the Confed. States Senate, Jan. 30, '65. pp. 13.

3633. OLDHAM, W. S.   Speech in the Confederate Senate, September 4, 1862, on the Conscript Law.   Richmond, 1862.

3634. —— Speech, on January 3, 1865, on Peace and Reconstruction.

3635. "OLD JACK" and his Foot-Cavalry; or a Virginia Boy's progress to renown.   A Story of the War in the Old Dominion.
12mo. pp. 300.   NEW YORK: *John Bradburn*, 1864.

3636. OLDS, Hon. EDSON B.   Arbitrary Arrests.   Speech for which he was arrested, and his Reception Speeches on his return from the Bastile.   8vo. pp. 48.

3637. OLMSTED, F. LAW.   A Journey in the Seaboard and Slave States, with Remarks on their Economy.
12mo. pp. xv, 723.   NEW YORK: *Dix & Edwards*, 1856.

3638. —— A Journey in the Back Country.
12mo. pp. 492.   NEW YORK: *Mason Brothers*, 1860.

3639. —— A Journey through Texas; or a Saddle Trip on the Southwestern Frontier.   With a Statistical Appendix.
12mo. pp. 516.   NEW YORK: *Mason Brothers*, 1860.

3640. —— The Cotton Kingdom.   A Traveller's Observations on Cotton and Slavery in the American Slave States.   Based upon former volumes of Journeys.
2 vols. 12mo.   Map.   NEW YORK: *Mason Brothers*, 1861.

3641. OPINIONS of the early Presidents, and the Fathers of the Republic, upon Slavery.   Including Washington, Adams, Jefferson, Monroe, Madison, J. Q. Adams, Jackson and others.
8vo. pp. 19.   *Loyal Publication Society, No.* 18, 1863.

3642. OPTIC, OLIVER.   The Young Lieutenant; or the Adventures of an Army Officer.   A Story of the Great Rebellion.
12mo. pp. 373.   BOSTON: *Lee & Shepard*, 1865.

3643. —— Fighting Joe; or the Fortunes of a Staff Officer.   A Sequel to the "Young Lieutenant."
12mo. pp.   BOSTON: *Lee & Shepard*, 1865.

3644. —— The Sailor Boy; or Jack Somers in the Navy.   A Story of the Great Rebellion.
12mo. pp. 336.   BOSTON: *Lee & Shepard*, 1865.

3645. —— The Yankee Middy; or the Adventures of a Naval Officer.   A Sequel to "the Sailor Boy."
12mo. pp.   BOSTON: *Lee & Shepard*, 1865.

3646. ORDNANCE. A Review of the Report of the Commission on Ordnance and Ordnance Stores; with Comments upon the present Administration of the War Department, by a Gun Manufacturer. 8vo. pp. 11.

3647. —— Report of the Chief of the Bureau of Ordnance, Navy Department. (H. A. Wise.) October 20, 1863. 8vo. pp. 23.   WASHINGTON: 1863.

3648. —— Report of the same, November, 1864. 8vo. pp. 40.   NEW YORK: *D. Van Nostrand*, 1865.

3649. —— Statement from the Bureau of Ordnance and Hydrography, relative to the Claim of Wm. W. Hubbell, for remuneration for the use of an explosive Shell, April, 1862. pp. 23.

3650. ORDNANCE DEPARTMENT. Report to the Navy Department, by Captain Dahlgren, Chief of Bureau. December 1, 1862. 8vo. pp. 16. WASHINGTON: *Government Printing Office*, 1862. ORDNANCE, see also, *Hubbell, Williams, Parrott, Hotchkiss.*

3651. O'REILLY, HENRY BROOKS. A Brief Memento of, Captain of the First Excelsior Regiment, who fell at the Battle of Williamsburg, May 5, 1862. pp. 7.

3652. O'REILLY, HENRY. Origin and Objects of the Slaveholders Conspiracy against Democratic Principles, illustrated in the Speeches of Col. A. J. Hamilton, in the Statements of Lorenzo Sherwood, and in the publications of the Democratic League. 8vo. pp. 22.

3653. —— First Organization of Colored Troops in the State of New York, to aid in suppressing the Slaveholders' Rebellion. Statements concerning the Origin, Difficulties and Success of the Movement. 8vo. pp. 24.   NEW YORK: *Baker & Godwin*, 1864.

3654. —— The Real Motives of the Rebellion. The Slaveholders' Conspiracy depicted by Southern Loyalists, in its Treason against Democratic Principles; showing the Contest of Slavery versus a Free Government. 8vo. pp. 16. Mr. O'Reilly has edited and published a number of valuable pamphlets relating to the rebellion, which do not bear his name.

3655. —— American Anthems, on the Triumph of Liberty and Union, on Slavery and Treason. Written for the Sumter Anniversary, April 14, 1865. pp. 4.

3656. Oreto. The Chace of the Rebel Steamer of War Oreto, J. N. Maffit, C. S. N., into the Bay of Mobile, by the U. S. Sloop Oneida, Commander, George Henry Preble, U. S. N., Sept. 4, 1862.
8vo. pp. 60.   Cambridge : *For private circulation,* 1862.

3657. ORR. Letter from Governor James L. Orr, of South Carolina, to the President of the United States, in reference to the Sea Island Lands, January 19, 1866. pp. 8.

3658. OSGOOD, Rev. Samuel. The People and the Government. *Harpers' Magazine, November,* 1862.

3658.* —— The Home and the Flag. Ibid. *April,* 1862.

3659. O. S. L. The Great Northern Conspiracy of the O. S. L. 8vo. pp. 15. No place or date.

3660. OTTMAN, Rev. S. God always Right, and against Wrong. A Fast Day Sermon, delivered January 4, 1861.
8vo. pp. 15.   Penn Yan: *S. C. Cleveland,* 1861.

3661. Our Military Experience ; and What it suggests.
8vo. pp. 24.   Baltimore: *Cushing & Baily,* 1863.

3662. Overthrow of the Ballot. History of the Election in Kentucky. August 3, 1862. Richmond, 1863. 8vo.

3663. OWEN, Robert Dale. Agent to purchase Arms for the State of Indiana. Report of September 4, 1865.
8vo. pp. 21.   Indianapolis : *Joseph J. Bingham,* 1863.

3664. —— The Claims to Service and Labor. *Atlan. Monthly, July,'63.*

3665. —— The Future of the Northwest; in connection with the Scheme of Reconstruction without New England. Addressed to the People of Indiana.
8vo. pp. 15.   *Loyal Publication Society No.* 1, 1863.

3666. —— The same. pp. 15. Philadelphia : *Crissy & Markley,* 1863.

3667. —— Emancipation is Peace.
8vo. pp. 7.   *Loyal Publication Society, No.* 22.

3668. —— The Policy of Emancipation ; in three Letters to the Secretary of War, the President of the U. S. and the Sec. of Treasury.
12mo. pp. 48.   Philadelphia : *J. B. Lippincott & Co.,* 1863.

3669. —— Conditions of Reconstruction; in a Letter to the Secretary of State, the Hon. Wm. H. Seward.
8vo. pp. 24.   *Loyal Publication Society, No.* 25, 1863.

3670. —— Letter from Robert Dale Owen, to the Hon. Salmon P. Chase. The Cost of Peace. November 10, 1862.

3671. OWEN, R. D. The Wrong of Slavery, the Right of Emancipation: and the Future of the African Race in the United States.
12mo. pp. 246. PHILADELPHIA: *J. B. Lippincott & Co.*, 1864.

PACHECO. Question de Mexico. Cartas de D. Jose Ramon Pacheco, al Ministro de Negocios Estrangeros de Napoleon III. M. Drouyn de Lhuys.
8vo. pp. 82. NEW YORK: *S. Hallett*, 1862.

3673. PADDOCK, Rev. BENJ. H. Our Cause, our Confidence, and our Consequent Duty. A Sermon preached May 12, 1861, before Co. A, 1st Regiment Michigan Volunteers. pp. 15.

3674. PADDOCK, Rev. WILBUR F. A Great Man Fallen. A Discourse on the Death of Abraham Lincoln. Delivered in Philadelphia, April 23, 1865.
8vo. pp. 24. PHILADELPHIA: *Sherman & Co.*, 1865.

3675. —— God's Presence and Purpose in War. A Discourse, in Philadelphia, November 26, 1863.
8vo. pp. 27. PHILADELPHIA: *C. Sherman, Son & Co.*, 1863.

3676. PAGE, DAVID COOK, DD. The Quadrennial Confederacy; or "A Haughty Spirit before a Fall." A Sermon preached on occasion of a Thanksgiving for National Victories.
8vo. pp. PITTSBURGH: *James M'Millan*, 1865.

3677. PAINE, LEVI L. Political Lessons of the Rebellion. A Sermon delivered at Farmington, Connecticut, April 1862.
8vo. pp. 19. FARMINGTON: *Samuel S. Cowles*, 1862.

3678. PAINTER, Rev. H. M. Brief Incidents in the War in Missouri; and of the Personal Experience of one who has suffered.
8vo. pp. 28. BOSTON: *Courier Press*, 1863.

3679. —— The Duty of the Southern Patriot and Christian in the Present Crisis. A Sermon preached in the First Presbyterian Church, Boonville, Missouri, January 4, 1861.
8vo. pp. 16. BOONVILLE: *Caldwell & Stahl*, 1861.

3680. PALFREY, Col. F. W. The Ambulance System. *North American Review, January,* 1864.

3681. PALMER, B. M., DD., and W. T. Leacock, DD., of New Orleans. The Rights of the South defended in the Pulpits.
8vo. pp. 16. MOBILE: *J. Y. Thompson*, 1860.

41

3682. PALMER, B. M., DD. The South; her Peril and her Duty. A Discourse delivered in New Orleans, November 29, 1860.
8vo. pp. 16.   NEW ORLEANS: *True Witness Office,* 1860.

3683. —— Slavery, a Divine Trust. The Duty of the South to preserve and perpetuate the Institution as it now exists.
8vo. pp. 20.   NEW YORK: *Geo. F. Nesbitt & Co.,* 1861.

3684. —— Discourse before the General Assembly of South Carolina, December 10, 1863. 8vo. Columbia, 1864.

3685. PALMER, Sir ROUNDELL, M. P. A Speech delivered in the House of Commons, in the Debate on the North American Blockade, March 7, 1862.
8vo. pp. 29.   LONDON: *James Ridgway,* 1862.

3685.* THE PALMETTO DICTIONARY, etc.
12mo. pp. 730.   RICHMOND: (Va.) *J. W. Randolph,* 1864.

3686. PAPER. Why the Duty on, should be removed. From the Journal of Commerce, and other Papers. (April, 1863.) pp. 19.

3687. PARKE, Rev. N. G. The Assassination of the President of the United States, overruled for the Good of our Country. A Discourse preached in Pittston, Penn., June 1, 1865.
8vo. pp. 20.   PITTSTON: (Pa.) *Gazette Office,* 1865.

3688. PARKER, Rev. HENRY E. Discourse, the day after the reception of the tidings of the Assassination of President Lincoln, preached in Concord, N. H., April 16, 1865.
8vo. pp. 15.   CONCORD: *McFarland & Jencks,* 1865.

3689. PARKER, Rev. HENRY W. The Despised Race. A Discourse preached in New Bedford, December 28, 1862.
8vo. pp. 15.   NEW BEDFORD: *Mercury Press,* 1863.

3690. PARKER, JOEL. Constitutional Law, with reference to the Present Condition of the United States.
8vo. pp. 35.   CAMBRIDGE: *Welch, Bigelow & Co.,* 1862.

3691. —— Non-Extension of Slavery, and Constitutional Representation. An Address before the Citizens of Cambridge, Oct. 1, '56.
8vo. pp. 92.   CAMBRIDGE: *James Munroe & Co.,* 1856.

3692. —— Personal Liberty Laws, (Statutes of Massachusetts) and Slavery in the Territories. (Case of Dred Scott.)
8vo. pp. 97.   BOSTON: *Wright & Potter,* 1861.

3693. PARKER, J. The Right of Secession. A Review of the Message of Jefferson Davis to the Congress of the Confederate States. 8vo. pp. 39. CAMBRIDGE: *Welch, Bigelow & Co.*, 1861.

3694. —— Habeas Corpus and Martial Law. A Review of the Opinion of Chief Justice Taney, in the case of John Merriman. Second edition. 8vo. pp. 55, PHILADELPHIA: *John Campbell*, 1862.

3695. —— The same. pp. 58. Cambridge: *Welch, Bigelow & Co.*, '61.

3696. —— The same. *North American Review, October*, 1861.

3697. —— International Law. Ibid. *July*, 1862.

3698. —— The Character of the Rebellion, and the Conduct of the War. Ibid. *October*, 1862.

3699. —— International Law. Case of the Trent. Capture and Surrender of Mason and Slidell. 8vo. pp. 66. CAMBRIDGE: *Welch, Bigelow & Co.*, 1862.

3700. —— The Domestic and Foreign Relations of the United States. 8vo. pp. 74. CAMBRIDGE: *Welch, Bigelow & Co.*, 1862.

3701. —— The same. *North American Review, January*, 1862.

3702. —— A Letter to the People of Massachusetts. 8vo. pp. 12. CAMBRIDGE: *H. O. Houghton*, 1862.

3703. —— Constitutional Law, and Unconstitutional Divinity. Letters to Henry M. Dexter and Rev. Leonard Bacon. 8vo. pp. 63. CAMBRIDGE: *H. O. Houghton*, 1863.

3704. —— The War Powers of Congress, and of the President. An Address delivered at Salem, March 13, 1863. 8vo. pp. 60. CAMBRIDGE: *H. O. Houghton*, 1863.

3705. —— The Character of the Rebellion, and the Conduct of the War. 8vo. pp. 42. CAMBRIDGE: *Welch, Bigelow & Co.*, 1862.

3706. PARKER, Rev. JOSEPH. American War and American Slavery. A Speech. 8vo. pp. 8. MANCHESTER: *Union and Emanc. Society*, 1863.

3707. PARKER, THEODORE. A Letter to the People of the United States, touching the matter of Slavery. 12mo. pp. 120. BOSTON: *James Munroe & Co.*, 1848.

3708. —— The Boston Kidnapping. A Discourse to commemorate the Rendition of Thomas Simms, delivered before the Committee of Vigilance, Boston, April 12, 1852. 8vo. pp. 72. BOSTON: *Crosby, Nichols & Co.*, 1852.

3709. PARKER, T. The Nebraska Question. Some Thoughts on the New Assault upon Freedom in America, and the general State of the Country in relation thereto.
8vo. pp. 72. BOSTON: *B. B. Mussey & Co.*, 1854.

3710. —— The New Crime against Humanity. A Sermon preached in Music Hall, Boston, June 4, 1854.
8vo. pp. 76. BOSTON: *B. B. Mussey & Co.*, 1854.

3711. —— The Trial of Theodore Parker, for the "Misdemeanor" of a Speech in Faneuil Hall, against Kidnapping; before the Circuit Court of the U. S., at Boston, April 3, '55. With his Defence.
8vo. pp. xx and 221. BOSTON: 1855.

3712. PARMENTER, Rev. FREDERICK A. God's Leadership of our Nation. A Discourse delivered Nov. 24, 1864, in Elizabeth, N. J.
8vo. pp. 15. PROVIDENCE: *R. Manning*, 1864.

3713. PARR's Improvement in Monitor and Armor-Plated Vessels. Patented October 25, 1864.
8vo. pp. 12. BOSTON: *Wright & Potter*, 1865.

3714. PARROTT GUNS, Ranges of, with Notes for Practice.
12mo. pp. 29. NEW YORK: *D. Van Nostrand*, 1863.

3715. PARROTT, R. P. Facts as to Hooped Guns. pp. 12.

3716. PARSONS, THEOPHILUS. Slavery; its Origin, Influence and Destiny.
12mo. pp. 36. BOSTON: *Wm. Carter & Brother*, 1863.

3717. —— The Constitution; its Origin, Function and Authority. A Lecture, Introductory to the subject of Constitutional Law, delivered at Harvard University, March 7, 1861.
8vo. pp. 30. BOSTON: *Little, Brown & Co.*, 1861.

3718. LE PARTI REPUBLICAIN, ses Doctrines et ses Hommes. Aux Français.
8vo. pp. 24. NEW YORK: *Club Republicain Francais*, 1860.

3719. PARTON, JAMES. General Butler in New Orleans. Being a History of the Administration of the Department of the Gulf in 1862. With an account of the Capture of New Orleans.
12mo. pp. 661. NEW YORK: *Mason Brothers*, 1864,

3720. —— The same work in German.
8vo. pp. 368. NEW YORK: *Mason Brothers*, 1864.

3721. PARTRIDGE, Rev. ALFRED. The Memory of the Just. A

Memorial of the Hon. William Jay, who died October 4, 1858. Preached in Bedford, N. Y., September 18, 1859.

8vo. pp. 20. NEW YORK: *R. Lockwood & Sons*, 1860.

3722. PARVIN, Rev. R. J. Soldier-Life and Every-Day Battles. With Biographical Illustrations, Anecdotes, etc.

18mo. pp. 107. *Evangelical Knowledge Society, N. Y.*, 1863.

3723. PASTORAL LETTER of the Synod of Michigan. 8vo. pp. 11. 1862.

3724. PASTORAL LETTER from the Bishops of the Protestant Episcopal Church, to the Clergy and Laity in the Confederate States. Delivered before the Gen. Council in Augusta, Ga., Nov. 22, 1862. Augusta, Georgia, *Chronicle Press*, 1862.

3725. —— The same. pp. 4. New York: *Rebellion Record.*

3726. —— The same. pp. 16. (No imprint.) 1863.

3727. —— The same. pp. 15. BALTIMORE: *W. M. Innis*, 1863.

3728. PATENT OFFICE FAIR. Proceedings at the Opening of, under the Auspices of the Ladies' Relief Association, District of Columbia, February 22, 1864.

8vo. pp. 30. WASHINGTON ; *Printed for the Fair*, 1864.

3729. PATRIOTISM, IN POETRY AND PROSE ; Being Selected Passages from Lectures and Patriotic Readings, by James E. Murdock. Also, Poems by T. B. Read, George H. Boker and others, commemorative of the Gallant Deeds of our Noble Defenders.

12mo. pp. 172. PHILADELPHIA : *J. B. Lippincott & Co.*, 1865.

3730. PATTERSON, JOHN STAHL. American Destiny. *Continental Monthly, January and February*, 1863.

3731. —— The Issues of the War. Ibid. *March*, 1864.

3732. PATTERSON, Hon. JAMES W. Memorial Address on the Life and Character of Abraham Lincoln, delivered at Concord, New Hampshire, June 1, 1865, at the request of the State Authorities.

8vo. pp. 24. CONCORD ; (N. H.) *Cogswell & Sturtevant*, 1865.

3733. PATTERSON, ROBERT, Maj. General. A Narrative of the Campaign in the Valley of the Shenandoah, in 1861.

8vo. pp. 128. Plan. PHILADELPHIA : *Sherman & Co.*, 1865.

3734. —— The same. 4to. 106 copies printed. *Campbell*, 1865.

3735. PATTON, Rev. WILLIAM. Correspondence between, and the Secretaries of the Evangelical Alliance, on the American War. From the *New Englander*, *April*, 1864.

3736. PAULDING, J. K.   Slavery in the United States.
        18mo. pp. 312.   NEW YORK: *Harper & Brothers*, 1836.
3737. ——— State Sovereignty, and the Doctrine of Coercion, by the
        Hon. Wm. D. Porter ; together with a Letter from J. R. Pauld-
        ing, former Sec. of Navy· The Right to secede by " States."
        8vo. pp. 36.   CHARLESTON : *Evans & Cogswell,* 1860.
3738. PAULINE, the Female Spy.
        18mo. pp. 104.   NEW YORK: *T. R. Dawley,* 1865.
3739. PAXTON, Rev. Wm. W.   The Nation's Gratitude and Hope.
        A Sermon preached in Pittsburgh, Penn., November 27, 1862.
        Thanksgiving day.
        8vo. pp. 38.   PITTSBURGH: *W. G. Johnston & Co.,* 1862.
3740. PAYNE, ABRAHAM.   Remarks [connected with the Political
        Contest] at Central Falls, Rhode Island, November 1, 1864.
        12mo. pp. 16.   PROVIDENCE: *S. S. Rider, & Bro.,* 1864.
3741. PAYNE, Rev. DANIEL A., Bishop of the African M. E. Church.
        Welcome to the Ransomed; or Duties of the Colored Inhabitants
        of the District of Columbia.
        8vo. pp. 16.   BALTIMORE : *Bull & Tuttle,* 1862.
3742. "PEACE, The Empire of Christ is."   N. York, Jan.,1862. p. 12.
3743. PEACE, System of Means in; or the Chief Instrumentalities em-
        ployed in the Cause of Peace. *American Peace Society.*   pp. 4·
3744. THE PEACE CAUSE, A Sketch of.   Ibid.   pp. 4.
3745. PEACE, to be enduring, must be Conquered.   pp. 7.   1864.
3746. "PEACE! PEACE!!"   "But there is no Peace."   Dated, New
        York, May 11, 1861.   8vo. pp. 31.
3747. PEACE.   The Programme of Peace.   By a Democrat of the Old
        School.
        8vo. pp. 22.   BOSTON ; *Ticknor & Fields,* 1862.
3748. THE PEACE CONVENTION, at Washington, and the Virginia
        Convention at Richmond.
        8vo. pp. 18.   NEW YORK: *Dodge & Grattan,* 1861.
3749. PEACE CONVENTION. Proceedings on the Death of J. C. Wright,
        one of the Commissioners.   February 14, 1861.
        8vo. pp. 14.   WASHINGTON: *R. A. Waters,* 1861.
3750. ——— Proceedings of, held in the City of N. York, June 3, 1863,
        Speeches, Addresses, Resolutions and Letters from Leading Men.
        8vo. pp. 63.

3751. PEACE COMMISSIONERS. Message from the President of the U. S., with Information relative to a Conference held at Hampton Roads, with Messrs. A. H. Stephens, R. M. T. Hunter and J. A. Campbell. p. 10, *Con. Doc.*, *39th Cong.*, *2d Ses.*, *Ex. Doc.*, *No.* 59.

3752. PEARSON, EMILY C. Ruth's Sacrifice; or Life on the Rappahannock.
12mo. pp. iv, 259.   BOSTON: *Graves & Young*, 1863.

3753. PEARSON, HENRY B. Letters to Rufus Choate, on his Letter to the Whig Committee of the State of Maine, on the subject of Freedom vs. Slavery.
8vo. pp. 16.   PORTLAND: *Daley & Lufkin*, 1856.

3754. PECK, GEORGE, DD. Our Country; its Trials and its Triumphs. A Series of Discourses suggested by the Varying Events of the War for the Union.
12mo. pp. 300.   NEW YORK: *Carlton & Porter*, 1865.

3755. PECK, J. G. R. Under Fire at Charleston. *Harpers' Magazine, August,* 1865.

3756. PELL, ALFRED. Forward and Backward.
8vo. pp. 12.   NEW YORK: *James Miller*, 1863.

3757. PELLETAN, EUGENE. An Address to King Cotton.
8vo. pp. 19.   *Loyal Publication Society, No.* 12, 1863.

3758. —— The same. Translated by Leander Starr.
8vo. pp. 19.   NEW YORK: *H. de Mareil*, 1863.

3759. —— Addresse au Roi Coton. NEW York: *H. de Mareil*, 1863.

3760. PENDLETON, Hon. GEORGE H. Speech on the Enlistment of Negro Soldiers, delivered in the H. of Rep., Jan. 31, '63. p. 8.

3761. —— Power of the President to Suspend the Privilege of Habeas Corpus. Speech in House of Reps., Dec. 10, 1861. pp. 8.

3762. —— The Resolution to expel Mr. Long of Ohio. Speech in House of Representatives, April 11, 1864. 8vo. pp. 8.

3763. —— Speech [on proposed Amendment to the Constitution] delivered in the House of Reps., June 15, 1864. pp. 8.

3764. PENNIMAN, Major. The Tanner-Boy, and how he became Lieutenant General.
18mo. pp. 316.   BOSTON: *Roberts Brothers*, 1864.

3765. —— Winfield, the Lawyer's Son, and how he became a Major General.
12mo. pp. 323.   PHILADELPHIA: *Ashmead & Evans*, 1864.

3766. PENNSYLVANIA. Message of Gov. Packer, Jan., 1861. pp. 18.

3767. —— Message of Governor Curtin, January, 1862. pp. 14.

3768. —— Annual Report of the Adjutant General for 1862. pp. 36.

3769. —— Report of the Quartermaster General for 1862. pp. 26.

3770. —— Report of the Commissary General for 1862. pp. 7.

3771. —— Report of the Surgeon General for 1862. pp. 19.

3772. —— Message of Governor Curtin, January 7, 1863. pp. 14.

3773. —— Report of the Commissioner on Federal Relations relative to a Call for a National Convention. pp. 8.

3774. —— Annual Report of the Adjutant General for 1863. 8vo. pp. 675. HARRISBURG : *Singerly & Myers*, 1864.

3775. —— Report of the Commissary General for 1863. pp. 4.

3776. —— Report of the Surgeon General for 1863. pp. 67.

3777. —— Report of Col. R. Biddle Roberts, State Agent at Washington, December 31, 1863. pp. 6.

3778. —— Report on Military Claims for the year 1863. pp. 142.

3779. —— Proceedings of the Commissioners of the Soldiers' National Cemetery at Gettysburg, December, 1863. pp. 5.

3780. —— Special Message of Governor Curtin, August, 1864. p. 13.

3781. —— Report of the Superintendent of Soldiers' Orphans, made to the Governor for the year 1864. pp. 22.

3782. —— Annual Report of the Executive Office, Military Department, for the year ending December 1, 1864. 8vo. pp. 263. HARRISBURG: *Singerly & Myers*, 1865.

3783. —— Report of the Quartermaster General for 1864. pp. 177.

3784. —— Report of the Surgeon General for 1864. pp. 52.

3785. —— Report of State Agent at Washington, 1864. pp. 6.

3786. —— Report of Col. James Chamberlain, State Agent at the Southwest. pp. 7.

3787. —— Report of the Board of Military Claims, for 1864. p. 119.

3788. —— Report of the Select Committee relative to Frauds upon the Soldiers, the People and Government. pp. 44.

3789. —— Report of the Select Committee relative to the Soldiers' National Cemetery, Gettysburg, with accompanying Documents 8vo. pp. 212. HARRISBURG : *Singerly & Myers*, 1865.

3790. —— Message of Governor Curtin, January 4, 1865. pp. 16.

3791. —— Report of the Adjutant General for 1864. 8vo. pp. 269. HARRISBURG: *Singerly & Myers*, 1865.

3792. Pennsylvania. List of Soldiers (Prisoners of War) belonging to Pennsylvania Regiments, who died at the Military Prison at Andersonville, Ga., from Feb. 26, 1864, to Mar. 20, 1865. 4to. p. 24.

3793. —— Message of Governor Curtin, January 30, 1865. pp. 18.

3794. —— Address of the Democratic State Committee of, to the People. *Age Office*, 1863. pp. 13.

3795. —— Address of the Union State Central Committee of. pp. 15.

3796. Pennsylvania Reserves in the Peninsula. Gen. McCall's Official Reports for 1862. pp. 10.

3797. Pensions, Pay and Bounty Lands, A Compilation of. Together with full Instructions, Forms and Decisions.
8vo. pp. 96. Chicago : *Tribune Company*, 1862.

3798. Pensions. Instructions and Forms to be observed in applying for Army Pensions. Act of July 14, 1862. 8vo. pp. 14. 1863.

3799. Gen. PERHAM'S Platform. The most feasible Plan yet offered for suppressing the Rebellion. " God Bless Abraham Lincoln."
8vo. pp. 12. Boston : *A. Mudge & Son*, 1862.

3800. PERHAM, Sidney, of Maine. The Slaveholders' Rebellion and Modern Democracy. Speech in H. of Rep. May 3, '64. p. 8.

3801. PERRIN, Lavalette. The Claims of Cæsar. A Sermon preached in New Britain, May 19, 1861.
8vo. pp. 27. Hartford : *Case, Lockwood & Co.*, 1861.

3802. PERRY, Aaron F. Speech before the National Union Association, Cincinnati, September 20, 1864.
8vo. pp. 15. Cincinnati : *Caleb Clark*, 1864.

3803. —— Vallandigham ; Habeas Corpus; United States Circuit Court. 8vo. pp. 97 to 168.

3804. PERRY, N., of New Jersey· The Omissions and Commissions of the Administration. Speech in H. of Reps., Feb. 28, '63. p. 8.

3805. —— The Constitution and the Union. Let them together be maintained. Speech in the H. of Reps., March 6, 1862.

3806. —— Rebellious States. Spech in H. of Reps., May 3, '64. p. 8.

3807. Personal Liberty and Martial Law. A Review of some of the Pamphlets of the Day.
8vo. pp. 38. Philadelphia : *April*, 1862.

3808. PETERHOFF. Argument of E. Delafield Smith, U. S. Attor-

42

ney, addressed to the United States Court at New York, in the case of the Prize Steamer Peterhoff, July 10, 1863.

8vo. pp. 25. NEW YORK: *John W. Amerman*, 1863.

3809. PETERHOFF. The United States, et al., Libellants and Captors, vs. The Steamship Peterhoff. In Prize. Argument of Lorenzo Sherwood, Advocate for Almond & Redgate, Owners, Consignees and Agents of Claimants of.

8vo. pp. 42. NEW YORK: *Westcott & Co.*, 1863.

3810. PETERS, Rev. B. The Reëlection of President Lincoln. *Universalist Quarterly Review, January*, 1865.

3811. PETERSON, FRED'K A. Military Review of the Campaign in Virginia and Maryland, under Generals Fremont, Banks, McDowell, Franz Sigel, John Pope and others, in 1862.

8vo. pp. 55. NEW YORK: *Sinclair Toucey*, 1862.

3812. —— Part 2d of the same. pp. 69. Ibid. 1863.

3813. PETERSON, HENRY. Address on American Slavery, before the Junior Anti-Slavery Society of Philadelphia, July 4, 1838.

8vo. pp. 28. PHILADELPHIA: *Merrihew & Gunn*, 1838.

3814. PETTEE, ROBERT. Funeral Discourse on. See *McGiffert*.

3815. PEUGH, SAMUEL A. Vindication of the District. Speech in the Common Council of Washington, D. C., Jan. 2, 1866. pp. 6.

3816. PEYTON, Hon. R. L. Y., of Missouri. Proceedings and Speeches on the Announcement of the Death of, in the House of Reps., of the Confederate States, December 19, 1864. pp. 8.

3817. PHELPS, AMOS A. Lectures on Slavery and its Remedy.

18mo. pp. 284. BOSTON: *N. E. Anti-Slavery So.*, 1834.

3819. PHELPS, Lieut. EGBERT, U. S. A. *Continental Monthly*, 1863.

3820. —— The Cause and Results of the War. Ibid. *April*, 1863.

3821. —— Our Future. Ibid. *August*, 1863.

3822. —— American Civilization. Ibid. *July and August*, 1864.

3823. PHELPS, JOHN S., of Missouri. Confiscation of Property and Emancipation of Slaves. Speech in H. of Rep., May 22, '62. p. 8.

3824. PHELPS, Mrs. LINCOLN. Our Country, in its Relations to the Past, Present and Future.

12mo. pp. 423. BALTIMORE: *John D. Toy*, 1864.

3825. PHELPS, S. D. National Symptoms. A Discourse preached in New Haven, April 18, 1862.

8vo. pp. 16. NEW YORK: *Sheldon & Co.*, 1862.

3826. PHELPS, S. D. Military Power a Blessing. A Discourse preached in New Haven, November 24, 1864.
8vo. pp. 16. NEW HAVEN; *Thomas H. Pease*, 1864.

3827. PHILADELPHIA. Rules of the Government of the National Union Party of. pp. 16. 1863.

3828. —— Immense Meeting in favor of the Union, the 11th instant, in Musical Fund Hall. pp. 15.
Contains Speeches by Gov. Curtin, Mr. Doolittle of Wisconsin, Hon. Andrew Johnson, Hon. H. B. Wright and others.

3829. —— Report of the City Bounty Fund Commission, December 31, 1864. 8vo. pp. 16.

3830. —— Sanitary Fair Catalogue and Guide.
4to. pp. 30. PHILADELPHIA : *Magee*, 1854.

3831. PHILADELPHIA CENTRAL FAIR. Catalogue of the Museum of Flags, Trophies and Relics, forming the most complete Collection ever brought together in the United States.
8vo. pp. 32. PHILADELPHIA: *Crissey & Markley*, 1864.

3832. —— Catalogue of Paintings, Drawings, Statuary, etc. 8vo. pp. 32. 1864.

3833. —— A priced Catalogue of Autographs, Relics and Curiosities, Books, Pictures and Engravings.
8vo. pp. 50. PHILADELPHIA: *H. B. Ashmead*, 1864.

3834. —— Memorial of the William Penn Parlor. pp 14.

3835. PHILADELPHIA. Report of the Special Relief Committee, March 1, 1865, 8vo. pp. 4.

3836. —— Report of the City Bounty Fund Commission, July 1, 1865. pp. 15.

3837. THE PHILANTHROPIC RESULTS of the War in America. Collected from Official and other authentic Sources, by an American Citizen. (Dr. L. P. Brockett.)
18mo. pp. 160. NEW YORK: *Sheldon & Co.*, 1864.

3838. PHILLIPS, Capt. EDWIN D. Texas and its late Military Occupation and Evacuation. By an Officer of the Army.
8vo. pp. 35. NEW YORK: *D. Van Nostrand*, 1862.

3839. PHILLIPS, Rev. GEORGE S. The American Republic and Human Liberty.
12mo. pp. 234. CINCINNATI: *Poe & Hitchcock*, 1864.

3840. PHILLIPS, WENDELL. The Constitution, a Pro-Slavery Compact; or Extracts from the Madison Papers, etc.
12mo. pp. 208. NEW YORK: *Am. Anti-Slavery Society,* 1856.

3841, —— The Philosophy of the Abolition Movement.
12mo. pp. 47. NEW YORK: *Am. Anti-Slavery Society,* 1860.

3842. —— The Infidelity of Abolitionism.
12mo. pp. 12. NEW YORK: *Am. Anti-Slavery Society,* 1860.

3843. —— Disunion. Two Discourses, Jan. 20 and Feb. 17, 1861. (Boston.)
12mo. pp. 46. BOSTON: *Robert F. Walcut,* 1861.

3844. —— The War for the Union. A Lecture delivered in New York and Boston, December, 1861.
12mo. pp. 30. NEW YORK: *E. D. Barker,* 1862.

3845. —— The same work. (Pulpit and Rostrum, No. 25.)

3846. PHILLIPS, WM. The Conquest of Kansas, by Missouri and her allies. A History of the Troubles in Kansas, from the Passage of the Organic Act, until the close of July, 1856.
12mo. pp. xii and 414. BOSTON: *Phillips, Sampson & Co.,* '56.

3847. PICARD, M. A. Le Conflit Américain et la Solution Probable.
8vo. pp. 32. PARIS: *E. Dentu,* 1862.

3848. PICKETT, CHARLES E. Gwinism in California.
8vo. pp. 8. SAN FRANCISCO, *October,* 1860.

3849. —— The Existing Revolution; its Causes and Results.
8vo. pp. 24. SACRAMENTO, (Cal.) 1861.

3850. PIERCE, E. L. The Negroes at Port Royal. Report of (E. L. P.) Government Agent, to the Hon. Salmon P. Chase, Secretrry of the Treasury.
8vo. pp. 36. BOSTON: *R. F. Wallcut,* 1862.

3851. PIERCE, EDWARD L. The Freedmen of Port Royal. *Atlantic Monthly, August,* 1863.

3852. PIERCE, H. N. Sermons preached on the National Fast [at the South] December 13, 1861. 8vo. Mobile, 1861.

3853. PIERPOINT, Gov. To the People of Virginia. 8vo. pp. 7.

3854. —— Reorganization of Civil Government. Speech delivered in the city of Norfolk, February 16, 1865. pp. 7.

3855. PIERREPONT, EDWARDS. Speech at the Convention of the

Democracy opposed to the Chicago Platform, held at New York, November 1, 1864.

8vo. pp. 11.   NEW YORK : *D. Van Nostrand*, 1864.

3856. PIERREPONT, E.   A Review of Gen. Butler's Defence, before the House of Representatives, in relation to the New Orleans Gold.

8vo. pp. 27.   NEW YORK : *W. C. Bryant & Co.*, 1865.

3857. PIKE, The Scout and Ranger ; being the Personal Adventures of Corporal Pike, of the 4th Ohio Cavalry. Cincinnati : *Hawley.*

3858. PIKE, F. A., of Maine.   The Currency and the War.   Speech in the House of Reps., February 5, 1862.   pp. 8.

3859. PILLSBURY, PARKER.   The Church as it is; or the Forlorn Hope of Slavery.

12mo. pp. 90.   BOSTON : *Bela Marsh*, 1847.

3860. PILSEN, Lieut. Col.   Reply to Emil Schalk's Criticisms of the Campaign in the Mountain Department, under Gen. Fremont, June, 1863.   pp. 14.

3861. PISANI, Lieut. Col., Aid-de-Camp du Prince Napoleon.   Lettres sur les Etats Unis d'Amérique.

12mo. pp. 452.   PARIS : *Hachette & Co.*, 1862.

3862. PITTENGER, WM   Daring and Suffering.   A History of the Great Railroad Adventure.

18mo. pp. 288.   PHILADELPHIA : *J. W. Daughaday*, 1863.

3863. THE PLANTER'S ALMANAC for 1864.   pp. 24.

3864. A PLATFORM for all Parties.   By Austro-Borealis.

8vo. pp. 21.   BALTIMORE : *J. P. Des Forges*, 1860.

3865. PLEASANTON, Brig. Gen. A. J., Commanding the Home Guards of Philadelphia.   Third Annual Report to the, for 1863.

8vo. pp. 111.   PHILADELPHIA : *King & Baird*, 1864.

3866. A POEM, comprising a few thoughts suggested by the Assault on our Glorious Flag in 1860–61.

12mo. pp. 32.   NEW YORK : *John F. Trow*, 1861.

3867. POLITICAL DIALOGUES.   Soldiers on their Right to Vote, and the Men they should support.   Scene : The Army of the Potomac, near the Weldon Railroad.

8vo. pp. 16.   WASHINGTON : *Chronicle Print* 1864.

3868. POLITICAL ECONOMY in a Nut-Shell.   The difference between

Money and Capital, and a practical Plan for paying the National
Debt without increasing the public burdens.

8vo. pp. 27.   NEW YORK: *G. Bartlett*, 1865.

3869. POLITICAL ECONOMY. Read and ponder. pp. 9. PROVIDENCE.

3870. THE POLITICAL STATUS of the Rebellious States, and the Action
of the President in respect thereto. By the Reporter of the New
York Court of Appeals. pp. 3.

3871. POLITICAL TRANSACTIONS of the Rip Van Winkle Club of
Westchester Co., N. Y. No. 1. The Vision of Judgement.

8vo. pp. 8.   TARRYTOWN: *For the Club*, 1864.

3872. POLLARD, EDWARD A. The Southern Spy. Letters on the
Policy and Inauguration of the Lincoln War.

8vo. pp.   RICHMOND: *West & Johnstone*, 1862.

3873. —— The First Year of the War. Richmond, 1862.

3874. —— The same. 8vo. pp. 368. N. Y.: *C. B. Richardson*, 1863.

3875. —— The Second Year of the War. Richmond, 1863.

3876. —— The same. 8vo. pp. 386. N. Y.: *C. B. Richardson*, 1863.

3877. —— The Third Year of the War.

8vo. pp. 391. Portraits. NEW YORK: *C. B. Richarson*, 1864.

3878. —— The Two Nations; a Key to the History of the War. Richmond, 1864.

3879. —— Observations on the North. Eight Months in Prison and
on Parole.

8vo. pp. 142.   RICHMOND: *E. W. Ayres*, 1865.

3880. —— Letter on the State of the War. Richmond, 1865.

3881. POMEROY, S. C., of Kansas. Speech on the Homestead Bill.
Senate, May 5, 1862. pp. 8.

3882. —— The Platform and Party of the Future, and National Freedom secured by an Amended Constitution. Senate, March 10,
1864. pp. 8.

3883. POOR WHITE; or The Rebel Conscript. By the Author of
Ruth's Sacrifice; or Life on the Rappahannock.

12mo. pp. 320.   BOSTON: *Graves & Young*, 1864.

3883.* POPE, Maj. Gen. Report concerning the operations of the Army
of Virginia while under his command, Jan. 27, 1863. pp. 256.
37th Cong. 3d Session, Ex. Doc. No. 81.

3884. —— The Campaign in Virginia of August, 1862.

8vo. pp. 74.   MILWAUKIE: *Jermain & Brightman*, 1863.

3885. POPE'S CAMPAIGN IN VIRGINIA. Its Policy and Results. And the Relations of the Army of the Potomac to the campaign, exposed. By a General Officer. pp. 32.

3886. POPE, SAMUEL. Legal View of the Alabama Case, and Ships building for the Confederates.
8vo. pp. 8. MANCHESTER: *Un. and Emanc. Soc.*, 1863.

3887. —— The American War. Secession and Slavery. A Lecture delivered at Timstall, Staffordshire. (England.)
12mo. pp. 16. MANCHESTER: *Emancipation Society*, 1863.

3888. PORTER, Hon. A. G., of Indiana. State of the Union. Speech delivered in the House of Reps., February 19, 1861.
8vo. pp. 8. WASHINGTON: *H. Polkinhorn*, 1861.

3889. PORTER, CHARLES S. A Fast, implies a duty. Sermon preached in Philadelphia, Fast day, April 3, 1863.
8vo. pp. 22. PHILADELPHIA: *Sherman & Co.*, 1863.

3890. PORTER, Hon. JOHN K. Democrats and the War. Speech at the Democratic Meeting at the Capitol, New York, April 22, 1861. 8vo. pp. 4.

3891. —— Speech at the Union Ratification Meeting at Glens Falls, October 21. pp. 14.

3892. —— Treasury Notes a Legal Tender. Argument in the Court of Appeals of the State of New York, in the case of the Metropolitan Bank and others, June 27, 1863.
8vo. pp. 37. ALBANY: *Weed, Parsons & Co.*, 1863.

3893. PORTER, Commodore W. D. Defence of, before the Naval Retiring Board, convened at Brooklyn, November, 1863.
8vo. pp. 22. NEW YORK: *John A. Gray & Greene*, 1863.

3894. PORTER, Major Gen. FITZ JOHN. Proceedings at a General Court Marshal for the Trial of. pp. 317. *37th Congress, 3d Session, Executive Document, No. 71.*

3895. —— A Reply to the Review of Judge Advocate General Holt, of the Proceedings in the case of Gen. Porter, and a vindication of that Officer, by Reverdy Johnson.
8vo. pp. 88. BALTIMORE: *John Murphy & Co.*, 1863.

3896. —— Reply of Hon. Reverdy Johnson to the Paper which Judge Advocate Holt furnished to the President, urging Gen. Porter's condemnation. pp. 56.

3897. PORTER, Maj. Gen. F. J. A Reply to the Hon. Reverdy Johnson's Attack on the Administration, in the case of Fitz John Porter. 8vo. pp. 19.   BALTIMORE : *Sherwood & Co.*, 1863.

3898. PORTER, Hon. WM. D. State Sovereignty, and the Doctrine of Coercion ; together with a Letter from Hon. J. K. Paulding, former Secretary of the Navy. The Right to secede by " States." 8vo. pp. 36.   CHARLESTON : (S. C.) *Evans & Cogswell*, 1860.

3899. POST, Hon. GEORGE I. Speech in House of Assembly, N. Y., March 3, 1863, on the Cause of the War, Abitrary Arrests. 8vo. pp. 10.

3900. POST, Rev. JACOB. Discourse on the Assassination of President Lincoln, preached in Camp, at Harrison's Landing, Va., April 23, 1865.
8vo. pp. 11.   OSWEGO : *S. H. Parker & Co.*, 1865.

3901. POST, TRUMAN M., DD. Our National Union. A Discourse delivered at St. Louis, November 29, 1860.
8vo. pp. 20.   ST. LOUIS : *R. P. Studley & Co.*, 1860.

3902. —— Palingenesy. National Regeneration. An Address delivered at Washington University, (Mo.) November 4, 1864.
8vo. pp. 17.   ST. LOUIS : *George Knapp & Co.*, 1864.

3903. —— Free Missouri. *North American Review, April*, 1865.

3904. POTTER, Hon. E. R. Speech in support of the Union, delivered in the General Assembly of Rhode Island. pp. 15. 1861.

3905. —— Speech on the present National Difficulties ; with an Appx. 8vo. pp. 53.   PROVIDENCE : *Cooke, Jackson & Co.*, 1861.

3906. POTTER. HORATIO, Bishop of New York, Annual Address of. 8vo. pp. 56.   NEW YORK : *James Pott*, 1863.

3907. —— A Form of Prayer to be used in the Diocese of New York, November 30, 1863, National Fast Day. pp. 15.

3908. —— A Form of Prayer to be used in the Diocese of New York, November 26, 1863, National Thanksgiving. pp. 16.

3909. POTTER, Rev. WM. J. The National Tragedy. Four Sermons delivered at New Bedford, on the Life and Death of Abraham Lincoln.
8vo. pp. 67.   NEW BEDFORD : *Abraham Taber & Bro.*, 1865.

3910. POTTS, Rev. WM. D., DD. Freeman's Guide to the Polls, and a Solemn Appeal to American Patriots.
12mo. pp. 125.   NEW YORK : *For the author*, 1864.

3911. POTTS, Rev. W. D., DD. Campaign Songs for Christian Patriots and True Democrats, accompanied with Notes.
16mo. pp. 24.   NEW YORK : *For the author*, 1864.

3912. POULAIN, ERNEST. La Crise Américaine. Recueil de Documents pouvant servir a l'histoire de la guerre des Etats Unis, 1859, 1860, 1861, 1862.
8vo. pp. 180.   PARIS : *Dentu*, 1863.

3913. POUSSIELGNE, M. Homme ou Singe ; ou la Question de L'Esclavage aux Etats Unis, par un ex-attaché d'ambassade à Washington.
8vo. pp. 24.   PARIS : *Dentu*, 1861.

3914. POWELL, GEO. MAY. Facts and Figures for the Hour.
8vo. pp. 16.   WASHINGTON : *McGill & Witherow*, 1864.

3915. POWELL, LAZARUS W. Speech on the State of the Union. Delivered in the Senate of the United States, January 22, 1861.
8vo. pp. 16.   WASHINGTON : *Globe Office*, 1861.

3916. —— Speech on Executive Usurpation, delivered in the Senate of the United States, July, 1861. pp. 15.

3917. POWER AND POLICY of Exclusion. By a Kentuckian. pp. 16.

3918. POWERS of the President of the U. S. in Times of War.
8vo. pp. 31.   MUSCATINE : (Iowa) *Journal Office*, 1863.

3919. POWERS, Rev. HORATIO N. The Soldiers' Claims upon the People. An Address before a Convention of Loyal Women of Iowa, at Muscatine, October, 1863.
8vo. pp. 11.   DAVENPORT : (Iowa) *Gazette Office*, 1863.

3920. —— Attitude of Iowa Copperheads towards the Soldier. A Glimpse of the Field of Victory. An Oration before the Soldiers of Scot County, October 4, 1865.

3921. PRATT, HORACE L. EDGAR. A Sermon for the Times. Civil War, no Remedy for Secession. Preached in Castleton, L. I.
8vo. pp. 12.   NEW YORK : *George F. Nesbitt & Co.*, 1861.

3922. PRATT, Rev. JAMES, DD. Our National Blessings and Duties. A Sermon preached at Chicago, August 31, 1862.
8vo. pp. 16.   CHICAGO : *Tribune Office*, 1862.

3923. PRATT, GEORGE. The Contest and its Duties. An Oration before the Delta Kappa Epsilon Fraternity, at Yale College, July 30, 1862.
8vo. pp. 25.   NORWICH : *Manning, Platt & Co.*, 1862.

43

3924. PRENTISS, Geo. L., DD. The Free Christian State, and the Present Struggle. An Address before the Alumni of Bowdoin College, August 8, 1861.
8vo. pp. 38.   New York: *John A. Gray*, 1861.

3925. —— The National Crisis; being an Address before the Phi Beta Kappa Society, Dartmouth College, N. H., July 30, 1862.
8vo. pp. 32.   New York: *H. H. Bidwell*, 1862.

3926. —— Some of the Providential Lessons of 1861. How to meet the Events of 1862. Two Discourses, preached December 29, 1861, and January 5, 1862.
8vo. pp. 19.   New York: *W. H. Bidwell*, 1862.

3927. —— Lessons of Encouragement, from the Times of Washington.
8vo. pp. 20.   New York: *Anson D. F. Randolph*, 1863.

3928. Presbyterian Church in the Confederate States. Address of the General Assembly to all the Churches of Jesus Christ throughout the Earth. Adopted at Augusta, Ga., Dec., 1861.
8vo. pp. 17.

3929. Presbyterian Church. Action of the General Assembly of, in the United States, at Brooklyn, N. Y., May 27, 1863, on the State of the Country. 8vo. pp. 8.

3930. PRESCOTT, George B. The United States Armory. *Atlantic Monthly, September*, 1863.

3931. The Present Attempt to dissolve the American Union. A British Aristocratic Plot. By B.
8vo. pp. 42.   New York: *For the author*, 1862.

3932. The Preservation of the Union. A National Economic Necessity. 8vo. pp. 7.   *Loyal Publication Society, No.* 14, 1863.

3933. Presidency. Whom do English Tories wish elected to the Presidency? *Loyal Publication Society, No.* 69,   pp. 4.

3934. President, Examination of the Power of, to Remove from Office during the Recess of the Senate.
8vo. pp. 23.   New York: *Wyncoop, Hallenbeck & Thomas*, '61.

3935. PREUSS, H. Clay. God save our Noble Union! and other Poems for the Times; also Reply to Charges of Disloyalty by the Potter Investigating Committee. 8vo. pp. 8.

3936. —— Patriotism and Provincialism. *Con. Mo'ly, Vol. iv, pp.* 40.

3937. PREVOST, F. Le Blocus Américaine (droit des Neutres.)
8vo. pp. 30.   Paris: *Castel*, 1861.

3938. PRICE, Rev. T., DD. A Narrative of the Adventures and escape of Moses Roper, from American Slavery.
18mo. pp. 89. BOSTON: *I. Knapp*, 1838.

3939. PRICE, Hon. THOMAS L. Speech on the Origin and Objects of the War. House of Reps., May 26, 1862. pp. 8.

3940. PRICE, WILLIAM, of Baltimore. The Position of Maryland. A Letter to the Editors of the Baltimore American. 8vo. pp. 8.

3941. PRIM, General JUAN, of the Spanish Army. General McClellan and the Army of the Potomac.
12mo. pp. 23. NEW YORK: *John Bradburn*, 1864.

3942. PRIME, Rev. G. WENDELL. A Sermon delivered in Detroit, April 16, 1865, after the Death of President Lincoln.
8vo. pp. 16. DETROIT: *Tribune Office*, 1865.

3943. THE PRINCETON REVIEW. The State of the Country. Rev. Charles Hodge, DD. January, 1861.
The Church and the Country. Ibid. April, 1861.
The General Assembly,—The State of the Country. Dr. Hodge. July, 1861.
American Nationality. Rev. J. H. McIlvaine, DD. Oct., 1861.

3944. —— England and America. Rev. Chas. Hodge, DD. Jan. '62.
Slavery and the Slave Trade. Rev. S. J. Baird, DD. July, '62.

3945. —— The War. Dr. Charles Hodge. January, 1863.
Religious Instruction in the Army. Rev. Jas. Matthews. July, '63.

3946. —— The War and National Wealth. Rev Lyman H. Atwater. July, 1864.
Abraham Lincoln. Rev. Dr. Hodge. July, 1865.

3947. PRINDLE, Hon. M., of Chenango. Arbitrary Arrests. Speech in the Assembly of New York, February 10, 1863. pp. 8.

3948. PRISONERS. Tracts on the Exchange of Poisoners. N. Y., 1862.
1. Massachusetts Historical Society Report, December 12, 1861.
2. Judge Daly's Letter to Hon. Ira Harris, December 21, 1861.
3. New York Historical Soc., Mr. Bancroft's Letter to Mr. Bradish.
4. "Mr. Bancroft and his Boston Critics." February–May, 1862.

3949. —— Report of a Committee of the Massachusetts Historical Society, on Exchanges of Prisoners during the American Revolutionary War. Presented December 19, 1861.
8vo. pp. 26. BOSTON: *Printed for the Society*, 1861.

3950. —— Letter from the Secretary of War in relation to the List of

Names of State or Political Prisoners, furnished to the Judge of the Court of the United States. *38th Congress, 2d Session, Senate Executive Document, No.* 23, 1865. pp. 9,

3951. PRISONERS IN THE PENITENTIARY, District of Columbia, by Sentence of Courts Martial. Letter from the Attorney General on the Legality of the Confinement of. *House of Reps., Miscellaneous Document, No.* 83, 37*th Congress,* 2*d Session,* 1862. pp. 6.

3952. PRISONERS OF WAR ; or Five Months among the Yankees. By a Rifleman. Richmond, 1865. 8vo.

3953. —— Report of H. W. Halleck, General-in-Chief, on the Treatment of Kansas Troops by the Rebels. *Senate Executive Document No.* 4, 37*th Congress,* 1*st Session,* 1864.

3954. —— Correspondence had by Major General Wool in relation to Exchange of prisoners.
8vo. pp. 12. *H. of Rep., Ex. Doc. No.* 124, 37*th Con.,* 2*d Ses.,'*62.

3955. —— The Report of Col. Key reative to the Exchange of. pp. 3.

3956. —— Letter from the Sec. of War relative to the Exchange of.
8vo. pp. 182. *Cong. Doc.,* 38*th Cong,, ,* 2*d Sess., Ex. Doc. No.* 32.

3957.• PRISONERS. Report -of the Committee on the Conduct of the War, on the Condition of Union Prisoners at Annapolis and Baltimore, who have been returned from Rebel Captivity.
8vo. pp. 30. *Sen. Rep. Com. No.* 68, 38*th Cong.,* 1*st Sess.,* 1864.

3958. PRISONERS OF WAR. Narrative of the Privations and Sufferings of United States Officers and Soldiers, while Prisoners of War in the hands of the Rebel Authorities. Report of a Commission appointed by the U. S. Sanitary Commission ; with the Testimony.
8vo. pp. 383. PHILADELPHIA : *For the U. Sanitary Com.,* '64.

3959. —— The same. pp. 86. *Loyal Publication Society No.* 76, '64.

3960. —— Report of the Joint Select Committee of the Confederate Congress, appointed to investigate the Condition and Treatment of Prisoners of War. Richmond, 1865.

 Printed by the Congress of the Confederate States, and, with the exception of a few copies, destroyed by the Great Fire in Richmond. Reprinted in the New York Tribune of June 29, 1865.

3961. PRISONS. A Voice from Rebel Prisons. Giving an account of some of the Horrors of the Stockade at Andersonville, Millen and other Prisons. By a Returned Prisoner of War. pp. 16. Boston : *Rand & Avery,* 1865.

3962. PRIZE CASES. Letter from the Secretary of the Navy, in relation to the Distribution of Prize Cases in New York. April 20, 1864. *38th Cong., 1st Sess., House Ex. Doc.* 74. pp. 595.

3963. PRIZE MATTERS. Letter of the Sec. of the Navy in reference to. 8vo. pp. 132. *H. of Reps. Ex. Doc. No.* 73, 37*th Con.*, 3*d Ses.*,'63.

3964. PROBLEM OF GOVERNMENT. By Analytica. Richmond, '62. 8vo.

3965. PROCEEDINGS of the Chamber of Commerce of the State of New York, on the continued Piracies of Vessels fitted out in Great Britain, upon American Commerce. February 24, 1863. 8vo. pp. 27. NEW YORK: *J. W. Amerman*, 1863.

3966. PROGRESS and Prospects of the Great Struggle for Freedom in America. Address to the People of Great Britain. September 6, 1864. pp. 2. Manchester.

3967. PROOFS FOR WORKING MEN of the Monarchic and Aristocratic Designs of the Southern Conspirators and their Northern Allies. pp. 8.

3968. PROPHECY AND FULFILLMENT. Speech of A. H. Stephens, of Georgia, in opposition to Secession in 1860. Address of E. W. Gantt, in favor of Re-Union, in 1863. 8vo. pp. 45. *Loyal Publication Society No.* 36, 1863.

3969. PROPOSAL. A private Citizen's Proposal for the Settlement of all the Differences between the Northern and Southern States. December 17, 1860. pp. 11.

3970. PROTEST of the Alabama Delegation. pp. 4. Charleston.

3971. PROUDFIT, JOHN, DD. The Sanctuary of God consulted in the Present Crisis. A Sermon preached at New Brunswick, N. J., April 21, 1861. 8vo. pp. 22. NEW BRUNSWICK: *Terhune & Van Anglen*, 1861.

3972. PROVOST MARSHAL GENERAL, Washington, D. C., Circulars of. Numbers 1 to 106. From May 15, to December 31, 1863 James B. Fry, Provost Marshal General.

3973. —— The same. Circulars, numbers 1 to 42. January 5, 1864, to December 5, 1864.

3974. —— The same. Circulars, numbers 1 to 9. Jan. 2, to Mar. 27,'65.

3975. PRYOR, Hon. ROGER A., of Virginia. Independence of the South. Speech on the Resolutions reported by the Committee of Thirty-three. 8vo. pp. 8. WASHINGTON: *H. Polkinhorn*, 1861.

3976. PUBLIC DEBT and the Public Credit of the Un'd States. I. A. H.
12mo. pp. 24.   NEW YORK : *Wynkoop & Hallenbeck,* 1864.

3977. PUTNAM, GEO., DD. An Address delivered at Roxbury, on
occasion of the Death of Abraham Lincoln April 19, 1865.
8vo. pp. 15.   ROXBURY . *L. B. & O. E. Weston,* 1865.

3978. PUTNAM, KATE. Our Future. *Northern Monthly, April,* 1864.

3979. —— Our Martyrs. *Continental Monthly, August,* 1864.

3980. PUTNAM, G. P. Before and after the Battle. A Day and
Night in " Dixie." pp. 20.

3981. PYNE, Rev. SMYTH, DD. Intercessory Prayer. A Sermon
preached in Washington, November 18, 1860. pp. 16.

3982. —— Thanksgiving Sermon preached in Washington, Aug. 6, '63.
8vo. pp. 8.   WASHINGTON: *Chronicle Office,* 1863.

3983. —— Sermon preached on the Day of Fasting, January 4, 1861,
in Washington, District of Columbia.
8vo. pp. 11.   WASHINGTON ; *McGill & Witherow,* 1865.

QUANTRELL, The Terror of the West. By Alouette.
12mo. pp. 59.   NEW YORK : *T. R. Dawley,* 1865.

3985. QUARLES, Hon. JAMES M., of Tennessee. State of the Union.
Speech in House of Reps., February 1, 1861. pp. 15.

3986. QUESTIONS for the Times. pp. 3. (No date.)

3987. LA QUESTION de l'Esclavage aux Etats Unis par un ancien
Fonctionnaire des Indes Nierlandaises.
8vo. pp. 61.   LA HAYE : *Martines Nijhoff,* 1862.

3988. —— Américaine suivie d'un appendice sur le Coton, le Tabac, etc.
8vo. pp. 74.   PARIS : *Dentu,* 1861.

3989. THE QUESTION before us.
8vo. pp. 12.   BOSTON : *John Wilson & Son,* 1862.

3990. QUINT, Rev. ALONZO H. The Christian Patriot's Present Duty.
A Sermon, 1861.

3991. —— The Potomac and the Rapidan. Army Notes, from the
Failure at Winchester, to the reënforcement of Rosecrans, '61-3.
12mo. pp. 407. Map.   BOSTON : *Crosby & Nichols,* 1864.

3992. —— National Sin must be expiated by National Calamity. What
President Lincoln did for his Country. Southern Chivalry, and

what the Nation ought to do with it. Three Sermons preached in New Bedford, Massachusetts.

8vo. pp. 45. NEW BEDFORD: *Mercury Press*, 1865.

3993. QUINT, Rev. A. H. History of the Second Massachusetts Regt. (In press.)

R AFF, GEORGE W. A Manual of Pensions, Bounty and Pay.

8vo. pp. viii and 477. CINCINNATI: *Robert Clarke & Co.*, 1862.

3995. RANDALL, Rev. GEORGE M., DD. The Benefits of the Rebellion. A Sermon preached in Boston, June 2, 1861.

18mo. pp. 48. BOSTON: *E. P. Dutton & Co.*, 1861.

3996. RANKIN, JOHN C. Our Danger and Duty. A Sermon preached at Basking Ridge, N. J., Fast Day, June 4, 1861.

8vo. pp. 7. JERSEY CITY: *John H. Lyon & Co.*, 1861.

3997. RANNEY, Rev. J. A. The Present Condition and Hopes of our Nation. A Thanksgiving Sermon, at Three Rivers, Michigan, November 28, 1861· pp. 8.

3998. RAPHALL, Rev. M. J. Bible View of Slavery. A Discourse delivered at the Jewish Synagogue, New York, Jan. 4, 1861.

8vo. pp. 41. NEW YORK: *Rudd & Carleton*, 1861.

3999. RAYMOND, CHARLES A. The Religious Life of the Negro Slave. *Harpers' Mag., August, October and November*, 1863.

4000. RAYMOND, HENRY J. Disunion and Slavery. A Series of Letters to W. L. Yancey, of Alabama. 8vo. pp. 36. New York.

4001. —— The Issues of the Canvass. The Extension and Increase of Slavery. Position of the Two Parties. Speech at Rochester, New York, October 31, 1860. pp. 9.

4002. —— The Financial Necessities and Policy of the National Government. Remarks in Assembly of N. York, Jan. 28, '62. p. 11.

4003. —— The Administration and the War. The Duty of supporting the Government. Arbitrary Arrests. The Question of Reconstruction. Remarks at Wilmington, Del., Nov. 6, 1863. pp. 15.

4004. —— The Life of Abraham Lincoln.

12mo. pp. 83. NEW YORK: *Derby & Miller*, 1864.

4005. —— History of the Administration of President Lincoln; including his Speeches, Letters, Addresses, Proclamations and Messages; with a preliminary Sketch of his Life.

12mo. pp. 496. NEW YORK: *Derby & Miller*, 1864.

4006. READ, Rev. C. H., DD. National Fast. A Discourse delivered on the day appointed by the President of the U. S., Jan. 4, 1861. 8vo. pp. 25.   RICHMOND : (Va.) *West & Johnson*, 1861.

4007. READ, Rev. HOLLIS. The Negro Problem Solved ; or Africa as she Was, as she Is, and as she Shall Be. Her Curse and her Cure. 12mo. pp. 418.   NEW YORK : *A. A. Constantine*, 1864.

4008. READ, Hon. JOHN M. Opinion in favor of the Constitutionality of the Act of Congress of March 3, 1863, " For enrolling and calling out the National Forces," etc. 8vo. pp.   PHILADELPHIA : *C. Sherman & Son*, 1864.

4009. ―――― Opinion in favor of the Constitutionality of the Acts of Congress, declaring Treasury Notes a Legal Tender in payment of debts. May 24, 1865. 8vo. pp. 20.   PHILADELPHIA : *Sherman & Co.*, 1865.

4010. READ, T. B. The Siege of Cincinnati. *Atlan. Mo'ly, Feb.,* '63.

4011. REBEL BARBARITIES. Official Account of the Cruelties inflicted upon Union Prisoners and Refugees at Fort Pillow, Libby Prison, etc. 8vo. pp. 98.   NEW YORK : *Rebellion Record*, 1864.

4012. REBEL BRAG and British Bluster. A Record of unfulfilled Prophecies, Baffled Schemes and Disappointed Hopes; with Echoes of very Insignificant Thunder, very pleasant to read and instructive to all who are capable of learning. By Owls-Glass. 12mo. pp. 111.   NEW YORK : *American News Co.*, 1865.

4013. REBEL Conditions of Peace, and the Mechanics of the South. *Loyal Publication Society, No.* 30. pp. 4.

4014. THE REBEL STATES. The President and Congress. Reconstruction and the Executive Power of Pardon. 8vo. pp. 15.   NEW YORK : *E. S. Dodge & Co.*, 1866.

4015. ―――― The President and Congress. Reconstruction and the Executive Power of Pardon. New York : *Dodge & Co.*, 1866.

4016. REBELLION. The Light and Dark of the Rebellion. 8vo. pp. 303.   PHILADELPHIA : *George W. Childs*, 1863.

4017. THE REBELLION of the Cavaliers. A Poem. 12mo pp. 28.   NEW YORK : *Sinclair Toucey*, 1865.

REBELLION RECORD, see *Frank Moore.*

4018. RECEPTION of the Oneida Volunteers at the City of New York, June, 1861.
8vo. pp. 10. NEW YORK: *George F. Nesbitt & Co.*, 1861.

4019. RECIPROCITY TREATY with Great Britain. Report of the Committee on Commerce, of the State of N. Y., in relation to.
8vo. pp. 36. *H. of Rep. Reps. No. 22, 37th Cong., 2d Sess.,* '62.

4020. RECLUS, ELISEE. De l'Esclavage aux Etats Unis. *Revue des Deux Mondes, January*, 1861.

4021. —— Le Coton et la Crise Américaine. Ibid. *January*, 1862.

4022. —— Les Noirs Américains depuis la Guerre Civile des Etats Unis. Ibid. *March*, 1863.

4023. —— La Guerre Civile aux Etats Unis. Ibid. *October*, 1864.

4024. RECONCILIATION. What are the Conditions of a candid and lasting Reconciliation between the two Sections of the Country?
8vo. pp. 69. NEW YORK: *Ross & Toucey*, 1861.

4025. RECONSTRUCTION. Universal Suffrage in the Rebel States. Justice to the Negro and Safety to the Republic. Reconstruction; A Manifesto of the German " Unionbund," of New York. Translated from the German for the *Commonwealth*. Bost., July 2, 65.

4026. —— in America. By a Member of the New York Bar.
8vo. pp. 134. NEW YORK: *W. I. Pooley*, 1860.

4027. RECONSTRUCTION of the Union. Suggestions to the People of the North on. By a Citizen of Iowa.
8vo. pp. 23. NEW YORK: *J. Bradburn*, 1863.

4028. RECONSTRUCTION. November, 1862. pp. 11. N. York: *Doolady.*

4029. —— The National Club on the Reconstruction of the Union. February 4, 1864.
8vo. pp. 16. Map. NEW YORK: *G. B. Teubner*, 1864.

4030. RECRUITING. Memorial to Congress from the Union League of Philadelphia, on the System of Recruiting by means of Local Bounties. December, 1864. pp. 6.

4031. REDINGTON, JAMES. Remarks on the Governor's Message, in Assembly, New York, February 18, 1863. 8vo. pp. 12.

4032. REDDEN, LAURA C. (Howard Glyndon.) Idyls of Battle, and Poems of the Rebellion.
12mo. pp. vi, 152. NEW YORK: *Hurd & Houghton*, 1864.

4033. REDFIELD, J. W., M. D. New Views of the Cause, Prevention and Cure of Diseases produced by Miasma and Mephitic Vapors. Presented for the Safety of the Army of Occupation in the Southern States.

8vo. pp. 16.   NEW YORK: *John A. Gray*, 1863.

4034. REDPATH, JAMES. The Public Life of Capt. John Brown; with an Autobiography of his Childhood and Youth.

8vo. pp. 407.   BOSTON: *Thayer & Eldridge*, 1860.

4035. —— Echoes of Harper's Ferry.

12mo. pp. 513.   BOSTON: *Thayer & Eldridge*, 1860.

4036. RED-TAPE and Pigeon-Hole Generals, as seen from the Ranks during a Campaign in the Army of the Potomac.

12mo. pp. 318.   NEW YORK: *Carlton*, 1864.

4037. REED, HENRY. Southern Slavery, and its relations to Northern Industry. A Lecture delivered in Cincinnati, January 24, 1862.

8vo. pp. 36.   CINCINNATI: *Enquirer Press*, 1862.

4038. REED, JAMES. Sermon on War. 8vo. pp. 7. (No date.)

4039. —— The Duty of the Citizen in these Times. A Sermon preached at Albany, April 21, 1861.

8vo. pp. 15.   ALBANY: *Munsell & Rowland*, 1861.

4040. REED, Rev. N. A. National Thanksgiving. A Discourse delivered in Zanesville, August 6, 1863.

12mo. pp. 17.   ZANESVILLE: *Beer & Hurd*, 1863.

4041. REED, P. FISKE. Incidents of the War; or the Romance and Realities of Soldier Life.

8vo. pp. 112.   NEW YORK: *Long & Co.*, 1862.

4042. REED, Rev. S. A Discourse delivered upon the occasion of the Obsequies of President Lincoln, April 19, 1865.

8vo. pp. 24.   BOSTON: *Rand & Avery*, 1865.

4043. REED, Capt. THEODORE. Letter from Col. Hardie to the Secretary of War, in regard to the Murder of Capt. Reed of Philadelphia, by the Citizens of Accomack County, Va., May 25, 1864. *38th Congress, 1st Session, Executive Document, No. 93.*

4044. REED, WILLIAM B. A Paper containing a Statement and Vindication of certain political Opinions.

8vo. pp. 32.   PHILADELPHIA: *John Campbell*, 1862.

4045. —— The Diplomatic Year; being a Review of Mr. Seward's Foreign Correspondence of 1862. By a Northern Man.

8vo. pp. 71.   PHILADELPHIA: *John Campbell*, 1863.

4046. REFUGEES. Report of the Western Sanitary Commission, on the White Union Refugees of the South ; their Persecutions, Sufferings and Destitute Condition.
8vo. pp. 44. ST. LOUIS : *Western Sanitary Commission,* 1864.

4047. REICHARDT, THEODORE. Diary of Battery A, First Regiment Rhode Island Light Artillery.
12mo. pp. 153. PROVIDENCE : *N. B. Williams,* 1865.

4048. REICHENBACH, BOGDEN GRAF. Die Krisis in Nord Amerika. Auf Grund eines im Evangelischen Verein für kirkliche zwecke am 23 Marz, 1863, gebaltenen Vortrags.
8vo. pp. 40. BERLIN : *Edward Beck,* 1863.

4049. REID, ALEXANDER. Government, a Divine Ordinance. A Discourse delivered at Salisbury, Conn. (Fast Day.)
8vo. pp. 24. HARTFORD : *Case, Lockwood & Co.,* 1863.

4050. REJECTED STONE ; or Insurrection vs. Resurrection in America. By a Native of Virginia. Third Edition.
8vo. pp. 131. BOSTON : *Walker, Wise & Co.,* 1862.

4051. REMAK, STEPHEN S. La Paix en Amérique.
8vo. pp. 160. PARIS : *Henri Plon,* 1865.

4052. RENOUF, SIDNEY. L'Union Américaine et l'Europe.
8vo. pp. 16. PARIS : *E. Dentu,* 1861.

4053. REPRESENTATIVE Government and Electoral Reform. A Review of recent Publications on that subject.
8vo. pp. 38. BOSTON : *Prentiss & Deland,* 1863.

4054. REPUBLICAN CAMPAIGN SONGSTER, for 1864.
12mo. pp. 64. CINCINNATI : *J. R. Hawley & Co.,* 1865.

4055. REPUBLICAN IMPERIALISM. 8vo. pp. 40. (No date.)

4056. REPUBLICAN IMPERIALISM is not American Liberty. [Pub. June, 1863.] 8vo. pp. 43.

4057. REPUBLICAN UNION FESTIVAL, New York, Feb. 22, 1862. Liberty and Union, One and Inseparable. Speeches on the occasion.
8vo. pp. 27. NEW YORK : *G. P. Putnam,* 1862.

4058. RESOURCES, (Our.) New York, March, 1864.
8vo. pp. 36. NEW YORK : *Wynkoop, Hallenbeck & Thomas,* '64.

4059. RESULTS of the Serf Emancipation in Russia.
8vo. pp. 30. *Loyal Publication Society, No.* 47, 1864.

4060. REVELATIONS. A Companion to the "New Gospel of Peace," according to Abraham.
12mo. pp. 36. NEW YORK : *Feeks & Bancker,* 1863.

4061. REVENUE. The New Internal Revenue Law, approved June 30, 1864; with copious marginal References, and Index.

8vo. pp. 122.   NEW YORK: *D. Appleton & Co.*, 1864.

4062. REVERE, Brig. General JOSEPH W. Tried by Court Martial, and dismissed from the Service of the United States, August 10, 1863. A Statement.

8vo. pp. 48.   NEW YORK: *C. A. Alvord*, 1863.

4063. —— A Review of the case of Gen. Revere.

8vo. pp. 19.   BOSTON: *J. H. Eastburn*, 1864.

4064. LA REVOLUTION Américaine Devoilée.

8vo. pp. 31.   PARIS: *Dentu*, 1862.

4065. REVUE DES DEUX MONDES, Paris.

Des Esclavage aux Etats, par E. Reclus. January, 1861.

La Question du Coton en Angleterre depuis la crise Américaine, par J. Ninet. March, 1861.

Les Causes et les caractères de la guerre civile aux Etats Unis, par A. Langel. November, 1861.

4066. REVUE DES DEUX MONDES, 1862.

Le Coton et la crise Américaine, par E. Reclus. January, 1862.

Les Finances et les Banques des Etats Unis depuis la Guerre, par A. Cochut. September, 1862.

Une Station sur les Côtes d'Amérique, etc., par E. Du Hailly. October, November and December, 1862.

4067. REVUE DES DEUX MONDES, 1863.

Les Noirs Américains depuis la Guerre civile des Etats Unis, par E. Reclus. March, 1863.

Les Noirs Américains depuis la Guerre civile des Etats Unis. No. 2, par Les Clauteurs. April, 1863.

La Guerre Civile aux Etats Unis—le Gouvernment Fédéral, etc., par A. Langel. October, 1863.

4068. REVUE DES DEUX MONDES, 1864.

La Guerre Civile aux Etats Unis, par Elisée Reclus. October, 1854.

Les Etats Unis pendant la Guerre—l'Election Présidentielle en 1864, par A. Langel. December, 1864.

4069. REVUE DES DEUX MONDES, 1865.

La Guerre d'Amérique et le marchê du Coton, par L. Reybaud. March, '65.

Les Etats Unis pendant la Guerre, par A. Langel. April, 1865.

Le Président des Etats Unis, Abraham Lincoln, par A. Langel. May, 1865.

Les Etats Unis pendant la Guerre, No. 3, un border-state, les états du Centre, par A. Langel. July, 1865.

Huit mois en Amérique a la fin de la Guerre lettres et notes de Voyage, par E. Duvergier de Hauranne.

Lettres et Notes la Convention. 3 parts. August and September, 1865.

4070. REYNOLDS, G.   A Fortnight with the Sanitary. *Atlantic Monthly, February,* 1864.

4071. REYNOLDS, Rev. Dr., of Chicago. Our National Crisis. *Evangelical Quarterly Review, Vol.* xiii.

4072. REYNOLDS, Rev. E. W. The Relation of Slavery to the War, and the Position of the Clergy. Three Discourses preached at Watertown, New York.
8vo. pp. 48.   WATERTOWN, New York, 1861.

4973. —— The True Story of the Barons of the South; or the Rationale of the American Conflict.
12mo. pp. 240.   BOSTON: *Walker, Wise & Co.,* 1862.

4074. REYNOLDS, JOHN. "The Balm of Gilead." An Enquiry into the Rights of American Slavery.
8vo. pp. 48.   BELLEVILLE, Illinois, 1860.

4075. REYNOLDS, Lieut. Col. J. G. Proceedings of a Marine General Court Martial on, convened at Washington City, May 7, '62.
8vo. pp. 21.   WASHINGTON: *H. Polkinhorn,* 1862.

4076. REYNOLDS, Rev. J. N. A Thanksgiving Sermon, (relating to the War) delivered in Meadville, Penn., Nov. 26, 1863.

4077. —— Sermon in commemoration of the Virtues of Abraham Lincoln, in Meadville, June 1, 1865.
8vo. pp. 36.   MEADVILLE: (Pa.) *R. L. White,* 1865.

4078. REYNOLDS, Dr. LAWRENCE. A Poetical Address before the Irish Brigade, in Camp near Falmouth, Va., March 17, 1863.
12mo. pp. 24.   ALBANY: *Weed, Parsons & Co.,* 1863.

4079. RHODE ISLAND. Report of the R. I. Peace Commissioners, who attended the Convention at Washington, February 4, 1861.

4080. —— Report of Col. A. E. Burnside, commanding the First Regiment Rhode Island Volunteers, May 23, 1861. pp. 7.

4081. —— Message of Gov. Sprague, with accompanying Documents, made to the General Assembly, January, 1862. pp. 8.

4082. —— Report of the Finance Committee, on the Military Expenses of the State, January, 1862. pp. 10.

4083. —— Report of the Adjutant General, for 1861. pp. 40.

4084. —— Report of the Quartermaster General for 1861. pp. 22.

4085. —— Report of Dr. Lloyd Morton on the physical Condition of the R. I. Regiments in the field, January, 1863. pp. 21.

4086. RHODE ISLAND. Report of Mrs. C. Dailey upon the disabled R. I. Soldiers, made to Gov. Sprague, January, 1863. pp. 24.

4087. —— Report of the U. S. Provost Marshal of R. I., Jan. 1863.

4088. —— Report of J. R. Bullock, Commissioner for adjusting the Claims of Rhode Island against the U. S., Jan., 1863. pp. 11.

4089. —— Report on the Accounts of the Adjutant Gen., Quartermaster Gen. and Paymaster General, (War Expenses,) Jan., 1863.

4090. —— Report of Adjutant Gen. Mauran, for 1862. pp. 64.

4091. —— Message of Governor Smith, January 11, 1864. pp. 8.

4092. —— Report of Quartermaster Gen. Cooke, for 1863. pp. 64.

4093. —— Report of Adjutant General Mauran, for 1863. pp. 94.

4094. —— Report of the State Allotment Commissioner, Jan. '64. p. 5.

4095. —— Message of Gov. Smith, January 9, 1865. pp. 11. With accompanying Documents. pp. 12.

4096. —— Special Message of Gov. Smith, January 31, 1865. pp. 8.

4097. —— Report of Col. Charles E. Bailey, relative to the Quota of the State, February 13, 1865. pp. 8.

4098. —— Report of Joint Special Committee, to proceed to Washington to procure extension of Draft, January, 1865. pp. 7.

4099. —— Report of Quartermaster Gen. Remington, for 1864. p. 82.

4100. —— Report of Adjutant Gen. Mauran, for 1864. pp. 73.

4101. —— Report of Commutation Commission. pp. 28.

4102. —— Report of the Special Committee on Finance of the House of Representatives, on Bounty Frauds, January, 1865.
8vo. pp. 411. PROVIDENCE: *H. H. Thomas & Co.*, 1865.

4103. —— Message of Governor Smith, January, 1866. pp. 22.

4104. —— Special Message of Gov. Smith, (relative to War expenses) with accompanying Documents, January, 1866. Providence: *Press Company*, 1866.

4105. —— Report of Joint Special Committee upon the Governor's Special Message.
8vo. pp. 107. PROVIDENCE: *Press Company*, 1866.

4106. —— Minority Report on Governor's Special Message. pp. 11.

4107. —— Affidavits and Letters laid before the Senate Committee, with the Majority and Minority Reports. pp. 16.

4108. —— Report of John R. Bartlett, Commissioner on the Soldiers' National Cemetery at Gettysburg, January, 1866. pp. 6.

4109. RHODE ISLAND. Letter from the Sec. of War to the U. S. Senate, with information relating to the Quota of Rhode Island. pp. 16. *38th Congress, 2d Session, Document* 17.

4110. —— My First Campaign. Twelfth Regiment R. I. Volunteers. 18mo. pp. 152. BOSTON : *Wright & Potter,* 1863.

4111. RICE, Hon. ALEXANDER H. Speech in the U. S. House of Reps., February 3, 1865, in reply to Henry Winter Davis, upon his Proposition to establish a Board of Naval Administration. pp. 16.

4112. RICE, Rev. DANIEL. The President's Death. Its Import. A Sermon preached in Lafayette, Indiana, April 19, 1865. 8vo. p. 7.

4113. —— Harper's Ferry. Its Lessons. A Discourse. 1860.

4114. RICE, DAVID. A Kentucky Protest against Slavery. Slavery inconsistent with Justice and Good Policy. 8vo. pp. 13. NEW YORK : 1812. Reprinted, N. Y., 1863.

4115. RICE, Rev. N. L., DD. Our Country and the Church. 12mo. pp. 93· NEW YORK : *C. Scribner,* 1861.

4116. —— The Pulpit ; its relations to our National Crisis. 8vo. pp. 71. NEW YORK : *Charles Scribner,* 1863.

4117. RICHARDS, Rev. GEO. Grounds for Gratitude. A Discourse delivered on Thanksgiving Day, Nov. 28, '61, in Litchfield, Ct. 8vo. pp. 12. LITCHFIELD : (Conn.) *Enquirer Office,* 1861.

4118. —— The Memory of Washington. A Sermon preached in Litchfield, Connecticut, February 22, 1863. 8vo. pp. 32. PHILADELPHIA : *H. B. Ashmead,* 1863.

4119. RICHARDSON, D. M. How Specie Payments may be resumed within three years, without contraction of the Currency or Commercial Revulsion. 8vo. pp. 10. PHILADELPHIA : *Ringwalt & Brown,* 1866.

4120. RICHARDSON, Hon. W. A. Speech of. The Abolition Schemes of Negro Equality, exposed. In the House of Representatives, May 19, 1862. 8vo. pp. 4.

4121. RICHEY, Rev. THOMAS. On Moral Unity, and the way of its attainment. A Sermon. 8vo. pp. 16. BALTIMORE : *John F. Wiley,* 1861.

4122. RICHMOND, The Defence of, against the Federal Army, under Gen. McClellan. By a Prussian Officer in the Confed. service. 8vo. pp. 16. NEW YORK : *George F. Nesbitt & Co.,* 1863.

4123. RIDDLE, Hon. A. G. Speech on the Bill to Abolish Slavery in the Dist. of Columbia, in the House of Reps., Apr. 11, '62. p. 5.

4123.* —— Speech in the House of Representatives, February 28, 1863, on the Bill to Indemnify the President. pp. 8.

4124. —— Speech on the Military Academy Bill. House of Representatives, January 27, 1862. pp. 16.

4125. RIDDLE, Rev. M. S. Principle and Passion in Conflict. A Thanksgiving Sermon, Nov. 28, 1861, at New Brunswick, N. J. 8vo. pp. 24. NEW BRUNSWICK : (N. J.) *Fredonian Office,* '61.

4126. [RICHARDSON, N., and G. Sinnott.] Suggestions upon the Bill introduced by Mr. Dawes of Massachusetts, to amend the Acts of Congress approved March 2, 1863 and 1864. 8vo. pp.

4127. RIFLE SHOTS at Passing Events. A Poem ; being hits at the Time, by an Inhabitant of the Comet of 1861. 8vo. pp. 112. PHILADELPHIA : *T. B. Peterson & Bro.,* 1862.

4128. RIGHTS, Prerogative and Public Law. 8vo. pp. 24. BOSTON : *William Guild & Co.,* 1863.

4129. THE RIGHTS OF STATES ; or the Union a Revocable Compact. pp. 16.

4130. THE RIGHT OF RECOGNITION. A Sketch of the Present Policy of the Confederate States. London, 1862. pp. 30.

4131. RIGHT OF SEARCH. Reply to an "American's Examination" of the "Right of Search ;" with Observations on the Questions at issue between Great Britain and the U. S., by an Englishman. 8vo. pp. 109, lxii. LONDON : *John Rodwell,* 1862.

4132. THE RIGHT, or the Wrong, of the American War. A Letter to an English Friend. Second edition. 8vo. pp. 28. NEW YORK : *Anson D. F. Randolph,* 1864.

4133. THE RIGHTFUL POWER of Congress to Confiscate and Emancipate. (Law Reporter, June, 1862.) 8vo. pp. 24. BOSTON : *Charles H. Crosby,* 1862.

4134. RIPLEY, Gen. JAMES W. Statement regarding certain Charges against. Washington, December, 1861. pp. 16.

4135. RISK, T. F. A View of the Impending Political Crisis, from a Western Standpoint. Address before the St. Louis Literary and Phil. Association, January 6, 1861. pp. 7.

4136. RITCHIE, Rev. ANDREW. The Sins of the Land. A Sermon preached at Cincinnati, Sept. 26, 1861, being Fast Day. pp. 16.

4137. ROBERTSON, Wm. Speech on the State of the Country, in the House of Delegates of Virginia, 5th and 6th March, 1860. 8vo. pp. 39. Richmond : *Whig Office*, 1860.

4138. ROBBINS, Rev. Frank L. A Discourse on the Death of Abraham Lincoln, delivered April 23, 1865. 8vo. pp. 21. Philadelphia : *H. B. Ashmead*, 1865.

4139. ROBINSON, Charles P. The Martyr President. A Sermon preached in Brooklyn, New York, April 15, 1865. 8vo. pp. 31. New York : *John F. Trow*, 1865.

4140. ROBINSON, Rev. Charles S. A Memorial Discourse, occasioned by the Death of Lieut. Col. J. M. Green, 48th N. Y. Vols. 8vo. pp. 15. Troy : (N. Y.) *Times Office*, 1864.

4141. ROBINSON, Rev. E. T. Christianity and War. A Discourse delivered in Cincinnati, December 11, 1861. 12mo. pp. 16. *Am. Book and Tract Society, Cincinnati*.

4142. ROBINSON, Lucius. The State and National Banks. The Question of Taxation. Correspondence between Bank Officers and the Comptroller. 8vo. pp. 14. Albany : *Weed, Parsons & Co.*, 1864.

4143. ROCHEFORT, Henri. Un Homme du Sud. 12mo. pp. 36. Paris : 1862.

4144. RODGERS, Ravaud K., DD. Thanksgiving. A Sermon preached in Round Brook, New Jersey, November 28, 1861. 8vo. pp. 18. New Bruns. : (N. J.) *Terhune & Van Anglen,* '61.

4145. ROELKER, Bernard. Argument in favor of the Legal Tender Clause in the Act of Congress of February 25, 1862. 8vo. pp. 42. New York : *F. W. Christern*, 1863.

4146. ROGNIAT, M. Calvet. Discours dans la Discussion du projet d'addresse, 13 Mars, 1862. 12mo. pp. 18. Paris : *Pankoucke & Cie.*, 1862.
Chiefly in relation to the American Blockade.

4147. The Roll Call. A Periodical 4to. Washington, Feb., 1864.

4148. ROLLINS, Hon. E. H., of New Hampshire. Slavery in the Capitol of the Republic. Speech, H. of Rep., April 11, '62. p. 8.

4149. ROLLINS, James S. One Union ; One Constitution ; One Destiny. Speech, House of Reps., April 24, 1862. pp. 16.

4150. —— Speech on the proposed Amendment to the Constitution of the United States, January 18, 1865. pp. 15.

4151. ROMERO, Senor. Speech on the Situation of Mexico. New York, 16th of December, 1863.
8vo. pp. 12. New York: *Wm. C. Bryant & Co.*, 1864.

4152. ROOKER, A. Does it answer? Slavery in America. A History.
8vo. pp. 34. London: *Virtue Brothers & Co.*, 1864.

4153. ROSECRANS, General. Letters to the Democracy of Indiana. Action of the Ohio Regiments, at Murfreesboro', regarding the Copperheads. pp. 8.

4154. —— Resolutions of Thanks to, with General Rosecrans' Reply; and the Address of the Ohio Soldiers to the People of Ohio, together with the Correspondence connected therewith. pp. 8.

4155. ROSS, Charles J. Chronicles of the Rebellion of 1861.
8vo. pp. 23. New York: *Frank McElroy*, 1861.

4156. ROSS, Frederick A., DD. Slavery ordained of God.
12mo. pp. 186. Philadelphia: 1843.

4157. —— Sermon delivered in Huntsville, Alabama, on Fast Day, November 29, 1860. The Separation of Israel.
8vo. pp. 11. Huntsville: (Ala.) *W. B. Figures*, 1860.
Relates to Secession and Disunion.

4158. ROSS, Fitzgerald. A Visit to the Cities and Camps of the Confederate States.
8vo. pp. 300. London: *William Blackwood & Sons*, 1865.

4159. ROSS, John. Communication of the Delegation of the Cherokee Nation, to the President of the United States, submitting the Memorial of their Council, with the Correspondence between John Ross and Officers of the Rebellious States.
8vo. pp. 48. Washington: *Gibson Brothers*, 1866.

4160. ROSS, Lewis W. Speech in House of Representatives, June 15, 1864, on the proposed Amendment to the Constitution. pp. 8.

4161. ROUSE, E. S. S. The Bugle Blast; or Spirit of the Conflict. Comprising Naval and Military Exploits.
18mo. pp. 336. Philadelphia: *James Challen & Son*, 1864.

4162. RUBEK, Sennoia. The Burden of the South, in verse; or Poems on Slavery, grave, humorous, didactic and satirical.
8vo. pp. 96. New York: *Everardus Walker*, 1864.

4163. RUDDER, Rev. Wm. The Educational Powers of our Present National Troubles. A Sermon preached in Albany, Jan. 13, '61.
8vo. pp. 35. Albany: *Munsell & Rowland*, 1861.

4164. RUFFIN, Hon. THOMAS, of North Carolina. State Rights and State Equality. Speech, House of Reps., February 20, 1861.

4165. RUGGLES, A. G. A National System of Finance, suited to a War or Peace Establishment ; regulating Exchanges.
8vo. pp. 14.   FOND DU LAC, Wisconsin, August, 1862.

4166. RUGGLES, SAMUEL B. Resources of the United States. Report to the International Statistical Congress, at Berlin ; with the accompanying Communication to the State Department, Sep., '63.
8vo. pp. 30.   *Loyal Publication Society, No.* 48.

4167. —— The same. pp. 23. Washington: *Govt. Pr. Office,* 1864.

4168. —— Report on the enlargement of the Canals for National Purposes, April 8, 1863.
8vo. pp. 105.   ALBANY : *Comstock &* *Cassidy,* 1863.

4169. —— The English Heptarchy and the American Union. 8vo. pp. 8. 1864.

4170. —— Address at the Opening of the Metropolitan Fair, New York, April 8, 1864.

4171. RUSH, BENJAMIN. Letter to a Citizen of Washington, on the Rebellion, May, 1862.
8vo. pp. 23.   PHILADELPHIA : *C. Sherman & Son,* 1862.

4172. RUSH, BENJ., M. D. Directions for preserving the Health of Soldiers. Published in 1777, for the American Army. Republished in 1865 for the Union Army, waging the Second War of Independence. 18mo. pp. 30. *Am. Tract Society.*

4173. RUSLING, Capt. JAMES F. The War for the Union. *Methodist Quarterly Review, April,* 1864.

4174. RUSSELL, CHARLES. Our Domestic Relations ; or How to treat the Rebel States. *Continental Monthly, May,* 1864.

4175. RUSSELL, EARL. The Slave Power.
8vo. pp. 11.   MANCHESTER : *Un. and Emanc. Society,* 1863.

4176. RUSSELL, HENRY EVERETT. Reconstruction. *Continental Monthly, December,* 1863.

4177. —— The War, a Contest for Ideas. Ibid. *May,* 1864.

4178. —— Negro Troops. Ibid. *August,* 1864.

4179. —— The Constitutional Amendment. Ibid. *September,* 1864.

4180. —— The Two Platforms. Ibid. *November,* 1864.

4181. RUSSELL, Rev. PETER. Two Sermons preached in Eckley,

Penn., on the occasion of the Funeral Solemnities of President
Lincoln, and Fast Day.

8vo. pp. 30.   PHILADELPHIA : *King & Baird*, 1865.

4182. RUSSELL, WILLIAM H.   Letter (to the London Times) on the
Battle of Bull Run : with Notes from the Rebellion Record.

8vo. pp. 14.   NEW YORK: *G. P. Putnam*, 1861.

4183. —— The Battle of Bull Run.

12mo. pp. 30   NEW YORK: *Rudd & Carlton*, 1861.

4184. —— Pictures of Southern Life, Social, Political and Military.
Written for the London Times.

12mo. pp. 143.   NEW YORK : *J. G. Gregory*, 1861.

4185. —— My Diary, North and South.

2 vols. post 8vo. p. 424 & 442.   LOND.: *Bradbury & Evans*,'63.

4186. —— The same work.

8vo. pp. 224.   NEW YORK: *Harper & Brothers*, 1863.

4187. —— The same work.

12mo. pp. 603.   BOSTON : *T. O. H. P. Burnham*, 1863.

4188. RUTH'S VISION : or Chronicle of the War.

18mo. pp. 8.   PITTSBURGH : (Pa.) *J. T. Sample*.

SABINE, Rev. WM. T.   " A Nation saved by the Lord."   A Sermon
preached at Philadelphia, Dec. 7, 1865.   pp. 16.   Phila., 1865.

4190. —— "The Land Mourneth" the Death of Abraham Lincoln. A
Sermon delivered in Philadelphia, April 16, 1865. 12mo. p. 18.

4191. SABLÉ CLOUD, (The.) A Southern Tale, with Northern Comments.

12mo. pp. 275.   BOSTON : *Ticknor & Fields*, 1861.

4192. SABRE, Lieut. G. E. (R. I. Cavalry.)   Nineteen months a
Prisoner of War.   Narrative of experiences in the War Prisons
and Stockades of Mobile, Atlanta, Libby, Belle Island, Andersonville, etc.

12mo. pp. 207.   NEW YORK : *American News Co.*, 1865.

4193. SADTLER, Rev. B.   " A Rebellious Nation Reproved."   A
Sermon preached at Easton, Penn.. September 26, 1861.

8vo. pp. 12.   EASTON : (Pa.) *Davis & Eichman*, 1861.

4194. SAFFORD, Rev. J. P., DD.   Reverence for Law ; from a Consideration of the Source of Authority in Government.

8vo. pp. 32.   PIQUA : (Ohio) *Register Office*, 1858.

4195. SALA, G. A.   My Diary in America in the Midst of War.
2 vols. 8vo. pp. 849.   LONDON: *Tinsley*, 1865.

4196. SALISBURY, Rev. S.   Sermon preached at West Alexandria,
Ohio, April 30, 1865, on the Assassination of Abraham Lincoln.
8vo. pp. 12.

4197. SALTER, WM.   The Gt. Rebellion, in the Light of Christianity.
12mo. pp. 63.   CINCINNATI: *Am. Reform Tract Society*, 1864.

4198. —— The Death of the Soldier of the Republic.   A Sermon
preached at Ottumwa, Iowa, May 18, 1862, with reference to the
Death of Capt. C. C. Cloutman, 3d Iowa, who fell at Fort Donelson.   pp. 8.

4199. SAMPLE, Rev. ROBERT F.   Our National Origin, Progress
and Perils.   A Sermon preached Nov. 28, 1861, in Bedford, Pa.
8vo. pp. 30.   PHILADELPHIA: *Wm. S. & A. Martien*, 1862.

4200. —— The Curtained Throne.   A Sermon on the Death of President Lincoln, at Bedford, April 23, 1865, repeated April 30, '65.
8vo. pp. 32.   PHILADELPHIA: *James S. Claxton*, 1865.

4201. SANBORN, F. B.   Emancipation in the West Indies.
8vo. pp. 15.   CONCORD: (Mass.) March, 1862.

4202. SANBORN, Rev. S.   A Discourse on the Terrible, yet Sublime,
Logic of Events, as suggested by the Assassination of President
Lincoln, etc., delivered in Ripon, Wis., April 23, 1865. pp. 7.

4203. SANDER, CONSTANTIN.   Geschichte des vierjährigen Bürger-
krieges in den Vereinigten Staaten von Amerika.
8vo. pp. 587.   Maps.   FRANKFURT: *J. D. Sauerländer*, 1865.

4204. —— Der Amerikanische Bürgerkrieg von seinem Beginn bis
zum Schluss des Jahres 1862.
8vo. pp. 121.   FRANKFURT: *Wilhelm Küchler*, 1863.

4205. SANDERS, GEO. N.   Address to the Democracy of the Northwest.   Dated, Nashville, Tennessee, January 8, 1862.   pp. 4.

4206. SANDERSON, Capt. JAMES M.   Camp Fires and Camp Cooking; or Culinary Hints for the Soldiers.
8vo. pp. 14.   WASHINGTON: *Government Printing Office*, 1862.

4207. SANFORD, HENRY S.   Letter to Thurlow Weed, on Free Cotton and Free Cotton States, December 15, 1860.   pp. 4.

4208. SANFORD, MILES.   Treason, and the Punishment it deserves.
A Sermon preached at Sandisfield, October 8, 1862.
8vo. pp. 27.   BOSTON: *J. M. Hewes*, 1862.

4209. SANGSTON, Lawrence. The Bastiles of the North. By a Member of the Maryland Legislature.

8vo. pp. 136. Baltimore : *Kelly, Hedian & Piet,* 1863.

Sanitary Commission, see *U. S. Sanitary Com., North West Sanitary Com., Illinois Sanitary Bureau, Western Sanitary Com., Chicago Sanitary Com.*

4210. Sanitary Fair, History of the Great Western.

8vo. pp. 578. Cincinnati : *C. F. Vent & Co.,* 1865.

4211. SARGENT, A. A. Confiscation of Rebel Property. Speech in the House of Reps., May 23, 1862. pp. 16.

4212. —— Speech on Pacific Railroad, as a Military Necessity, January 31, 1862. pp. 16.

4213. SARGENT, Epes. Peculiar.

12mo. pp. 500. New York : *Carlton,* 1864.

4214. SARGENT, F. W., DD. England, the United States, and the Southern Confederacy. Second edition, revised.

8vo. pp. 184. London : *Hamilton, Adams & Co.*

4215. SARMIENTO, F. L. Life of Pauline Cushman, the celebrated Union Spy and Scout.

12mo. pp. 374. Philadelphia : *John E. Potter,* 1865.

4216. SASS, Job. A Trackt for the Soldiers. Written at Wallpole, Mass., May Fust, 1863. pp. 4.

4217. SAUER, George. La Traite et l'Esclavage des Noirs.

8vo. pp. 26. Paris : *Dentu,* 1863.

4218. —— L'Affranchissement des Nègres.

8vo. pp. 26. Aix-la-Chapelle : *M. Ulrichs,* 1863.

4219. SAUNDERS, Maria L., of Paducah, Ky. Memorial to Congress for remuneration for Losses by reason of the destruction of her Property, as a Military Necessity. pp. 12.

4220. SAVAGE, John. The Life of Abraham Lincoln.

12mo. pp. 85 to 136. New York : *Derby & Miller,* 1864.

4221. —— Life and Public Services of Andrew Johnson.

12mo. pp. 408, 130. New York : *Derby & Miller,* 1866.

4222. SAXTON, Luther C. History of Liberty and Slavery, in all Ages and Nations,

8vo. pp. 44. New York : *Union Book Company.*

4223. SAYLER, Hon. Milton. The Right of Personal Liberty. Speech, House of Reps., of Ohio, January 29, 1863. pp. 24.

4224. SAYVE, le Comte de. Etude sur la révolution des Etats Unis. 8vo. pp. 47. Paris: *E. Dentu,* 1863.

4225. SCHADE, Louis. A Book for the Impending Crisis. Appeal to the Common Sense and Patriotism of the People of the U. S. "Helperism" annihilated. 8vo. pp. 16. Washington; *Little, Morris & Co.,* 1860.

4226. SCHAFF, Rev. Philip, DD. Slavery and the Bible. 8vo. pp. 32. Chambersburg: (Pa.) *Kieffer & Co.,* 1861.

4227. —— Der Bürgerkreig und des christliche Leben in N. Amerika. 8vo. pp. 72. Berlin: *Wiegandt und Grieben,* 1866.

4228. SCHAFFNER, Col. Tal. P. The War in America; being an Historical and Political Account of the Southern and Northern States, showing the Origin and Cause of the recent Secession War. 8vo. pp. vi, 416. Map. London: *Hamilton, Adams & Co.,*'62.

4229. SCHALK, Emil A. O. Summary of the Art of War. 8vo. pp. 182. Philadelphia: *J. B. Lippincott & Co.,* 1862.

4229.* SCHALK, Emil. Campaigns of 1862 and 1863, illustrating the Principles of Strategy. 8vo. pp. 252. Philadelphia: *J. B. Lippincott & Co.,* 1863.

4230. SCHENCK, Maj. Gen. Robert C., U. S, A. Life of. pp. 16.

4231. —— and Gen. F. P. Blair. Report in relation to the Commissions held by them as Major Generals, and as Members of Congress. 8vo. pp. 12. *Sen. Rep. Com. No.* 84, *38th Cong.,* 1*st Ses.,* 1864.

4232. SCHENCK, Mr., of Ohio. No Compromise with Treason. Reply to Fernando Wood. House of Reps., April 11, 1864. pp. 8.

4233. SCHENCK, Rev. B. S. The Burning of Chambersburg, Pennsylvania. By an Eye Witness and a Sufferer. 12mo. pp. 72. Philadelphia: *Lindsay & Blakiston,* 1864.

4234. SCHENCK, Rev. Noah Hunt. Christian Moderation; the Word in Season, to the Church and Country. A Sermon, May 19, 1861. 8vo. pp. 27. Baltimore: *Entz & Bash,* 1861.

4235. —— The Memory of Washington. An Oration delivered in Baltimore, February 22, 1861. 8vo. pp. 32. Baltimore: *Entz & Bash,* 1861.

4236. —— Songs in the Night. A Thanksgiving Sermon preached in Baltimore, November 26, 1863. 8vo. pp. 16. Baltimore: *Entz & Bash,* 1863.

4237. SCHENCK, Rev. N. H. The Grateful Sacrifice. A Thanksgiving Sermon preached in Baltimore, Nov. 24, 1864. pp. 15.

4238. SCHMIDT, Rev. Dr. Slavery among the Ancient Hebrews. Translated from the German. *Evang. Quar. Review, Vol.* xiii.

4239. SCHOBERT, Le Baron. Paix a L'Amérique.
8vo. pp. 32. Paris: *Dentu,* 1862.

4240. SHIRREFF, Emily. The Chivalry of the South.
12mo. pp. 14. London: *Ladies' Emancipation Society,* 1864.

4241. SCHMUCKER, Rev. Dr., and Gerritt Smith, Esq., Letters of. From the *Colonization Herald.* pp. 7.

4242. SCHURZ, Carl. Republican Nominations. Speech at Milwaukie, May 30, 1860. 8vo. pp. 8.

4243. —— Judge Douglas. The Bill of Indictment. Speech at the Cooper Institute, New York, September 13, 1860.
8vo. pp. 23. New York: *Tribune Office,* 1860.

4244. —— Die Anklage—Acte gegen Stephen A. Douglas.
8vo. pp. 18. New York: *Democrat Office,* 1860.

4245. —— The Life of Slavery, or the Life of the Nation. Speech at New York, March 6, 1862. pp. 11.

4246. —— "For the Great Empire of Liberty, Forward!" Speech delivered at Philadelphia, September 16, 1864. pp. 16.

4247. —— Speeches of, Collected by the Author.
12mo. pp. 392. Philadelphia: *J. B. Lippincott & Co.,* 1865.

4248. —— Reports on the States of South Carolina, Georgia, Alabama, Mississippi and Louisiana; also the Report of Lieut. General Grant. *39th Congress, 1st Sess., Executive Doc. No.* 2. pp. 108.

4249. SCHUTZ, Dr. Frederick. Für die Freiheit Aller! Für die Einheit des Vaterlandes! Reden von F. Schutz und Weil von Gernsbach. Philadelphia. 8vo. pp. 11.

4250. SCOFIELD, B. B. The Philosophy of Money; or a System of Finance based on Natural and Common Sense Principles. pp. 8. Genesee, 1862.

4251. SCOFIELD, Glenni W. Suffrage in the District of Columbia. Speech in House of Reps., January 10, 1866. pp. 8.

4252. SCOFIELD, Rev. Wm. C. A Nation's Joy and Jeopardy. An Address at Koskonong, Wisconsin, July 4, 1865.
8vo. pp. 16. Milwaukie: *Daily Wisconsin Office,* 1865.

4253. SCOTT, Lieut. General. The Private Letters of, and Reply of President Buchanan. State Secrets for the People.
8vo. pp. 24. NEW YORK: *Hamilton, Johnson & Farrelly*, 1862.

4254. SCOTT, T. PARKIN. Authority and Free Will. A Lecture before the Catholic Institute, Baltimore, Feb. 11, 1863. pp. 10.

4255. SCOVEL, JAMES M. New Jersey for the Union. Speech upon the Bill prohibiting the Enlistment of Negro Troops in New Jersey, under a Penalty of $500. March 16, 1864. pp. 16.

4256. —— Speech before the Anti-Monopoly Convention, at Trenton, New Jersey, February 1, 1865. pp. 12.

4257. SCOVEL, SYLVESTER F. Always Thankful. A Discourse delivered in Springfield, Ohio, November 27, 1862. pp. 15.

4258. SCROGGS, Gen., G. A. The Duty of Americans. Speeches and a Letter from Hon. James O. Putnam. pp. 15.

4259. SEABURY, SAMUEL. American Slavery distinguished from the Slavery of English Theorists, and justified by the Law of Nature.
12mo. pp. 319. NEW YORK: *Mason Brothers*, 1861.

4260. SEAMAN, EZRA C. Commentaries on the Constitutions and Laws, Peoples and History, of the United States, and upon the Great Rebellion and its Causes.
8vo. pp. 287. ANN ARBOR: *Journal Office*, 1863.

4261. SEARING, EDWARD, A. M. President Lincoln in History. An Address delivered in Milton, Wisconsin, June 1, 1865.
8vo. pp. 20. JANESVILLE: *Veeder & Devereux*, 1865.

4262. SEARLE, JANUARY. A Great Social Problem. Our Great America. *Continental Monthly, October*, 1864.

4263. SEARLE, Mrs. L. C. Washington an Example. The Father of a Nation will restore it to Peace.
8vo. pp. 121. PHILADELPHIA: *J. Challen & Sons*, 1864.

4264. SEARS, Rev. CLINTON W. A Sermon on the occasion of the National Fast, September 26, 1861, at Urbana, Ohio.
8vo. pp. 17. SPRINGFIELD: (Ohio) *Republican Office*, 1861.

4265. SEARS, EDMUND H. Revolution in Reform. A Discourse preached at Wayland, Mass., June 15, 1856.
8vo. pp. 16. BOSTON: *Crosby, Nichols & Co.*, 1856.

4266. LA SECESSION aux Etats Unis et son Origine par un Journaliste Américaine. (T. M.)
8vo. pp. 30. PARIS: *E. Dentu*, 1861.

46

4267. SECESSION; or "Borrowed Plumes," in three Acts. By "Peter Pindar, Jr." Second volunteer edition.

8vo. pp. 39. AURORA: *J. Pendleton Snell*, 1861.

4268. SECESSION; or Prose in Rhyme, and East Tennessee. A Poem by an East Tennesseean.

12mo. pp. 64. PHILADELPHIA: *For the author*, 1864.

4269. SECESSION. The Political Right of, a Reserved Power under the Constitution. Printed for personal friends.

8vo. pp. 16. NEW YORK: 1862.

4270. SECESSION TROUBLES. Legal Effect of, on the Commercial Relations of the Country. Privately printed New York, 1861.

4271. SECESSION, (The,) of the Whole South an Existing Fact. A Peaceable Separation the True Course. Its Effect on Peace and Trade between the Sections. From the Cincinnati *Press*. pp. 15.

4272. SECESSION, Concession and Self-Possession— Which? By a Massachusetts Citizen. BOSTON: *Walker, Wise & Co.*, 1861.

4273. SECESSIONISTS; their Promises and Performances; the Condition into which they have brought the Country; the Remedy, etc. A Voice from North Carolina.

8vo. pp. 21. NEW YORK: *Anson D. F. Randolph*, 1863.

4274. SECRET CORRESPONDENCE, illustrating the Condition of Affairs in Maryland. Baltimore, 1863. pp. 42.

4275. SEDGWICK, C. B. Speech on Government Contracts. House of Representatives, April 28, 1862. pp. 16.

4276. —— Emancipation and Enrollment of Slaves in the Service of the U. S. Speech in House of Reps., May 23, 1862. pp. 11.

4277. —— An Eulogy on Abraham Lincoln, on the occasion of the Obsequies, at Syracuse, April 19, 1865.

8vo. pp. 16. SYRACUSE: *Daily Journal Office*, 1865.

4278. SEGAR, Hon. JOSEPH. Speech in the House of Delegates of Virginia, March 30, 1861, on the Resolutions directing the Governor of Virginia to seize the United States Guns at Bellona Arsenal, and on the Secession of Virginia. pp. 23.

4279. —— Letter to a Friend in Virginia, in vindication of his course in declining to follow his State into Secession.

8vo. pp. 48. WASHINGTON: *W. H. Moore*, 1862.

4280. —— Letter to Robert Saunders, Esq., of Williamsburg.

8vo. pp. 15. HAMPTON, June 28, 1861.

4281. SEGAR, Hon. J. Vindication of the Union. Speech before the Union Meeting in Portsmouth, Virginia, May 31, 1862. 8vo. pp. 14. WASHINGTON: *W. H. Moore,* 1862.

4282. SEGAR, Hon. JOSEPH. Speech in the House of Reps., February 7, 1863, upon the Construction of a Ship Canal from the Mississippi to Lake Michigan. 8vo. pp. 13.

4283. —— and Hon. L. H. Chandler. Speeches in the House of Reps., May 17, 1864, in defence of their Claim to a Seat in the 38th Congress. pp. 28 and 23.

4284. SEISS, JOSEPH A., DD. The Threatening Ruin ; or our Times, our Prospects and our Duty. A Discourse delivered in Philadelphia, January 4, 1861.
18mo. pp. 38. PHILADELPHIA : *Smith, English & Co.,* 1861.

4285. —— Government and Christianity. A Sermon for the Times. 8vo. pp. 35. PHILADELPHIA : *C. Sherman & Son,* 1861.

4286. —— Remarks at the Funeral of Henry Bohlen, Brig. General, U. S. A., September 12, 1862, in St. John's Ch., Phila. pp. 16.

4287. —— The Assassinated President; or the Day of National Mourning for Abraham Lincoln. Philadelphia, June 1, 1865. 8vo. pp. 43. PHILADELPHIA, 42 North Ninth street, 1865.

4288. SELECT COMMITTEE OF THIRTY-THREE. Reports of the, on the Disturbed State of the Country.
8vo. pp. 71. WASHINGTON: *Thomas H. Ford,* 1861.

4289. SEMMES. The Cruise of the Alabama and the Sumter ; from the Private Journals and other Papers of Commander R. Semmes, C. S. N., and other Officers.
2 vols. 12mo. LONDON: *Saunders & Otley,* 1864.

4290. —— The same. 12mo. pp. 328. New York: *Carlton,* 1864.

4291. —— Croisières de l'Alabama et du Sumter.
12mo. pp. 471. PARIS : *E. Dentu,* 1864.

4292. SEMMES, the Pirate.
18mo. pp. 105. NEW YORK : *T. R. Dawley* 1865.
For other works relating to Semmes and his vessel, see *Alabama* and *British Parliamentary Papers.*

4293. SENOUR, Rev. F. The Hand of God in the present Great Rebellion, the Hope of our Country and a Reason for Thanksgiving.
8vo. pp. 12. ROCKFORD : (Ill.) *Register Press,* 1862.

4294. SENOUR, Rev. F.   The Christian Soldier.

   32mo. pp. 96.   Cincinnati: *C. F. Vent & Co.*, 1861.

4295. —— Morgan and his Captors.

   8vo. pp. 389.   Cincinnati: *C. F. Vent & Co.*, 1865.

4296. The Sequestration Cases before the Hon. A. G. Magrath, under the Act of the Confederate States, in the District Court of South Carolina, October Term, 1861.   8vo. pp. 68.

4297. The Services of the Protestant Episcopal Church in the United States of America, as ordered by the Bishops during the Civil War.

   4to. pp. 27.   Brooklyn, February 22, 1864.

   An engraved facsimile is given of the various prayers and services, as written by the Bishops themselves, thus giving copies of the autographs of each contributor.

4298. SEWARD, Hon. William H.   Speech against the Lecompton Constitution.   Senate, March 3, 1858.   pp. 48.

4299. —— Speech on the Admission of California, and the subject of Slavery ; in the United States Senate, March 11, 1850.

   8vo. pp. 26.   Boston: *Redding & Co.*, 1850.

4300. —— Freedom in Kansas.   Speech in the Senate of the United States, March 3, 1858.   pp. 15.

4301. —— Political Issues of the Day.   Speech delivered at Detroit, September 4, 1860.   8vo. pp. 14.

4302. —— The Union.   Speech in the Senate, Jan. 12, 1861.   pp. 8.

4303. —— Correspondence with the Governments of Great Britain, France, Spain, Brazil and Netherlands, relative to Insurgent Privateers in Foreign Ports, April 26, 1862.

   8vo. pp. 211.   *37th Congress, 2d Sess., Ex. Doc. No.* 104.

4304. —— Correspondence with William L. Dayton, U. S. Minister to France, and Mons. Drouyn de l'Huys, on the subject of " Mediation, arbitration, and other measures looking to the Termination of the existing Civil War."

   8vo. pp. 16.   *37th Cong., 3d Sess., Ex. Doc., No.* 38, 1863.

4305. —— Papers relating to Foreign Affairs, (embracing the Correspondence of the State Department,) communicated to Congress, December 1, 1862.

   8vo. 3 parts, pp. 910, 439.   Washington: *Gov. Pr. Office,* '63.

4306. —— Papers relating to Foreign Affairs, etc.   December, 1863.

   8vo. 2 parts, pp. 1389.   Washington: *Govt. Pr. Office,* 1864.

4307. SEWARD, Hon. W. H. Papers relating to Foreign Affairs, etc. December, 1864.

8vo. 2 parts, pp. 896, 814. WASHINGTON : *Gov. Pr. Office*, '65.
These Papers, which embrace the Correspondence of the Hon. Wm. H. Seward, Secretary of State, accompany the Messages of the President of the United States, and relate chiefly to the Rebellion, or matters growing out of that event.

4308. —— Issues of the Conflict. Terms of Peace. Speech on the occasion of the Fall of Atlanta, at Auburn, Sept. 3, 1864.

8vo. pp. 8. WASHINGTON : *McGill & Witherow*, 1864.

4309. —— Review of Mr. Seward's Diplomacy, by a Northern Man. pp. 60.

4310. SHANKS, Rev. G. H. Freedom and Slavery. An Explanation of the Principles and Issues involved in the American Conflict, and the Duty of the People of Britain in relation to that momentous Struggle.

8vo. pp. 63. BELFAST : *William McComb.*

4311. SHANKS, Hon. JOHN P. Vindication of Major Gen. Fremont, against the attacks of the Slave Power and its Allies. House of Representatives, March 4, 1862. pp. 21.

4312. —— Confiscation of Rebel Property. H. of Reps., May 23, '62.

4313. SHARP, PINDAR B. The Reconstruction of the American Union ; or Confederation of N. American Republics. 12mo. p. 24.

4314. SHAVER, Mr. Papers relating to the Imprisonment of, at Fort Warren, Boston. *British Parliamentary Papers*, 1862.

4315. SHAW, Rev. LINUS H. The War and its Cause. A Sermon preached at Sudbury, Mass., November 21, 1861.

8vo. pp. 21. WALTHAM : *Josiah Hastings*, 1861.

4316. —— The Black Man and the War. A Sermon preached at Sudbury, Massachusetts, November 24, 1864.

8vo. pp. 24· WALTHAM : *Sentinel Office*, 1864.

4317. SEWELL, ROBERT. Practice in the Executive Departments of the Government, under the Pension, Bounty and Prize Laws.

8vo. pp. 358. NEW YORK : *D. Appleton & Co.*, 1865.

4318. SEYMOUR, Hon. HORATIO, and John Van Buren. Speeches at the Grand Ratification Meeting, October 13, 1862 : with Gen. Scott's Prophetic Letter. pp. 16.

4319. —— Speeches at the Conventions held at Albany, January 31, 1861, and September 10, 1862. 8vo. pp. 13.

4320. SEYMOUR, Hon. H. Speech at Brooklyn, October 22, 1862.
8vo. pp. 7.

4321. —— Speech in the Democratic State Convention, at Albany,
September 10, 1862 ; also his Speech at the Albany Convention,
January 31, 1861. pp. 15.

4322. —— "The Union, the Constitution and the Laws," vindicated.
January, 1863.
8vo. pp. 11. NEW YORK : *Comstock & Cassidy,* 1863.

4323. SEYMOUR, Brig. General T. Military Education. A Vindication of West Point and the Regular Army. pp. 7.

4324. SHAKERS. Memorial from the United Society of Believers, or
Shakers, asking for Exemption from Service of such members as
may be drafted. 8vo. pp. 8.

4325. SHEA, JOHN GILMARY. The Fallen Brave. A Biographical
Memorial of the American Officers who have given their lives for
the preservation of the Union.
4to. pp. 128. Portraits. NEW YORK : *C. B. Richardson,* 1861.

4326. —— The American Nation ; Illustrated in the Lives of her
Fallen Brave and Living Heroes.
Vol. 1, 4to. pp. 443. NEW YORK : *T. Farrell & Son,* 1864.

4327. SHEDD, Rev. WM. G. T., DD. The Union and the War. A
Sermon preached November 27, 1862.
12mo. pp. 40. NEW YORK : *C. Scribner,* 1863.

4328. SHEFFIELD, Hon. WM. P. of R. I. Speech in Congress upon the
Power and Duties of the Government in suppressing the Rebellion. January 27, 1862.

4329. —— Speech upon the Bill to Confiscate the Property and to
free the Slaves of Rebels from servitude, May 23, 1862.

4330. SHELDON, J. Thomas Jefferson, as seen by the Light of 1863.
Continental Monthly, February, 1864.

4331. SHELDON, W. D. The "Twenty-Seventh," a Regimental
History.
8vo. pp. 44. NEW HAVEN : *Morris Benham,* 1866.

4332. SHELLABARGER, Hon. SAMUEL. Relations of the Constitution and of Public Laws, to the Rebellion. A Speech delivered
in the House of Representatives, February 24, 1862.

4333. —— Speech on the Habeas Corpus, May 12, 1862.

4334. SHELLABARGER, Hon. S. Who are the authors of the Rebellion? Speech in Reply to Messrs. Vallandigham, Richardson and Cox, Jan. 27, '63. p. 16.

4335. —— Reconstruction. Speech, House of Reps., Jan. 8, '66. p. 8.

4336. SHEPARD, S. E. The Duty of Christians to Civil Government. 12mo. pp. 24. CINCINNATI: *H. S. Bosworth.*

4337. SHERIDAN, Gen. P. H. The Life of, by Julian K. Larke. 12mo. pp. 108. NEW YORK: *T. R. Dawley,* 1864.

4338. SHERMAN vs. HOOD. A Low Tart, inclined to be very Sweet. Something for Douglas Democrats to Remember. 8vo. pp. 4. *Loyal Publication Society, No.* 61, 1864.

4339. SHERMAN, Hon. JOHN. Letter in Reply to S. Teacle Wallis, Esq., of Maryland. pp. 8. Baltimore, 1863.

3340. —— Correspondence with S. Teacle Wallis, concerning the Arrest of Members of the Maryland Legislature, and the Mayor and Police Commissioners of Baltimore, in 1861. pp. 31.

4341. —— Slaves and Slavery. How affected by the War. Remarks in Senate, April 2, 1862. 8vo. pp. 15. WASHINGTON: *Scammell & Co.,* 1862.

4342. —— Taxation of Bank Bills. Speech, January 2, 1863. 8vo. pp. 15. WASHINGTON: *Globe Office,* 1863.

4343. —— Uniform National Currency. Speech, Feb. 10, '63. p. 16. 8vo. pp. 16. WASHINGTON: *Gideon & Pearson.*

4344. —— Speech on Emancipation as a Compensation for Military Service rendered by Slaves. Senate, February 2, 1864. p. 16.

4345. —— Speech in the U. S. Senate, on the General Policy of the Government. February 27, 1865. pp. 8.

4346. SHERMAN, General WM. T. The Life of, by T. R. Dawley. 12mo. pp. 108. NEW YORK: *T. R. Dawley,* 1864.

4347. —— Reply to the Mayor of Atlanta, and Speeches of Maj. Gen. Hooker, Brooklyn and New York, September 22, 1864. Letter of Lieut. Gen. Grant. pp. 8.

4348. —— The Hero's Our Story. General Sherman's Official Account of his Great March through Georgia and the Carolinas. 12mo. pp. 214. NEW YORK: *Bunce & Huntington,* 1865.

4349. —— Story of the Great March. See *Bowman, Nichols.*

4350. —— Description of the Sword made by Tiffany & Co., for presentation to Gen. Sherman, by gentlemen of New York. pp. 7.

4351. SHERMAN, Surgeon S. N., U. S. V. Eulogy upon President Lincoln, April 19, 1865, at Grafton, West Virginia. pp. 14.

4352. SHERWOOD, Hon. LORENZO. The Great Questions of the Times, exemplified in the antagonistic Principles involved in the Slaveholders' Rebellion against Democratic Institutions.
8vo. pp. 31. NEW YORK: *C. S. Westcott & Co.*, 1862.

4353. —— Argument in the case of the U. S. et al., Libellants and Captors vs. the Steamship Peterhoff. In Prize. U. S. District Court for the Southern District of New York.
8vo. pp. 42. NEW YORK: *C. S. Westcott & Co.*, 1863.

4354. —— Speech respecting the Slaveholders' Conspiracy against Democratic Principles. pp. 8.

4355. —— Pretext of the Rebels and their sympathizers refuted by a Logic of Facts. Rebellion against Free Government, as well as against the National Union. pp. 16.

4356. SHERWOOD, Miss VIRGINIA. Southern Hate of New England. *Continental Monthly, September*, 1863.

4357. SHIP CANAL. Proceedings of the National Ship Canal Convention, held at the City of Chicago, June 2 and 3, 1863.
8vo. pp. 218. CHICAGO: *Tribune Office*, 1863.

4358. —— Memorial to Congress from the Canal Convention at Chicago, to facilitate Commerce between the East and West. p. 16.

4359. —— Report on a Ship Canal between Lake Michigan and the Mississippi River, for War purposes.
8vo. pp. 13. *H. of Reps., Rep. No,* 37, *37th Cong., 2d Sess.,* '62.

4360. —— Proposed Ship Canal at Sturgeon Bay, Wisconsin, to connect Green Bay with Lake Michigan. pp. 4. Washington.

4361. —— Report by C. B. Stuart, upon proposed Improvements, to pass Gunboats from Tide-Water to the Great Lakes.
8vo. pp. 28. *H. of Rep., Ex. Doc., No,* 61, *38th Con., 1st Ses.,* '64.

4362. —— Extracts from the above Report. pp. 16. Washington, '65.

4363. —— Speech by Hon. Ezra Cornell, on the Question of a Ship Canal connecting Cayuga Lake with Lake Ontario.
8vo. pp. 34. ALBANY: *Weed & Parsons*, 1864.

4364. —— Report relative to the Enlargement of the Erie, Oswego and Champlain Canals, so as to admit Vessels of War.
8vo. pp. 5. ALBANY: *C. Van Benthuysen*, 1862.

4365. SHIP CANAL. The Necessity of a Ship Canal between the East and the West. Proceedings of the Board of Trade, Chicago, Feb., '63. 8vo. pp. 30.   CHICAGO: *Tribune Office*, 1863.

4366. —— The Necessity of a Ship Canal between the East and the West. Report of the Com. on Statistics, Chicago, June 2, 1863. 8vo. pp. 45.   CHICAGO: *Tribune Office*, 1863.

4367. —— Memorial in behalf of the State of New York, in respect to adapting its Canals to the defence of the Lakes. Washington, June, 1862. pp. 15.

4369. —— Memorial to Congress from the Chamber of Commerce, N. Y., in favor of enlarging the Canals for the defence of the Lakes. 8vo. pp. 14.   NEW YORK: *W. C. Bryant & Co.*, 1863.

4370. —— The Niagara Ship Canal; its Military and Commercial Necessity. 8vo. pp. 15. 2 Maps.   NEW YORK: 1863.

4371. —— The Niagara Ship Canal Proposition. Speech of A. X. Parker, of St. Lawrence, N. Y. In Assembly. 1864. pp. 7.

4372. —— Report of the Committee on Commerce, on the Bill to incorporate the Niagara Ship Canal Company, New York. *Senate Document No. 22, 1864.* pp. 16.

4373. —— Report of Samuel B. Ruggles, Commissioner in respect to the enlargement of the Canals, for National Purposes. 8vo. pp. 105.   ALBANY: *Comstock & Cassidy*, 1863.

4374. —— Report of the Committee on Naval Affairs, on "the cheapest, most expeditious, and reliable mode of placing vessels-of-war upon the Great Lakes." 8vo. pp. 16. *H. of Rep., Rep. No.* 4, *37th Cong., 3d Sess.*, 1863.

4375. —— The Defence of the Great Lakes; its necessity, and the quickest and best way to accomplish it. 8vo. pp. 16. ITHACA: (N. Y.) *Andros, McChain & Co.*, 1863.

4376. —— Northwestern Ship Canal Convention. Memorial to Congress from the Convention at Dubuque, Iowa, May 4, 1864. *38th Congress, 2d Session, House Miscellaneous Doc., No.* 23.

4377. SICKLES, Hon. DANIEL E. Speech on the State of the Union, delivered in the House of Reps., December 10, 1860. pp. 8.

4378. —— The Republic is Imperishable. Speech on the State of the Union. House of Reps., January 16, 1861. pp. 16.

47

4379. SICKLES, Hon. D. E. New Phases of the Revolution. How to
     meet them. Speech in House of Reps., Feb. 5, 1861. pp. 8.

4380. SIGNAL CORPS. Annual Report of the Acting Signal Officer of
     the Army, to the Secretary of War. Washington, 1864.

4381. SIGNALS. A Manual of, for the use of Signal Officers in the
     field, by Col. Albert J. Myer.

     8vo. pp. 148.   WASHINGTON: D. C. 1864.

4382. SIMMONS, Rev. ICHABOD. Our Duty in the Crisis. A Dis-
     course delivered September 20, 1861.

     8vo. pp. 24.   HARTFORD: *Case, Lockwood & Co.*, 1861.

4383. —— The Funeral Sermon of Capt. Joseph R. Toy, delivered at
     Simsbury, July 16, 1862.

     12mo pp. 24.   HARTFORD: *Case, Lockwood & Co.*, 1861.

4384. SIMMONS, Rev. JAMES B. The Cause and Cure of the Re-
     bellion ; or How far the People of the Loyal States are responsi-
     ble for the War.

     8vo. pp. 12.   INDIANAPOLIS: *Werden & Co.*, 1861.

4385. SIMMS, WM. GILMORE. The Morals of Slavery ; Being a brief
     Review of the Writings of Miss Martineau, and other persons, on
     the subject of Negro Slavery, as it now exists in the United
     States. Charleston, 1838.

4386. —— The Poetry of the South relating to the War. (In press.)

4387. SIMPSON, JOHN. Horrors of the Virginia Slave Trade, and of
     the Slave Rearing Plantations.

     12mo. pp. 64.   LONDON: *A. W. Bennett*, 1863.

4388. SIMPSON, Rev. MATTHEW. Funeral Address at the Burial of
     President Lincoln, at Springfield, Illinois, May 4, 1865.

     12mo. pp. 21.   NEW YORK: *Carlton & Porter*, 1865.

4389. SINCLAIR, PETER. Freedom or Slavery, in the United States,
     being Facts and Testimonies for the consideration of the British
     People.

     8vo. pp. 160.   LONDON: *Job Caudwell*, 1862.

4390. SISTERS OF THE GOOD SAMARITAN. Constitution and By-Laws
     of, together with Reports of the Officers, 1863.

     8vo. pp. 12.   QUINCY: (Ill.) *Whig Press.*

4391. SKETCH of the Origin and Progress of the Causes which have led
     to the overthrow of our Union. By a Man who has been an

actor in many Scenes, for more than fifty years past. Washington, 1861. pp. 33.

4392. SIZER, Thomas J. The Crisis; Its Rationale. I. Our National Force, the proper Remedy. II. Restoration of legitimate Authority, the end and object of the War.
8vo. pp. 100. Buffalo: *Reed, Butler & Co.*, 1862.

4393. SKINNER, Rev. T. H. J. Light in Darkness. A Discourse delivered at Stapleton, S. I., November 27, 1862.
8vo. pp. 20. Stapleton: (S. I.) *Gazette Office*, 1862.

4394. —— Comfort in Tribulation. An Address delivered at Stapleton, S. I., (on National Fast Day.)
8vo. pp. 28. New York: *Anson D. F. Randolph*, 1861.

4395. SLATER, Edward C., DD. The Nation's Loss. A Sermon upon the Death of Abraham Lincoln. Preached April 19, 1865, at Paducah, Kentucky.
8vo. pp. 20. Paducah: (Kentucky) *Brelock & Co.*, 1865.

4396. SLAUGHTER, Rev. P. The Virginian History of African Colonization.
8vo. pp. 20 and 116. Richmond: *McFarland & Ferguson,* '55.

4397. Slavery, the mere Pretext for Rebellion, not its Cause. Andrew Jackson's Prophecy of 1833. His Last Will and Testament in 1843. Bequests of the Swords. Picture of the Conspiracy drawn in 1863, by a Southern Man.
8vo. pp. 16, Philadelphia: *Sherman & Co.*, 1863.

4398. —— (Southern,) considered upon General Principles; or a Grapple with Abstractionists. By a North Carolinian.
8vo. pp. 24. New York: *D. Murphy & Son*, 1861.

4399. —— The Abolition of, the Right of the Government under the War Power.
12mo. pp. 24. Boston: *R. F. Wallcut*, 1861.

4399.* —— Separation from Slavery. A Premium Essay.
18mo. pp. 46. Boston: *American Tract Society.*

4400. —— The Ethics of American Slavery; being a Vindication of the Word of God and a pure Christianity in all Ages, from complicity with involuntary Servitude.
12mo. pp. 146. New York: *Ross & Toucey*, 1861.

4401. —— Aux Pasteurs et Ministres de toutes les denominations

Evangeliques de la Grande-Bretagne.   Paris, le 12 fevrier, 1862.
8vo. pp. 12.

Address from the Protestant Clergy of France of all denominations, relative to the abolition of Slavery and the American War.

4402. SLAVERY. Address of the New York Young Men's Anti-Slavery Society, to their Fellow Citizens.

8vo. pp. 38.   NEW YORK: *W. T. Coolidge & Co.*, 1834.

4403. —— By a Marylander. 8vo. pp. 8.   *J. P. Des Forges.*

4405. —— An Appeal of the People of West Virginia to Congress, for its immediate Action, and their Acceptance of the Nation's Proposal for the gradual Abolition of Slavery.   Wheeling, May 22, 1862.   pp. 8.

4406. —— The Abrogation of the Seventh Commandment by the American Churches.

18mo. pp. 33.   NEW YORK: *David Ruggles*, 1835.

4407. —— The Abolition of Slavery, the Right of Government, under the War Power.

12mo. pp. 24.   BOSTON: *R. F. Wallcutt*, 1861.

4408. —— A serious Address to the Rulers of America, on the inconsistency of their Conduct respecting Slavery.   Forming a Contrast between the encroachments of England on American Liberty and American Injustice in tolerating Slavery.

8vo. pp. 24.   TRENTON: *Printed.* LONDON: *Reprinted*, 1783.

4409. —— The Pro-Slavery Argument, as maintained by the most distinguished Writers of the Southern States.

12mo. pp. 490.   PHILADELPHIA: *Lippincott & Co.*, 1853.

4410. —— The Suppressed Book about Slavery.

12mo. pp. 432.   NEW YORK: *Carlton*, 1864.

4411. —— Address to the Friends of Constitutional Liberty, on the Violation, by the U. S. House of Reps., of the Right of Petition.
8vo. pp. 12.

4412. —— The Condition of the Free People of Color in the U. S.
8vo. pp. 23.   NEW YORK: 1839.

4413. —— Address of the N. E. Anti-Slavery Convention, to the Slaves of the U. S.; with an Address to President Tyler, adopted in Faneuil Hall, May 31, 1843.   pp. 16.

4414. —— Address to Non-Slaveholders of the South, on the Social and Political Evils of Slavery.

12mo. pp. 58.   NEW YORK: *Am. Anti-Slavery Society*, 1847.

4415. SLAVERY. Report of the Boston Anti-Slavery Society; being a concise History of the cases of the Slave Child, Med, and of the Women demanded as Slaves of the Supreme Court of Mass. 12mo. pp. 90. BOSTON: *Isaac Knapp*, 1836.

4416. —— American Slavery as it is. Testimony of a Thousand Witnesses. 8vo. pp. 224. NEW YORK: *Am. Anti-Slavery Society*, 1839.

4417. —— An Appeal to the Women of the Nominally Free States, from the Anti-Slavery Convention of African Women. 12mo. pp. 70. BOSTON: *Isaac Knapp*, 1838.

4418. —— The American Churches, the Bulwarks of Am. Slavery. 12mo. pp. NEWBURYPORT: *Charles Whipple*, 1842.

4419. SLAVERY in America. An Essay. By R. H. Mason. 8vo. pp. 34. BOSTON: *Crocker & Brewster*, 1853.

4420. —— The Bible against Slavery; or an Inquiry into the Genius of the Mosaic System and the Teachings of the Old Testament, on the subject of Human Rights. 12mo. pp. 154. PITTSBURGH: *Presb. Board of Education,* '64.

4421. —— A Second Dialogue of the Dead; between Ferdinand Cortez and Wm. Penn; to which is added a Scheme for the Abolition of Slavery. 12mo. pp. 14. WORCESTER: *J. Holt*, 1789.

4422. —— The Chattel Principle, the Abhorrence of Jesus Christ and the Apostles; or no Refuge for American Slavery in the New Testament. 8vo. pp. 71. *American Anti-Slavery Society*, 1839.

4423. —— Debate on Slavery, at Boston, May, 1841, between the Rev. Nath. Clover, of Boston, and the Rev. Jonathan Davis, of Georgia. 18mo. pp. 120.

4424. —— A Review of the Official Apologies of the American Tract Society, for its silence on the subject of Slavery. 8vo. pp. 16. NEW YORK: *American Abolition Society*, 1856.

4425. —— Selections from the Speeches and Writings of prominent Men in the U. S., on the subject of Abolition and Agitation, and in favor of the Compromise Measures of Congress. 8vo. pp. 69. NEW YORK: *J. P. Wright*, 1851.

4426. —— Address to the Inhabitants of New Mexico and California, on the omission by Congress to provide them with Territorial Governments, and on the Social and Political Evils of Slavery. 12mo. pp. 56.   NEW YORK : *Am. Anti-Slavery Society,* 1849.

4427. SLAVERY. Despotism in America ; or an Inquiry into the Nature and Results of the Slave-Holding System in the United States. 12mo. pp. 186.   BOSTON : *Whipple & Damrell,* 1840.

4428. —— Democratic Opinions of Slavery. 1776—1863. pp. 8.

4429. —— Address of the New York City Anti-Slavery Society. 8vo. pp. 46.   NEW YORK : *West & Trow,* 1833.

4430. —— Being Birney's Vindication of Abolitionists. Protest of the American A. S. Society. Outrage upon Southern Rights, etc. 12mo. pp. 80.   BOSTON : *Isaac Knapp,* 1836.

4431. —— The Fugitive Slave Law and its Victims. 12mo. pp. 48.   *American Anti-Slavery Society,* 1856.

4432. —— The same, enlarged. 12mo. pp. 168. Ibid. 1861.

4433. —— The Gospel of Slavery. A Primer of Freedom. By Iron Gray. 12mo. pp. 28. Plates.   NEW YORK : *T. W. Strong,* 1864.

4433.* —— Doom of Slavery in the Union ; its Safety out of it. Charleston, 1860.

4434. —— The Extinction of Slavery a National Necessity, before the present Conflict can be ended. pp. 8. (No date.)

4435. —— A Reproof of the American Church, by the Bishop of Oxford. Extracted from a " History of the Protestant Episcopal Church in America." By Samuel Wilberforce. 8vo. pp. 59.   NEW YORK : *William Harned,* 1846.

4436. —— Is Slavery a Blessing ? A Reply to Professor Bledsoe's Essay on Liberty and Slavery. With Remarks on Slavery as it is. By a Citizen of the South. 8vo. pp. 120.   BOSTON : *John P. Jewett,* 1857.

4437. —— Liberty, or Slavery ; the Great National Question. Three Prize Essays on American Slavery. By Rev. E. B. Thurston, Rev. A. C. Baldwin, and Rev. Timothy Williams. 18mo. pp. 138.   BOSTON : *Cong. Board of Education,* 1857.

4438. SLAVERY, The Abolition of, the Right of the Government, under the War Power. 8vo. pp. 24.   BOSTON : *R. T. Walcutt,* 1861.

4439. SLAVERY. A Letter of Inquiry to Ministers of the Gospel on Slavery. By a Northern Presbyter.
8vo. pp. 32. BOSTON : *Fetridge & Co.*, 1854.

4440. —— Letters on American Slavery, from Victor Hugo, De Toqueville, Emile de Girardin, Humboldt, La Fayette, etc.
12mo. pp. 24. BOSTON : *Anti-Slavery Society*, 1860.

4441. —— The Life of Slavery, or the Life of the Nation ? Mass Meeting at New York, March 6, 1862.
8vo. pp. 11. *From the Rebellion Record*, 1862.

4442. —— The Majority and Minority Reports of the Committee of the Meth. Epis. Church, on Slavery, May, 1860. pp. 24. Buffalo.

4443. —— The Nail hit on the Head ; or the Two Jonathans agreeing to settle the Slave Question with, or without, more Fighting, as the South pleases. By Pacificator.
8vo. pp. 24. NEW HAVEN : *T. H. Pease*, 1862.

4444. —— The Nutshell. The System of American Slavery " Tested by Scripture." Being a " short Method " with Pro-Slavery DD's, whether Doctors of Divinity, or of Democracy.
12mo. pp. 72. NEW YORK : *For the author*, 1865.

4445. —— Pictures of the " Peculiar Institution," as it exists in Louisiana and Mississippi. By an Eye Witness.
12mo. pp. 24. BOSTON : *J. B. Yerrington*, 1850.

4446. —— Picture of Slavery in the United States of America.
18mo. pp. 227. MIDDLETOWN ; *Edwin Hunt*, 1834.

4447. —— A Picture of Slavery drawn from the Decisions of Southern Courts. What is it Judge Woodward thinks. pp. 16.

4448. —— Proceedings of the Anti-Slavery Convention of American Women, at Philadelphia, May, 1838. pp. 18.

4449. —— Proceeding of the Anti-Slavery Conven., Phil., Dec., 1833.
8vo. pp. 28. NEW YORK : *Dorr & Butterfield*, 1833.

4450. —— Proceedings of the Indiana Convention to organize a State Anti-Slavery Society, at Milton, September 12, 1838.
8vo. pp. 28. CINCINNATI : *S. A. Alley*, 1838.

4451. —— La Question de l'Esclavage aux Etats Unis, par un ancien fonctionnaire des Indes Neérlandaises.
8vo. pp. 61. LA HAGE : *Martinus Nijhoff*, 1862.

4452. SLAVERY. Proceedings of the New England Anti-Slavery Convention, held in Boston, May 27, 1834.

8vo. pp. 72. BOSTON : *Garrison & Knapp,* 1834.

4453. —— Proceedings of the Rhode Island Anti-Slavery Convention, held in Providence, February 2, 1836.

8vo. pp. 88. PROVIDENCE : *H. H. Brown,* 1836.

4454. —— Platform of the American Anti-Slavery Society.

12mo. pp. 35. *American Anti-Slavery Society,* 1853.

4455. SLAVERY in Rebellion. An Outlaw. How to deal with it.

12mo. pp. 12. CINCINNATI : *American Reform Society.*

4456. —— Free Remarks on the Spirit of the Federal Constitution. The Practice of the Federal Government respecting the exclusion of Slavery from the Territories and New States.

8vo. pp. 116. PHILADELPHIA : *A. Finley,* 1819.

4457. —— Report of the Select Committee on Slavery and the Treatment of Freedmen, asking for the Repeal of the Fugitive Slave Act of 1850.

8vo. pp. 34. *Sen. Rep. Com. No.* 24, 38*th Cong.,* 1*st Ses.,* 1864.

4458. —— Report and Treatise on Slavery and the slavery Agitation. Printed by Order of the H. of Reps. of Texas, December, 1857.

8vo. pp. 81 and vi. AUSTIN : *John Marshall & Co.,* 1857.

4459. —— Resolutions of the Legislature of the State of New York, relative to the Proclamation of the President of the U. S., for the Extinction of Slavery. *House of Reps. Miscellaneous Document, No.* 79, 38*th Congress,* 1*st Session,* 1864.

4460. —— Revolution, the only Remedy for Slavery. *Anti-Slavery Tracts, No.* 7.

4461. —— The South. A Letter from a Friend in the North. With special Reference to the Effects of Disunion upon Slavery.

8vo. pp. 46. PHILADELPHIA : *For the author,* 1856.

4462. —— Some thoughts concerning Domestic Slavery, in a Letter to ——, Esq., of Baltimore.

18mo. pp. 115. BALTIMORE : *Joseph N. Lewis,* 1838.

4463. SLAVERY in the Southern States. By a Carolinian.

12mo. pp. 53. CAMBRIDGE : *John Bartlett,* 1852.

4464. —— in the Confederate States. By a Missionary. 8vo.

4465. —— The Tables Turned. Letter to the Congregational Association of N. York, reviewing the Report of their Committee on the subject of Slavery.

8vo. pp. 44.   BOSTON: *Crocker & Brewster.*

4466. SLAVERY. Testimony of the Society of Friends, against Slavery.
12mo. pp. 12.   BOSTON: *S. N. Dickinson & Co.,* 1847.

4467. —— Twenty Millions thrown away and Slavery perpetuated.
12mo. pp. 20.   BOSTON: *Isaac Knapp.*

4468. —— The Tract Society and Slavery. Speeches of Chief Justice Williams, Judge Parsons and Ex-Governor Ellsworth, at Hartford, before the American Tract Society, January, 1859.
8vo. pp. 26.   HARTFORD: *Elisha Geer,* 1859.

4469. —— The Unanimous Remonstrance of the Fourth Cong. Church, Hartford, against the Policy of the Am. Tract So., on Slavery.
12mo. pp. 34.   NEW YORK: 1855.

4470. —— Union and Liberty. Powers of Congress in relation to the Slaves; with a form of Enactment in conformity thereto. Addressed to a Congressman. pp. 8.

4471. —— The War on Slavery; or Victory only thro' Emancipation.
12mo. pp. 8.   BOSTON: *R. F. Wallcutt,* 1861.

4472. —— Where will it End? A View of Slavery in the United States, in its Aggressions and Results.
12mo. pp. 23.   PROVIDENCE: *Knowles, Anthony & Co.,* 1863.

4473. SLAVES. Ordinance organizing and establishing Patrols for the Police of Slaves in the Parish of St. Landry.
8vo. pp. 29.   OPELOUSAS: *Patriot Office,* 1863.

4474. —— Influence of Catholic Christian Doctrines on the Emancipation of Slaves. By a Member of the B. V. Mary Church, East Boston.
8vo. pp. 35.   BOSTON: *Patrick Donahoe,* 1863.

4475. SLAVES IN DISLOYAL STATES. Letter from the Secretary of the Treasury, on the employment and Sustenance of.
8vo. pp. 11.   *Ex. Doc. No. 72, 37th Cong., 3d Session,* 1865.

4476. SLAVEHOLDER ABROAD; or Billy Buck's Visit with his Master to England. Letters from Dr. Pleasant Jones to Major Joseph Jones, of Georgia.
12mo. pp. 512.   PHILADELPHIA: *J. B. Lippincott & Co.,* 1860.

48

4477. SLAVEHOLDING STATES. The New Reign of Terror in the Slaveholding States, for 1859–60.

12mo. pp. 144. *American Anti-Slavery Society*, 1860.

4478. SLAVE-HUNTING. No Slave-Hunting in the Old Bay State. An Appeal to the People and Legislature of Massachusetts.

12mo. pp. 23. NEW YORK: *Am. Anti-Slavery Society*, 1860.

4479. —— Report of the Select Committee on the Petition to prevent, in the State of New York, February 11, 1860.

8vo. pp. 11. ALBANY: *Van Benthuysen*, 1860.

4480. SLAVERY AND THE CHURCH. Two Letters addressed to Rev N. L. Rice, in Reply to his Letters to the Congregational Deputation, on Slavery.

8vo. pp. 44. BOSTON: *Crocker & Brewster*, 1856.

4481. SLAVE POWER. A Chapter of American History. Five Years Progress of the Slave Power. From the Bost. " Commonwealth."

8vo. pp. 84. BOSTON; *Benj. B. Mussey*, 1852.

4482. SLAVES. On receiving Donations from Holders of Slaves.

12mo. pp. 20. BOSTON: *Perkins & Marvin.*

4483. SLAVE REPRESENTATION. By Boreas. Awake! O Spirit of the North. pp. 28.

4484. SLAVE TRADE. Remarks on the Colonization of the Western Coast of Africa, by the Free Negroes of the United States.

8vo. pp. 67. NEW YORK: *W. L. Burroughs*, 1850.

4485. —— An Exposition of the African Slave Trade, from the year 1840 to 1850, prepared from Official Documents, for the Religious Society of Friends.

8vo. pp. 160. PHILADELPHIA: *J. Rakestraw*, 1851.

For other works relating to American Slavery, see their respective authors.

4486. SLOANE, Rev. J. R. W. Review of Rev. Henry J. Van Dyke's Discourse on " The Character and Influence of Abolitionism."

8vo. pp. 40. NEW YORK: *William Ewing*, 1861.

4487. —— The Three Pillars of a Republic. An Address at the Annual Commencement, Jefferson College, Canonsburg, Aug. 6, '62.

8vo. pp. 31. NEW YORK: *Phair & Co.*, 1862.

4488. SLOCUM, WM. N. The War, and How to end it.

8vo. pp. 48. 3d edition, revised. SAN FRANCISCO, 1861.

4489. SMALLEY, Judge, U. S. Circuit Court, Vermont, 1861. In

the matter *ex parte,* Anson Field. Application for Habeas Corpus.
    8vo. pp. 27. BURLINGTON : (Vt.) *W. H. & C. A. Hoyt & Co.,*'62.

4490. SMART, Rev. JAMES S. A Fast Day Sermon, delivered in the
    City of Flint, Michigan, January 4, 1861.
    8vo. pp. 22.   FLINT : (Mich.) *W. Stevenson,* 1861.

4491. SMART, Rev. J. S. The Political Duties of Christian Men and
    Ministers. A Sermon for the Times. Jackson, July 28, 1854.
    8vo. pp. 23.   DETROIT : *Baker & Conover,* 1854.

4492. SMEDES, W. C., of Vicksburg. Letter justifying Secession, '61.

4493. SMITH, E. DELAFIELD. Brief Appeals for the Loyal Cause.
    8vo. pp. 16.   NEW YORK : *John W. Amerman,* 1863.

4494. SMITH, G. CLAY, of Ky. Speech on the Confiscation Bill,
    House of Representatives, February 5, 1864. pp. 8.

4495. SMITH, FRANKLIN W. The Prosecution of, by the Navy Depart-
    ment. Report of the Boston Board of Trade, including the
    Memorial from Massachusetts, to the President of the United
    States. Opinion of the Hon Charles Sumner on the case.
    8vo. pp. 60.   BOSTON : *John Wilson & Son,* 1865.

4496. SMITH, GERRIT, and the Vigilant Association of the city of N. Y.
    12mo. pp. 29.   NEW YORK : *John A. Gray,* 1860.

4497. —— The Country. Speech delivered in N. Y., Dec. 21, '63. p. 8.

4498. —— McClellan's Nomination and Acceptance.
    8vo. pp. 15. NEW YORK : *Loyal Publication Soc'y, No.* 63, '64.

4499. —— Speeches and Letters on the Rebellion, delivered in 1863.
    8vo. pp. 70.   NEW YORK : *John A. Gray & Greene,* 1864.

4500. —— Speeches and Letters on the Rebellion, 1864.
    8vo. pp. 76.   NEW YORK : *American News Company,* 1865.

4501. —— No Treason in Civil War. Speech, N. York, June 8, '65.
    8vo. pp. 25.   NEW YORK : *American News Company,* 1865.

4502. SMITH, GOLDWIN. Does the Bible sanction Amer. Slavery ?
    8vo. pp. 73. OXFORD and LONDON : *J. H. & James Parker,* '63.

4503. —— The same work.
    12mo. pp. 107.   CAMBRIDGE : *Sever & Francis,* 1863.

4504. —— On the Morality of the Emancipation Proclamation. With
    W. E. Forster's Speech on the " Slaveholder's Rebellion."
    8vo. pp. 15.   MANCHESTER : *Union Emanc. Society,* 1863.

4505. SMITH, Goldwin. A Letter to a Whig Member of the Southern Independence Association.

12mo. pp. 184. London, 1864.

4506. —— The same. pp. 64. Boston: *Ticknor & Fields*, 1864.

4507. —— England and America. *Atlantic Monthly, December*, 1864.

4508. —— Welcome to, by the Citizens of New York, at a Breakfast given at the Rooms of the Un. League Club, N. Y., Nov. 12, '64.

8vo. pp. 56. New York: *Baker & Godwin*, 1864.

4509. —— Reception of, by the Union League Club of New York,(the evening before his departure for Europe.) With the Remarks on the occasion, December, 1864. pp. 11.

4510. SMITH, Rev. Henry, DD. God in the War. A Discourse in behalf of the U. S. Christian Commission, August 6, 1863, at Buffalo, New York.

8vo. pp. 34. Buffalo: *Wheeler, Mathews & Co.*, 1863.

4511. —— The Religious Sentiments proper for our National Crisis. A Sermon delivered April 23, 1865.

8vo. pp. 32. Buffalo: *Matthews & Warren*, 1865.

4512. SMITH, Henry B., DD. British Sympathy with America. A Review of the Course of the Leading Periodicals of Great Britain, upon the Rebellion in America. *Am. Theolog. Rev., July*,'62.

4513. SMITH, Jeremiah. Is Slavery sinful? Being partial Discussions on the Proposition, between Ovid Butler, Bishop, at Indianapolis, and Hon. Jeremiah Smith and others.

12mo. pp. 396. Indianapolis; *H. H. Dodd & Co.*, 1863.

4514. SMITH, John Cotton. Two Discourses on the State of the Country.

8vo. pp. 48. New York: *John A. Gray*, 1861.

4515. —— Patriotism. A Sermon delivered before the Ancient and Honorable Artillery Company, June 7, 1858.

8vo. pp. 33. Boston: *Wm. White*, 1858.

4516. SMITH, John Y. Address on the State of the Country, Madison, Wisconsin, March 14, 1861. pp. 15.

4517. —— Depreciation of the Currency. Essay on the Financial Condition and Prospects of the Country. pp. 15.

4518. —— Review of Senator Doolittle's Speech, Madison, Wisconsin, Sept. 30, 1865, on the Reconstruction of the Rebel States. p. 24.

4519. SMITH, L. M., Practical Phrenologist. The Great American Crisis ; or Cause and Cure of Rebellion.
8vo. pp. 36. CINCINNATI : *Johnson, Stevens & Co.,* 1862.

4520. SMITH, Rev. MOSES. Our Nation not Forsaken. A Thanksgiving Discourse preached at Plainville, Ct., Nov. 27, 1862.
8vo. pp. 20. HARTFORD : *D. B. Moseley,* 1863.

4521. —— God's Honor, Man's Ultimate Success. A Sermon preached Sept. 27, 1863, when about to enter the Army of his Country.
8vo. pp. 20. NEW HAVEN ; *Thomas J. Stafford,* 1863.

4522. —— Past Mercies ; Present Gratitude ; Future Duty. A Discourse delivered at the Camp of the 8th Connecticut Vols., near Fort Harrison, Virginia, November 24, 1864.
8vo. pp. 24. NEW HAVEN ; *J. H. Benham,* 1865.

4523. SMITH, Rev. M. B. The Nation's Danger, and the Nation's Duty. A Sermon preached at Passaic, N. J., April 21, 1861.
8vo. pp. 14. NEW YORK : *John A. Gray,* 1861.

4524. —— Thanksgiving for Victory. A Sermon preached in the Ref. Dutch Church, Passaic, N. J., August 6, 1863.
8vo. pp. 15. NEW YORK : *John A. Gray,* 1863.

4525. —— God's Mighty Doings for the Nation. A Sermon preached November 24, 1864, in Passaic, N. Jersey.
8vo. pp. 19. NEW YORK : *John A. Gray & Greene,* 1864.

4526. SMITH, Rev. MATSON M. He Thanked God and took Courage. A Sermon, Thanksgiving Day, 1861, at Bridgeport, Conn.
8vo. pp. 18. BRIDGEPORT ; *Samuel B. Hall,* 1861.

4527. SMITH, Adjt. M. W., Memorial of. A Tribute to a Beloved Son and Brother. pp. 47. (Privately printed.)

4528. SMITH, PHILIP A. The Seizure of the Southern Commissioners considered, with reference to International Law.
8vo. pp. 45. LONDON : *J. Ridgeway,* 1862.

4529. SMITH, Hon. ROBERT H. An Address to the Citizens of Alabama, on the Constitution and Laws of the Confederate States of America, delivered in Mobile, March 30, 1861.
8vo. pp. 24. MOBILE : *Register Office,* 1861.

4530. SMITH, TRUMAN. Considerations on the Slavery Question. Addressed to President Lincoln. 8vo. pp. 15.

4531. —— Anthracite Coal, and the proposed Tax of Fifteen Cents per ton, examined and considered. pp. 7. Washington, 1862.

4532. SMITH, W. L. G. Life at the South; or "Uncle Tom's Cabin" as it is. Being Narratives, Scenes and Incidents.

    12mo. pp. 519.   BUFFALO: *George H. Derby & Co.*, 1852.

4533. SMITH, WM. Trial of, for Piracy, as one of the crew of the Confederate Privateer, the Jeff. Davis.

    8vo. pp. 100.   PHILADELPHIA : *King & Baird,* 1861.

4534. SNETHEN, W. G. The Black Code of the District of Columbia, in force September 1, 1848.

    8vo. pp. 61. NEW YORK : *A. & F. Anti-Slavery Society*, 1848.

4535. SNIVELY, Rev. WM. A. The Chastisement of War, and its alleviation. A Sermon preached at Pittsbugh. 12mo. pp. 26. '62.

4536. —— The Recognition of God in the Facts of our History. A Sermon. 12mo. pp. 25. 1863.

4537. —— The National Fast Day, and the War, 1864.

4538. —— The Nation's Bereavement. pp. 26. 1865.

4539. —— Past and Future. The Return of Peace, 1865.

4540. —— Reconstruction. Thanksgiving Sermon, 1865.

4541. SNOW, W. D. Letter to J. C. Pomeroy, showing the History of the Reorganized Government of Arkansas. pp. 11. 1865.

4542. SOCIETY FOR THE DIFFUSION OF POLITICAL KNOWLEDGE, New York, 1863.

    The Constitution. Address of Prof. Morse, Geo. Ticknor Curtis and S. J. Tilden, at the organization. 8vo. pp. 16.

4543. —— Speech of Mr. Turpie, U. S. Senate, Feb. 7, 1853. pp. 10.

4544. —— Speech of the Hon. James Brooks, Dec. 30, 1862. pp. 16.

4545. —— The Letter of a Republican, Edward N. Crosby, Esq., to Prof. S. F. B. Morse, Feb. 25, 1863, and Mr. Morse's Reply. pp. 12.

4546. —— The True Conditions of American Loyalty. Speech of Geo. T. Curtis, March 28, 1863. pp. 11.

4547. SOLDIERS AND SAILORS, Twelve Hospital Tracts for. By a Chaplain.

    12mo. pp.   *American Tract Society.*

4548. SOLDIERS. Twenty-four Pocket Tracts for Soldiers. *Am. Tr. Soc.*

4549. —— To the Soldiers of the Union. pp. 14.

4550. SOLDIERS' TEXT BOOK ; or Confidence in Time of War. By the Rev. J. Macduff, DD.

    18mo. pp. 64.   NEW YORK : *American Tract Society.*

4551. SOLDIERS' VOTING, Law of Ohio relative to.
8vo. pp. 12. COLUMBUS: *Richard Nevins*, 1863.

4552. SOLDIERS and SAILORS' ALMANAC, for 1865.
18mo. pp. 48. NEW YORK: *Evangelical Knowledge Soc.*, 1865.

4553. SOLDIERS' AID SOCIETY of Cleveland. To the U. S. San. Com.
8vo. pp. 40. CLEVELAND: *Fairbanks, Benedict & Co.*, 1861.

4554. SOLDIERS' ARMOR of Strength. A Brief Course of Non-Sectarian Devotional Exercises, Proverbs and Aphorisms, adapted to the present Calamitous Times of Rebellion. By Pilgrim John.
16mo. pp. 96. BROOKLYN: *D. S. Holmes*, 1864.

4555. SOLDIER'S COMPANION. Short Stories for Leisure Moments.
24 stories. *American Tract Society*.

4556. SOLDIER'S POCKET BIBLE. A Reprint of the original edition of 1643; with a Preface by George Livermore. 12mo. pp. 16.
Cambridge, 1861.

The original edition of this work, which consists of selected Passages from the Scriptures, was distributed by Cromwell to his soldiers. A few copies were reprinted in facsimile by the late George Livermore, of Cambridge. It was subsequently reprinted and distributed in large numbers among the Soldiers of the Union Army.

4557. THE SOLDIER'S COMPANION. Dedicated to the Soldiers in the Field, by their Friends at Home.
12mo. pp. 48. BOSTON: *Walker, Wise & Co.*, 1862.

4558. THE SOLDIER'S POCKET COMPANION. pp. 11. New York: *Dodge & Grattan*, 1862.

4559. SOLDIERS OF INDIANA, Proceedings and Resolutions of. To the Indiana Legislature. With Letters of Gen. Rosecrans and others. pp. 8.

4560. SOLDIERS OF OHIO. Address of the Union Members of the Legislature of the State of Ohio, to the Soldiers. pp. 4.

4561. SOLDIERS' PAY. Instructions in preparing. Washington, 1862.

4562. SOLDIERS' LETTERS from Camp, Battle Field and Prison. Edited by Lydia M. Post. (For the U. S. Sanitary Commission.)
12mo. pp. 472. NEW YORK: *Bunce & Huntington*, 1865.

4563. SOLDIERS AND SAILORS' Patriotic Songs.
8vo. pp. 24. *Loyal Publication Society No.* 49, 1864.

4564. SOLDIERS AND SAILORS' SABBATH. (With President Lincoln's Order for the Observance of the Sabbath in the Army and Navy.) pp. 4.

SOLDIERS.　Sixteen envelope Tracts for. *Am. Tact Soc'y.* 18mo.

4565. —— Masked Batteries, by the Rev. R. S. Cook, New York.

4566. —— Widow's Only Son enlisting, by the Rev. Wm. M. Thayer, Franklin, Massachusetts.

4567. —— The Great Rebellion, by the Rev R. Fisher, New Jersey.

4568. —— The Grand Army, by the Rev. P. C. Headley.

4569. —— The Christian Hero, by the Rev. F. A. Crafts, Maine.

4570. —— The Social Glass, by the Rev. S. Williams, Ohio.

4571. —— Albert Layton, by Miss Sarah E. Smith, Milltown, Maine.

4572. —— Fight for the Flag, and Live by the Cross; by Miss E. L. Newbold, Bellevue, Ohio.

4573. —— Emery Magbin, by Miss Lydia A. Tompkins. Ohio.

4574. —— The Great Warfare, by Rev. Tryon Edwards, N. London.

4575. —— "Thou God seest me." By Rev. Calvin Terry, Weymouth, Massachusetts.

4576. —— To Officers and Soldiers of the United States Army, by the Rev. Samuel Cutler, Hanover, Massachusetts.

4577. —— "I can drink or let it alone," by Rev. H. V. Warren.

4578. —— The Sick Soldier, by Mrs. Mary O. Darrah, St. Louis.

4579. —— A Light in the Window, by Rev. W. N. Wyeth, Ohio.

4580. —— The Eloquent Senator, by the Rev. S. Williams, Ohio.

4581. SOLDIERS. Twenty-five Army Tracts for the Pocket. *Am. Tr. So.*

4582. THE SOLDIER'S SACRIFICE. A Poem for the Times. By M. S. H. 16mo. pp. 38.　　　　STOUGHTON : *The author,* 1865.

4583. SOLDIERS. A List of the Union Soldiers buried at Andersonville. Copied from the Official Record in the Surgeon's Office. Royal 8vo. pp. 74.　　　NEW YORK : *Tribune Association,* 1866.

4584. A SOLUTION of our National Difficulties, and the Science of Republican Government, by a Citizen of the United States. 8vo. pp. 60.　　　　CINCINNATI : *G. S. Blanchard,* 1863.

4585. SONGS FOR WAR TIME. German Airs, with English Words. For the Army, the Family and the School. 12mo. pp. 32.　　　　BOSTON : *Gould & Lincoln,* 1863.

4586. SONGS AND BALLADS of Freedom : inspired by incidents and scenes of the Present War. 12mo. pp. 48. N. Y.: *J. E. Feeks.*

4587. SORET, H. Histoire du Conflit Américaine, de les Causes et les Résultats. 8vo. pp. 46.　　　　TARBES : *Th. Salmon,* 1863.

4588. SOULE, Rev. F. A. The Great Rebellion. An Address delivered at Nassau, New York, August 6, 1863.
8vo. pp. 20. ALBANY ; *J. Munsell*, 1863.

4589. THE SOUTH. A Letter from a Friend in the North. With reference to the Effects of Disunion upon Slavery.
8vo. pp. 46. PHILADELPHIA : *For the author*, 1856.

4590. THE SOUTH VINDICATED from the Treason and Fanaticism of the Northern Abolitionists.
12mo. pp. 314. PHILADELPHIA : *H. Manly*, 1836.

4591. SOUTH CAROLINA. The Report, Ordinance and Addresses of the Convention of the People of S. Carolina, adopted Nov. 24,'32.

4592. —— The Reports and Ordinances of the People of South Carolina, adopted March, 1833.
8vo. pp. 19. COLUMBUS: (S. C.) *A. S. Johnson & Bo.*, 1833.

4593. —— The Mission of South Carolina to Virginia. From *DeBow's Review, December*, 1860. 8vo. pp. 34.

4594. —— Disunion, and a Mississippi Valley Confederacy. 8vo. pp. 15. (No date.)

4595. —— Declaration of the Immediate Causes which induce and justify the Secession of South Carolina from the Federal Union ; and the Ordinance of Secession.
8vo. pp. 13. CHARLESTON : *Evans & Cogswell*, 1860.

4596. —— Ordinances and Constitution of the State of South Carolina, with the Constitution of the Provisional Government, and of the Confederate States of America.
8vo. pp. 93. CHARLESTON : *Evans & Cogswell*, 1861.

4597. THE SOUTH alone should govern the South. And African Slavery should be controlled by those only who are friendly to it.
8vo. pp. 62. CHARLESTON: *Evans & Cogswell*, 1860.

4598. SOUTHARD, W. Why Work for the Slave? A Manual for the Collectors of the Anti-Slavery Cent-a-Week Societies.
18mo. pp. 24. NEW YORK : *Am. Anti-Slavery Society*, 1838.

4599. SOUTHERN AID SOCIETY, Annual Report of, Nov. 25, 1860.
8vo. pp. 48. NEW YORK : *Geo. F. Nesbitt & Co.*, 1861.

4600. SOUTHERN COMMERCIAL CONVENTION, Assembled at Knoxville, Tennessee, August 10, 1857. Official Report of the Debates and Proceedings of.
8vo. pp. 96. KNOXVILLE : (Tenn.) *Kinsloe & Rice*, 1857.

49

4601. SOUTHERN GENERALS ; Who they are, and What they have done.
8vo. pp. 473. Portraits. NEW YORK : *C. B. Richardson*, '65.

4602. SOUTHERN HATRED of the American Government, the People of
the North and Free Institutions.
8vo. pp.   BOSTON : *R. F. Wallcut*, 1862.

4603. SOUTHERN HISTORY OF THE WAR. Official Reports of Battles,
published by order of the Confederate States.
8vo. pp. 578.   RICHMOND : *Enquirer Press*, 1862.

4604. ——— Official Reports of Battles.
8vo. pp. 578. NEW YORK : *C. B. Richardson*, 1863.

4605. SOUTHERN MONTHLY. The Battle of Manassas. Sept., 1861.

4606. ——— General G. T. Beauregard. November, 1861.

4607. ——— Philosophy of the Revolution. January, 1862.

4608. ——— The Protective System, a Necessity. February, 1862.

4609. SOUTHERN NOTES for National Circulation.
8vo. pp. 132.   BOSTON : *Thayer & Eldridge*, 1860.

4610. SOUTHERN OUTRAGES upon Northern Citizens. A Fresh Catalogue of.   New York : *American Anti-Slavery Society*, 1860.

4611. "SOUTHERN RIGHTS " and "Union" Parties in Maryland contrasted.
8vo. pp. 30.   BALTIMORE : *W. M. Innes*, 1863.

4612. SOUTHERN RIGHTS CONVENTION, held in Baltimore. Addresses
and Resolutions of.   pp. 14. Baltimore : *J. B. Rose & Co.*, '61.

4613. THE SOUTHERN SPY, (Weekly, No. 1, June 29, 1861. pp. 20.
—a few numbers issued,—E. A. Pollard & Co., Baltimore.)

4614. SPAULDING, Rev. GEORGE B. The Presence and Purpose
of God in the War. A Sermon preached at Vergennes, Vermont, November 26, 1863.
8vo. pp. 21.   BURLINGTON : *Free Press*, 1863.

4615. SPAULDING, RUFUS F. Confiscation of Rebel Property.
Speech in House of Reps., January 22, 1864. 8vo. pp. 8.

4616. SPAULDING, Hon. E. G. The Republican Platform. Speech
at Washington and Buffalo, at Meetings to Ratify the Nomination of Abraham Lincoln. pp. 8.

4617. ——— Speech in House of Representatives, January 28, 1862, on
the Finances, and the Power of Congress to issue demand Treasury Notes. pp. 16.

4618. SPAULDING, Hon. E. G. Speech on the Senate's Amendment to the Treasury Note Bill. House of Reps., Feb. 19. '62. pp. 8.

4619. SPAULDING, Rev. WILLARD. The Pulpit and the State. A Discourse preached February 15, 1863, at Salem, Mass.
8vo. pp. 22.   SALEM: *Charles A. Beckford*, 1863.

4620. SPEAR, SAMUEL T., DD. Two Sermons for the Times. Obedience to the Civil Authority; and Constitutional Government against Treason. Preached in Brooklyn, April 28 and May 5,'61.
8vo. pp. 56.   NEW YORK: *Nathan, Lane & Co.*, 1861.

4621. —— Radicalism, and the National Crisis. A Sermon preached in Brooklyn, October 19, 1862.
8vo. pp. 23.   BROOKLYN: *Wm. W. Rose*, 1862.

4622. —— The Nation's Blessing in Trial. A Sermon preached in Brooklyn, November 27, 1862.
8vo. pp. 39.   BROOKLYN: *Wm. W. Rose*, 1862.

4623. —— The Duty of the Hour.
8vo. pp. 16.   NEW YORK: *A. D. F. Randolph*, 1863.

4624. —— Radicalism and the National Crisis.
8vo. pp. 23.   BROOKLYN: *Wm. W. Rose*, 1862.

4625. —— Our Country and its Cause. A Discourse Oct. 2, 1864.
8vo. pp. 37.   BROOKLYN: *Union Steam Press*, 1864.

4626. —— The Death of the President. Our Duty in the emergency. Address delivered April 16, 1865.

4627. —— The Punishment of Treason. A Discourse preached at Brooklyn, April 23, 1865.
8vo. pp. 38.   BROOKLYN: *Union Steam Press*, 1865.

4628. SPECIE PAYMENTS, How to resume, without contraction. A Letter to the Secretary of the Treasury.
8vo. pp. 18.   NEW YORK: *W. C. Bryant & Co.*, 1865.

4629. SPEED, JAMES, Attorney General. Opinion on the Constitutional Power of the Military to Try and Execute the Assassins of the President.
8vo. pp. 16.   WASHINGTON: *Government Printing Office*, 1865.

4630. SPEER, Rev. WILLIAM. The Lessons of 1860. Discourse before the Young Men's Chr. Ass., St. Paul, Minn., Feb. 3, '61.
8vo. pp. 36.   ST. PAUL: *Press Company*, 1861.

4631. SPENCE, JAMES. The American Union; its Effect on National

Character and Policy; with an Inquiry into Secession as a Constitutional Right, and the Causes of Disruption.

8vo. pp. xvi and 391. LONDON: *R. Bentley,* 1862.

4632. SPENCE, J. L'Union Américaine; ses Effets sur le Caractère Nationale et la Politique, Causes de la Disunion, etc., de l'Anglaise.

8vo. pp. 434. PARIS: *Michel Levy Frères,* 1862.

4633. —— Der Amerïkanische Union etc., translated by Wetter.

8vo. pp. 272. BARMEN: *M. Langewiesche,* 1863.

4634. SPENCER, W. S. Maryland and the Union.

8vo. pp. 6. ANNAPOLIS: (Md.) *January* 16, 1861.

4635. SPOONER, LYSANDER. The Constitutionality of Slavery.

12mo. pp. 281. BOSTON: *Bela March,* 1847.

4636. —— A Defence for Fugitive Slaves, against the Acts of Congress of February 12, 1793, and Sept. 18, 1850.

8vo. pp. 72. BOSTON: *Bela Marsh,* 1850.

4637. —— A New System of Paper Currency, 1861.

8vo. pp. 64 and 58. BOSTON: *A. Williams & Co.,* 1861.

4638. SPRAGUE, Miss A. W. I still Live. A Poem for the Times.

12mo. pp. 19. OSWEGO: *Oliphant & Brother,* 1862.

4639· SPRAGUE, Major J. T. The Treachery in Texas; and the Arrest of the United States Officers and Soldiers serving in Texas.

8vo. pp. 110 to 142. NEW YORK: *Rebellion Record,* 1862.

4640. SPRAGUE, PELEG. What is Treason? A Charge addressed to the U. S. District Court of Mass., March Term, A. D. 1863.

8vo. pp. 17. SALEM: *C. W. Swasey,* 1863.

4641. SPRAGUE, WM. B., DD. An Address on the occasion of the Raising of the National Flag upon the Second Presbyterian Church, Albany, June 17, 1861.

8vo. pp. 8. ALBANY: *C. Van Benthuysen,* 1861.

4642. —— Glorifying God in the Fires. A Discourse delivered at Albany, November 28, 1861.

8vo. pp. 58. ALBANY: *C. Van Benthuysen,* 1861.

4643. —— A Discourse delivered in Albany, April 16, 1865, the Sunday succeeding the Assassination of the President.

12mo. pp. 18. ALBANY: *Weed & Parsons,* 1865.

4644. SPRATT, L. W. The Foreign Slave Trade the Source of Political Power,—of Material Progress,—of Social Integrity, and of Social Emancipation at the South.

8vo. pp. 31.   Charleston; *Walker, Evans & Co.*, 1858.

4645. SPRING, Rev. Gardiner, DD.   State Thanksgiving during the Rebellion.   A Sermon preached Nov. 28, 1861, in N. York. 8vo. pp. 48.   New York: *Harper & Brothers*, 1862.

4646. SPROULL, Professor.   Christianity and the Commonwealth. A Lecture delivered at Alleghany, Penn., November 4, 1862. 8vo. pp. 15.   Pittsburgh: *U. S. Haven*, 1862.

4647. SPURR, Lieut. Thomas Jefferson.   In Memoriam.   A Sermon preached in Worcester, Oct. 5, 1862, by Rev. Alonzo Hill. 8vo. pp. 32.   Boston: *John Wilson & Son*, 1862.

4648. SQUIER, Hon. E. G.   Is Cotton King?   Sources of Cotton Supply.   Letter to H. B. Anthony, N. Y., Jan. 25, '61. 8vo. p. 4.

4649. —— Tropical Fibres; their Production and economic Extraction. 8vo. pp. 64.   16 engravings.   New York: *Scribner & Co.*, '61.
The object of the author is to point out the various countries from which cotton can be produced, besides the Slaveholding States, as well as to show other fibrous materials available.

4650. St. Albans Raiders.   Trial of Hezekiah Payne, charged with the Murder of Elinus J. Morrison, at St. Albans, October 19, 1864.   Franklin County Court, Vermont.   *Vermont Transcript, June 30, July 7 and 14,* 1865.

4651. Standish.   A Story of Our Day.
8vo. pp. 185.   Boston: *Loring*, 1865.

4652. STANLEY, Hon. Edward, of N. Carolina.   Speech exposing the Causes of the Slavery Agitation.   House of Representatives, March 6, 1860.   pp. 16.

4653. —— Letter to Col. Henry A. Gilliam, refuting Charges and Insinuations made by Hon. George E. Badger, in behalf of the Southern Confederacy. July 17, 1862.   pp. 10.

4654. —— A Military Governor among Abolitionists.   A Letter to Charles Sumner.
8vo. pp. 48.   New York: 1865.

4655. STANLEY, Rev. E. S.   A Sermon on Civil Government, and the Relative Duties of Subjects.   Preached at Fisherville, Connecticut, September 26, 1861.

4656. STANTON, Lieut. Governor, of Ohio.   Letter in Reply to Hon. Thomas Ewing, November, 1862.   Columbus.   pp. 25.

4657. STANTON, E. M., Secretary of War. Report of, accompanied by the Annual Report of H. W. Halleck, General-in-Chief, dated November 15, 1863. pp. 46.
Annual Reports of the Secretary of War.

4658. —— Dec. 1, 1861. pp. 569. 37th Cong., 2d Ses. Ex. Doc. No. 1.

4659. —— Dec. 1, 1862. pp. 117. 37th Cong., 2d Ses. Ex. Doc. No. 1.

4660. —— Dec. 5, 1863. pp. 510. 38th Cong., 1st Ses. Ex. Doc. No. 1.

4661. —— Mar. 1, 1865. pp. 235. 38th Cong., 2d Ses. Ex. Doc. No. 83.

4662. —— Nov. 22, 1865. pp. 1305. 39th Con., 1st Ses. Ex. Doc. No. 1.

4663. STANTON, F. P. The Causes of the Rebellion. *Continental Monthly, November and December,* 1862.

4664. —— The Freed Men of the South. Ibid. *December,* 1862.

4665. —— Consequences of the Rebellion. Ibid. *Jan. and Feb.,* 1863.

4666. —— European Opinion. Ibid. *March,* 1863.

4667. —— How the War affects Americans. Ibid. *April,* 1863.

4668. —— The Third Year of the War. Ibid. *July,* 1863.

4669. —— The Restoration of the Union. Ibid. *October,* 1863.

4670. —— The Defence and Evacuation of Winchester. Ibid. *Nov.* '63.

4671. —— Union not to be maintained by Force. Ibid. *Jan.,* 1864.

4672. —— The Treasury Report of Secretary Chace. Ibid. *Feb.,* '64.

4673. STANTON AND LANE. In the matter of Contest between F. P. Stanton and Gen. J. H. Lane, United States Senate. pp. 4.

4674. STANTON, HENRY B. Remarks, February 23, 1837, before the Committee of the House of Representatives of Massachusetts, on the subject of Slavery.
12mo. pp. 90. BOSTON: *Isaac Knapp,* 1837.

4675. STANTON, Rev. R. L., DD. Civil Government of God. Obedience, a Duty. A Discourse upon the present National Crisis, December 3, 1860. Chillicothe, Ohio.
8vo. pp. 36. CINCINNATI: *John D. Thorpe,* 1860.

4676. —— Causes for National Humiliation. A Discourse, on Fast Day, September 26, 1861.
8vo. pp. 48. CINCINNATI: *Moore, Wilstace, Keys & Co.,* 1861

4676.* —— The Church and the Rebellion. A Consideration of the Rebellion against the Government of the United States, and the Agency of the Church, North and South, in relation thereto.
12mo. pp. xiv, 562. NEW YORK: *Derby & Miller,* 1864.

4677. STAPLES, Rev. N. A.   A Sermon, July 4, 1862, the Chastisement of War.   Preached in Brooklyn.
8vo. pp. 16.   NEW YORK : *Stearns & Beale*, 1862.

4677.* STAR OF THE WEST.   Protest of the Master against the Seizure of the Steamship " Star of the West."
8vo. pp. 23.   NEW YORK : *Wynkoop, Hallenbeck & Co.*, 1861.

4678. STARBUCK, Rev. C. C.   Emancipation in Jamaica.   *Continental Monthly, July*, 1863.

4679. STARKWEATHER, Brig. General J. C.   Statement of Military Services of, since the 4th of March, 1861. p. 14. Milwaukie.

4680. STARR, Rev. FREDERIC, Jr.   What shall be done with the People of Color in the United States ?   A Discourse delivered in Penn-Yan, New York, November 2, 1862.
8vo. pp. 29.   ALBANY : *Weed, Parsons & Co.*, 1862.

4681. —— The Loyal Soldier.   A Discourse delivered in Penn Yan, at Funeral of Major John Barnet Sloan, of the 179th Regiment, New York Volunteers, June 27, 1861.
8vo. pp. 28.   PENN YAN : *G. D. A. Bridgman*, 1864.

4682. —— The Martyr President.   A Discourse delivered in Penn Yan, New York, April 16, 1865, on the Death of A. Lincoln.
8vo. pp. 19.   ST. LOUIS : *Sherman Spencer*, 1865.

4683. STARS AND STRIPES IN REBELDOM.   A Series of Papers written by Federal Prisoners (Privates) in Richmond, Tuscaloosa, New Orleans and Salisbury, N. C.
8vo. pp. 137.   BOSTON : *T. O. H. P. Burnham*, 1862.

4684. STATE SOVEREIGNTY.   A Dialogue,   pp. 8.   (No date.)

4685. THE STATE OF THE COUNTRY.   From the *Princeton Review*, January, 1861.   pp. 36.

4686. STATES *vs.* TERRITORIES,   A True Solution of the Territorial Question.   By an Old Line Whig.   August 15, 1860. pp. 20.

4687. STATES, The Rights of ; or the Union a Revocable Compact. 1862.   pp. 11.

4688. STEARNS, CHARLES.   Narrative of Henry Box Brown, who escaped from Slavery, enclosed in a box.   Written from a Statement of Facts, made by himself.
12mo. pp. 90.   BOSTON : *Brown & Stearns*, 1849.

4689. STEARNS, Edward J.   The Sword of the Lord.   A Sermon preached in Newark, New Jersey, September 26, 1861.
8vo. pp. 15.   BALTIMORE : *J. S. Waters,* 1861.

4690. —— The Powers that be.   A Sermon preached in Centerville, Maryland, February 2, 1862.   pp. 15.

4691. STEARNS, Geo. L.   A few Facts pertaining to Currency and Banking, adapted to the present Position of our Finances, January 19, 1864.   pp. 15.

4692. —— The same.   pp. 16.   Boston: *A. Williams & Co.,* 1864.

4693. STEARNS, Rev. W. A.   Slavery, in its present Aspects and Relations.   A Sermon preached April 6, '54, at Cambridge, Mass.
8vo. pp. 47.   BOSTON : *James Munroe & Co.,* 1854.

4694. —— Necessities of the War, and the Conditions of Success in it.   A Sermon preached September 26, 1861.
8vo. pp. 23.   AMHERST : (Mass.) *Henry A. Marsh,* 1861.

4695. STEBBINS, G. B.   " British Free Trade," a Delusion.   Detroit, July 1, 1865.   pp. 8.

4696. STEBBINS, Hon. HENRY G.   Finances and Resources of the United States.   Speech in the House of Reps., March 3, 1864.
8vo. pp. 22.   *Loyal Publication Society, No.* 45, 1864.

4697. STEDMAN, Edmund C.   The Battle of Bull Run.
12mo. pp. 42.   NEW YORK : *Rudd & Carlton,* 1861.

4698. STEECE, Lieut. TECUMSEH, U. S. N.   A Republican Military System.
8vo. pp. 39.   NEW YORK : *John A. Gray & Green,* 1863.

4699. STEELE, Rev. DANIEL.   De Profundis Clamavi.   The Cause, the Crime, and the Cure of our National Suicide.   A Sermon delivered in Springfield, September 26, 1861.
8vo. pp. 30.   SPRINGFIELD : *Samuel Bowles & Co.,* 1861.

4700. STEELE, JOHN B., of New York.   Speech on the Slavery Question.   House of Reps., January 20, 1862.   pp. 8.

4701. STEINER, LOUIS H., M. D.   Diary kept during the Rebel •Occupation of Frederick, in Maryland.
8vo. pp.   NEW YORK : *Anson D. F. Randolph,* 1862.

4702. STELLING, Rev. G. J.   The Great Rebellion.   A Discourse delivered at Camp Meigs, October 18, 1861.
8vo. pp. 16.   LEBANON ; (Pa.) *H. Roedel,* 1862.

4703. STEPHENS, ALEXANDER H. Extract from a Speech delivered in the Secession Convention of Georgia, January, 1861. pp. 4.

4704. —— Speech for the Union, delivered at Milledgeville, Georgia, Nov., 1860, before the Members of the Legislature. pp. 8.

4705. —— The same. *Loyal Publication Society, No.* 56.

4706. —— African Slavery, the Corner-Stone of the Southern Confederacy. A Speech delivered at the Athenæum, Savannah, March 22, 1861. (Pulpit and Rostrum, No. 27.)

4707. —— Speech in Opposition to Secession in 1860, and Address of E. W. Gantt of Ark. in favor of Reünion in 1863. pp. 45. N. Y.

4708. —— Speech in Opposition to Secession in 1860.
8vo. pp. 21. *Loyal Publication Society, No.* 36, 1863.

4709. STERN, SIMON. The Tariff; its Evils and their Remedy.
12mo. pp. 22. NEW YORK: *G. A. Whitehorne,* 1861.

4710. STEVENS, THADDEUS. Speech at Gettysburg, Oct. 3 '65. p. 8.

4711. —— Reconstruction. Speech in Lancaster, September 7, 1865.

4712. STEVENSON, DAVID. Indiana Roll of Honor.
Vol. 1, pp. 654. INDIANAPOLIS: *Pub. by the Author,* 1864.

4713. STEVENSON, WM. G. Thirteen Months in the Rebel Army; being a Narrative of Personal Adventures.
12mo. pp. 232. NEW YORK: *A. S. Barnes & Burr,* 1862.

4714. STEWART, ALVAN. Writings and Speeches on Slavery.
12mo. pp. 426. NEW YORK: *A. B. Burdick,* 1860.

4715. STEWART, Rev. A. M. Camp, March and Battle Field; or Three Years and a half with the Army of the Potomac.
12mo. pp. viii and 413. PHILADELPHIA: *James B. Rodgers,* '64.

4716 STEWART, CHARLES. Immediate Emancipation safe and Profitable for Masters, Happy for Slaves, Right in Government, Advantageous to the Nation, etc. From the (English) Quarterly Magazine, April, 1832.
8vo. pp. 35. NEWBURYPORT: *Charles Whipple,* 1838.

4717. STUART, Rev. DANIEL, DD. A Discourse on the Death of Abraham Lincoln, delivered in Johnstown, New York, April 16 and 19, 1865.
8vo. pp. 20. JOHNSTOWN: *J. D. Haughtaling,* 1865.

4718. STUART, Rev. WM. B. The Nation's Sins and the Nation's Duty. A Sermon preached in Pottstown, Pa., April 30, 1863.
8vo. pp. 15. PHILADELPHIA: *W. S. & A. Martien,* 1863.

50

4719. STUART, Rev. W. B. The Southern Rebellion a Failure. A Sermon November 27, 1862.

8vo. pp. 23. PHILADELPHIA: *W. S. & A. Martien*, 1863.

4720. STILES, JOSEPH C. The National Controversy; or the Voice of the Fathers, unpon the State of the Country.

12mo. pp. 108. NEW YORK: *Rudd & Carleton*, 1861.

4721. STILLE, ALFRED, M. D. War as an Instrument of Civilization. An Address before the Society of the Alumni of the University of Pennsylvania, November 27, 1861.

8vo. pp. 62. PHILADELPHIA: *Collins*, 1862.

4722. STILLE, CHARLES J. The Historical Development of American Civilization. An Address before the Graduates of Yale College, July 29, 1863.

8vo. pp. 38. NEW HAVEN: *E. Hayes*, 1863.

4723. —— Northern Interests and Southern Independence. A Plea for United Action.

8vo. pp. 50. PHILADELPHIA: *W. S. & A. Martien*, 1863.

4724. —— How a Free People conduct a Long War. A Chapter from English History.

8vo. pp. 34. NEW YORK: *A. D. F. Randolph*, 1863.

4725. —— The same, pp. 16. New York: *A. D. F. Randolph.*

4726. —— The same. pp. 37. PHILADELPHIA: *Collins*, 1862.

4727. —— The same, 9th thousand. pp. 40. Phila.: *Martien*, 1863.

4728. —— Memorial of the Great Central Fair, held at Phil., June, '64.

4to. pp. 211. PHILADELPHIA: *U. S. Sanitary Commision*, '64.

4729. STILWELL, SILAS M. National Finances. Philosophical Examination of Credit. Gold and Paper are equally subject to the great Law of Supply and Demand.

8vo. pp. 30. NEW YORK: *J. A. Gray & Green*, 1866.

4730. STIMER, ALBAN C His Report of the Last Trial Trip of the "Passaic." Unparalleled attempt to throw Discredit upon Superiors. Language unbecoming an Officer. His Dismissal from the Service demanded. pp. 15. 1862.

4731. —— Defence of Engineer Stimers against Charges made by Rear Admiral DuPont, U. S. N., before a Naval Court of Inquiry, October 19, 1863.

8vo. pp. 15. NEW YORK: *John W. Oliver*, 1863.

4732. STERLING, JAMES. Letters from the Slave States.
Post 8vo. pp. 374. LONDON: *J. W. Parker*, 1857.

4733. STOCK, Rev. JOHN. The Duties of British Christians, in relation to the Struggle in America.
8vo. pp. 28. MANCHESTER: *Un. and Emanc. Society*, 1861.

4734. STOCKTON, Rev. T. H. American Sovereignty. A Sermon delivered in the Hall of Reps., July 28, 1861. pp. 8.

4735. —— Address in House of Reps., Fast Day, January 4, 1861.

4736. STODDARD, MOSES. Letter to Gen. Ripley and Capt. Dahlgren, Chief of Navy Ordnance, etc. Buffalo, Sept. 30, '62. p. 8.

4736.* —— Correspondence with Capt. John A. Dahlgren, 1862.

4737. STODDARD, R. H. Abraham Lincoln. A Horatian Ode.
8vo. pp. 12. NEW YORK: *Bunce & Huntington*, 1865.

4738. STOEVER, Prof. M. L. Abraham Lincoln. *Cong. Quar.*, 1865.

4739. —— The United States Christian Commission. Ibid. *Vol.* 16.

4740. STONE, Rev. A. L., DD. The War, and the Patriot's Duty. A Discourse delivered in Boston, April 21, 1861.
12mo. pp. 24. BOSTON: *Henry Hoyt*, 1861.

4741. —— The Divineness of Human Government. A Discourse on occasion of the National Fast, September 26, 1862.
12mo. pp. 55. BOSTON: *Henry Hoyt*, 1861.

4742. —— God the Governor. A Discourse delivered in Providence, October, 1861.
8vo. pp. 15. PROVIDENCE: *Knowles, Anthony & Co.*, 1861.

4743. —— Praise for Victory. A Sermon preached Feb. 13, 1862.
8vo. pp. 15. BOSTON: *T. R. Marvin & Son*, 1862.

4744. —— The War, and the Patriot's Duty. A Discourse delivered in Park street Church, April 21, 1861.
12mo. pp. 24. BOSTON: *Henry Hoyt*, 1861.

4745. —— Emancipation. A Discourse delivered April 3, 1862.
12mo. pp. 28. BOSTON: *Henry Hoyt*, 1862.

4746. —— The same. 12mo. pp. 28. CINCINNATI: *Tract Soc'y*, 1862.

4747. —— The Work of New England in the Future of our Country. A Sermon delivered before the Legislature of Mass., Jan. 4, '65.
8vo. pp. 48. BOSTON: *Wright & Potter*, 1865.

4748. —— A Discourse occasioned by the Death of Abraham Lincoln. Preached in Boston, April 14.
8vo. pp. 21. BOSTON: *J. K. Wiggin*, 1865.

4749. STONE, A. T.   Letter on Reconstruction, to Gov. Oglesby, of Illinois.   8vo. pp. 12.   (Without date.)

4750. STORKE, and L. P. Brocket.   A Complete History of the Great American Rebellion.
2 vols. 8vo.   Maps and Plates.   AUBURN: (N. Y.) *Au. Pub. Co.*

4751. STORMS, Gen. HENRY.   Petition to Gov. Seymour, for the Office of Commissary General of the State of New York.
8vo. pp. 24.   TARRYTOWN: *George Q. Farraud*, 1863.

4752. STORRS, Rev. R. S., Jun., DD.   A Sermon preached in Brooklyn, New York, in Memory of Robert Sedgwick Edwards.
8vo. pp. 21.   BROOKLYN: *Union Press*, 1864.

4753. —— An Oration commemorative of Abraham Lincoln, delivered at Brooklyn, New York, June 1, 1865.
8vo. pp. 65.   Portrait.   BROOKLYN: *Union Print*, 1865.

4754. STORY, W. W.   The American Question.
8vo. pp. 68.   LONDON: *George Manwaring*, 1862.

4755. STOWE, HARRIET BEECHER.   Uncle Tom's Cabin.
2 vols. 12mo.   BOSTON: *J. B. Jewett & Co.*, 1852.

4756. —— The same, illustrated.   8vo.   Boston.   Ibid.   1852.

4757. —— The same.   8vo.   London: *Ingram, Cooke & Co.*, 1853.

4758. —— The same, illustrated.   8vo.   London, *N. Cooke*, 1863.

4759. —— The same, with Introduction by the Rev. J. Sherman.
12mo. pp. xx and 483.   LONDON: *H. G. Bohn*, 1862.

4760. —— La Case de L'Oncle Tom.
12mo. 2 vols.   PARIS: *Michel Levy Frères*, 1863.

4761. —— The same.   Trad. par Adolphe Joanne.
Royal 8vo.   PARIS: *Magasin Pittoresque*, 1863.

4762. —— The same.   Trad. par Louis Enault.
12mo. pp. 440.   PARIS: *Hachette et Cie.*, 1865.

4763. —— The same.   Trad par Mme. L. S. W. Belloc.
12mo. pp. 596.   PARIS: *Charpentier*, 1862.

4764. —— The same.   Trad. par L. de Wailly and E. Texier.
12mo. pp. 456.   PARIS: *Perrotin*, 1853.

4765. —— L'Oncle Tom raconté aux Enfans par Mlle. de Constant.
12mo. pp. 420.   PARIS: *Borrani et Droz*.

4766. —— La Choza de Tom.   Trad. par W. A. de Izco.
8vo. pp. 478.   MADRID: *Ayguals de Izco*, 1863.

4767. STOWE, H. B. La Cabaña del Tio Tom. Trad. par A. A. Oriburla.
12mo. pp. 322. BARCELONA: *Juan Oliveres*, 1863.

4768. —— The same. (Spanish.) Paris, 1852.

4769. —— Onkel Tom's Hütte. Ein Roman aus dem Leben der Sklaven in Amerika. 6 wood Cuts.
8vo. 2 vols. BERLIN: *Albert Sacco.*

4770. —— The same. 12mo. pp. 55. BERLIN: *L. Hassar*, 1853.

4771. —— The same. 12mo. 4 vols. LEIPZIG: *Otto Wigand*, 1852.

4772. —— The same. 12mo. 4 vols. LEIPZIG: *Otto Wigand*, 1853.

4773. —— The same. With 50 Illustrations.
8vo. pp. 430. LEIPZIG: *J. J. Weber*, 1854.

4774. —— The same. Translated by J. G. Lowe.
12mo. 2 vols. HAMBURG: *Robert Rittler*, 1853.

4775. —— The same. Translated by L. Du Bois.
12mo. 3 vols. STUTTGART, 1853.

4776. —— The same. Translated by Ungewitter.
8vo. pp. 238. WIEN UND LEIPZIG: *Hartleben*, 1853.

4777. —— The same. 12mo. pp. 326. LEIPZIG: *G. H. Friedlein*, 1853.

4778. —— The same. Translated by Moriz Gans.
12mo. pp. 216. PESTH: *Gustav Heckenast.*

4779. —— Schlüssel zu Onkel Tom's Hütte.
12mo. 4 vols. BERLIN: *Duncker & Humblot*, 1853.

4780. —— The same 8vo. pp. 439. Leipzig, *G. H. Friedlein*, 1853.

4781. —— Chata Wuja Tom, in Polish and French.
12mo. pp, 253. WARSAW: *A. Nowoleckiego*, 1856.

4782. —— Same. Dutch. 2 vols. 8vo. HARLEM: *A. C. Kruseman.*

4783. —— Same. Dutch. 8vo. BATAVIA, E. Indies: *Van Dorp,* '63.

4784. —— Same. Dutch. 2 vols. 12mo. SOERABAYA: *E. Fuhri,* '53.

4785. —— Same. Italian. 2 vols. 12mo. FIRENZE: *Giacomo Ferni,* '53.

4786. —— Same. Italian. 4 vols. 18mo. NAPOLI: *G. Nobile*, 1853.

4787. —— Same. Illyrian. 12mo. 1853.

4788. —— Same. Armenian. 2 vols. 12mo. ST. LAZARO, 1854.

4789. —— Same. Welsh. 12mo. ABERTAWY.

4790. —— Same. Portuguese. PARIS: *Rey & Belhatte.*

In addition to the foregoing, there are known to be editions in the Wallachian, Russian and Hindostanee Languages. Nor in other respects is the List complete.

4791. —— Uncle Tom, adapted to Young Persons, by Mrs. Crowe.
London, 1853,

4792. STOWE, H. B.　Uncle Tom in England ; or a Proof that Black's White.　An Echo to the American Uncle Tom.　12mo.　London, 1853.

4793. —— Uncle Tom's Companions.　By J. P. Edwards.　12mo. London, 1853.

4794. —— Uncle Tom at Home ; or Review of the Reviewers, and Repudiation of Uncle Tom's Cabin.　By F. C. Adams.　12mo. London, 1853.

4795. —— A Key to Uncle Tom's Cabin, presenting the original Facts and Documents upon which the story is founded.
8vo. pp. 262.　　　　　　　　BOSTON : *J. P. Jewett & Co.,* 1853.

4796. —— The same.　12mo.　London, *Clarke, Beeton & Co.,* 1853.

4797. —— The same.　Royal 8vo.　London, 1853.

4798. —— La Clef du Case de l'Oncle Tom.　London, *Cassell,* 1853.

4799. —— Uncle Sam's Emancipation.　12mo.　*W. P. Hazard,* 1852.

4800. —— Dred.　A Tale of the Great Dismal Swamp.
2 vols. 12mo.　　　　　　BOSTON : *Phillips, Sampson & Co.,* 1856.

4801. —— A Voice from the Mother Land, answering Mrs. H. Beecher Stowe's Appeal.　By Civis Anglicus.
8vo. pp. 56.　　　　　　　　　LONDON : *Trübner & Co.,* 1862.

4802. —— A Reply to the Affectionate and Christian Address of many Thousands of Women in Great Britain and Ireland to their Sisters, the Women of the United States.　*Atlantic Mo'ly, Jan. '63.*

4803. STREET, ALFRED B.　Lookout Mountain.　*Cont. Mo'ly, July,* 64.

4803.* —— Averill's Raid.　Ibid.　*September,* 1864.

4804. STREET, Rev. THOMAS.　Sermon at York, Penn., March 9, 1860, occasioned by the Death of Capt. J. S. Slaymaker, Second Iowa Regiment, who fell at Fort Donelson.
8vo. pp. 16.　　　　　　　YORK : (Penn.) *W. H. Albright,* 1862.

4805. THE STRENGTH OF THE BATTLE.　A Discourse delivered in Worcester, Fast Day, September 26, 1851.
8vo. pp. 20.　　　　　　　WORCESTER : *Transcript Office,* 1861.

4806. STRICKLAND, Rev. W. P., Chaplain, U. S. A.　Methodism and the War.　*Methodist Quarterly Review, July,* 1863.

4807. STRINGFELLOW, Rev. T.　Slavery ; its Origin, Nature and History.　Its relations to Society, to Government, and to True Religion ; Human Happiness and Divine Glory.
8vo. pp. 32.　　　　　　ALEXANDRIA : (Va.) *Sentinel Office,* 1860.

4808. STRINGFELLOW, Rev. T.   The same.
8vo. pp. 56.   New York: *John F. Trow*, 1861.

4809. STRONG, Rev. EDWARD.   The Duty of a Christian Citizen in the present Crisis of our Country.   A Discourse in New Haven, December 9, 1860.
8vo. pp. 15.   NEW HAVEN: *S. H. Elliot*, 1860.

4810. STRONG'S Washington and the War.   The City, and the Great Battles near Washington.
8vo. pp. 16.   NEW YORK: *Wynkoop, Hallenbeck & Thomas*, '63.

4811. STRONG, Rev. J. D.   The Nation's Sorrow.   A Discourse on the Death of Abraham Lincoln, delivered in San Francisco, April 16, 1865.
8vo. pp. 14.   SAN FRANCISCO: *George L. Kenny & Co.*, 1865.

4812. STRONG, MOSES M.   Speech on the State of the Country. Madison, Wisconsin, April 2, 1861.   8vo. pp. 7.

4813. STRONG, RICHARD MARION, Adjt. 177th Regiment New York Vols. who died at Bennett Carré, La., May 12, '63. A Memoir of.
8vo. pp. 45.   ALBANY: *J. Munsell*, 1863.

4814. —— Sermon commemorative of, by Rev. A. S. Twombly.
8vo. pp. 22.   ALBANY: *J. Munsell*, 1863.

4815. STROUD, Judge.   Southern Slavery and the Christian Religion.
12mo. pp. 7.   PHILADELPHIA: 100 North Tenth Street.

4816. STROUD, GEORGE M.   A Sketch of the Laws relating to Slavery in the several States of the United States.   2d edition.
12mo. pp. 125.   PHILADELPHIA: 1856.

4817. STROUSE, MYER, of Pennsylvania.   Speech in House of Representatives, on "The Reconstruction Bill," May 2, 1864.   pp. 7.

4818. STUART, Capt. A. A.   Iowa Colonels and Regiments.   Being a History of Iowa Regiments in the Rebellion.
8vo. pp. 656.   DES MOINES: *Mills & Co.*, 1865.

4819. STUART, CHARLES B.   Report on the proposed Improvements to pass Gunboats from Tide-Water to the Northern Lakes. March 21, 1864.   pp. 16.

4820. STUART, MOSES.   Conscience and the Constitution; with Remarks and Speech of Daniel Webster in the United States Senate on Slavery.
8vo. pp. 119.   BOSTON: *Crocker & Brewster*, 1850.

4821. STURTEVANT, Rev. J. M.   The Destiny of the African Race in the United States. *Continental Monthly, April,* 1863.

4822. —— The Lessons of our National Conflict.   Address to the Alumni of Yale College, July 24, 1861.

> 8vo. pp. 21.   New Haven : *Thomas J. Stafford,* 1861.

4823. Subnegation. The Theory of the Normal Relation of the Races. An Answer to " Miscegenation."

> 8vo. pp. 72.   New York : *J. Bradburn & Co.,* 1864.

4824. Sumter, Fort, The Battle of, and First Victory of the Southern Troops, April 13, 1861.

> 8vo. pp. 32.   Charleston : *Evans & Cogswell,* 1861.

4825. —— Within Fort, by One of the Company ; or a View of Major Anderson's Garrison Family, for 110 days.

> 8vo. pp. 72.   New York : *N. Tibbals & Co.,* 1861.

4826. The Sumter Anniversary, 1863.   Opinions of Loyalists concerning the Great Questions of the Times, expressed in Speeches and Letters at the Inauguration of the Loyal National Leagues, New York, April 11, 1863.

> 8vo. pp. 144.   New York : *C. S. Westcutt & Co.,* 1863.

4827. Sumter, The Cruise of, from the *Cornhill Magazine,* for August, 1862.   London.

4828. —— Cruise of the Alabama and the Sumter, from the private Journals and other Papers of Commander R. Semmes, C. S. N., and other Officers.

> 12mo. pp. 328.   New York : *Carlton,* 1864.

4828.* Sumter. Programme of the Order of Exercises at the Re-Raising of the U. S. Flag on Fort Sumter, April 14, 1865.

> 8vo. pp. 4.   Port Royal : (S. C.) *New South Office,* 1865.

4829. SUNDERLAND, Rev. Byron, DD.   The Crisis of the Times. A Sermon preached in Washington, April 30, 1863.

> 8vo. pp. 36.   Washington : *Banner Office,* 1863.

4830. —— Loyalty vs. Copperheadism.   An Address before the National League, Washington, June 30, 1863.   pp. 8.

4830.* SUNDERLAND, La Roy.   The Testimony of God against Slavery.

> 18mo. pp. 177.   New York : *R. G. Williams,* 1836.

4831. SUMNER, Charles.   The True Grandeur of Nations.   An

CATALOGUE. 397

Oration delivered before the Authorities of the City of Boston, July 4, 1845.

8vo. pp. 104. BOSTON: *William D. Ticknor & Co.,* 1845.

4832. SUMNER, CHARLES. The same, second edition.

8vo. pp. 96. BOSTON: *American Peace Society,* 1845.

4833. —— The War System of the Commonwealth of Nations. An Address before the Amer. Peace Society, Boston, May 28, 1849.

8vo. pp. 80. BOSTON: *American Peace Society,* 1849.

4834. —— The same. 2d edition. 8vo. Boston, *Am. Peace So.,* '54.

4835. —— Freedom, National; Slavery, Sectional. Speech on his Motion to Repeal the Fugitive Slave Bill, in the Senate of the United States, August 26, 1852.

8vo. pp. 31. WASHINGTON: *Buell & Blanchard,* 1852.

4836. —— A Finger-Point from Plymouth Rock. Remarks at the Plymouth Festival, on the First of August, 1853.

8vo. pp. 11. BOSTON: *Crosby, Nichols & Co.,* 1853.

4837. —— The Landmarks of Freedom. Speech against the Repeal of the Missouri Prohibition of Slavery North of 36° 30′. Senate, February 21, 1854. pp. 16.

4838. —— Final Protest for himself and the Clergy of New England, against Slavery in Kansas and Nebraska. Speech in the United States Senate, May 25, 1854. pp. 8.

4839. —— Defence of Massachusetts. Speeches on the Boston Memorial for the Repeal of the Fugitive Slave Bill, and in Reply to Messrs. Jones of Tennessee, Butler of South Carolina, and Mason of Virginia. In the Senate of the United States, June 26 and 28, 1854. pp. 16. WASHINGTON, 1854.

4840. —— Duties of Massachusetts at this Crisis. A Speech delivered at the Republican Convention, Worcester, Sept. 7, 1854. pp. 8.

4841. —— The Demands of Freedom. Speech in the Senate of the United States on his Motion to Repeal the Fugitive Slave Law, February 23, 1855. pp. 8.

4841.* —— The Anti-Slavery Enterprise; its Necessity, Practicability and Dignity; with Glimpses at the Special Duties of the North. An Address before the People of N. York, May 9, 1855. *Portland Inquirer, May* 4, 1855.

4842. —— American Slavery. A Reprint of an Article on "Uncle

51

Tom's Cabin," of which a portion was inserted in the 26th number of the " Edinburg Review," and of Mr. Sumner's Speech of the 19th and 20th May, 1856, (in the U. S. Senate) with a Notice of the Events which followed that Speech.

8vo. pp. 164.   LONDON : *Longman & Co.*, 1856.

4843. SUMNER, C.   Recent Speeches and Addresses.

12mo. pp. 562.   BOSTON : *Ticknor & Fields*, 1856.
This volume contains, among others, Mr. Sumner's Speech on American
Slavery; the Struggle for the Repeal of the Fugitive Slave Law; the Kansas
and Nebraska Question; the Slave Oligarchy and its Usurpations, etc.

4844. —— The Crime against Kansas.   The Apologies for the Crime.
The True Remedy.   Speech, U. S. Senate, 19 – 20 May, 1856.
8vo. pp. 32.   WASHINGTON : *Buell & Blanchard*, 1856.

4845. —— The Barbarism of Slavery.   Speech of, on the Bill for the
Admission of Kansas as a Free State, in the United States Senate, June 4, 1860.
8vo. pp. 32.   WASHINGTON : *Buell & Blanchard*, 1860.

4846. —— The same.   New edition, with a Dedication.
8vo. pp. iv and 80.   NEW YORK : *Yng. Men's Repub. Asso.*, '63.

4847. —— The same.   pp. 115.   Boston, *Thayer & Eldridge*, 1860.

4848. —— The same.   pp. 118 and Appx.   Bost., *Thayer & Eldg.*, '60.

4849. —— The Republican Party ; its Origin, Necessity and Permanence.   Speech before the Young Men's Republican Union, New York, July 11, 1860.
8vo. pp. 16.   NEW YORK : *J. A. H. Hasbrouck & Co.*, 1860.

4850. —— Usurpation of the Senate.   Two Speeches on the Imprisonment of Thaddeus Hyatt.   Senate, 12th March and 15th June, '60.
Mr. Hyatt was imprisoned in Washington for refusing to appear and testify
before the Harpers' Ferry Investigating Committee, on the John Brown raid.

4851. —— Speech at the State Convention at Worcester, Massachusetts, September 1, 1860.   *Boston Atlas*, September 1, 1862.

4852. —— Douglas-Thayer Popular Sovereignty.   Speech at Mechanics' Hall, Worcester, Nov. 1, 1860.   *Boston Journal, Nov. 2.*

4853. —— Speech at a Republican Mass Meeting, in Framingham, Massachusetts, October 11, 1860.

4854. —— Union and Peace.   How shall they be restored?   Speech before the Repub. State Convention, Worcester, October 1, 1861.
8vo. pp. 8.   BOSTON : *Wright & Potter.*

4855. SUMNER, C. The Rebellion ; its Origin and Main-Spring. An Oration delivered under the Auspices of the Young Men's Republican Union of New York, November 27, 1861.
Royal 8vo. pp. 16. New York : *Yng. Men's Repub. Assoc.* '61.

4856. —— The same. Boston, *Wright & Potter*, 1861.

4857. —— Bingham and Baker. Two Speeches in the Senate, December 10 and 11, 1861. 8vo. pp. 7.

4858. —— The Expulsion of a Senator. Speech in the Senate of the United States, January 20, 1862. pp. 8.

4859. —— Treasury Notes a Legal Tender. Speech in the Senate of the United States, February 13, 1862. pp. 7.

4860. —— A short Consideration of Senator Sumner's Resolutions, and a Plan of Treating the subject, on Principles of American Law and Liberty, suggested. February 11, 1862. pp. 13.

4861. —— Maritime Rights. Speech in Senate, Jan. 9, 1862. p. 14.

4862. —— Resolutions declaring the Rule in ascertaining the three-fourths of the several States, required in the ratification of a Constitutional Amendment. Submitted to the United States Senate, February 4, 1865.

4863. —— Resolutions declaratory of the relations between the United States and the Territory once occupied by certain States, and now Usurped by pretended Governments, without Constitutional or Legal Right. Submitted to the Senate, February 11, 1862.

4864. —— Immediate Emancipation, a War Measure. Speech on Emancipation in Missouri. Senate, February 12, 1863. pp. 3.

4865. —— Letters of Marque and Reprisal. Speech on the Bill to authorize the President, in all Domestic and Foreign Wars, to issue Letters of Marque and Reprisal. Senate, Feb. 17, '63. p. 8.

4866. —— Speech on the Bill for the Abolition of Slavery in the District of Columbia. Senate, March 31, 1862. pp. 13.

4867. —— Indemnity for the Past, and Security for the Future. Speech on his Bill for the Confiscation of Property and the Liberation of Slaves belonging to Rebels. Senate, May 19, 1862. pp. 16.

4868. —— Rights of Sovereignty, and Rights of War. Two Sources of Power against the Rebellion.
8vo. pp. 16. New York : *Young Men's Repub. Union*, 1864.

4869. —— Independence of Hayti and Liberia. Speech on the Bill to authorize the Appointment of Diplomatic Representatives to those Republics. Senate, April 23 and 24, 1862. pp. 14.

4870. SUMNER, C. Speech on the Bill to maintain the Freedom of the Inhabitants in the States declared in Insurrection and Rebellion, by the Proclamation of the President of July 1, 1862. 8vo. pp. 15.

4871. —— Our Foreign Relations. Showing present Perils from England and France; the Nature and Conditions of Intervention by Mediation; and also by Recognition; the Impossibility of any Recognition of a New Power with Slavery as a Corner-Stone; and the wrongful Concession of Ocean Belligerency. Speech before the Citizens of New York, Sept 10, 1863.

8vo. pp. 80. NEW YORK: *Young Men's Repub. Union,* 1863.

4872. —— The same. pp. 78. Boston, *W. V. Spencer,* 1863.

4873. —— Les Relations Extérieurs des Etats Unis. Préface et Traduction. Par A. Malespine.

8vo. pp. 32. PARIS: 1863.

4874. —— Emancipation; its Policy and Necessity as a War Measure for the suppression of the Rebellion. Speech at Fanueil Hall, October 6, 1862. pp. 23.

4875. —— Our Domestic Relations. *Atlantic Monthly, Sept.,* 1863.

4876. —— Resolution defining the Character of the National Contest, and protesting against any Premature Restoration of Rebel States, without proper Guarantees and Safeguards against Slavery, and for the Protection of Freedmen. Submitted February 8, 1864. pp. 3.

4877. —— The Prayer of One Hundred Thousand. Speech on the Presentation of the First Instalment of the Emancipation Petition of the Women's National League. Senate, Feb. 9, 1863.

4878. —— Report from the Select Committee on Slavery and the Treatment of Freedmen, to which were referred sundry Petitions for the Repeal of the Fugitive Slave Act of 1850. March 7, 1864. *38th Congress, 1st Sess., Senate Report No.* 24.

4879. —— Report of the Committee on Slavery, etc., on " A Bill to secure Equality before the Law in the Courts of the United States, March 17, 1864. *38th Cong., 1st Sess., Report No.* 25.

4880. —— Universal Emancipation, without Compensation. Speech on the proposed Amendment to the Constitution Abolishing Slavery through the United States. Senate, April 8, 1864. p. 18.

4881. SUMNER, C. No Property in Man. (Same as above.)
  8vo. pp. 23.   *Loyal Publication Society, No.* 51, 1864.

4882. —— The National Finances in Time of War. Speech on the Bill to establish a National Currency. Senate, April 27 and May 4, 1864. pp. 15. WASHINGTON, 1860.

4883. —— Reconstruction of the Rebel States. Speech on the Credentials of Mr. Fishback, as Senator of Arkansas, June 13, 1864.

4884. —— The Position and Duties of the Merchant. [Life and Character of Granville Sharp.] An Address before the Mercantile Library Association of Boston, November 13, 1854.
  8vo. pp. 30.   BOSTON : *Ticknor & Fields*, 1855.
  This Address contains much relating to Slavery and the Slave Trade.

4885. —— A Bridge from Slavery to Freedom. Speech on Bill to establish a Bureau of Freedmen. Senate, June 13 and 15, '64. pp. 15. WASHINGTON, 1864.

4886. —— The Case of the Florida, illustrated by Precedents from British History.
  8vo. pp. 19.   NEW YORK : *Young Men's Repub. Union*, 1864.

4887. —— Slavery and the Rebellion, One and Inseparable. Speech before the New York Young Men's Republican Union, at Cooper Institute, New York, November 5, 1864.
  8vo. pp. 30.   BOSTON : *Wright & Potter*, 1864.

4888. —— Slavery and the American War. (The same as the above.)
  12mo. pp. 32.   LONDON : *Bacon & Co.*, 1865.

4889. —— Reciprocity Treaty. Speech on the Resolution for the Termination of the Reciprocity Treaty. Senate, December 24, 1864, and January 12 and 13, 1865.
  8vo. pp. 8.   NEW YORK : *Young Men's Repub. Union*, 1865.

4890. —— Joint Resolution to terminate the Treaty of 1817, regulating the Naval Force on the Lakes, January 17, 1865.

4891. —— Joint Resolution providing for the termination of the Reciprocity Treaty of the 5th June, 1854, between the United States and Great Britain,

4892. —— Resolutions declaring three Conditions precedent to the Reception of Senators from Rebel States, March 8, 1865. *Miscellaneous Document No.* 3.

4893. —— Treatment of Prisoners of War. Speech in Senate, January 29, 1865, on the Resolution of the Committee on Military Affairs, advising Retaliation for Rebel Cruelties to Prisoners.

12mo. pp. 8.   NEW YORK: *Young Men's Repub. Union*, 1865.

4894. SUMNER, C. The Equal Rights of All; the Great Guarantee and Present Necessity, for the sake of Security and to Maintain a Republican Government. Speech in Senate, Feb. 6 and 7, '65. p. 32.

4895. —— Railroad Usurpation in New Jersey. Speech on the Act to regulate Commerce among the several States. Sen., Feb. 14,'65.

8vo. pp. 12.   NEW YORK: *Young Men's Repub. Union*, 1865.

4896. —— The Promises of the Declaration of Independence. Eulogy on Abraham Lincoln, delivered before the Municipal Authorities of Boston, June 1, 1865.

8vo. pp. 67.   BOSTON: *J. E. Farwell & Co.*, 1865.

4897. —— The same. pp. 62. Boston, *Ticknor & Fields*, 1865.

4898. —— Opinion on the case of Franklin W. Smith, "lately convicted of Fraud against the Government of the United States, by a Court Martial, at Charlestown," Report of the Special Committee of the Boston Board of Trade.

12mo. pp. 61.   BOSTON: *John Wilson & Son*, 1865.

4899. —— Security and Reconciliation for the Future. Propositions and Arguments on the Reorganization of the Rebel States.

8vo. pp. 32.   BOSTON: *Geo. C. Rand & Avery*, 1865.

4900. —— The National Security and National Faith. Guarantees for the National Freedmen and the National Creditor. Speech at the Republican State Convention, Worcester, Sept. 14, 1865.

8vo. pp. 21.   BOSTON: *Wright & Potter*, 1865.

4901. —— The same. 2d edition. pp. 21. Bost.: *Ticknor & Fields*,'65.

4902. —— Clemency and Common Sense. A Curiosity of Literature, with a Moral. *Atlantic Monthly, December*, 1865.

4903. —— A Republican Form of Government, our First Duty and the essential Condition of Peace. Bills and Resolutions in the United States Senate, December 4, '65, embracing the following:

1. A Bill to carry out the principles of a republican form of Government in the District of Columbia.
2. A Bill to preserve the right of trial by jury, by securing impartial jurors, in the Courts of the United States.
3. A Bill in part execution of the guarantee of a republican form of government in the Constitution of the United States.

4. A Bill to enforce the guarantee of a republican form of government in certain States whose governments have been usurped or overthrown.

5. A Bill to prescribe an oath to maintain a republican form of government in the rebel States.

6. Concurrent Resolutions declaratory of the adoption of the constitutional amendment abolishing Slavery.

7. A Bill supplying appropriate legislation to enforce the amendment to the Constitution prohibiting slavery.

8. Joint Resolution proposing an amendment to the Constitution of the United States.

9. Resolutions declaratory of the duty of Congress in respect to guarantees of the national security and the national faith in the rebel States.

10. Resolutions declaratory of the duty of Congress, especially in respect to loyal citizens in the rebel States.

11. A Bill to warrant and confirm the land titles of grantees under the field order of Major-General Sherman at Savannah, January sixteen, eighteen hundred and sixty-five.

4904. SUMNER, C. Protection of Freedmen ; Actual Condition of the Rebel States. Speech on the Bill to maintain the Freedom of the Inhabitants of the States declared in Insurrection and Rebellion, by the Proclamation of the President, of July 1, 1862. Senate, December 20, 1865. pp. 15.

4905. —— The Equal Rights of All, the Great Guarantee and Present Necessity, for the sake of Security, and to maintain a republican government. Speech in the Senate of February, 1866. 8vo. WASHINGTON ; *Mansfield & Martin.* (Suppressed edition.)

4905.* —— The same. pp. 32. Wash., *Cong. Globe Office*, 1866.

4906. THE SUNNY SOUTH ; or the Southerner at Home. Five Years of a Northern Governess in the Land of Sugar and Cotton. 8vo. pp. 526. PHILADELPHIA : *G. G. Evans*, 1860.

4907. SURGEON GENERAL'S OFFICE. Reports on the Extent and Nature of the Materials available for the preparation of a Medical and Surgical History of the Rebellion. Imp. 4to. pp. 166. PHILADELPHIA : *J. B. Lippincott & Co.*, '65.

4908. SURRY, OF EAGLE'S NEST ; or the Memoirs of a Staff Officer serving in Virginia. Edited by John Esten Cooke. 12mo. pp. 484. NEW YORK : *Bunce & Huntington*, 1866.

4909. SUSQUEHANNA, (U. S. Ship.) Journal of the Cruise of, during the years 1860–63. By Amos Burton. 8vo. pp. 177. NEW YORK : *E. O. Jenkins*, 1863.

4910. SUTPHEN, Rev. MORRIS C.   Discourse on the Death of Abraham Lincoln, in Philadelphia.
8vo. pp. 19.   PHILADELPHIA : *James B. Rodgers,* 1865.

4911. SWAIN, Rev. LEONARD.   God in Strife.   A Sermon preached in Providence, Rhode Island, April 28, 1861.
8vo. pp. 13.   PROVIDENCE : *Knowles, Anthony & Co.,* 1861.

4912. —— Our Banner set up.   A Sermon, Providence, April 21, '61.
8vo. pp. 16.   PROVIDENCE : *Knowles, Anthony & Co.,* 1861.

4913. —— A Nation's Sorrow.   A Sermon preached at Providence, on the Sabbath after the Assassination of President Lincoln, April 15, 1865. pp. 11.

4914. SWEETSER,. Rev. SETH, DD.   A Commemorative Discourse at Worcester, on the Death of Abraham Lincoln.   pp. 29.

4915. SWING, Prof. D., of Miami University.   A Discourse in Memory of Col. Minor Milliken, Feb. 8, 1863.   Oxford, Ohio. pp. 8.

4916. —— The Death of the President.   A Sermon preached at Hamilton, Ohio, April 16, 1865.
12mo. pp. 18.   HAMILTON : *Telegraph,* 1865.

4917. SWINTON, WILLIAM.   The "Times" Review of McClellan.   His Military Career reviewed and exposed.
8vo. pp. 32.   NEW YORK : *Pub. by the N. Y. Tribune,* 1864.

4918. —— Armee und ihre ruhmreichen Thaten.   pp. 8.

4918.* —— The War for the Union.   *Loyal Pub. Society, No.* 62.

4919. SWINTON, WM.   Campaigns of the Army of the Potomac, from its organization to the close of the War.
8vo. pp. 600.   Maps and Plans.   N. YORK : *C. B. Richardson,* '66.

4920. Dr. SYNTAX, Jr.   A New "Sartor Resartus."   Being a Critical Analysis of a pamphlet entitled "A Review of Mr. Seward's Diplomacy."   1862.   8vo. pp. 24.

4921. SYPHER, J. R.   History of the Pennsylvania Reserve Corps.   Complete Record of the Organization, and of the different Companies, Regiments and Brigades, containing descriptions of Expeditions, Marches, Skirmishes and Battles, etc.
8vo. pp. 723.   Maps.   LANCASTER : (Pa.) *Elias Barr & Co.,* '65.

4922. SZOLD, BENJAMIN.   Vaterland und Freiheit.   Predigt bei der Erinnerungsteier des verstorbenen Präsidenten, Abraham Lincoln am Juni 1, 1865, in Baltimore.
12mo. pp. 10.   BALTIMORE : *W. Polmeyer,* 1865.

TAGGART, JOHN H.   Free Military School, for Applicants for commands of Colored Troops, Philadelphia.

8vo. pp. 12.   PHILADELPHIA: *King & Baird*, 1863.

4924. —— Second edition, with names of students. 8vo. pp. 43.

4925. TALBOT, THOMAS H.   The Constitutional Provision respecting Fugitives from Service or Labor, and Act of Cong. of Sept. '50.

8vo. pp. 128.   BOSTON: *Bela Marsh*, 1852.

4926. TALCOTT, W. H.   Report on a Marine Railway around the Falls of Niagara.

8vo. pp. 31.   NEW YORK: *W. C. Bryant & Co.*, 1864.

4927. TALES OF THE PICKET GUARD; or the Blue Devils driven from Camp.   A Collection of Stories.

8vo. pp. 84.   PHILADELPHIA: *Barclay & Co.*, 1864.

4928. TALMADGE, Rev. GOYN.   Admonitions for the Times.   A Discourse preached at Green Point, (Brooklyn, E. D.) March 10, 1861.   pp. 22.

4929. TANEY, Hon. ROGER B.   The Proceedings in the Habeas Corpus Case of John Merryman, of Baltimore County, Maryland.

8vo. pp. 24.   BALTIMORE: *Lucas Brothers*, 1861.

4930. —— Decision in the Merriman Case.

8vo. pp. 16.   PHILADELPHIA: *John Campbell*, 1862.

4931. —— The Unjust Judge.   A Memorial of Roger Brooke Taney, late Chief Justice of the United States.

8vo. pp. 68.   NEW YORK: *Baker & Godwin*, 1865.

4932. TAPLEY, RUFUS P.   Eulogy on Abraham Lincoln, April 19, 1865, at Saco, Maine.

8vo. pp. 27.   BIDDEFORD: *Journal Office*, 1865.

4933. TAPPAN, HENRY P., LL. D.   A Discourse on the Death of Abraham Lincoln.   Delivered May 2, 1865, in the Dorotheen Church, Berlin, [Prussia.]

8vo. pp. 46.   BERLIN: *G. Lange*, 1865.

4934. —— The same in German.

8vo. pp. 36.   FRANKFURT AM MAIN: *H. Keller*, 1865.

4934.* TARIFF.   The United States Tariff of 1861.

8vo. pp. 109.   NEW YORK: *Merchants' Magazine*, 1861.

4935. —— of Duties under the Act of March 2, 1861, as amended by the Acts of August and December 24, 1861.   pp. 27.

52

4936. TAX. Draft of an Act to provide Internal Revenue to support the Government; with Remarks by the Boston Board of Trade. 8vo. pp. 45.   WASHINGTON: *H. Polkinhorn*, 1862.

4937. —— U. S. Stamp Tax Law, applicable to Banking. Dated, New York, September 20. 1862. pp. 8.

4938. TAX COMMITTEES of New York, Boston and Philadelphia Clearing House Associations. Dated, August 7, 1863. 8vo. pp. 16.

4939. TAX LAW DECISIONS, alphabetically arranged; together with a complete Stamp Directory. Dime series.
12mo. pp. 77.   NEW YORK: *Beadle & Co.*, 1863.

4940. TAX. Instructions concerning the Tax on Legacies, Distributive Shares, and Gifts and Assignments. April 1863. pp. 6.
TAX, see also *Income Tax.*

4941. TAXATION. Boston Board of Trade. Report on Internal Taxation, made to the Government, April 10. pp. 14.

4942. —— Report of Committee of New York Chamber of Commerce to prepare Memorial to Congress, April 24, 1862. pp. 4.

4943. —— Memorial of the Chamber of Commerce of New York, on Taxation by the General Government. N Y., Apr. 4, '62. p. 4.

4944. —— Report of a Committee of the Philadelphia Board of Trade, on National Finances and Taxation.
8vo. pp. 15.   PHILADELPHIA: *King & Baird*, 1862.

4945. —— National and State Taxation; their operation and results as affecting Life Insurance.
8vo. pp. 20.   NEW YORK: *John A. Gray*, 1862.

4946. —— OF BANK STOCKS Constitutional Law. Decisions of the Supreme Court of the United States, relating to.
8vo. pp. 63.   NEW YORK: *J. Smith Hamans*, 1863.

4947. —— Laws relating to the Direct and Excise Taxes, passed at the 1st and 2d Sessions of the 37th Congress. 8vo. pp. 115. Washington, 1862.

4948. —— Principles of. Public Finances. The New Tax Bill. pp. 16.

4949. —— Seventeen Decisions of the Supreme Court of the United States, relating to Taxation of Government Loans and Property, by States and Cities. N. Y., *Office of Bankers' Magazine*, 1864.

4950. —— A Nation, to become rich and prosperous, must protect its Producing Classes. Reasons for taxing High Wines.
Folio, pp. 11.   CHICAGO: *Beach & Barnard*, 1864.

4951. TAXATION. Essays on Taxation and Reconstruction. By Diversity. 8vo. pp. 22. NEW YORK : *C. B. Richardson*, 1865.

4952. —— The New Internal Revenue Law of June 30, 1864, with the Amendments of March, 1865. Index and Tables of Taxation. 8vo. pp. 150. NEW YORK : *Bankers' Magazine Office*, 1865.

4953. TAXES. The New and Complete Tax-Payers' Manual. 8vo. pp. 148. NEW YORK : *D. Appleton & Co.*, 1863.

4954. —— IN INSURRECTIONARY DISTRICTS. Letter of the Secretary of the Treasury relating to. April 7, 1864. pp. 3.

4955. TAYLOR, Rev. A. A. E. Israel against Benjamin. A Sermon for the Times, preached at Dubuque, Iowa, May 26, 1861.

4956. —— Eulogy on the Death of President Lincoln, delivered at Georgetown, D. C., June 1, 1865.

4957. TAYLOR, Rev. ALFRED. Our Nation not Dead yet. Thanksgiving Sermon, preached Nov. 26, 1863, in Bristol, Penn. 12mo. pp. 36. PHILADELPHIA : *H. B. Ashmead.*

4958. TAYLOR, JAMES W., Alleghania. Memoir, exhibiting the Strength of the Union, and the Weakness of Slavery, in the mountainous Districts of the South. 8vo. pp. 24. ST. PAUL : *James Davenport*, 1862.

4959. TAYLOR, Hon. N. G. Relief of East Tennessee. Meeting at Cooper Institute, March 10, 1864. Address. 8vo. pp. 32. NEW YORK : *W. C. Bryant & Co.*, 1864.

4960. TAYLOR, Mrs. P. A. Professor Huxley on the Negro Question. Tract No. 10. 12mo. pp. 14. LONDON : *Ladies' Emancipation Soc.*, 1864.

4961. TAYLOR, WM. Cause and probable Result of the Civil War in America. Facts for the People of Great Britain. 8vo. pp. 32. LONDON : *Simpkin, Marshall & Co.*, 1863.

4962. TEFFT, Rev. B. F., DD. Letter to the Hon. John Sherman, in relation to his Bill of Reduction in the Pay of Army Officers. Augusta, Maine, January 22, 1862. pp. 4.

4963. —— The National Crisis. Address at Bangor, May, 1861. 8vo. pp. 22. BANGOR : *Samuel S. Smith*, 1861.

4964. TEN EYCK, JOHN C. Speech in Senate, April 2, 1860, on Resolutions relative to State Rights, Slavery, Fugitive Slave Law, etc. 8vo. pp. 7.

4965. TEN EYCK, J. C.　Speech on the State of the Union, Feb. 1, 1861.　pp. 8.

4966. —— Remarks on the Motion to postpone the Confiscation Bills. Senate, May, 21, 1862.　pp. 8.

4967. —— Reconstruction in the States.　Speech delivered in the United States Senate, January 5, 1864.　pp. 8.

4968. —— Railroads in New Jersey.　Power of the United States over State Charters.　Speech in the U. S. Senate, Feb. 16, '65.　p. 16.

4969. TENNESSEE.　Gov. Harris's Message to the General Assembly, Extra Session, Jan. 7, 1861. With the Public Acts of that Session. 8vo. pp. 127.　　NASHVILLE : *E. G. Eastman & Co.*, 1861.

4970. —— Senate Journal of the Extra Session of the General Assembly, which convened at Nashville, January, 1861.
8vo. pp. 189.　　NASHVILLE : *J. O. Griffith & Co.*, 1861.

4971. —— House Journal, Extra Session, Gen. Assembly, Jan., 1861. 8vo. pp. 256.　　NASHVILLE : *J. O. Griffith & Co.*, 1861.

4972. —— Senate Journal of the Second Extra Session, April 21, '61. With the Message of Governor Harris.
8vo. pp. 294.　　NASHVILLE : *J. O. Griffith & Co.*, 1861.

4973. —— House Journal, Second Extra Session, April, 1861.
8vo. pp. 224.　　NASHVILLE ; *J. O. Griffith & Co.*, 1861.

4974. —— Message of Gov. Wm. G. Brownlow, April 6, 1865.
8vo. pp. 23.　　　NASHVILLE : *S. C. Mercer*, 1865.

4975. —— Report of the Contributors to the Pennsylvania Relief Association for East Tennessee, by a Commission sent to that region, and forward supplies to the Loyal and Suffering Inhabitants.　Philadelphia, 1864.　pp. 45.

4976. —— Police Record of the Spies, Smugglers and Rebel Emissaries in Tennessee.　By an Officer.
8vo. pp. 652.　　PHILADELPHIA : *J. B. Lippincott & Co.*, 1864.

4977. TENNEY, WM. J.　The Military and Naval History of the Rebellion in the United States.
Royal 8vo. pp. 850.　　NEW YORK : *D. Appleton & Co.*, 1866.

4978. TERRILL, WM. R., Brig. General.　Remarks of Rev. Alexander G. Cummings, at the Burial of, Oct. 16, 1862, at Reading. 8vo. pp. 10.　　PHILADELPHIA : *C. Shearman & Son*, 1862.

4979. THE TERRITORIAL QUESTION.　By A Volunteer.　National Democratic Volunteers.　8vo. pp. 38.　(No date.)

4980. THAVIN. Arbitrary Arrests in the South; or Scenes from the Experience of an Alabama Unionist.
12mo. pp. 245. NEW YORK: *John Bradburn*, 1863.

4981. THATSACHEN aus der politischen Geschichte der Vereinigten Staaten. Zur Verständigug ueber die am 6 November, 1860, zu entscheidenden Fragen.
8vo. pp. 62. NEW YORK: *Abend Zeitung*, 1860.

4982. THAYER, M. RUSSELL. A Reply to Mr. Charles Ingersoll's " Letter to a Friend in a Slave State," May 5, 1862.
8vo. pp. 26. PHILADELPHIA: *John Campbell*, 1862.

4983. —— Speech in the House of Representatives, April 30, 1864, on the Bill to guarantee to certain States a Republican form of Government.
8vo. pp. 16. WASHINGTON: (D. C.) *McGill & Witherow*, 1864.

4984. —— The Great Victory; its Cost and its Value. An Address delivered in Philadelphia, July 4, 1865.
8vo. pp. 18. PHILADELPHIA: *King & Baird*, 1865.

4985. THAYER, THATCHER, DD. The State. An Oration before the Phi Beta Kappa Society, at Brown University, Sept. 2, '62.
8vo. pp. 30. PROVIDENCE: *Sidney S. Rider*, 1862.

4986. THAYER, W. M. The Pioneer Boy and how he became Pres.
12mo. pp. 310. BOSTON: *Walker, Wise & Co.*, 1863.

4987. —— A Youth's History of the Rebellion.
8vo. pp. 347. BOSTON: *Walker, Wise & Co.*, 1864.

4988. —— The Ferry Boy and the Financier.
12mo. pp. 332. BOSTON: *Walker, Wise & Co.*, 1864.

4989. THE TWO WAYS OF TREASON; or the Open Traitor of the South face to face with the Skulking Abettor at the North.
8vo. pp. 12. *Loyal Publication Society No.* 33, 1863.

4990. THIRTEEN MONTHS in the Rebel Army. By an impressed New Yorker.
8vo. pp. 282. LONDON: *Sampson, Low, Son & Co.*, 1862.

4991. THOMAS, Rev. ALFRED C. Prayerful Sympathy invoked for America. A Sermon preached at Islington, Eng., Dec. 21, '62.
8vo. pp. 20. LONDON: *W. Mitchena*, 1862.

4992. —— The same. pp. 32. PHILADELPHIA: *Martien*, 1863.

4993. THOMAS, Rev. A. G. Our National Unity perfected in the

Martyrdom of our President. A Discourse delivered in the United States General Hospital, April 19, 1863.

8vo. pp. 16. PHILADELPHIA: *Smith, English & Co.*, 1865.

4994. THOMAS, BENJ. F. The Treasury Note Bill. Remarks in House of Reps., February 6, 1862. pp. 8.

4995. —— Speech on Confiscation, May 24, 1862. pp. 8.

4996. —— Remarks on the relation of the seceded States to the Union, and the Confiscation of Property, and Emancipation of Slaves in such States. House of Representatives, April 10, 1862.

8vo. pp. 37. BOSTON: *John Wilson & Son*, 1862.

4997. —— The same. pp. 14. Washington: *Globe Office*, 1862.

4998. —— Speeches in the Second and Third Sessions of the 37th Congress, and in the Vacation.

8vo. pp. 217. BOSTON: *John Wilson & Son*, 1863.

The following are the titles of the Speeches relating to the War: The Relation of the "Seceded States" (so called) to the Union, and the Confiscation of Property, and Emancipation of Slaves, in such States. Confiscation. The Treasury Note Bill. Case of the "Trent." Speech at the Mass Meeting for Recruiting, on Boston Common. The Army of the Reserve. Speech at Chelsea. Remarks on the Border States. On the Bill "To raise additional Soldiers for the service of the government. The Louisiana Election Cases. The Conscription. New England and the Union.

4999. THOMAS, Rev. CHARLES B. A Sermon for the Hour. Preached February 23, 1862, in the First Unitarian Church, Chicago.

8vo. pp. 19. CHICAGO: *Dunlop, Lowell & Spaulding*, 1862.

5000. THOMAS, JAMES S. The Case of Gen. Fremont. Remarks suggested by the Speech of F. P. Blair, in House of Representatives, March 7, 1862. pp. 32.

5001. THOMAS, JOHN L., of Maryland. Speech on amending the Constitution, in the House of Reps., January 31, 1866.

5002. THOMPSON, Rev. D. R. The War. Correspondence between the Young Men's Christian Associations of Richmond, Virginia, and of the City of New York.

8vo. pp. 16. NEW YORK: *G. P. Putnam*, 1861.

5003. THOME, JAMES A. Emancipation in the West Indies. A Six Months' Tour in Antigua, Barbadoes and Jamaica, in the year '37.

8vo. pp. 128. *American Anti-Slavery Society*, 1838.

5004. —— The Future of the Freed People.

8vo. pp. 47. CINCINNATI: *Tract and Book Society*, 1863.

5005. THOME, J. A. The same. 8vo. pp. 32. (No date.)

5006. —— What are we Fighting for ? Occasional, No. 2.

5007. THOMPSON, GEO. Discussion on American Slavery, with the Rev. Robert J. Breckinridge, at Glasgow, Scotland, June, 1836. 8vo. pp. 23. BOSTON : *Isaac Knapp*, 1836.

5008. —— Letters and Addresses, during his Mission in the United States, from October 1, 1834, November 27, 1835. 12mo. pp. 126. BOSTON : *Isaac Knapp*, 1847.

5009. —— Speech on the Divisions among American Abolitionists, at the Annual Meeting of the Glasgow Emancipation Society, 2d August, 1841. pp. 8.

5010. —— Prison Life and Reflections ; or a Narrative of the Arrest, Trial, &c., of Work, Burr and Thompson, who suffered imprisonment in Missouri for attemping to aid some Slaves to Liberty. 12mo. pp. 377. NEW YORK : *S. W. Benedict*, 1848.

5011. THOMPSON, HUGH MILLER. The Nation. *Con. Mo'ly, Dec.'*63.

5012. —— Some uses of a Civil War. Ibid. *October*, 1864.

5013. THOMPSON, REV JOHN B. Signs of Promise. A Discourse preached at Metuchen, N. J., Nov. 24, '64. (Pulpit & Rostrum.)

5014. THOMSON, WM. ALEXANDER. Essay on Production, Money and Government. 8vo. pp. 47. BUFFALO : *Wheeler, Mathews & Co.*, 1863.

5015. THOMPSON, REV. JOHN C. In Memoriam. A Discourse upon the Character of Abraham Lincoln, at Pottstown, Pa., June 1, '65. 8vo. pp. 20. PHILADELPHIA : *Stein & Jones*, 1865.

5016. —— The President's Fast. A Discourse upon our National Crimes and Follies, preached in New York, January 4, 1861. 8vo. pp. 26. NEW YORK : *Thomas Holman*, 1861.

5017. —— Anniversary Address delivered at the Annual Meeting of the African Colonization Society, May 19, 1861. 8vo. pp. 39. NEW HAVEN : *T. J. Stafford*, 1861.

5018. —— Christianity and Emancipation ; or the Teachings and Influence of the Bible against Slavery. 8vo. pp. 86. NEW YORK : *Anson D. F. Randolph*, 1863.

5019. —— Bryant Gray ; the Student, the Christian, the Soldier. 8vo. pp. 148. NEW YORK : *Anson D. F. Randolph*, 1864.

5020. THOMPSON, Rev. J. C. Revolution against Free Government, not a Right, but a Crime. Address before the Un. League Club. 8vo. pp. 46. NEW YORK : *Club House,* 1864.

5021. —— Abraham Lincoln ; his Life and its Lessons. A Sermon preached on Sabbath, April 30, 1865.
8vo. pp. 38. NEW YORK : *Loyal Publication Society,* 1865.

5022. THOMPSON, J. P., DD. England during the War. *New Englander, July,* 1862.

5023. —— The Hour of Popular Liberty and Republican Government. 8vo. pp. 30. NEW HAVEN : *T. J. Stafford,* 1862.

5024. —— Peace through Victory. A Sermon.
8vo. pp. 16. *Loyal Publication Society No.* 60, 1864.

5025. —— Memorial Service for three hundred thousand Soldiers, with the Communicative Discourse.
8vo. pp. 28. *Loyal Publication Society, No.* 88, 1866.

5027. THOMPSON, Senator, of New Jersey. Speech on the State of the Union. United States Senate, Feb. 7, 1861. 8vo. pp. 14.

5028. THOMPSON, Rev. M. L. P., DD. The Sword, a Divine Judgment for Sin. Discourse preached at Cincinnati, Sept. 26, and Nov. 28, 1861, on the occasions of Thanksgiving and National Fast.
8vo. pp. 25 and 22. CINCINNATI : *Gazette Company,* 1861.

5029. THOMSON, Rev. E., DD. The Confederated Republic of Israel. A Sermon preached in N. Y., Thanksgiving Day, Nov. 27, '62.
12mo pp. 27. NEW YORK : *Carlton & Porter,* 1863.

5030. THORNE, Rev. JAMES A. What are we Fighting for?
12mo. pp. 8. CINCINNATI : Ohio, (No date.)

5031. THORNWELL, Rev. J. H., DD. Report on Slavery presented to the Synod of S. Carolina, Nov. 6, '51. pp. 16. Charleston, 52.

5032. —— The State of the Country. An article republished from the Southern Presbyterian Review.
8vo. pp. 32. COLUMBIA : (S. C.) *Southern Guardian Press,*'60.

5033. THE THREE VOICES ; the Soldier, Farmer and Poet, to the Copperheads.
8vo. pp. 12. NEW YORK : *Loyal Publication Society, No.* 4,'63.

5034. THRILLING STORIES of the Great Rebellion ; comprising Heroic Adventures and Hair-Breadth Escapes of Soldiers, Spies, Refugees, etc. By a Disabled Officer.
12mo. pp. 384. PHILADELPHIA : *John E. Potter,* 1864.

5035. THROOP, MONTGOMERY H.   The Future.   A Political Essay. 8vo. pp. 343.   NEW YORK: *James G. Gregory*, 1864.

5036. TILDEN, SAMUEL J.   The Union.   Its Dangers, and How can they be averted.   Letter to Hon. William Kent.   8vo. pp. 16.

5037. TILLINGHAST, Rev. N. P.   A Thanksgiving Sermon delivered at Georgetown, D. C., December 7, 1865. 8vo. pp. 16.   WASHINGTON: *McGill & Witherow*, 1865.

5038. TILTON, THEODORE.   The Negro.   A Speech at Cooper Institute, New York, May 12, 1863, before the Am. Anti-Slavery So. 18mo. pp. 16.   BOSTON: *Anti-Slavery Office*, 1863.

5039. THE TIMES.   [In four chapters.]   Chapter 1 ; A Million of Men taken from the Field of Labor for the Field of Battle !   War ! War ! War !   Carnage !   Free Negroes to compete with White Labor !   Debt, Taxation and Demoralization ! etc.   Chapter 2 : Democratic Rule, etc.   pp. 4.   (Philadelphia.)

5040. TIMLOW, Rev. HEMAN.   A Discourse occasioned by the Death of Abraham Lincoln, at Rhinebeck, New York, April 19, 1865. 12mo. pp. 42.   RHINEBECK, New York, 1865.

5041. TOBACCO.   Petition of the Receivers and Exporters of American Leaf Tobacco, to Congress.   (1863.)   N. Y., Dec. 19, '63. p. 11.

5042. —— Report of Committee of the Board of Trade of Baltimore, relative to a Tax on Tobacco.   8vo. pp. 8.

5043. —— A Word about the Tax on Tobacco.   Balt., Jan., '64. p. 7.

5044. —— Preamble and Resolutions passed at a Meeting of the Receivers and Exporters of American Leaf Tobacco, January 12, 1865, with Petition to Congress of December, 1863. 8vo. pp. 14.   NEW YORK: *Barton & Son*, 1865.

5045. TOBITT, JOHN H.   What I heard in Europe during the "American Excitement ;" illustrating the difference between Government and People abroad, in their Habits and Good Wishes to the Perpetuity of the Great Republic. 8vo. pp. 132.   NEW YORK: *H. M. Tobitt*, 1865.

5046. TOLLES, Lieut. Col. C. W.   An Army ; its Organization and Movements.   *Cont. Monthly, June, July, Aug., Sept. and Dec.* '64.

5047. TOMES, ROBERT, M. D.   The War with the South.   A History of the Great American Rebellion ; being a complete Narrative of the Origin and Progress of the War, with Biographical

53

Sketches of Leading Statesmen, Naval and Mil. Commanders, etc. 4to. 2 vols. Steel engravings. NEW YORK : *Virtue & Co.,* '62–5.

5048. TOMES, R., M. D. The Fortunes of War. *Harpers' Mag., July,*'64.

5049. TORREY, JESSE. A Portraiture of Domestic Slavery in the U. S., with Reflections on the Practicability of Restoring the Moral Rights of the Slave. Philadelphia : *For the author,* 1817.

5050. TORREY, H. D. America; or Visions of the Rebellion. A Poem in Four Cantos.
18mo. pp. 67. READING : (Penn.) *B. F. Owen,* 1862.

5051. TOURNIQUET. A Description of the newly-invented Elastic Tourniquet, for the use of Armies.
8vo. pp. 31. NEW YORK : *G. F. Nesbitt & Co.,* 1862.

5052. TOWER, Rev. PHILO. Slavery Unmasked; Being a truthful Narrative of a Three Years' Residence in Eleven Southern States, to which is added the Invasion of Kansas.
18mo. pp. 432. ROCHESTER : *E. Darrow & Brother,* 1856.

5053. TOWLE, G. M. Our Recent Foreign Relations. *At. Mo., Aug.,*'64.

5054. —— Some Secession Leaders. *Harpers' Mag., April,* 1863.

5055. TOWNE, Rev. JOSEPH H., DD. The Harvest Festival. A Thanksgiving Discourse delivered in Milwaukee, Nov. 28, 1861.
8vo. pp. 24. MILWAUKEE : *Ben. Franklin,* 1861.

5056. TOWNSEND, S. P. Speech delivered before the Union League, at New Providence, New Jersey, November 9, 1863. pp. 16.

5057. —— Great Speech, at Plainfield, New Jersey, Oct. 30, 1862, on Conservatism, Abolitionism, Sham Democracy, Paper Money, the War, etc. pp. 15.

5058. TRAIN, GEO. FRANCIS. The Facts; or at Whose door does the Sin (?) lie ? Who profits by Slave Labor ? Who initiated the Slave Trade ?
12mo. pp. 144. NEW YORK : *R. M. De Witt,* 1860.

5059. —— Union Speeches delivered in England during the Present American War. Second series. Phila. : *Peterson & Bro.,* 1862.

5060. —— The Downfall of England. His Great Speech before the Brotherhood of St. Patrick, in London. Phil., *Peterson & Bro.,*'62.

5061. —— Unionist on T. C. Grattan, Slanderer. Defence of America.
8vo. pp. 48. BOSTON : *Lee & Shepard,* 1862.

5062. TRAIN, Unionist, on T. Colley Grattan, Secessionist.
8vo. pp. 60. LONDON : *John Adams Knight,* 1862.

5063. **TRAIN** among the Pennsylvanians. The Union Train smashing up the Chicago Wigwam! pp. 13.

5064. **TRAPNELL**, Rev. JOSEPH, Jr. A Word from the West. Our Duty as American Citizens in this, our Country's Imminent Peril. A Discourse at Keokuk, Iowa, January 4, 1861.
8vo. pp. 16· KEOKUK : *Rees & Delaplain*, 1861.

5065. **TRAVER**, Rev. A. D., DD. Address at the Burial of the late G. Sibbald Wilson, Adjt. 17th Regt., N. Y. S. V., Poughkeepsie.
8vo. pp. 8. POUGHKEEPSIE : *Osborne & Otis*, 1863.

5066. **TREADWELL**, DANIEL. Rifled Cannon. 8vo. pp. 7.

5067. —— The Construction of Improved Ordnance.
8vo. pp. 28. CAMBRIDGE : *Welch, Bigelow & Co.*, 1862.

5068. —— On the Construction of Hooped Cannon.
8vo. pp. 40. BOSTON : *Little, Brown & Co.*, 1865.

5069. **TREADWELL**, FRANCIS C. Secession an Absurdity. It is Perjury, Treason and War.
16mo. pp. 32. NEW YORK : *Ross & Toucey*, 1861.

5070. **TREASURY REPORTS**. Report of the Secretary, Dec., 1862.

5071. —— Review of the Report of the Secretary of the Treasury, December 4, 1862. pp. 16. Washington.

5072. —— Report for the year ending June 30, 1863. pp. 439.

5073. —— Report for the year 1864. pp. 351.

5074. —— Report of W. P. Fessenden, Sec'y, Dec. 6, 1864. pp. 45.

5075. **TREASURY NOTES A LEGAL TENDER**. Argument of John R. Porter, in the Court of Appeals of the State of New York, in the Case of the Metropolitan Bank and others, Respondents, against H. H. Van Dyck, Sup't of the Bank Department, June 27, 1863.
8vo. pp. 37. ALBANY : *Weed, Parsons & Co.*, 1863.

5076. —— Arguments of Counsel. (Same Case.)
8vo. pp. 239. NEW YORK : *W. C. Bryant & Co.*, 1863.

5077. **TREMENHEERE**, HUGH SEYMOUR. The Constitution of the United States compared with our own. London, 1854.

5078. **TRENT**, Steamer. Case of the Seizure of the Southern Envoys.
8vo. pp. 26. LONDON : *J. Ridgeway*, 1861.

5079. —— The Seizure of the Southern Commissioners considered, with reference to International Law, and the Question of War and Peace.
8vo. pp. 45. LONDON : *J. Ridgeway*, 1862.

5080. TRENT. The Case of the Trent examined.
  8vo, pp. 24. LONDON: *James Ridgway*, 1862.

5081. TRENT AFFAIR. Memoir on. By An. Michele Costi, Publicist of Venice, Italy.
  8vo. pp. 23. WASHINGTON; (D. C.) *McGill & Witherow*, 1865.

5082. THE TRIALS FOR TREASON at Indianapolis. Disclosing the Plans for establishing a Northwestern Confederacy.
  8vo. pp. 340. CINCINNATI: *Moore, Wilstach & Baldwin*, 1865.

5083. TRIP of the Steamer Oceanus to Fort Sumter and Charleston, with the Exercises at the re-Raising of the Flag over the Ruins of Sumter, April 14, 1865.
  8vo. pp. 174. BROOKLYN: *Privately printed*, 1865.

5084. TRIMBLE, ROBERT. Slavery in the United States. A Lecture delivered in Liverpool, December, 1861.
  8vo. pp. 31. LIVERPOOL: *Henry Young*, 1863.

5085. —— Popular Fallacies relating to the American Question. A Lecture delivered in November, 1863.
  8vo. pp. 36. LONDON: *Whitaker & Co.*, 1863.

5086. —— The Negro and the South. The Status of the Colored Population in the Northern and Southern States of Amer., compared.
  8vo. pp. 34. LONDON: *Whitaker & Co.*, 1864.

5087. —— Peace and its Consequences. *Amer. Monthly, Sept.*, 1864.

5088. —— A Review of the American Struggle, in its Military and Political Aspects, from the Inauguration of President Lincoln, 4th March, 1861, till his reëlection, November, 1864.
  8vo. pp. 48. LONDON: *Whitaker & Co.*, 1864.

5089. —— The Present Crisis in America.
  8vo. pp. 10. LONDON: *Whitaker & Co.*, 1865.

5090. TROLLOPE, ANTHONY. North America.
  2 vols. 8vo. LONDON: *Chapman & Hall*, 1862.

5091. —— The same. Philadelphia: *Lippincott & Co.*, 1862.

5092. TROWBRIDGE, J. T. Cudjo's Cave.
  12mo. pp. 504. BOSTON: *J. E. Tilton & Co.*, 1864.

5093. —— We are a Nation. *Atlantic Monthly, December*, 1864.

5094. —— The Three Scouts.
  12mo. pp. 381. BOSTON: *J. E. Tilton & Co.*, 1865.

5095. THE TRUE ISSUES now involved. Shall the Republic stand on the Foundation laid by our Patriotic Fathers, or shall the Nation be sacrificed to the Covetousness and Knavery of the Confederates in Treason ? Letter of N. B. Browne to C. J. Biddle. p. 24.

5096. TRUMAN, Hon. Mr. Bounties to Soldiers. Provision for their Families. Copperheads. Secessionists, etc. Remarks in Senate of New York. March 19, 1863. pp. 6.

5097. TRUMBULL, Lyman, of Illinois. Speech on the Bill to Confiscate the Property and Free the Slaves of Rebels. Senate, December 5, 1861.

5098. —— The Constitutionality and Expediency of Confiscation, vindicated. April 7, 1862.
8vo. pp. 15.   WASHINGTON: *Cong. Globe Office*, 1862.

5099. —— The Constitutionality and Expediency of Confiscation, vindicated. Speech in Senate, April 7, 1862. pp. 15.

5100. —— The Freedmen's Bureau. Veto Message. Speech in Senate, February 20, 1866. pp. 16.

5101. TUCKER, Hon. Beverly, of Virginia. Prescience. Speech in the Southern Convention, held at Nashville, April 13, 1850.
8vo. pp. 38.   RICHMOND : (Va.) *West & Johnson*, 1862.

5102. TUCKER, John. Reply to the Report of the Select Committee of the Senate, on Transports for the War Depart'nt, Feb. 27, 63.
8vo. pp. 57.   PHILADELPHIA : *Moss & Co.*, 1863.

5103. TUCKER, Rev. J. T. The Southern Insurrection ; its Elements and Aspects. *Boston Review*, November, 1861. 8vo. pp. 20.

5104. —— A Discourse in Memory of President Abraham Lincoln, in Holliston, Massachusetts, June 1, 1865.
8vo. pp. 21.   HOLLISTON : *Plimpton & Clark*, 1865.

5105. TUCKER, St. George. A Dissertation on Slavery ; with a Proposal for the Gradual Abolition of it in the State of Virginia.
8vo. pp. 104.   PHILADELPHIA : *Mathew Carey*, 1796.

5106. —— The same work.
8vo. pp. 104.   NEW YORK : *Reprinted*, 1863.

The author was Professor of Law in the University of William and Mary, and one of the Judges of the General Court in Virginia.

5107. TUCKERMAN, Charles K. The Legend of the Corner Stone. A Political Allegory. *Boston Transcript, April 25*, 1865.

Mr. Tuckerman also is the author of several patriotic Poems, which appeared in the New York Evening Post; among them, " Raising the Flag at Sumter;" " Burying the Dead."

5108. TUCKERMAN, Henry T.   The Rebellion; its Latent Causes
and True Significance.   In Letters to Friends abroad.
8vo. pp. 48.   New York: *James G. Gregory,* 1861.

5109. —— Our Wounded.   *Continental Monthly, October,* 1862.

5110. —— Virginia.   Ibid.   *December,* 1863.

5111. TURPIE, Mr.   Speech in the Senate of the United States, February 7, 1863.   8vo. pp. 12.

5112. Twenty-Second Reg't, N. G., S. N. Y.   The Last Campaign
of June and July, 1863.
8vo. pp. 47.   New York: *C. S. Westcott & Co.,* 1864.

5113. TWISS, Horace, D. C. L.   Law of Nations, considered as Independent Political Communities.   On the Rights and Duties of
Nations in Time of War.
8vo. pp. xi, 526.   London: *Longman,* 1863.

5114. Two Months in Fort LaFayette.   By a Prisoner.
18mo. pp. 53.   New York: *For the author,* 1862.

5115. Two Months in the Confederate States; including a Visit to
New Orleans, under the Domination of Gen. Butler, by an English Merchant.
8vo. pp. 299.   London: *Richard Bentley,* 1863.

5116. TWOMBLY, Rev. A. S.   A Sermon commemorative of Adjutant R. M. Strong, 177th Regt., N. Y. S. V., who died in Louisiana, May 12, 1863.   Preached at Albany, June 7, 1863.
8vo. pp. 22.   Albany: *J. Munsell,* 1863.

5117. —— A Thanksgiving Plea for Free Labor, North and South.
8vo. pp. 30.   Albany: *J. Munsell,* 1864.

5118. —— The Assassination of Abraham Lincoln.   A Discourse delivered at Albany, April 16, 1865.
8vo. pp. 18.   Albany: *J. Munsell,* 1865.

5119. TYLER, Prof.   The Universal Fatherhood of God and the Universal Brotherhood of Man, God's Argument against Oppression.
Evangelical Quarterly Review, Vol. xiv.

5120. TYLER, Rev. G. P.   The Successful Life.   A Discourse on the
Death of Pres. Lincoln, April 19, '65, at Brattleboro', Vt.   p. 12.

5121. TYLER, Rev. Moses.   Our Solace and our Duty in this Crisis.
A Sermon for the Last Night of Mr. Buchanan's Administration,
preached in Poughkeepsie, New York, March 3, 1861.
8vo. pp. 24.   Poughkeepsie: *Platt & Schram,* 1861.

5122. TYNG, Stephen H., DD. Christian Loyalty. A Discourse delivered in New York, April 30, 1863.
18mo. pp. 83.　　　　　Boston: *American Tract Society.*

5123. —— The same.　New York: *John A. Gray & Greene*, 1863.

5124. TYNG, Rev. Dudley A. Our Country's Troubles. A Sermon preached in Philadelphia, June 29, 1856.
8vo. pp. 32.　　　　Philadelphia: *W. S. & A. Martien*, 1864.

5125. —— Our Country's Troubles; or National Sins and National Retribution. A Sermon preached July 5, 1857.
8vo. pp. 15.　　　　Philadelphia: *W. S. & A. Martien*, 1864.

5126. TYSON, Bryan, of North Carolina. The Institution of Slavery in the Southern States, religiously and morally considered in connection with our Sectional Troubles.
8vo. pp. 60.　　　Washington: (D. C.) *H. Polkinhorn*, 1863.

5127. —— A Ray of Light; or a Conservative Treatise on the Sectional Troubles, religiously and morally considered.

ULSTER Historical Society. The Ulster Regiment in the Great Rebellion. Vol. 1, Part 3.

5129. Uncle John's Cabin, (next door to Uncle Tom's Cabin;) containing an Answer to Pro-Slavery Men, an Answer to others, and an Impeachment. By a Neutral.
12mo. pp. 87.　　　London: *Simpkin, Marshall & Co.*, 1865.

5130. —— A Reply to a Critique on "Uncle Tom's Cabin," which appeared in the "Dundee Advertiser," April 1, 1865.
12mo. pp. 43.　　Liverpool: *Edward Howell*, 1865.

5131. UNDERWOOD, John C. Speech at Alexandria, July 4, '63.

5132. UNDERWOOD, T. H. Our Flag. A Poem in four Cantos. New York, *Carleton*, 1862.

5133. UNDYE, Lieut. Col. Charles Redington, who fell at the Battle of Gettysburg, July 1, 2 and 3, 1863. In Memoriam. (A private Memorial.) Boston, 1863.

5134. The Union, the Constitution and Slavery. From the *American Quarterly Church Review, January*, 1864, pp. 36.

5135. The Union as it was, and the Constitution as it is. pp. 12.

5136. The Union; Being a Condemnation of Mr. Helper's Scheme, with a Plan for the Settlement of the "Irrepressible Conflict." By One who has considered both sides of the Question. 8vo. pp. 32.   NEW YORK : *F. A. Brady.*

5137. UNION. Facts for the Times. Dissolution of American Union Question. pp, 28. Boston, *Redding & Co.,* 1850.

5138. —— for the sake of the Union. Constitution of S. B. as promulgated by order of the Board of Control. 12mo. pp. 23.   CHICAGO : *C. J. Ward,* 1864.

5139. UNION DOCUMENT. pp. 16. Albany, *Standard Office.*

5140. THE UNION ALPHABET, for Children. 8vo. Boston, *Sampson & Farrar,* 1862.

Each letter of the alphabet is followed by the name of a distinguished military officer or statesman, with a brief notice of him.

5141. UNION DEFENCE COMMITTEE of the Citizens of New York. Reports and Docs., Board of Aldermen, September 9, '61. Doc. 18. 8vo. pp. 71.   NEW YORK : *Edmund Jones & Co.,* 1861.

5142. UNION LEAGUE CLUB, New York. Articles of Association, By-Laws, Officers and Members of, 1863. 8vo. pp. 17.   NEW YORK : *W. C. Bryant & Co.,* 1863.

5143. —— Report of the Special Committee on Emigration. Presented May 12, 1864. pp. 19.

5144. —— Report of Executive Committee, July, 1864. pp. 48.

5145. —— Report on Volunteering. Presented October, 13, 1864. 8vo. pp. 55.   NEW YORK : *Club House,* 1864.

5146. —— The Charter, By-Laws and List of Members, July, 1865. 8vo. pp. 29.   NEW YORK : *Club House,* 1865.

5147. —— Report of Executive Committee, Constitution, By-Laws and List of Members, January, 1865. pp. 35.

5148. —— Report of Executive Committee and Treas., Jan.,'65. p. 43.

5149. —— Report of Special Committee on the Passage, by the House of Reps., of the Constitutional Amendment for the Abolition of Slavery, January 31, 1865. pp. 22.

5150. UNION LEAGUE OF PHILADELPHIA, Articles of Association and By-Laws of. Organized December 27, 1862. 8vo. pp. 16.

5151. —— Address and Resolutions, September 16, 1863. pp. 8.

5152. —— First Annual Report of the Board of Directors of, December 14, 1863. 8vo. pp. 16.

5153. —— Second Annual Report, December 12, 1864. pp. 16.

5154. UNION LEAGUE of Philadelphia, Rules adopted by the Board of Directors, Rules of the League House, and a List of Committees. 8vo. pp. 22. PHILADELPHIA: *H. B. Ashmead,* 1865.

5155. —— Proceedings in Commemoration of the 89th Anniversary of American Independence, 1865. Oration by Chas. Gibbons, Esq. 8vo. pp. 32. PHILADELPHIA: *King & Baird,* 1865.

5156. —— Proceedings regarding the Assassination of Abraham Lincoln, President of the United States. 8vo. pp. 22. PHILADELPHIA: *H. B. Ashmead,* 1865.

5157. UNION LEAGUE, 24th WARD, PHILADELPHIA. Address at the Opening Celebration, May 9, 1863. By N. B. Brown. Lord Lyons in Council with the Democracy. pp. 16.

UNION LEAGUE OF PHILADELPHIA. Publications of. These Pamphlets are not numbered. They are here arranged alphabetically for convenience of reference.

5158. *Abraham Lincoln.*

5159. *Amnesty Proclamation,* and Third Annual Message of President Lincoln.

5160. *Agnew.* Our National Constitution; its adaptation to a State of War.

5161. *About the War.* Plain Words to Plain People. The same, in German.

5162. *African Slave Trade, The.*

5163. *Address* and Resolutions of the Union League.

5164. *Address* of the State Central Committee of Pa., Sept., 1863.

5165. *Butler, General B. F.* Speech.

5166. *Bellows, H. W.* Unconditional Loyalty.

5167. *Bible Views* of Polygamy.

5168. *Bible Views of Slavery;* or Bishop Hopkins Reviewed by a Layman.

5169. *Breckenridge, R. J.* The Nation's Success. A Sermon.

5170. *Boot on the other Leg, The;* or Loyalty above Party.

5171. *Browne, N. B.* Address of. Lord Lyons in Council, etc.

5172. *Boker, G. H.* Hymn for the 87th Anniversary of American Independence.

5173. *Boker, G. H.* The Second Louisiana. English and German.

54

UNION LEAGUE of Philadelphia, Publications of.

5174. *Binney Horace*, A Letter from.

5175. *Bokum.*   The Testimony of a Refugee from E. Tennessee.

5176. *Conscription, The ;* also Speeches of the Hon. Wm. D. Kelley.

5177. *Cooper.*   The Loyalty demanded by the Present Crisis.

5178. *Democratic Peace.*   English and German.

5179. *Democratic Opinions* on Slavery, 1776–1863.

5180. *Davis, Henry Winter.*   Speech,

5181. *Designs* of the Southern Conspiritors and their Norther Allies.

5182. *Duties* of Adopted Citizens, The.   In German.

5183. *English Neutrality.*

5184. *Elder, William.*   The Debt and Resources of the United States.   English and German.

5185. *Few Words, A,* for Honest Pennsylvania Democrats.

5186. *Future* of the North-West, The.

5187. *First Duty* of the Citizen.   The Grandeur of the Struggle, etc.

5188. *Gantt.*   Address of General Gantt, C. S. A.

5189. *Great Auction Sale* of Slaves.   Sequel to Mrs. Kemble's Journal.

5190. *Grund's* Speech, in the North American.

5191. *Holmes, Oliver Wendell.*   Oration.

5192. *Howard, Robert,* on Military Interference at Elections.

5193. *Irish Patriot, The.*   O'Connell's Legacy to Irish Americans.

5194. *John Jay.*   The Great Conspiracy.

5195. *Jackson,* President.   Proclamation, December 11, 1832.

5196. *Letter* to the President of the United States, by a Refugee.

5197. *Letter* of the President.   Truth from an Honest Man.

5198. *Loyalists.*   Ammunition, The.

5199. *Lieber,* Dr.   Plantations for Slave Labor, the Death of the Yeomanry.

5200. *Lowell, James Russell.*   The President's Policy.

5201. *Loyalty* for the Times, The.

5202. *Maynard.*   Extracts from Judge Maynard's Charge.

5203. *No Party* now, but all for our Country.

5204. *Narrative* of the Sufferings of the Union Soldiers while Prisoners.

5205. *Old Continental,* and the New Greenback Dollar.   Uncle Sam's Debts, and his ability to pay them.

Union League of Philadelphia, Publications of.

5206. *Planters' Almanac* for 1864.

5207. *Proofs of Workingmen* of the Monarchic and Aristocratic Designs of the Southern Conspirators and their Northern Allies.

5208. *Paddock, Rev. Wilbur F.* God's Presence and Purpose in our War.

5209. *Picture of Slavery,* from the Decisions of the Southern Courts.

5210. *Porter, Rev. Charles S.* A Fast Day implies a Duty.

5211. *Rival* Platforms.

5212. *Rosecrans,* General. Letter to the Democracy of Indiana.

5213. *Rebuke* of Secession Doctrines.

5214. *Shanafelt, Rev. J. R.* The End of the Slave Controversy.

5215. *Swinton, William.* The War for the Union.

5216. *Sumner, Charles.* Our Foreign Relations.

5217. *Smith, Goldwin.* Does the Bible sanction American Slavery?

5218. *Stewart, Rev. W. B.* The Nation's Sins and the Nation's Duty.

5219. *Southern Slavery* and the Christian Religion. A Letter of Judge Stroud's.

5220. *Stillé.* Northern Interests and Southern Independence.

5221. *Stillé.* How a Free People conduct a Long War.

5222. *Slavery,* the mere Pretext for the Rebellion.

5223. *Speeches* at the Inauguration Meeting of the Union Club.

5224. *Savoury* Dish for Loyal Men. English and German.

5225. *The True Issues* now Involved.

5227. *To the Soldiers* for the Union.

5228. *To the Men* of the South. By a Texan.

5229. *Thompson, Rev. J. P.* Christianity and Emancipation.

5230. *Washington* and Jackson on Negro Soldiers.

5231. *Whiting, Hon. William.* The War Powers of the President.

5232. *Whiting, Hon. Wm.* The Return of the Rebellious States.

5233. *Will,* (The,) of the People.

5234. *Woodward,* Judge, on Foreigners. English and German.

5235. *Woodward,* in 1860 and 1863.

5236. *Woodward.* Extracts from his Speech, December 13, 1860.

5237. *Woodward.* Views of Judge Woodward and Bishop Hopkins, on Negro Slavery, illustrated by Extracts from Mrs. Butler's Journal.

5238. *Workingman's,* A, Reasons for the Reëlection of Abraham Lincoln.

5239. UNION LEAGUE MELODIES. A Collection of Patriotic Hymns and Tunes. Original and Selected, by Rev. J. W. Dadman.
16mo. pp. 32.   BOSTON : *B. R. Russell,* 1864.

5240. UNITED STATES vs. Franklin W. Smith. Argument for the Defence, by Benjamin H. Thomas.
8vo. pp. 127.   BOSTON : *Alfred Mudge & Son,* 1865.

5241. UNITED STATES vs. Franklin W. Smith. A Review of the Argument of the Judge Advocate, by F. W. Smith, with an App.
8vo. pp. 144.   BOSTON : *Alfred Mudge & Son,* 1865.

5242. UNITED STATES vs. F. W. Smith. Memorial of the Senators and Reps. in Congress from Mass., to the President of the U. S. p. 11.

5243. UNITED STATES CHRISTIAN COMMISSION for the Army and Navy. Work and Incidents. First Annual Report.
8vo. pp. 126.   PHILADELPHIA : February, 1863.

5244. —— Second Annual Report. For the year 1863.
8vo. pp. 284.   PHILADELPHIA, April, 1864.

5245. —— Second Report of the Committee of Maryland, Sept., 1863.
8vo. pp. 146.   BALTIMORE : *Sherwood & Co.,* 1863.

5246. —— Third Report of the Committee of Maryland. 8vo. pp. 286.

5247. —— The War and the Chr. Commission. By A. B. Cross. p. 56.

5248. —— Battle of Gettysburg and the Christian Commission. By Andrew B. Cross. Baltimore, *Sherwood & Co.* pp. 32.

5249. —— Report of the Committee of the Christian Commission in charge of the District of Maryland. pp. 15.

5250. —— Christian Commission for the Army and Navy of the United States of America. (Address and Circular.)
12mo. pp. 52.   PHILADELPHIA : *Ringwalt & Brown,* 1862.

5251. —— Report of the Army Committee of the United States Christian Commission. Pittsburgh, Pennsylvania. 12mo. pp. 13.

5252. —— Facts, Principles and Progress, October, 1863.
12mo. pp. 36.   PHILADELPHIA : *C. Sherman & Son,* 1863.

5253. —— Organization, By-Laws, Objects and Plan for Volunteer Chaplains, March 3, 1863. 8vo. pp. 8.

5254. UNITED STATES Christian Commission. A Delegate's Story. By Rev. H. Q. Butterfield. pp. 8.

5255. —— Union Prayer Meeting, held by the Christian Commission, on the Night of the National Fast, April 30, 1863, in Light St. Methodist Episcopal Church, Baltimore.
12mo. pp. 24.   BALTIMORE : *James Young*, 1863.

5256. —— Information for Army Meetings, August, 1864. pp. 35. Philadelphia, *J. B. Rogers*, 1864.

5257. —— do. September, 1864. pp. 35.   Philada., *J. B. Rogers*, 1864.

5258. —— do. October, 1864. pp.   do.   do.   1864.

5259. —— do. November, 1864. pp.   do.   do.   1864.

5260. —— do. December, 1864. pp. 36.   do.   *Alfred Martien*, 1864.

5261. —— do. January, 1865. pp. 34.   do.   *Jas. B. Rogers*, 1865.

5262. —— do. February, 1865. pp. 34.   do.   do.   1865.

5263. UNITED STATES SERVICE MAGAZINE, for 1864.   Vol. 1.
Chattanooga; with a Map.—A Few Facts about Artillery. January.
The Burial at Gettysburg. (Poetry.) January.
The use of Iron in Fortification. Lieut. Col. J. G. Barnard. January.
Modern War, in Theory and Practice. January.
Later Rambles over the Field of Gettysburg. Dr. M. Jacobs. January.

5264. UNITED STATES SERVICE MAGAZINE, for 1864.
Organization of the Staff.—The African Color Sergeant. February.
Later Rambles over the Field of Gettysburg. Dr. M. Jacobs. February.
Three Months around Charleston Bar; or the Great Siege as we saw it. Robert Stewart Davis. February.

5265. UNITED STATES SERVICE MAGAZINE, for 1864.
Missouri.—Railroads in War.—Volunteering and Conscription. March.
Three Months around Charleston Bar. Robert Stewart Davis. March.
The Siege of Charleston. From the French *Journal des Sciences Militaires.* March.

5266. UNITED STATES SERVICE MAGAZINE, for 1864.
What the Navy has done during the War. W. V. McKean. April.
Practical Campaigning.—Secession at the Naval School. April.
Where Sherman went and what he did. April.

5267. UNITED STATES SERVICE MAGAZINE, for 1864.
Three Months around Charleston Bar; or the Great Siege as we saw it. Robert S. Davis. May.
Homes for Discharged Invalid Soldiers. May.
Organization of United States Artillery. General John Gibbon. May.
General McClellan's Campaigns. May.

5268. UNITED STATES SERVICE MAGAZINE, for 1864.
Lieutenant General Grant. Professor Coppée. June.

The probable Influence of the new Military Element of our Social and National Character. C. A. Bristed. June.

Naval Staff Rank. June.

5269. UNITED STATES SERVICE MAGAZINE, for 1864.

Reorganization. The Confederacy through French Spectacles. July.

5270. UNITED STATES SERVICE MAGAZINE, for 1864.

Major General Wm. T. Sherman.—The Florida Expedition. August.
Reorganization, No. 2.—Love and Loyalty, No. 2. August.
The Lay of the Light Artillery. By Professor Coppée. August.

5271. UNITED STATES SERVICE MAGAZINE, for 1864.

The Militia.—Love and Loyalty, No. 3. September.
Maj. Gen. Wm. T. Sherman, No. 2.—The Naval Hospital Establishment. Sept.
Brigadier General Alexander Hays. September.

5272. UNITED STATES SERVICE MAGAZINE, for 1864.

Philanthropy and the War. October.
Life and Character of Major General James B. McPherson. October.

5273. UNITED STATES SERVICE MAGAZINE, for 1864.

The Red River Campaign.—Love and Loyalty, No. 4. November.

5274. UNITED STATES SERVICE MAGAZINE, for 1864.

The New York State Militia.—Love and Loyalty.—Expeditions. December.

5275. UNITED STATES SERVICE MAGAZINE, for 1865.

Battle of Pittsburg Landing.—Letter from General Sherman. January.
Farragut.—The Romance of a Raid. January.
Ana of the War.—Pickings and Picketings. January.
Notes on the May Campaign on the James River. January.
The Campaign in Missouri against Price. January.
The Military Situation, with a View to Peace. January.
A Word for the Quartermaster's Department. January.

5276. UNITED STATES SERVICE MAGAZINE, for 1865.

The Victory at Nashville. Captain J. F. Rusling. February.
A Word for the Quartermaster's Department. February.
Ana of the War.—Pickings and Picketings. February.
Sherman's Winter Campaign through Georgia. February.

5277. UNITED STATES SERVICE MAGAZINE, for 1865.

Reorganization of the Army. March.
New York State Militia, No. 2.—Services in 1861. March.
Notes of the May Campaign on the James River, No. 2. March.
A Word for the Quartermaster's Department, No. 3. March.
Captures and Prize Money.—Women in the War. March.
The Army of the Dead. (Poetry.) March.

5278. UNITED STATES SERVICE MAGAZINE, for 1865.

Sherman's Atlanta Campaign; with Map. April.
Seeking the Bubble, No. 2. By Lieut. Colonel Irwin. April.
Naval Staff Rank.—Relieved Guard. (Poetry.) H. P. Leland. April.
Our Moral Weakness.—Fort Fisher; with a Plan. April.

5279. UNITED STATES SERVICE MAGAZINE, for 1865.
Grant.—Major General Philip Henry Sheridan. May.
Sherman's Georgia Campaign. By Colonel Bowman. May.
A Word for the Quartermaster's Department, No. 4. May.
The Fall of Richmond. Professor Coppée. May.

5280. UNITED STATES SERVICE MAGAZINE, for 1865.
Sherman's Truce.—What the Coast Survey has done for the War. June.
Sherman's Sixty Days in the Carolinas. By J. E. Parker Doyle. June.
Army Movements. Lt.Col. Tolles.—My Capture and Escape from Moseby. June.

5281. UNITED STATES SERVICE MAGAZINE, for 1865.
What to do with our Generals. Prof. Coppée.—Maj. Gen. Jno. A. Logan. July.
Seeking the Bubble, No. 5.—Lieutenant Colonel R. B. Irwin. July.
Brig. Gen. James S. Wadsworth.—The Yankee as a Fighter. July.
What the Coast Survey has done for the War. July.
The Homeward March of the Sixth Corps through Richmond. July.

5282. UNITED STATES SERVICE MAGAZINE, for 1865.
Sheridan's Mode of Fighting. August.
Seeking the Bubble, No. 6. Lieutenant Colonel Irwin. August.
Ana of the War. C. G. Leland. August.

5283. UNITED STATES SERVICE MAGAZINE, for 1865.
Drill and Discipline.—Women in the War. September.
The Quartermaster General's Report.

5284. UNITED STATES SERVICE MAGAZINE, for 1865.
Story of a Brigade.—Reminiscences of the War, Wilmington. October.
Snicker's gap.—A Welcome to the Army. October.
Ana of the War, No. 6. Charles G. Leland. October.

5285. UNITED STATES SERVICE MAGAZINE, for 1865.
Who may kill in War, and who may not. November.
Siege of Morris Island.—Seeking the Bubble, No. 7. November.
Brevet Major General Hugh Judson Fitzpatrick. November.

5286. UNITED STATES SERVICE MAGAZINE, for 1865.
Military Organization. Major General T. J. Wood. December.
Seeking the Bubble, No. 8.—Four Years. By E. Y. Z. December.
Ana of the War, No. 7.—The Draft. Charles G. Leland. December.
Sketches of Army Life. Annie E. Faxen. December.

5287. UNITED STATES SERVICE MAGAZINE, for 1866.
Major General Sherman.—Ana of the War, No. 8. January.
Reminiscences of the War, No. 2, Wilmington. January.

5288. UNITED STATES SERVICE MAGAZINE, for 1866.
Nineteenth Army Corps. By Colonel Gouverneur Carr. February.
Seeking the Bubble. Lieutenant Colonel Irwin. February.

5289. UNITED STATES SERVICE MAGAZINE, for 1866.
The Sixth Army Corps. From Yorktown to Gettysburg. March.
Military Courts.—Up the Arkansas. March.
The Army Bill.—Grant. March.

5290. UNITED STATES SERVICE MAGAZINE, for 1866.
  The Sixth Army Corps. From Gettysburg to the end. April.
  National Guard Bill. Major General H. W. Slocum. April.
  Notes on Naval Courts, by Charles Cowley. April.
  Up the Arkansas.—Ana of the War, by C. G. Leland. April.

  UNITED STATES SANITARY COMMISSION, Papers published by, or
      relating to.

5291. —— Brief Outline of What the U. S. Sanitary Commission has
  done and is doing. Contributions received, $11,214. 1861. p. 24.

5292. —— Circular Letter to the Loyal Women of America. Dated,
  Washington, October 1, 1861. With Note from Prest. Lincoln.

5293. —— Letter from Rev. Dr. Bellows to Gov. Morgan of New
  York, relative to the Plans and Wants of the Com., Oct. 22, '61.

5294. —— Appeal to the People of Pennsylvania, for the Sick and
  Wounded Soldiers. Philadelphia, November 29, 1861. pp. 40.

5295. —— Proceedings of a Meeting of the Associate Members of the
  Sanitary Commission, at New York, January 29, 1862.

5296. —— Brief Reports of Operations in Tennessee, May, 1862. By
  Dr. J. S. Newberry, Secretary Western Department. pp. 12.

5297. —— Statement from the Executive Committee of What has been
  done, and What is required. With Extracts of Letters, New
  York, September 1, 1862.

5298. —— What they have to do who stay at home. Dated, Washington, October 21, 1862. Signed, F. Law Olmsted, Sec'y. pp. 4.

5299. —— Resolutions suggested by Mr. Olmsted, in Executive Committee, October 31, 1862, and ordered to be printed. pp. 5.

5300. —— Letter from J. H. Douglass, Asso. Secretary, giving " some
  idea of the extent of our Operation and Plans to be pursued.
  December 8, 1862.

5301. —— Blank Receipt for Contributions to the Sanitary Commission, with an Acconnt of its Operations, Dec. 25, 1862. pp. 14.

5302. —— Letter on the Sanitary Condition of the Troops in the neighborhood of Boston, to Gov. Andrew, from S. G. Howe, M. D.
  8vo. pp. 16. WASHINGTON: *Government Printing Office*, 1861.

5303. —— Report of Delegates from the General Aid Society, for the
  Army at Buffalo, to visit the Agencies of the Sanitary Commission. By Rev. G. W. Hosmer. Buffalo, 1862. pp. 16.

United States Sanitary Commission, etc.

5304. —— Queries about the Sanitary Commission, by " Index ;" and the Reply of the New York Evening Post, March 30, 1864.

5305. —— The United States Sanitary Commission. Reprinted from the North American Review, No. cciii, for April, 1864.
8vo. pp. 52.   Boston: *Crosby & Nichols*, 1864.

5306. —— The United States Sanitary Commission. A Sketch of its Purposes and its Work.
12mo. pp. xiii and 299.   Boston: *Little, Brown & Co.*, 1863.

5307. —— The same. pp. 300.   N. York: *For the San. Com.*, 1864.

5308. —— Hospital Transports. A Memoir of the Embarkation of the Sick and Wounded, from the Peninsula of Virginia in the Summer of 1862.
12mo. pp. 167.   Boston: *Ticknor & Fields*, 1863.

5309. —— Report on Military Hygiene and Therapeutics. Dated, June 21, 1861. 8vo. pp. 27.

5310. —— Speech of the Rev. Dr. Bellows, made at the Academy of Music, Philadelphia, February 24, 1863.
8vo. pp. 32.   Philadelphia: *C. Sherman & Sons*, 1863.

5311. —— Monthly Bulletin of the Operations of the Cincinnati Branch of the United States Sanitary Com., for May, '63. Cincinnati,'63.

5311.* —— The same, for September, 1863. pp. 16. 1863.

5312. —— Correspondence between James C. Wetmore, Ohio State Military Agent, Washington, and Frederick N. Knapp, Agent U. S. Sanitary Commission, on the subject of alleged Fraudulent Sale of Railroad Tickets, on the part of the Com. 8vo. pp. 15.

United States Sanitary Commission, Official Publications of, all printed in 8vo. form.

5213. A. Report Military Hygiene and Therapeutics. Report of Committee on Military Surgery, to the Surgical Section of the New York Academy of Medicine. pp. 27.

5314. B. Directions to Army Surgeons on the Field of Battle. By G. J. Guthrie, Surgeon General to the British Forces, during the Crimean War. pp. 8.

5315. C. Rules for preserving the Health of the Soldiers. p. 10.

55

UNITED STATES SANITARY COMMISSION, Publications.

5316. D. Report of a Committee of the Sanitary Commission, to prepare a Paper on the use of Quinine as a Prophylactic against Malarious Diseases.
8vo. pp. 19.   WASHINGTON : *McGill & Witherow,* 1862.

5317. E. Report of a Committee of the Sanitary Commission, to prepare a Paper on the value of Vaccination in Armies. p. 34.

5318. F. Report of a Committee of the Associate Medical Members, on the subject of Amputations. 8vo. pp. 8.

5319. G. Report of a Committee, on the subject of Amputations through the Foot, and at the Ankle Joint.
8vo. pp. 28.   New York : *Baillière Brothers,* 1862.

5320. H. Report of a Committee, on Venereal Diseases, with special reference to Practice in the Army and Navy.
8vo. pp. 19.   WASHINGTON : *McGill & Witherow,* 1862.

5321. J. Report of a Committee on the subject of Pneumonia.
8vo. pp. 24.   WASHINGTON : *McGill & Witherow,* 1862.

5322. K. Report of the Com., on the subject of Continued Fevers.
8vo. pp. 23.   WASHINGTON : *J. E. Farwell & Co.,* 1862.

5323. L. Report of a Committee on the subject of Excision of Joints for Traumatic Causes.
8vo. pp. 23.   CAMBRIDGE : *Welch, Bigelow & Co.,* 1862.

5324. M. Report of a Committee, on Dysentery. 8vo. pp. 40.

5325. N. Report of a Committee, on the subject of Scurvy, with special reference to Practice in the Army and Navy.
8vo. pp. 29.   WASHINGTON : *Govt. Printing Office,* 1862.

5326. O. Report of a Committee, on the subject of the Treatment of Fractures in Military Surgery.
8vo. pp. 15.   PHILADA. : *J. B. Lippincott & Co.,* 1862.

5327. P. Report of a Committee, on the subject of the Nature and Treatment of Miasmatic Fevers.
8vo. pp. 23.   NEW YORK : *Baillierè Brothers,* 1862.

5328. Q. Report of Com., on the Nature and Treatment of Yellow Fever. 8vo. pp. 25. N. YORK : *Wm. C. Bryant & Co.,* '62.

5329. R. Hemorrhage from Gun-Shot Wounds, and the best means of arresting it. By Valentine Mott, M. D. pp. 16.

It is proper to state that the above reports were from the Associate Medical Members of the United States Sanitary Commission.

CATALOGUE431

UNITED STATES SANITARY COMMISSION, Publications.

5330. S. Hints for the control and prevention of Infectious Diseases, in Camps, Transports and Hospitals.
8vo. pp. 36. NEW YORK: *Wm. C. Bryant & Co.*, 1862.
5331. 1. Address to the Sec. of War, May 18, 1861. pp. 6.
5332. 2. Letter from the Surgeon General to the Secretary of War. Draft of Powers asked for. Order the Commission. Approval of the President.
5333. 3. Plan of Organization, with Approval of the Secretary of War, June 13, 1861.
5334. 4. Address to the People of the U. S., June 21. pp. 4.
5335. 5. Address to Life Insurance Companies, June 21, 1861.
5336. 6. Resolutions appointing Finance Committee, June 22, 1861. pp. 2.
5337. 7. (Circular Letter, asking for Contributions to aid the Commission in carrying out the objects for which it is formed.) pp. 3.
5338. 8. (Circular Letter to the Governors of the several States. Dated, July 13, 1861; with Inquiries relative to the Soldiers, Officers, Surgeons, Nurses, Hospitals, etc., connected with the Organization of Regiments. pp. 4.
5339. 9. (Circular to Regiments, requesting information respecting Hygiene, Food, Medicines, Camp Police, etc.) pp. 6.
5340. 10. Letter announcing the Election of Persons as Associate Members of the Sanitary Commission, June 22, 1861. p. 2.
5342. 12. Associate Members of the Comm., June 29, 1861. pp. 7.
5343. 13. Address of the Central Finance Committee. pp. 2.
5344. 14. Directions to Army Surgeons on the Field of Battle. By G. J. Guthrie, Surgeon General to the British Forces during the Crimean War. pp. 9.
5345. 15. Letter of the President to the Executive Committee of the Central Finance Com., in N. Y., July 9, 1861. pp. 7.
5346. 16. Appeal of the Executive Finance Committee, in the City of New York. pp. 3.
5347. 17. Rules for preserving the Health of the Soldiers. By W. H. Van Buren, M. D. pp. 12
5349. 19*a*. Camp Inspection Return. pp. 15.

UNITED STATES SANITARY COMMISSION, Publications.

5350. 20. Resolutions passed by the Sanitary Committee, July 29, and ordered to be sent to the President, Heads of the Departments, and to both Houses of Congress. pp. 2.

5351. 21. Record of certain Resolutions. pp. 10.

5352. 22. Statements of the Considerations which led to the appointment of the Sanitary Commission by the War Department. pp. 10.

5353. 23. Report of the Committee, (Drs. Van Buren and Agnew,) to visit the Military General Hospitals, in and around Washington, and to ascertain their Condition and the Wants of the Sick and Wounded Volunteers, July 31, 1861. p. 12.

5354. 24. General Instructions to Sanitary Inspectors. pp. 13.

5355. 25. Collection of the Papers of the Sanitary Commission, September 1, 1861. pp. 93.

5356. 26. Notes of a Preliminary Sanitary Survey of the Forces of the United States, in the Ohio and Mississippi Valleys, near midsummer, 1861. By H. W. Bellows, President of the Sanitary Commission. pp. 18.

5357. 27. Report on the Sanitary Condition of the United States Troops in the Mississippi Valley, August. By J. S. Newberry, M. D. pp. 11.

5358. 28. Advice as to Camping, by the British Government Sanitary Commission. Addressed to Lord Panmure, A. C. B., Minister of War. Dated December 1, 1856. pp. 11.

5359. 29. Report concerning the Aid and Comfort given by the Sanitary Commission to Sick Soldiers found at the Railroad Station. By Fred'k N. Knapp, Sept., 23, 1861. pp. 13.

5360. 30. Outline of What the Sanitary Commission has done.

5361. 31. Report of Committee, on the use of Quinine as a Prophylactic against Malarious Diseases. pp. 21.

5362. 32. Report concerning the Woman's Central Association of Relief, at New York, October 12, 1861. pp. 44.

5363. —— Appeal to the Public. Operations and Results. November 25, 1861. pp. 24.

5364. 33. A List of the Associate Members of the United States Sanitary Commission, March 15, 1862. pp. 16.

UNITED STATES SANITARY COMMISSION, Publications.

5365. 34. List of same, December 7, 1861. pp. 16.

5366. 35. Two Reports concerning the Aid and Comfort given by the Sanitary Commission to Sick Soldiers passing through Washington. By Fred'k N. Knapp, Sept. 23, 1861. p. 23.

5367. 36. Report on the Condition of the Troops, and the Operations of the Commission in the Valley of the Mississippi, for three months, ending Nov. 30, 1861. By Dr. Newberry. 8vo. pp. 48. CLEVELAND: *Fairbanks, Benedict & Co.,* '61.

5368. 37. Report of the Soldiers' Aid Society of Cleveland, Ohio, and its auxiliaries, November 30, 1861. pp. 40.

5369. 38. Report on the condition of Camps and Hospitals at Cairo and vicinity, St. Louis, etc. By Drs. Patton and Isham, October, 1861. pp. 12.

5370. 39. Third Report concerning aid and comfort to Sick Soldiers passing through Washington, March 21, 1862. pp. 29.

5371. 40. Report to the Secretary of War, on the operation of the Commission and upon the Sanitary Character of the Army, Dec. 21, '61. By F. L. Olmsted, Gen. Supt. p. 107.

5372. —— Meeting of Associate Members in N. Y., Jan. 19, '62.

5373. —— Extracts from Minutes,—8th Session. Mar., '62. pp. 6.

5374. 41. Two Reports on the Military Hospitals of Grafton, Va., and Cumberland, Md., March 10, 1862. pp. 40.

5375. 42. Visit to Fort Donelson for the Relief of the wounded. By Dr. Newberry, February, 1862. pp. 10.

5376. —— Brief Reports of operations in Tenn., May, '62. p. 12.

5377. 43. Letter to the President of the U. S., July 21, '62. p. 8.

5378. 44. Report at the Cincinnati Branch, March 1, '62. p. 13.

5379. 44*b*. Appeal to the Public for Funds, July 4, 1863. pp. 8.

5380. 45. Regulations of the N. Y. Agency, and for its Hospital Transport Service on the Atlantic Coast. pp. 10.

5381. 46. Report on the Mortality and Sickness of the U. S. Volunteer Forces. By E. B. Elliott, May 18, 1862. pp. 80.

5382. 47. Letter to President Lincoln, August 5, 1862, (relative to the great loss of life during the Peninsular Campaign. p. 8.

5383. —— Appeal to the Public, September 11, 1862. pp. 8.

5384. 48. Statement from Dr. Bellows, with Letters on Battles and Relief Work in Maryland, Sept. 24, 1862. pp. 18.

United States Sanitary Commission, Publications.

5385. 49. Letter from Dr. Bellows to S. G. Perkins, relative to the future of Disabled Soldiers, August 15, 1862. pp. 8.

5386. 50. What they have to do who stay at home. pp. 12.

5387. 51. Revised Instructions for Camp Inspections. pp. 18.

5388. 52. Instructions to Inspectors on Campaign Duties. p. 4. Camp Inspection Returns, with Forms. pp. 11, 26, 28.

5389. 53. Rules of the Central Office, September 22, 1862. p. 8.

5390. 54. Statement from Rev. Dr. Bellows as to the Labor and Wants of the Commission, October 22, 1862. pp. 7.

5391. 55. Reports from the Western Department. pp. 16.

5392. —— Reports, (the same.) 2d edition, enlarged. pp. 24.

5393. —— Resolution on the Relation of the Sanitary Commission to its Branches, October 31, 1862. pp. 6.

5394. —— Letter from Dr. Bellows to J. S. Newberry, M. D., Secretary of the Western Department, Nov. 5, '62. pp. 10.

5395. —— Report on the relation of the Auxiliaries to the Central Board, November 17, 1862. pp. 20.

5396. 56. Inspection of the General Hospitals. First Report. By Henry G. Clark, M. D., November 18, 1862. pp. 15.

5397. 57. Report of the operations of the Inspectors and Relief Agents, after the Battle of Fredericksburg, Dec. 13, '62. p.31.

5398. 58. Dr. Ordronaux on the Relief of Disabled Soldiers. p. 8.

5399. 59. Fourth Special Relief Report. Dec. 5, 1862. pp. 24.

5400. 59*a*. Supplement to the 2d edition of the Relief Report, containing additional memoranda. pp. 14.

5401. 60. Executive Organization, Dec. 18, 1862. pp. 138.

5402. —— Acknowledgment of Receipts from Pacific Coast. p. 14.

5403. 61. General Order for the Executive Service, Jan. '63. p. 6.

5404. 62. Rules for the Supply Department, Jan. 27, '62. pp. 4.

5405. 63. Letter to the Women of the Northwest from H. W. Bellows, D. D., October 29, 1863. pp. 7.

5406. 64. What the Commission is doing in the Mississippi Valley. Letter from Dr. J. S. Newberry, Feb. 16, '63. pp. 31.

5407. 65. Inspection of the General Hospitals. Second Report. By H. G. Clark, M. D., January 21, 1863. pp. 10.

5408. 66. Regulations of the Supply Department. pp. 18.

UNITED STATES SANITARY COMMISSION, Publications.

5409. —— The Work of the Sanitary Commission. Address of the Rev. Dr. Bellows, at Philad., October 29, 1863. pp. 8.

5410. —— Letter to the Surgeon General of the State of New York, March 11, 1862.

5411. —— How can we best help our Camps and Hospitals. Women's Central Asso. of Relief, March 27, 1863. pp. 42.

5412. 67. Report on the Pension Systems and Invalid Hospitals in Europe. By Stephen H. Perkins, May 22, '63. pp. 52.

5413. 68. Preliminary Reports on Operations of the Commission in the Army of the Potomac, during June and July,'63. p. 8.

5414. 69. Objects and Methods of the Sanitary Commission, June 7, 1863. By G. T. Strong, Treasurer. pp. 64.
Supplement to the same, being an Appeal to the Public. p. 4.

5415. 70. Operations of the Commission before Charleston. pp. 4.

5416. 71. Report on Operations during and after the Battles at Gettysburg, July, 1863. By J. H. Douglass, M. D. pp. 29.

5417. —— Three Weeks at Gettysburg. By two Ladies, July, 1863. pp. 24.

5418. —— Operations of the Commission at Beaufort and Morris Island, S. C., September 17, 1863. pp. 8.

5419. 72. Organization of the Field Relief Corps, in the Army of the Potomac. By Dr. Steiner, September 19, '63. p. 12.

5420. 73. Letter to the President of the United States. Removal of the Surgeon General. pp. 4.

5421. 74. List of Associate Members, March, 1864. pp. 22.

5422. 75. Report on Operations in the Mississippi Valley. By J. S. Newberry, M. D., September, 1863. pp. 24.

5423. 76. Preliminary Reports on the Campaign in Northern Virginia. By Dr. Agnew, May, 1864. pp. 12.

5424. 77. Fifth Relief Report, December 15, 1862, to October 1, 1863. By F. N. Knapp. pp. 68.

5425. —— Executive Organization, adopted Oct. 8, 1863. pp. 8.

5426. 78. Answer to the Question, "Why does the Sanitary Commission need so much Money?" January 1, 1864.

5427. —— United States Sanitary Commission,—Origin, Struggles and Principles. From the *N. Am. Rev.*, *Jan.*, 64. p. 42.

United States Sanitary Commission, Publications.

5428. 79. Inspection of General Hospitals. Third Report. By H. G. Clark, M. D., May, 1863. pp. 42.

5429. —— Relief of Disabled Soldiers. By J. Ordronaux, M. D. April 6, 1864. pp. 164.

5430. —— United States Sanitary Commission,—Plans, Methods and Results. April, 1864. *N. American Review.* pp. 52.

5431. 80. Letters from the Army of the Potomac, May, '64. p. 70.

5432. 81. Regulations for Field Relief Corps, July, 1864. pp. 4.

5433. 82. Rules for Executive Service, July, 1866. pp. 8.

5434. 83. Financial Report, with Supplement. pp. 16.

5435. 84. Report on the Operations in the Mississippi Valley, October 1, 1864. By Dr. Newberry. pp. 30.

5436. —— Brief Statement of the Sanitary Commission Work. October, 1864. California Branch. pp. 16.

5437. —— Observations in Hospitals in Shenandoah Valley, October, 1864. By Elisha Harris, M. D. pp. 12.

5438. 85. Case and Opinion. The Trust on which the Sanitary Commission holds its Funds. By Prof. T. W. Dwight, November, 1864. pp. 26.

5439. 86. Executive Organization and Service, Oct., '64. p. 18.

5440. 87. Preliminary Report on Operations in North Carolina, and on the Condition of Exchanged Prisoners lately received at Wilmington. By Dr. Agnew. pp. 18.

5441. 88. Address of Mrs. Hoge at the Packer Institute, Brooklyn, New York, March, 1865. pp. 22.

5442. 89. Extracts from Special Report concerning the Rebel Hospitals in Richmond, April 20, 1865. pp. 8.

5443. —— Outlines of Enquiry,—Hygienic, Medical and Surgical Experiences in the War. By Elisha Harris, M. D. p. 16.

5444. 90. Circular to Branches and Aid Societies, May, '65. p. 8.

5445. —— Supplement to No. 90. Bureau of Information and Employment, with blanks, A to F. pp. 26.

5446. —— Hygienic Observations. By Dr. E. Harris. pp. 4.

5447. 91. Report of the Auxiliary Finance Committee, January, 1865. pp. 4.

5448. 92. Report concerning the Field Relief Service, with the Army of the Potomac, July 7, 1865. pp. 28.

UNITED STATES SANITARY COMMISSION, Publications.

5449. 93. Circular to Branches and Aid Socs., July 4, '65. p. 8.
5450. —— Circular respecting the Army and Navy Claim Agency.
5451. 94. Special Relief Report for the Quarter ending June 30, 1865. By F. N. Knapp. pp. 46.
5452. 95. Pensions required for the Relief and Support of Disabled Soldiers and Sailors and their dependents. A Report to the Standing Committee, United States Sanitary Commission. By H. W. Bellows, DD., President, New York, December 15, 1865. pp. 26.
5453. —— Report of the Secretary with regard to the probable Origin of the Demoralization of the Volunteer Army at Washington, and the Duty of the Sanitary Commission. 1861. (Confidential.) pp. 46.
5454. —— Report of the Committee appointed in New Haven, to aid in furnishing supplies to the Sick and Wounded Soldiers of our Army, October, 1861. pp. 7.
5455. —— First Annual Report of the General Aid Society for the Army. Buffalo, N. York, January 1, 1863. pp. 15.
5456. —— Soldiers' Aid Society of Northern Ohio. Annual Report to the U. S. Sanitary Com., July 1, 1862. pp. 40.
5457. —— The English Branch of the United States Sanitary Commission. The Motive of its establishment and Results of its Work. By Edmund C. Fisher. London. pp. 31.
5458. —— Constitution and By-Laws of the New England Women's Auxiliary Association, Branch of the United States Sanitary Commission, January, 1864. pp. 7. Boston.
5459. —— First annual Report of the same. Boston, 1864.
5460. —— Second annual Report of the same. Boston, '64. p. 19.
5461. —— Third annual Report of the same. Boston, '65. p. 28.
5462. —— Second Semi-Annual Report of the Women's Central Association of Relief, November 1, 1862. pp. 19.
5463. —— Second An. Report of same, May 1, 1863. pp. 35.
5464. —— Third Annual Report of same, May 1, 1864. pp. 35.
5465. —— Fourth An. Report of same, July 7, 1865. pp. 41.
5466. —— Annual Report of the Women's Branch of the U. S. Sanitary Commission, April 1, 1864. pp. 32.

56

UNITED STATES SANITARY COMMISSION, Publications.

5467. —— The Army Ration. How to diminish its Weight and Bulk. By Prof. E. N. Hosford. pp. 44.

5468. —— Nelly's Hospital. Reprinted from "Our Young Folks," for the Sanitary Commission.

5469. —— Officers and Associates of the U. S. Sanitary Commission, Phila.; Record of the Women's Branch, Jan. 1, 1864.

5470. —— First Report of the Solicitor of the Protective War Claim and Pension Agency, of the United States Sanitary Commission, in Philadelphia, January 1, 1865. pp. 24.

5471. —— Statistics of Operations from Executive Committee of Boston Associates, October 20, 1864. pp. 4.

5472. —— Report of the General Superintendent of the Philadelphia Branch of the U. S. San. Com., Feb. 1, 1864. pp. 28.

5473. —— Report of same, January 1, 1865. pp. 81.

5474. —— Report concerning the Special Relief Service of the Sanitary Commission in Boston, March 31, 1864. pp. 28.

5475. —— Report of same, for the year ending March 31, '65. p. 8.

5476. —— Classified Statement of Expenditures and Receipts of the Gen. Treasury, from June 27, 1861, to July 1, '65. p. 8.

5477. —— Letter from the General Secretary, with List of the Agents of U. S. Sanitary Com., July 15, 1865. pp. 3.

5477.* —— The Sanitary Commission Bulletin, Nos. 1 to 40. Nov. 1, 1863, to Aug. 1, 1865. N. Y., Philada. and Wash.

5478. UPFOLD, GEO., Bishop of Indiana. National Sins the Cause of National Calamity. A Sermon delivered at La Porte, Ind. 8vo. pp. 29. NEW YORK: *D. Appleton & Co.*, 1863.

5479. UPHAM, J. B., M. D. Epidemic Cerebro-Spinal Menengitis. Hospital Notes and Memoranda; in illustration of the Congestive Fever, (so called,) as it occurred in 1862–3, in the Camps around Newbern. 8vo. pp. 38. BOSTON: *David Clapp*, 1863.

5480. UPHAM, Hon. NATH'L G. Letter on the Present Crisis; addressed to Hon. Gilman Marston, Member of Congress from New Hampshire, February 20, 1861. 8vo. pp. 20. CONCORD: *McFarland & Jencks*, 1861.

5481. UPHAM, Hon. N. G.   Rebellion,—Slavery,—Peace.   An Address delivered at Concord, New Hampshire, March 2, 1864. 8vo. pp. 40.   CONCORD : *E. C. Eastman*, 1864.

5482. —— The same. pp. 24. *Loyal Publication Society No.* 52, 1864.

5483. —— Views on Reconstruction.   *Bost. Daily Adv., Aug.* 31, '65.

5484. —— British Complicity in the Final Expedition of the Alabama. *Boston Daily Advertiser, November* 11, 1865.

5485. UPSHUR, ABEL P.   A brief Enquiry into the True Nature and Character of our Federal Government ; being a Review of Judge Story's Commentaries on the Constitution. 8vo. pp. 131.   PHILADELPHIA : *John Campbell*, 1863.

5486. UPSON, CHARLES, of Michigan. The Missouri Election. Speech in the House of Representatives, May 6, 1864. pp. 15.

5487. UTLEY, H. T.   The History of Slavery and Emancipation. Speech before the Democratic Ass., Dubuque, Iowa, Feb. 12, '63. 8vo. pp. 31.   PHILADELPHIA : *John Campbell*, 1863.

VALLANDIGHAM, Hon. CLEMENT L., and Mr. McClernand. Justice to the Northwest.   Remarks on the Motion to excuse Mr. Hawkins of Florida, from serving on the Committee of Thirty-Three.   House of Representatives, December 10, 1860.   pp. 8.

5489. —— The Great American Revolution of 1861. Speech in the House of Representatives, February 20, 1861. pp. 21.

5490. —— Letter to Messrs. R. H. Hendrickson, N. G. Oglesby and others [in reply to their request for Mr. V.'s Opinion upon the present " inglorious and, it may be, bloody War."]   Dated, May 15, 1861. *Broadside.*

5491. —— "After some time be past."   Speech on Executive Usurpation, in the House of Representatives, July 10, 1861. pp. 8.

5492. —— Speech on the " United States Note " Bill, in the House of Representatives, February 3, 1862. pp. 15.

5493. —— Reply to Mr. Hickman, on Democratic Loyalty to the Union.   House of Reps., February 19, 1862. pp. 8.

5494. —— Public Debt, Liability and Expenditures. Speech, House of Representatives, June 30, 1862. pp. 8.

5495. —— Speech at the Democratic State Convention, held in Columbus, July 4, 1862. *Broadside.*

5496. VALLANDIGHAM, C. L. Speech [on the State of the Country] at Dayton, Ohio, August 2, 1862. pp. 12.

5497. —— The Great Civil War in America. Speech in the House of Representatives, January 14, 1863. pp. 16.

5498. —— Speech in Newark, New Jersey, February 14, 1863. *Freeman's Journal, February* 28, 1863.

5499. —— Peacè, the Way to Union. Speech before the Democratic Union Association, New York, March 7, 1863. *New York Caucasian, March* 14, 1863.

5500. —— Address to the Students of the University of Michigan, November 14, 1863. pp. 8.

5501. —— Speech in reply to Mr. Lowe, on receiving a gold-headed cane, at his residence near Dayton, Ohio, Nov. 21. *Broadside.*

5502. —— Letter to the Young Men's Democratic Association of Lancaster, Penn., May 5, 1865. *Daily Empire, May* 24, 1865.

5503. —— Trial of, by a Military Commission, and the Proceedings under the Application for a Writ of Habeas Corpus, in the Circuit Court of the U. S. for the Southern District of Ohio. 8vo. pp. 72   CINCINNATI: *Rickey & Carroll,* 1863.

5504. —— Habeas Corpus, United States Circuit Court. Argument of Hon. Aaron F. Perry. pp. 97–168.

5505. —— Decision of Judge Leavitt, of Ohio, in the Vallandigham Habeas Corpus Case. pp. 16. Philadelphia: 1863.

5506. —— Speech at Peoria, Illinois, October 24, 1864, on Secret Societies; the War and the Effects of Uniformity and Diversity on Political Institutions. Dayton, Ohio, 1864.

5507. VALLANDIGHAM als Congress—Mitglied Seine Stellung in der Kriegsfrage. Thatsachen aus den officiellen Protokollen. Wichtige Enthüllungen fur die loyale Bevölkerung. 8vo. pp. 8.

5508. —— The Congressional Record of. His course in the War, from Offi. Records. Important Information for Loyal People. p. 7.

5509. —— The Record of the Hon. C. L. Vallandigham on Abolition, the Union, and the Civil War. 8vo. pp. 256.   COLUMBUS: (Ohio) *J. Walter & Co.,* 1863.

5510. VAN ALSTINE, Rev. N. Thanksgiving Sermon. A Specific Remedy for National Calamities. Preached in Meriden, New York, November 28, 1861. 8vo. pp. 32.   ALBANY: *S. R. Gray,* 1862.

5511. VANANDA, C. A.   A Discourse delivered to the Ross County Volunteers, April 21, 1861.   Chillicothe, Ohio.   pp. 15.   1861.

5512. VANDENHOFF, George.   Life; or Men, Manners, Modes and Measures.   A Poem for the Union. Delivered at St. Louis and other cities of the West, and in N. York, 29th Jan., 1861.   12mo. pp. 41.   NEW YORK: *For the author,* 1861.

5513. VANDEMARK, J. R., (of Lancaster, Ill.)   An Epic Poem, upon the Troubles in the United States of America.   18mo. pp. 48.   VIRGINIA: (Ill.) *La F. Briggs,* 1861.

5514. VAN DEUSEN, Rev. E. M., of Pittsburg.   Address to his Parishioners, (relative to Bishop Hopkins and Slavery.) pp. 15.

5515. VAN DYKE, Rev. HENRY J.   The Character and Influence of Abolitionism.   A Sermon preached in Brooklyn, Dec. 9, 1860.   8vo. pp. 81.   NEW YORK: *G. F. Nesbitt & Co.,* 1860.

5516. —— Giving Thanks for all Things.   A Thanksgiving Sermon preached November 29, 1860.   8vo. pp. 24.   NEW YORK: *G. F. Nesbitt & Co.,* 1860.

5517. VAN DYKE, Rev. JOSEPH S.   Elements and Evidences of National Decay.   A Lecture delivered in Bloomsbury, New York, August 7, 1862.   8vo. pp. 16.   PHILADELPHIA: *McLaughlin Brothers,* 1862.

5518. VAN EVRIE, J. H., M. D.   Negroes and Negro "Slavery." The First, an Inferior Race,—The Latter, its Normal Condition.   8vo. pp. 32.   NEW YORK: *Day Book Office,* 1853.
Prefixed to this Pamphlet is the following letter.
Washington, 3d June, 1853.
Dr. VAN EVRIE,—Dear Sir: I have read the enclosed pages with great interest; and not as a Southern man merely, but as an American, I thank you for your able and manly exposure of a fallacy which more than any or all other causes has disturbed the tranquility of our people, and endangered the perpetuity of our Constitutional Union.—JEFFERSON DAVIS.

5519. —— The same work complete.   12mo. pp. 339.   NEW YORK: *Van Erie, Horton & Co.,* 1861.

5520. VAN HORN, J. C.   The Civil War in America; its Causes and Objects.   pp. 8.

5521. VAN HORN, Hon. B.   The War and its Management. Speech, House of Representatives, January 23, 1862.   pp. 14.

5522. VAN WINKLE, Hon. P. G.   Reorganization of Virginia, and Admission of West Virginia.   Speech in the United States Senate, April 21, 1864.   pp. 32.

5523. VAN WYCK, C. H.   Fraud upon the Treasury is Treason against the Government.   Speech, H. of Rep., Feb. 7, '62. p. 8.

5524. VARNELL, George H.   Outline of an Address at Ashley, Washington County, Illinois, November 3, 1862. pp. 7.

5525. Vermont.   Executive Address of Erastus Fairbanks, Governor of Vermont, extra session, April 23, 1861. 8vo. pp. 8.

5526. —— Valedictory Address of Gov. Fairbanks, Oct. '61. pp. 16.

5528. —— Message of Gov. Holbrook, October, 1862. pp. 38.

5529. —— Report from the Quartermaster Gen. for the year '62. p. 27.

5530. —— Report of the Adjutant and Inspector General for the year ending November 1, 1862. 8vo. pp. 110.

5531. —— Report of John Howe, Jr., relative to State Aid for Soldiers' Families in Vermont, September, 1863.

5532. —— Message of Governor J. G. Smith, Oct. 1863. pp. 32.

5533. —— Report of the Adjutant and Inspector General, November 1, 1862, to Otober 1, 1863.
8vo. pp. 106.   Montpelier : *Walton's Press*, 1863.

5534. —— Report of the Quartermaster General, Oct. 1, 1863. pp. 56.

5535. —— Register of the Commissioned Officers of the Vermont Volunteers in the service of the United States, June, 1863. pp. 37.

5536. —— Message of Governor Smith, October, 1864. pp. 39.
Documents accompanying the Governor's Message:
Treasurer's Report,—State Finances. pp. 6.
Report of John Howe, Jr., relative to State Aid for Soldiers' Families, from September 1, 1863, to September 1, 1864.
Correspondence relative to arms and equipments for the Militia of Vermont.
Correspondence relative to Hospital for sick and wounded Vermont Soldiers.
Report of W. G. Veazey, agent to visit Gettysburg, in relation to the Soldiers' National Cemetery, November 2, 1863.
Report of the Hon. Paul Dillingham, on the Soldiers' National Cemetery at Gettysburg, September 28, 1864.
Surgeon General's Report, October 1, 1864.

5537. —— Opinion of the Judges of the Supreme Court of Vermont, on the Constitutionality of " An Act providing for Soldiers Voting." pp. 36.

5538. —— Report of the Quartermaster General, Sept., 1864. pp. 38.

5539. —— Report of the Adjutant and Inspector General, from October 1, 1863, to October 1, 1864. Roster of Vermont Volunteers. Reports of Engagements.
8vo. pp. 229, 666 & 61.   Montpelier, 1865.

5540, VERMONT. Message of Gov. Smith, October 12, 1865. pp. 44.

5541. —— Message of Gov. Dillingham, October 13, 1865. pp. 14.

5542. —— Report of the Adjutant and Inspector General, from October 1, 1864, to October 1, 1865.
8vo. pp. 130. Appendix, 80 and 762. MONTPELIER, 1865.

5543. VASSA, GUSTAVUS, The Life of. The African.
12mo. pp. 288. BOSTON : *Isaac Knapp*, 1837.

5544. VAUGHAN, VIRGINIA. Recognition. *Cont. Monthly, July,* '64.

5545. VEILE, Mrs. Brig. General. Following the Drum.
12mo. pp. 262. PHILADELPHIA : *Peterson & Brothers,* 1864.

5546. THE VENOM and the Antidote.
8vo. pp. 4. *Loyal Publication Society No.* 9, 1863.

5547. —— The same. 8vo. pp. 4. *Loyal Reprints, No.* 2.

5548. VERNON, MERLE. Hints to Officers in the Army and Navy.
18mo. pp. 64. *American Tract Society.*

5549. VERTOT, Rev. A., of Florida. Slavery and Abolitionism. A Sermon, January 4, 1861.

5550. VETERAN RESERVE CORPS. Field Record of the Officers of, from the Commencement to the Close of the Rebellion.
8vo. pp. 39. WASHINGTON : *Scriver & Swing.*

5551. —— Letter from the Secretary of War in regard to invalids being recruited. *Ex. Doc. No.* 80, 38*th Congress,* 1*st Session.*

5552. VICKSBURG. My Cave Life in Vicksburg.
12mo. pp. 196. NEW YORK : *D. Appleton & Co.,* 1864.

5553. VICTOR, Mrs. M. V. The Unionist's Daughter. A Tale of the Rebellion in Tennessee.
12mo. pp. 223. NEW YORK : *Beadle & Co.,* 1862.

5554. VICTOR, ORVILLE J. The History ; Civil, Political and Military, of the Southern Rebellion, from its incipient stages to its close.
2 vols. Royal 8vo. NEW YORK : *James D. Torrey.*

5555. —— The Life of Maj. Gen. George B. McClellan.
12mo. pp. 98. NEW YORK : *Beadle & Company.*

5556. VIEWS OF THE WAR. The Administration and the People ; with Special Remarks on McClellan's Campaign. By a Soldier.
8vo. pp. 24. MANCHESTER : (N. H.) *C. F. Livingston,* 1864.

5557. VINCENT, Rev. MARVIN R. Our National Discipline. A Thanksgiving Sermon preached in Troy, N. Y., Nov. 26, 1863.
8vo. pp. 47. TROY : *A. W. Scribner,* 1863.

5558. VINCENT, Rev. M. R.   The Lord of War and Righteousness. Sermon preached at Troy, N. Y., November 24, 1864. pp. 45.

5559. —— A Sermon on the Assassination of Abraham Lincoln. Troy, New York, April 23, 1865.

8vo. pp. 50.   TROY : *A. W. Scribner,* 1865.

5560. VINTON, ALEXANDER H., DD.   God in Government. A Sermon preached at Philadelphia, January 4, 1861.

8vo. pp. 24.   PHILADELPHIA : *Prot. Epis. Book Society,* 1861.

5561. —— Thanksgiving Sermon, November 29, 1860.

8vo. pp. 23.   PHILADELPHIA : *Prot. Epis. Book Society,* 1860.

5562. ——- Man's Rule and Christ's Reign. A Sermon. Nov. 22, '62.

8vo. pp. 26.   NEW YORK : *John A. Gray,* 1862.

5563. —— The Sabbath and its Relations to the State. A Sermon preached in New York, March 9, 1862.

8vo. pp. 23.   NEW YORK : *E. E. Barker,* 1862.

5564. —— The same work. (Pulpit and Rostrum, No. 30.)

5565. —— Cause for Thanksgiving. A Sermon, Nov. 24, 1864. p. 24.

5566. —— The Mistakes of the Rebellion. A Thanksgiving Sermon preached November 26, 1863.   pp. 28.

5567. —— The Duties of Peace. The Nation's Third Thanksgiving. A Sermon preached December 7, 1865.   pp. 25.

5568. VINTON, FRANCIS, DD.   The Christian Idea of Civil Government.   A Sermon preached in New York, on the occasion of the Prov. Bishop's Pastoral Letter.

8vo. pp. 12.   NEW YORK : *Nesbitt & Co.,* 1861.

5569. —— Thanksgiving Sermon, November 29, 1860.

8vo. pp. 23.   PHILADELPHIA : *Prot. Epis. Book Society,* 1860.

This sermon was preached in December, 1860. It was printed by gentlemen of the Democratic Party, and circulated by them throughout the country. The writer received letters from Georgia, Alabama and other southern States, asking for copies to be circulated among the southern people. Many of these letters abounded in patriotic and loyal sentiments. From South Carolina, however, Dr. Vinton got abuse.

5570. —— The Philosophy of the War ; or the Cause and Cure of the Rebellion. A Sermon preached before the Ancient and Honorable Artillery Company, Boston, June 2, 1862.

8vo. pp. 78.   BOSTON : *Wright & Potter,* 1862.

5571. VIRGINIA.   Status of Jefferson and Berkeley Counties. A Question of Territory between Virginia and West Virginia. *Large Broadside.*

5572. VIRGINIA. Communication from the Executive of Virginia, (John Floyd,) to the Governor of Maryland, enclosing Resolutions relative to the Federal Relations. pp. 7.

5573. —— The Past, the Present and the Future of our Country. Correspondence between the Opposition Members of the Legislature of Virginia, and John Minor Botts, Jan. 17, 1860. pp. 16.

5574. —— Constitution and Ordinances adopted by the Convention at Alexandria, February 13, 1864.
8vo. pp. 27.   ALEXANDRIA: *D. Turner*, 1864.

5575. —— Message of the Governor of Virginia, (John Letcher,) with accompanying Documents. pp. 55. RICHMOND: 1861.

5576. —— Journal of the House of Delegates, Ex. Ses., '61. pp. 104.

5577. —— Acts passed at the Extra Session, 1861. pp. 65.

5578. —— Acts passed at the Extra Session, May, 1862. pp. 31.

5579. —— Message of Gov. Pierpoint, December 7, 1863. pp. 7.

5580. —— Message of Gov. Pierpoint, December 6, 1864. pp. 7.

5581. —— Reorganization of Civil Government. Speech of Governor Pierpoint in Norfolk, February 16, 1865. pp. 7.

5582. VOICES from the Army. The Soldiers open their Batteries on the Copperheads. The President cordially sustained.
8vo. pp. 7.   *Loyal Publication Society No.* 5, 1863.

5583. VOLUNTEER TEACHERS, Washington. First Report of, November, 1864. pp. 15.

5584. VOORHEES, Hon. D. W. Speech [on the Financial Policy of the Government.] House of Representatives, May 21, '62. p. 16.

5585. —— The Pledges of the Government. House of Representatives, February 20, 1862. pp. 16.

5586. —— The Rights of the Citizen. Speech on the Indemnity Bill, House of Representatives, February 18, 1863. pp. 15.

5587. —— The Liberty of the Citizen. pp. 15. Washington, 1863.

5588. VOTERS' CATECHISM. Plain Questions and Answers for the Campaign. pp. 4.

5589. VOTERS' CATECHISM. Number 2. pp 4.

W. W. W.   The Battle Field of Shiloh.
         8vo. pp. 8.   Dated, April 14, 1862.

5591. W. J. M.   The Fall of Man; Rebellion, and War, and the Importance of Peace.   Minisink, New York, 1861.   pp. 11.

5592. W. R. G.   Forward, March!   April 19, 1861.   pp. 3.

5593. WABASH.   Abstract of the Cruise of the Steam Frigate Wabash, bearing the Flag of Rear-Admiral S. F. Dupont, 1861–63.
      12mo. pp.   NEW YORK: *E. O. Jenkins*, 1863.

5594. WADE, Hon. B. F.   Speech in Young Men's Hall, Detroit, on Saturday, October 18, 1862.   8vo. pp. 8.

5595. —— Traitors and their Sympathizers.   Speech in Senate, April 21, 1861.   pp. 8.

5596. —— Speech on the Confiscation Bill, May 2, 1862.   pp. 8.

5597. —— Speech against the Immediate Restoration of the Seceded States, in answer to Mr. Doolittle and others, Jan. 18, '66.   pp. 8.

5598. WADE, BEN, on McClellan, and Gens. Hooker and Heintzelman's Testimony.   A Crushing Review of Little Napoleon's Military Career.   pp. 8.   Cincinnati, 1864.

5599. WADSWORTH.   Proceedings of the Century Association, in honor of the Memory of Brig. Gen. J. S. Wadsworth and Col. Peter A. Potter; with the Eulogies by W. J. Hoppin and F. S. Cozzens, December 3, 1864.
      Royal 8vo. pp. 88.   NEW YORK: *D. Van Nostrand*, 1865.

5600. WADSWORTH, WM. H., of Kentucky.   Concord, Fraternity, and the Constitution.   Speech, House of Reps., Jan. 15, 1862.

5601. —— Speech on the Confiscation Bill, Feb. 3, 1864.   pp. 16.

5602. WAINWRIGHT, J. H.   Letter to H. G. Stebbins, on Gold Currency and Funded Debt.   March 24, 1864.   pp. 20.

5603. WAKEMAN, ABRAM.   "Union," on Dis-Union Principles! The Chicago Platform.   McClellan's Letter of Acceptance, and Pendleton's Haskin Letter, Reviewed and exposed.
      8vo. pp. 31.   NEW YORK: *Daniel W. Lee*, 1864.

5604. WALBRIDGE, Gen. HIRAM.   Oration on the Political and Industrial Interests of the United States, delivered in New York, July 4, 1862.   4to. pp. 16.

5605. —— Speech on the Proposed Amendment to the Federal Constitution, forever Prohibiting Slavery in the United States, at Albany, January 27, 1865. pp. 16.

5606. WALBRIDGE, Gen. H. The same.

pp. 20.   NEW YORK : *W. O. Bourne*, 1865.

5607. WALCUTT, R. F. The Spirit of the South towards Northern Freemen and Soldiers, defending the American Flag against Traitors of the Deepest Dye.

12mo. pp. 24.   BOSTON : *R. F. Walcutt*, 1861.

5608. WALDEN, Rev. TREADWELL. The National Sacrifice. A Sermon preached on the Sunday before the Death of the President, and Two Addresses following, in Philadelphia.

8vo. pp. 41.   PHILADELPHIA : *Sherman & Co.*, 1865.

5609. WALKER, Hon. AMASA. Cotton, not Slavery, the Immediate Cause of the Rebellion. Speech, H. of Reps., Feb. 18, '63. p. 8.

5610. —— The Advocate of Peace. An Address before the American Peace Society, Boston, May 25, 1863. *Am. Peace Society*.

5611. —— The Suicidal Folly of the War System.

8vo. pp. 24.   BOSTON : *American Peace Society*, 1863.

5612. —— The National Finance. An Article from Hunt's *Merchants' Magazine*, January, 1865. pp. 16.

5613. WALKER, E. A. Our First Year of Army Life. An Address to the First Regiment of Connecticut Heavy Artillery, at their Camp near Gaines' Mills, June, 1862.

8vo. pp. 95.   NEW HAVEN : *Thomas H. Pease*, 1862.

5614. WALKER, Rev. GEORGE LEON. A Sermon preached in Portland, Thanksgiving Day, November 21, 1861.

8vo. pp. 16.   PORTLAND : *Brown Thurston*, 1861.

5615. —— The Offered National Regeneration. A Sermon preached in Portland, September 26, 1861.

8vo. pp. 24.   PORTLAND : *Little, Brother & Co.*, 1861.

5616. WALKER, Rev. JAMES, DD. The Spirit proper to the Times. A Sermon preached at King's Chapel, Boston, May 12, 1861.

12mo. pp. 12.   BOSTON : *George C. Rand & Avery*, 1861.

5617. —— An Address delivered before the Alumni of Harvard College, July 16, 1863. pp. 28.

5618. —— A Sermon delivered before the Executive and Legislative Departments of Massachusetts, Wednesday, Jan. 7, 1863. p. 29.

5619. WALKER, Jonathan. A Brief View of American Chattelized Humanity, and its Supports.
18mo. pp. 36.   Boston : *Dow & Jackson,* 1846.

5620. WALKER, Peter. Thoughts on the Pacification of the Country, for the consideration of the North and South.   pp. 16.

5621. WALKER, Hon. Robert J. The Union. *Continental Monthly, Oct., Nov., Dec..* 1862, and *Jan., March, April, May,* 1863.

5622. —— Our National Finances. Ibid. *Feb.,* 1863.

5623. —— Nullification and Secession. Ibid. *February,* 1863.

5624. —— Flag of Our Sires. Ibid. *April,* 1863.

5625. —— Jefferson Davis and Repudiation. Ibid. *Aug. & Sept.,* '63.

5626. —— American Finances and Resources. Ibid. *October,* 1863.

5627. —— The Great Struggle.— American Finances and Resources. Ibid. *January, March and May,* 1864.

5628. —— Jeff. Davis and Repudiation of Ark. Bonds. Ibid. *Apr.,*'64.

5630. —— American Slavery and Finances. Ibid. *July,* 1854.

5631. —— Letter in favor of the Reëlection of Abraham Lincoln. Ibid. *December,* 1864.

5632. —— American Finances and Resources, No. 1.
8vo. pp. 26 and 45.   London : *W. Ridgway,* 1863.

5633. —— Letter No. II, on Jefferson Davis, Repudiation, Recognition and Slavery. London, July, 1863.
8vo. pp. 12.   London : *Wm. Ridgway,* 1863.

5634. —— Same. 2d edition. pp. 58. London, *Ridgway,* 1863.

5635. —— American Finances and Resources, No. 2.
8vo. pp. 24.   London : *Wm. Ridgway,* 1863.

5636. —— The same. pp. 16. No date.

5637. —— Letter No. III, on American Finances and Resources.
8vo. pp. 26.   London : *William Ridgway,* 1865.

5638. —— Familiar Epistle to Robert J. Walker, formerly of Pennsylvania, later of Mississippi, more recently of Washington, and last heard of in Mr. Coxwell's Balloon. From an Old Acquaintance.
8vo. pp. xiii and 57.   London : *Saunders & Otley,* 1863.

5639. WALL, James W. The Constitution. An Address delivered at the City Hall, Burlington, February 20, 1862.
8vo. pp. 60.   Philadelphia : *King & Baird,* 1862.

5640. WALL, J. W.   The same.   pp. 22.   Burlington, 1862.

5641. WALLACE, Rev. CHARLES C.   The Situation, the Duty and the Hour.   A Discourse at Perth Amboy, N. J., Aug. 6, 1863. 8vo. pp. 24.   NEW YORK : *J. A. Gray & Greene,* 1863.

5642. —— A Prince and a Great Man has fallen.   Address in Memory of Abraham Lincoln, at Placerville, Cal., April 19, '65.   p. 8.

5643. WALLACE, W. ROSS.   A Psalm of the Union. *Harpers' Magazine, December,* 1861.

5644. WALLACE, Major General LEW.   Communication in relation to the Freedmen's Bureau, to the General Assembly of Maryland. 8vo. pp. 95.   ANNAPOLIS ; *Richard P. Bayly,* 1865.

5645. WALTHAM UNION LEAGUE, Report of Committee on. 8vo. pp.   BOSTON : *John Wilson & Son,* 1863.

5646. WALTON, Hon. E. P.   Speech on the Bill for the Admission of Kansas.   House of Reps., March 31, 1859.   pp. 15.

5647. —— Speech upon the Report of the Thirty-Three upon the State of the Union.   House of Reps., Feb. 16, 1861.   8vo. pp. 8.

5648. —— Confiscation of Rebel Property.   H. of Rep., May 24, '62.

5649. WAR, A Remedy for ; or Stipulated Arbitration as a Substitute for the Sword.   pp. 4.   *American Peace Society.*

5650. WAR, Articles of, for the Government of the Armies of the Confederate States. 8vo. pp. 24.   CHARLESTON : (S. C.) *Evans & Cogswell,* 1861.

5651. —— Laws of War and Martial Law.   Extracts from General Halleck's Work on International Law, and their Application to passing events. 12mo. pp. 15.   BOSTON : *A. Williams & Co.,* 1863.

5652. —— Report on Contracts of the War Department for the year 1861.   37*th Cong.,* 2*d Sess., Ex. Doc. No.* 102.   pp. 145.

5653. WAR DEPARTMENT.   Report on Military and Naval Defences, made to Congress in 1836, and ordered to be printed, March, 1862.   37*th Congress,* 2*d Sess., Ex. Doc. No.* 92.   pp. 415.

5654. WAR.   Report from Brig. General Ripley, with Statement of Arms purchased and contracted for, February 20, 1862.   37*th Congress,* 2*d Session, Executive Document, No,* 67.   pp. 235.

5655. —— Report of Quartermaster Gen. Meigs, relative to the purchase of Horses for Penn. Cavalry.   Ibid.   *Doc. No.* 60.   pp. 38.

5656. THE WAR AND ITS END; or its Cause and Cure.
8vo. pp. 16.   NEW YORK : *Samuel Hopper & Co.*, 1865.
5657. THE WAR. Shall it be prosecuted ? (No date.) pp. 4.
5658. WAR CLAIMS AT ST. LOUIS. Letter from the Secretary of War, with the Final Report made by the Commission.
8vo. pp. 41. *Ex. Doc. No.* 94, *H. of Reps.*, 37*th Con.*, 2*d Ses.*,'62.
5659. WAR DEBTS of the Loyal States. Report of the Select Com. on. 39*th Congress, 1st Session, Report No.* 16, 1865.
5660. THE WAR EAGLE. A Periodical. Columbus, Kentucky, 1863.
5661. WAR LETTERS of a Disbanded Volunteer. Embracing his experience as Honest Old Abe's Bosom Friend and Unofficial Adviser.
12mo. pp. 312.   NEW YORK : *F. A. Brady*, 1864.
5662. WAR LYRICS. A Selection of. With Illustrations by Darley.
Small 4to. pp. 32.   NEW YORK : *J. G. Gregory*, 1864.
5663. WAR POWER of the President. Summary Imprisonment,—Habeas Corpus.
8vo. pp. 10.   *Loyal Publication Society, No.* 32, 1863.
5664. WAR SONGS for Freemen.
12mo. pp. 56.   BOSTON : *Ticknor & Fields*, 1863.
5665. WAR SONGS of the South. Edited by " Bohemian," of the Richmond Despatch. Richmond : *West & Johnson*, 1863.
5666. THE WAR AND SLAVERY. Victory only through Emancipation.
12mo. pp. 8.   BOSTON : *R. F. Wallcutt*, 1863.
5667. WAR SHIPS for the Southern Confederacy.
8vo. pp. 36.   MANCHESTER : *Union and Emanc. Soc.*, 1863.
5668. WARD, DURBIN. Of the Government of the Territories. The Constitutional Right of the General Government; and the People in the Federal Territories.
8vo. pp. 20.   CINCINNATI : *Daily Enquirer*, 1860.
5669. WARD, E. B. Reasons why the Northwest should have a Protective Tariff; and why the Republican Party is the safest Party to trust with the Government. Detroit, 1860. pp. 8.
5670. WARD, ELIJAH, of New York. The Financial Condition of the Union. Speech, House of Reps., January 15, 1863. pp. 8.
5671. —— Bankrupt Law; its present Necessity, and Importance as a permanent Act. Speech, House of Reps., June 3, 1862. pp. 15.
5672. WARD, THOMAS. War Lyrics. 12mo. pp. 16. New York : *French & Wheat*, 1865.

5673. **WARDEN,** T. B., and J. M. Catlett. Battle of Young's Branch or Manassas Plain. Fought July 31, 1861. With Maps from actual survey, and the various Positions of the Regiments. 12mo. pp. 156. RICHMOND: *Enquirer Office,* 1862.

5674. **WARE,** JOHN F. W. The Danger of To-Day. A Sermon preached in Baltimore, February 5, 1865. pp. 16.

5675. —— Mustered out. A Few Words with the Rank and File, when parting. BOSTON: *American Unitarian Association,* '65.

5676. —— The Home to the Camp. Address to the Soldiers of the Union.
12mo. pp. 19. BOSTON: *American Unitarian Asso.,* 1861.

5677. —— The Home to the Hospital. Address to the Sick and Wounded of the Army of the Union. *Am. Unitarian Asso.,* 1862.

5678. —— Manhood, the Want of the Day. A Sermon preached in Cambridgeport Parish, March 1, 1863.
8vo. pp. 19. BOSTON: *Leonard C. Bowles,* 1863.

5679. —— The Rebel. pp. 9. BOSTON: *Am. Unitarian Asso.,* 1864.

5680. —— To the Color. pp. 10. BOSTON: *Am. Unitarian As.,* '64.

5681. —— The Recruit. pp. 12. BOSTON: *Am. Unitarian As.,* '64.

5682. —— A Few Words with the Convalescent. Ibid. 1865.

5683. —— On Picket. pp. 11. BOSTON: *Am. Unitarian Asso.,* '65.

5684. —— The Reconnoissance. Ibid. 1865.

5685. —— The Reveille. pp. 12. Ibid. 1865.

5686. —— Rally upon the Reserve. pp. 12. Ibid. 1865.

5687. —— A Day at Annapolis. *Monthly Religious Mag., Feb.,* 1864.

5688. **WARNER,** Rev. J. R. Our Times and our Duty. An Oration delivered at Gettysburg, July 4, 1861.
8vo. pp. 16. GETTYSBURG: *H. C. Neinstadt,* 1861.

5689. A **WARNING VOICE**; or What is the Object of this War. Being a Few and Desultory Observations on same Things that concern us all. By Quaesitor.
12mo. pp. 56. BOSTON: 1861.

5690. **WARREN,** Maj. General G. K. Battle of Five Forks, Va.
8vo. pp. 53. NEW YORK: *D. Van Nostrand,* 1866.

5691. **WARREN,** J. THOMAS. The Traitor's Doom; or the Heiress of Bella Vista. A Tale of the Gt. Rebellion in the Crescent City.
8vo. pp. 38. NEW YORK: *American News Co.,* 1864.

5692. WARREN, J. T. Old Hal Williams; or the Spy of Atlanta. A Tale of Sherman's Georgia Campaign.

8vo. pp. 42.   NEW YORK: *American News Co.*, 1865.

5693. WARRINER. E. A. The Battle of the Wilderness. *Continental Monthly, August,* 1864·

5694. WASHBURN, Major ANDREW, 14th Regiment Massachusetts Vols. Heavy Artillery. Documents in the case of, 1862. pp. 27.

5695. WASHBURN, EMORY. Can a State secede? Sovereignty in its bearing upon Secession and State Rights.

8vo. pp. 36.   CAMBRIDGE: *Dakin & Metcalf,* 1865.

5696. WASHBURN, Hon. ISRAEL, Jun., of Maine. The Issues; The Dred Scott Decision; The Parties. Speech delivered in the House of Representatives, May 19, 1860. 8vo. pp. 16.

5697. WASHINGTON'S BIRTH DAY, Celebration of, at Hoosick Falls, 1862. pp. 6.

5698. —— Celebration at the Cooper Institute, under the Auspices of the Union Defence Committee. Speeches, Resolutions, etc.

8vo. pp. 46.   NEW YORK: *George F. Nesbitt & Co.,* 1862.

5699. WASHINGTON, B. F. The Spoils and the Crisis. Correspondence with the Attachés of the San Francisco Custom House, April 29, 1861. pp. 16.

5700. WASHINGTON DESPOTISM, Depicted in articles from the Metropolitan Record.

12mo. pp. 130.   NEW YORK: *Metropolitan Record,* 1863.

5701. WASHINGTON MILITARY UNION of the American Army, Constitution and By-Laws of. Quincy, Illinois, 1861. pp. 33.

5702. WASSON, D. A. Shall we Compromise? *Atl. Month., May,* '63.

5703. WATERBURY, Rev. J. B. Something for the Knapsack.

18mo. pp. 48.   NEW YORK: *American Tract Society.*

5704. —— Friendly Councils for Freedmen. New York. pp. 32.

5705. —— The Soldier on Guard.

18mo. pp. 64.   NEW YORK: *American Tract Society.*

5706. —— Mustered out; or the Soldier at Home.

18mo. pp. 31.   NEW YORK: *American Tract Society.*

5707. —— Ship, ahoy! pp. 64. N. York: *American Tract Society.*

5708. —— Something for the Locker. 18mo. pp. 36. Ibid.

5709. —— The Christian Soldier. 12mo. pp. 32. N. Y. Ibid.

5710. —— The Soldier from Home. 18mo. pp. 63. N. Y. Ibid.

5711. WATERBURY, D., and others. Remarks in Assembly, January 25, 1862. Butter as an Army Ration. pp. 8.

5712. WATKINS, FRANCES E. Poems on Miscellaneous Subjects. 18mo. pp. 40.   BOSTON: *J. B. Yerrington*, 1855.

5713. WATSON, Rev. W. C. Eulogium on Lieut. Colonel Gorton T. Thomas, 22d Regiment New York Volunteers, delivered at Keeseville, New York, September 10, 1862. pp. 26.

5714. WATTS, Rev. ROBERT. The Scripture Doctrine of Civil Government, applied to the present Crisis. A Discourse delivered in Philadelphia, June 9, 1861. pp. 24.

5715. WAYLAND, FRANCIS. Domestic Slavery considered as a Scriptural Institution; in a Correspondence with Rev. Richard Fuller, of Beaufort, South Carolina. 12mo. pp. 254.   NEW YORK: *Lewis Colby*, 1845.
For a Review of this correspondence, see *Hague.*

5716. WAYLAND, F., JR. Our State Militia. A Series of Articles originally contributed to the "Connecticut War Record." 8vo. pp. 24.   NEW HAVEN: *J. H. Benham*, 1864.

5717. —— Letter to a Peace Democrat. *Atlantic Monthly, Dec.*, 1863.

5718. —— No Failure for the North. *Atlantic Monthly, July*, 1863.

5719. WAYMAN, Rev. JAMES. The Passing away of Human Greatness. A Sermon on the Death of President Lincoln, preached May 7, 1865, in the Newington Chapel, Liverpool. 8vo. pp. 8.   LIVERPOOL: *Henry Young*, 1865.

5720. WEDGWOOD, WM. B. The Destruction of the Government of the United States of America. A Democratic Empire Advocated, and an Imperial Constitution proposed. 8vo. pp. 30.   NEW YORK: *John A. Tingley*, 1861.

5721. WEEKS, GRENVILLE M. The Last Cruise of the Monitor. *Atlantic Monthly, March*, 1863.

5722. WEAVER, ABRAM B. The Policy of the War, and Arbitrary Arrests. Speech, House of the Assembly of the State of New York, March 10, 1863. pp. 20.

5723. WEBB, THOMAS H. Information for Kansas Immigrants. 12mo. pp.   BOSTON: *Alfred Mudge & Co.*, 1857.

5724. WEBSTER, Hon. DANIEL. Speech upon the subject of Slavery, delivered in the U. S. Senate, March 7, 1850. 8vo. pp. 39.   BOSTON: *Redding & Co.*, 1860.
58

5725. WEBSTER, Hon. D. Speech to the Young Men of Albany, May 28, '51. pp. 29.

5726. —— Speech at Capon Springs, Virginia, together with those of Sir H. L. Bulwer and W. L. Clarke, June 28, 1851. pp. 18.

5727. —— Address at the laying of the Corner Stone of the addition to the Capitol, [at Washington,] July 4, 1851. pp. 29.

5728. —.— The Union not a Compact. A Speech on the Force Bill in the United States Senate, February 16, 1833. (In reply to John C. Calhoun;) and Jackson's Proclamation to South Carolina, in 1833. (Pulpit and Rostrum, Nos. 15 and 16.)

5729. WEBSTER, Hon. EDWIN H. Speech on the Prosecution of the War, delivered in the House of Reps., Feb. 28, 1863. pp. 8.

5730. WEBSTER, Rev. JOHN C. The Gospel, the World's Disturber. A Sermon preached in Hopkinton, Mass., Nov. 2, 1862. pp. 14.

5731. WEISS, Rev. JOHN. A Discourse on Causes for thanksgiving. Preached at Watertown, Mass., November 30, 1862.
8vo. pp. 24. BOSTON : *Wright & Potter,* 1862.

5732. WEISS, JOHN. Northern Strength and Weakness. An Address at Watertown, on occasion of the National Fast, April 30, 1863. pp. 23.

5733. —— The Four Necessities. A New Years' Sermon, delivered at Watertown, Mass., January 4, 1863. pp. 21.

5734. —— Eulogy on President Lincoln, April 19, 1865. *The Friend of Progress, June,* 1865.

5735. WELLS, DAVID A. Our Burden and Our Strength ; or a comprehensive and popular examination of the Debt and Resources of our Country, present and prospective.
8vo. pp. 39. *Loyal Publication Society No.* 54, 1864.

5736. —— The same. New York: *Young & Benson,* 1864.

5737. WELLS, THEODORE W. A Sermon on the Assassination of Abraham Lincoln, preached at Bayonne, N. J., April 23. p. 23.

5738. WELLS. WM. P. Address on the Position of the Democracy, before the Detroit Democratic Association, March 11, '63. p. 8.

5739. WELCH, Hon. ISAAC. Loyalty to the Government. Speech in the Senate of Ohio, March 3, 1863. pp. 8.

5740. WENTWORTH, Rev. J. B., DD. A Discourse on the Death of President Lincoln, delivered in Buffalo, N. Y., April 23, '65.
8vo. pp. BUFFALO : *Matthews & Warren,* 1865.

5741. WENZEL, Rev. G. A.   Ministers of the Gospel in the time of War.   Translated from the German.   *Evan. Qr. Rev., Vol.* xiii.

5742. —— Christianity and Politics.   Ibid.   *Vol.* xiv.

5743. WEST, Rev. N., Jr.   Establishment in National Righteousness; and present Cause for Thanksgiving.   A Sermon preached in Brooklyn, New York, November 28, 1861.   pp. 39.

5744. WEST, Rev. NATH'L.   A Lecture on the Causes of the Ruin of Republican Liberty in the Ancient Roman Republic, etc., delivered at West Philadelphia, January 4, 1861.   pp. 20.

5745. —— History of Satterlee U. S. A. General Hospital, at West Philadelphia, Pa., from October 8, 1862, to October 8, 1863.
8vo. pp. 36.   *Printed by the Hospital Press,* 1863.

5746. WEST, Rev. N.   Victory and Gratitude.   A Thanksgiving Discourse delivered in the Second Presbyterian Church, Brooklyn, New York, November 24, 1864.
8vo. pp. 42.   NEW YORK: *E. B. Clayton's Sons,* 1864.

5747. WEST, W. H.   Speech on Military Arrests, delivered in the House of Representatives of Ohio, January, 1863.   pp. 12.

5748. WESTERN SANITARY COMMISSION.   A Sketch of its Origin, History, Labors for the Sick and Wounded of the Western Armies, and Aid given to Freedmen and Refugees.
8vo. pp. 144.   ST. LOUIS: *R. P. Studley & Co.,* 1864.

5749. —— What it does with its Funds.   Why it should be aided in its work.   March 16, 1864.   pp. 8.

5750. —— Report on the General Military Hospitals of St. Louis, Missouri, August 1, 1862.
8vo. pp. 75.   ST. LOUIS: *R. P. Studley & Co.,* 1863.

5751. —— Report for the year ending June 1, 1863.   pp. 32.

5752. —— Report on the White Refugees of the South.
8vo. pp. 44.   ST. LOUIS: *R. P. Studley & Co.,* 1863.

5753. WESTERN SANITARY REPORTER.   A Periodical published at St. Louis and Louisville.   May, 1863, to May, 1865.   4to.

5754. WESTCOTT, THOMPSON.   The Tax-Payers' Guide.   An Analytical and Comprehensive Digest of the Internal Revenue and Excise Tax Laws of the United States.
12mo. pp. 112.   PHILADELPHIA: *A. Winch,* 1864.

5755. WESTMINSTER REVIEW.   American Slavery, and the Impending Crisis.   January, 1861.

5756. WESTMINSTER REVIEW. The Rival American Confederacies. Oct., 1861.

5757. —— The American Belligerents. Rights of Neutrals. Jan., '62.

5758. —— The Anti-Slavery Revolution in America. July, 1865.

5759. WESTON, EDWARD PAYSON. The Pedestrian's Adventure, while on his Walk from Boston to Washington, in fulfillment of an Election Wager. Baltimore in disguise at the commencement of the Rebellion of 1861. pp. 48.

5760. WESTON, GEORGE M. The Progress of Slavery in the U. S. 8vo. pp. 80.   WASHINGTON: *For the author*, 1858.

5761. WESTON, Rev. H. G. Incentives to Prayer. Fast Day Sermon, delivered before the Baptist Churches of the City of New York, September 26, 1861. pp. 10.

5762. WEST PHILADELPHIA Hospital Register. Printed and published at the United States Army General Hospital. 4to.

5763. WEST POINT and the War. St. Louis, March, 1863. pp. 11.

5764. WEST VIRGINIA. An Appeal of the People of, to Congress, for its immediate Action, and their Acceptance of the " Nation's Proposal " for the Gradual Abolition of Slavery, May, 1862. pp. 8.

5765. —— Constitution of the State of, proposed by the Convention assembled at Wheeling, on the 26th November, 1861, and ratified by a vote of the People. pp. 28.

5766. WHARTON, Rev. FRANCIS. A Military Reünion not impossible. A Thanksgiving Sermon, preached at Brookline, November 26, 1863. 8vo. pp. 24.   BOSTON: *E. P. Dutton & Co.*, 1863.

5767. WHARTON, G. M. Remarks on Mr. Binney's Treatise on the Writ of Habeas Corpus. Second edition. 8vo. pp. 20.   PHILADELPHIA: *John Campbell*, 1862.

5768. —— An Answer to Mr. Binney's Reply to his " Remarks " on the Habeas Corpus. pp. 8.

5769. WHAT ARE THE CONDITIONS of a Candid and Lasting Reconciliation between the Two Sections of the Country? 8vo. pp. 69.   NEW YORK: *Ross & Toucey*, 1861.

5770. WHAT ARE WE FIGHTING FOR? A Letter to Horace Greeley 12mo. pp. 11.   NEW YORK: *Carlton*, 1862.

5771. WHAT THE SOUTH is Fighting for. 8vo. pp. 8.   LONDON: *British & For. Anti-Slavery Soc.*, 1862

5772. **WHEAT, M. T.** The Progress and Intelligence of Americans. Collateral Proof of Slavery from Genesis, as founded on Organic Laws, and from the fact of Christ being a Caucasian, owing to his peculiar Parentage. Progress of Slavery South, etc.
Post 8vo. pp. xx. 595. LOUISVILLE, Kentucky, 1863.

5773. **WHEELER, Capt., U. S. A.** The Track of Fire; or a Cruise with the Pirate Semmes.
16mo. pp. 110. NEW YORK : *P. Beadle & Co.*, 1863.

5774. **WHEELER, EVERETT P.** The Supreme Court as a coördinate Branch of the United States Government.
8vo. pp. 12. NEW YORK : *Baker & Godwin*, 1860.

5775. —— The Character and Conduct of the War.
8vo. pp. 24. N. YORK : *Christopher, Morse & Skippon*, 1863.

5776. **WHIPPLE, CHARLES R.** Relation of the American Board of Commissioners for Foreign Missions, to Slavery.
12mo. pp. 247. BOSTON : *R. F. Walcutt*, 1861.

5777. **WHIPPLE, E. P.** The Causes of Foreign Enmity to the United States. *Atlantic Monthly, March,* 1864.

5778. **WHITBY, Rev. WM.** American Slavery. A Sketch.
8vo. pp. 210. LONDON : *Richard Davies*, 1864.

5779. **WHITE ACRE vs. BLACK ACRE.** A Case at Law. Reported by J. G., Esq., a Retired Barrister of Lincolnshire, England.
12mo. pp. 251. RICHMOND : (Va.) *J. W. Randolph*, 1856.

5780. **WHITE, ANDREW DICKSON.** Letter to W. Howard Russell, on Passages in his "Diary, North and South." From the Lond. ed.
8vo. pp. 32. SYRACUSE : *Summers & Brother*, 1863.

5781. **WHITE, A. L.,** of Indiana. Speech on the Confiscation Bill. House of Representatives, May 26, 1862. pp. 7.

5782. **WHITE, Rev. ERSKINE N.** The Personal Influence of Abraham Lincoln. A Sermon preached June 1, 1865.
8vo. pp. 25. NEW YORK : *John A. Gray & Green*, 1865.

5783. **WHITE.** In Memoriam. Lieut. Wm. G. White, killed at Antietam, September 17, 1862. pp. 15.

5784. **WHITE, JOHN.** Philosophy of the War of Secession, illustrated by Historical Facts, showing the Destiny of the Union. By J. W., a Discharged Soldier of the 72d Illinois Volunteers.
8vo. pp. 47. CHICAGO : *For the author*, 1863.

5785. WHITE, Rev. PLINY H.   A Sermon occasioned by the Assassination of Abraham Lincoln, at Coventry, Vt., April 28, 1865.
8vo. pp. 20.   BRATTLEBORO': (Vt.) *Record Office,* 1865.

5786. WHITE, RICHARD GRANT.   National Hymns.   How they are written and how they are not written.   A Lyric and National Study for the Times.
8vo. pp. 152.   NEW YORK: *Rudd & Carlton,* 1861.

5787. —— The New Gospel of Peace, according to St. Benjamin.
12mo. pp. 42.   NEW YORK: *Sinclair Toucey,* 1863.

5788. WHITE, Rev. WM. O.   Our Struggle, Righteous in the Sight of God.   A Sermon preached at Keene, N. H., April 13, 1862.
8vo. pp. 14.   KEENE: *G. & G. H. Tilden,* 1862.

5789. WHITE SLAVE, The; or Memoirs of a Fugitive,
12mo. pp. 408.   BOSTON: *Tappan & Whittemore,* 1862

5790. WHITEHEAD, JOHN.   The Currency Question made plain, in a Comparison of the Currency supplied by Banks with the National Currency, introduced by Mr. Chase.
8vo. pp. 72.   NEW YORK: *Ross & Toucey,* 1862.

5791. WHITEHEAD, L., Sr.   The New House that Jack built.   An Original American Version.   Designs by Stephens and White.
12mo. pp. 29.   NEW YORK: *Beadle & Co.,* 1865.

5792. WHITING, WM.   The War Powers of the President and the Legislative Powers of Congress, in relation to the Rebellion, Treason and Slavery.
8vo. pp. 143.   BOSTON: *John L. Shorey,* 1862.

5793. —— War Powers under the President of the U. S.   10th ed.
8vo. pp. xvii, 342.   BOSTON: *Little, Brown & Co.,* 1864.

5794. —— Military Arrests in Time of War.
8vo. pp. 59.   WASHINGTON: *Government Printing Office,* 1863.

6795. —— The Return of the Rebellious States to the Union.   A Letter to the Union League, Philadelphia.
8vo. pp. 15.   PHILADELPHIA: *C. Sherman & Son,* 1864.

5796. WHITMAN AND TRUE.   Maine in the War for the Union.   A History of the Part borne by Maine Troops in the Suppression of the American Rebellion.
8vo. pp. viii, 592.   LEWISTON: *Nathan Dingley, Jr.,* 1865.

5797. WHITNEY, DANIEL S.   Echoes and Glimpses of Prophecy.
18mo. pp. 24.   BOSTON: *Bela Marsh,* 1859.

5798. WHITNEY, Lorenzo H. The History of the War for the Preservation of the Union.

8vo. pp. 516.   Philadelphia : *For the author*, 1863.

5799. WHITTIER, John Greenleaf. In War time, and other Poems.

12mo. pp. 152.   Boston : *Ticknor & Fields*, 1864.

5800. —— National Lyrics ; with Illustrations.

12mo. pp. 104.   Boston : *Ticknor & Fields*, 1865.

5801. WHITTINGHAM, W. R., Bishop of Maryland. A Form of Prayer and Thanksgiving, composed for use in the Diocese of Maryland, on Thursday, August 6, 1863.

8vo. pp. 11.   Baltimore : *John D. Toy*, 1863.

5802. —— A Form of Prayer and Thanksgiving, composed for use in the Diocese of Maryland, on occasion of the Day of National Thanksgiving, Thursday, November 26, 1863.   pp. 7.

5803. —— A Form of Prayer for use in the Diocese of Maryland, on the occasion of the Day of Humiliation and Prayer, appointed to be observed the 4th of August, 1864.   pp. 8.

5804. —— Form of Prayer for the Day of National Thanksgiving, 24th November, 1864.   pp. 7.

5805. WHITTLESEY, C. H. Personal Liberty. *American Monthly Magazine, September & October*, 1864.

5806. WIARD, Norman. Memorial to Congress accompanied by four Pamphlets, entitled, 1, Great Guns ; the Cause of their Failure. 2, Field Artillery. 3, Marine Artillery. 4, Small Arms.

8vo. pp. 12.   New York : *Holman*, 1863.

5807. —— Memorial etc., with eight Pamphlets on Artillery, etc. p. 50.

5808. —— The Manufacture of Small Arms at Home *vs.* their Purchase abroad.

8vo. pp. 29.   New York : *Holman*, 1863.

5809. —— Field Artillery, as improved to meet the requirements of the Service.

8vo. pp. 38.   New York : *Holman*, 1863.

5810. —— Great Guns ; the Cause of their Failure, and the True Method of Constructing them.

8vo. pp. 98.   New York : *Holman*, 1863.

5811. —— Marine Artillery, as adapted for service on the Coast and on Inland Waters.

8vo. pp. 57.   New York : *Holman*, 1663.

5812. WIARD, N. Communication addressed to the Committee on the Conduct on the War, upon the subject of Great Guns. *Cong. Doc.* 38*th Congress, 2d Sess., Mis. Doc. No.* 47. pp. 29.

5813. —— Memorial of. A Few Words in advance. Dated, Feb. 27,'65.

5814. WICKLIFFE, Hon. C. A., of Kentucky. Speech on the Resolution : " That the United States ought to coöperate with any State which may adopt the Gradual Abolishment of Slavery, giving to such State pecuniary aid, to be used by such State in its discretion, to compensate for the inconvenience, public and private, produced by such change of System." House of Representatives, March 11, 1862. pp. 16.

5815. WIECZOREK, Dr. RUDOLPH. An Open Letter to the Thirty-Eighth Congress of the United States, May. 1864. pp. 12.

5816. WIE DER KRIEG angefangen wurde. Eine Verufung auf die Dokumente.
8vo. pp. 15.   *Loyal Publication Society No.* 53, 1864.

5817. WIGHAM, ELIZA. The Anti-Slavery Cause in America, and its Martyrs.
8vo. pp   LONDON : *A. W. Bennett,* 1866.

5818. WILCOX, ANDREW J. The Powers of the Federal Government over Slavery. Baltimore, 1862. pp. 23.

5819. —— of the Baltimore Bar. A Remedy for the Defects of the Constitution. pp. 40. (No date.)

5820. WILKES, CHARLES, U. S. N. Late Acting Rear Admiral in Command of the West India Squadron. Defence read before a General Court Martial, on Charges preferred by the Secretary of the Navy.
8vo. pp. 56. WASHINGTON ; (D. C.) *McGill & Witherow,* 1864.

5821. WILKES, GEORGE. McClellan, from Ball's Bluff to Antietam.
8vo. pp. 40.   NEW YORK : *Sinclair Toucey,* 1863.

5822. —— McClellan; Who he is, and What he has done.
12mo. pp. 12.   NEW YORK : *Sinclair Toucey,* 1862.

5823. WILKESON, SAMUEL. How our National Debt may be a National Blessing. The Debt is Public Wealth, Political Union,etc.
8vo. pp. 16.   PHILADELPHIA : *McLaughlin Brothers,* 1865.

5824. WILKS, WASHINGTON. English Criticism on President Lincoln's Anti-Slavery Proclamation and Message. London : *J. Kenny.* pp. 8.

5825. WILKINSON, M. S., of Minn. Speech on the Expulsion of Mr. Bright from the Senate. January 20, 1862. pp. 8.

5826. —— Speech of, on the Abolition of Slavery in the District of Columbia, March 26, 1862. pp. 16.

5827. —— On the Discharge of State Prisoners. Senate, Jan. 12, '63 pp. 8. *L. Towers.*

5828. WILKINSON, PASSMORE. Report of the Proceedings on the Writ of Habeas Corpus, issued by the Hon. J. K. Kane, Judge of the District Court of the United States, of Pennsylvania, with Arguments of Counsel.
8vo. pp. 190. PHILADELPHIA: *Uriah Hunt & Son,* 1856.

5829. THE WILL OF THE PEOPLE. (No date.) pp. 8.

5830. WILLARD, EMMA. Via Media. A Peaceful and Permanent Settlement of the Slavery Question.
8vo. pp. 10. WASHINGTON: *C. H. Anderson,* 1862.

5831. WILLARD, G. L. Comparative Value of Rifled and Smooth Bored Arms. pp. 13.

5832. WILLARD, Major SIDNEY, Tribute to, by C. A. Bartol, December 21, 1862.
8vo. pp. 58. BOSTON: *Walker, Wise & Co.,* 1862.

5833. WILLARD, SYLVESTER D., M. D. Regimental Surgeons of the State of N. York, in the War of the Rebellion, 1861-3. p. 33.

5834. —— Conservative Surgery; with a List of the Medical and Surgical Force of New York, in the War of the Rebellion, 1861-2.
8vo. pp. 41. ALBANY: *Charles Van Benthuysen,* 1862.

5835. WILLETT, EDWARD. A Tale of the War in the West. Bob Brant, Patriot and Spy.
8vo. pp. 46. NEW YORK: *Sinclair Toucey,* 1864.

5836. —— The Vicksburg Spy; or Found and Lost. A Story of the Siege and Fall of that great Rebel Stronghold.
8vo. pp. 48. NEW YORK: *American News Co.,* 1864.

5837. —— Old Bill Woodworth, The Scout of the Cumberland.
8vo. pp. 48. NEW YORK: *American News Co.,* 1864.

5838. —— Crazy Dan; or Fight Fire with Fire. A Tale of E. Tenn.
8vo. pp. 44. NEW YORK: *American News Co.,* 1864.

5839. —— Kate Sharp. A Tale of Chattanooga. pp. 44.

5840. —— The Loyal Spectre; or the True Hearts of Atlanta. New York. pp. 44.

59

5841. WILLEY, Hon. W. T., of Virginia. Object of the War. Speech in the Senate, December 19 and 20, 1861. pp. 15.

5842. —— Speech on the Abolition of Slavery in the District of Columbia. Senate, March 20, 1862. pp. 16.

5843. WILLIAMS, Hon. Geo. H., of Oregon. Speech on Apportionment of Representation. U. S. Senate, Feb. 5, 1866. pp. 29.

5844. WILLIAMS, J. Narrative of James Williams, an American Slave, who was for several years a driver on a Cotton Plantation in Alabama. New York, *Anti-Slavery Society.* pp. 118.

5844.* WILLIAMS, James. Hurrah für die Union! Eine Widerlegung der Vertheidigung der Südstaaten.
8vo. pp. 32.   Zurich, 1864.

5845. WIILLIAMS, Hon. James. The South vindicated; being a Series of Letters written for the American Press, during the Canvass for the Presidency in 1860, with a Letter to Lord Brougham on the John Brown Raid.
8vo. pp. 444.   London: *Longman, Green & Co.*, 1862.

5846. —— Die Rechtfertigung der Südstaaten Nord Amerika's, etc. Mit einem Vorworte von E. M. Hudson.
8vo. pp. 326.   Berlin: *A. Charisius*, 1863.

5847. —— Rise and Fall of "The Model Republic."
8vo. pp. xiv, 424.   London: *Bentley*, 1863.

5848. WILLIAMS, Col. John. Sanitary Report of, to Gov. Richard Yates, of Illinois, Springfield, 1862. pp. 19.

5849. WILLIAMS, John. Immigration. A Letter to Peter Cooper, Esq., New York, 1864. pp. 12.

5850. WILLIAMS, John E., and John L. Everitt. Report on the National Bank Currency Act; its Defects and its Effects. New York, November 28, 1863. pp. 18.

5851. WILLIAMS, John Mason. Nullification and Compromise. A Retrospective View.
8vo. pp. 32.   *Loyal Publication Society No.* 27, 1863.

5852. —— The same. pp. 29. New York: *Frances & Loutrel*, 1863.

5853. Williams' Patent Bullet. Reports of Experiments with.
8vo. pp. 15.   New York: *Baker & Godwin*, 1862.

5854. WILLIAMS, Rev. J. T. Sermon delivered in the Lutheran Churches of the Blain Charge, Fast Day, September 26, 1861.
8vo. pp. 24.   Gettysburg: *H. C. Neimstedt*, 1861.

5855. WILLIAMS, Rev. R. H.   The Good Land.   A Thanksgiving Sermon, delivered November 24, 1864, at Frederick, Md. p. 20.

5856. —— A Time to Weep.   A Sermon on the Death of President Lincoln, April 29, 1865, at Frederick.   pp. 11.

5857. —— God's Chosen Ruler.   A Sermon delivered on a day of National Humiliation and Prayer, Frederick, Md., June 1, 1865. pp. 14.

5858. WILLIAMS, Hon. THOMAS.   Speech on the Restoration of the Union.   House of Representatives, April 28, 1864.   pp. 16.

5859. —— Eulogy on the Life and Public Services of Abraham Lincoln, delivered at Pittsburgh, Penn., June 1, 1865.   pp. 36.

5860. —— Speech on the Reconstruction of the Union, in the House of Representatives, February 10, 1866.   pp. 31.

5861. WILLIAMS, Rev. THOMAS.   The Evils and End of the War. 8vo. pp. 15.   PROVIDENCE: *Alfred Anthony*, 1862.

5862. WILLIAMS, WILLIAM R.   National Renovation; its Source, its Channels and its Results. 12mo. pp. 24.   NEW YORK: *A. D. F. Randolph*, 1863.

5863. —— God Timing all National Changes in the Interest of His Christ.   A Discourse delivered in Providence, R. I., May 29,'62. 12mo. pp. 56.   NEW YORK: *Sheldon & Co.*, 1862.

5864. WILLIAMSON, D. B.   The Volunteers' Roll of Honor.   The Noble and Praiseworthy Deeds performed in the Cause of the Union, by the Heroes of the Army and Navy of the United States.   Philadelphia: *Barclay & Co.*   pp. 100.

5865. WILLIS, Rev. SAMUEL B.   Sermon on the Death of Abraham Lincoln, delivered at Charleston, S. C., April 23, 1865.   pp. 8.

5866. WILMOT, Mr., of Pennsylvania.   Speech on his Amendment restricting Slavery from Territory hereafter acquired, delivered in the House of Representatives, February 8, 1847.   pp. 8.

5867. WILSON, Rev. EDMUND B.   Reasons for Thanksgiving.   A Sermon preached in Salem, April 20, 1862. 8vo. pp. 22.   SALEM: *"Observer Office,"* 1862.

5868. —— The Proclamation of Freedom.   A Sermon preached in the North Church, Salem, January 4, 1863. 8vo. pp. 16.   SALEM: *T. J. Hutchinson*, 1863.

5869. WILSON, Adj. GEORGE S.   Address at the Burial Service of. By Rev. A. D. Traver, DD.   Poughkeepsie, N. Y., 1863. p. 8.

5870. WILSON, JAMES GRANT. Biographical Sketch of Illinois Officers engaged in the War against the Rebellion in 1861.
8vo. pp. 104·   CHICAGO : *James Barker,* 1862.

5871. WILSON, Hon. HENRY, of Mass. Speech in the Senate, March
27, 1862, on the Bill to Abolish Slavery in the District of Columbia, introduced by him December 16, 1861. pp. 8.

5872. —— The Death of Slavery, the Life of the Union. Speech in
Senate, May 1, 1862. 8vo. pp. 7.

5873. —— History of the Anti-Slavery Measures of the Thirty-Seventh and Thirty-Eighth U. S. Congresses, 1861–64.
8vo. pp. 384.   BOSTON : *Walker, Wise & Co.,* 1864.

5874. —— The Crittenden Compromise—A Surrender. Speech de-
livered in the Senate, February 21, 1861, on the Resolutions of
Mr. Crittenden proposing Amendments to the Constitution of the
United States. pp. 16.

5875. —— The Death of Slavery is the Life of the Nation. Speech in
the Senate, March 28, 1864, on the proposed Amendment to the
Constitution Prohibiting Slavery within the United States. p. 16.

5875.* —— Military Measures of the U. S. Congress, 1861–65.
Royal 8vo. pp. 88.   NEW YORK : *Van Nostrand,* 1860.

5876. WILSON, JOSEPH R., DD. Mutual Relation of Master and
Slave, as taught in the Bible. A Discourse preached at Augusta,
Georgia, January 6, 1861.
8vo. pp. 21.   AUGUSTA : (Ga.) *Chronicle Office,* 1861.

5877. WILSON, THOMAS L. A Brief History of the Cruelties and
Atrocities of the Rebellion, compiled from Authentic Sources. p. 8.

5878. WILSON, Rev.W., DD. The Great American Question. Democracy vs. Doulocracy ; or Free Soil, Free Labor and Free Speech,
against the Extension and Domination of Slaveholding Interests.
8vo. pp. 40.   CINCINNATI : *E. Shepard,* 1848.

5879. —— The Cause of the United States against the Rebel Confederacy ; and the Cause of Jehovah identical. A Sermon preached
in Cincinnati, January 27, 1861.
8vo. pp. 39.   CINCINNATI : *B. Frankland,* 1861.

5880. —— A Nation Nonplussed, but Enlightened, Extricated and Vic-
torious, by turning its waiting Eyes upon God. A Sermon
preached in Xenia, January 4, 1861.
8vo. pp. 32.   CINCINNATI : *B. Frankland,* 1861.

5881. WILSON, Rev. W., DD. The Day of Small Things—the Precursor and the Cause of the Day of Great Things. A Sermon preached in Cincinnati.
8vo. pp. 40.   CINCINNATI : *Frankland & Tidball*, 1862.

5882. —— The Curse of Meroz ; or the Curse of the Neutral or Hostile toward the complete Extirpation of the Great American Rebellion, together with Slavery, which is its Cause and its source.
8vo. pp. 41.   CINCINNATI : *Frankland & Tidball*, 1862.

5883. —— The Man for the Hour. A Sermon preached in the Church of the Covenanters, Cincinnati, January 22, 1863.   pp. 44.

5884. WILSON, W. D., DD., of Hobart College.   Attainder, Treason and Confiscation of the Property of Rebels.   A Letter to Hon. S. A. Foote ; with Judge Foote's Answer.
8vo. pp. 30.   ALBANY : *Weed, Parsons & Co.*, 1863.

5885. WILSON, Rev. WM. T., (Rector.)   The Death of President Lincoln.   A Sermon preached in Albany, N. Y., April 19, 1865.
8vo. pp. 25.   ALBANY : *Weed, Parsons & Co.*, 1865.

5886. WINDER, W. H.   Secrets of the American Bastile.
8vo. pp. 47.   PHILADELPHIA : *John Campbell*, 1863.

5887. WINDSOR, WM.   Justice and Mercy.   A Sermon delivered at Davenport, Iowa, on the National Fast Day, June 1, 1865. p. 12.

5888. WINSLOW, Hon. WARREN, of North Carolina.   The Critical Condition of the Country.   Remarks in House of Representatives, January 29, 1861, upon the Report of the Committee of the States.   pp. 16.

5889. WINSOR, Rev. J. H.   The Surety of the Upright.   A Discourse on National Fast Day, at Saco, Maine, June 1, '65.   8vo. pp. 20.

5890. WINTER CAMPAIGNS, the Test of Generalship.
12mo. pp. 24.   NEW YORK : *Charles G. Stone*, 1862.

5891. WINTHROP, JOHN.   The Story of "Ham."   From Major Winthrop's John Brent.   New York, 1862.   pp. 11.

5892. WINTHROP, THEODORE. Life in the Open Air, and other Papers.
12mo. pp. 374.   BOSTON : *Ticknor & Fields*, 1863.
Among the papers in this volume are, "The March of the New York Seventh Regiment to Washington," in 1861.   "Washington as a Camp."   "Fortress Monroe."

5893. WISCONSIN.   Annual Message of the Governor of Wisconsin, (Alexander W. Randall,) September 30, 1861.   pp. 35.

5894. WISCONSIN. Annual Report of the Adjutant General of the State of Wisconsin, for the year 1861. pp. 57.

5895. —— Message of Gov. Louis P. Harvey, Jan. 8, 1862. pp. 22.

5896. —— Message of Governor Solomon, January 15, 1863. pp. 28.

5897. —— An. Report of the Sec'y of State, Sept. 30, 1862 ; containing Report on War Fund, Volunteer Aid and Allotment Fund. 8vo. pp. 73 to 1014. MADISON : *W. G. Roberts*, 1862.

5898. —— Quartermaster General's Report for the year ending December 31, 1862. pp. 200.

5899. —— Surgeon General's Report, February 27, 1863. pp. 8.

5900. —— Message of James T. Lewis, Governor of Wisconsin, January 14, 1864, with accompanying Documents. 8vo. pp. xiii and 1213. MADISON : *Wm. J. Park*, 1864.

5902. —— An. Report of the Quartermaster Gen., Sep. 30, '63. p. 30.

5903. —— Surgeon General's Report, December 31, 1863. pp. 19.

5904. —— An. Report of the Adjutant General, September 30, 1863. 8vo. pp. 337. MADISON: (Wis.) *W. J. Peck*, 1863.

5905. —— Annual Reports of the Adjutant General, Quartermaster General and Surgeon General, for the year 1864. 8vo. pp. 418. MADISON: *Atwood & Rublee*, 1865.

5906. WISE, HENRY A. Correspondence with Fernando Wood, February, 1866. pp. 4.

5907. WISWELL, Rev. GEO. F. Federal Sovereignty. An Oration in Wilmington, Delaware, July 4, 1861.

5908. —— Our Troubles and their Causes. A Fast Day Discourse, delivered at Wilmington, Del., September 26, 1861.

5909. —— The Republic, How to Save it. A Discourse preached in Wilmington, November 28, 1861. pp. 8.

5910. —— Thanksgiving Discourse, Wilming., Del., Nov. 27, '62. p. 8.

5921. —— Victory Recognized. A National Discourse delivered in Wilmington, Del., July 12, 1863. pp. 14.

5922. —— The Providential Government of God in the Affairs of Nations. A Discourse preached at Wilmington, Nov. 26, '63. p. 8.

5923. WOART, Rev. JOHN. Thanksgiving Discourse delivered in St. John's Church, Norristown, November 29, 1863. pp. 15.

5924. WOMAN'S CENTRAL ASSOCIATION of Relief at New York, to the U. S. Sanitary Commission at Washington, Oct. 12, '61. pp. 43.

5925. WOMAN's Central Association of Relief. Second Semi-Annual Report, November 1, 1862. pp. 19.

5926. —— Third Semi-Annual Report, November 1, 1863. pp. 23.

5927. —— Fourth Annual Report.

5928. WOOD, BENJAMIN, of New York. The State of the Union. Speech in the House of Reps., May 16, 1862. pp. 14.

5929. —— Peace. Speech, House of Reps., Feb. 27, 1863. pp. 12.

5930. —— Government Finances. Speech on the Bill to provide Internal Revenue. House of Reps., April 19, 1864. pp. 24.

5931. WOOD, FERNANDO. A History of the Private, Political and Official Misdeeds and Offences of Fernando Wood to Brown Brothers, Goodhue & Co., W. B. Astor and other, [1863.] p. 58.

5932. WOOD, FERNANDO. Expulsion of Alexander Long. Speech in the House of Representatives, April 11, 1864. pp. 7.

5933. —— Speech on the Naval Appropriation Bill. And the Negotiations held between the President and Commissioners from Richmond, for Peace. House of Reps., Feb. 4, 1865. pp. 8.

5934. WOOD, GEORGE I. We must carry this War through. A Sermon preached in Guilford, Conn., on the Sunday succeeding the Battle near Richmond, July 6, 1862.

5935. WOODBURY, Rev. AUGUSTUS. Courage. A Sermon which was to have been preached on Sunday morning, April 21, 1861. 8vo. pp. 8. PROVIDENCE: *Cooke & Danielson*, 1861.
Mr. Woodbury was suddenly called to act as Chaplain of the First Rhode Island Regiment of Volunteers, which left Providence for the defence of Washington, April 20, 1861.

5936. —— The Preservation of the Republic. An Oration delivered before the Municipal Authorities and Citizens of Providence, July 4, 1862.
8vo. pp. 23. PROVIDENCE: *Knowles, Anthony & Co.*, 1862.

5937. —— A Narrative of the Campaign of the First Rhode Island Regiment, in the Spring and Summer of 1861. By the Chaplain. 12mo. pp. 260. PROVIDENCE: *S. S. Rider*, 1862.

5938. —— The same. Royal 8vo. 25 copies printed, 1862.

5939. —— The Camp and the Field. Bost., *Am. Unit. As.* 8vo. p. 18.

5940. —— The Help of God, (with reference to the Campaign of the First R. I. Volunteers, at Washington and Bull Run.) A Sermon preached at Providence, Aug. 5, 1861. *Providence Press.*

5941. WOODBURY, Rev. A. Speech in the Rhode Island House of Representatives, on the Bill for the Reimbursement of Drafted Men, March 11, 1863. *Providence Journal.*

5942. —— Fast Day Sermon, Nov., 1861. *Chr. Enquirer, Nov.*, 23.

5943. —— General Halleck and General Burnside. A Reprint, with Additions of two Articles originally communicated to the Providence Journal, December 18, 1863, and Jan. 6, 1864.

  8vo. pp. 23.   BOSTON : *John Wilson & Son*, 1864.

5944. —— The Son of God calleth the Dead to Life. A Sermon suggested by the Assassination of Abraham Lincoln, preached in Providence, R. I., April 16, 1865.

  12mo. pp. 27.   PROVIDENCE : *S. S. Rider & Bro.*, 1865.

5945. —— The same. 4to. large paper. pp. 27. *Rider*, 1865.

5946. —— A Sketch of the Character of Abraham Lincoln. A Disconrse preached in Providence, June 1, 1865.

  12mo. pp. 28.   PROVIDENCE : *S. S. Rider & Bro.*, 1865.

5947. —— The same. 4to. large paper. Ibid. 1865.

5948. —— General Burnside and the Ninth Army Corps.

  8vo. With Maps and Portraits. (In press.)

5949. —— A Memoir of Major General Ambrose E. Burnside.

  25 copies, (privately printed.) 4to.

5950. WOODS, JOHN R. Report on the Condition of sick and wounded Soldiers in Military Hospitals, at Chicago, Keokuk, Quincy and St. Louis, 1862. pp. 19.

5051. WOODMAN, CHARLES. Argument in favor of a Marine Railway round the Falls of Niagara, February, 1865. pp. 19.

5952. WOODRUFF, J. B. The Future of a Cotton State Confederacy. *Methodist Quarterly Review, July*, 1861.

5953. WOODWARD, ASABEL, M. D. Life of Gen. Nathaniel Lyon.

  12mo. p. 360. Portrait. HARTFORD : *Case, Lockwood & Co.*,'62.

5954. WOODWARD, E. M., Adjutant 2d Penn. Reserves. Our Campaigns; or the Marches, Bivouacs, Battles, Incidents of Camp Life, and History of our Regiment during its three years of Service, etc.

  12mo. pp. 362.   PHILADELPHIA : *J. E. Potter*, 1865.

5955. WOODWARD, Major GEO. A. Letter to T. J. Bingham, Pittsburgh, Penn., September 23, 1863. Letter of Judge Woodward.

Address of the Democratic State Central Committee, by C. J. Biddle. pp. 8.

5956. WOODWARD, Hon. GEO. W. Speech at the Great Union Meeting in Philadelphia, December 13, 1860. With the Democratic Platform adopted by the State Convention at Harrisburg, June 19, 1863. pp. 16.

5957. WOODWARD. Opinions of a Man who wishes to be Governor of Pennsylvania. Extracts from a Speech of Judge Woodward, delivered Dec. 13, '60, at Independence Square, Phil. 8vo. p. 7.

5958. WOODWARD, in 1860 and 1863. 8vo. pp. 7.

5959. WOODWARD ON FOREIGNERS. pp. 8.

5960. WOODWARD, Judge, and Bishop Hopkins. Views on Negro Slavery at the South, illustrated from Mrs. Kemble's Journal. p. 32.

5961. WOOL, Major General JOHN E. Report on the number, age and condition of the Africans in Fort Monroe Military District, March 25, 1862.
8vo. pp. 13. *H. of Reps., Ex. Doc. No. 85, 37th Con., 2d Ses. '62.*

5962. WORCESTER, Rev. THOMAS. A Discourse delivered in the New Jerusalem Church, Boston, September 26, 1861.
12mo. pp. 24. BOSTON: *William Carter & Brother.*

5963. WORDS FOR THE PEOPLE. 1, Civil Government. 2, Government of the United States. 3, Social Duties. By Origen.
18mo. pp. 295. HARTFORD: *Case, Lockwood & Co.,* 1865.

5964. WORTHINGTON, G. F. A Plea for Horse Claims ; or shall Officers of the Army receive the Compensation for their lost Horses, to which they are entitled by law ? Dec., 1862. pp. 17.

5965. WORTHINGTON, T., Col. 46th Regt. Ohio Vols. Extracts from a Diary of the Tennessee Expedition, 1862. (Confidential.) pp. 8.

5966. —— Abstract of Evidence, etc., in the Proceedings of the Court Martial for Trial of, at Memphis, August 14, 1862. pp. 8.

5967. WORTMAN, Rev. DENIS. A Discourse on the Death of President Lincoln, delivered in Schenectady, N. Y., April 16, 1865.
8vo. pp. 22. ALBANY: *Weed, Parsons & Co.,* 1865.

5968. WRIGHT, CHARLES, (Mountaineer.) Political Letters in Aid of Integrity, 1861.

5969. —— The Prospect. A View of Politics.
8vo. pp. 52. BUFFALO: *Rockwell & Baker,* 1862.

5970. WRIGHT, C. An Appeal for Rectitude in Primary Politics.
8vo. pp. 18.   BOSTON : *Alfred Mudge & Son,* 1863.

5971. —— A Plea for Equity in Church Maintenance. pp. 86.

5972. —— Our Political Practice. The Usurpation of Vice through Popular Negligence. In Three Parts. 1864. pp. 8.

5973. —— Part Second of Our Political Practice. Containing a Letter of Protest to General Henry Wilson.
8vo. pp. 58.   BOSTON : *Alfred Mudge & Son,* 1865.

5974. —— Section II, Part Second of Our Political Practice. On the War-Time Ways of a Modern Statesmen. pp. 24.

5975. WRIGHT, ELIZUR. An Eye Opener for the Wide Awakes.
8vo. pp. 59.   BOSTON : *Thayer & Eldridge,* 1860.

5976. WRIGHT, HENRY C. The Natick Resolution ; or Resistance to Slaveholders the Right and Duty of Southern Slaves and Northern Freemen.
12mo. pp. 36.   BOSTON : *For the author,* 1859.

5977. WRIGHT, Hon. HENDRICK B., of Penn. Objects of the War ; and How it should be conducted. Speech, House of Representatives, January 20, 1862. pp. 8.

5978. —— Speech in Reply to Mr. Vallandigham, on Peace Resolutions offered by the latter. H. of Rep., Jan. 14, 1863. pp. 8.

5979. —— Speech on the Bill to authorize the Enrollment of one hundred and fifty Negro Regiments in the Military Service. House of Representatives, January 30, 1863. pp. 8.

5980. WRIGHT, J. A., of Indiana. Speech on the Discharge of State Prisoners. Senate, December 6, 1862. pp. 16.

5981. —— Speech on Slavery in the District of Columbia. Senate, April 1, 1862. pp. 8.

5982. WRIGHT, J. S., and J. H. Agnew. Citizen Sovereignty.
8vo. pp. viii and 208. CHICAGO : *For American Citizens,* 1864.

5983. WRIGHT, WM. A Word of Warning to Democrats, from a Life Long Voter of the Party. pp. 16.

5984. WROTNOWSKI, STANISLAS. Discours a ses Citoyens de Baton Rouge, Louisiana, prononcé a la Société de l'Union. p. 43.

5985. WURTS, GEO. Our Domestic Affairs. *Con. Monthly, Sept.,* 64.

5986. WYLIE, Rev. Dr. Washington, a Christian. A Discourse preached February 23, 1862, in Philadelphia.
18mo. pp. 68.   PHILADELPHIA : *W. S. & A. Martien,* 1862.

YARD, Rev. ROBERT B. The Providential Significance of the Death of Abraham Lincoln. A Discourse delivered in Newark, N. J., June 1, 1865.

8vo. pp. 23. NEWARK: (N. J.) *H. Harris*, 1865.

5988. YATES, EDWARD. A Letter to the Women of England, on Slavery in the Southern States of America.

8vo. pp. 68. LONDON: *John Snow*, 1863.

5988.* YATES, EDWARD, (of St. John's College, Cambridge, England.) A Letter to the Women of England, on Slavery in the Southern States of America; considered especially in reference to the Female Slaves.

8vo. pp. 68. NEW YORK: *Calvin Blanchard*, 1863.

5989. YATES, WM. Rights of Colored Men to Suffrage, Citizenship and Trial by Jury. Facts, Arguments and Authorities.

8vo. pp. 104. PHILADELPHIA: *Merrihew & Gunn*, 1838.

5990. YANCEY, WILLIAM L., of Alabama. Constitutional Rights. Speech at Weiting Hall, Syracuse, N. Y., Oct. 15, '60. 8vo. p. 16.

5991. YATES, Hon. RICHARD. The Only Salvation, Equality of Rights. Speech in the U. S. Senate, February 19, 1866.

5992. YEAMAN, Hon. GEO. H., of Kentucky. Speech on the President's Proclamation, delivered in the H. of Rep., Dec. 18, 1862

8vo. pp. BALTIMORE: *John Murphy & Co.*, 1863.

5993. —— Speech on the Proposition to Amend the Constitution of the United States. House of Reps., January 9, 1865. pp. 15.

5994. YEATMAN, JAMES E. Report on the Condition of the Freedmen of the Mississippi, presented to the Western Sanitary Commission, December 17, 1863. pp. 16.

5995. YOKUM. Letter of the Secretary of War communicating information concerning the case of William Yokum, confined in the Penitentiary at Albany, New York, June 14, 1864.

Senate Ex. Doc. No. 51, 38*th Congress*, 1*st Session*, 1864. p. 20.

5996. —— Report of the Committee on the Judiciary on the case of, June 24, 1864. *H. of Rep. Report*, 118, 38*th Cong.*, 1*st Ses*, '64.

5997. YOUNG, DANIEL S., M. D. Field Observations in Surgery; being the Surgical Aspects of the War in the Army of the West, 1861–65. 4to. CINCINNATI: *R. Clarke & Co.*, 1866.

4998. YOUNG, Harrison Perry.　Indestructibility of the American Union.　A Lecture before the Parker Fraternity, Boston.
12mo. pp. 59.　　　　　　　　Boston: *R. H. Blodgett,* 1864.

5999. YOURTEE, Rev. S. L.　A Sermon delivered at Springfield, Ohio, on the occasion of the Death of the President of the United States.　pp. 16.

5999.* —— A Sermon preached on the Day of National Thanksgiving, at Springfield, Ohio, December 7, 1865.　pp. 16.

ZABRISKIE, Col. Abram, Memorial of, by the Bar of Hudson County, New Jersey.　(Privately printed.)
8vo. pp. 34.　　　　　　　Jersey City: *John Logan,* 1864.

6001. ZABRISKIE, Rev. F. N.　God's Battle.　A Sermon for the Fourth of July, preached in Coxsackie, June 30, 1861.
12mo. pp. 30.　　　　　Albany: *William B. Sprague, Jr.*

6002. —— Weighed in the Balance. A Fast Day Sermon, Apr. 30,'63.
12mo. pp. 26.　　　　　Albany: *Wm. B. Sprague, Jr.,* 1863.

6003. —— The Post of Duty.　A Funeral Discourse in Memory of Capt. Lansing Hollister, 120th Regt. New York Volunteers.
11mo. pp. 20.　　　　Coxsackie: (N. Y.) *F. C. Dedrick.*

6004. ZEIGLER, Prof.　Politics and the Pulpit.　*Evangelical Quarterly Review, Vol.* xvi.

6005. ZERMAN, J. Napoleon.　Memorial to the U. S. Senate, in relation to the Confirmation of his Appointment as Brigadier General, June 2, 1862.　pp. 4

ADDITIONS.

ADAMS, F. Colburn.　The Story of a Trooper.　With much of Interest concerning the Peninsula, not before written.
12mo. pp. 616.　　　　　New York: *Dick & Fitzgerald,* 1866.

6007. America und seine jetzige Bewegung.
12mo. pp. 32.　　　　Berlin: *Reinhold Schlingmann,* 1861.

6008. ARNAUD, Achille.　Abraham Lincoln.　Sa Naissance, sa Vie, sa Mort, avec un récit de la Guerre d'Amérique.
Folio, pp. 96.　　　　　　Paris: *Charlien Fréres,* 1865.

6009. ARTHUR, William.　English Opinion on the Am. Rebellion.
8vo. pp. 4.　　Manchester: *Union and Emancipation Society.*

6010. BARNEY, Capt. C.   Recollections of Field Service with the 20th Iowa Infantry Vols.; or What I saw in the Army.
12mo. pp. 323.   DAVENPORT: *The author*, 1866.

6011. BIGELOW, JOHN.   Collana di Storie e Memorie Contemporaine gli Stati Uniti nel 1863.
12mo. pp. 470.   MILAN: *Corona e Caimi*, 1863.

6012. BISHOP, JOEL P.   Secession and Slavery; or the Constitutional Duty of Congress to give the Elective Franchise and Freedom to all Loyal Persons, in response to the Act of Secession.
8vo. pp. 112.   BOSTON: *A. Williams & Co.*, 1866.

6013. BLACK, JEREMIAH S.   Military Trials of Civilians.   The Indiana Conspiracy Cases.   *Washington Reporter, March* 26, '66.

6014. BONDRYE, Rev. LOUIS N.   Historic Records of the Fifth N. Y. Cavalry; with accounts of Prison Life and the secret Service.
16mo. pp. 358.   ALBANY: *S. R. Gray*, 1866.

6015. BROCKETT, L. P.   Our Great Captains.   12mo.   New York, *C. B. Richardson.*

6016. —— The Great Rebellion; its History, Biography and Incidents.
2 vols. 8vo.   AUBURN: *American Publishing Company*, 1865.

6017. —— The History of the Civil War.
Royal 8vo. pp. 1020.   PHILADELPHIA: *Jones & Brothers*, 1866.

6018. BROOM, W. W.   Great and Grave Questions for American Politicians.   With a Topic for Amer. Statesmen.   By Eboracus.
8vo. pp. 122.   BOSTON: *Walker, Fuller & Co.*, 1866.

6019. BROWN, W. W.   Clotelle; a Tale of the Southern States.
12mo. pp. 104.   BOSTON: *J. Redpath*, 1864.

6020. CAREY, H. C.   The Resources of the Union.   A Lecture read Dec., 1865, before the Am. Geographical and Statistical Society,
8vo. pp. 26.   PHILADELPHIA: *H. Carey Baird*, 1866.

6021. —— Contraction or Expansion?   Repudiation or Resumption? Letters to the Hon. Hugh McCulloch, Sec'y of the Treasury.
8vo. pp. 47.   PHILADELPHIA: *Henry Carey Baird*, 1866.

6021.* CIBO, S. FRENFANELLI.   Cenni Storici sugli Stati Uniti D'America.   12mo.   FOLIGNO, 1865.

6022. CHASE, WARREN.   The American Crisis; or Trial and Triumph of Democracy.
8vo. pp. 82.   BOSTON: *Bela Marsh*, 1862.

6023. CLAXTON, Rev. Dr.   In Memoriam.   Sermon, in Rochester,

New York, at the Funeral of Capt. C. S. Montgomery, 5th Regiment New York Volunteers. 8vo.

6024. COOKE, JOHN ESTEN. Stonewall Jackson. A Military Biography. 12mo. New York, *D. Appleton & Co.*, 1866.

6025. COLLINS, Rev. N. G. Speech to Regiments in Gen. Dodge's Division, on the Intellectual Condition of the South, compared with the North ; with its bearing upon the present Rebellion. No. 1. 12mo. pp. 24. CHICAGO : *Church & Goodman.*

6026. —— Same. No. 2. pp. 24. Chicago.

6027. COOPER, PETER. Letters on the Necessity of a wise, discriminating Tariff to protect American Labor, and maintain a harmonious Interest, as the Means to insure a return to Specie Payments, etc. 8vo. pp. 14. NEW YORK : *Office of " Iron Age,"* 1866.

6028. COLONEY, MYRON. Manomin. A Rhythmical Romance of Minnesota, the Great Rebellion, and the Massacre. 12mo. pp. 297. ST. LOUIS : *The author,* 1866.

6029. CONFEDERATE STATES, Acts and Resolutions of the First Session of the Provisional Congress of '61. Montgomery, Ala.,'61. p. 131.

6030. DAVIS, GARRETT. Speech on District of Columbia Suffrage, delivered in the U. S. Senate, January 16, 1866. pp. 16.

6031. DAVIS, Hon. THOMAS T. Speech on Equality and Equal Rights, in House of Reps., February 28, 1866. pp. 12.

6032. DEMING, Hon. H. C. Insurgent Relations and Insurgent Armies. A Speech in the House of Reps., Jan. 19, 1866. p. 8.

6033. DIE EREIGNISSE IN AMERIKA in ihrer Rückwirkung auf Deutschland. 8vo. pp. 80. BERLIN : *Ferdinand Schneider,* 1861.

6034. DOSTIE, Hon. A. P. A Loyal Voice from Louisiana. Speech before the Union Association, New Orleans, Jan. 27, 1865. p. 4.

6035. DOUGLASS, Mr., and the Doctrine of Coercion ; with Letters from Hon. Herschell V. Johnson and Hon. J. K. Paulding. p. 24.

6036. DYE. JOHN SMITH. History of the Plots and Crimes of the Great Conspiracy to overthrow the Liberty of America. 8vo. pp. 368. NEW YORK : *The author,* 1866.

6037. ELDRIDGE, Hon. CHARLES A. Has the Revolt destroyed the Union. Speech in the House of Reps., Jan. 25, 1866. pp. 8.

6038. ESTVAN, B. Kreigsbilden aus Amerika. 2 vols. 8vo. LEIPZIG : *F. A. Brockhaus,* 1864.

6039. FOOTE, Henry S. War of the Rebellion.
12mo. pp. 440.   New York: *Harper & Brothers,* 1866.

6040. FULLER, Richard. A City or House divided against itself.
A Discourse at Baltimore, Fast Day, June 1, 1865. pp. 20.

6041. Gazelle. A True Tale of the Gt. Rebellion, and other Poems.
16mo. pp. 258.   Boston: *Lee & Shepard,* 1866.

6042. GESSNER, L. Le Droit des Neutres sur Mer.
Royal 8vo. pp. xiv and 437. Berlin: *Stilke et Van Muyden,*'65.

6043. GITTERMANN, J. Ch. H. Revolution oder Abolition frei
bearbitet nach H. R. Helper's die dem Süden bevorsteheude Crisis.
8vo. pp. 112.   Stuttgart: *J. G. Cotta.*

6044. GREGG, Rev. T. Chandler. Life in the Army, in the Departments of Virginia and the Gulf, including New Orleans, etc.
12mo. pp. 271. Philadelphia: *Perkinpine & Higgins,* 1866.

6045. GRABE. Ueber die Bedeutung des Ersten Kampfes von Panzerschiffen für die Künftig gebotene bauart der Kriegsschiffe.
8vo. pp. 73.   Berlin: *Strikken,* 1862.

6046. GRIESINGER, T. Land und Leute in Amerika.
12mo. 2 vols.   Stuttgart: *A. Kröner,* 1863.

6047. HENDERSON, J. B. The Missouri Test Oath. Argument in
the Supreme Court of the United States, March, 1866. *Washington Reporter, March* 19. pp. 16.

6048. HOTCHKISS, Jed., and W. Allan. The Battle Fields of Virginia; embracing the Operations of the Army of Northern Va.
8vo. Maps.   New York: *Van Nostrand,* 1866.

6049. HUGHES, Denver and Peck. Review of the Opinion of
Charles O'Conor, Esq., on what he styles the "Treasury Agent
System of Cotton Seizures at the South," addressed to Hon.
Hugh McCulloch, Sec. of the Treasury. Washington, '66. p. 19.

6050. HUDSON, E. M. Der Zweite Unabhängigkeits–Krieg in Amerika.
8vo. pp. 99.   Berlin: *A. Charisius,* 1862.

6051. INGERSOLL, L. D. Iowa in the Rebellion. A History of the
Troops furnished by the State of Iowa to the Volunteer Armies
of the 1861–5.
8vo. pp. 743. Philadelphia: *J. B. Lippincott & Co.,* 1866.

6052. LIEBER, Dr. Remarks on the Final Adjournment of the Loyal
Publication Society, February 15, 1866. pp. 3.

6053. LINCOLN. La Médaille de la Liberté, avec les Lettres de Flocon, Edgar Quinet, Victor Hugo, Schœler, Louis Blanc, et la vie d'Abraham Lincoln. PARIS : *A. Lacroix,* 1866.

6054. LINCOLN, ABRAHAM. Illustrated Life, Services, Martyrdom and Funeral of.
12mo. pp. 329.　PHILADELPHIA : *T. Peterson & Bros.,* 1866.

6055. LUNT, GEORGE. Origin of the late War traced from the beginning of the Constitution, to the Revolt of the Southern States.
12mo.　NEW YORK : *D. Appleton & Co.,* 1866.

6056. MARGRAF, J. Kirche und Sklaverei seit der Entdeckung Amerikas, etc. 8vo. pp. 230. Tubingen, 1865.

6057. MARQUARDSEN, Dr. HEINRICK. Der Trent-Fall. Zur Lehre von der Kriegscontrebande und dem Transportdienst der Neutralen.
8vo. pp. 196.　ERLANGEN : *Ferdinand Enke,* 1862.

6058. MILBERG, J. H. Ueber die Werthlosigkeit Eiserner Panzerschiffe.
8vo. pp. 38.　MÜNCHEN, 1862.

6059. MOORE, GEORGE H. Slavery in Massachusetts.
8vo. pp.　NEW YORK : *D. Appleton & Co.,* 1866.

6060. REED, SAMUEL R. The Currency and the Finances. A Policy for the Present Expansion of Currency and Public Debt. The Way to Specie Payments. 8vo. Cincinnati : *Gazette Office,*'66.

6061. SAUER, G. Ueber den Einfluss des Separatismus auf die Handelsbeziehungen zwischen den nördlichen und südlichen Staaten der Union, etc.
8vo. pp. 29.　AACHEN : *Benrath & Vogelgefang,* 1861.

6062. SIMPSON, J. HAWKINS. Horrors of the Virginia Slave Trade, and the Slave-bearing Population. The Story of Dinah, an Escaped Slave.
12mo. pp.　LONDON : *A. W. Bennett,* 1866.

6063. SHERMAN, JOHN. Speech on Representation of Southern States, in the United States Senate, February 26, 1866. pp. 22.

6064. SMEDES, WM. C. Letter in vindication of the Southern Confederacy. pp. 12. Jackson, Mississippi, 1861.

6065. THE SOUTH alone should govern the South. And African Slavery should be controlled by those only who are friendly to it.
8vo. pp. 62.　CHARLESTON : *Evans & Cogswell,* 1860.

6066. STIGER, JOSEPH LEOPOLD. Die Nord und Sudländer der Vereinigten Staaten Amerikas. Zurich, 1864.

6067. —— Ist die Auswanderung nach den Vereinigten Staaten Nord-Amerikas inter den jetzigen Verhältnissen anzurathen? 8vo. ZURICH: 1864 pp. 48 and 8.

6068. —— Die Rechtfertigung der Nordstaaten in dem jetzigen Kampfe mit den Südstaaten der amerikanischen Union. 8vo. ZURICH, 1864. pp. 72.

6069. —— Nieder mit der Sklaverei. 8vo. pp. 32. ZURICH, 1862.

6070. STONE, Rev. RICHARD C. Duties and Responsibilities of the Christian Citizen in the Present Crisis. A Discourse delivered at St. Louis, Missouri.
8vo. pp.   ST. LOUIS : *M'Kee & Fishback*, 1861.

6071. STREUBEL, W. Die Panzerschiffe ein nautischer und artilleristischer—Rückschritt.
8vo. pp. 69.   DARMSTADT : *Edward Zernin*, 1862.

6072. WHITE, RICHARD GRANT. Poetry ; Lyrical, Narrative and Satirical, on the Civil War.
12mo. pp.   *American News Company*, 1866.

6073. ZERFALL DER VEREINIGTEN STAATEN von Nord-Amerika. Verfasst von einem Deutzchen.
8vo. pp. 480.   MUNSTER : *C. J. Fahle*, 1864.